CW00350983

The World Bank

'Superior ... a broad-ranging guide that explains the global power structure over the last eight decades. The history of the World Bank and its frequent support of dictatorships in the Global South clarifies the nexus between high finance and power politics.'

—Carlos Marichal, El Colegio de México

'Could not be more opportune as the world enters a dangerous period of potential geopolitical conflict. Toussaint exposes, the role of the World Bank (and other Bretton Woods institutions) as tools for the financial control of the world – in particular, the exploitation of the Global South through the manipulation of debt. The World Bank is found not to be a great institution to reduce global poverty, but on the contrary, to perpetuate it.'

—Michael Roberts, economist and co-author of
Capitalism in the 21st Century: Through the Prism of Value

'The record of lending to authoritarian regimes ... invites fresh thinking on the need to streamline human rights considerations into development lending. Recommended reading to get a different view of the Bretton Woods institutions.'

—Andrés Solimano, founder,
International Center for Globalization and Development

'The World Bank's many critics usually urge institutional redemption through reforms. In this harsh and thorough indictment, Eric Toussaint blasts those hopes. Covering the history of the Bank from its early days as a prop to European colonialism through the Rwandan genocide, the Washington Consensus and the Iraq war, he argues that the Bank is incorrigible and should, therefore, be abolished. Read and judge for yourselves.'

—James K. Galbraith, author of *Welcome to the Poisoned Chalice:
The Destruction of Greece and the Future of Europe*

The World Bank

A Critical History

ÉRIC TOUSSAINT

With a contribution by Camille Bruneau

Foreword by Gilbert Achcar

Pluto Press

First published as *Banque mondiale, une histoire critique* 2022 by Éditions Syllepse
Parts of this edition are based on *The World Bank: A Critical Primer*, 2008

This edition first published 2023 by Pluto Press
New Wing, Somerset House, Strand, London WC2R 1LA
and Pluto Press, Inc.
1930 Village Center Circle, 3-834, Las Vegas, NV 89134

www.plutobooks.com

Copyright © Éric Toussaint 2022, 2023

The right of Éric Toussaint to be identified as the author of this work has been asserted in accordance with the Copyright, Designs and Patents Act 1988.

Translated by the CADTM translation team.

British Library Cataloguing in Publication Data
A catalogue record for this book is available from the British Library

ISBN 978 0 7453 4828 5   Hardback
ISBN 978 0 7453 4829 2   PDF
ISBN 978 0 7453 4830 8   EPUB

This book is printed on paper suitable for recycling and made from fully managed and sustained forest sources. Logging, pulping and manufacturing processes are expected to conform to the environmental standards of the country of origin.

Typeset by Riverside Publishing Solutions, Salisbury, England

Printed in the United Kingdom

Dedication

I would like to dedicate this book to all those who fight for human dignity and social justice.

And to those who attempt to cross the Mediterranean Sea, the English Channel, the Rio Grande despite all the shameful barriers that the governments of rich countries have put up to prevent people from circulating freely.

Contents

Tables and Figures

FIGURES

Foreword

Gilbert Achcar

The World Bank and its fraternal twin, the International Monetary Fund (IMF), have earned an execrable reputation in the Third World since the start of the neoliberal era in the 1980s. That is because these two intergovernmental financial institutions – the two main pillars of the international economic order put in place after the Second World War under the domination of the United States of America, a domination clearly visible in the fact that both institutions are headquartered in Washington – have been the primary vectors of the extension of the capitalist system in its neoliberal mutation in the Global South.

That mutation has visited even more pain on the poor nations than it has on the poorest citizens of the wealthy countries. Let us take the example of one of the key measures of that neoliberal mutation: the privatization of state-owned companies. The gap between the working conditions prevalent in the private sector and in the public sector is much greater in countries of the Global South than in the economically advanced countries. In the latter countries, the power of trade unions, the rule of law as regards labour legislation and the generalization of compulsory social coverage reduce the gap between the two sectors. On the other hand, in poor nations where there is an enormous 'informal sector' deprived of any rights, the move from the public sector to the private sector is accompanied by a considerable deterioration of working conditions.

It is well known that increased precarity of the workforce is one of the major damaging consequences of neoliberalism in the economically advanced countries. But precarious workers in those countries – excepting the relatively small number of victims suffering in the hell that is clandestine work – generally enjoy more rights and social benefits than the great majority of workers in the private sector in the poor nations, whose status has always been precarious in practice, if not in legality.

Another example is the sacrosanct principle of drastically reducing budgetary deficits, which necessarily results in reduced social spending and public investment, despite the hypocritical pronouncements made by the international financial institutions in favour of expenditures for education and health. Combine that principle with that of privatization and you will understand that the governments of the Third World, in the absence of strong labour and socio-political resistance, tend to sacrifice those two vital sectors in favour of private-sector providers whose only principle is maximizing profit and who provide services that are very poor in quality or else whose prices are prohibitive for the great majority of the population.

Public investments, generally guided by the needs of the society and the economy as a whole, lose ground to private investments that are more and more 'free' – that is, free of public regulation, and guided by the hunger for rapid profit in a context of growing corruption and rigged markets. The result is the development of crony capitalism and speculative activities of all types. Social inequality is inexorably aggravated by these changes. The unbridled enrichment of a minority of the privileged is accompanied by the deterioration of social conditions and the relative or absolute impoverishment of the great majority.

It then becomes understandable that while neoliberalism may have maintained the pretence of being the natural corollary of liberal democracy in the northern hemisphere at the time of its extension into Eastern Europe following the collapse of the so-called 'socialist' dictatorships, in the countries of the Global South the imposition of the full range of neoliberal measures often requires ironclad despotism. There is an unbroken line over four decades from that first champion of the neoliberal mutation, General Augusto Pinochet – who headed the bloody US-fostered coup that ended democracy in Chile in 1973 – to Marshal Abdel Fattah al-Sissi, author of the even bloodier coup that ended the democratic experiment in Egypt in 2013 as the prelude to the first full-scale application of the directives of the international financial institutions in his country.

The main economic lever with which the new neoliberal order concocted in Washington was imposed on the countries of the Third World was the mechanism of debt. The peak of indebtedness that followed the skyrocketing of oil prices on the worldwide market in the 1970s was the main instrument of the blackmail exercised on the countries of the Global South to force them to apply the programmes of the neoliberal mutation under the mask of the technocratic term 'structural adjustment'.

And so it is no accident that Éric Toussaint has become one of the most knowledgeable people concerning the World Bank and the IMF outside the inner circles of power in those institutions. For some 30 years now he has been studying them closely – a task he set for himself in 1990 in founding the Committee for the Abolition of Third World Debt, which has since been re-named Committee for the Abolition of Illegitimate Debt, keeping the acronym of its original name: CADTM. Éric began his study of the World Bank as a critical observer, and over the years has accumulated a formidable and rare knowledge of the Third World, whose length and breadth he has travelled – that Third World which is the primary field of activity of the World Bank in the neoliberal era. In the process Éric has uncovered many aspects that were originally intended to remain hidden behind the opaque veil that conceals the workings of international finance and of the intergovernmental economic institutions.

A tireless militant for the cause of the Third World and of other dominated countries, Éric Toussaint has become an internationally known expert on all questions related to foreign debt. This book is the fruit of decades of research, practical experience and commitment to militancy. And as one would expect, it is written for the great majority. It is an instructional work in which Éric's primary profession, that of teacher in technical and professional education, is evident – a book free of the usual jargon encountered in technocratic and academic publications and which makes them inaccessible to the great majority of the people whose lives are affected by the subjects they deal with. It is to those people that this book is addressed, and not to the members of the elite of worldwide economic power.

Preface

This book is the result of an undertaking that began 30 years ago. The writing itself was begun in March 2004. It led to an initial edition of the book in French in 2006 in the form of a co-publication by the Paris publisher Syllepse, the Cetim in Geneva and the CADTM in Liège. The book met with success and was translated into English, Spanish, Japanese, Indonesian, Arabic and Portuguese. In Spanish, it appeared in four different editions (Viejo Topo in Barcelona, Spain; Centro Internacional Miranda in Caracas, Venezuela; Abya-Yala in Quito, Ecuador; and DESC in La Paz, Bolivia). There are two different editions in English (Pluto in London, UK and VAK in Mumbai, India). This edition is an expanded and updated version of the work published in 2008 by Pluto.

My main source consisted of documents produced by the World Bank itself, totalling over 15,000 pages. I also consulted numerous reports and studies published by other international institutions, principally the International Monetary Fund (IMF), the United Nations Development Programme (UNDP), the United Nations Conference on Trade and Development (UNCTAD), the Organization for Economic Cooperation and Development (OECD) and the Bank for International Settlements (BIS). Also of great use were the publications and studies by some 50 authors whose analyses are related to the subject (see Bibliography). Over the last 30 years I have undertaken – mainly on behalf of the CADTM – more than 100 missions and journeys in the Global South, mainly in Latin America, but also in Africa, Asia, and Central and Eastern Europe. The analysis developed in the pages of this book owes much to these missions and to the people I have had occasion to meet.

Many direct contacts with the authorities of various developing countries also helped me develop this analysis. Outstanding among them were the invitations I received from the Ministry of the Economy of East Timor in March 2003 and from the Venezuelan parliament – the first in 1997 followed by another in 2003 – from Venezuela's Ministry for Economy and Planning in 2008, from the government of Ecuador several times between 2007 and 2011, from the president of Paraguay in 2008 and 2011, as well as regular contacts with Luis Inácio Lula da Silva between 1990 and 2003, when his term as Brazil's president began.[1] Since 1995, in my capacity as president of CADTM Belgium, I have also had several meetings and engaged in debate with three successive Belgian Finance Ministers: Philippe Maystadt (Minister of Finance from 1988 to 1998, then chairman of the European

---

1   See Éric Toussaint, *Your Money or Your Life: The Tyranny of Global Finance* (Chicago: Haymarket Books, 2005), chapter 16, 'Case study: Brazil', pp. 292–313.

Investment Bank (EIB) from 2000 to 2011), Jean-Jacques Viseur (Minister of Finance in 1998–99) and Didier Reynders (Minister of Finance from 1999 to 2011, then European Commissioner for Justice beginning in 2019). Between 1998 and 2014, I also met regularly with Belgian administrators of the World Bank and the IMF posted in Washington. Finally, I have taken part in public debates with top officials of the World Bank and the IMF in Prague, Geneva and Brussels.

Numerous contacts at grassroots level in developing countries and ongoing relations in the context of their social movements have been the compass that has constantly confirmed my course in the writing of this work.

Three chapters of this book are taken from my doctoral thesis in political science, which I defended in November 2004 at the Universities of Liège and Paris VIII.[2]

This book takes a chronological approach in analyzing the World Bank from its beginnings to 2021. Care has been taken to place World Bank policy in its political and geostrategic context. In addition, seven studies of different countries are presented to illustrate World Bank policy: the Philippines (1946–86), Turkey (1980–90), Indonesia (1947–2005), South Korea (1945–98), Mexico (1970–2005), Ecuador (1990–2019) and Rwanda (1980s–1990s). A critical analysis of how the World Bank interprets the Arab Spring, which began in 2011, is given. At many points in the book, the policies conducted by the International Monetary Fund (IMF) are also analyzed. The actions of the World Bank with regard to the environmental crisis and climate change are also dealt with. This book aims to show clearly the political, economic and strategic motives of the United States government with regard to the World Bank. Thanks to the contribution of Camille Bruneau, a feminist and member of the CADTM team, the book includes a chapter proposing a feminist reading of the policies of the World Bank. In the last part of the book, the question of the justiciability of the World Bank is raised. The book ends with a proposal for replacing the World Bank, the IMF and the WTO with new, multilateral and democratic institutions. The book contains charts and graphs, a World Bank–IMF data sheet, an index of the principal names cited and a glossary. If a concept is not clear, consulting the latter will make reading easier.

As stated in the Acknowledgements, this book could not have been written without the help of others who are close to me. But the analyses developed here are entirely my own personal responsibility. My dearest wish is that they should be taken, completed, amended and of course applied as widely as possible in the effort to free the oppressed people of the Earth, which is, after all, a lifelong struggle.

Éric Toussaint,
Liège, 7 March 2023

2　They are chapters 3, 5 and 6, taken from Éric Toussaint, 'Enjeux politiques de l'action de la Banque internationale pour la Reconstruction et le Développement et du Fonds monétaire international envers le tiers-monde' ('Political implications of the actions of the IBRD and the IMF towards the Third World'), doctoral thesis in political science (Universities of Liège and Paris VIII, academic year 2003–04).

Acknowledgements

Special thanks go to Camille Bruneau for authoring the chapter devoted to a feminist reading of the World Bank's policies.

The author thanks Snake Arbusto, Omar Aziki, Vicki Briault Manus, Anaïs Carton, Virginie de Romanet, Christine Pagnoulle, Maxime Pierrot, Brigitte Ponet and Claude Quémar for reading the manuscript. Thanks to Tina D'angelantonio for the preliminary layout.

Rémi Vilain and Daniel Munevar provided invaluable help in researching documents and statistical data. We would like to thank the following for research assistance with the English version: Lauren Reinhalter and Monique Libby at the Council on Foreign Relations in Washington and New York; Nina Clements at the University of Wisconsin Library in Madison.

Thanks also to all who contributed to translating into the various languages (English, Arabic, Spanish and Portuguese): Snake Arbusto, Omar Aziki, Vicki Briault Manus, Alain Geffrouais, Mike Krolikowski, Maria da Liberdade, Alberto Nadal, Christine Pagnoulle, Griselda Pinero and Rui Viana Pereira.

Terminology: South/North – Developing/ Developed. Just What Are We Talking About?

The terms chosen to designate the different categories of countries convey the theoretical and political divergences that exist when it comes to analysis and strategy. Generally, these divergences are related to the social content of the economic concepts: the economic categories are often presented as reflecting natural laws in which social relations and power struggles have a limited place. In the dominant view, underdevelopment, for example, is perceived as being a simple time lag, sometimes ascribed to natural causes. Let us have a look at some of these terms:

1. *Underdeveloped countries*: this old term has become obsolete because of its derogatory overtones.
2. *Developing countries*: this expression is less derogatory than the first but subscribes to the same biased notion of a simple time lag. Moreover, it presumes a trajectory of improvement of the situation that is not always verifiable. The World Bank still classifies countries as 'developed' or 'developing'.[1]
3. *Least advanced countries*: a term used in the classifications of international authorities, but it combines all the preceding defects.
4. *Third World*: a term invented by Alfred Sauvy in 1952 (by analogy with the Third Estate) and which was popular during the Cold War as a means of naming all the countries taking an independent stand, whether with regard to the United States or to the USSR.[2] Two facts have rendered the use of the term more problematic, although the habit still persists: on the one hand, the disappearance of the USSR and the Soviet bloc, and on the other hand the growing heterogeneity of the former countries of the Third World, several of which have experienced

---

1 Tariq Khokar, 'Should we continue to use the term "developing world"?', Worldbank.org, November 2015 <blogs.worldbank.org/opendata/should-we-continue-use-term-developing-world> [accessed 23/11/2021].

2 Alfred Sauvy: 'We readily speak of two opposing worlds [the capitalist world and the socialist world – author's note], of their possible war, of their coexistence, etc., all too often forgetting that there exists a third one, the most important, and in fact the first one in chronological terms. This is the body of those that we call, in United Nations fashion, the underdeveloped countries. […] The underdeveloped countries, the third world, have entered into a new phase […]. Because at last this ignored, exploited Third World, looked down on as was the Third Estate, also wants to be acknowledged.' (*L'Observateur*, 14 August 1952, No. 118; translation CADTM).

actual economic development, or even, in some cases, have joined the group of 'developed' countries in the World Bank's classification. In the early twenty-first century, China became the world's second-ranking economic power.

> In 1951, in a Brazilian journal, I mentioned three worlds, yet without using the term 'Third World'. I coined and used the term for the first time in writing in the French weekly *L'Observateur* on 14 August 1952. This is how the article ended: 'Because at last this ignored, exploited Third World, looked down on as was the Third Estate, also wants to be acknowledged.' I was referring to the well-known words of *Siéyès*[3] on the Third Estate during the French Revolution.
>
> – Alfred Sauvy, demographer and economist[4]

5. *Poor countries*: a term that focuses on the economic poverty of the majority of the population in the countries concerned and obscures the blatant inequalities that exist there. Moreover, a number of countries considered poor are actually very rich in natural resources, not to mention their cultural wealth. These countries should be called 'exploited' or 'impoverished' countries.

6. *Countries of the South*: a convenient term to stigmatize the break with the countries in the northern hemisphere, often developed and dominant, but which has the twofold defect of ignoring the numerous exceptions to this geographical classification and of implying that geography is somehow a determining factor. This is why in Latin America 'Global South' and 'Global North' are used, in order to distinguish them from geographical realities. We also speak of 'the Souths' in the plural, to highlight the heterogeneity among many countries of the South.

7. *Peripheral countries*: a term belonging to the Structuralist and Marxist vocabulary which stresses the domination that is at the heart of a global capitalism run by the most industrialized countries and their imperialist policies.

8. *Emerging countries*: a term designating the economies that have initiated an undeniable development process which distinguishes them from the body of the formerly more homogenous Third World – China, India and Brazil being the principal examples. This term is often enough replaced by 'emerging markets', a substitution that clearly reflects the neoliberal vision of a development that can only be achieved through insertion into the international division of labour imposed by capitalist globalization. It should be noted that five countries labelled 'emerging countries' have developed mutual collaboration in a context called 'BRICS', after their respective initials: Brazil, Russia, India, China and South Africa.

---

3   '1. Qu'est-ce que le tiers-état ? – TOUT. 2. Qu'a-t-il été jusqu'à présent dans l'ordre politique? – RIEN. 3. Que demande-t-il? – À ÊTRE QUELQUE CHOSE' ('What is the Third Estate? Everything. What has it been hitherto in the political order? Nothing. What does it desire to be? Something'). Abbé Sieyès, *Q'est-ce que le tiers-état? précédé de l'Essai sur les privilèges* (1788) <alphahistory.com/frenchrevolution/sieyes-what-is-the-third-estate/> [accessed 24/11/2021].

4   Collège de France, 'Anciennes Chaires – Alfred Sauvy' <college-de-france.fr/site/anciennes-chaires/alfred_sauvy.htm> [accessed 05/04/2023].

9. *Countries in transition towards a market economy*: a euphemism for countries of Eastern Europe which, after the collapse of the USSR and the explosion of the Soviet bloc, underwent a process of capitalist revival.

> For the CADTM, the distinction North/South, developed/developing countries also covers the domination by international financial institutions (IFI) such as the World Bank, the IMF and other creditors that enforce imperialist and neocolonial policies under the control of the major powers in the North.

In this book, in spite of their various shortcomings, the following terms are used as synonyms: *countries of the South, South(s), Periphery, impoverished countries, developing countries, Third World.*

They are usually contrasted with: *countries of the North, North, Centre or Core countries* – also used as synonyms. This group is dominated by the main industrialized countries or imperialist countries. The United States, Western Europe and Japan are also referred to in this book as the 'Triad'.

In spite of our reluctance and because of statistical data, the CADTM feel we have no choice but to use categories established by the World Bank. That is because the CADTM do not have the resources to set up our own database on a global scale, one that would take into account more relevant standards than those the World Bank use to establish categories of countries.

In 2020, according to the World Bank, 'developing countries' comprises three categories, according to the countries' incomes, namely:

- 31 'low-income economies' (countries where the GDP per capita is lower than or equal to $1,025 per year);
- 47 'lower-middle-income economies' (countries where the GDP per capita stands between $1,026 and $3,995 per year);
- 60 'upper-middle-income economies' (countries where the GDP per capita stands between $3,996 and $12,375 per year).[5]

This classification ranks as 'developing' countries with economies as different from each other as Thailand and Haiti, Brazil and Niger, Russia and Bangladesh. The World Bank includes China among the 60 'higher-middle-income' economies. We have decided to treat China on its own considering the country's economic significance and the size of its population. According to our approach there are 137 countries of the South in 2020 (vs 138 according to the World Bank).

Schematically speaking, the South includes Latin America, the Caribbean, the Middle East, North Africa, Sub-Saharan Africa, South Asia, South-East Asia and the Pacific, Central Asia, Turkey and Central and Eastern European countries outside the EU, as well as Bulgaria and Romania, which are members of the EU (see the lists at the end of this Terminology section).

---

5   World Bank, 'World Bank country and lending groups', 2020 <datahelpdesk.worldbank.org/knowledgebase/articles/906519-world-bank-country-and-lending-groups> [accessed 24/11/2021].

When we use the term 'North' we mean the group of 80 countries identified by the World Bank as high-income economies, namely countries where the GDP per capita is over $12,375 per year.

The North thus includes Western European countries, Central and Eastern European countries that are members of the EU (except Bulgaria and Romania), the United States of America, Canada, Japan, South Korea, Australia, New Zealand and some 40 countries at various latitudes. Not all of these countries are 'industrialized' in the sense that their economies comprise a significant manufacturing sector. Indeed, some of those countries are hardly industrialized at all, but they are regarded by international bodies as having achieved a high level of income either because they managed to attract foreign capital, notably through their status as tax havens (such as Panama, the Seychelles, the Bahamas and the Cayman Islands), or because they can rely on income from oil extraction (such as the Arab States of the Persian Gulf or Brunei in South-East Asia).

WORLD DISTRIBUTION OF POPULATION, WEALTH AND CO2 EMISSIONS

Of a world population estimated at about 7.8 billion in 2020, countries of the South account for about 66 per cent, China for about 18 per cent and countries of the North for about 16 per cent (see Figure 0.1).[6]

Gross domestic product (GDP) is traditionally the index used by many economists to assess the production of wealth in the world. However, it only provides an imperfect, biased and disputable perception, for at least five reasons:

- unpaid labour, mainly that of women, which is vital for social reproduction, is not taken into account;

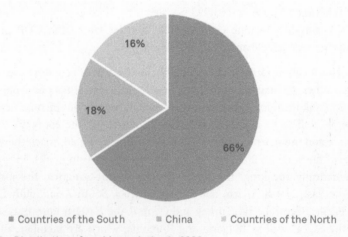

Figure 0.1   Distribution of world population in 2020
Source: United Nations, 2019

---

6   United Nations Organization, Department of Economic and Social Affairs, Population Division, *World Population Prospects 2019, Online Edition*, Rev. 1 <population.un.org/wpp/> [accessed 25/11/2021].

- environmental damage is not recorded as negative (see 'Geographical breakdown of CO2e emissions' below);
- the account unit used is the price of a good or service, not the amount of work required to produce it;
- inequalities within countries are not taken into account;
- the impact of debt on the progression of economic, political, social and cultural indices is excluded.

In spite of these shortcomings, the GDP reveals deep economic imbalances between the North and the South. The GDP, as well as other economic indices used in this study, is expressed in US dollars (USD) – except when otherwise specified – since nowadays about 60 per cent of foreign exchange reserves,[7] 88 per cent of international trade[8] and the majority of loans are denominated in that currency.

The accumulation of wealth is largely concentrated in the North, in almost inverse proportion to the distribution of population. While the share of the North in the accumulation of world wealth has decreased over the past years, it should be noted that the reason for this is not the accumulation of a larger share by countries of the South, but China's strong economic growth (see Tables 0.1 and 0.2).

The per capita GDP figures shown in Table 0.2 reveal the huge economic gap between North and South.

Table 0.1   Breakdown of gross world product by country category

Regions	Distribution of gross world product		
	In 2010	In 2018	In 2020
Gross world GDP	$66,108.9 billion	$85,968.7 billion	$84,456.2 billion
Countries of the North (high-income economies)	68.8%	63.5%	63.3%
China	9.2%	16.2%	17.4%
Countries of the South	22%	20.4%	19.3%
incl. higher-middle-income economies (except China)	13.2%	11.3%	10%
incl. lower-middle-income economies	7.9%	8.5%	8.7%
incl. low-income economies	0.9%	0.5%	0.5%

Source: World Bank (totals and subtotals may not be consistent due to rounding)[9]

The Gross world product (GWP) is equal to the total of all gross domestic products (GDP) of all the states on the planet. It is expressed in US dollars (USD).

---

7   International Monetary Fund, 'World Currency Composition of Official Foreign Exchange Reserves, 3rd term 2019' <data.imf.org/?sk=E6A5F467-C14B-4AA8-9F6D-5A09EC4E62A4> [accessed 25/11/2021].

8   Bank for International Settlements, *Triennial Central Bank Survey, Foreign Exchange Turnover in April 2019* (Bank for International Settlements, 16 September 2019) <bis.org/statistics/rpfx19_fx.pdf> [accessed 25/11/2021].

9   *World Bank Open Data* <data.worldbank.org> [accessed 07/04/2022].

Table 0.2   GDP per capita by country category

Region	GDP per capita (in USD)		
	In 2010	In 2018	In 2020
World	9,605.6	11,347.3	10,918.7
North *(high-income economies)*	39,411.9	45,240.6	44,003.4
China	4,550.5	9,905.3	10,434.8
South	3,590.2	4,933.1	4,754.8
incl. higher-middle-income economies (China included)	6,324.5	9,468.9	9,177.8
incl. lower-middle-income economies	1,806.5	2,267.6	2,217.2
incl. low-income economies	1,125.4	674.4	691.2

Source: World Bank[10]

Geographical breakdown of CO2e emissions[11]

We know that the countries currently emitting the most greenhouse gases are countries of the North, China, Brazil and India. Political leaders and CEOs in countries of the North frequently reiterate the notion that China now emits the most greenhouse gases (GHG) and should thus make the greatest effort to reduce those emissions and fight climate change. That discourse is actually a way of avoiding any acknowledgement of the historical responsibility of the countries of the North for GHG emissions going back to the Industrial Revolution in the nineteenth century (GHG remain present for decades in the atmosphere, and their consequences on climate change can persist 40 years after their emission). It also ignores the part played by China in the international division of labour: much of China's GHG emissions result from its manufacture of goods that are sold worldwide – and notably in the North where the domestic purchasing power is higher – by multinational corporations based in countries of the North.

A more detailed analysis of CO2e emissions, taking 'imported emissions' into account,[12] further widens the gap between countries of the North and countries of the South (see Figures 0.2 and 0.3).

World population in 2019: Low-income countries: 668.45 million inhabitants, or 8.71%; Lower-middle-income countries: 2.91 billion inhabitants, or 37.97%; Higher-middle-income countries: 2.86 billion inhabitants, or 37.22%; High-income countries: 1.23 billion inhabitants, or 16.11%.

---

10   *World Bank Open Data* <data.worldbank.org> [accessed 07/04/2022].
11   CO2e, which stands for 'CO2 equivalent', accounts for greenhouse gases (GHG) that are not taken into account if we only refer to CO2.
12   An example of 'imported emissions' would be a US textile company that produces in China but whose products are sold in the USA.

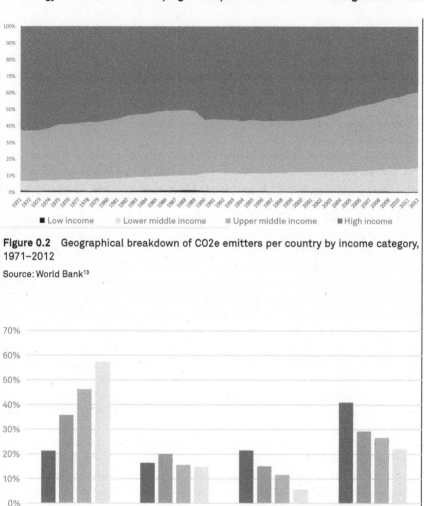

Figure 0.2   Geographical breakdown of CO2e emitters per country by income category, 1971–2012

Source: World Bank[13]

Figure 0.3   Breakdown of carbon emissions worldwide, 2010–18[14]

13   World Bank, 'World Development Indicators' <databank.worldbank.org> [latest data available 16/12/2021].
14   Chart from Thomas Piketty, *Capital and Ideology* (Cambridge, MA: The Belknap Press of Harvard University Press, 2020), chapter 13 <piketty.pse.ens.fr/en/ideologie> [accessed 25/11/2021].

Reading the chart: The share of North America (US and Canada) in total carbon emissions (direct and indirect) is 21% on average for 2010–18; it represents 36% of individual emissions greater than the world average (6.2t CO2e per year), 46% of emissions greater than 2.3 times the world average (or the top 10% of individual emissions worldwide, responsible for 45% of total emissions, vs 13% for the least-emitting 50%), and a huge 57% of emissions greater than 9.1 times the world average (in other words, the top 1% of individual emissions worldwide are responsible for 14% of all emissions).

Similarly, the Global Footprint Network has developed an indicator which combines the Human Development Index (HDI) and countries' environmental footprints. The purpose of the HDI is to attempt to measure the level of countries' development not simply in terms of their economic weight as measured by the GDP, whose shortcomings have been pointed out; the HDI combines three series of data: health/longevity, knowledge or level of education, and standard of living. The HDI is calculated by the United Nations Development Programme (UNDP). Taking those two variants (the HDI and countries' environmental footprints) into account results in a very different analysis of 'development': in 2015, no single country in the world combined a high HDI and a sustainable environmental footprint. On the other hand, countries that were close to doing so were mainly located in Latin America, with Cuba in the lead.[15]

What this means is that the countries of the North have been able to achieve economic development and relatively high living standards at the cost of high GHG emissions. In the struggle against climate change, countries of the North have to reduce a much higher proportion of their emissions than do countries of the South if we are to achieve a transition to an energy system using 100 per cent renewable resources, but also improve living standards in countries of the South within the strictures of the necessary drastic reduction of emissions at a global level. It is essential to call out the responsibility of large capitalist corporations over the past two centuries. Very large corporations that emerged during the nineteenth century or at the beginning of the twentieth have a huge responsibility for GHG emissions. They include Cargill (founded in 1865), Coca-Cola (1886), Pepsi-Cola (1898), Monsanto (1901) and Unilever (1930) in the agri-food sector; ExxonMobil (1870), Chevron (1879), Shell (1907), BP (1909) and Total (1924) in the oil industry; ThyssenKrupp (1811) and ArcelorMittal (made up of various groups that developed in the first half of the twentieth century) in the steel and metal industry; in the automotive industry, Renault-Nissan-Mitsubishi (a group of three companies founded between 1870 and 1932), Ford (1903), General Motors (1908) and Volkswagen (1937); in the mining sector, Rio Tinto (1873) and BHP Billiton (1895). If we were to calculate the amount of GHG that these corporations have produced since they were founded, we would realize that it covers a very high proportion of the GHG that have accumulated in the atmosphere – a time bomb that eventually exploded. More recently we have to add to that a number of private or public companies in emergent capitalist

15   See *Sustainable Development: Making it Measurable*, 'Human Development Index & ecological footprint per person for nations' (Global Footprint Network, 2015) <footprintnetwork.org/content/images/article_uploads/2015_HDI_poster_final_low_res.pdf> [accessed 25/11/2021].

countries which also have a highly damaging effect on the environment, such as Gazprom and Rosneft in Russia, Sinopec and PetroChina in China, Petrobras and Vale do Rio Doce in Brazil, and Coal India and Tata in India. Basically, whether in the North or in the South, the capitalist mode of production is responsible for the destruction of the Earth. Rather than blaming humankind at large for the ecological crisis, as is implicit in the use of the term 'anthropocene' to designate our epoch, we should instead use 'capitalocene', because it is the capitalist mode of production that is responsible for climate change.

BEYOND THE NORTH–SOUTH DIVIDE: CLASS EXPLOITATION IN ALL COUNTRIES

Yet such a survey of the global economic situation is incomplete, since it bypasses the huge inequalities in income and wealth accumulation within nations. Capitalism has spread over the entire planet. It is a system under which the capitalist class, which accounts for a tiny minority of the population, gets richer and richer due to the wealth produced by the labour of the majority of the population, but also due to the exploitation of nature, without any concern for its physical limits. Dispossessed of ownership of the means of production, most people are forced to sell their labour power to capitalists (the owners of the means of production), who try to pay the workforce as little as possible, thus preventing the majority of the population from escaping the social conditions in which they find themselves. Conversely, wealth accumulated by capitalists makes it possible for them to invest in various sectors so as to diversify the sources of the profit they derive from exploiting both humans and nature.

In order to keep profits at their highest level and to make sure that this mode of production endures, the capitalist class try not only to pay the lowest wages possible, but also to prevent redistribution of wealth by paying as little tax as possible and by opposing social policies such as public services (whether housing, transport, health care or education). Capital also tries to prevent workers from organizing, in particular by attacking labour rights – the right to form trade unions, to go on strike, to engage in collective bargaining, etc. Conversely, workers must organize if they want to acquire social rights and fight those inequalities. This means that there is a class struggle at the international level, the intensity of which depends on the level of collective organization of working people in the face of blatant injustices in a given place and at a given time.

Economic inequalities between various groups can be measured in terms of the wealth possessed by individuals and the income they earn (income from labour – wages, pensions, various social benefits – and income from capital such as corporate profits, dividends received by shareholders, etc.)

The poorest groups among the world population own literally less than nothing: they are indebted and owe money to their creditors – generally banks; in other words, to the richest segment of the population. In the United States, about 12 per cent of the population, over 38 million inhabitants, are indebted beyond what they can ever hope to repay.[16] Their debts (mostly student loans and mortgages) are so high that the cumulated assets of the poorer 50 per cent are negative (−0.1 per cent).[17]

That is why we should never oppose North and South as though they were homogeneous entities, but rather create a global 'geography': most decisions are made by a tiny minority in both the North and South (the 1 per cent) but have heavy negative consequences for the overwhelming majority of the population in the South as in the North (the 99 per cent). The system of domination and exploitation exists and is being reproduced within each country and each region (see Tables 0.3 and 0.4).

In India, for instance, a tiny minority is becoming phenomenally rich thanks to labour performed by hundreds of thousands of poor Indians. In January 2020 and in another region of the world, the International Consortium of Investigative Journalists (ICIJ) exposed the mechanisms of predation and spoliation used by

Table 0.3   Inequality in the distribution of wealth

Respective shares of various groups in total wealth	USA (2014)	France (2014)	China (2014)	India (2012)
Top 10%	73%	55.3%	66.7%	62.8%
Top 1%	38.6%	23.4%	27.8%	30.7%
Next 9%	34.4%	31.9%	38.9%	32.1%
Middle 40%	27.1%	38.4%	26.7%	30.8%
Poorest 50%	−0.1%	6.3%	6.6%	6.4%

Source: World Inequality Database (the total in some columns may not equal 100% because of rounding)

Table 0.4   Inequality in the distribution of income

Respective shares of total income held by various groups	World (2016)	EU28 (2016)	USA (2014)	China (2015)	India (2015)
Top 10%	52.1%	33.4%	47%	41.4%	56.1%
Top 1%	20.4%	10.3%	20.2%	13.9%	21.3%
Next 9%	31.7%	23.1%	26.8%	27.5%	34.8%
Middle 40%	38.2%	44.6%	40.4%	43.7%	29.2%
Poorest 50%	9.7%	22%	12.6%	14.8%	14.7%

Source: World Inequality Database (the total in some columns may not equal 100% because of rounding)

---

16   Chuck Collins, 'Negative Wealth Matters', Inequality.org, 28 January 2016 <inequality.org/great-divide/negative-wealth-matters/> [accessed 25/11/2021].

17   World Inequality Database <wid.world> [accessed 25/11/2021].

Isabel dos Santos to become the richest woman in Africa, at the expense of the people in her country, Angola.[18]

In the United States, the world's leading economy, over 14 million households were unable to repay their mortgages and were evicted following the subprime crisis in 2006 (but massive foreclosures had occurred before and still occur today).

Beyond the distinction between geographical blocs, what is at stake is the exploitation of the overwhelming majority of the population, in the South as in the North, by a tiny minority of the capitalist class, also sometimes called the 1 per cent. This ruling class is motivated by a quest for maximum short-term profit. We have to understand and fight this division, otherwise we run the risk of not perceiving relevant alternatives in our struggle for the emancipation of the majority who are victims of exploitation and oppression.

PATRIARCHAL DOMINANCE

Similarly, the oppression and exploitation of women everywhere in the world must be pointed to. The oppression of women goes back a long way and existed before capitalism, but the capitalist system has transformed and reinforced certain of its traits. We use the term 'patriarchy' to designate a form of social organization – the dominant form today – under which there is a binary division between 'men' and 'women', with constraining gender norms imposed on each. Under it, power – economic, political, familial, etc. – is mainly held by men. Women, and also minorities in terms of gender and sexual orientation, are subjected to a long list of forms of oppression. In the context of capitalism, patriarchy means that women and gender minorities are assigned most of the tasks related to 'social reproduction' (also referred to by the term 'care work' – see chapter 27 and the Glossary). These tasks (such as education, care-giving, food acquisition and preparation, etc.) produce and regenerate the living conditions of the labour force, and thus perpetuate capitalism. They are usually performed within the family, and are unpaid and unseen, but they are also performed by underpaid and undervalued workers in the health and education sectors, for example. That oppression is reproduced in several ways beyond strictly economic aspects: through language, filiation, stereotypes, religions, culture, etc. The oppression of women and the patriarchal system are part and parcel of capitalist exploitation, whether in the South or in the North, along with other mechanisms of domination such as racism. The consequences of illegitimate public and private debt reinforce the oppression of women.

---

18   See Joan Tilouine, "'Luanda Leaks': la mainmise d'Isabel dos Santos, la femme la plus riche d'Afrique, sur les finances de l'Angola' ('Luanda Leaks: the control of Isabel dos Santos, Africa's richest woman, over Angola's finances') *Le Monde*, 19 January 2020 (in French) <lemonde.fr/afrique/article/ 2020/01/19/luanda-leaks-la-mainmise-d-isabel-dos-santos-la-femme-la-plus-riche-d-afrique-sur-les-finances-de-l-angola_6026507_3212.html> [accessed 25/11/2021].

CENTRE–PERIPHERY RELATIONS IN THE NORTH AND IN THE SOUTH

Brazil's large private corporations exert imperialist relationships of dominance on neighbouring countries in Latin America; China's big corporations similarly dominate other countries in Africa and Southern and South-East Asia. Such relationships are sometimes called 'sub-imperialism', 'peripheral imperialism' or 'regional imperialism'.

Within the European Union, whose member states are almost all part of the North (except for Romania and Bulgaria), peripheral countries are dominated by countries with stronger economies and their large private corporations. This applies to countries in the so-called South Periphery such as Greece, Cyprus, Spain and Portugal and to countries in the so-called East Periphery, in Central and Eastern Europe. Within the United States, people in Puerto Rico are subjected to a neocolonial relationship.

We must therefore add the concept of economic centres and peripheries at a regional and continental level to enable a better understanding of international relationships.[19] The Centre–Periphery model clarifies the system of oppression by a Centre consisting of dominant economies that enforce their conditions on the peripheral economies. That system, based on unequal relationships and dependency mechanisms, operates in the service of capital accumulation.

LIST OF SOUTHERN AND NORTHERN COUNTRIES
(ACCORDING TO WORLD BANK CLASSIFICATION)

LOW-INCOME ECONOMIES (GDP PER CAPITA: $1,025 OR LESS):

Afghanistan, Benin, Burkina Faso, Burundi, Central African Republic, Chad, Democratic Republic of Congo (Congo-Kinshasa), Eritrea, Ethiopia, Gambia, Guinea, Guinea-Bissau, Haiti, North Korea, Liberia, Madagascar, Malawi, Mali, Mozambique, Nepal, Niger, Rwanda, Sierra Leone, Somalia, South Sudan, Syria, Tajikistan, Tanzania, Togo, Uganda, Yemen

LOWER-MIDDLE-INCOME ECONOMIES (GDP PER CAPITA: $1,026 TO $3,995):

Angola, Bangladesh, Bhutan, Bolivia, Cambodia, Cameroon, Cape Verde, Comoros, Republic of Congo (Congo-Brazzaville), Côte d'Ivoire, Djibouti, Arab Republic of Egypt, El Salvador, Eswatini, Ghana, Honduras, India, Indonesia, Kenya, Kiribati, Kyrgyzstan, Laos, Lesotho, Mauritania, Federated States of Micronesia, Moldova, Mongolia, Morocco, Myanmar, Nicaragua, Nigeria, Pakistan, Papua New Guinea, Philippines, São Tomé and Príncipe, Senegal, Solomon Islands, Sudan, East Timor, Tunisia, Ukraine, Uzbekistan, Vanuatu, Vietnam, West Bank and Gaza, Zambia, Zimbabwe

---

19   See François Houtart, 'Rapports Nord-Sud ou la rigueur des concepts' ('North–South relations or the rigorousness of concepts'), *Alternatives Sud*, 2016, Vol. 23, No. 2, pp. 157–78 (in French).

HIGHER-MIDDLE-INCOME ECONOMIES (GDP PER CAPITA: $3,996 TO $12,375):

Albania, Algeria, American Samoa, Argentina, Armenia, Azerbaijan, Belarus, Belize, Bosnia and Herzegovina, Botswana, Brazil, Bulgaria, China, Colombia, Costa Rica, Cuba, Dominica, Dominican Republic, Ecuador, Equatorial Guinea, Fiji, Gabon, Georgia, Grenada, Guatemala, Guyana, Iran, Iraq, Jamaica, Jordan, Kazakhstan, Kosovo, Lebanon, Libya, Malaysia, Maldives, Marshall Islands, Mauritius, Mexico, Montenegro, Namibia, Nauru, Northern Macedonia, Paraguay, Peru, Romania, Russian Federation, Saint Lucia, Saint Vincent and the Grenadines, Samoa, Serbia, South Africa, Sri Lanka, Suriname, Thailand, Tonga, Turkey, Turkmenistan, Tuvalu, Venezuela

HIGH-INCOME ECONOMIES (GDP PER CAPITA: $12,376 OR MORE):

Andorra, Antigua and Barbuda, Aruba, Australia, Austria, Bahamas, Bahrain, Barbados, Belgium, Bermuda, Brunei Darussalam, Canada, Cayman Islands, Channel Islands, Chile, Cyprus, Croatia, Curaçao, Czech Republic, Denmark, Estonia, Faroe Islands, Finland, France, French Polynesia, Germany, Gibraltar, Greece, Greenland, Guam, Hong Kong, Hungary, Iceland, Ireland, Isle of Man, Israel, Italy, Japan, South Korea, Kuwait, Latvia, Liechtenstein, Lithuania, Luxembourg, Macao, Malta, Monaco, Netherlands, New Caledonia, New Zealand, Northern Mariana Islands, Norway, Oman, Palau, Panama, Poland, Portugal, Puerto Rico, Qatar, San Marino, Saudi Arabia, Seychelles, Singapore, Saint Martin (French part), Sint-Maarten (Dutch part), Slovakia, Slovenia, Spain, Sweden, Switzerland, Taiwan, Trinidad and Tobago, Turks and Caicos Islands, United Arab Emirates, United Kingdom, United States, Uruguay, Virgin Islands (United States)

Introduction

The list of governments resulting from military coups supported by the World Bank is an impressive one.

Among the better-known examples are the dictatorship of the Shah of Iran after the overthrow of Prime Minister Mohammad Mossadegh in 1953; the military dictatorship in Guatemala put in place by the USA after the 1954 overthrow of the progressive government of democratically elected president Jacobo Árbenz; that of the Duvaliers in Haiti beginning in 1957; the dictatorship of General Park Chung-hee in South Korea from 1961; the dictatorship of the Brazilian generals starting in 1964; of Mobutu in the Congo (Zaire) and Suharto in Indonesia beginning in 1965; the military dictatorship in Thailand starting in 1966; the regimes of Idi Amin Dada in Uganda and General Hugo Banzer in Bolivia in 1971; the rule of Ferdinand Marcos in the Philippines beginning in 1972; those of Augusto Pinochet in Chile, the Uruguayan generals, and Juvénal Habyarimana in Rwanda starting in 1973; the junta in Argentina from 1976; the Arap Moi regime in Kenya starting in 1978; the dictatorship in Pakistan from 1978; Saddam Hussein's coup in 1979; and the military dictatorship in Turkey starting in 1980. We could add Ben Ali in Tunisia from 1987 to 2011. And Mubarak in Egypt from 1981 to 2011.

Among the other dictatorships supported by the World Bank, we should also mention Somoza's in Nicaragua until his fall in 1979 and Ceaușescu's in Romania. Some are still in place today: the dictatorship of Idriss Déby in Chad, that of Abdel-Fattah al-Sissi in Egypt, and many more. Neither should we forget the Bank's support for dictatorships in Europe – Franco's in Spain and Salazar's in Portugal.

Very clearly, the World Bank has methodically supported despotic regimes – whether or not they came into power via coups – who conduct or conducted antisocial policies and commit crimes against humanity. The Bank has shown a total lack of respect for the constitutional principles of some of its member countries. It has never hesitated to support criminal military putschists who are economically docile at the expense of democratic, but less submissive, governments. And with good reason: the World Bank does not consider respect for human rights to be part of its mission.

The World Bank's support for the apartheid regime in South Africa from 1951 until 1968 must not be forgotten. The World Bank explicitly refused to apply a resolution of the General Assembly of the United Nations adopted in 1964 (see chapter 3), which required all the agencies of the UN to cease financial support for South Africa because the country was in violation of the Charter of the United Nations. That support, and the violation of international law it implies, must not go unpunished.

Lastly, as shall be seen in these pages, during the 1950s and 1960s the World Bank systematically granted loans to colonial powers and their colonies for projects that increased exploitation of natural resources and of colonized peoples for the benefit of the ruling classes in the colonizer countries. It is in that context that the World Bank refused to apply a United Nations resolution adopted in 1965 calling on the Bank to refrain from supporting Portugal financially and technically until the country's government abandoned its colonialist policies.[1]

The debts contracted with the World Bank on decision of the colonial powers by the African colonies of Belgium, Britain and France were subsequently imposed on the newly independent countries.

The World Bank's support for dictatorial regimes takes the form of financial support as well as technical and economic assistance. That financial support and that assistance have helped these dictatorial regimes maintain power and perpetrate their crimes. The World Bank has also contributed to ensuring that these regimes are not isolated on the international scene, since the loans and technical assistance have always facilitated relations with private banks and transnational companies. The neoliberal model was gradually imposed in the world beginning with the dictatorship of Augusto Pinochet in 1973 in Chile and Ferdinand Marcos in the Philippines in 1972. Both regimes were actively supported by the World Bank. Whenever such dictatorial regimes come to an end, the World Bank has systematically required any democratic government that succeeds them to take on the burden of the debts contracted by their predecessors. In other words, the Bank's financial complicity with dictatorships is transformed into a burden for the respective peoples. And those peoples are forced to continue paying, even today, for the weapons purchased by the dictators and used to oppress them.

In the 1980s and 1990s, and again in a second wave between 2011 and 2020, many dictatorships collapsed, some of them under the battering ram of powerful democratic movements. The regimes that replaced them have generally submitted to the policies recommended or imposed by the World Bank and the IMF and have continued repaying debts that are odious in nature. The neoliberal model, imposed with the aid of dictatorships, is now maintained through the yoke of debt and ongoing 'structural adjustments'. This is because after the overthrow or collapse of the dictatorships, the democratic governments that replace them have continued

---

1   The World Bank continued to grant loans to Portugal until 1967.

applying policies that in fact impede attempts to implement a development model based on autonomy. The new phase of globalization that began in the 1980s at the time of the explosion of the debt crisis is generally accompanied by increased subordination of developing (Periphery) countries to the more industrialized (Core) countries, which now include China. We have also seen the emergence of new authoritarian regimes with Jair Bolsonaro in Brazil (2019–22), Jeanine Áñez (2019–20) in Bolivia, Sebastián Piñera in Chile (2018–22), Iván Duque in Colombia (2018–22) and Rodrigo Duterte in the Philippines (2016–22). All these governments are supported by the World Bank and the IMF. Not to mention the Saudi regime, which is a pillar of both institutions.

THE HIDDEN AGENDA OF THE WASHINGTON CONSENSUS

Since the World Bank and the IMF first began their activities, the major decisions of the Bank and the Fund have remained aligned with the orientations of the US government via a mechanism that is both simple to understand and complex to put in place. At times, certain European governments (in particular those of the UK, France and Germany) and that of Japan have had a voice, but such cases are rare. Friction sometimes emerges between the White House and the leadership of the World Bank and IMF, but a rigorous analysis of history since the end of the Second World War shows that until now, the US government has always had the last word where its direct interests are concerned.

The agenda of the Washington Consensus, as stated, is to reduce poverty through growth, the free operation of market forces, free trade, and minimum intervention by public authorities. But the Washington Consensus has a hidden agenda: guaranteeing that US dominance is maintained worldwide and freeing capitalism from the limits that had been placed on it in the post-1945 period – limits established under pressure from a combination of powerful social mobilizations both in the South and in the North, the incipient emancipation of certain colonized peoples and attempts at finding an exit from capitalism. The Washington Consensus is also bent on imposing and intensifying the productivist-extractivist model.

Over recent decades, in the context of this Consensus, the World Bank and the IMF have strengthened their ability to exert pressure on a great many countries by taking advantage of the situation created by the debt crisis. The World Bank has developed subsidiaries (the International Finance Corporation – IFC, the Multilateral Investment Guarantee Agency – MIGA, the International Centre for Settlement of Investment Disputes – ICSID) as it weaves a tighter and tighter web that is more and more difficult to escape from.

An example of how this works: the World Bank grants a loan on condition that a water treatment and distribution system be privatized. As a result, the public company is sold to a private consortium among whose members just happens to be the IFC, a subsidiary of the World Bank. When the population impacted by the privatization revolts against the drastic rate increases and the reduction in the quality of services and the public authorities seek redress from the predatory transnational, the case is entrusted to the ICSID, also a subsidiary of the Bank, which serves as both judge and jury. The result is a situation where the World Bank Group has influence at all levels: 1) the imposition and financing of privatization (World Bank); 2) investment in the privatized company (IFC); 3) insurance and guarantees for that company (MIGA); 4) arbitration of disputes (ICSID). And that is exactly what happened in 2004–05 at El Alto in Bolivia (see Annex 1: The World Bank: An ABC, at the end of this volume).

Collaboration between the World Bank and the IMF is also fundamental for exercising maximum pressure on public authorities. And to complete the process of putting the public sphere and public authorities under its control and further extending the dominance of the model, World Bank/IMF collaboration now extends to the World Trade Organization (WTO) since that entity's creation in 1995.

Thus, there is a fundamental difference between the agenda proclaimed by the Washington Consensus and its hidden reality.

The hidden agenda, the one that is actually applied, is to subordinate the public and private spheres of all human societies to the capitalist imperative of seeking maximum profit. The implementation of this hidden agenda results in reproducing poverty rather than reducing it and in increasing inequalities rather than reducing them. It results in stagnation, if not deterioration, of the living conditions of a great majority of the world's population, concurrently with greater and greater concentration of wealth in the hands of a smaller and smaller elite. A further result is the continued deterioration of ecological balances, which means that the very future of humanity is in danger.

One of the numerous paradoxes of this hidden agenda is that in the name of ending the dictatorship of the state and liberating the forces of the market, governments – allied with transnational corporations – use the coercive action of multilateral public institutions (World Bank–IMF–WTO) to impose their model on the people.

THE WAY OUT IS TO MAKE A CLEAN BREAK

It is for these reasons that there needs to be a radical break with the Washington Consensus and the model the World Bank applies.

The mechanism of power that is the Washington Consensus must not be understood as being a project that is limited to the government in Washington and its 'infernal trio'. The European Commission, most European governments and the Japanese government are also committed to the Washington Consensus and have translated its programme into their languages, constitutional projects and political programmes.

Breaking with the Washington Consensus, if that is limited to ending domination by the US via the World Bank–IMF–WTO troika, is not an alternative, because the other major powers are ready to take the place of the US in order to pursue similar goals. Let's imagine for a moment that the European Union might supplant the US as worldwide leader. That would not fundamentally alter the situation of the peoples of the planet because it would amount to simply replacing one Northern capitalist bloc (one pole of the Triad – that is, North America, Western Europe and Japan) with another. Let's imagine another possibility: the China–Brazil–India–South Africa–Russia bloc gains strength and supplants the Triad countries. If that bloc's motivations are in line with the current attitude of the governments in place and the dominant economic system they submit to, again there would be no real improvement. No, the Washington Consensus must be replaced by a consensus of peoples founded on rejection of capitalism.

The belief that development and the productivist model are interdependent must be radically challenged. Such a development model excludes any protection of cultures and their diversity; it exhausts natural resources and irremediably damages the environment. That model considers the protection of human rights to be at best a long-term goal (when in fact in the long term we will all be dead). Most often, human rights are perceived as an obstacle to growth. The productivist model considers equality an obstacle, if not a danger.

BREAK THE INFERNAL SPIRAL OF INDEBTEDNESS

The attempt to improve living conditions for peoples via public indebtedness is a failure. The World Bank claims that in order to develop, countries must rely on external debt and attract foreign investments.[2] The debt serves mainly to purchase equipment and consumer goods from the industrialized countries. For decades the facts have demonstrated, over and over again, that this does not lead to development.

According to the dominant economic theory, development in the South is held back by a shortage of domestic capital (that is, local savings). Still according to dominant economic theory, countries who want to launch business projects or accelerate their development must rely on external capital via three channels: first, contracting external debt; second, attracting foreign investments; third, increasing exportation to bring in the hard currency necessary for purchasing foreign goods that enable growth. The poorest countries supposedly also need to attract aid by conducting themselves in ways that gain the favour of the developed countries.

---

2   The vocabulary used to designate the countries to which the World Bank offers its development loans has evolved over the years: at first the term 'backward regions' was used; then the term 'underdeveloped countries' was adopted, and finally the 'developing countries' used today, with 'emerging countries' applied to some.

Reality contradicts that theory: in fact, the developing countries provide the capital to the industrialized countries,[3] and to the economy of the USA in particular. The World Bank said so itself in a report published in 2003: 'Developing countries, in aggregate, were net lenders to developed countries.'[4]

If popular political movements were able to gain governmental power in several developing countries and create their own development bank and their own international monetary fund, they would be quite able to do without the World Bank, the IMF and the private financial institutions in the highly industrialized countries. It is not true that developing countries must resort to indebtedness to finance their development. Today, indebtedness serves essentially to continue the flow of debt repayments. Despite the existence of large foreign reserves, the governments and ruling classes of the South do not increase investments in local production and social spending.

The dominant view that sees indebtedness as an absolute need must be challenged and rejected. Further, countries must not hesitate to cancel or repudiate odious and illegitimate debts.

CANCEL ODIOUS DEBTS

According to the odious debt doctrine formulated in 1927 by Alexander Nahum Sack (1890–1955), a debt may be considered odious if it fulfils two conditions:

1. The population does not enjoy the benefits of the loan: the debt was incurred not in the interests of the people or the state but against their interest and/or in the personal interest of the leaders or persons holding power.
2. Lenders' complicity: the lenders had foreknowledge, or could have had foreknowledge, that the funds concerned would not benefit the population.

According to Sack's doctrine the democratic or despotic nature of a regime does not influence this general rule.

The father of the odious debt doctrine clearly states that 'regular governments [may] incur debts that are incontestably odious'. Sack defines a regular government as follows:

By a regular government is to be understood the supreme power that effectively exists within the limits of a given territory. Whether that government be monarchical (absolute or limited) or republican; whether it functions by 'the grace of God'

---

3   Milan Rivié, 'Illicit financial flows: Africa is the world's main creditor', CADTM5 November 2020 <cadtm.org/Illicit-Financial-Flows-Africa-is-the-world-s-main-creditor> [accessed 30/12/2021].
4   World Bank, *Global Development Finance 2003* (Washington, DC: World Bank, 2003), p. 13. In the 2005 edition of GDF, the Bank wrote: 'Developing countries are now capital exporters to the rest of the world.' (World Bank, *Global Development Finance 2005*, p. 56).

or 'the will of the people'; whether it express 'the will of the people' or not, of all the people or only of some; whether it be legally established or not, etc., none of that is relevant to the problem we are concerned with.[5]

In Sack's words, a debt may be considered odious if: 'a) the purpose which the former government wanted to cover by the debt in question was odious and clearly against the interests of the population of the whole or part of the territory, and b) the creditors, at the moment of the issuance of the loan, were aware of its odious purpose.' He continues: 'Once these two points are established, the burden of proof that the funds were used for the general or special needs of the state and were not of an odious character would be upon the creditors.'[6]

This doctrine, which has been applied several times in history by various governments, is also useful for denouncing as odious the debts whose repayment is currently being demanded of countries of the South and countries such as Greece by the World Bank and the IMF.

MAKE USE OF LEGITIMATE LOANS AND FINANCE THE STATE THROUGH SOCIALLY JUST TAXES

That being said, public indebtedness is not in itself a bad thing if it is envisaged in a radically different way than under the current system. Public borrowing is quite legitimate if it serves legitimate projects and if those who contribute to the loan do so legitimately.

Public debt could be used to finance ambitious programmes of ecological transition instead of to enforce antisocial, extractivist, productivist policies that foster competition between nations. Public authorities can use bond issues to, for example:

- finance the complete closure of thermal and nuclear power plants;
- replace fossil energies with renewable sources of energy that respect the environment;
- finance a conversion from current farming methods, which contribute to climate change and use large amounts of chemical inputs which decrease biodiversity, to methods that favour local production of organic food to make farming compatible with the fight against climate change;
- radically reduce air and road transport and develop collective transport and the use of railways;

---

5   Alexander Nahum Sack, *Les effets des transformations des états sur leurs dettes publiques et autres obligations financières* (*The Effects of the Transformation of States on Their Public Debt and Other Financial Obligations*), (Paris: Recueil Sirey, 1927). Abridged document freely available (in French) on the CADTM website: <http://cadtm.org/IMG/pdf/Alexander_Sack_DETTE_ODIEUSE.pdf> [accessed 30/12/2021].

6   See Éric Toussaint, 'The doctrine of odious debt: from Alexander Sack to the CADTM', CADTM 24 November 2016 <cadtm.org/The-Doctrine-of-Odious-Debt-from> [accessed 05/04/2023].

- finance an ambitious programme of low-energy social housing;
- finance public medical research and expenditures for public health to deal with the serious health problems that affect humanity.

A government of the people will not hesitate to force corporations (whether national, foreign or multinational), as well as richer households, to contribute to the bond issue without drawing any profit from it, i.e. with zero interest and without compensation for inflation.

At the same time, a large portion of working-class households will easily be persuaded to entrust their savings to the public authorities to fund the legitimate projects mentioned above. This voluntary funding by the working classes would be remunerated at a positive actual rate, for instance 4 per cent. This means that if annual inflation reached 3 per cent, the public authorities would pay a nominal interest rate of 7 per cent, to guarantee an actual rate of 4 per cent. Such a mechanism would be perfectly legitimate since it would finance projects that are really useful to society and would help reduce the wealth of the rich while increasing the income of the working classes.

Other measures can also be taken to finance the budget of the state in a legitimate way: obtaining credit from the central bank at zero interest, establishing a tax on large fortunes and very high incomes, levying fines on companies guilty of large-scale tax evasion, radically reducing military expenditures, ending subsidies to banks and major corporations, increasing taxes on foreign companies, in particular in the raw-materials sector, and still more.

PEOPLES WILL LIBERATE THEMSELVES

In 2021, with the exception of Cuba's, no government is raising the question of profoundly changing the rules of the game in favour of the people. The governments of China, Russia and the major developing countries (India, Brazil, Nigeria, Indonesia, Thailand, South Korea, Mexico, Algeria, South Africa, etc.) express no intention of changing, in practice, the world situation for the benefit of their peoples.

And yet, politically, if they wanted to do so, governments of the major developing countries together could constitute a powerful movement capable of imposing fundamental democratic reforms of the entire multilateral system. They could adopt a radical policy: repudiate debt and apply a set of policies that break with neoliberalism.

I am convinced, however, that this will not materialize. The radical scenario will not be put in place in the short term. The overwhelming majority of current leaders of developing countries are totally caught up in the neoliberal model. In most cases, they are in full allegiance with the interests of the local ruling classes, who have no vision of actually distancing themselves from (let alone breaking with) the policies conducted by the major industrial powers, which today include China.

The great majority of capitalists in the South remain within a rentier lifestyle, or at best they endeavour to increase their market shares by maximizing their exploitation of working people and of nature. That is true of the capitalists in Brazil, South Korea, China, Russia, South Africa, India, etc., who pressure their governments to obtain concessions from the industrialized countries during bilateral or multilateral trade negotiations. In addition, competition and conflicts between governments of developing countries, between capitalists in the South, are real and may exacerbate. The aggressive trade attitude of capitalists in China, Russia, India, South Africa and Brazil towards their competitors in the South causes stubborn divisions. And yet generally, they make arrangements (between themselves and between the South and the North) to impose a deterioration of the conditions of working people in their countries under the pretext of increasing their competitiveness to the maximum.

But sooner or later the peoples will free themselves from the slavery of debt and oppression imposed on them by the ruling classes in the North and South. Through struggle, they will succeed in imposing policies that redistribute wealth and put an end to the productivist model that is so destructive of nature. Public authorities will then be forced to give absolute priority to guaranteeing fundamental human rights.

EXIT THE VICIOUS CYCLE OF INDEBTEDNESS

For that to happen, an alternative approach is required: the vicious cycle of indebtedness must be ended while avoiding the trap of a politics of charity aimed only at perpetuating a worldwide system dominated entirely by capital and by a few major powers and transnational companies. The solution is to set up an international system of redistribution of revenue and wealth in order to repair the centuries of looting to which the dominated peoples of the Periphery have been and still are subjected. These reparations, in the form of donations, would not give the industrialized countries any right to interfere in the affairs of the populations receiving compensation. In the South, mechanisms for deciding and overseeing how these funds would be used need to be invented and put in the hands of the people concerned and their public authorities. That opens up a vast area of reflection and experimentation.

The mobilization of farmers and fishermen in Gujarat (western India) who are victims of the environmental and social effects of a coal-fired power plant financed by the IFC, whose role within the World Bank Group is to finance private companies, led to an important ruling of the Supreme Court of the USA on 27 February 2019.[7] The justices ruled that the IFC is no longer entitled to the immunity given international organizations when financing commercial activities. This shows that popular action can get results.

---

7   United States Supreme Court, JAM ET AL. v. INTERNATIONAL FINANCE CORP. (2019), No. 17-1011 <caselaw.findlaw.com/us-supreme-court/17-1011.html> [accessed 30/12/2021].

ABOLISH THE WORLD BANK AND THE IMF

We need to go further and abolish the World Bank and the IMF and replace them with other international institutions that operate democratically. The new world bank and the new international monetary fund – whatever names they might be given – must have missions that are radically different from their predecessors'. They must guarantee adherence to international treaties on human rights (political, civil, social, economic and cultural) in the sphere of international credit and international monetary relations. These new global institutions must be part of a worldwide institutional system overseen by a radically reformed United Nations. It is essential, and must be a priority, that developing countries associate to create regional entities with a shared bank and monetary fund as soon as possible. During the crisis in South-East Asia and Korea in 1997–98, the creation of an Asian monetary fund had been envisaged by the countries concerned. The discussion was aborted following intervention by Washington. A lack of determination on the part of the governments concerned did the rest. In South America, under the leadership of the government of Hugo Chávez, the foundations of a Bank of the South were laid in 2008, but in the end the project did not become reality. In 2007–09, the government of Ecuador stood up to its creditors and won a victory, but the other governments of the left in the region did not follow.

RESTORE HEALTH SYSTEMS THAT THE WORLD BANK AND THE IMF HAVE CONTRIBUTED TO WEAKENING

In 2020, the worldwide health crisis caused by the Covid-19 pandemic has shown the extent to which the policies dictated by the World Bank/IMF and applied by governments have deteriorated public health services and allowed the disease to ravage populations. If governments had rejected the Washington Consensus and neoliberalism and strengthened the essential instruments of a sound public-health policy regarding personnel employed, infrastructures, stocks of medicines, equipment, research, production of medicines and treatments and health coverage for populations, the Coronavirus crisis would not have reached such proportions.

If governments had broken with the logic of austerity of the World Bank and the IMF, a radical increase in expenditures for public health would have also had highly beneficial effects on the fight against other diseases that mainly affect countries of the Global South. Instead, today, many states devote more resources to debt repayment than to health. For example, Congo devotes 2.5 times as many resources to repayment of external debt (11.3 per cent) than to health expenditures (4.4 per cent).[8]

---

8   Jubilee Debt Campaign, 'Comparing debt payments with health spending', April 2020 <jubileed-ebt.org.uk/wp-content/uploads/2020/04/Debt-payments-and-health-spending_13.04.20.pdf> [accessed 30/12/2021].

According to the latest *World Malaria Report*, published in December 2019, 228 million cases of malaria were detected in 2018 and the number of deaths from the disease was estimated at 405,000.[9] Tuberculosis, meanwhile, is one of the ten leading causes of death in the world. In 2018, ten million persons contracted tuberculosis and one million died from it (including 251,000 HIV-positive individuals). These diseases could be fought successfully if only governments would allocate the necessary resources.

Additional measures could successfully fight the malnutrition and hunger that are destroying the daily lives of one out of nine human beings (more than 800 million inhabitants of the planet). Approximately 2.5 million children die each year around the world of malnutrition, either directly or from diseases related to reduced immunity due to malnutrition. Similarly, if investments were made to massively increase supplies of clean water and wastewater removal and treatment, the number of deaths from diarrhoeal diseases, which is as high as 430,000 per year, would be reduced radically.

While the illegitimate debts that populations are being forced to repay should simply be cancelled, the World Bank, the IMF and the majority of government leaders mention only postponement and new formulas for further indebtedness. Covid-19 is being used as a pretext for reinforcing yet another cycle of massive indebtedness with conditions that ramp up austerity even more and compromise the well-being of future generations.

IMMEDIATELY SUSPEND REPAYMENT OF PUBLIC DEBTS

An immediate suspension of the repayment of public debts must be combined with an audit of the debts with citizen participation in order to identify the portions that are illegitimate and cancel them. One thing must be clear: if populations are to be emancipated and guaranteed their rights as humans, the new financial and monetary institutions, both regional and international, must be at the service of a social project that breaks with neoliberalism, extractivism, productivism ... in other words, with capitalism.

As much as possible must be done so that a new and powerful social and political movement can assist in the convergence of social struggles and contribute to working out a programme for breaking with capitalism by promoting anti-capitalist, antiracist, environmentalist, feminist, internationalist and socialist solutions.

It is of fundamental importance to work toward the socialization of banks with expropriation of their major shareholders; suspension of repayment of public debt until audits with citizen participation can be conducted in order to repudiate the illegitimate portion of the debts; imposition of a high crisis tax on the wealthiest

---

9   *World Malaria Report 2019* (World Health Organization, 2019) <who.int/publications/i/item/9789241565721> [accessed 08/02/2022].

individuals and entities; cancellation of illegitimate debts enforced against the working classes (student debt, abusive mortgage debts, abusive microcredits, etc.); closing down of stock and security exchanges, which enable speculation; radical reduction of working hours (with wages maintained) in order to create a large number of socially useful jobs; a radical increase in public expenditures for health and education; socialization of pharmaceutical companies and the energy sector; relocation of as much production as possible and development of short supply circuits; and many more essential demands.

1

The Origins of the
Bretton Woods Institutions

In order to prevent a recurrence of economic crises like the crash of 1929, but also to ensure world leadership in the post-war era, the United States government began to plan for the creation of international financial institutions as early as 1941. The World Bank and the International Monetary Fund (IMF) saw the light of day at the Bretton Woods Conference of 1944 in New Hampshire, USA. Initially, the administration of Franklin Roosevelt was in favour of creating strong institutions capable of imposing rules on the private financial sector, including Wall Street. But Roosevelt backed down in the face of the hostility of the banking world. Indeed, the distribution of votes within the World Bank and the IMF clearly illustrates the will of certain major powers to exert domination over the rest of the world.

IN THE BEGINNING[1]

It was in 1941, the year the United States entered the Second World War, that discussions were initiated concerning the international institutions to be set up once this major conflict was over. In May 1942, Harry White, chief international economist at the US Treasury, presented Franklin Roosevelt (US president from 1933 to 1945) with a blueprint entitled *Plan for a United and Associated Nations Stabilization Fund and a Bank for Reconstruction and Development of the United Nations.* One of its

---

1   This section is largely based on: 1) Robert W. Oliver, *International Economic Co-operation and the World Bank* (London: Macmillan Press, 1975); 2) Edward S. Mason and Robert E. Asher, *The World Bank since Bretton Woods* (Washington, DC: The Brookings Institution, 1973), chapter 1, pp. 11–35; 3) Devesh Kapur, John P. Lewis and Richard Webb, *The World Bank: Its First Half Century, Volume 1: History* (Washington, DC: Brookings Institution Press, 1997), specifically chapter 2, pp. 57–84; 4) Susan George and Fabrizio Sabelli, *Faith & Credit: The World Bank's Secular Empire* (New York: Routledge, 1994), chapter 1; 5) Bruce Rich, *Mortgaging the Earth* (Boston: Beacon Press, 1994), chapter 3, pp. 49–80; 6) Michel Aglietta and Sandra Moatti, *Le FMI. De l'ordre monétaire aux désordres financiers (The IMF: Monetary Order and Financial Disorder)* (Paris: Editions Economica, 2000), chapter 1, pp. 8–31; 7) Catherine Gwin, 'U.S. relations with the World Bank, 1945–1992,' in Devesh Kapur, John P. Lewis, and Richard Webb, *The World Bank: Its First Half Century, Volume 2: Perspectives* (Washington, DC: Brookings Institution Press, 1997), pp. 195–200.

objectives was to convince the Allied nations currently at war with the Axis powers (Germany, Italy and Japan) that once peace was established, certain systems would need to be adopted to prevent the world economy entering a depression similar to that of the 1930s.

Between 1941 and July 1944, when the Bretton Woods Conference assembled, several of the proposals contained in the initial plan were abandoned. But one of them came to fruition: the creation of the IMF and the IBRD (International Bank for Reconstruction and Development), better known as the World Bank.

To fully understand the roles attributed to these two institutions, we must go back to the late 1920s and the 1930s. The severe economic depression that gripped the United States during this period had a profound effect on world capitalism in general. One of the consequences was that in 1931 Germany stopped repayment of its war debt to France, Belgium, Italy and Great Britain. In a domino effect, these countries stopped repayment of their external debt to the United States.[2] As for the United States, it drastically reduced capital exports in 1928 and even more so in 1931.[3] At the same time, it cut down on imports. The result was that the flow of dollars from the United States to the rest of the world dried up, and countries with debts to the world's leading power did not have the dollars to repay them. Nor did they have the dollars they needed to buy North American products. The machinery of world capitalism was grinding to a halt. Competitive devaluations ensued as each country attempted to win market shares at the expense of the others. The developed capitalist world was caught in a downward spiral.

In 1932 John Maynard Keynes made this ironic remark about the attitude of the United States: 'The rest of the world owes them money. They will not take payment in goods; they will not take it in bonds; they have already all the gold there is. The puzzle which they have set to the rest of the world admits logically of only one solution, namely, that some way must be found of doing without their exports.'[4]

One of the conclusions drawn by the United States government under Roosevelt was that a great creditor nation must make currency available to debtor countries to be used for repayment of their debt. Another, bolder conclusion was that in certain cases, it is preferable to offer donations instead of loans if a state wants its exporting industries to gain maximum and lasting profit. This question will be dealt with later in the pages devoted to the Marshall Plan for the reconstruction of Europe (1948–51).

---

2   Éric Toussaint, *Your Money or Your Life*, chapter 7, pp. 131–36.
3   Robert W. Oliver, *International Economic Co-operation and the World Bank*, pp. 72–75, p. 109.
4   John Maynard Keynes, *Collected Writings*, Vol. XXI (London: Macmillan, 1982) quoted by Cheryl Payer, *Lent and Lost: Foreign Credit and Third World Development* (London: Zed Books, 1991), p. 20.

Let us take a closer look at the 1930s before going on to the founding of the Bretton Woods institutions during the Second World War.

FOUNDING OF THE EXPORT-IMPORT BANK OF WASHINGTON (1934)

The Export-Import Bank of Washington (the US public agency for export credit, later called Exim Bank) was created in 1934 to protect and promote US exporters. It guaranteed US exports and at the same time granted long-term credit to foreign buyers for the purchase of US goods and services. Each dollar lent had to be spent on merchandise produced in the United States. The Export-Import Bank released funds only on receipt of proof of shipment of goods abroad. At the start, the total amount of loans granted by the Export–Import Bank was a very modest one: $60 million in the first five years. But the volume of loans increased rapidly from then on. In 1940, the Bank's lending capacity was $200 million, and in 1945 it had reached $3,500 million. During its first years of operation, the Export-Import Bank targeted Latin America and the Caribbean, China and Finland, a reflection not only of the economic but also the geostrategic interests at stake.

FOUNDING OF THE INTER-AMERICAN BANK (1940)

In 1940 another financial institution was established: the Inter-American Bank. This was an inter-state bank founded on US initiative in the context of the Pan-American Union (the ancestor of the Organization of American States (OAS)). The original members included Bolivia, Brazil, the Dominican Republic, Ecuador, Mexico, Nicaragua, Paraguay and the United States. In some respects, this bank was the forerunner of the World Bank, which came into being four years later.

The main architect on the US side was a fervent partisan of public intervention in the economy, an advocate of the New Deal: Emilio Collado, number two in the Department of State.[5] He played a prominent role in the discussions leading up to the Bretton Woods Conference and in 1944 was appointed as the US's first executive director of the World Bank. The Department of State was not the only player involved in the launch of the Inter-American Bank in 1940. The US Treasury was also represented in the persons of Henry Morgenthau and his assistant Harry White.

Four basic reasons led the Roosevelt administration to approve the founding of the Inter-American Bank.

---

5   The United States Department of State is the department responsible for administering the country's foreign policy.

Firstly, the US government realized that it must not only lend money to foreign buyers of US products, but that it must also buy exports from those to whom it wished to sell its goods. Nazi Germany, with its dominance over part of Europe, was in the process of buying goods from, and investing in, Latin America.[6] The establishment of the Inter-American Bank would tighten the bonds between the United States and all its Southern neighbours.

Secondly, Washington considered that it could not count on the US private financial sector to lend capital to countries south of the Rio Grande when 14 Latin American countries were in partial or total default on payment of their external debt. In Washington's view, the big US banks were responsible for the 1929 crisis and its continuing effects. The formation of a public agency would enable the government to take serious action.

Thirdly, to convince the governments of Latin America to actively engage in reinforced relations with the United States, they must be offered an instrument which, officially at least, pursued objectives not directly answerable to the United States.

Adolf A. Berle, deputy secretary of the Department of State, put it plainly:

In the past, movements of capital have been regarded as, frankly, imperialist. They usually led later to difficulties of one sort and another. The other country did not like to pay; the interests built up were frequently supposed to be tyrannous. We are still liquidating many of the nineteenth-century messes which were occasioned by the somewhat violent and not too enlightened moves of capital.'[7]

Fourthly, a bank had to be set up in which the borrowing countries played a part and had a voice. The reasoning was very simple: if borrowers were to repay their debts, it would be better for them to be part of the bank. The same principle was applied when planning the founding of the World Bank and the IMF.

---

6   The Chilean representative of the Inter-American Bank, Carlos Davila, wrote on 8 January 1940: 'In 1938, Germany absorbed 2 percent of the cacao exported by our countries; 25 percent of the cattle hides; 16 percent of the coffee; 19 percent of the corn; 29 percent of the cotton; 6 percent of the wheat; and 23 percent of the wool. [...] A new and closer form of association will be necessary in order to develop and exploit the mineral and agricultural resources of Latin America with a view to supplying and increasing the products saleable in the United States without domestic competition. A financial, technical and commercial collaboration which can be extended to the industrial field also, and which would permit creating or augmenting the production in Latin America of that large variety of manufactured articles which the United States now cannot or does not wish to import from other continents.

It is advisable from every point of view that the necessary capital to carry out this program come from the United States and Latin America investors. Only thus would a page be turned over the history of the difficulties which United States investments by themselves have encountered.' Cited in Robert W. Oliver, *International Economic Co-operation*, p. 95.

7   Cited in Oliver, *International Economic Co-operation*, pp. 96–97.

As regards the distribution of votes within the Inter-American Bank, the criteria used were subsequently to be adopted by the World Bank and IMF. The 'one country, one vote' principle was rejected in favour of a voting system based on the economic weight of a country (in this case, export volume).

The system implied an extra bonus for Latin American countries: the existence of a multilateral banking institution would protect them from strong-arm tactics on the part of creditors anxious to recover their funds. After all, it was not so very long ago that the United States and other powerful creditors intervened militarily or took control over the customs and tax administrations of indebted countries in order to recover what they claimed to be their due.[8]

It should be noted that the firm stand taken by a large number of Latin American countries (14 in all, including Brazil, Mexico, Colombia, Chile, Peru and Bolivia) which had decided to discontinue, either totally or partially, repayment of their external debt, scored a resounding victory. Three positive results ensued: their economic growth was higher than in countries that continued to repay the debt; they won back a significant degree of autonomy vis-à-vis the rich countries; far from being excluded from sources of financing, they were wooed by various governments in the North eager to offer them public financing. An instructive lesson in the advantages of standing one's ground.

DISCUSSIONS WITHIN THE ROOSEVELT ADMINISTRATION

As of 1942, the Roosevelt administration pursued discussions concerning the economic and financial order to be established after the war. A number of ideas were regularly brought up on the subject of debt and capital movements: it was considered advisable to set up a number of public, multilateral institutions which, to counteract the risky nature of private international investments, would provide public capital. These institutions should 'police international investment by private capital, so as to provide judicial or arbitral facilities for settlements of disputes between creditor and debtor, and to remove the danger of the use by creditor countries of their claims as a basis for illegitimate political or military or economic demands.'[9]

HARRY WHITE'S AMBITIOUS PROJECT

As mentioned above, in 1941 Harry White at the Treasury was already preparing the groundwork for a plan to set up two major multilateral institutions. Franklin Roosevelt received a first draft in May 1942 based on the premise that before the war ended, it would be necessary to set up an Exchange Rate Stabilization Fund

---

8   Éric Toussaint, *Your Money or Your Life*, chapter 7.
9   Jacob Viner, 'Problems of International Long-term Investment', in *Council on Foreign Relations, Memorandum on Postwar Economic Problems*, April 1942, p. 15. Cited in Oliver, *International Economic Co-operation*, p. 106.

(the future International Monetary Fund) and an international bank to provide capital. He explained: 'Two separate, though linked agencies would be better than one, since one agency dealing with both tasks would have too much power and would run the risk of greater errors of judgment.'[10] The Fund and the Bank would bring together all nations, starting with the Allies. The relative weight of each member nation would be a function of its economic weight. Borrower countries would belong to the Bank, as this would motivate them to repay their loans. The two institutions would favour policies designed to ensure full employment.

The Fund would work to stabilize exchange rates, bring about a gradual discontinuance of exchange controls and the end of export subsidies. As for the Bank, it would provide capital for the reconstruction of the countries affected by the war and for the development of backward regions; it would help stabilize commodity prices. The Bank would lend money from its own capital and have its own currency: the *unitas*.

Harry White's ambitious project was drastically cut down to size in the years to come. Wall Street and the Republican Party were particularly hostile to several fundamental aspects of the White plan. They wanted nothing to do with two strong public institutions designed to regulate the flow of private capital, and which would in fact be in competition with them. Franklin Roosevelt decided to come to terms with them, with the result that in 1945, Congress eventually ratified, by a large majority, the Bretton Woods agreements of July 1944. The concessions made by Roosevelt were generous to the point of changing the nature of the original plan. Yet Wall Street effectively withheld its support of the Bank and the Fund until 1947.

Among the original proposals withdrawn before the Bretton Woods Conference were:

- The creation of a currency specific to the Bank. As we have seen, Harry White proposed calling it the *unitas*. John Maynard Keynes had meantime made a similar proposal, the *bancor*, which was no more successful.
- The Bank's use of its own capital when making loans. It was finally decided that the Bank would borrow the capital it needed to make loans from the private banking sector.
- The stabilization of commodity prices.[11]

The two most influential countries in discussions with the US about the adoption of a final proposal were Great Britain and the USSR. Great Britain demanded

---

10   Cited in Oliver, *International Economic Co-operation*, pp. 111–12.
11   For a full list of the proposals put forward by Harry White and that were abandoned or seriously amended, see Oliver, *International Economic Co-operation*, pp. 157–159.

privileged terms from Washington. For Churchill, any negotiations between Washington and London must be bilateral and secret.[12] Washington preferred to negotiate with all the Allies separately, on the principle of 'divide and rule'.

It seems that Franklin Roosevelt, seconded by Harry White and Henry Morgenthau (Secretary of the Treasury), genuinely wished to guarantee Soviet Russia's participation in the establishment of the Bank and the Fund. In January 1944 Henry Morgenthau publicly disclosed that two Soviet delegates had arrived in Washington to discuss the formation of these two institutions.

THE GEOPOLITICAL AND GEOSTRATEGIC DIMENSION

Between 1 and 22 July 1944, the United Nations Monetary and Financial Conference, better known as the Bretton Woods Conference,[13] was attended by representatives of 44 countries.

The United States delegation was headed by Henry Morgenthau and Harry White, the British delegation by Lord John Maynard Keynes. These two delegations directed the work of the Conference.

The Soviets were also in attendance. As a result of bargaining between Washington, Moscow and London, the USSR was to obtain third place in terms of voting rights, whereas it had wanted second place. Finally, Moscow did not ratify the final agreements and in 1947, at the UN General Assembly, denounced the Bretton Woods institutions as 'branches of Wall Street'. For the Soviet representative, the World Bank was 'subordinated to political purposes which make it the instrument of one great power'.[14]

The distribution of votes clearly reflected the US and British desire to dominate the two institutions. In 1947, the two countries together had almost 50 per cent of the votes (34.23 per cent for the United States and 14.17 per cent for the United Kingdom on 30 August 1947).

The distribution of votes by major categories of countries and regions paints a telling picture of the balance of power in the Allied camp (not counting the USSR) immediately after the war. Eleven of the most industrialized countries held more than 70 per cent of votes.[15] All the countries of the African continent together held no more than 2.34 per cent. Only three African countries had voting rights because

---

12 Winston Churchill was uneasy about the United States' intentions. He told President Roosevelt: 'I believe you want to abolish the British Empire. [...] Everything you say is confirmation of this fact. Yet we know that you are our only hope. And you know we know it. Without America, the British Empire will perish.' Quoted by George and Sabelli, *Faith & Credit*, p. 31.

13 Bretton Woods is located in the mountains of New Hampshire.

14 Mason and Asher, *The World Bank since Bretton Woods*, p. 29.

15 At 30 August 1947: Australia (2.41%), Belgium (2.67%), Canada (3.74%), Denmark (0.99%), France (5.88%), Greece (0.53%), Luxembourg (0.37%), Netherlands (3.21%), Norway (0.80%), United Kingdom (14.17%), United States (34.23%).

practically all the others were still under colonial rule.[16] These three countries were Egypt (0.70 per cent of votes), the Union of South Africa (1.34 per cent) – governed by a white racist power that would introduce apartheid a year later – and Ethiopia (0.30 per cent). In other words, black Africa under black government (Emperor Haile Selassie) held just one-third of 1 per cent of the votes.

The entire Asian continent held 11.66 per cent. Only three countries were members: Chiang Kai-shek's nationalist China (6.68 per cent) – a US ally; the Philippines (0.43 per cent) – a US colony until 1946; India (4.55 per cent) – which gained independence from the British crown in 1947.

Central and Eastern Europe held 3.90 per cent of the votes (Poland and Czechoslovakia each held 1.60 per cent and Tito's Yugoslavia 0.70 per cent).

The Near East and Middle East had 2.24 per cent (Turkey, 0.73 per cent; Lebanon, 0.32 per cent; Iran, 0.52 per cent; Syria, 0.34 per cent; Iraq, 0.33 per cent).

The whole of Latin America and the Caribbean, a region considered to be firmly allied with the United States, held 8.38 per cent of the votes, spread over 18 countries: Bolivia (0.34 per cent), Brazil (1.39 per cent), Chile (0.64 per cent), Colombia (0.64 per cent), Costa Rica (0.29 per cent), Cuba (0.64 per cent), Dominican Republic (0.29 per cent), Ecuador (0.30 per cent), El Salvador (0.28 per cent), Guatemala (0.29 per cent), Honduras (0.28 per cent), Mexico (0.96 per cent), Nicaragua (0.28 per cent), Panama (0.27 per cent), Paraguay (0.28 per cent), Peru (0.45 per cent), Uruguay (0.38 per cent) and Venezuela (0.38 per cent).

---

16   Damien Millet, *L'Afrique sans dette* (*Africa Without Debt*) (Liège: CADTM/Paris: Syllepse, 2005), chapter 1 (in French).

2
The First Years of the World Bank
(1946–62)

Contrary to common belief, the mission of the World Bank is not to reduce poverty in developing countries. The Bank's mission, as originally conceived by the victors of the Second World War, the United States and Great Britain in particular, was to help rebuild Europe, and secondarily to promote the economic growth of the countries in the South, many of which were still under colonial rule. It was this second mission that went by the name of 'development' and which constantly increased in scope. The World Bank lent money first of all to the colonial powers (Great Britain, France and Belgium) to help them more effectively exploit their colonies. Then, when the colonies became independent, the Bank made them liable for the debt contracted by their former colonizers.

In the first 17 years of its existence, the projects supported by the World Bank focused on improving communication infrastructures and power production. The money lent by the World Bank was to be spent essentially in industrialized countries. The projects approved by the Bank were designed to improve the South's ability to export to the North, thereby meeting the needs of Northern countries and enriching a handful of transnational companies in the relevant sectors. During this period, no projects were undertaken in the areas of education, health, clean water supply or wastewater treatment.

From the start, the Bank's missions served essentially to increase its ability to influence the decisions taken by the authorities of a given country in a way that would benefit the shareholding powers and their companies.

World Bank policy evolved in response to the threat of spreading revolution and the Cold War. For the directors of the Bank, the political stakes were a central issue: their internal debates were heavily biased towards the interests of Washington or other industrialized world centres.

The World Bank effectively began operations in 1946. On 18 June of that year, Eugene Meyer, editor of the *Washington Post* and formerly a banker, became the Bank's first president. He lasted six months.

Admittedly the early days of the Bank were difficult. The hostile attitude of Wall Street was still acute even after Franklin Roosevelt's death in April 1945. The banking world mistrusted an institution that, in its view, was still too influenced by the excessively interventionist, excessively public policy of the New Deal. They would have preferred the United States to concentrate on developing the Export-Import

The witch-hunt

Operations at the World Bank and the IMF were strongly influenced by the Cold War and the witch-hunt launched in the US and largely orchestrated by a Republican Senator from Wisconsin, Joseph McCarthy. Harry White, the 'father' of the World Bank and executive director of the IMF, was placed under investigation by the Federal Bureau of Investigation (FBI) as early as 1945, accused of spying for the USSR.[1] In 1947, his case was put before a federal grand jury, which refused to prosecute. In 1948, he was questioned by the House Committee on Un-American Activities. Hounded by a spiteful and unrelenting campaign, he died of a heart attack on 16 August 1948, three days after appearing before the committee.[2] In November 1953, during Eisenhower's presidency, Attorney General Herbert Brownell Jr brought posthumous charges against Harry White as a Soviet spy. He also accused President Truman of appointing Harry White executive director of the IMF in the knowledge that he was spying for Russia.

The witch-hunt also had repercussions throughout the United Nations and its specialized agencies, since, at the end of his term of office, on 9 January 1953, President Truman adopted an Executive Order ordering the UN Secretary-General and the directors of specialized agencies to inform the United States of all applications made by US citizens for jobs at the UN.[3] The United States would then carry out a full investigation to determine if the applicant was likely to engage in espionage or subversive activities (such as 'advocacy of revolution [...] to alter the constitutional form of government of the United States'). During this period, the term 'un-American' was a common euphemism used to describe subversive behaviour. A subversive element could not be hired by the UN. Interference in the internal business of the UN went very far, as demonstrated by the tone and content of a letter sent by Secretary of State John Foster Dulles of the Eisenhower[4] administration to the president of the World Bank, Eugene Black:

> Secretary Dulles has asked me [wrote his assistant secretary] to express to you the extreme importance he attaches to obtaining the full cooperation of all heads of the Specialized Agencies of the United Nations in the administration of Executive Order 10422. He believes it is manifest that without this full cooperation the objectives of the order cannot be achieved, and without such achievement, continued support of these Organizations by the United States cannot be assured.[5]

---

1   According to Robert W. Oliver, Harry White was a progressive in political terms, sympathizing with workers' causes throughout the world and fraternizing with communists. See Oliver, *International Economic Co-operation and the World Bank*, pp. 81–85.
2   During this hearing, he had a first warning attack.
3   Executive Order 10422 of 9 Jan. 1953, Part II, 2. c <archives.gov/federal-register/codification/executive-order/10422.html> [accessed 25/11/2021].
4   Dwight D. Eisenhower, a general and a Republican politician, succeeded Harry S. Truman as US president in January 1953. He was re-elected in 1957 and ended his second term of office in 1961.
5   Letter, John D. Hickerson, Assistant Secretary of State, to President Eugene Black, 21 February 1953, in Kapur, Lewis and Webb, *The World Bank: Its First Half Century, Volume 1*, p. 1173.

Bank. They were overjoyed when Henry Morgenthau left the Treasury,[6] and were not particularly averse to Eugene Meyer's appointment as president of the Bank; but by no means did they welcome the enthusiastic supporters of public control Emilio Collado and Harry White, who were appointed executive directors of the World Bank and the IMF respectively.

However, in 1947 a number of changes were made in the Bank's higher echelons, and a new trio favourable to Wall Street took the reins: John J. McCloy was made president of the World Bank in February 1947, seconded by Robert Garner, vice-president, while Eugene Black was brought in to replace Emilio Collado. Before their appointment, McCloy had been a prominent business lawyer on Wall Street, Robert Garner vice-president of General Foods Corporation and Eugene Black vice-president of the Chase National Bank. Meanwhile, at the IMF, Harry White had been fired. Wall Street was most happy about this. With the ousting of Emilio Collado and Harry White, the last proponents of public intervention and control of capital movements were gone. The financial world could 'get down to business'.

To lend money to its member countries, the World Bank had first to borrow from Wall Street by way of bonds.[7] Private banks required guarantees before lending to a public organization, especially since at the beginning of 1946, 87 per cent of European bonds were in default of payment, as were 60 per cent of Latin American bonds and 56 per cent of Asian bonds.[8]

With the McCloy–Garner–Black triumvirate at the helm of the Bank, private bankers were willing to loosen the purse strings because they counted on recovering their outlay and making a profit too. They were not wrong.

During its first years of operation, the Bank lent mainly to industrialized countries in Europe. It was only with the greatest caution that it began to grant loans to developing countries. Between 1946 and 1948, it granted loans for a total amount of just over $500 million to countries in Western Europe ($250 million to France, $207 million to the Netherlands, $40 million to Denmark and $12 million to Luxembourg), while only one loan was made to a developing country ($16 million to Chile).

The World Bank's lending policy to Europe was radically destabilized and curtailed by the introduction of the Marshall Plan in April 1948. The scope of the Plan far exceeded the Bank's capacities (see chapter 4). For the World Bank, the 'reconstruction' part of its name was over, and only the 'development' part remained. One of the immediate consequences of the introduction of the Marshall Plan was the resignation a month later of the Bank's president, John J. McCloy, who went to

---

6   Henry Morgenthau, a close collaborator of Franklin Roosevelt, clashed with his successor, Harry Truman, before the Potsdam Conference of July 1945 and handed in his resignation.

7   From 1953, the World Bank did not only borrow from within the United States: it also issued bonds in Europe, then in Japan. In the 1970s, when oil prices surged, the Bank also borrowed from Venezuela and from oil-producing Arab countries.

8   Kapur, Lewis and Webb, *The World Bank: Its First Half Century, Volume 1*, p. 917.

Europe to take up the post of US High Commissioner for Germany. Eugene Black replaced him at the Bank and occupied the post until 1962.

With the Chinese revolution of 1949 the United States lost a valuable ally in Asia, causing the leaders in Washington to incorporate the 'underdevelopment' dimension into their strategy in order to prevent communist 'contagion'. The terms of Point IV of President Truman's inaugural address in 1949 are very illuminating:

[W]e must embark on a bold new program for making the benefits of our scientific advances and industrial progress available for the improvement and growth of underdeveloped areas. More than half the people of the world are living in conditions approaching misery. Their food is inadequate. They are victims of disease. Their economic life is primitive and stagnant. Their poverty is a handicap and a threat to them and to more prosperous areas. [...] I believe that we should make available to peace-loving peoples the benefits of our store of technical knowledge in order to help them realize their aspirations for a better life. [...] With the cooperation of business, private capital, agriculture, and labour in this country, this program can greatly increase the industrial activity in other nations and can raise substantially their standards of living. [...] Greater production is the key to prosperity and peace. And the key to greater production is a wider and more vigorous application of modern scientific and technical knowledge. [...] we hope to create the conditions that will lead eventually to personal freedom and happiness for all mankind.[9]

On the first page of the World Bank annual report that appeared after Truman's inaugural address, the Bank announced that it would henceforth work in the spirit of Point IV of Truman's speech: 'As of the date of this report the full implications of the Point IV program, and the precise method of its implementation, are not yet entirely clear. From the standpoint of the Bank, however, the program is of vital interest. [...] The Bank's basic objectives in this field are essentially the same as those of the Point IV program.'[10]

The words read like the minutes of a party meeting intent on executing an order from its central committee. This being said, this fourth annual report, written under the dual impact of the Chinese revolution and Harry Truman's speech, was the first to point out that the political and social tensions caused by poverty and unequal distribution of wealth were an obstacle to development, as were poor distribution of land and its twin effects of inefficiency and oppression.

---

9   Harry S. Truman, Inaugural Address, Point IV <en.wikisource.org/wiki/Harry_S._Truman%27s_ Inaugural_Address>. The other points of Truman's address concerned support for the United Nations system, the creation of NATO and the introduction of the Marshall Plan.

10   *Fourth Annual Report 1948–1949* (Washington, DC: IBRD [World Bank]) <documents1.world-bank.org/curated/zh/910741468739300603/pdf/multi-page.pdf> [accessed 25/11/2021].

The report went on to say that diseases like malaria must be eradicated,[11] the rate of school attendance increased and public health services improved. In addition, said the report, the development of the South was also important for developed countries because their own expansion depended on the markets that these under-developed countries represented.

In subsequent reports, the social themes gradually disappeared and a more traditional view became prevalent.

In any event, as regards its lending policy, the World Bank did nothing to embrace the social dimension evoked in Truman's Point IV. It failed to support any project aimed at redistributing wealth and granting land to landless peasants. And as regards improvements in health, education and provision of drinking water, it was not until the 1960s and 1970s that the Bank supported a small number of projects, and even then with the greatest circumspection.

SOME CHARACTERISTICS OF THE BANK'S LENDING POLICY

High costs for the borrower

The loans made by the World Bank to developing countries were very costly. A high interest rate (equal to that practised in the market or close to it) was levied, plus a management commission, and the period for repayment was relatively short. This very quickly brought protests from the developing countries, who proposed that the UN should set up an alternative, less costly means of financing than that offered by the World Bank (see the next chapter). Like any conventional bank, the World Bank is careful to select profitable projects, and makes sure that it imposes drastic economic reforms.

In 2020, the situation has not changed. The IBRD lends to developing countries at market rates (the LIBOR) plus an additional rate of interest that varies depending on the category the country belongs to, plus a commission of between 0.25 and 1 per cent of the total amount of the loan. The categories (A, B, C and D) are defined by the World Bank itself.[12]

The money lent comes mainly from bonds issued on the financial markets ($80 billion in 2020[13]). The solidity of the World Bank, guaranteed by the rich countries that are its biggest shareholders, allows it to procure these funds at a favourable rate

---

11   More than seventy years later, the World Bank is still concerned with the eradication of malaria, the fatal disease of the poor. See Julie Castro and Damien Millet, 'Malaria and Structural Adjustment: Proof by Contradiction' in Christophe Boëte, *Genetically Modified Mosquitoes for Malaria Control*, (Georgetown, TX: Landes Bioscience), 2006.

12   See 'IBRD Financial Products' and the various sub-pages ('IBRD Flexible Loan', 'IBRD Hedges', 'Guarantees', 'Retired Loan Products') at <treasury.worldbank.org/en/about/unit/treasury/ibrd-financial-products/> [accessed 29/11/2021].

13   $75 billion for IBRD and 5 billion for IDA. 'Supporting Countries in Unprecedented Times', *Annual Report 2020*, World Bank, p. 67 <openknowledge.worldbank.org/bitstream/handle/10986/34406/9781464816192.pdf> [accessed 29/11/2021].

(its bonds are rated triple-A). Repayment of loans is made over periods varying from 15 to 20 years, with a grace period of three to five years during which there is no repayment of capital. This lending business is very lucrative. The World Bank makes profits to the tune of several billion dollars per year at the expense of developing countries and their populations.

Even in the case of less costly loans, those granted by the International Development Association (IDA), which is part of the World Bank group, the interest rates are far from being low. Depending on the category the country is in, they range between 2.5 and 7.5 per cent. Taking an example based on the official document from the IDA concerning so-called concessional credits dating from October 2020,[14] we see that there is a commission or 'service charge' of 0.75 per cent on all credits (see note 6 of the document in question). Added to this commission is the interest rate, which depends on the type of country and the duration of the loan (as shown in the table in the document). For example, a country classified as 'Blend' in the jargon of the World Bank (as is Pakistan) may borrow over a period of 30 years. On reception of the loan from the IDA branch of the World Bank, Pakistan immediately pays the commission of 0.75 per cent of the total value of the loan. Then, the first five years constitute a period of grace during which no repayment needs to be made. From the sixth year on, Pakistan will pay a rate of 3.3 per cent up until the twenty-fifth year, and between the twenty-sixth and thirtieth years a rate of 6.8 per cent.

Not one loan for a school until 1962

The World Bank lends money for specific projects: a road, a port infrastructure, a dam, an agricultural project, etc.

In its first 17 years of operation, the Bank did not grant a single loan for a school, health unit, drainage system, or drinking-water conveyance!

Until 1962, all loans, without exception, were put into electrical power infrastructure, transportation routes (roads, railways, etc.), dams, agricultural machinery, promotion of export crops (tea, cocoa, rice, etc.) or, to a marginal extent, modernization of processing industries.

Investments oriented towards exports

It is easy to see where the priorities lay. The idea was to increase the capacity of developing countries to export the raw materials, fuel and tropical agricultural products needed for ensuring the well-being of the most industrialized countries.

An analysis of projects accepted or rejected by the World Bank clearly shows that, with rare exceptions, the Bank was unwilling to support industrial projects designed to satisfy the domestic demand of developing countries because this

---

14   'IDA Terms (Effective as of October 1, 2020)', Worldbank.org <ida.worldbank.org/sites/default/files/pdfs/ida_terms_effective_10.1.2020.pdf> [accessed 29/11/2021].

would result in reduced imports from the most industrialized countries. The exceptions to the rule concern a handful of strategically important countries possessing real bargaining power. India was one of these.

Money lent to the South found its way back North

The World Bank made its loans on condition that the money be spent by the developing countries on goods and services from industrialized countries. During the first 17 years, more than 90 per cent of the money lent came back each year to the most industrialized countries in the form of purchases.

That's 96 per cent to industrialized capitalist countries and 4 per cent for other countries.

These annual figures were provided by the World Bank until 1962. From the following year to the present, this kind of data has no longer been publicly available. The explanation is simple: up to 1962, the rich countries with the most influence in the Bank were happy enough to show that the money lent by the Bank came back to them immediately. They were proud to demonstrate that the Bank was an extremely profitable business for them. But as time went by, more and more recently independent countries joined the World Bank and it became embarrassing to show, in the Bank's annual report, that its activities in fact benefited the wealthiest countries most (see Tables 2.1, 2.2 and Figure 2.1).

Odious loans to colonial powers ...

Ten years after its creation, the World Bank counted only two members in Sub-Saharan Africa: Ethiopia and South Africa. In strict violation of the right of peoples to self-determination, the World Bank granted loans to Belgium, France and Great Britain to finance projects in their colonies. The right of peoples to self-determination is a principle recognized in a number of international instruments

Table 2.1 Geographical distribution of expenditures made with funds loaned by the World Bank, 1946–55

	1946–51	1951–52	1952–53	1953–54	1954–55
United States	73.1%	65.3%	63.5%	58.7%	47.1%
Europe	11.3%	25.3%	30.1%	38.1%	48.8%
Canada	6.6%	8.8%	4.3%	2.4%	2.9%
Subtotal, industrialized countries	91.0%	99.4%	97.9%	99.2%	98.8%
Latin America	8.3%	0.5%	1.1%	0.4%	0.1%
Middle East	0.4%	0.0%	0.0%	0.0%	0.0%
Africa	0.3%	0.1%	0.8%	0.2%	1.0%
Asia	0.0%	0.0%	0.2%	0.2%	0.1%
	100%	100%	100%	100%	100%

Source: World Bank, *Annual Reports*, 1946 to 1962

Table 2.2 Geographical distribution of expenditures with amounts lent by the World Bank, 1946–62

	Until 1955	1956	1957	1958	1959	1960	1961	1962
Germany	4.1%	14.1%	18.6%	17.2%	16.3%	16.9%	13.5%	10.9%
Belgium	3.7%	2.9%	2.8%	2.9%	3.3%	2.1%	2.5%	1.6%
Canada	5.6%	7.0%	6.0%	1.1%	2.0%	2.3%	1.5%	1.1%
United States	63.4%	50.5%	44.3%	38.8%	29.7%	29.8%	29.6%	33.2%
France	2.7%	3.3%	3.5%	1.2%	5.2%	6.7%	12.0%	12.3%
Italy	0.9%	1.7%	3.0%	5.8%	6.3%	7.7%	6.6%	8.3%
Japan	0.%	0.2%	2.2%	8.3%	6.2%	3.9%	6.1%	5.0%
Netherlands	0.0%	0.0%	0.0%	0.0%	0.0%	0.0%	0.0%	2.5%
Sweden	0.7%	1.5%	2.7%	0.9%	2.1%	2.3%	3.1%	2.6%
Switzerland	2.1%	2.3%	1.9%	1.3%	2.7%	4.3%	4.5%	3.6%
United Kingdom	11.1%	13.2%	10.9%	18.8%	20.5%	16.5%	13.7%	13.7%
Sub-total, industrialized countries	94.2%	96.7%	95.9%	96.3%	94.4%	92.5%	93.1%	94.7%
Other countries	5.8%	3.3%	4.1%	3.7%	5.6%	7.5%	6.9%	5.3%
Total	100.0%	100.0%	100.0%	100.0%	100.0%	100.0%	100.0%	100.0%

Source: World Bank, *Annual Reports*, 1946 to 1962

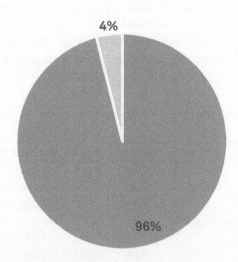

■ Industrialized countries   ■ Other countries

Figure 2.1 Geographical distribution of expenditures made with funds lent by the World Bank, 1946–62

Source: World Bank, *Annual Reports*, 1946 to 1962

(in the Charter of the United Nations of 1945, in the Declaration on the Granting of Independence to Colonial Countries and Peoples of 14 December 1960, in the two International Covenants on Civil and Political Rights of 1966, in the Declaration on Principles of International Law concerning Friendly Relations and Cooperation among States of 24 October 1970) and in numerous regional instruments. The colonies affected by these World Bank loans were, for Belgium, the Belgian Congo, Rwanda and Burundi; for Great Britain, East Africa (including Kenya, Uganda and the future Tanzania), Rhodesia (to become Zimbabwe and Zambia), Nigeria and British Guiana in South America; for France, Algeria, Gabon and French West Africa – that is, Mauritania, Senegal, French Sudan (which became Mali), Guinea, Côte d'Ivoire, Niger, Upper Volta (which became Burkina Faso) and Dahomey (which became Benin). As World Bank historians have recognized: 'These loans, which served to alleviate the dollar shortages of the European colonial powers, were largely directed to colonial interests, especially mining, either through direct investments or indirect assistance, as in the development of transport and mining.'[15]

These loans enabled colonial powers to reinforce their domination over the peoples they had colonized. And in so doing, states violate the right of peoples to self-determination – a right which imposes a twofold obligation: to engage in no military or other cooperation with a view to repressing a national liberation movement, as well as the duty to promote decolonization and self-determination by providing appropriate diplomatic and material support. The loans helped supply the colonial powers with minerals, agricultural products and fuel. In the Belgian Congo, the millions of dollars loaned to the colony for projects determined by Belgium were almost entirely spent by the colonial administration of the Congo on products exported by Belgium. The Belgian Congo received a total of $120 million in loans (in three phases), $105.4 million of which were spent in Belgium.[16]

... that create a heavy burden for young independent nations

When the aforementioned colonies gained independence, the main shareholders came to an agreement to transfer the debt contracted by the colonial power to these new nations.

A blatant example can be seen in the case of Mauritania. On 17 March 1960, France guaranteed a loan of $66 million contracted by the Société Anonyme des Mines de Fer de Mauritanie (MIFERMA). Mauritania was living its last months

---

15   Kapur, Lewis and Webb, *The World Bank: Its First Half Century, Volume 1*, p. 687.
16   The fact that Belgium was the beneficiary of loans to the Belgian Congo can be deduced from a chart published in the fifteenth annual report of the World Bank for 1959–60. *World Bank Fifteenth Annual Report 1959–1960* (Washington, DC: IBRD [World Bank]), p. 12 <documents.worldbank.org/en/publication/documents-reports/documentdetail/287421468739540161/international-bank-for-reconstruction-and-development-world-bank-annual-report-1959-1960> [accessed 29/11/2021].

as a colony, as independence was proclaimed on 28 November of the same year. This loan was to be repaid between 1966 and 1975. According to the Bank's annual report six years later, independent Mauritania had a debt to the Bank of $66 million.[17] The debt incurred at France's request while Mauritania was its colony had become Mauritania's debt a few years later. Transferring debts contracted by a colonial power to the new independent state was common practice at the World Bank.

The Treaty of Versailles had cancelled the debts of Poland and African colonies

Yet a similar case had already occurred in the past and had been decided by the Treaty of Versailles in 1919. When Poland was reconstituted and made an independent state after the First World War, it was decided that the debts contracted by Germany to colonize the part of Poland under its domination would *not* be passed on to the new independent state. The Treaty of Versailles of 18 June 1919 stipulated:

There shall be excluded from the share of such financial liabilities assumed by Poland that portion of the debt which, according to the finding of the Reparation Commission referred to in the above-mentioned Article [Article 254], arises from measures adopted by the German and Prussian Governments with a view to German colonisation in Poland.'[18]

The Treaty stated that the creditors that had lent money to Germany for projects in Polish territory could only claim their due from that power, and not from Poland.

Under the Treaty of Versailles, the German Empire lost the territories it had colonized in Africa and the debts of those colonies were cancelled. The German side was unhappy with that and tried to convince the victorious powers to reconsider the debt cancellation, since it implied that Germany would have to repay the debt. The Allies responded:

The colonies should not bear any portion of the German debt, nor remain under any obligation to refund to Germany the expenses incurred by the Imperial administration of the protectorate, In fact, it would be unjust to burden the natives with expenditure which appears to have been incurred in Germany' own interest, and that it would be no less unjust to make this responsibility rest upon the Mandatory Powers which, in so far as they may be appointed trustees by the League of Nations, will derive no benefit from such trusteeship.[19]

---

17   *World Bank Fifteenth Annual Report*, p. 52; *Annual Report 1965–1966* (Washington, DC: IBRD [World Bank]), appendix 2 <documents.worldbank.org/curated/en/786661468765027751/ World-Bank-and-IDA-annual-report-1965-1966> [accessed 29/11/2021].

18   <https://www.census.gov/history/pdf/treaty_of_versailles-112018.pdf>, quoted by Sack, *Les effets des transformations des Etats*, p. 159.

19   Cited by Sack, *Les effets des transformations des Etats*, p. 162 as: 'Treaty Series, n° 4, 1919, p. 26.'

Alexander Nahum Sack, the theoretician of odious debt, states in his treatise of 1927: 'When the government contracts debts for the purpose of subjugating part of the people's territory or of colonizing it by nationals of the dominant nationality, etc., these debts are odious for the native population of this part of the territory of the debtor State.'[20] This principle applies in every respect to the loans made by the World Bank to Belgium, France and Great Britain for the development of their colonies. Consequently, the Bank acted in violation of international law by making the new independent states liable for debts incurred for the purpose of colonizing them. The Bank, with the connivance of its main colonial shareholders and with the blessing of the United States, committed an act that should not go unpunished. These debts are null and void and the Bank should answer for them before the law. The states that have been victims of this violation should demand reparations and use the sums in question to repay the social debt owed to their people.[21]

Beginning in the years 1950–60 the World Bank and the IMF acted as enforcers for the former private creditors

As the author's analysis in *The Debt System* shows,[22] during the nineteenth century and through the Second World War a number of governments of former Spanish colonies in Latin America ceased repaying or repudiated debts they considered to be odious, illegal and/or illegitimate. Such was the case of Mexico in 1861, in 1867 and in 1883; of Guatemala in 1829; Peru in 1886; Costa Rica in 1922; Cuba in 1909 and again in 1934; and Brazil beginning in 1932. The United States also repudiated debts judged to be odious and illegitimate during the 1830s, in 1865, during the 1870s and in 1898. Soviet Russia, in 1918, repudiated the debts contracted by the tsarist regime. In addition to the cancellation of debts contracted by Germany to colonize territory in Poland and Africa in 1919, mentioned above, there is the Bolshevik government's repudiation in 1920–21 of the debt of the three Baltic states that had been part of the tsarist empire along with that of Poland, Persia and Turkey. These various cancellations, suspensions and repudiations led to many conflicts and arbitrations and to unilateral acts, leading to the emergence of the legal doctrine of odious debt, mentioned above. Clearly, the World Bank and the IMF acted to

---

20 Sack, *Les effets des transformations des Etats*, p. 158 (translation CADTM).
21 Reparations should be demanded from the former colonial powers via the International Court of Justice in The Hague. It should be noted that as long as the UN agencies, of which the World Bank is one, continue to enjoy immunity, and as long as the Bank's statutes are not modified, the member states of the World Bank will have difficulty initiating legal proceedings against it. On the other hand, citizens' associations representing the victims can take the Bank to court either in their own country or in a country where the Bank has an agency or where it has issued loans. This point will be developed later in the book.
22 Éric Toussaint, *The Debt System: A History of Sovereign Debts and their Repudiation* (Chicago: Haymarket Books, 2019), first published in French in 2017.

re-establish creditors' power and attempted to persuade the various states that the doctrine of odious debt was a relic of the past.

As Julia Juruna wrote in the monthly *Le Monde diplomatique*, when a member country first made a request for credit from the IMF and the World Bank, the two institutions imposed two prior conditions: repayment of all previously contracted international debts and 'adequate' compensation for any foreign holdings that had been nationalized. According to Bank historians Edward S. Mason and Robert E. Asher, this requirement of repayment of old debts revived disputes between certain Latin American governments and their Western creditors that were several decades old or even went back to the nineteenth century.[23] Julia Juruna, basing her claims on their work, writes that 'The most striking case was that of Guatemala, where the World Bank resuscitated the question of repayment of securities issued in 1829. The country was not able to obtain loans from the Bank until the Guatemalan courts had ruled in favour of the holders of bonds that were over a hundred years old.'[24]

> We should make our terms clear: by **cancellation** of debt, we mean that the creditor waives any claim to repayment of a debt. **Suspension** or **moratorium** means a temporary halting of repayment. **Repudiation** is a unilateral decision by a debtor to no longer repay the capital and the interest on a debt.

THE WORLD BANK'S MISSIONS

The World Bank is in the habit of sending specialists on missions to certain member countries. In its first 20 years, in most cases these specialists were sent from the United States.

In the beginning, the 'test' country most visited was undoubtedly Colombia. It was a key country from the point of view of strategic US interests. One of Washington's priorities was to prevent Colombia falling into the Soviet camp or heeding the call of revolution.

In 1949, the Bank sent a well-manned survey mission to Colombia, including experts from the Bank, the IMF, the FAO (Food and Agriculture Organization of the United Nations) and the WHO (World Health Organization). Its task was to study needs and determine a global development strategy for the country. The concrete projects supported by the Bank involved the purchase from the United States of 70 bulldozers, 600 tractors and equipment for three hydroelectric power stations! In 1950, it was learned that the Colombian government was studying the report delivered by the Bank's commission with a view to formulating a development programme based on it. The next year – 1951 – a commission of independent Colombian

---

23   Mason and Asher, *The World Bank since Bretton Woods*, p. 367.

24   Julia Juruna, 'Le Fonds monétaire et les banques privées. Le "gendarme" du grand capital' ('The Monetary Fund and the private banks: big capital's "enforcer"'), *Le Monde diplomatique*, October 1977, pp. 1, 20–21 (translation CADTM) <monde-diplomatique.fr/1977/10/JURUNA/34425> [accessed 05/01/2021 (by subscription)].

experts finished drawing up such a development programme, which the government then put into action: budgetary and bank reforms; reduction and relaxing of import restrictions; relaxing of exchange controls; adoption of a liberal and accommodating attitude with regard to foreign capital.

Consultants designated jointly by the Bank and the Colombian government also drew up proposals concerning the railways, civil aviation, industrial investment and the issuing of public-debt bonds. An economic adviser nominated by the Bank was taken on by the Colombian National Board of Economic Planning. This is what one of the top people at the IMF, Jacques Polack,[25] had to say about his participation in a mission to Colombia: 'The oral instructions that I received as head of a Fund (IMF) mission to Colombia in 1955, formulated in a meeting between the vice-president of the Bank and the deputy managing director of the Fund, conveyed the same notion, expressed in the heartier language of these days: "You twist their right arm and we'll twist their left arm."'[26]

As can be seen, in general these missions served essentially to increase the ability of the Bank (and other institutions, in particular the IMF) to influence the decisions made by the authorities of a given country in a way that would benefit the shareholding powers and their companies.

World Bank policy evolved in response to the threat of spreading revolution and the Cold War

In 1950, the US and its allies in the World Bank effectively expelled China when it became a communist state and gave its seat to the anti-communist government of General Chiang Kai-shek, which had set up headquarters on the island of Taiwan.[27] To prevent contagion spreading to the rest of Asia, various strategies were used and certain countries were the focus of systematic intervention by the World Bank. Such was the case of India,[28] Pakistan, Thailand, the Philippines and Indonesia. Up to 1961, the Bank was not authorized to deal with South Korea, which was the exclusive domain of the United States (see chapter 11).

Poland and Czechoslovakia, which were part of the Soviet bloc, left the Bank early on.[29] On its expulsion from the Soviet camp, Yugoslavia received financial support from the Bank.

---

25 Jacques Polack participated in the Bretton Woods Conference of 1944. He was director of the research department of the IMF from 1958 to 1980, and IMF executive director for the Netherlands from 1981 to 1986.

26 Kapur, Lewis and Webb, *The World Bank: Its First Half Century, Volume 2*, p. 477.

27 This situation lasted until 1980, the year China returned to the World Bank and the IMF. At the United Nations, the situation lasted until 1971.

28 See Damien Millet and Éric Toussaint, 'India, 60 years after the long struggle for independence when will India's new liberation come?', in *Tsunami Aid or Debt Cancellation! The Political Economy of Post Tsunami Reconstruction* (Mumbai: VAK, 2005), chapter 4.

29 Poland withdrew from the World Bank in March 1950 and Czechoslovakia in December 1954, the Bank having refused to grant them a single loan.

In 1959 a tremendous revolutionary hurricane shook the Americas: in Cuba the struggle for revolution finally triumphed under Uncle Sam's very nose.[30] Washington was obliged to grant concessions to the governments and people of Latin America to try to prevent revolution spreading like wildfire to other countries.

Bank historian Richard Webb, ex-president of the Central Bank of Peru, recalled the effects of this phenomenon:

Between 1959 and 1960, Latin America received the full benefit of Fidel Castro's revolution. The first effects had already appeared with the decisions to establish an Inter-American Development Bank and to surrender – after a long resistance – to Latin American demands for a commodity price stabilization, a coffee agreement was signed in September 1959. The aid momentum increased in early 1960, following Cuba's sweeping expropriation, its trade pact with the USSR, and Eisenhower's trip to South America. 'Upon my return' he wrote 'I determined to begin ... historic measures designed to bring about social reforms for the benefit of all the people of Latin America.'[31]

President Eisenhower himself added:

Constantly before us was the question of what could be done about the revolutionary ferment in the world. [...] We needed new policies that would reach the seat of the trouble, the seething unrest of the people. [...] One suggestion was [...] to raise the pay of the teachers and start hundreds of vocational schools. [...] [We] had to disabuse ourselves of some old ideas [...] to keep the Free World from going up in flames.[32]

Richard Webb continues:

In April, Secretary of State Christian A. Herter informed the Pan American Union of a sharp change in American foreign policy toward Latin America, including a decision to support land reform. Dillon presented a new aid program to Congress in August, which called for $600 million in funding for soft loans by the Inter-American Development Bank and stressed social expenditures to contend with income inequality and outdated institutions, two serious impediments to progress. The bill was promptly enacted.

The perception of crisis in the region continued into 1961, and Kennedy escalated the response: 'Next to Berlin it's the most critical area. [...] The whole place could blow up on us. [...] I don't know if Congress will give it to me. But now's the time, while they're all worried that Castro might take over the

---

30   Havana is less than 200 kilometres from the coast of the United States, which had been effectively controlling Cuba since 1898.

31   Kapur, Lewis and Webb, *The World Bank: Its First Half Century, Volume 1*, p. 163.

32   Dwight D. Eisenhower, *Waging Peace* (Garden City, NY: Doubleday, 1965), pp. 530–37.

hemisphere.' In March 1961 Kennedy demanded action to avert chaos in Bolivia. His staff decided to 'ignore proposals by both the International Monetary Fund and State Department that Bolivia needed a good dose of an anti-inflationary austerity, and instead should offer immediate economic assistance. [...] Things were grim enough without calling for further sacrifice from those who had nothing to give.' A week later Kennedy announced the Alliance for Progress with Latin America, a ten-year program for cooperation and development, stressing social reform, with large-scale aid to countries that 'did their part'.[33]

The announcement of major reforms did not prevent the Bank and the United States from supporting corrupt and dictatorial regimes like that of Anastasio Somoza in Nicaragua, as demonstrated in the following example. On 12 April 1961, just five days before the United States was due to launch a military expedition against Cuba from Nicaraguan territory,[34] the directors of the Bank decided to grant a loan to Nicaragua although fully aware that the money would be used to reinforce the dictator's economic power. It was the price to pay for his support for the assault on Cuba. Below is an excerpt from the official minutes of the discussion between the Bank's directors on 12 April 1961:

- Mr. [Aron] Broches. I am told that the Somoza Family is in everything and it would be difficult to find anything in Nicaragua which did not raise this problem.
- Mr. [Robert] Cavanaugh. I am concerned that we would appear to be fostering an arrangement under which people will be urged to sell land that the President wants ...
- Mr [Simon] Cargill. If the project itself is satisfactory I don't believe that the interest of the President is such a problem that the whole thing should be held up ...
- Mr Rucinski. I agree that it is too late to turn it down.
- Mr. Aldewereld. The problem of the land holding and Somoza ownership is an unfortunate one but it is one we have been aware of from the very start and I think it is too late to raise the question now.[35]

A few months later, in June 1961, the same Bank directors were debating the question of a loan to Ecuador. The contents of their discussion are eloquent reminders of the global political stakes behind the Bank's action:

- Mr. Knapp. Ecuador would appear to be the next country on the list to go 'Fidelistic.' [...] What is the political risk of the submerged Indians, representing half or two-thirds of the population, who are still completely out of the political and economic picture? [...]

---

33 Kapur, Lewis and Webb, *The World Bank: Its First Half Century, Volume 1*, pp. 163–64.
34 The expedition took place on 17 April 1961. More than 1,500 anti-Castro mercenaries disembarked at the Bay of Pigs. The expedition was a monumental fiasco.
35 Kapur, Lewis and Webb, *The World Bank: Its First Half Century, Volume 1*, p. 165.

- Mr. [John] de Wilde. Ecuador has a good record. [...] Isn't this a strategic time for the agencies [...] such as the Bank to step into the picture [...] and [...] prevent a deterioration in the political situation?
- Mr. Knapp. [...] That is the sort of salvage job that the United States must perform.
- Mr. Broches. Where does Ecuador stand on the index of social injustices Mr. Kennedy has been referring to?
- Mr [Orvis] Schmidt. While there is great disparity in the distribution of wealth in Ecuador, this is less so than in other countries in Latin America. [...] The Indians up on the mountains are still quiet although the Government has not really been doing very much on their behalf.
- Mr. Demuth. In looking at the Latin American feudal countries [...] to be realistic we must assume that revolutions are going to occur and only hope that the new governments will honour the obligations of former Governments. [...]
- Mr. Aldewereld. Colonialism is certainly bad in Ecuador [...] even [...] worse than in the Far East. Something violent is going to happen. [...] I think that our projects do serve to relieve internal pressures. [...] I agree that we might consider more IDA money because of these political risks.
- Mr. Knapp. [...] But political situations do lead to defaults.[36]

It could hardly have been put more clearly.

---

36   Ibid., p. 166.

3

Difficult Beginnings between the UN and the World Bank

The World Bank and the IMF are specialized institutions of the United Nations, comparable in theory to the International Labour Organization (ILO) or the Food and Agriculture Organization (FAO). As such, they are supposed to cooperate closely with the various UN bodies and the other specialized institutions to achieve the objectives set out in the Charter of the United Nations and in the Universal Declaration of Human Rights.

From the outset, the World Bank and the IMF attempted to extricate themselves to a large extent from the obligations that bind member organizations of the United Nations system. In the case of the Bank, while its development aid mission should have led it to seek a rapprochement with the UN, its directors consistently managed to place the Bank outside the UN's sphere of authority. The Bank and the IMF were instrumental in heightening the Cold War, and later, in playing on the reactions of leaders in the most industrialized countries to the growing influence of developing countries calling for a new world economic order.

Having no Marshall Plan to promote their growth, the developing countries proposed that a new UN body be created, based on a 'one country, one vote' system designed to facilitate loans to their industries: SUNFED (Special United Nations Fund for Economic Development). The industrialized countries were fiercely opposed to this move, and successfully imposed a counter-proposal, the International Development Association (IDA), a branch of the World Bank, thus effectively putting an end to SUNFED.

EARLY RELATIONS WITH THE UN

In March 1946, on the occasion of the first meeting of the governors of the World Bank and the IMF, the president of the Economic and Social Council of the United Nations (known by the acronym ECOSOC)[1] handed a letter to the directors

---

1 The Economic and Social Council of the United Nations makes recommendations with a view to coordinating the programmes and activities of the specialized institutions of the UN (Article 58 of the United Nations Charter). To this end, ECOSOC enjoys powers which are granted to it by virtue of the terms of Chapter X of the Charter. Article 62, Paragraph 1 states: 'The Economic and Social Council may make or initiate studies and reports with respect to international economic, social, cultural, educational, health, and related matters and may make recommendations with respect to any such matters to the General Assembly, to the Members of the United Nations, and to the specialized agencies concerned.' <un.org/en/about-us/un-charter/chapter-10> [accessed 29/11/2021].

of the World Bank asking it to set up liaison facilities with its organization. The Bank postponed discussion of this issue until the executive directors' meeting to be held in May 1946. In fact, the Bank dragged its feet so successfully that it was only in November 1947 that an agreement between the two parties was arrived at. According to Mason and Asher, the Bank's historians, the negotiations were not particularly cordial.[2] The first letter from ECOSOC having gone unanswered, a second letter was sent, to which the executive directors of the Bank replied that, in their view, a meeting on the subject would be premature. Meanwhile, the United Nations had already signed cooperation agreements with the ILO, UNESCO and the FAO.

In July 1946 a third attempt was made when the UN Secretary-General proposed that the Bank and the IMF begin negotiations in September 1946. The directors of the IMF and the World Bank subsequently met and decided that such a meeting was still not timely. This is what Mason and Asher have to say about these stalling tactics: 'The Bank was very fearful that becoming a specialized agency of the UN would subject it to undesirable political control or influence and hurt its credit rating in Wall Street.'[3] The Bank finally adopted a draft text to be submitted for discussion with the United Nations; this text was more a declaration of independence than a declaration of cooperation. Then followed a day of discussions at UN headquarters, during which the Bank's president, John J. McCloy, agreed to exercise a little more moderation.

The resulting agreement was accepted by ECOSOC's negotiating committee, but it raised a furore within ECOSOC itself and at its General Assembly. During ECOSOC's 1947 session, the Soviet Union delegate described the draft agreement as a flagrant violation of at least four articles of the UN Charter. Even more embarrassing for the Bank's directors, and obliquely, for the United States, was the attack led by the delegate from Norway (the native country of then UN Secretary-General Trygve Lie). He declared that Norway could not tolerate such privileges being granted to the Bank and the IMF, because it would undermine UN authority. To which the United States delegate retorted that nothing would undermine UN authority more than the impossibility of its coming to an agreement with the Bank and the IMF. Finally, ECOSOC adopted (13 for, three against and two abstentions) the draft text which was ratified in September 1947 by the Bank's governors (the governor representing Yugoslavia abstained). The agreement was approved by the UN General Assembly in November 1947.[4]

This agreement ratified the Bank's status as a UN specialized agency but, at the Bank's request, allowed it to operate as an 'independent international organization'.

2   Mason and Asher, *The World Bank since Bretton Woods*, p. 55.
3   Mason and Asher, *The World Bank since Bretton Woods*, p. 56.
4   Agreement between the United Nations and the International Bank for Reconstruction and Development, 15 Nov. 1947, *United Nations Treaty Series (UNTS)*, Vol. 16, p. 346 <treaties.un.org/doc/Publication/UNTS/Volume%2016/v16.pdf> [accessed 05/01/2021].

Following the same line, it authorized the Bank to use its own judgement as to what information could be usefully communicated to ECOSOC, which constituted a departure from Article 17, Paragraph 3 and Article 64 of the United Nations Charter (Article 64 gives ECOSOC the right to obtain regular reports from specialized agencies). It was also a departure from Article 70, which allows for reciprocal representation at each deliberation. Yet in spite of this, the Bank and the IMF reserved the right to invite UN representatives only to the meetings of the Board of Governors. In reviewing these events, the Bank's historians declare that this agreement was considered unsatisfactory by the United Nations secretariat, but that it felt obliged to accept it. They go on to say that the World Bank's president, McCloy, 'could not be classified as an admirer of the United Nations, and Garner [the Bank's vice-president] was considered anti-UN'.[5]

THE CREATION OF THE IFC AND IDA[6]

From the beginning of World Bank operations, the governments of developing countries, starting with Latin America and followed by India, complained that their countries did not enjoy aid facilities like those of the Marshall Plan, which was restricted to Europe. Indeed, World Bank loans were granted at current market interest rates, while Marshall Plan aid was mainly given in the form of grants. A small proportion of Marshall Plan aid was in the form of interest-free loans or loans with interest rates lower than those of the market (see chapter 4).

In 1949, an Indian economist proposed creating a new international organization within the framework of the UN. He suggested it be called the 'United Nations Administration for Economic Development'. Some years later, the same idea took shape within ECOSOC, and SUNFED (Special United Nations Fund for Economic Development) was set up. From 1950 to 1960, several Third World countries, as well as the USSR and Yugoslavia, waged a systematic campaign within the UN to consolidate and reinforce SUNFED. For the US government and the governments of the other major industrial powers, the idea of a special fund controlled by the UN and separate from the World Bank was unacceptable.

Among the reasons behind the developing countries' demand for a specialized UN agency to finance their development was the question of voting rights. They wanted a UN specialized agency in order to ensure that the 'one country, one vote' rule was applied, as opposed to the census-type rule applied within the Bank. The same reason – but in reverse – was behind US and other major powers' opposition to the proposal: the small number of rich countries were afraid of becoming minority voters.

---

5   Mason and Asher, *The World Bank since Bretton Woods*, p. 59.
6   This section is largely based on Aart Van de Laar, *The World Bank and the Poor* (Boston/The Hague/London: Martinus Nijhoff Publishing, 1980), pp. 56–59; Mason and Asher, *The World Bank since Bretton Woods*, pp. 380–419; Gwin, 'U.S. relations with the World Bank, 1945–1992', pp. 205–09; and Rich, *Mortgaging the Earth*, p. 77.

As recounted by the Bank historians Mason and Asher, and later by Catherine Gwin, in 1954 the United States made a first counter-proposal which the Bank put into practice in 1956 with the creation of the International Finance Corporation (IFC), whose role was to grant loans to private-sector companies in developing countries.[7] This new initiative failed to quell dissatisfaction and the developing countries' campaign in favour of SUNFED gained strength: in 1958, the Special United Nations Fund was authorized to finance pre-investments in developing countries.

Unfortunately, the Third World camp quickly became divided. India, which had originally supported SUNFED, switched allegiances and declared itself favourable to the second US counter-proposal. This proposal involved the creation of an International Development Association (IDA), linked to the World Bank, as an alternative to SUNFED.[8] The pro-Washington Indian lobby was convinced that India would benefit from IDA since the major powers predominating in the Bretton Woods institutions would understand the necessity of giving India special treatment in view of its strategic position. And India was right: in the first year of IDA activity, it received 50 per cent of IDA loans.

By proposing the creation of IDA, the US government had a dual objective: on the one hand to prevent the United Nations continuing to reinforce SUNFED and thereby satisfying the needs of developing countries; on the other hand to find a way of using the currency reserves of developing countries that the US Treasury had been piling up since 1954 through the sale of its agricultural surpluses under Public Law 480.[9] Several authors agree that it was Senator Mike Monroney of Oklahoma who first floated the idea: he put a resolution before the Senate for the establishment of an IDA in cooperation with the World Bank and proposing that non-convertible currency reserves should be paid into this agency in order to grant long-term, low-interest loans that would be paid back in local currency. Basically, it meant that loans would be made to poor countries so that they could buy North American agricultural surpluses.[10] Eugene Black, president of the World Bank, would later say that the IDA 'was really an idea to offset the urge for SUNFED'.[11] It is worth quoting Mason and Asher here: 'As an international organization affiliated with the World Bank, IDA is an elaborate fiction. Called an "association" and possessed of Articles of Agreement, officers, governmental members galore, and all the trappings of other international agencies, it is as yet simply a fund administered by the World Bank.'[12]

---

7   Mason and Asher, *The World Bank since Bretton Woods*, pp. 384–85; Gwin, 'U.S. relations with the World Bank', p. 206; Van de Laar, *The World Bank and the Poor*, p. 57.
8   Kapur, Lewis and Webb, *The World Bank: Its First Half Century, Volume 1*, p. 1127.
9   Van de Laar, *The World Bank and the Poor*, p. 57; Gwin, 'U.S. relations with the World Bank', p. 206; Mason and Asher, *The World Bank since Bretton Woods*, pp. 386–87.
10   Kapur, Lewis and Webb, *The World Bank: Its First Half Century, Volume 1*, p. 1128.
11   Mason and Asher, *The World Bank since Bretton Woods*, p. 386.
12   Mason and Asher, *The World Bank since Bretton Woods*, pp. 380–81.

The United States provided 42 per cent of IDA's initial funding, thus ensuring US predominance within the agency.

At the same time that IDA was founded, the DAC (Development Assistance Committee of the OECD) was being set up in Paris. This was a structure designed to 'coordinate' bilateral development aid from the most highly industrialized countries. This spelt the final demise of SUNFED, the United States having imposed institutions where US control could be guaranteed.

IDA FINANCING

IDA does not borrow on the financial markets. The money it lends comes from donations made regularly by member countries (mainly the wealthiest industrial countries, and also the Petroleum Exporting Countries (OPEC) since the 1970s) and from the repayments it receives.

Every three or four years, the contributing countries haggle over the kitty. It is the stuff of great debates in the US Congress, which is where the payouts are decided. Bargaining proceeds smartly between Congress, the Washington government and the US presidency of the World Bank/IDA. Yet the amounts at stake are actually very modest. What is really important is to ensure that money loaned by IDA comes back to the donors in the form of purchases (linked aid).[13]

THE WORLD BANK'S REFUSAL TO COMPLY WITH UN DEMANDS CONCERNING PORTUGAL AND SOUTH AFRICA

From 1961, when most colonial countries had won their independence and become UN members, the General Assembly on several occasions adopted resolutions condemning the apartheid regime in South Africa and Portugal's iron dominance over several African and Asian countries.[14] In 1965, in view of the continued financial support of the World Bank and the IMF for these regimes, the UN made a formal demand:

to all the specialized agencies of the United Nations, and in particular the International Bank for Reconstruction and Development and the International Monetary Fund [...] to refrain from granting Portugal any financial, economic or

---

13   Kapur, Lewis and Webb, *The World Bank: Its First Half Century, Volume 1*, p. 1149.

14   See the following General Assembly resolutions, among others: A/RES/1761, 6 November 1962; A/RES/1881 (XVIII), 11 October 1963; A/RES/1978 (XVIII) A and B, 16 December 1963; A/RES/2054 (XX) A and B, 15 December 1965; A/RES/2060 (XX), 16 December 1965; A/RES/2202 (XXI) A and B, 16 December 1966; A/RES/2307 (X X II), 13 December 1967; A/RES/2396 (X X III), 2 December 1968; A /RES/2397 (X X III), 2 December 1968 <worldlii.org/int/other/UNGA/1962/> (and <worldlii.org/int/other/UNGA/1963/>, -/1965/, -/1966/, /1967/, /1968/) [accessed 29/11/2021]. The Security Council also unanimously condemned the apartheid regime on 4 December 1963 with the adoption of its Resolution S/182 (1963) <unscr.com/en/resolutions?y=1963> [accessed 29/11/2021].

technical assistance so long as the Portuguese Government fails to renounce its colonial policy, which constitutes a flagrant violation of the provisions of the Charter of The United Nations[15]

It issued a similar demand concerning South Africa.

The Bank's directors met to take a position and a majority of its executive directors decided to continue making loans. To justify this decision, they invoked Article IV, Section 10 of the Bank's Articles of Agreement,[16] which forbids political involvement! All the most industrialized countries, backed by a certain number of Latin American countries, voted to continue the loans. That interpretation of Article IV of its own founding statutes led the Bank to adopt an official (or ostensible) policy of not taking into account the status of civil and political rights in its member states when deciding whether or not to grant a loan. And yet in practice the World Bank has repeatedly sidestepped that argument regarding its constitutional limitations (see chapter 6). In 1966, the Bank approved a $10 million loan to Portugal and a $20 million loan to South Africa. Subsequently, under further pressure, the Bank stopped making new loans to these countries. However, a UN body, the Decolonization Committee,[17] continued for 15 years to denounce the fact that the Bank allowed South Africa and Portugal to apply for World Bank financing for projects in other countries. In addition, the Bank curried favour with South Africa to obtain donations to IDA.[18]

---

15   Telegram dated 17/06/1965 from the Chairman of the Special Committee on the Situation with Regard to the Implementation of the Declaration on the Granting of Independence to Colonial Countries and Peoples addressed to the President of the Security Council, 21 June 1965 <digitallibrary.un.org/record/609928> [accessed 16/03/2022].

16   Article IV, Section 10 stipulates: 'The Bank and its officers shall not interfere in the political affairs of any member; nor shall they be influenced in their decisions by the political character of the member or members concerned. Only economic considerations shall be relevant to their decisions, and these considerations shall be weighed impartially in order to achieve the purposes (set by the Bank) stated in Article I.'

17   The Special Committee on the Implementation of the Declaration on the Granting of Independence to Colonial Countries and Peoples, created in 1961.

18   Kapur, Lewis and Webb, *The World Bank: Its First Half Century, Volume 1*, p. 692.

4

The Post-1945 Context: The Marshall Plan and the London Agreement on Germany's Debt

This chapter presents an analysis of the bilateral economic policies developed by Washington towards its allies in the Cold War context. The Marshall Plan replaced the World Bank's intervention since the US came to the conclusion that reconstruction grants to Europe would be more efficient and cost-effective than loans. This bilateral policy aimed to buttress the capitalist Western bloc spearheaded by Washington against the Eastern bloc dominated by the USSR.

The United States cancelled the debts of some of its allies. The most obvious instance of this kind was the way German debt was largely cancelled by the 1953 London Agreement. In order to make sure that the economy of West Germany would thrive and thus become a key element of stability in the Atlantic bloc, the creditor allies led by the United States made major concessions to German authorities and corporations – concessions that went beyond debt relief. A comparison between the way West Germany was treated after the Second World War and the current attitude to developing countries is telling.

THE US GOVERNMENTS HAD LEARNED FROM THE MISTAKES MADE IN THE 1920S AND 1930S

With the Treaty of Versailles at the end of the First World War, the victors demanded that Germany pay huge amounts as war debt and reparations.[1] Germany soon found it difficult to pay and social discontent grew as a consequence. The Wall Street crash of 1929 had led to a global economic crisis. The US drastically reduced capital outflow. Germany stopped repaying its debt to France, Belgium and Britain, and these countries in turn stopped repaying their debts to the United States. The more industrialized world sank into recession and massive unemployment. International trade plummeted.

---

1 John Maynard Keynes, who worked for the British Treasury, had participated in the negotiations leading to the Treaty of Versailles (1919), the peace settlement that was signed after the First World War ended. As he was against demanding such large amounts from Germany, he resigned from the British delegation and subsequently published a book called *The Economic Consequences of the Peace* (New York: Harcourt, Brace and Howe, 1920).

To prepare for a different outcome after the Second World War, Washington decided on policies that were completely different from those implemented after the First World War and until the early 1930s. Seeing to it that the international institutions – the Bretton Woods institutions and the United Nations – were set up was one aspect of those policies.

Let us now analyze the bilateral economic policy advocated by the United States.

GIVE RATHER THAN LEND MONEY

The US government's major concern at the end of the Second World War was to maintain the full employment that had been achieved thanks to the tremendous war effort. It also wanted to guarantee that there would be a trade surplus in relations between the US and the rest of the world.[2] But the major industrialized countries that could import US commodities were literally penniless. For European countries to be able to buy US goods, they had to be provided with lots of dollars. But how? Through grants or through loans?

To put it simply, the US reasoning went as follows: if we lend European countries on our side the money they need to rebuild their economy, how are they going to pay us back? They will no longer have the dollars we lent them since they will have used them to buy from us. So there are only three possibilities. First possibility: they pay us back in kind. Second possibility: they pay us back with dollars. Third possibility: we give them the money for as long as it takes for them to recover.

In the first hypothesis, if they pay us back in kind, their goods will compete with ours on our home market, full employment will be jeopardized, and profits will fall. This is not a good solution.

In the second hypothesis, they cannot use the dollars they received on loan to pay us back since they will have used them to buy our goods. Consequently, if they are to pay us back, we have to lend them the same amount (which they owe us) again, with interest added. The risk of being caught in an infernal cycle of indebtedness (which puts a stop to or slows down the smooth running of business) is added to the risk attached to the first possibility. If Europeans try not to accumulate debt towards us, they will try to sell their goods on our home market. They will thus earn some of the dollars they need to pay us back. But this will not be enough to rid them of their debts. *And* it will lower the rate of employment in the US.[3]

We are left with the third possibility: rather than lend money to Europeans (whether or not via the World Bank), it seems appropriate to give them the amount

---

2   This is indeed what happened: the US trade balance, which used to be in the red, remained in the black until 1971. In other words, the US exported more than they imported.

3   'Repayment in the form of imports has been traditionally opposed in this country on the ground that it causes competition for domestic producers and contributes to unemployment'. Randolph E. Paul, *Taxation for Prosperity* (Indianapolis: Bobbs-Merrill, 1947), quoted by Payer, *Lent and Lost: Foreign Credit and Third World Development*, p. 20.

of dollars they need to build up their economy within a fairly short time. Europeans will use the donated dollars to buy goods and services from the US. This will guarantee an outlet for US exports, hence full employment at home. Once economic reconstruction is achieved, Europeans will not be riddled with debt and will be able to pay for what they buy from us.

The US authorities thus concluded that grants were the preferable approach, and launched the Marshall Plan.

THE MARSHALL PLAN[4]

Between 1948 and 1951 the United States devoted over $13 billion ($11 billion of which were in the form of aid) to restore the economy of 17 European countries in the context of the Organization for European Economic Cooperation (OEEC, today the OECD). The total of US aid amounted to approximately $140 billion in 2020 terms. The United States demanded a number of commitments in exchange for their aid: first, European countries had to coordinate reconstruction expenses within the OEEC. The United States thus contributed to European cooperation – a prelude to Europe's subsequent union – in order to reinforce the Western bloc against the Soviet bloc. Then they demanded that the money received be used to buy goods produced by US industry.

To the aid granted under the Marshall Plan must be added the partial cancellation of France's debt to the US in 1946 ($2 billion were written off). Similarly, Belgium benefited from a reduction of its debt to the US as compensation for the uranium provided to make the first two atomic bombs, which it dropped on the Japanese cities of Hiroshima and Nagasaki, resulting in the first nuclear holocaust. The uranium had been extracted in the mines of Shinkolobwe (near Likasi, then called Jadotville) located in the province of Katanga in the Belgian Congo. Thanks to its colony, from which it extracted such valuable natural resources, Belgium was granted debt cancellation. Then, some 15 years later, Belgium illegally transferred the entire burden of the debts it had incurred in exploiting the resources and the population of that colony to the people of the newly independent Congo (see chapter 2).

THE 1953 LONDON DEBT AGREEMENT ON GERMANY'S DEBT

It should be kept in mind that Nazi Germany had suspended repayment of its external debt beginning in 1933 and never resumed repayment. Yet that was no obstacle to the Hitler regime receiving financial support from and doing business with major private corporations in the United States: Ford, who financed the launch of Volkswagen (the 'People's Car' created by the regime); General Motors, who

4   Information and table taken from the English *Wikipedia* page: <en.wikipedia.org/wiki/Marshall_Plan> [accessed 02/03/2022].

owned Opel; and IBM, accused of providing, through a fully managed subsidiary, technology that was used in managing the Nazis' persecution and extermination of targeted populations before and during the Second World War.[5]

The amount of debt cancelled did not take into account whether a debt was related to Nazi Germany's aggression and destruction during the Second World War or the reparations to which countries who were the victims of that aggression were entitled. The war debts were simply set aside, which amounted to an enormous gift to West Germany.

Despite the fact that they had played a major role in supporting the Nazi regime and were accomplices in the genocide of the Jewish and Roma people, big German corporations such as AEG, Siemens, IG Farben (AGFA, BASF, Bayer and Hoechst), Krupp, Volkswagen, BMW, Opel and Mercedes-Benz, and also major financial firms such as Deutsche Bank, Commerzbank and the insurer Allianz were protected and strengthened. The power of Germany's big capital emerged intact from the Second World War thanks to the support of the governments of the major Western powers.

In short, West Germany was able to redeem its debt and rebuild its economy so soon after the Second World War thanks to the political will of its creditors, i.e. the United States and its main Western allies (the United Kingdom and France). In October 1950 the three countries drafted a project in which the German federal government acknowledged debts incurred before and during the war. They added a declaration to the effect that:

The three Governments are agreed that the plan should provide for the orderly settlement of the claims against Germany, the total effect of which should not dislocate the German economy through undesirable effects on the internal financial situation, nor unduly drain existing or potential German foreign exchange resources. [...] The three Governments feel certain that the Federal Government shares their view as to the desirability of restoring Germany's credit and of providing for an orderly settlement of German debts which will ensure fair treatment to all concerned, taking full account of Germany's economic problems.[6]

---

5   See Oliver Burkeman, 'IBM "dealt directly with Holocaust organisers"', *The Guardian*, 29 March 2002 <theguardian.com/world/2002/mar/29/humanities.highereducation>; and Michael D. Hausfeld, 'IBM technology helped facilitate the Holocaust', *Los Angeles Times*, 19 February 2001 <latimes.com/archives/la-xpm-2001-feb-19-me-27417-story.html> [both accessed 30/11/2021].

6   William Z. Slany, Charles S. Sampson and Rogers P. Churchill (eds), *Foreign Relations of the United States, 1950, Central and Eastern Europe; The Soviet Union, Volume IV* (Washington, DC: US Government Printing Office, 1980), Document 410-762A.00/3–151, 'The Chairman, of the Allied High Commission for Germany (Kirkpatrick) to the Chancellor of the Federal Republic of Germany (Adenauer)' <history.state.gov/historicaldocuments/frus1950v04/d410> [accessed 30/11/2021].

Germany's pre-war debt amounted to DM22.6 billion including interest. Its post-war debt was estimated at DM16.2 billion. In the agreement signed in London on 27 February 1953,[7] these sums were reduced to DM7.5 and DM7 billion respectively.[8] This amounts to a 62.6 per cent reduction.

The agreement set up the possibility of suspending payments and renegotiating conditions in the event of a substantial change limiting the availability of resources.[9]

To make sure that the West German economy was effectively doing well and represented a stable key element in the Atlantic bloc against the Eastern bloc, Allied creditors granted the indebted German authorities and companies major concessions that far exceeded debt relief. The starting point was that Germany had to be able to pay everything back while maintaining a high level of growth and improving the living standards of its population. They had to pay back without getting poorer. To achieve this, creditors agreed, firstly, that Germany could repay its debt in its national currency; secondly, that Germany could reduce importations (manufacturing at home those goods that were formerly imported);[10] and thirdly, that it could sell its manufactured goods abroad so as to achieve a positive trade balance. These various concessions were set down during meetings held in London in July 1951:

Germany's capacity to pay involves not only the ability of private and governmental debtors to raise the necessary Deutschemark without inflationary consequences but also the ability of the country's economy to cover foreign debt service in its balance of payments on current account; [...]

The analysis of Germany's capacity to pay calls for the study of a number of difficult problems among which are:

a. the future productive capacity of Germany, with particular emphasis on the capacity to produce goods for export and to replace goods now imported;
b. the opportunities for the sale of German goods abroad;

---

7   *Agreement on German External Debts of 27 February 1953 [with Annexes and Subsidiary Agreements] London, February 27, 1953* (London: Her Majesty's Stationery Office, 1959), <assets. publishing.service.gov.uk/government/uploads/system/uploads/attachment_data/file/269824/ German_Ext_Debts_Pt_1.pdf> [accessed 30/11/2021]. Signatories of the 27 February 1953 Agreement: Federal Republic of Germany, United States of America, Belgium, Canada, Ceylon, Denmark, Spain, France, United Kingdom of Great Britain and Northern Ireland, Greece, Ireland, Liechtenstein, Luxembourg, Norway, Pakistan, Sweden, Switzerland, Union of South Africa and Yugoslavia.

8   1 USD was worth 4.2 DM at the time. West Germany's debt after reduction (i.e. DM14.5 bn) was thus equal to USD3.45 bn.

9   Creditors systematically refuse to include this kind of clause in agreements with developing countries.

10 In allowing Germany to replace imports by home-manufactured goods, creditors agreed to reduce their own exports to the country. As it happened, for the years 1950–51, 41 per cent of German imports came from Britain, France and the United States. If we add the share of imports coming from other creditor countries that participated in the conference (Belgium, Netherlands, Sweden and Switzerland), the total amount reached 66 per cent.

c.   the probable future terms of trade of Germany;

d.   the internal fiscal and economic policies required to ensure an export surplus[11]

Another significant aspect was that the debt service depended on how much the German economy could afford to pay, taking the country's reconstruction and the export revenues into account. The debt service/export revenue ratio was not to exceed 5 per cent. This meant that West Germany was not to use more than one twentieth of its export revenues to repay its debt. In fact, it never used more than 4.2 per cent (except once in 1959).

Another exceptional measure was that interest rates were substantially reduced (to between 0 and 5 per cent).

Finally, we have to consider the dollars the United States gave to West Germany: $1,173.7 million as part of the Marshall Plan from 3 April 1948 to 30 June 1952 (see Table 4.1) with at least $200 million added from 1954 to 1961, mainly via USAID.

Table 4.1   Expenditures involved in Marshall Plan economic assistance, 3 April 1948 to 30 June 1952 (USD million of the time)

Countries	Total	Grants	Loans
Total for all countries	13,325.8	11,820.7	1,505.1
Austria	677.8	677.8	–
Belgium-Luxembourg[a]	559.3	491.3	68.0
Denmark	273.0	239.7	33.3
France	2,713.6	2,488.0	225.6
Germany (FR)	1,390.6	1,173.7	216.9
Greece	706.7	706.7	–
Iceland	29.3	24.0	5.3
Ireland	147.5	19.3	128.2
Italy (including Trieste)	1,508.8	1,413.2	95.6
Netherlands (Indonesia)[b]	1,083.5	916.8	166.7
Norway	255.3	216.1	39.2
Portugal	51.2	15.1	36.1
Sweden	107.3	86.9	20.4
Turkey	225.1	140.1	85.0
United Kingdom	3,189.8	2,805	384.8
Regions[c]	407.0	407.0	–

[a] The loan included $65 million for Belgium and $3 million for Luxembourg.
[b] Marshall Plan support to the Dutch East Indies (Indonesia) extended to the Netherlands after the former became independent on 30 December 1949.
[c] Included the US contribution to the European Payments Union (EPU), a European social fund: $361.4 million.

11   'Preliminary Consultations on German Debts – London, July 1951', in Bundesrepublik Deutschland, Auswärtiges Amt et al., *Deutsche Auslandsschulden; Dokumente zu den internationalen Verhandlungen Oktober 1950 bis Juli 1951; englisches Sonderheft* (Hameln: C.W. Niemeyer, 1952), pp. 64–65.

Thanks to such exceptional conditions Germany had redeemed its debt by 1960. In record time. It even anticipated on maturity dates.

SOME ELEMENTS TOWARDS A COMPARISON

It is enlightening to compare the way post-war West Germany was treated with the way developing countries are treated today. Although bruised by war, Germany was economically stronger than most developing countries. Yet it received in 1953 what is currently denied to developing countries.

Proportion of export revenues devoted to paying back the debt

Germany was allowed to limit the share of its export revenues devoted to repaying its debt to 5 per cent. In actual fact, Germany never devoted more than 4.2 per cent of its export revenue to debt repayment (that percentage was reached in 1959).

And in any case, since a large portion of Germany's debt was repaid in German marks, the German central bank could simply issue currency – in other words, monetize the debt.

In 2019, according to data supplied by the World Bank, developing countries were forced to devote an average of 15.41 per cent of their revenue from export to repayment of external debt (14.1 per cent for the countries of Sub-Saharan Africa; 26.84 per cent for Latin America and the Caribbean; 11.02 per cent for the countries of East Asia and the Pacific; 22.3 per cent for the European and Central Asian countries; 13.27 per cent for North Africa and the Middle East; and 11.16 per cent for the countries of Southern Asia).

Here are a few examples of specific countries, including developing ones and economies of Europe's periphery: in 2019, the percentage of income from exports devoted to debt service was 26.79 per cent for Angola, 53.13 per cent for Brazil, 11.01 per cent for Bosnia, 12.85 per cent for Bulgaria, 32.32 per cent for Colombia, 12.35 per cent for Côte d'Ivoire, 28.94 per cent for Ethiopia, 26.06 per cent for Guatemala, 39.42 per cent for Indonesia, 88.21 per cent for Lebanon, 12.33 per cent for Mexico, 19.95 per cent for Nicaragua, 35.35 per cent for Pakistan, 11.45 per cent for Peru, 27.19 per cent for Serbia, 15.74 per cent for Tunisia, and 34.29 per cent for Turkey.

Interest rates on external debt

As stipulated in the 1953 London Agreement on German External Debts, the interest rate was between 0 and 5 per cent.

By contrast, the interest rates paid by developing countries are much higher. And the great majority of agreements set rates that are upwardly variable. From 1980 to 2000 the average interest rate for developing countries fluctuated between 4.8 and 9.1 per cent (between 5.7 and 11.4 per cent for Latin America and the Caribbean, and even between 6.6 and 11.9 per cent for Brazil from 1980 to 2004).

In 2019, for example, the average interest rate was 7.08 per cent for Angola, 7.11 per cent for Ecuador, 7.8 per cent for Jamaica, 9.76 per cent for Argentina and 11.15 per cent for Lebanon.

Currency in which the external debt had to be paid

Germany was allowed to use its national currency.

No country of the South is allowed to do the same, except in exceptional cases for ludicrously small sums. All major indebted countries must use hard currencies (dollars, euros, yen, Swiss francs, pounds sterling).

Review clause

In the case of Germany, the agreement set up the possibility of suspending payments and renegotiating conditions in the event that a substantial change should curtail available resources.

Creditors see to it that loan agreements with developing countries do not include such a review clause, despite the fact that a recent judgment of the Court of Justice of the European Union confirms that a state may modify its debt obligations in response to exceptional circumstances.[12]

Jurisdiction over disputes

The German courts were allowed to refuse to execute rulings of foreign courts or arbitration bodies concerning repayment of external debt if their execution might threaten public order.

No such allowance is made by creditors for developing countries. It must be said that debtor countries are wrong to surrender their own jurisdictions when there is this example of Germany's courts being allowed to have the final word.

Import substitution policy

The agreement on Germany's debt explicitly grants the country the right to manufacture commodities that it once imported.

By contrast, the World Bank and the IMF generally recommend that developing countries not manufacture anything they can import.

Cash grants in hard currency

Although it was largely responsible for the Second World War, Germany received significant grants in hard currency as part of the Marshall Plan and beyond.

---

12 Court of Justice of the European Union, Judgment of the General Court (Third Chamber) of 23 May 2019 <curia.europa.eu/juris/document/document.jsf?docid=214384&text=&dir=&doclang=EN&part=1&occ=first&mode=DOC&pageIndex=0&cid=8474255>; see Éric Toussaint, 'Exceptional circumstances can help indebted States', CADTM, 14 January 2021 <cadtm.org/Exceptional-circumstances-can-help-indebted-States> [accessed 30/11/2021].

While the rich countries have promised developing countries assistance and cooperation, the latter merely receive a trickle by way of currency grants. Between 2000 and 2018, developing countries repaid an annual average of $214 billion – much more than the $100 billion they had received in the form of 'aid' and 'cooperation'. The largest indebted countries in the Third World receive no cash aid whatsoever.

Unquestionably, the refusal to grant indebted developing countries the same kind of concessions as were granted to Germany indicates that creditors do not really want these countries to get rid of their debts. Creditors consider it in their better interest to maintain developing countries in a permanent state of indebtedness so as to extract maximum revenues in the form of debt reimbursement, but also to enforce policies that serve their interests and to make sure that these countries remain loyal partners within the international institutions.

What the United States did via the Marshall Plan for industrialized countries that had been ravaged by war, they also did during the post-war period for certain Allied developing countries at strategic locations on the peripheries of the Soviet Union and China. They gave them much greater amounts than those lent by the World Bank to the rest of the developing countries. This particularly applies to South Korea and Taiwan, which were to receive significant aid beginning in the 1950s – aid that largely contributed to their economic success.

From 1954 to 1961, for example, South Korea received more from the United States than *the total amount of the loans* the World Bank granted to all the independent countries in the Third World (India, Pakistan, Mexico, Brazil and Nigeria included) – over $2.5 billion vs $2.3 billion. During the same period Taiwan received about $800 million.[13] Because it was strategically located in relation to China and the USSR, a small farming country like South Korea with a population of less than 20 million benefited from US largesse. The World Bank and the United States were tolerant of economic policies in Korea and Taiwan that they banned in Brazil or Mexico. This will be developed in chapter 11 on Korea.

---

13   Calculations by the author based on: 1) World Bank annual reports 1954–61, and 2) *US Overseas Loans and Grants (Greenbook)* <catalog.data.gov/dataset/u-s-overseas-loans-and-grants-greenbook> [accessed 30/11/2021].

5

A Bank Under the Influence

The book commissioned by the World Bank to recount its first 50 years of existence shows that the concept of the Bank as a huge bureaucracy that has gradually freed itself from the influence of the US is actually a far cry from reality.[1] This mistaken notion is revealed by the North American environmentalist Bruce Rich in his insightful book on the World Bank.[2] In reality the institution is firmly under the control of the US government, which negotiates – with the governments of other major capitalist powers – the policies to be adopted, under its leadership, within the World Bank. It has frequently failed to make any effort to reach a consensus with its principal partners (since the end of the 1950s, these are Japan, Germany, Great Britain and France) and it imposes its views directly on the Bank.

Relations have sometimes been tense between the US government and the Bank's president and/or its management in the wider sense. One must also consider the intervention (more or less active depending on the period) of Congress. On several occasions, the US Executive has had to make a deal with Congress concerning the attitude to be taken with reference to the Bank and its activities.[3]

Although the World Bank is systematically subjected to US influence, it does nevertheless enjoy a certain measure of autonomy. It possesses a certain logic of its own which sometimes comes into conflict with the immediate interests of the US government. The Bank's autonomy is very limited, however, and the US government imposes its will on all issues that it considers important. Also, one must take into consideration the close links that exist between the US business world (big capital) and the World Bank.

THE INFLUENCE OF THE UNITED STATES ON THE BANK

Throughout the history of the International Bank for Reconstruction and Development (the World Bank), the United States has been the largest shareholder and the most influential member country. US support for, pressure on,

---

1   Kapur, Lewis and Webb, *The World Bank: Its First Half Century*, Volumes 1 and 2.

2   'But the only fully consistent hypothesis to reconcile the discordant elements of the Bank's actions, performance, and stated goals was that of a bureaucracy that had become an end in itself, driven by an institutional culture of expansion and a will to power for its own sake.' Rich, *Mortgaging the Earth*, p. 103.

3   This is a unique position in the world. No other legislature has played as active a role as that of the United States in the World Bank Group (and the IMF). Besides the part of this chapter devoted to this question, chapter 19 on the Meltzer Commission will address the subject again.

and criticisms of the Bank have been central to its growth and the evolution of its policies, programs, and practices.[4]

These are the opening lines of the chapter on relations between the US and the World Bank from 1945 to 1992 in the aforementioned history commissioned by the Bank. The book's authors, who had free access to the World Bank's archives, produced a work whose overall tone is fundamentally critical. That explains, by the way, why the Bank did not widely publicize the book and why it was not published until late in 1997.

Other excerpts from the same text, reproduced below, are so explicit as to need no comment:

And the top management of the Bank spends much more time meeting with, consulting, and responding to the United States than it does with any other member country. Although this intense interaction has changed little over the years, the way the United States mobilizes other member countries in support of its views has changed considerably. Initially, it was so predominant that its positions and the decision of the board were virtually indistinguishable.[5]

The United States has viewed all multilateral organizations, including the World Bank, as instruments of foreign policy to be used for specific US aims and objectives.[6]

The United States is often impatient with the processes of consensus building on which multilateral cooperation rests.[7]

A preoccupation with containing communism, and the change in the relative US power in the world explain much of the evolution in US relations with the World Bank over the past fifty years.[8]

The debt crisis in the south and the collapse of communism in eastern Europe led to renewed US interest in the Bank.[9]

RETRACING THE ORIGIN OF THE WORLD BANK AND THE US INFLUENCE

In contrast to the IMF which is the result of intense negotiation between the United States and Britain, the Bank is largely an American creation. The role of the United States was acknowledged by John Maynard Keynes in his opening remarks at the Bretton Woods Conference.[10]

---

4   Gwin, 'U.S. relations with the World Bank, 1945–1992', p. 195.
5   Gwin, 'U.S. relations with the World Bank, 1945–1992', p. 248.
6   Ibid., p. 195.
7   Ibid.
8   Ibid., p. 196.
9   Ibid.
10   Ibid.

The result was a strong and enduring American imprint on all aspects of the Bank, including its structure, general policy direction, and the manner of granting loans.[11]

Among the issues that divided the participants at the Bretton Woods Conference was the location of the headquarters of the Bank and the IMF. The US Treasury wanted it to be established in Washington, within the reach of its influence, while several foreign delegations preferred New York – on the one hand to put it at a distance from the US government, and on the other hand to move it closer to the future headquarters of the United Nations. John Maynard Keynes explicitly asked that the Bank and the IMF be kept at a distance from the US Congress and, he added, from the influence of the embassies; New York must therefore be the choice of headquarters. In fact, Keynes initially tried to persuade the participants to choose London. Realizing it was a losing battle, he then tried to avoid Washington by proposing New York. The US Treasury Secretary, Henry Morgenthau, replied that it was necessary to move the centre of the world from London and Wall Street towards the US Treasury. Morgenthau's line of argument was clever with respect to other delegations since at the end of the Second World War, the British Empire, though shaky, was still dominant – hence the desire not to locate the headquarters of the new financial institution in London, close to the leading financial centre, the City of London. The second part of his argument was also clever in that Wall Street was synonymous with the domination of the business world that had produced the 1929 crash.

Basically, Morgenthau wanted, as he declared, to place the centre of the new financial institutions under the control of the US Treasury Department and maintain a distance from Wall Street. Morgenthau, Harry White and Emilio Collado later left or would be dismissed under pressure from Wall Street (see chapter 2). In fact, the Bretton Woods institutions very quickly (from 1947 in fact) came under the twofold supervision of the Treasury and Wall Street.

In fact, of the thirteen presidents of the World Bank from 1946 until today, ten, including the first, have come directly from the business world.

Moreover, to avoid undue influence from the US, Keynes wanted the Bank's executive directors to divide their activity between their country of origin and World Bank headquarters. He therefore proposed that they work on a part-time basis.[12] But the US Treasury Department's proposal prevailed: the executive directors were to be permanent residents in Washington and the headquarters of the two institutions just a five-minute walk from the White House.

During the vote in Congress on US participation in the World Bank and the IMF, an overwhelming majority emerged (345 against 18 in the House of Representatives;

11   Ibid., p. 197.
12   Rich, *Mortgaging the Earth*, p. 64; Mason and Asher, *The World Bank since Bretton Woods*, p. 30.

61 against 16 in the Senate) – a very unusual state of affairs. This clearly proved that Congress was indeed satisfied with the choices made in the construction of these two institutions.

While the Bank was principally created to ensure reconstruction of the countries devastated by the Second World War, the US preferred to launch the Marshall Plan on its own initiative, because in this way it could totally control operations and also make donations to whomever it liked.

Although it in fact played a marginal role in reconstruction, the Bank nevertheless allocated certain loans to European countries, starting with the first in its history: $250 million to France in May 1947.[13] According to Catherine Gwin, the US government refused to grant any loan to France as long as the French Communist Party (PCF) was in the government. The State Department therefore took explicit and formal action in the matter: the PCF was pushed out of the governmental coalition and, in the days that followed, the representative of the World Bank announced that the loan of $250 million was granted. This clearly shows the direct influence exercised by the US Executive on the Bank and the political choices leading to this intervention. In the same study, the author indicates that in 1947, the US successfully prevented loans being granted to Poland and Czechoslovakia on the grounds that the governments of these countries included communists.[14]

From the start of its operations, the policies of the World Bank were determined by the context of the Cold War and related US interests.

THE PRESIDENT OF THE WORLD BANK

Since its origin and up to the present time, the president of the World Bank has always been a US citizen nominated by the US government. The members of the Board of Governors simply ratify that nomination. This privilege does not figure in the Bank's Articles of Agreement. Although the Articles allow it, no governor has ventured up to now – or at any rate, publicly[15] – to propose a candidate from another country or even an American candidate other than the one selected by the US government.[16]

---

13   This was the first and the biggest loan in its 50 years of existence (see Kapur, Lewis and Webb, *The World Bank: Its First Half Century, Volume 1*, p. 1218).
14   See Gwin, 'U.S. relations with the World Bank, 1945–1992', pp. 253–54. Note that Poland withdrew from the World Bank on 14 March 1950, as did Czechoslovakia on 31 December 1954. The Soviet Union, which was present at the beginning of the Bretton Woods Conference, did not participate in the system's implementation.
15   None of the sources that we have consulted mentions the existence of an internal debate in the Board of Governors during which a different candidate than that of the US government was proposed.
16   The US upheld this tradition so strongly that when it wished to propose a candidate who was not a US national – as happened in 1995 in the case of James Wolfensohn, an Australian – it quickly granted him citizenship to ensure it could offer him the position of president of the World Bank.

THE US RIGHT OF VETO AT THE WORLD BANK

From its beginnings till today, the US is the only country to have a de facto right of veto at the World Bank. With the creation of the Bank, the US had 35.07 per cent of the voting rights;[17] in 2020, the US had 16.41 per cent – which is still enough to exercise a veto since the required majority is 85 per cent. Since 1947 (the year the Bank began operating), the majority required to modify the Articles of Agreement was 80 per cent (held by at least 60 per cent of the member countries), which in fact gave the US a right of veto. The wave of newly independent countries in the South increased the number of member nations of the World Bank Group, gradually diluting the weight of the US vote. However, the US took care to preserve its right of veto: in 1966, it had only 25.50 per cent of voting rights but this percentage was still sufficient for the purpose.

When in 1987 the situation was no longer tenable for the US, the definition of the qualified majority was modified in its favour. That year, Japan negotiated a significant increase in its voting rights with the US, placing it as the second most important country, ahead of Germany and Great Britain.[18] In order to concede this increase to their Japanese allies, the US agreed to a reduction of its voting rights provided that the required majority was raised to 85 per cent. In this manner it gave full satisfaction to Japan while maintaining its right of veto.

According to Catherine Gwin, 'The United States is also the dominant member of the Bank's board – but only in part it is lead shareholder. Formally, most Bank decisions, including those affecting lending levels and loan allocations, require a simple majority vote of the board.' Which means that that the US could be made a minority. But the author continues:

Decisions are, however, often worked out between the United States and Bank management before they ever get to the Board, or among members of the Board before they get to a vote. And most Board decisions are taken by consensus. It is the weight of its voice, therefore, more than the exercise of its vote that gives the United States effective power on the Board.[19]

US INFLUENCE ON THE BANK IN SPECIFIC COUNTRIES

Here I will present the cases of five countries in order to illustrate the scope of the US influence on the choices made by the Bank. To do this, I draw on the two books commissioned by the World Bank to narrate its own history,[20] as well as on

---

17   The second-ranking country in terms of percentage of voting rights was Great Britain with 14.52 per cent.

18   Japan had joined the Bank in 1952 at the same time as the Federal Republic of Germany.

19   Gwin, 'U.S. relations with the World Bank, 1945–1992', p. 244.

20   Mason and Asher, *The World Bank since Bretton Woods* and Kapur, Lewis and Webb, *The World Bank: Its First Half Century*, Volumes 1 and 2.

the Bank's annual reports, while comparing the information provided with other sources, generally critical of the Bank. The choice has not been easy since there is a profusion of examples at our disposal. In fact, according to these two books, the instances in which the opinion of the US government did not prevail can be counted on the fingers of both hands.

Nicaragua and Guatemala

Central America is considered by the US government as part of its own exclusive sphere of influence. The policies adopted by the World Bank as regards granting loans to the countries of the region are directly influenced by the political choices of the US government. The case of Nicaragua and Guatemala during the 1950s makes this clear:

Thus one of the largest developing country borrowers, in number of loans, was Nicaragua, a nation with one million inhabitants, controlled by the Somoza family.[21] Washington and the Somozas found their relationship highly convenient. The United States supported the Somozas and the Somozas supported the United States – in votes at the United Nations, in regional councils, and by offering Nicaragua as a base for training and launching the Cuban exile forces that met disaster at the Bay of Pigs in 1961. Between 1951 and 1956 Nicaragua received nine World Bank Loans, and one in 1960. An American military base was established in 1953 from which was launched the successful overthrow, by the US Central Intelligence Agency (CIA), of Guatemalan President Jacobo Arbenz, who had legalized the Communist Party and threatened to expropriate the assets of the United Fruit Company. Guatemala itself, with three times the population of Nicaragua, and though it was one of the first countries to receive a survey mission (published in 1951), did not obtain a loan until 1955, after the overthrow of its 'communist' regime.[22]

After Somoza's fall in 1979, the US attempted, by various political, economic and military means, to destabilize and then overthrow the new Sandinista system. The US undertook several unilateral military interventions in Nicaragua in the 1980s, none of them with any legal justification. This led to a plea by Nicaragua against the US in the International Court of Justice of The Hague, which delivered a verdict in 1986. It condemned the United States for violating obligations imposed by international law, in particular the ban on the use of force (Article 2, Paragraph 4 of

---

21   The Somoza family ruled Nicaragua from 1935, the year it was put in power by a US military intervention, to 1979 when a popular insurrection brought about the fall of dictator Anastasio Somoza and his flight to Paraguay, also ruled by a dictator, Alfredo Stroessner.
22   Kapur, Lewis and Webb, *The World Bank: Its First Half Century, Volume 1*, p. 103.

the UN Charter) and on attempts to undermine the sovereignty of another state and intervention in the internal affairs of a state.[23]

Concerning the Bank's attitude with regard to the Sandinista regime during the 1980s and the influence that was brought to bear on it by the US government, we quote another excerpt from Catherine Gwin's study: 'A more recent example in which the Bank's refusal to lend clearly coincided with US policy is that of Nicaragua in the 1980s. The reason for the suspension of lending was the accumulation of arrears. However, in September 1984, the Nicaraguan government formally proposed a solution to its arrearages problem.'[24] Gwin details the concrete proposals formulated by Nicaragua and explains that although these proposals were acceptable, the Bank made no effort to help the Sandinista regime. She pointed out the contrast with the Bank's flexibility towards other regimes which were allies of the US.

Yugoslavia

In order to strengthen Marshal Tito's distancing of his regime from the Soviet Union, the US government incited the Bank to grant a loan to Yugoslavia at the end of the 1940s. As the following quotation shows, the US government preferred to assist Tito's Yugoslavia through the Bank rather than grant direct bilateral assistance, for fear of being criticized in Congress by the numerous members who opposed any support of a communist regime:[25]

The Bank lent to Yugoslavia soon after the break from the Soviet bloc in 1948. George Kennan[26] had recommended 'discreet and unostentatious support' by the West, fearing Russian reaction, and aware that Congress would be unwilling to assist a Communist country. The 'international Bank' was an appropriate vehicle for such a role, and a mission travelled to Belgrade the following year.[27]

The president of the Bank, Eugene R. Black, went in person to negotiate directly with Marshal Tito.

Chile

After the election of Salvador Allende in 1969 and the founding of the Popular Unity government, the Bank, under US pressure, suspended its loans to Chile from 1970 to 1973. The case of Chile shows that there can be a contradiction between the

---

23   International Court of Justice, *Case Concerning Military and Paramilitary Activities in and against Nicaragua, Judgment of 27 June 1986* <icj-cij.org/public/files/case-related/70/070-19860627-JUD-01-00-EN.pdf> [accessed 11/11/2021]. Following this conviction, the US officially announced that it would no longer acknowledge the competence of the ICJ.

24   Gwin, 'U.S. relations with the World Bank, 1945–1992', p. 258.

25   As we shall see later, on several occasions the US Executive used its direct influence on the Bank to bypass possible opposition from Congress or, in any case, to avoid a debate.

26   George Kennan represented the State Department.

27   Kapur, Lewis and Webb, *The World Bank: Its First Half Century, Volume 1*, p. 103.

Bank's judgement and the position of the US government, with the US finally getting the Bank to modify its position. Although the Bank's management considered that Chile fulfilled the conditions to receive loans, the US government made sure that no loan was granted to the Allende government. Catherine Gwin summarizes this emblematic case as follows:

The United States pressured the Bank not to lend to the Allende government after nationalization of Chile's copper mines. Despite the pressure, the Bank sent a mission to Santiago (having determined that Chile was in compliance with Bank rules requiring that for lending to resume after nationalization, procedure for compensation had to be under way). Robert McNamara subsequently met with Allende to indicate that the Bank was prepared to make new loans contingent upon government commitments to reform the economy. But the Bank and the Allende regime could not come to terms on the conditions for a loan. Throughout the period of the Allende regime, Chile received no new loans. Shortly after Allende's assassination in 1973 during a coup that brought General Pinochet's military junta to power, the Bank resumed lending, providing a fifteen-year credit for copper mine development. [...] The suspension of lending in 1970–73 was cited in the 1982 US Treasury report as a significant example of the successful exercise of US influence on the Bank and although the Bank reached an agreement in principle on new lending in June 1973, the loan proposals were not formally considered by the board until after the September coup that brought General Pinochet to power.[28]

As a complement to this information there is a document conserved in the archives of the World Bank in which the Chilean government, at the Bank's September 1972 meeting, protests the suspension of loans and points out that precisely defined projects had already been submitted to the Bank.[29] Under pressure from the US, the Bank took no action as long as Allende was in power.

Several internal working documents of the Bank are critical of the Bank's policies towards Chile under Allende and under Pinochet (see the following chapter).

Some ten years later, when the atrocities committed by the Augusto Pinochet regime were incurring wide protests in the US, and even within Congress, the US government asked the Bank to delay a discussion on granting loans to Chile in order to avoid opposition in Congress. This request was rejected by the president of the Bank, Barber Conable, in a letter addressed to James Baker, then Secretary of the Treasury, on 29 October 1986. One can deduce that the request of the

---

28   Gwin, 'U.S. relations with the World Bank', pp. 256–57.
29   International Bank for Reconstruction and Development, *Summary Proceedings of the 1972 Annual Meetings of the Boards of Governors* (Washington, DC: IBRD, September 1972), p. 55 <documents1.worldbank.org/curated/en/602141468156870809/pdf/534080BR0board101Official-0Use0Only1.pdf> [accessed 10/02/22].

US government was simply lip service to public opinion, designed to depict the government as being sensitive to expressed democratic concerns, while remaining fully aware that, in a well-rehearsed distribution of roles, the president of the Bank would keep to the political course recommended by the government. It was a question of pleasing everyone.

Vietnam

From the 1960s until the end of the Vietnam War in 1975, the US successfully encouraged the Bank, through its affiliate IDA, to grant loans regularly to the South Vietnam regime – an ally of the US. After the end of the war and the defeat of the US, the World Bank sent two successive survey missions which concluded that the Vietnamese authorities, although not pursuing a totally satisfactory economic policy, fulfilled the conditions required to receive concessional loans. Shahid Husain, director of the Bank's mission, specified that the performance of Vietnam's economy was not inferior to that of Bangladesh or Pakistan, which received aid from the Bank. In spite of this, the Bank management, under pressure from the US government, suspended loans to Vietnam and its president, Robert McNamara, affirmed in *Newsweek* (20 August 1979) that the suspension was based on a negative report by the mission. That is factually false, as Catherine Gwin points out: 'The mission's contention, in contrast to what McNamara said publicly in *Newsweek*, was that on substantive grounds there was no basis for stopping all lending to Vietnam.'[30]

Conclusion regarding specific country cases

The World Bank management justifies its allocation or non-allocation of loans on purely economic grounds. But we have seen that in reality, the policies governing the granting of loans are determined first and foremost by the intervention of the US government in the Bank's business, largely on the basis of political objectives.

This is not to say that economic objectives have no importance, but they are subordinate or complementary to political and strategic choices. Catherine Gwin, who defends the generally positive result of US influence on the World Bank, from the US standpoint, adopts a rigorous approach in which she does not conceal the contradictory aspects of the policies of both the US government and of the Bank's management. The following remark is particularly interesting: 'Although one need not dispute the Bank's economic policy assessments of Allende's Chile, Vietnam, and Nicaragua under the Sandinistas, it is worth noting that equally harsh assessments could have been made, but were not, of Somoza's Nicaragua, Marcos's Philippines, and Mobutu's Zaire, regimes that were all important cold war allies of the United States.'[31]

---

30   Gwin, 'U.S. relations with the World Bank', p. 258.
31   Gwin, 'U.S. relations with the World Bank', p. 258.

UNITED STATES INFLUENCE ON SECTORAL LOANS

From the 1970s, the US systematically used its influence in an attempt to convince the Bank not to grant loans which facilitated the production of goods that would compete with US products. For example, the US regularly opposed the production of palm oil, citrus fruits and sugar.[32] In 1987 the US got the Bank to drastically reduce loans granted to the steel-manufacturing industry in India and Pakistan. In 1985, the US successfully opposed an investment project by the International Financial Corporation (IFC – World Bank Group) in the Brazilian steel industry and later a loan from the Bank to support the restructuring of Mexico's steel-manufacturing sector. It also threatened to use its veto to block a loan for the Chinese steel industry in the 1980s. The US also blocked a loan from the IFC to a mining company for the extraction of iron ore in Brazil. It took similar action regarding an investment by the IFC in the Chilean copper industry.

In addition, the US actively influenced the Bank in its policy on the oil sector. The US was in favour of loans for oil drilling, but not refining. No comment is necessary.

CASES OF CONVERGENCE BETWEEN THE US
AND ANOTHER POWER (HERE THE UK)

On several occasions, US interests have coincided with those of other powers. In these cases the attitude adopted by the Bank was the result of close consultation between the United States, the other power(s) concerned and the Bank. Two examples: the Bank's attitude toward the Aswan Dam construction project under the regime of Gamal Abdel Nasser in Egypt, and in Iraq since the occupation of that territory by troops from the US, Britain and their allies in March 2003.

The Aswan Dam project in Egypt

The project to build the Aswan Dam on the Nile preceded Colonel Nasser's accession to power in 1952 but took its final form during that year. In January 1953, the Egyptian finance minister wrote to Eugene Black, president of the World Bank, proposing that the Bank co-finance the gigantic project. Although the execution of this infrastructure corresponded to the Bank's priorities, its management was reluctant to be involved because Britain, which at that time ranked second in terms of voting rights within the Bank's Board of Governors, considered the progressive military regime to be a threat to its strategic interests. And indeed, the Egyptian military in power challenged the occupation of the Suez Canal by British troops.[33]

---

32 The different examples concerning sectoral loans are from Gwin, 'U.S. relations with the World Bank,' pp. 223–24 and 259–63.

33 The British occupation of Egypt dated from 1882. The debt demanded of Egypt served as a pretext for this imperialistic occupation. See Éric Toussaint, *The Debt System*, chapter 6.

Black personally visited Egypt and discussed the project; the Bank sent engineers, etc. The project involved a dam whose capacity of 130 billion cubic metres would be four times greater than the largest artificial dams to date. The vast scope of the project offered huge prospects to international construction firms.

The negotiations between Egypt and Britain for the departure of British troops resulted in an agreement, which reduced Britain's reluctance and the pressures it was putting on Bank management not to grant loans. The North American and British governments gave the Bank management their go-ahead for negotiations, but they imposed restrictions by dividing the execution of the project into two phases. The financing of the first phase was guaranteed while the second phase would depend on how the Egyptian authorities evolved politically. Of course, this was not explicitly expressed in the agreements, but that was how the Egyptian government interpreted it. The Egyptians wanted to start the project in July 1957, which meant that the contract had to be signed in July 1956. Consequently, they asked the Bank to confirm the loans as quickly as possible.

In December 1955, a meeting of the executive directors of the Bank gave Eugene Black the green light to pursue negotiations with the Egyptians on the basis of the conditions laid down by the North American and British governments. The Egyptians gave the Bank's conditions a cool reception. Meanwhile, the British authorities learned that the Egyptians had signed a commercial agreement with the Soviet Union with a view to a cotton-for-arms exchange.[34] Historians Mason and Asher commented on the appearance of the Soviet Union on the scene as follows: 'These maneuvers had simply heightened the desire of the Western powers to associate themselves with the dam.'[35] Eugene Black, before going to Cairo to finalize the agreement with the Egyptians, contacted the US government, who confirmed the go-ahead. On his way to Cairo, Eugene Black also met British Prime Minister Eden in London. After ten days of negotiations in Cairo, one fundamental point of disagreement remained: the Egyptians would not accept the conditions fixed by the US and Britain. On his return to Washington, Black proposed pursuing negotiations because he was eager to reach an agreement. But in Washington and especially in London, hesitation was growing as the Egyptian regime took on an Arab nationalist orientation. British opposition increased further when King Hussein of Jordan, on 1 March 1956, sacked the entire British command of the Arab Legion. Eugene Black now found himself more and more isolated, but the governments let him pursue negotiations, implying that they could succeed, while it appears to the Bank historians that the decision to refuse had already been taken.

---

34   According to Mason and Asher, it is unlikely that Prime Minister Nasser actively desired the support of the Soviets to finance the dam before the withdrawal of American and British offers. After this withdrawal, 17 months passed before he signed an agreement with the Soviets to finance the first phase of the construction of the dam. (Mason and Asher, *The World Bank since Bretton Woods*, p. 642.)

35   Mason and Asher, *The World Bank since Bretton Woods*, p. 636.

At the beginning of July 1956, thanks to tenacious negotiation, Eugene Black got Nasser, the Egyptian prime minister, to declare his acceptance of the conditions fixed by the Western powers. Nevertheless, when the Egyptian ambassador officially announced Egypt's agreement on 19 July 1956, he was told that in the present circumstances the US government had decided not to participate in financing the Aswan Dam. On 20 July, the British Parliament was informed that the British government had withdrawn from the project. Mason and Asher point out that the State Department informed the Bank of its decision to withdraw from the project only one hour before the official communication was sent to the Egyptian ambassador. They add that in this communication, the US used the pretext of a negative economic assessment on the part of the Bank. With the printed version of the assessment already being circulated in the chancelleries, the Bank's president persuaded the US government to withdraw that argument from the text released to the press.

To come back to the fundamental political consequences, we once again refer to the judgement made by Mason and Asher:

The dramatic sequel is well known. On July 26, 1956, Premier Nasser announced that the government was taking control of the property and operations of the Suez Canal Company. On October 29, after a series of border incidents, Israeli troops invaded Egypt, and on December 2, British and French military action against Egypt began – ostensibly for the purpose of protecting the Canal Zone but, in the opinion of many observers, actually for the purpose of overturning Premier Nasser.[36]

The Aswan Dam affair shows how the US government can work with another government to influence the decisions of the World Bank when their interests coincide. It also reveals that the US can take refuge behind a so-called refusal of the Bank to oppose a project, thus making the Bank seem responsible for the failure.

In a limited number of cases, the US government has allowed other powers to use their means of influence on the Bank. This has happened when the strategic interests of the United States were not directly concerned. For example, France was able to exert influence on the Bank to persuade it to adopt a policy in accordance with 'French' interests in Côte d'Ivoire.

The occupation and reconstruction of Iraq

The military intervention of March 2003 against Saddam Hussein's Iraq, followed by the occupation of its territory, was carried out without any authorization from the UN to resort to the use of force, which constitutes a flagrant violation of Article 51

36   Mason and Asher, *The World Bank since Bretton Woods*, p. 641.

of the Charter of the United Nations. The invasion of Iraq took place against the opinion of several major powers such as France, Germany, Russia and China. The US, at the head of the coalition which launched the attack against Iraq, had the active support of three other members of the G7 (Britain, Japan and Italy) and of medium-size powers such as Spain and Australia.[37]

As early as April 2003, the US took the initiative of negotiating with the G7 and within the framework of the Paris Club a substantial reduction of the debts contracted by the Saddam Hussein regime. The idea was to reduce the burden of this debt so that the 'new' Iraq, an ally of the United States, would be in a position to contract new ones and repay them. In addition to this approach, which I have analyzed elsewhere,[38] the US government put pressure on the World Bank and the IMF to lend to the new Iraqi authorities who were directly under their control through the civilian administrator of Iraq, the American Paul Bremer. In several declarations from the end of March to the end of May 2003, it can clearly be seen that the president of the World Bank and the director of the IMF were very reluctant. The necessary conditions for granting loans were not met. What were the problems?

1. The legitimacy of the authorities at the head of Iraq was not recognized, particularly because they exercised no real sovereignty in view of the executive power held by Paul Bremer and the occupation authorities.
2. In principle, the World Bank and the IMF respect the following rule: they do not grant new loans to a country that has defaulted on payment of its sovereign debt. The pressure exerted by the US on the Bank and the IMF, on the one hand, and on the powers opposing the war, on the other, gradually removed the obstacles inasmuch as the UN Security Council, at its meeting on 22 May 2003, entrusted the US and its allies with the management of Iraq's oil and lifted the embargo against Iraq. The Security Council did not recognize the war but it recognized the fait accompli of the occupation. The US and its allies got the World Bank and the IMF to agree to actively participate in the donor conference for the reconstruction of Iraq held in Madrid on 23 October 2003.

---

37   For an overview of the position of the UN and various States regarding the invasion of Iraq, see (in French): Centre de droit international de l'Université Libre de Bruxelles, 'L'intervention america-no-britannique en Irak du 20 mars 2003 (Opération Iraqi Freedom)' ('The US–British intervention in Iraq of 20 March, 2003 [Operation Iraqi Freedom]') <iusadbellum.files.wordpress.com/2011/07/irak-2003.pdf> [accessed 01/12/2021]. The circumstances of the invasion of Iraq show how much influence the US has when it comes to determining questions of 'collective security', ignoring the resolutions of the Security Council and the other UN institutions. See (in French): Monique Chemillier-Gendreau, 'L'ONU confisquée par les grandes puissances' ('The UN Confiscated by the Major Powers'), Le Monde diplomatique, January 1996; and Olivier Corten, 'La sécurité collective, un rêve contrarié' ('Collective Security, a Shattered Dream'), Le Monde diplomatique, September 2005.
38   Toussaint, Your Money or Your Life, chapter 16, pp. 327–38.

The case of Iraq demonstrates the US's ability to form an alliance to determine the orientation of the Bank and the IMF – in this case, despite the reluctance of their principal directors, James Wolfensohn and Horst Köhler.[39] In October 2004, the United States managed to get the member nations of the Paris Club (to which it also belongs) to agree to a three-phase cancellation of 80 per cent of their $38.9 billion claim against Iraq.[40]

DIVERGENCES BETWEEN WORLD BANK MANAGEMENT AND THE UNITED STATES

In the early 1970s, divergences appeared between the US Executive and the Bank's management. This was due to the fact that Robert McNamara, president of the Bank since 1968, was directly aligned with the Democratic Party: he entered politics thanks to President John F. Kennedy, who made him his adviser in 1961; his career continued (as Defense Secretary) under the Democrat Lyndon B. Johnson, whose administration had him appointed president of the Bank in 1968. In 1969, the situation changed when a Republican president, Richard Nixon, took office while McNamara's term was still running. Several skirmishes between the Nixon administration and the management of the Bank occurred during 1971. For example, the US Executive ordered the executive director representing the United States to vote against a loan that the Bank had decided to grant to Guyana. In 1972, the option was to renew McNamara's term (a term of five years) or to replace him. The Republicans were favourable in principle to the appointment of one of their own but in the end, the executive reluctantly renewed Robert McNamara's term.

During his second term, tensions increased considerably. The government foiled an initiative to which Robert McNamara was strongly committed: he had negotiated with the OPEC member nations for the creation of a new development financing fund fuelled by petrodollars. The government, which wanted to break the OPEC monopoly, aborted this initiative. During this tense period, Secretary of State Henry Kissinger led the offensive against McNamara. As an alternative to the creation of a special fund fuelled by OPEC, Kissinger proposed increasing the funds made available for the International Finance Corporation and the World Bank.[41]

---

39 Horst Köhler resigned from his post on 4 March 2004 in order to accept the office of president of Germany proposed to him by Germany's CDU-CSU opposition. Once released from his responsibilities at the IMF, he made declarations in which he criticized the American occupation of Iraq. Rodrigo Rato, who was appointed on 4 May 2004 by the Board of Governors to succeed him, was until March 2004 Minister of Finance and Economy in Spain's José María Aznar government, a faithful ally of the US and the host of the conference of donors in October 2003. Note that in 2018 Rato was sentenced by a Spanish court to four and a half years in prison for embezzlement of funds from the banks he headed (see Raphael Minder, 'Rodrigo Rato, Ex-Chief of Spain's Bankia, Loses Bid to Avoid Prison', New York Times, 24 October 2018 <nytimes.com/2018/10/24/business/rodrigo-rato-bankia-prison.html> [accessed 10/02/2022].
40 The agreement was confirmed and signed one year later, on 27 October 2005.
41 These facts are related by Gwin, 'U.S. relations with the World Bank', p. 213.

Relations between McNamara and the US Executive improved substantially again with the arrival of the new Democratic president, Jimmy Carter, in the White House. McNamara was even invited to participate in the meetings of the National Security Council to discuss an increase in financial resources for the IDA.

The end of Robert McNamara's term was somewhat eventful due to the election of a new Republican president, Ronald Reagan, in January 1981. Ronald Reagan and the Republicans had campaigned in favour of a radical change in US foreign policy with immediate consequences for the World Bank. Reagan proposed a drastic reduction in multilateral aid – and therefore in the US's contribution to the IDA – in favour of bilateral aid, notably via a major increase in military assistance.

The bill presented in January 1981 by David Stockman, director of the Office of Management and Budget, eloquently reflects the spirit of the Ronald Reagan camp. Its adoption would have meant the end of US contributions to the IDA and to the United Nations and an increase in expenditures for military assistance. In 1986 David Stockman summed up in the following manner the contents of the bill that he presented jointly with Representative Phil Gramm to Congress in January 1981:

The Gramm–Stockman budget plan had called for deep cuts in foreign economic aid on the basis of pure ideological principle. Both Gramm and I believed that the organs of international aid and so-called Third World development [...] were infested with socialist error. The international aid bureaucracy was turning Third World countries into quagmires of self-imposed inefficiency and burying them beneath mountainous external debts they would never be able to pay.[42]

The situation improved greatly with the designation of a new Bank president. The administration chose Alden W. Clausen, who until then had been president of the Bank of America. He took office on 1 July 1981. Several hardcore neoliberals joined the staff of the Bank, including Anne Krueger, who was hired on 10 May 1982 as Chief Economist and Vice-President. The quotation given below from the letter written by President Reagan to the Republican Congressional leader is proof of the favourable change in the attitude of the US Executive regarding the Bank.

THE INFLUENCE OF THE UNITED STATES AS SEEN BY THE EXECUTIVE

A report from the US Treasury in 1982 praised the pre-eminence of the US in the multilateral financial institutions:

The United States was instrumental in shaping the structure and mission of the World Bank along Western, market-oriented lines [...] We were also responsible [...] for the emergence of a corporate entity with a weighted voting

---

42   David A. Stockman, *The Triumph of Politics: How the Reagan Revolution Failed* (New York: Harper and Row, 1986), pp. 116–19 (quoted by Gwin in 'U.S. relations with the World Bank', p. 229).

run by a board of directors, headed by a high-caliber American-dominated management, and well-qualified professional staff. As a charter member and major share-holder in the World Bank, the United States secured the sole right to a permanent seat on the Bank's Board of Directors. [...] Other significant actors – management, major donors, and major recipients – have recognized the United States as a major voice in the [multilateral development] banks. They know from past experience that we are capable and willing to pursue important policy objectives in the banks by exercising the financial and political leverage at our disposal.[43]

According to Walden Bello, another passage in this Treasury document specifies that 'in a study of fourteen of "the most significant issues" that sparked debate at the Bank – ranging from blocking observer status for the Palestine Liberation Organization (PLO) to halting Bank aid to the Vietnam and Afghanistan – the United States was able to impose its view as Bank policy in twelve cases'.[44]

A passage in another Treasury report dated the same year is also devoted to the World Bank and the other development banks:

On the whole, the policies and programs of the World Bank Group have been consistent with US interests. This is particularly true in terms of general country allocation questions and sensitive policy issues. The international character of the World Bank, its corporate structure, the strength of the management team, and the Bank's weighted voting structure have ensured broad consistency between its policies and practices and the long term economic and political objectives of the United States.[45]

Elsewhere in the same report, one reads: 'By promoting economic and social development in the Third World, fostering market-oriented economic policies, and preserving a reputation for impartiality and competence, the MDBs encourage developing countries to participate more fully in an international system based on liberalized trade and capital flows [...] This means expanding opportunities for US exports, investment, and finance.'[46]

In a letter from President Ronald Reagan to Robert Michel, Republican leader of the House of Representatives, asking him to support an increase in World Bank capital in 1988, one finds a very useful list of middle-income countries

43 *Assessment of US Participation in Multilateral Development Banks in the 1980s* (Washington, DC: Department of the Treasury, 1982), chapter 3, quoted by Walden Bello, *Deglobalization: Ideas for a New World Economy* (London/New York: Zed Books, 2002), pp. 59–60.
44 Bello, *Deglobalization*, p. 60.
45 *United States Participation in Multilateral Development Banks* (Washington, DC: Department of the Treasury, 1982), p. 59 (quoted by Gwin, 'U.S. relations with the World Bank', p. 270).
46 *United States Participation in Multilateral Development Banks*, pp. 48, 52 (quoted by Gwin, 'U.S. relations with the World Bank', p. 271).

that are strategic allies of the US and supported by the Bank. Here is an excerpt from that letter: 'The Bank commits the vast majority of its funds in support of specific investment projects in the middle income developing nations. These are mostly nations (such as the Philippines, Egypt, Pakistan, Turkey, Morocco, Tunisia, Argentine, Indonesia and Brazil) that are strategically and economically important to the United States.'[47]

THE FINANCIAL ADVANTAGES ENJOYED BY THE US THANKS TO THE EXISTENCE OF THE WORLD BANK AND ITS INFLUENCE ON THE BANK

Catherine Gwin estimates the benefits the Bank and its activities brought the US between 1947 and 1992.[48] Firstly, a distinction must be made between two contributions: first, income received by US citizens possessing bonds issued by the Bank (according to Gwin, this represents $20.2 billion for the said period); second, the operating expenditures of the Bank on US territory (this represents $11 billion for the same period). Then, Gwin writes, and above all, the lever effect of US investment in the World Bank and the IDA must be taken into account. Since the founding of the World Bank, Gwin says, the US made only a minimum outlay – $1.85 billion – while the World Bank granted loans for a total amount of $218.21 billion (more than a hundredfold increase). These loans generated major contracts for US firms. Gwin provides no estimate regarding the amounts of these contracts ('flow-back', in Bank jargon). In the case of the IDA, the United States has made a larger outlay than for the World Bank: $18 billion to finance IDA loans to the tune of $71 billion.

THE INFLUENCE OF US BUSINESS CIRCLES AND BIG CAPITAL ON THE WORLD BANK

The fact that the World Bank, since its creation, has obtained the bulk of its financial resources by issuing bonds keeps it in a permanent and privileged relationship with the big private US financial entities. The latter are among the biggest holders of Bank bonds and they exert a considerable influence.

The link between US business circles, big capital and the World Bank is also immediately perceptible when one looks more closely at the careers of the 14 American citizens who have succeeded each other at the head of the Bank up to the present day.

Eugene Meyer, the first president, who lasted only eight months, was the publisher of the *Washington Post* and a former banker. The second, John J. McCloy, was a leading business lawyer on Wall Street and was subsequently appointed High

---

47   Letter from President Ronald Reagan to Representative Robert Michel, 10 June 1988, p. 1 (quoted by Gwin, 'U.S. relations with the World Bank', p. 271).
48   Gwin, 'U.S. relations with the World Bank', pp. 271–72.

Commissioner of the Allies in Germany and later chairman of the Chase Manhattan Bank. The third, Eugene R. Black, was vice-president of Chase National Bank and later became Special Adviser to President Lyndon B. Johnson. The fourth, George D. Woods, also a banker, was president of the First Boston Corporation. Robert S. McNamara had been CEO of the Ford Motor Company, then Secretary of Defense under Presidents Kennedy and Johnson. His successor, Alden W. Clausen, was president of the Bank of America (one of the principal US banks deeply involved in the Third World debt crisis), where he returned on leaving the World Bank. In 1986, Barber Conable, a former Republican member of Congress, succeeded him. Lewis T. Preston, formerly CEO of the J.P. Morgan bank, arrived in 1991. James D. Wolfensohn, president from 1995, was a banker on Wall Street with Salomon Brothers. At the end of his presidency in May 2005, he joined the management of Citibank-Citigroup, the leading banking group worldwide. Paul Wolfowitz was Deputy Secretary for Defense until he took office as the tenth president of the World Bank in May 2005. Robert Zoellick, who succeeded him in 2007, had been vice-president of the board of directors of the bank Goldman Sachs, in charge of international affairs. At the end of his term as president of the World Bank, Zoellick returned to an executive position at Goldman Sachs. The twelfth president, from 2012 to 2019, Jim Yong Kim – also an American – resigned to work for a private investment fund specializing in the infrastructures sector. The thirteenth president, David Malpass, had worked at the US Treasury and State Departments under the Ronald Reagan and George H. W. Bush administrations (1989–93), then as head economist at Bear Stearns, a major investment bank until its failure during the 2008 crisis. Ajay Banga, the fourteenth president of the World Bank, was CEO of Citigroup for Asia and then CEO of Mastercard.

In summary, and in general, a close link has been established between US political power, business circles (or if one prefers, the hard core of the US capitalist class) and the presidency of the World Bank.

6

World Bank and IMF Support
for Dictatorships

After the Second World War, in a growing number of Third World countries, policies diverged from those of the former colonial powers. This trend encountered firm opposition from the governments of the major industrialized capitalist countries whose influence held sway with the World Bank and the IMF. World Bank projects have a strong political content: to curtail the development of movements challenging the domination/rule of major capitalist powers. The prohibition against taking 'political' and 'non-economic' considerations into account in the World Bank's operations, one of the most important provisions of its charter, is systematically circumvented. The political bias of the Bretton Woods institutions is shown by their financial support of the dictatorships ruling in Chile, Brazil, Nicaragua, Congo-Kinshasa and Romania.

ANTI-COLONIAL AND ANTI-IMPERIALIST MOVEMENTS
IN THE THIRD WORLD

After 1955, the spirit of the Bandung (Indonesia) Conference[1] and the ensuing Non-Aligned Movement unleashed a mighty wind across much of the planet. It followed in the wake of the French defeat in Vietnam (1954) and preceded Nasser's nationalization of the Suez Canal (1956). Then came the Cuban (1959) and Algerian (1954–62) revolutions and the renewed Vietnamese liberation struggle. In more and more Third World countries, the policies implemented were a rejection of the former colonial powers. This often meant import substitution and the development of policies turned towards the internal market. The approach met with firm opposition from the governments of the major industrialized capitalist countries,

---

1   Indonesian president Sukarno called the Bandung Conference in 1955, launching the Non-Aligned Movement. Sukarno, Tito and Nehru were leaders who gave a voice to Third World hopes to overcome the old colonial system of rule. Here is an excerpt from Sukarno's speech at the conference opening: 'We are often told "Colonialism is dead." Let us not be deceived or even soothed by that. I say to you, colonialism is not yet dead. How can we say it is dead, so long as vast areas of Asia and Africa are unfree. [...] Colonialism has also its modern dress, in the form of economic control, intellectual control, actual physical control by a small but alien community within a nation. It is a skilful and determined enemy, and it appears in many guises. It does not give up its loot easily. Wherever, whenever and however it appears, colonialism is an evil thing, and one which must be eradicated from the earth.' *Asia-Africa Speaks from Bandung* (Jakarta: Indonesian Ministry of Foreign Affairs, 1955), pp. 19–29.

who held sway at the World Bank and the IMF. A wave of bourgeois nationalist regimes carrying out populist policies (Nasser in Egypt, Nehru in India, Perón in Argentina, Goulart in Brazil, Sukarno in Indonesia, N'Krumah in Ghana, etc.) and outright socialist regimes (Cuba, the People's Republic of China) appeared on the scene.

In this context, World Bank projects have an underlying political purpose: to thwart movements challenging domination by major capitalist powers.

THE WORLD BANK'S POWER TO INTERVENE IN NATIONAL ECONOMIES

As early as the 1950s, the World Bank established a network of influence that was to serve it greatly in later years. In the Third World, the Bank sought to create demand for its services. The influence it enjoys nowadays is to a large extent the outcome of the networks of agencies it built up in states that became its clients and, by so doing, its debtors. The Bank exercises a real policy of influence to support its network of loans.

From the 1950s onward, one of the primary goals of World Bank policy was 'institution building'. This most often meant setting up para-governmental agencies based in the Bank's client countries.[2] Such agencies were expressly founded with relative financial independence with respect to their own governments and outside the control of local political institutions, including national parliaments. They became natural relays for the Bank and owed it a great deal – beginning with their very existence, and in some cases, their funding.

Establishing such agencies was one of the World Bank's primary strategies for getting a foothold in the political economies of Third World countries. These agencies, operating according to their own rules (often developed on the basis of World Bank suggestions) and staffed with Bank-backed technocrats, were used to create a stable and trustworthy source for what the Bank most needed: 'viable' loan proposals. They also provided the Bank with parallel power bases through which it succeeded in transforming national economies, and entire societies, without the bother of democratic control and open debate.

In 1956, the Bank founded the Economic Development Institute with significant backing from the Ford and Rockefeller Foundations.[3] The Institute offered six-month training courses to official delegates from member countries: 'Between 1957 and 1971, more than 1300 officials had passed through EDI, a number of them

---

2   Bruce Rich quotes as examples of agencies founded through the World Bank: in Thailand, Industrial Finance Corporation of Thailand (IFCT), Thai Board of Investment (BOI), the National Economic and Social Development Board (NESDB) and the Electrical Generating Authority of Thailand (EGAT); in India, National Thermal Power Corporation (NPTC) and Northern Coal Limited (NCL). See Rich, *Mortgaging the Earth*, pp. 13 and 41.

3   In 2000 the Economic Development Institute was re-named World Bank Institute. More recently it began offering online training: <classcentral.com/institution/worldbank> [accessed 01/12/2021].

already having risen to the position of prime minister or minister of planning or finance in their respective countries.'[4]

This policy had disturbing implications. The study of World Bank policy in Colombia from 1949 to 1972 conducted by the New York-based International Legal Center (ILC) concluded that the independent agencies founded by the World Bank had a profound impact on the political structure and social development of the entire region, undermining the political party system and minimizing the role of the legislative and judicial branches.[5]

From the 1960s on, the World Bank has certainly found singular and novel means of remaining continually involved in the internal affairs of borrower countries. And yet, the Bank vigorously denies that such involvement is political. It insists on the contrary that its policies are unrelated to power structures and that political and economic matters are separate spheres.

HOW POLITICAL AND GEOPOLITICAL CONSIDERATIONS INFLUENCE WORLD BANK LENDING POLICY

Article IV Section 10 of the World Bank's Articles of Agreement stipulates:

The Bank and its officers shall not interfere in the political affairs of any member; nor shall they be influenced in their decisions by the political character of the member or members concerned. Only economic considerations shall be relevant to their decisions, and these considerations shall be weighed impartially in order to achieve the purposes stated in Article I.

Nevertheless, the World Bank has systematically circumvented this prohibition on taking 'political' and 'non-economic' considerations into account in its operations – one of the most important conditions set down in its founding document – from its very beginnings. As mentioned in the preceding chapter, the Bank refused loans to post-liberation France as long as there were communists in the government. The day after PCF members left the government in May 1947 the loan France had requested, which had been blocked until then, was granted.[6]

The World Bank has repeatedly contravened Article IV of its own statutes. In reality the Bank has made many choices based on political considerations. The quality of governments' economic policies is not the determining element in its choices. The Bank has often lent money to the authorities in countries despite the dismal quality of their economic policies and a great deal of corruption: Indonesia

4   Rich, *Mortgaging the Earth*, p. 76. Also see Nicholas Stern and Francisco Ferreira, 'The World Bank as "intellectual actor"', in Kapur, Lewis and Webb, *The World Bank: Its First Half Century, Volume 2*, pp. 583–85.
5   Rich, *Mortgaging the Earth*, p. 75.
6   See Kapur, Lewis and Webb, *The World Bank: Its First Half Century, Volume 1*, p. 1218.

and Zaire are two cases in point. Specifically, World Bank choices relative to countries that play a major political role in the eyes of its major shareholders, first and foremost the United States, are regularly linked to these shareholders' interests and outlooks.

From 1947 to the collapse of the Soviet bloc,[7] World Bank and IMF decisions were determined in large part by the following criteria:

- to avoid shoring up self-reliant models;
- to provide funding to large-scale projects (World Bank) or policies (IMF) enabling the major industrialized countries to increase exports;
- to refuse to help regimes seen as a threat by the United States government or other important shareholders;
- to attempt to modify the policies of certain governments in the so-called socialist countries so as to weaken the cohesion of the Soviet bloc. This is why support was granted to Yugoslavia, which had dropped out of the Moscow-dominated bloc from 1948, or to Romania from the 1970s at the time when its president Nicolae Ceaușescu was attempting to distance himself from the Comecon and the Warsaw Pact;
- to support strategic allies of the Western capitalist bloc and in particular of the US, (e.g. Indonesia from 1965 to the present day, Mobutu's Zaire, the Philippines under Marcos, Brazil under the dictators after the 1964 coup, dictator Anastasio Somoza's Nicaragua, apartheid South Africa);
- to attempt to avoid, or to limit as far as possible, closer links between Third World countries and the Soviet bloc or China – for example, by distancing the USSR from India and Sukarno-era Indonesia;
- from 1980 on, to integrate China into the United States' system of alliances.

To carry out this policy, the World Bank and the IMF have generalized a tactic: greater flexibility towards right-wing governments (who are more tolerant of austerity measures damaging to the population) facing a strong left opposition than towards left-wing governments facing strong opposition from the right. Concretely, that means that the international financial institutions (IFI) are more demanding and make life more difficult for left-wing governments, to weaken them and ease the right's path to power. According to the same logic, the IFI have made fewer demands on right-wing governments facing a left-wing opposition to avoid weakening them and preventing the left from coming to power. Monetarist orthodoxy has variable geometrics, and the variations depend on many political and geopolitical factors.

Some concrete examples – Chile, Brazil, Nicaragua, Zaire and Romania – will serve as cases in point. They involve the choices of both the World Bank and the

---

7   The period coinciding with the Cold War.

IMF, since those choices are determined, overall, by the same considerations and subject to the same influences.

The IMF and World Bank do not hesitate to support dictatorships when they (and other major capitalist powers) find it opportune. The author of the *Human Development Report* published by the UNDP (1994 edition) says so in black and white:

But rhetoric is running far ahead of reality, as a comparison of the per capita ODA received by democratic and authoritarian regimes shows. Indeed, for the United States in the 1980s, the relationship between aid and human rights has been perverse. Multilateral donors also seem not to have been bothered by such considerations. They seem to prefer martial law regimes, quietly assuming that such regimes will promote political stability and improve economic management. After Bangladesh and the Philippines lifted martial law, their shares in the total loans given by the World Bank declined.[8]

IFI POLITICAL BIAS: EXAMPLES OF FINANCIAL SUPPORT TO DICTATORSHIPS

Support for General Augusto Pinochet's dictatorship in Chile

Under Salvador Allende's democratically elected government (1970–73), Chile received no World Bank loans. Under the Pinochet government put in place by the 1973 military coup, the country suddenly became credible. And yet, no World Bank or IMF leader could fail to be aware of the deeply authoritarian and dictatorial – in fact criminal – nature of the Pinochet regime. The link between lending policies and the geopolitical context is blatant in this case.

One of then Bank president Robert McNamara's principal assistants, Mahbub ul Haq, drafted a highly critical memorandum in 1976 with a view to modifying the orientation of the World Bank. It states: 'We failed to support the basic objectives of the Allende regime, either in our reports or publicly.'[9] McNamara decided to ignore it.[10] Ul Haq tried, unsuccessfully, to persuade World Bank management to suspend loans to Pinochet until such time as it should be 'reasonably satisfied that Pinochet's government is not merely restoring the unstable elitist economic society'. He stated later that Pinochet's policies had 'worsened the country's distribution of income'.[11]

---

8   UNDP, *Human Development Report 1994* (Oxford: Oxford University Press, 1994), p. 76.
9   Mahbub ul Haq, memorandum, 'The Bank's Mistakes in Chile', 26 April 1976, cited in Kapur, Lewis and Webb, *The World Bank: Its First Half Century, Volume 1*, p. 301.
10 Kapur, Lewis and Webb, *The World Bank: Its First Half Century, Volume 1*, p. 301.
11 Mahbub ul Haq, memorandum to Robert S. McNamara, 'Chile Country Program Paper – Majority Policy Issues', 12 July 1976, cited in Kapur, Lewis and Webb, *The World Bank: Its First Half Century, Volume 1*, p. 301.

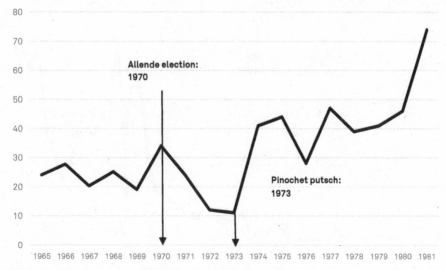

Figure 6.1 Chile: multilateral disbursements (USD million)

Source: World Bank, *Global Development Finance*, 2001

Support for the Brazilian military junta after the overthrow of President João Goulart

President João Goulart's democratic government was overthrown by the military in April 1964. World Bank and IMF loans, suspended for three years, resumed very soon afterwards.[12]

A brief timeline: in 1958, Brazilian president Kubitschek was about to undertake negotiations with the IMF to gain access to a loan of $300 million from the United States. In the end, Kubitschek refused the IMF-imposed conditions and did without the US loan. This earned him wide popularity.

His successor, Goulart, announced that he would implement a radical land reform programme and proceed to nationalize petroleum refineries. He was overthrown by the military. The United States recognized the new military regime one day after the coup. Not long afterwards, the World Bank and IMF resumed their suspended lending policy. As for the military, they rescinded the economic measures the United States and the IMF had criticized. Note that the international financial institutions were of the view that the military regime was taking sound

---

12   An analysis of the facts summarized below is found in Cheryl Payer, *The Debt Trap: The International Monetary Fund and the Third World* (New York/London: Monthly Review Press, 1974), pp. 143–65.

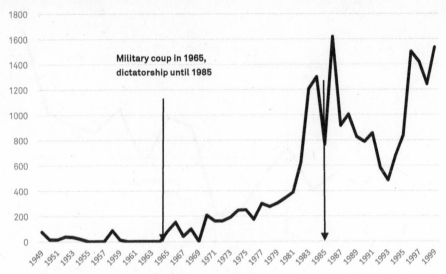

Figure 6.2   Brazil: World Bank disbursements (USD million)

Source: World Bank, *Global Development Finance*, 2001

economic measures.[13] Yet, the GDP fell 7 per cent in 1965 and thousands of firms declared bankruptcy. The regime organized harsh repression, outlawed strikes, caused a dramatic drop in real wages, eliminated direct ballot voting, disbanded trade unions and made systematic use of torture.

After his first trip in May 1968, Robert McNamara visited Brazil regularly and made a point of meeting with the military rulers. The World Bank's public reports systematically praised the policies of the dictatorship in reducing inequalities.[14] However, inside the World Bank, the discussions took a bitter turn. When Bernard Chadenet, Vice-President of Projects at the World Bank, declared that the Bank's image would suffer due to its support of the repressive government of Brazil, McNamara recognized that there was a tremendous amount of repression but he added that it

is not necessarily a great deal different from what it had been under previous governments, and it did not seem to be a lot worse than in some other member countries of the World Bank. Is Brazil worse than Thailand?[15]

---

13   In 1965 Brazil signed the Stand-By Agreement with the IMF, received new credits and had the United States, several European creditor nations and Japan restructure its debt. After the military coup, loans rose from zero to an average of $73 million for the rest of the 1960s and reached almost half a billion USD per annum in the mid 1970s.

14   Details in Kapur, Lewis and Webb, *The World Bank: Its First Half Century, Volume 1*, pp. 274–82.

15   World Bank, 'Notes on Brazil Country Program Review, December 2, 1971'. Details in Kapur, Lewis and Webb, *The World Bank: Its First Half Century, Volume 1*, p. 276.

Some days later, McNamara added that 'No viable alternative to the Government by generals seemed open.'[16] The Bank was well aware that inequalities would not diminish and that its loans in the agricultural sector would reinforce the big landowners. Nevertheless, it decided to maintain the loans because it absolutely wanted to get the government under its influence. But that tactic was a resounding failure. The military regime proved extremely wary of the World Bank's desire to strengthen its presence. Finally, at the end of the 1970s, they took advantage of a profusion of loans from international private bankers granted at a lower rate of interest than that of the Bank.

Support for Anastasio Somoza's dictatorship, and the refusal to provide loans to Sandinista Daniel Ortega

The Somoza clan had held power in Nicaragua since the 1930s with the help of United States military intervention. On 19 July 1979, a powerful popular movement overthrew the dictatorship and dictator Anastasio Somoza was forced to flee. The Somoza family had a stranglehold on a huge proportion of the country's wealth and encouraged large foreign firms, especially from the US, to locate there. The people hated them. The World Bank had showered loans on Somoza's dictatorship. After the dictatorship fell, an alliance government brought together the traditional democratic opposition (led by top businessmen) and the Sandinista revolutionaries.

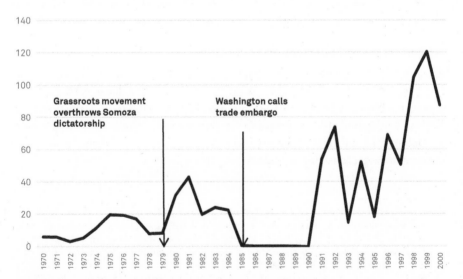

Figure 6.3   Nicaragua: World Bank disbursements (USD million)

Source: World Bank, *Global Development Finance*, 2001

---

16   Ibid.

The latter made no secret of their sympathy for Cuba nor their desire to undertake certain economic reforms (land reform, nationalization of certain foreign firms, confiscation of Somoza clan landholdings, a literacy programme and so on). Washington, which supported Somoza to the bitter end, feared that the new government might spread communism in Central America. Yet the Carter administration, in office when the dictatorship was overthrown, did not immediately take an aggressive stance.

But things changed overnight when Ronald Reagan moved into the White House. In 1981, Reagan announced his commitment to bring down the Sandinistas. He provided financial and military backing to a rebellion by former members of the National Guard (*contrarevolucionarios* or 'contras'). The US mined several of Nicaragua's harbours. Faced with such hostility, the Sandinista majority government opted for more radical policies. During the 1984 elections, the first democratic ones in half a century, the Sandinista Daniel Ortega was elected president with 67 per cent of the vote. The following year, the United States called a trade embargo against Nicaragua, isolating the country from foreign investors. As mentioned in the preceding chapter, the Sandinistas actively urged the World Bank to resume its loans.[17] They were even ready to accept a draconian structural adjustment plan. The World Bank decided not to follow up on this and did not resume the loans until the Sandinistas' electoral defeat in February 1990, when Violeta Barrios de Chamorro, the US-backed conservative candidate, won the vote. Note that the World Bank and the IMF supported the government of Daniel Ortega when he returned to power in 2007. That can be explained by the neoliberal and pro-Washington orientation adopted by the Ortega government.[18]

Support for the Mobutu dictatorship in Zaire

As early as 1962, a report by the United Nations Secretary-General revealed that Congolese dictator Mobutu had looted several million dollars, earmarked to finance his country's troops. In 1982, a senior IMF official, Erwin Blumenthal – a German banker and an ex-governor of the Bundesbank – wrote a damning report on Mobutu's administration of Zaire.[19] Blumenthal warned the foreign lenders not to expect repayment as long as Mobutu remained in power.

---

17   David Knox, vice-president of the World Bank for Latin America, wrote: 'One of my nightmares was what we would do were the Nicaraguans to start putting in place policies that we could support. I feared that political pressure, and not only from the United States, would be so great as to prevent us from helping the country.' Cited in Kapur, Lewis and Webb, *The World Bank: Its First Half Century, Volume 1*, p. 1058, note 95.

18   See Éric Toussaint, 'Nicaragua: from 2007 to 2018, Daniel Ortega had the Support of the IMF and conducted policies favourable to big national and international capital', CADTM, 6 November 2018 <cadtm.org/Nicaragua-From-2007-to-2018-Daniel-Ortega-Had-the-Support-of-the-IMF-and> [accessed 08/01/2021].

19   Colette Braeckman, 'L'amertume d'un expert' ('An expert's bitterness'), *Le Monde diplomatique*, November 1982 (in French) <monde-diplomatique.fr/1982/11/BRAECKMAN/37019> [accessed 08/01/2021].

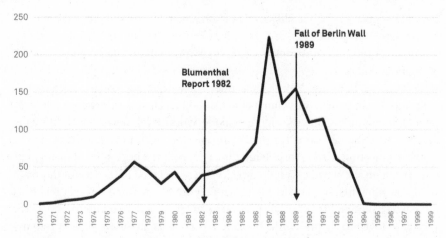

Figure 6.4   Congo-Kinshasa (Zaire under Mobutu): World Bank disbursements (USD million)
Source: World Bank, *Global Development Finance*, 2001

Between 1965 and 1981, the Zairian government borrowed approximately $5 billion abroad, and between 1976 and 1981 its foreign debt was rescheduled four times by the Paris Club for a total of $2.25 billion.

Mobutu's gross economic mismanagement and systematic misappropriation of a portion of the loans did not result in the IMF and World Bank halting aid to his dictatorial regime. It is striking to observe that after the Blumenthal report was submitted, World Bank payouts actually increased[20] (as did IMF payouts, though they are not shown on Figure 6.4). It is clear that sound economic management criteria are not the deciding factor in World Bank and IMF decisions. Mobutu's regime was a strategic ally of the United States and other influential powers in the Bretton Woods institutions (including France and Belgium) during the Cold War. After 1989–91, with the fall of the Berlin Wall, followed soon after by the implosion of the Soviet Union, Mobutu's regime was no longer worthy of interest. Moreover, in many African countries, including Zaire, national conferences were making democratic demands. World Bank loans started to dry up, and ceased completely in the mid-1990s.

World Bank support for the Ceaușescu dictatorship in Romania

In 1947, Romania was brought into the Soviet bloc. In 1972, Romania was the first Soviet satellite country to join the World Bank. Since 1965, Nicolae Ceaușescu had been secretary-general of the ruling Communist Party. In 1968, he criticized

20   The Bank historians write that in 1982: 'lured by Mobutu's guile and promises of reform and by pressures from the United States, France and Belgium, the Bank embarked on an ambitious structural adjustment lending program to Zaire'. Kapur, Lewis and Webb, *The World Bank: Its First Half Century, Volume 1*, p. 702.

the USSR's invasion of Czechoslovakia. Romanian troops did not take part in the Warsaw Pact operation there. This distancing from Moscow clearly made up Washington's mind to contemplate closer ties with the Romanian regime, through the World Bank.

As early as 1973, the World Bank undertook negotiations with Bucharest to determine a loan policy; the volume of loans soon reached a very appreciable level. In 1980, Romania became the eighth-ranking World Bank borrower. World Bank historian Aart Van de Laar tells a significant anecdote from 1973. Early that year, he attended a meeting of the World Bank directors, with the beginning of loan grants to Romania on the agenda. Certain directors were sceptical of the lack of thorough studies on Romania, but Robert McNamara reportedly declared he had great trust in the financial morality of socialist countries in terms of debt reimbursement. The story goes that one of the World Bank vice-presidents attending piped up to ask whether Allende's Chile had perhaps not yet become socialist enough.[21] McNamara reportedly responded with stony silence.

World Bank choices did not depend on reliable economic criteria. First, while the World Bank has regularly refused loans to countries that had failed to repay old sovereign debts, it began lending to Romania although the latter had not settled disputes over outstanding debts. Secondly, most of Romania's economic exchanges took place within the Comecon in non-convertible currency. How could the country

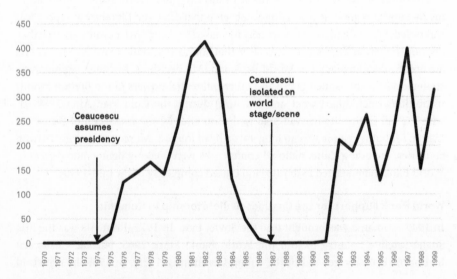

Figure 6.5   Romania: World Bank disbursements (USD million)

Source: World Bank, *Global Development Finance*, 2001

---

21   Van de Laar, *The World Bank and the Poor*, p. 40.

reimburse debts in hard currency? Thirdly, from the outset Romania refused to hand over the economic data the World Bank required.

Clearly then, political considerations were the reason for the World Bank developing close relations with Romania. The lack of internal democracy and systematic police repression were no greater stumbling blocks for the World Bank in this case than in others.

Romania in fact became one of the World Bank's biggest clients. The Bank financed large-scale projects (strip coal mines, fossil-fuel power plants) whose negative environmental impact was patently obvious. To operate the strip coal mines, the Romanian authorities displaced farming communities. In another area, the Bank supported a population-planning policy aimed at increasing the birth rate.

In 1982, when the debt crisis came to the fore internationally, the Romanian regime decided to impose shock therapy on its people. Romania slashed its imports to the bone to come up with the surplus in hard currency to pay off its foreign debt as soon as possible. The consequences were catastrophic for the population. But, as the authors of the book commissioned by the Bank to commemorate its first half-century of existence put it, 'Romania was, in a sense, a "model" debtor, at least from the creditors' point of view.'[22]

CONCLUSION

In violation of Section 10 of Article IV of the World Bank's own charter, the Bank and the IMF have systematically used lending to states as a way of influencing their policies. The examples given in this study show that the choices the institutions make are determined by the political and strategic interests of the major capitalist powers. Regimes with the backing of those powers have received financial aid even though their economic policies did not meet official IFI criteria and despite the fact that they failed to respect human rights. Furthermore, regimes seen as hostile to the major powers were deprived of IFI loans on the pretext that they were failing to respect the economic criteria set by these institutions.

These policies of the Bretton Woods institutions, far from being abandoned at the end of the Cold War, continue to the present day. Examples include the loans made to Boris Yeltsin's Russia to ensure the permanence of the restoration of capitalism; to the dictatorship of Mohamed Suharto in Indonesia until his fall in 1998; to Iraq while under foreign occupation; to the Ben Ali dictatorship in Tunisia from 1987 to 2011; to Mubarak's in Egypt from 1981 to 2011; to that of Marshal al-Sissi in Egypt since 2014; and to Idriss Déby's dictatorship in Chad from 1990 until his death on 20 April 2021.

22   Kapur, Lewis and Webb, *The World Bank: Its First Half Century, Volume 1*, p. 1061.

7
The World Bank and the Philippines (1946–90)

The 1946 US decision to grant the Philippines its independence inaugurated a period of prosperity in the country. For a number of geostrategic reasons, in the wake of the Second World War the Americans were willing to let the Philippine government pursue policies that they ruled out elsewhere.

The Philippine government was allowed to implement independent policies that fostered the country's economic development. However, American tolerance was short-lived. From 1962 onwards, and with the backing of the IMF and the World Bank, the Conservatives (who had won a majority of seats in the Philippine Congress in the 1959 elections) imposed radically different policies. These new policies sparked massive capital flight, crippling debts, devaluation and a drop in wages for the population. It was in this context of crisis that Ferdinand Marcos declared martial law in 1972. The dictator earned the admiration of the World Bank for pursuing policies very much in line with Washington's expectations. Massive corruption increased popular discontent and brought about the downfall of Ferdinand Marcos and his replacement by Corazon Aquino in 1986. Aquino was the leader of the democratic opposition but was also closely connected to the plantation owners. She carried out intransigently neoliberal economic policies bearing the unmistakable imprint of the World Bank. To be sure, this was a great disappointment to the people.

FROM THE COLONIAL PERIOD TO INDEPENDENCE IN 1946

The Philippines remained a Spanish colony until 1898, when Spain was defeated in a war declared by the United States. It was then the turn of the US to occupy the country; this occupation was interrupted by the Japanese occupation during the Second World War. In 1946, the US granted the Philippines independence in exchange for its acceptance of a number of conditions: a fixed exchange rate between the Philippine peso and the American dollar (to protect US companies against the effects of devaluation), free-trade agreements and so forth. At the beginning, the arrangement worked relatively well since the US was bringing in a large amount of dollars to the Philippines, primarily through its strong military presence in the country.

SUCCESS WAS RELATIVE DURING THE 1950S

However, in 1949 the flow of dollars slowed down dramatically. The Philippine government established strict exchange controls to avoid a heavy drain on the currency. Private companies were forbidden to borrow money from foreign investors. The US government and the IMF tolerated this measure in order to stay on good terms with their Philippine ally. The introduction of controls over currency exchange, capital flows and imports sparked an economic boom in the country, driven in particular by the growth of industry. This period of economic growth ended twelve years later, in 1962, when the control measures were abandoned under pressure from the United States, the IMF and the World Bank.

During the 1950s, the manufacturing sector grew annually from 10 to 12 per cent, the annual inflation rate was kept below 2 per cent, foreign-exchange reserves were strong and the external debt was extremely low. However, this was not to everyone's liking; American and other foreign companies complained about having to reinvest all their profits in the country's economy. Capitalist export firms were forced to deposit their hard-currency export earnings in the Central Bank, which returned them in pesos at an unfavourable rate. This was a source of enormous revenue for the state. In 1954, bolstered by its success, the Philippine government demanded that the US alter the rules of the game laid down in 1946 at the time of independence. Washington submitted to this demand, which strengthened the position of the Philippine authorities.

Of course, one has to be careful not to idealize the achievements of the Philippines in this period. It remained a profoundly unequal capitalist society, and industrialization did not go much beyond assembly and light manufacturing. Nevertheless, the situation of the 1950s was certainly promising in comparison with all that has transpired since 1962. Indeed, it was these promising developments that triggered the united offensive led by the US, the IMF and the World Bank – together with the most conservative sectors of the Philippine ruling classes – aimed at putting an end to the experiment.

ADOPTION OF CONSERVATIVE POLICIES AND AN INCREASE IN THE DEBT DURING THE 1960S

In 1962, the Conservatives, who had won a majority in the Philippine Congress after the elections of 1959, eliminated controls on capital movements. The IMF and the US government showed their approval by immediately granting a loan of $300 million. The elimination of controls led to massive capital flight towards foreign countries; the resulting deficit was financed by one set of external loans after another. The external debt increased sevenfold between 1962 and 1969 – from $275 million to $1.88 billion!

Transnational corporations and Philippine exporters of agricultural products and raw materials rejoiced as their profits jumped. On the other hand, the manufacturing sector oriented toward the domestic market rapidly declined. In 1970, the peso had to be sharply devalued. The incomes and earnings of small producers slumped.

It was in this context of a crisis of the policies supported by the United States, the IMF, the World Bank and the Conservatives that Ferdinand Marcos set up a dictatorship in 1972. His objective was to consolidate neoliberal policies through force.

One year later, on the other side of the Pacific, Augusto Pinochet took power in Chile with exactly the same objectives, the same overlords and the same backing.

THE ROLE OF THE WORLD BANK AND ITS SUPPORT FOR THE MARCOS DICTATORSHIP IN THE 1970S

The first loans granted by the World Bank to the Philippines date back to 1958. But the loans remained extremely low until Robert McNamara became World Bank president in 1968. McNamara argued that the Philippines – where there were American military bases, as in Indonesia and Turkey – was of such strategic importance that it was absolutely necessary to strengthen its ties to the World Bank. Lending money was a way to get greater leverage. World Bank historians do not mince words:

McNamara and his staff were annoyed at the way the Philippines legislature was stalemating policy reforms. Thus the Philippines was an instance in which martial law triggered the takeoff of Banking lending. Marcos dismissed the legislature and started ruling by presidential decree in August 1972. McNamara and the Bank staff welcomed the move.[1]

One of the first measures taken by the Marcos dictatorship was to remove the ceiling on public indebtedness, initially established by the Philippine Congress in 1970. The regulation had established a debt margin of $1 billion with an annual ceiling of $250 million. Marcos put an end to this limitation, to the great satisfaction of the World Bank.[2] McNamara announced that the World Bank was ready to at least double the amounts granted. The World Bank historians make public one of the internal reports of a high-level meeting between McNamara and his colleagues:

A rather surprising meeting! No more of the criticism of early years (politics, corruption, income inequality), but a rather general feeling that we should increase our lending program. And a flabbergasted Area Department trying to defend the cautious position taken in the Country Program Paper (CPP)! The order

---

1   Kapur, Lewis and Webb, *The World Bank: Its First Half Century, Volume 1*, p. 558.
2   See Payer, *Lent and Lost*, p. 82.

of the day is to work within the system. (Politics not necessarily worse than in Thailand but more publicized.) [...] We should aim to lend on average $120 million a year in FY74–78, 50 per cent more than proposed.[3]

At the time it was too late to increase the loans granted for 1973, much to McNamara's displeasure. That is why the Bank did the job in double-quick time and increased by 5.5 times the total amount for 1974 ($165 million instead of $30 million).[4]

The World Bank and the IMF publicly supported the dictatorship to such an extent that they held their 1976 annual general meeting in Manila. That year, Bernard Bell, vice-president of the Bank for East Asia and Pacific Region, declared: 'The risk in lending to the Philippines was lower than for Malaysia or Korea.'[5] Also note that the World Bank established one of the three Green Revolution research centres in the Philippines, in partnership with the Ford and Rockefeller Foundations (see 'The Green Revolution').

The Green Revolution

In certain developing countries, especially in Asia (India, Pakistan, Indonesia, the Philippines, Thailand, etc.), the Green Revolution was launched in the context of the Cold War and was largely financed by public funds in Western countries and private funds from big foundations (Rockefeller, Ford, Kellogg, etc.) It should be emphasized that the World Bank launched the Green Revolution in 1965 in India following a request for limited food aid after a drought. To qualify for the Green Revolution, India was forced to completely restructure its agricultural policy, devalue its currency and apply a set of structural measures. These required the use of agricultural techniques that were environmentally non-sustainable and an obligation to export accompanied by an obligation to import pesticides and chemical fertilizers. Only after complying with all that was India able to obtain food aid that was only necessary for a single season, whereas the profound agricultural transformation of the Green Revolution had negative effects that are still being suffered today.[6]

---

3   World Bank, 'Notes on the Philippines Country Program Review, July 28, 1972', prepared by H. Schulmann on 15 August 1972, cited by Kapur, Lewis and Webb, *The World Bank: Its First Half Century, Volume 1*, p. 303. 'A miracle has occurred in the Philippines. Philosophically, it is distressing, however, that the miracle occurred under the auspices of a military dictatorship. Mr. Cargill said he didn't believe the miracle would continue, "but while it does," interjected Mr McNamara, "and only as long as it does, let us continue to support it."' (Memorandum, Alexis E. Lachman to John Adler, 27 December 1973, with attachment, 'Philippines Country Program Review', 19 December 1973, quoted by Kapur, Lewis and Webb, *The World Bank: Its First Half Century, Volume 1*, p. 304.)

4   In 1980, the World Bank lent $400 million.

5   Quoted by Kapur, Lewis and Webb, *The World Bank: Its First Half Century, Volume 1*, p. 304

6   See Vandana Shiva, *The Violence of the Green Revolution* (Penang, Malaysia: Third World Network, 1991). For the application of the Green Revolution in Africa, see Rémi Vilain, 'The New Green Revolution', CADTM, 5 September 2016 <cadtm.org/The-New-Green-Revolution> [accessed 05/04/2023]; also see (in French) the two-part article 'La nouvelle révolution verte en Afrique subsaharienne' ('The new green revolution in Sub-Saharan Africa'), CADTM, December 2015–January 2016 <cadtm.org/La-nouvelle-revolution-verte-en-Afrique-subsaharienne-Partie-1-sur-2> [accessed 05/04/2023].

However, Ferdinand Marcos did not quite carry out the economic policy the World Bank had hoped for. The Bank was disappointed since it was on very good terms with the dictator and the team of academics he had gathered around himself – some of whom later became officials of the Bank, such as Gerardo Sicat, Secretary for Planning and then President of the Philippine National Bank, the main bank of the country.

THE WORLD BANK IN THE ECONOMIC AND POLITICAL CRISIS OF THE 1980S

The World Bank did not criticize in the slightest the regime's repressive measures. However, it was concerned about the slowness with which structural reforms were being implemented. It wanted the dictatorship to replace what remained of the import substitution industrialization model with the export-oriented industrialization model that it championed. It is important to stress the fact that import substitution consists in manufacturing products in-country that had been imported beforehand (see 'Import substitution industrialization (ISI)'). In order to exert greater influence on the Philippine government, the Bank decided to grant two huge structural-adjustment loans in 1981 and 1983, aimed at export promotion. The Bank was perfectly aware of the fact that most of these funds ended up in the bank accounts of Marcos and his generals; nevertheless, it considered it worthwhile to pay off members of the ruling clique in exchange for an acceleration of the neoliberal counter-reform.

Import substitution industrialization (ISI)

This strategy is mainly associated with the historical experience of Latin America in the 1930s and 1940s and with the work of the ECLAC (United Nations Economic Commission for Latin America and the Caribbean) in the 1950s, and in particular the writings of the Argentine Raúl Prebisch, who in 1964 became the first secretary-general of the United Nations Conference on Trade and Development (UNCTAD). The starting point is the observation that, in the face of a drastic reduction in trade due to the great crisis of the 1930s and the Second World War, the major Latin American countries were able to meet internal demand by developing local production in order to replace imported products with locally made ones. ECLAC theory aimed at successively extending this process to all sectors of industry, creating a 'disconnect' from the Centre. Making use of a fair degree of protectionism and coordinated intervention by the state, the aim was to enable nascent industries to get off the ground. South Korea applied this policy successfully, but under specific conditions (see chapter 11). In the 1950s and early 1960s, the government of the Philippines also partially applied the import substitution industrialization model.

At this juncture, in 1981, a banking crisis broke out in the Philippines due to a huge corruption scandal involving the capitalists and sections of the state bureaucracy. The crisis spread gradually to the whole financial system, threatening the two largest public banks with bankruptcy. The crisis spread from 1981 to 1983–84 and was exacerbated by the external debt crisis that broke out internationally in 1982. Foreign private banks stopped granting credit to the Philippines. This was a clear failure for the World Bank and its good friends, Ferdinand Marcos, Gerardo Sicat and Prime Minister Cesar Virata.

Popular discontent rose sharply. A number of key sectors of the ruling classes clashed with the Marcos regime. The crisis deepened following the murder of one of the members of the landed oligarchy opposed to Marcos: Senator Benigno Aquino, previously exiled to the United States, was shot down at Manila airport upon his return to the country in August 1983.

In spite of the growing opposition to Marcos, the World Bank opted to stand behind the dictator. Departing from its plans, it massively boosted its loans to the Philippines: $600 million in 1983, or more than double the previous year's loans of 251 million. World Bank historians write that it was a matter of 'loyalty to an old friend'.[7]

Popular mobilizations became more radical until the opposition within the ruling classes and the army removed Marcos and forced him into exile.[8] They did so with the assistance of the Americans – represented in Manila by Paul Wolfowitz,[9] who supported the Marcos regime until the end. Corazon Aquino, leader of the opposition among the middle-class and landed sectors and widow of Benigno Aquino, took over the reins of power in 1986.

The World Bank then hesitated over which course to follow. Its president for the East Asia and Pacific Region, Atilla Karosmanoğlu (see chapter 8 on Turkey), wrote a rather unenthusiastic internal memo on the new democratic regime: 'We expect that the decision making process will be more difficult than in the past, because of a more collegial nature of the new team, the enhanced role of the legislative branch and the populist tendencies of the new government.'[10]

THE WORLD BANK AND IMF FINALLY ABANDON FERDINAND MARCOS AND SUPPORT CORAZON AQUINO

Finally, the World Bank, the IMF and the US decided to make the best of a bad situation by backing President Corazon Aquino since she had agreed to keep her country on the right side, and even to deepen the neoliberal reforms. The World Bank lent $300 million in 1987 and $200 million in 1988: it was all about greasing the wheels of the privatization of state-owned firms. Between 1989 and 1992, the World Bank lent the Philippines $1.3 billion to finance structural adjustments. The US threatened to block these loans in the event that the Philippines carried out its plan to close American military bases on its territory.

---

7   Kapur, Lewis and Webb, *The World Bank: Its First Half Century, Volume 1*, p. 563.
8   Ferdinand Marcos was transferred to Honolulu by the US army and lived there until 1989.
9   Paul Wolfowitz became president of the World Bank in 2005.
10   Quoted by Kapur, Lewis and Webb, *The World Bank: Its First Half Century, Volume 1*, p. 565, note 102.

As for the land reform demanded by the powerful popular movement that led to the overthrow of Marcos and became even stronger in 1987, Corazon Aquino sided with the landed oligarchy she came from. Between 1986 and 1990, the state only acquired 122 hectares! In 1987 a World Bank team led by Martin Karcher envisaged the possibility of a radical land reform, similar to the ones carried out in Japan, South Korea and Taiwan after the Second World War, as a consequence of the radicalization of the rural workers' struggle. The document delivered by this team in March 1987 recommended the limitation of land ownership to seven hectares, which implied directly taking on the main growers of sugar cane (who included Corazon Aquino). This study by the World Bank suggested that landless workers should obtain the lands in exchange for a one-time payment of 600 pesos (around $30 at the time). Needless to say, the study was never followed by concrete measures.

All told, the government of Corazon Aquino went even further than Marcos in implementing neoliberal policy prescriptions. This was cause for great satisfaction at the World Bank.

8

The World Bank's Support for the Dictatorship in Turkey

The example of Turkey is another illustration of how thoroughly the World Bank's policies are determined by geostrategic interests, particularly those of the United States. The World Bank's strategy in Turkey closely resembles its policy towards Ferdinand Marcos's dictatorship in the Philippines from 1972 and Augusto Pinochet's in Chile from 1973, and the economic model the two regimes implemented. Geopolitics was once again a determining factor: Turkey, a hinge between Europe and Asia, is an essential pawn on the Middle East chessboard. Consequently the country's subordination to Washington's interests needed to be ensured via full and enthusiastic support for an authoritarian regime. The World Bank, along with the military leaders in power, applied a programme of neoliberal economic policies that opened the door wide to investments by transnational corporations and suppressed both trade unions and far-left parties. Such policies consolidated Turkey's role as a spearhead for the United States in a new historic context.

THE BANK'S DIFFICULT BEGINNINGS IN TURKEY

In the 1950s the World Bank got off to a bad start in Turkey. Its signing officer, Pieter Lieftinck, from the Netherlands, was expelled by the Ankara authorities on the grounds of excessive interventionism.

Under Robert McNamara, Turkey's geostrategic importance led the World Bank to increase its efforts to improve matters. A few months after becoming president, in July 1968, McNamara visited Turkey. He knew the country well since it had been a military ally of the United States. As Defense Secretary until 1967 he was in close contact with Ankara. Anxious not to repeat what had happened with Pieter Lieftinck, the World Bank took great care not to appear too openly intrusive in the 1970s.[1] At the end of the decade the Bank gradually increased its pressure on the Turkish government, notably in 1978 when the left-wing nationalist Bülent Ecevit became prime minister. In particular, the Bank tried to force an increase in the price of electricity.

---

1   'The Bank in the 1970s was at pains in Turkey not to overreach', in Kapur, Lewis and Webb, *The World Bank: Its First Half Century, Volume 1*, p. 547.

THE BANK'S SUPPORT FOR THE MILITARY COUP IN 1980

The September 1980 military coup, which resulted in a dictatorship that lasted until May 1983, was very convenient for the World Bank, since the military leaders agreed to maintain the neoliberal plan it had drawn up with Süleyman Demirel[2] and Turgut Özal.[3]

Demirel, Ecevit's successor as prime minister, had appointed Özal as state undersecretary for economic coordination. The two launched a neoliberal economic programme in January 1980. But its implementation was made difficult by trade-union actions, the sense of insecurity resulting from confrontations between right-wing and left-wing students, manoeuvres in the Muslim Party – which drove a hard bargain for its parliamentary support of Demirel's minority government – and the army's thirst for power, which motivated it to work behind the scenes to destabilize the government with the help of the US. Following the coup, the military regime dissolved parliament and put Demirel in jail in September 1980, yet agreed to appoint Turgut Özal deputy prime minister with full powers over economic affairs. He was then able to implement neoliberal policies unhindered for two years, until the financial crash that resulted in his eviction.

THE TURKEY PROGRAMME BECAME A PROTOTYPE FOR STRUCTURAL-ADJUSTMENT LOANS

The World Bank enthusiastically supported the policies developed by the military leaders and Turgut Özal, since they led the way to 'increasing export incentives, improving external debt management, eliminating the budget deficit [...], reducing the level of public investment.'[4]

The historians of the World Bank write: 'the Turkish program became a prototype for the institution's structural adjustment loan series.'[5] Several factors made such developments easier:

1. The close connections between Turkish political leaders and Turkish senior officers in the World Bank. In addition to the names already cited we can mention Atilla Karosmanoğlu[6] and Munir Benjenk,[7] men of the Bank par excellence.[8]

---

2   Süleyman Demirel (1924–) served several times as prime minister (1965–71; 1975–78; 1979–80). He was head of government again in 1991, then president of the Republic from 1993 to 2000.
3   Turgut Özal (1927–93) was prime minister from 1983 to 1989, then president of the Republic from 1989 to his death in 1993. He worked at the Bank in Washington from 1971 to 1973.
4   Kapur, Lewis and Webb, *The World Bank: Its First Half Century, Volume 1*, p. 548.
5   Ibid.
6   In the mid-1980s Attila Karosmanoğlu became vice-president of the World Bank for East Asia and the Pacific. He had been responsible for hiring Turgut Özal as head of planning in 1960 and was deputy prime minister immediately after the 1971 coup.
7   Munir Benjenk was vice-president of the World Bank for Europe, the Middle East and North Africa all through the 1970s. Benjenk was Robert McNamara's direct adviser for Turkey.
8   Later it would turn into quite a tradition with, for instance, Kemal Dervis, former vice-president of the World Bank, becoming Turkey's finance minister from March 2001 to August 2002. In 2005 Dervis became director of the UNDP.

2. In 1977 a heavily indebted Turkey experienced a crisis, and contrary to other indebted countries was granted significant aid by Western powers (the United States and Germany), the World Bank and the IMF so that it did not go under.[9]

Turkey's adoption of a neoliberal course was not easy, since the constitution that had been drafted in the early 1960s stipulated that the country develop an industrialization policy aiming at import substitution, and to that end implement both protectionism and public investment.

The military coup in September 1980 therefore had the World Bank's wholehearted sympathy. It is likely that Robert McNamara knew about preparations for the coup, for he entertained close relations with the Carter administration.

THE COUP WAS PREPARED WITH DIRECT AID FROM WASHINGTON

The World Bank's historians even acknowledge this openly: 'Personally as a global statesman, McNamara was not blind to Turkey's geopolitical salience.'[10] Faced with the danger of the 1979 Iranian revolution that was hostile to US policy, Turkey's stability had to be ensured by supporting an authoritarian regime.[11] The military coup in Turkey was prepared with the help of the United States.

In neighbouring Iraq, Saddam Hussein's 1979 coup against a pro-Soviet regime was part of the same convergence of strategic interests. Later Saddam would serve the interests of the United States and of Western Europe when he launched the war against Iran in 1980.

That is not something the historians of the World Bank ever mention. However, their comments on Turkey are clear enough: 'The Bank seemed to take special pains to attribute benign motives to the Turkish military and avoid exhibiting displeasure at its interventions. The institution's formal comments to the effect that the military takeover in 1980 would not displace the Bank's lending intentions were extremely polite.'[12]

When the military leaders handed power back to civilians, Turgut Özal and his Motherland party led the government.

THE WORLD BANK SEES TURKEY AS A SUCCESS

In subsequent years Turkey received five structural adjustment loans (until 1985). In 1988 the World Bank wrote: 'Among the Bank's clients, Turkey represents one of the most spectacular success stories.'[13]

---

9   This continued in the 1990s and early 2000s.
10 Kapur, Lewis and Webb, *The World Bank: Its First Half Century, Volume 1*, p. 549, note 62.
11 At the time of the coup, tensions between the United States and Iran were very high since about a hundred American hostages were being detained in Tehran. The issue was at the core of the election campaign opposing Ronald Reagan and Jimmy Carter (running for a second term of office).
12 Kapur, Lewis and Webb, *The World Bank: Its First Half Century, Volume 1*, p. 547.
13 Ibid., p. 550.

Such a self-congratulatory observation deserves comment. If we look at one of the Bank's major objectives, namely reducing inflation, there is little success to be celebrated: the annual inflation rate before structural adjustment was between 40 and 50 per cent at the end of the 1970s; under the military dictatorship that implemented adjustment, inflation reached 46 per cent in 1980–83, 44 per cent in 1984–88, and 60 per cent in 1989. In the following decades it reached an average of 70 per cent with peaks as high as 140 per cent.

In short, the objective of reducing inflation was definitely not achieved. The same applies to the public internal debt, which exploded, and the external debt, which increased even further.

But if we consider the Bank's hidden agenda, it can indeed be said that it achieved a remarkable victory in the 1980s:

1. Turkey remained one of the Western powers' staunch allies.
2. It completely relinquished the import substitution industrialization model, which implied a high level of protectionism and a high level of public investment.
3. It developed a model focusing on exports by increasing its competitiveness, forcing down real wages and devaluing its currency in significant proportions.
4. The trade-union movement and both the reformist and the revolutionary left were repressed thanks to the dictatorship.

From the end of 1979 to 1994 the relative value of the US dollar to the Turkish lira multiplied by 900; this process started with a 30 per cent devaluation in 1980. In the 1970s real wages had significantly increased as a result of the trade unions' influence and the political standing of the far left among young people and workers. The 1980 military coup made it possible to ban trade unions and strikes, reduce wages and increase profits.

Turkey thus became a veritable haven for corporate investments. Turgut Özal was rewarded and elected president from 1989 to 1993.

The World Bank steadily supported the military regime and the one that followed it through loans of close to $1 billion per year.

In 1991, in exchange for its services to the United States and its allies in the first Gulf War, Turkey benefited from reparations paid by a defeated Iraq.

We are justified in saying that the World Bank's strategy in Turkey clearly recalls its policy towards Ferdinand Marcos's dictatorship in the Philippines from 1972, Augusto Pinochet's in Chile from 1973 and the economic model those two dictators put in place.

We should add that in 1999–2001, Turkey went through a financial crisis as severe as Argentina's. Geostrategic interests again prevailed in the decisions taken: the IMF abandoned Argentina in December 2001 when it refused a new loan to

President Fernando de la Rúa while it simultaneously pursued its policy of loans to Turkey in order to prevent social disruption that would destabilize an essential pawn on the Middle East chessboard.

But as everywhere else, the aid provided by the IMF and the World Bank only increases the debt of recipient countries. Turkish citizens have a right to refuse further reimbursement to the Bretton Woods institutions. The debt that was contracted to the IMF and the World Bank is odious by any standards.

9
The Bank in Indonesia:
A Textbook Case of Intervention

The World Bank's policy on Indonesia is a textbook case in many ways. Everything is there: interference in a country's internal affairs, support for a dictatorial regime guilty of crimes against humanity, backing for a regime responsible for an aggression against a neighbouring country (the annexation of East Timor in 1975) and the development of mega-projects which simultaneously involved massive transfers of population, the plundering of natural resources for the profit of transnational corporations, and aggressions against indigenous populations.

In 1997, Indonesia was hit hard by the South-East Asian crisis. The remedies prescribed by the World Bank and the IMF worsened the economic situation and brought about social disasters. The tsunami tragedy in 2004 changed nothing for the Bank. The creditors maintained their pressure for repayment of Indonesia's debts and imposed an additional dose of neoliberal 'adjustment'.

THE WORLD BANK'S ODIOUS LOAN TO THE NETHERLANDS KEPT INDONESIA UNDER THE COLONIAL YOKE UNTIL 1949

In 1947, the World Bank granted a $195 million loan to the Netherlands – the second loan in the Bank's history. Two weeks before the loan was approved, the Netherlands launched its offensive against the Indonesian nationalists who were demanding independence. In the next two years, as many as 145,000 Dutch occupying troops were sent into the country. It was a large-scale operation that could hardly go unnoticed. Within the United Nations and in the US, criticism was voiced concerning Dutch policy in Indonesia and the World Bank's involvement. The Bank replied that the loan had been granted to the Dutch government for spending within the Netherlands. The critics objected in their turn that since money is fungible by nature, it was easy for the Dutch government to use the Bank loan to support its military effort in Indonesia.[1]

The US put pressure on the Netherlands, giving it $400 million under the Marshall Plan so that it could grant independence to Indonesia. The US objective was to open a new field of trade and investment for its companies. On 27 December 1949, the transfer of sovereignty was signed. Indonesia became a republic and the

---

1   Rich, *Mortgaging the Earth*, p. 69.

nationalist Sukarno was elected president. He set about maintaining a balance between the various factions in the country, while amassing personal power. In 1955, following the first elections, Sukarno decided to collaborate with the Communist Party (PKI) in order to establish his legitimacy. The PKI won 16 per cent of the votes and Sukarno's party, the PNI, 25 per cent.

SUKARNO PURSUES NATIONALIST POLICIES AND LEAVES THE WORLD BANK AND IMF

In external affairs, Sukarno made skilful use of the two opposing blocs in the Cold War, and there too, he managed to maintain an equilibrium until 1963; at that point the US, exasperated by the USSR's assistance to Indonesia, explicitly asked him to choose his camp. The IMF played the role of intermediary by proposing financial assistance strictly conditioned by terms of close cooperation. In March 1963, negotiations for loans got underway with the US, the IMF and the member states of the OECD, but everything went haywire in September 1963 when the British proclaimed the Federation of Malaysia without any outside consultation. Sukarno saw it as a destabilizing manoeuvre and retaliated by nationalizing the British companies, which led to the cancellation of the agreements with the IMF. Despite everything, the UN endorsed the creation of Malaysia, and Sukarno, unable to prevail, walked out of the UN in 1965.

At the height of the Cold War, Sukarno nationalized all foreign private companies except the oil companies. Indonesia left the IMF and the World Bank in August 1965 and decided to manage its affairs without them. On 30 September 1965, General Mohamed Suharto staged a military coup, supported by Washington. As chief of the armed forces, he launched a massive repression against the leftist parties, making the PKI his prime target: between 500,000 and one million civilians were murdered simply for being members or sympathizers of the PKI. In March 1966, Suharto finally forced Sukarno to make an official transfer of power. Six days later, the US government announced that it was opening a line of credit for Indonesia amounting to $8.2 million so that it could buy American rice.[2] On 13 April 1966, Indonesia joined the World Bank.[3] In 1966, US President Lyndon B. Johnson went to visit US troops in Vietnam and in one of his speeches praised the Indonesian model.[4] That model, the 'New Order' of the Suharto era, regularly resorted to terror and assassination, and basically aligned its policies with those of the United States.

---

2   See Payer, *The Debt Trap*.
3   See Kapur, Lewis and Webb, *The World Bank: Its First Half Century, Volume 1*, p. 467ff.
4   *Shadow Play: Indonesia's Years of Living Dangerously* (written, produced and directed by Chris Hilton; a co-production of Hilton-Cordell/Vagabond Films and Thirteen/WNET New York in association with Arte France, SBS, YLE, and the Australian Film Finance Corporation, 2002), 0:52:12: '[Johnson] told US troops that their exploits were the reason why people in Indonesia were enjoying freedoms that they didn't previously have.'

THE WORLD BANK AND SUHARTO'S DICTATORSHIP

When Robert McNamara became president of the World Bank in April 1968, he observed that Indonesia (with Mao's China) was the only highly populated country with which the Bank did not have an important relationship. It was necessary to make up for lost time and his first trip abroad as World Bank president was to Indonesia in June 1968. He felt quite at home there: the dictator Suharto had already surrounded himself with economists trained in the US, courtesy of the Ford Foundation.[5]

Relations between them were idyllic: 'He (McNamara) and President Suharto admired each other.'[6] 'While they were engaged in daily policy discussion, the Bank and the government acted like a couple of old cronies.[7] 'Indonesia was the presidentially designated jewel in the Bank's operational crown.'[8]

Moreover, the Bank's historians admit that: 'President Suharto (he had assumed the office in 1967) was a general, and his government, in good part, was a government of generals, many of whom were corrupt.'[9]

Indonesia officially rejoined the ranks of the IMF in February 1967 and the rewards were not long in coming: the Western countries immediately granted $174 million in aid in order to absorb the effects of the Indonesian crisis. Thereafter, in the early 1970s, the good relations between Indonesia, the US and the financial institutions took the form of a substantial debt reduction.

At the end of 1966, $534 million should have been repaid as debt servicing (interest, principal and arrears), a sum which represented 69 per cent of the estimated earnings from export. Without rescheduling, debt servicing would have destroyed the effect of financial assistance. The Western creditor countries agreed to a long-term moratorium until 1971 on repayment of the principal and interests on the debt contracted before 1966.[10] However, the effects of a moratorium are only temporary and, in 1971, repayments were supposed to start again. Consequently, the creditors signed the most favourable agreement ever granted at that time to a Third World country: the pre-1966 debt (contracted under Sukarno) must be repaid in 30 annual instalments over a period extending between 1970 and 1999.[11] The creditors agreed that Indonesia's repayments would not exceed 6 per cent of

---

5   Kapur, Lewis and Webb, *The World Bank: Its First Half Century, Volume 1*, pp. 467–71.

6   Ibid., p. 469.

7   Ibid., p. 470.

8   Ibid., p. 493.

9   Ibid., p. 469.

10 More than half of Indonesia's debt was contracted with the USSR, and when granting a moratorium on their debt, the Western creditors vouched for the repayment of the Soviet debt. In order to avoid any flow of capital towards the USSR, they granted this preferential treatment on condition that the Soviets did the same. The USSR accepted for fear of not being fully repaid should it refuse.

11 This new contract included the clause of most favoured nation, which implied that the Soviet debt was to be repaid at a faster rate.

the earnings from export. This operation had the effect of cancelling 50 per cent of the debt.

This reduction of debt was coupled with a reprehensible complacency regarding corruption. As soon as the World Bank returned to Indonesia to support the military dictatorship, its representatives became aware of the extent of the corruption. But Robert McNamara and the enormous Bank staff who settled in permanently in Jakarta decided not to make it grounds for divorce.[12] Thus, they were clearly accomplices.

Bernard Bell, who headed the Bank resident staff in Indonesia, recalls the question of the enormous misappropriation of funds caused by high-level government corruption. On 11 February 1972 he described this corruption to McNamara, as 'unacceptable to small but potentially vigorous elements of the public'.[13] And that was only the beginning. The 2004 *Global Corruption Report* by Transparency International estimated embezzlement by Suharto and his entourage at $15 billion to $35 billion.[14] The World Bank itself nurtured the corruption, since one of its own reports mentioned that 20 to 30 per cent of the budgets related to development funds were misappropriated.[15] The Bank continued its loans while knowing perfectly well that they were likely to be diverted.

THE PERTAMINA AFFAIR

During the 1970s, oil income exploded, and so did misappropriation of funds by corrupt generals for their own benefit. In 1975, a major crisis came to a head between the US and Indonesia. Ironically, the invasion and annexation of East Timor by Indonesia that year had nothing to do with it.

The Indonesian generals had developed the public oil company Pertamina so successfully that in February 1975 it had become the largest Asian company (Japan not included). The Pertamina conglomerate not only extracted and refined hydro-carbons, but it also possessed a chain of hotels and numerous oil tankers. Pertamina improved the country's harbour infrastructures and built roads and hospitals. The public company was active in the field of insurance with offices in Hong Kong, Los Angeles, Singapore and Tokyo. It played a key part in a strategy of import substi-tution industrialization. This was less and less to the liking of the US, and naturally, to the World Bank.

---

12 An 'atypically large resident staff' in Kapur, Lewis and Webb, *The World Bank: Its First Half Century, Volume 1*, p. 495.

13 Cable from Bernard Bell, cited in Kapur, Lewis and Webb, *The World Bank: Its First Half Century, Volume 1*, p. 490 and note 61.

14 Transparency International, *Global Corruption Report 2004* (London and Sterling, VA: Pluto Press, 2004), p. 1 and Table 1.1, p. 13 <images.transparencycdn.org/images/2004_GCR_PoliticalCorruption_EN.pdf> [accessed 17/03/2022].

15 World Bank, 'Summary of RSI staff views regarding the problem of "leakage" from the World Bank project budget', August 1997 <journal.probeinternational.org/1997/08/01/summary-rsi-staff-views-regarding-problem-leakage-world-bank-project-budgets/> [accessed 03/12/2021].

To put it bluntly, Pertamina was an obstacle to the development of the large US oil companies. Consequently, the US found it advisable to weaken and even dismantle Pertamina. Under pressure, Suharto bowed to its demands during the summer of 1975. Robert McNamara wrote to him: 'I applaud the comprehensive and systematic way in which you have moved to re-establish appropriate priorities.'[16] As a consolation prize, Robert McNamara added that he would see to it that the World Bank increased its loans.

It was only during his last visit to Indonesia on 15 May 1979 that Robert McNamara privately spoke his mind: 'It was also necessary to maintain the emphasis on reducing corruption. Outside Indonesia, this was much talked about and the world had the impression, rightly or wrongly, that it was greater than in any but perhaps one other country [...] It was like a cancer eating away at society.'[17]

However, at the end of 1980, the World Bank was still supporting Suharto's Indonesia to such an extent that it granted a loan without respecting (or imposing) the usual conditions. A similar situation can be seen nine years later when the Bank, anxious to maintain good relations with China, failed to distance itself after the repression of the Chinese spring of 1989.[18]

THE BANK'S SILENCE REGARDING THE ANNEXATION OF EAST TIMOR

Thirty years after Indonesia's invasion of Timor, certain US archives were made public. They establish indisputably what had long been suspected: Indonesia's invasion of East Timor in December 1975 was with the connivance of the American, British and Australian governments, and it resulted in 24 years of bloody occupation and systematic violations of human rights. According to these documents, as early as March 1975, the State Department, then headed by Henry Kissinger, aware of Indonesia's preparations for invasion, estimated that the US 'has considerable interests in Indonesia and none in Timor'. When he learned about the special operations leading up to the invasion, Kissinger asked his colleagues: 'Can I trust you to keep quiet about this?' His fear was that Congress would decree an embargo on arms deliveries to Indonesia, an ally of Washington in the Cold War.[19]

We understand better the World Bank's making no allusion to, let alone criticizing, the invasion and annexation of East Timor at the time! Submission to the interests of the US and its allies the UK and Australia, and complicity regarding the dictatorship were constant components of the Bank's behaviour.

---

16   Kapur, Lewis and Webb, *The World Bank: Its First Half Century, Volume 1*, p. 491.
17   Extract from Memorandum, Jean Baneth, 'Meeting with President Suharto, 15 May 1979', 22 May 1979, cited in Kapur, Lewis and Webb, *The World Bank: Its First Half Century, Volume 1*, p. 492, note 67 ('The other country may have been Zaire', the World Bank historians note).
18   Kapur, Lewis and Webb, *The World Bank: Its First Half Century, Volume 1*, p. 538.
19   Jacques Amalric, 'ONU, une réforme menacée' ('UN: a reform under threat'), *Daily Libération*, Paris, 26 January 2006 (translation CADTM).

Yet at the very start of the invasion, on 12 December 1975, the United Nations General Assembly condemned the actions of Indonesia's armed forces and demanded that it 'desist from further violation of the territorial integrity of Portuguese Timor [...] to enable the people of the Territory freely to exercise their right to self-determination and independence'.[20] This was recalled in 1995 by the International Court of Justice in its judgment of 30 June 1995 regarding the situation.[21]

Note that beginning in 2002, when the people of East Timor finally achieved independence, the World Bank set its sights on the new state. It managed to assert itself as the institution that coordinated most of the donations coming from the international community (see 'The World Bank kept East Timor in poverty', at the end of this chapter).

THE WORLD BANK'S SUPPORT FOR THE TRANSMIGRATION PROGRAMME

The World Bank actively collaborated in the disastrous transmigration project, certain facets of which constitute crimes against humanity. This project involved the displacement – in certain cases, forced – of millions of people from the islands of Java and Sumatra to other islands of the archipelago and the dispossession of the indigenous people of these islands.

The World Bank, especially during the 15 years of the programme's heyday (1974–89), was its principal source of external financing. The historians recognize this responsibility of the Bank: 'During the middle and later 1970's, the Bank, as well, supported and assisted the government's controversial program of official and subsidized transmigration of families from Java to the outer islands.'[22] This contribution was not limited to financial and technical support. The Bank also supported the project politically.

Between 1950 and 1974, the government displaced 664,000 people under the transmigration programme. But from 1974 on, with the World Bank's support, millions more were displaced. And the World Bank contributed directly to these displacements and relocations. World Bank loans almost totally financed the 'official' migrations of 2.3 million people, and 'catalysed' the relocation of some two million more people who transmigrated 'spontaneously'.

It soon appeared that what the World Bank called 'one of the largest resettlement programs in the world'[23] was also used to rid Java of undesirable inhabitants.

---

20 General Assembly resolution 3485 (XXX), 12 December 1975 <etan.org/etun/genasRes.htm> [accessed 11/01/2021].

21 ICJ, 'Case concerning East Timor' (Portugal v. Australia), judgment of 30 June 1995, *ICJ Reports 1995*, p. 90ff. <icj-cij.org/public/files/case-related/84/084-19950630-JUD-01-00-EN.pdf> [accessed 11/01/2021].

22 Kapur, Lewis and Webb, *The World Bank: Its First Half Century, Volume 1*, p. 489 (see note 60 for reference to the Board's decision on this matter in January 1979).

23 World Bank, *ED Précis*, September 1994 (World Bank, Operations Evaluation Department) <documents1.worldbank.org/curated/en/187401468042260249/pdf/28489.pdf> [accessed 12/01/2022].

The Bank's insistence that the resettlement was voluntary is significant. It erases the political nature of the practice and exonerates Indonesia, as well as itself, of the violations that went along with the displacements. For example, in the principal Javanese cities, 'nonconformists', elderly people, sick people (including those with leprosy), beggars and vagrants were forced either to disappear into the countryside (where their chances of survival were slim) or to transmigrate. In the latter case, they were herded into army trucks during the night and brought to 'transit camps' where they were given training for their relocation.[24] Marriage was an obligatory criterion for selection: the authorities organized forced marriages of single people before their departure. One should note that the World Bank played a large role in operations to recruit homeless people and political prisoners to be sent to the remotest and least desirable transmigration sites.

The transmigration projects most heavily supported by the World Bank were those involving private domestic or foreign firms likely to promote foreign trade and attract more ambitious transnational investments (particularly projects for industrial plantations).

Unrestricted foreign exploitation of the resources of the outer islands was pursued for the benefit of the central government and firms operating in the country, but to the detriment of the local populations, who saw a great portion of their habitat and their means of subsistence destroyed forever. The lands of the outer islands were regarded as 'empty' because the natives who had lived there for millennia did not have ownership certificates. These lands were then declared to be 'at the state's service' and were forcibly confiscated, most often without compensation. In fact, the World Bank supported the government in its acts of expropriating land belonging to indigenous people, although it never acknowledged it officially.

The people of the transmigration programme were given land that was not reserved for forest concessions and that was generally far from productive. For the government officials appointed to locate the sites to be cleared, it did not matter whether they were cultivable or not. Their job was to fill up a chart with information relating to site access, the number of acres to be cleared and the number of families that could possibly be located there.

The forest – a vital resource for the native dwellers – gradually disappeared due to the operations of forestry companies and commercial plantations on the one hand, and government teams entrusted with clearing the areas intended for agriculture and the installation of migrants, on the other. In addition, mining companies (see the case of the American mining company Freeport-McMoRan)[25] destroyed whole mountainsides and daily poured tons of mining waste into the rivers, polluting them beyond recovery. These rivers being the only source of water

---

24   One of these camps is a small island off Java from which it was impossible to escape, and where the people known as 'undesirables' were indoctrinated with agricultural techniques and state ideology.
25   Millet and Toussaint, *Tsunami Aid or Debt Cancellation!*, chapter 3.

for native dwellers, major medical disasters occurred. Oil extraction along the coasts also caused great damage to the marine fauna and flora, another source of food for the indigenous populations.

The real culprits in this matter were those who devised, carried out and financed the project. Primarily they were the Indonesian authorities and the international institutions (the World Bank first and foremost), as well as certain Western governments (the US, the UK, Germany and Israel, for example) and the national and foreign companies involved in the project's materialization. Among the devastating effects of programmes financed by international loans under the project were the development and proliferation of intensive exploitation of natural resources and a rapid increase in the surface areas intended for commercial plantations. These loans were always conditioned by the opening up of markets at all levels – removal of tariff barriers, attraction of foreign capital, priority on monocultures for export, liberalization and privatization of the goods and services distribution sectors, etc.

At the end of 1980, vociferous criticism increased, as much inside as outside the archipelago, accusing the World Bank of having taken part in a project of geopolitical domination typified by social and ecological blunders and infringing human rights in the course of its procedures.[26] The World Bank indeed played a major part in this project, with harmful and irreversible consequences: control of the indigenous populations of the outer islands and violation of their right to land ownership; the exorbitant cost of displacements (at least $6,638 per family according to World Bank estimates)[27] in relation to the results achieved, because according to a 1986 World Bank study, 50 per cent of the displaced families were living below the poverty level and 20 per cent below subsistence level; persistent problems of density in Java; massive deforestation of the outer islands, etc.

The World Bank, accused on all sides, decided to cease financing the installation of new transmigration sites and the costs of transmigration travel. Nevertheless, it concentrated its loans on the reinforcement of already existing villages[28] and on

---

26 Among the criticisms aimed at the Bank concerning the damage to and non-observance of human rights caused by its support for the actions of the government in West New Guinea, the best known are: the letter addressed in 1984 to A.W. Clausen, then president of the Bank, by the Minority Rights Group (New York); the sentence declared by the World Council of Indigenous Peoples at its regional meeting in 1984; and a petition addressed to the Inter-Governmental Group of Indonesia in 1984–85 by the Australian Council for Overseas Aid and by many associations for the defence of native rights. These complaints were taken into account neither by the Indonesian government nor by the Bank, which maintained its support for the abuse of the rights of New Guinea's native populations.

27 World Bank, *Indonesia – Transmigration Sector Review*, Report No. 6506, 24 October 1986, Table 3.1, p. 41. <documents1.worldbank.org/curated/en/806001468052135322/pdf/multi-page.pdf> [accessed 03/03/2022].

28 This reinforcement, called 'Second Stage Development', consisted in improving infrastructures and general living conditions in the transmigration villages, as well as rehabilitating sites with a high rate of desertion by transmigrants.

maintenance of the commercial plantations, thus only partially renouncing its participation in the programme.

The World Bank obviously denied all the allegations brought by observers. In 1994, it decided to carry out internal evaluation studies of the projects it financed, in order to determine any responsibilities. In one report, the World Bank accepted a very small share of responsibility, stating that the project in Sumatra had 'a major negative and probably irreversible impact'[29] on the Kubu, a nomadic people whose survival relied on swidden agriculture (shifting cultivation) and hunting and gathering in the forest. Another report admits that 'although the existence of the Kubu in the area has been known since project planning little effort has been made to deal with their problems'.[30]

In all respects, the World Bank's loans for the transmigration programme constitute odious debt: they were contracted by a despotic regime, which used them for repression and not for the well-being of the population. Consequently, this debt is null and void: it must be cancelled. But it should not stop there. The transmigration project supported by the World Bank implied the displacement, sometimes forced, of certain populations. The World Bank cannot simply claim that it was not aware of this. It was also an accomplice to the violation of the rights of the indigenous people who lived in the zones colonized by the transmigration project. These very serious acts should not go unpunished.

THE CRISIS OF 1997–98 IN INDONESIA AND ITS CONSEQUENCES

From the 1980s, and especially during the first half of the 1990s, the World Bank and the IMF got the Indonesian government to agree to free circulation of capital. This had the effect of placing Indonesia (like the Philippines, Thailand, Malaysia and South Korea) at the mercy of international speculation.

The IMF's annual report for the year 1997 compliments the Indonesian authorities: 'Directors commended the authorities for Indonesia's economic achievements of recent years, especially the sizable reduction in poverty and the improvement in many social indicators'.Further on, the IMF directors compliment the Indonesian authorities' 'emphasis on maintaining an open capital account' while having just pointed out the risks themselves: 'large capital inflows had raised important policy challenges'. They continue their analysis by praising the authorities, implying that they are capable of controlling the situation: 'The authorities' flexibility in adapting the policy mix to meet changing circumstances had been an important

---

29 'Indonesia Transmigration Program: a review of five Bank-supported projects', World Bank, Operations Evaluation Department, 26 April 1994 <documents1.worldbank.org/curated/en/823551468752430966/pdf/multi-page.pdf> [accessed 12/01/2022].

30 'Impact evaluation report: Transmigration I, Transmigration II, Transmigration III', World Bank, Operations Evaluation Department, Report No. 12874-IND, 22 March 1994, p. xiii <documents1.worldbank.org/curated/en/588091468915015089/pdf/12874-PPAR-PUBLIC.pdf> [accessed 12/01/2022].

aspect of their success over the years and would remain essential in addressing those challenges.'[31]

In 1997, a massive economic and financial crisis broke out in South-East Asia. After appearing in Thailand in February 1997, it had spread to Malaysia, Indonesia and the Philippines by July 1997. These four countries, described previously by the IMF, the World Bank and the private banks as role models for having opened up to the world market, their low rate of inflation and high growth rate, were now unable to resist the onslaughts of speculators. Between 2 July 1997 and 8 January 1998, the Indonesian rupee was depreciated by 229 per cent in relation to the US dollar.

After having been praised to the skies by the World Bank and the IMF, the Indonesian authorities were now strongly criticized for leaving too much power in the hands of the state; the state would in fact have been wrong had it allowed private financial and industrial institutions to go into debt and speculate.

The South-East Asia crisis of 1997 dealt a hard blow to Indonesia. In the space of less than a year, foreign capital was withdrawn from the country. Mass unemployment set in. At the end of 1998, according to government statistics, 50 per cent of the population lived below the poverty line, estimated in Indonesia at $0.55 per day for cities and $0.40 for the countryside.

The IMF imposed its 'shock' measures to resolve the crisis of 1997. They worsened the situation, particularly by causing the bankruptcy of a large section of the banking sector and of many entrepreneurs. The IMF and the World Bank pressed the government to transform the banks' private debt into public debt. Indonesia's public debt, which accounted for 23 per cent of the gross domestic product (GDP) before the crisis, literally exploded as a consequence of the policies imposed by the IMF and the Bank. In 2000, public debt amounted to 93 per cent of GDP.

Real wages plunged: whereas there had been an increase of 46 per cent between 1990 and 1996, they lost 25.1 per cent of their value in 1998.[32]

The population directly suffered the effects of these measures and started protesting vigorously. On 5 May 1998, under the agreements signed with the IMF, Suharto eliminated the subsidies on basic commodities so that the price of kerosene, electricity and petrol increased by 70 per cent. This intensified the huge popular mobilization that had begun several months before. Two weeks later, deserted by Washington and denounced by the people, Suharto was forced to step down, bringing an end to a dictatorial regime of 32 years.

Today, the largest portion of the state budget is devoted to debt repayment. In 1999 and 2000, 50 per cent and 40 per cent respectively were devoted to debt servicing. In 2004, the figure was close to 28 per cent.

---

31 IMF, *Annual Report 1997*, p. 80 <imf.org/~/media/Websites/IMF/imported-flagship-issues/external/pubs/ft/ar/97/pdf/_file06pdf.ashx> [accessed 03/03/2022].

32 UNCTAD, *Trade and Development Report 2000* (New York/Geneva: United Nations Conference on Trade and Development, 2000), pp. 65–66, cited by Toussaint, *Your Money or Your Life*, chapter 17.

After the tragedy of the tsunami, which resulted in the death of 150,000 people in the Indonesian province of Aceh in 2004, the World Bank and the governments of the creditor countries had promised to show generosity. The reality is quite different: financial aid, at first turned into a huge media event, has been provided in a chaotic and transitory way. While making a show of providing financial resources for reconstruction, the creditors in the Paris Club (who in addition direct the World Bank and the IMF) decided to deduct late-payment interest from the portion of debt servicing which was not remitted in 2005.[33] The moratorium granted by the Paris Club is thus only a show of generosity, since the states that accept it will make their populations pay, right down to the last cent. The Indonesian government, under pressure from its creditors, imposed a steep increase (29 per cent) on the price of fuel on 1 March 2005, which occasioned deep popular discontent. The tax revenue resulting from this rise was intended mainly for replenishing the budget deficit and repaying the debt.[34]

BY WAY OF CONCLUSION

The 1965 military coup d'état deprived the Indonesian people of the possibility of determining their own future. Yet with the Bandung Conference in 1955, Indonesia had begun to assert itself on the international scene. It was the threat of seeing one of the most populous countries on Earth play a key role in establishing a new world order that led the United States and the Bretton Woods institutions to provide active support for the Suharto dictatorship.

These institutions based their choice on political and geostrategic factors. Their financial support enabled Suharto to carry out policies that ran counter to human rights. Suharto served the interests of the major Western powers in the region and allowed transnational corporations based in the industrialized countries to siphon up Indonesia's natural resources. The World Bank and the IMF were active accomplices in these policies. The local ruling class supported Suharto and did not seek to invest in the country's development. It preferred to abet the plundering of Indonesia's natural resources by transnational corporations.

Starting from the crisis in 1997, IMF-imposed measures aggravated the economic situation and brought about a sharp increase in the internal and external public debt. The historical balance sheet of the IMF's and World Bank's role in Indonesia is an unqualified disaster. In consequence, the claims they hold against the country must be cancelled in full. Moreover, the World Bank and the IMF must be brought to account for their complicity in the Suharto regime and for projects like the transmigration, which in many respects constitute a crime against humanity.

The bilateral debts are in the hands of countries that directly backed the Suharto dictatorship, and they too must be cancelled. The same applies to debts owed to foreign

33   The decision of the Paris Club was announced on 10 March 2005 <clubdeparis.org/en/communications/page/exceptional-treatments-in-case-of-crisis> [accessed 03/12/2021].
34   *Financial Times*, 1 March 2005.

private companies that played a part in the corruption of the Indonesian regime, the pillaging of the country's natural resources and the exploitation of its workers.

A review of Indonesia's debt shows a totally negative result in terms of human development. Between 1970 and 2020, Indonesia's external debt increased by a factor of 93.9.[35] Over that same period, the total amount of debt repayment represents 19.9 times the amount of the initial debt stock. In every year except 1998, Indonesia has repaid more than it has received in the form of loans. The net transfer for that period stands at −$45.8 billion.

This is irrefutable proof that the debt system is a fatal mechanism for extracting a country's wealth.

The World Bank kept East Timor in poverty

East Timor, located 500 km from the coast of Australia, won independence in May of 2002 after several decades of struggle. In 2003, when I went there at the request of the Timorese authorities, the country had a population of a little over 800,000; in 2021, it stands at 1.3 million, of which 60 per cent are under 16 years of age. In 2003, two out of five Timorese were living on less than $0.55 per day. Three-quarters of the population had no access to electricity, and half had no clean water. In 2021, 19 years after independence, the situation has not really improved: 46 per cent of children under age five suffer from malnutrition, and 50 per cent of the population has no access to wastewater treatment.[36]

A Portuguese colony until 1975, East Timor was annexed to Indonesia under the Suharto dictatorship. The high points of the liberation struggle were in the 1970s, at the end of Portuguese rule, and in 1998–99 following Suharto's overthrow by the people of Indonesia. The Carnation Revolution in Portugal in 1974 led to the independence of Portugal's colonies Guinea-Bissau, Cape Verde, Angola and Mozambique.

The leading Timorese liberation movement, Fretilin, which engaged in armed struggle for nearly 30 years, had a comfortable majority in the legislature in 2002. President of the Republic Xanana Gusmão was a historic Fretilin figure. The liberation struggle after the fall of Suharto left more than 100,000 Timorese dead. From 1999, following a referendum in which the population voted overwhelmingly for independence, the country was placed under UN administration.

The country is very poor. Its economy lacked diversity and there was no industry. The main activity was agriculture (more than 75 per cent of the population is rural). Aside from coffee for export, agricultural production was oriented towards meeting internal demand, which in reality was an advantage. The challenge for any economic policy aimed at improving living conditions for the population was to take the realities of that local agriculture into account. Yet after independence, oil and gas gradually became the engine of East Timor's economy. There are large oil and gas reserves out at sea, where the

---

35   Calculations by the author based on World Bank, *International Debt Statistics 2020*.

36   French Treasury Department (Direction générale du Trésor de la France), 'Situation économique – Timor Oriental', 4 March 2021 <tresor.economie.gouv.fr/Pays/TL/situation-economique> [accessed 03/03/2022].

Australian and Timorese territorial waters meet. Powerful Australian financial and economic interests managed to take over the lion's share under the Suharto dictatorship. When Timor became independent and sought to renegotiate the agreements in order to recover its rightful share, Australia refused. The Timorese authorities considered appealing to the International Court of Justice in The Hague, but finally gave up the idea in the face of threats of economic reprisals by Australia. In the end there was an agreement with Australia and the Timorese authorities granted operating rights on the main offshore oilfield to the US firm ConocoPhillips. The country has become completely dependent on oil revenues. In 2020, revenues from hydrocarbons accounted for 76 per cent of the state's revenue and 99 per cent of currency revenue.[37] That is an extremely high level of dependence.

In 2003 the government was against indebtedness for the country
The new state had the good fortune to come into being without debt and at first the government had made the wise decision to refuse to borrow. It was in that context that I was invited to meet with the country's authorities. When I went there in March of 2003, the government was only accepting grants from the international community. The World Bank was frustrated because it had tried to impose an indebtedness plan. The Bank had to adopt a new strategy in order to convince the authorities to fall in line with the Washington Consensus. It managed to get itself appointed as the institution which coordinated the majority of grants coming from the international community. The Bank took a 2 per cent cut of each grant for itself – a true scandal. It took advantage of its function as intermediary to coerce the Timorese authorities into applying neoliberal policies – eliminating customs barriers (to the detriment of local farmers, in particular rice producers), imposing a policy of cost recovery (high registration fees in higher education, payment for health care), privatization of management of the electricity sector and installation of prepayment electricity meters, etc.

There is also another very grave phenomenon: only a small part of each grant (10 to 20 per cent) actually reached the local economy. The World Bank managed to see to it that the majority was spent outside Timor, either in the form of remunerations paid to foreign experts or purchases of goods and services on the international markets.

The World Bank managed to impose the use of international consultants (some of them coming directly from the Bank) whose fees ate up 15 to 30 per cent of the grants. The inequality of the fees paid is particularly striking. An international expert was paid at least $500 per day (not counting coverage of all their expenses in the country), which is at least a hundred times what Timorese workers earn ($3 to $5 per day). The representative of the World Bank, whom I met in her office in Díli, the capital, earned something like $15,000 per month. And her colleague from the IMF, who was paid the same kind of money, actively opposed the adoption of legislation that would have established a legal minimum wage. He even wrote, without hesitation, that a wage of $3 to $5 a day was far too high.

---

37   Ibid.

Here are a few examples of the scandalous level of the fees paid to external consultants. They are taken from an article in the daily *The Australian*, published in April of 2009:

> Ines Almeida is a media flak for East Timor's Ministry of Finance. This year, she will earn a lot more than her Prime Minister, Xanana Gusmao, who has a base salary of $US1000 a month with a $US500 allowance.

> Ms Almeida, a joint Australian-Timorese citizen who lives mostly in Timor, is treated as an outsider, paid in US dollars out of World Bank funds and grant money from individual nations. In her 2008–09 package, she earns a base of $US182,400 and picks up a further $US41,365 in travel expenses and living allowances, taking the package to $US219,765.

> [...]

> Another Australian, Graham Daniel, is on a 12-month contract as a senior management adviser to the Finance Minister. For his 180 days' work through 2008–09, he is being paid $US236,160, plus $US60,361 in reimbursible [sic] expenses and contingencies, bringing his package to $US296,521. Asked if he thinks the East Timorese would be shocked at how much he earned if they were aware of it, Mr Daniel says: 'They shouldn't be made aware of it. I wouldn't be the most highly paid person in Timor. It's consistent with what I've been paid in other countries. My contract is certainly fairly high, but others are getting a lot more.'

> [...]

> A US citizen, Francis Ssekandi, is another senior adviser to the Finance Minister. His 2008–09 package, including remuneration and travel expenses, is $US424,427 for 272 days' work.[38]

Note that at that time, Francis M. Ssekandi was a judge at the World Bank Administrative Tribunal, a position he held from 2007 to 2013.[39]

The same article in *The Australian* continues, citing Timor's then Minister of Finance Emilia Pires, among others:

> 'I earn $US700 a month,' Ms. Pires says.

> 'I personally think the money (advisers are paid) is too high ... Some of my advisers have been working in Afghanistan and Iraq and I had to compete to get them over here. It is way out of my control; we go by market standards. [...] In post-conflict countries it is a complex job. Timorese people have not had the opportunity and education to do this. We need expertise. I am very much aware that technical assistance comes at a high price.'

> Asked if she thinks the ordinary East Timorese people would understand the high pay packages, Ms Pires says: 'I'm trying to explain to them. This is the world we live in. We all want to change the world, but I'm realistic.'

---

38   Paul Toohey, 'East Timorese go begging as foreign advisors rake it in', *The Australian*, 25 April 2009 <etan.org/et2009/04april/26/25forei.htm> [accessed 29/03/2022].

39   World Bank Administrative Tribunal, 'Appointment of new tribunal judges' <tribunal.worldbank. org/index.php/news/appointment-new-tribunal-judges> [accessed 21/03/2022].

Fretilin MP and party vice-president Arsenio Bano says they would not understand. 'A lot of Timorese often cannot even get $1 a day,' he says. 'Fifty cents a day is a big thing. Even in a month some of them cannot get $5.

The country is very poor and they (consultants) are paid too much. $US200,000 is more than the money that is invested in roads in the district of Oecussi this year. It's more than some of the school-feeding projects for 4000 students in one district of Ermera.'[40]

The Australian daily asked Nigel Roberts, World Bank Director for East Timor, New Guinea and the Pacific Islands, about the situation and he answered:

'Timor-Leste needs to pay these rates if it is to attract first-rate talent, which I believe it is entitled to and needs in order to make the transition out of poverty [...] Using cheaper expertise isn't going to help develop the country. In an ideal world, this type of expertise would be provided on a voluntary basis, but unfortunately no employment market anywhere in the world works on this principle, and people don't discount their services when they work in places like Dili or Moresby or Honiara.'[41]

The paper adds that in March 2009, President José Ramos-Horta had said that 'since independence about $3 billion has been spent on Timor but not in Timor'.[42] This is what I was referring to above when I explained that the World Bank had pressured the Timorese authorities to agree to using the grants for Timor mainly to pay for goods and services purchased abroad. Nearly 20 years after independence, the bottom line is entirely negative. The advice given by the World Bank and the experts it recommended led only to the development of East Timor's underdevelopment.

During the lectures I gave in 2003, I compared the attitude of the World Bank to that of Christopher Columbus and other conquistadors who, to gain a foothold in a territory, began by handing out gifts – beads and trinkets, for example – before beginning their pillage. The first time I made that comparison, I expected the audience to protest. No-one did. In Timor, many people who are sincerely committed to rebuilding the country were very disturbed at the influence the World Bank had gained. They had the impression that their government itself had fallen under the influence of the neoliberal credo and were wondering how to set things right. In the years that followed, the Bank's thinking indeed predominated and the country was locked onto the path of total dependence on fossil fuels exported without any processing. The result is that very few skilled jobs are being created for the Timorese and the country must import fuel, since it has no refinery. Not to mention the fact that the reserves are quickly being used up and the country is going further and further into debt. All with no benefit to the majority of the population, 35 per cent of whom are illiterate.[43]

40   Toohey, 'East Timorese go begging as foreign advisors rake it in'.
41   Ibid.
42   Ibid.
43   French Treasury Department (Direction générale du Trésor de la France), 'Situation économique – Timor Oriental'.

10
The World Bank's Theoretical Falsehoods Regarding Development

The World Bank claims that in order to progress, developing countries must rely on external borrowing and attract foreign investments. The main aim of thus running up debt is to buy basic equipment and consumer goods from the highly industrialized countries. The facts show that day after day, for decades now, that idea has failed to bring about progress. The models which have influenced the Bank's vision can only result in making developing countries heavily dependent on an influx of external capital, particularly in the form of loans, which creates the illusion of a certain level of self-sustained development. The lenders of public money (the governments of the industrialized countries and especially the World Bank) see loans as a powerful means of control over indebted countries. Thus the Bank's actions should not be seen as a succession of errors or bad management. On the contrary, they are a deliberate part of a coherent, carefully thought-out, theoretical plan, taught with great application in most universities. It is expounded in hundreds of books on development economics. The World Bank has produced its own ideology of development. When facts undermine the theory, the Bank does not question the theory. Rather, it seeks to twist the facts in order to protect the dogma.

In the first ten years of its existence, the Bank was not much given to reflecting upon the type of economic policy that might best be applied to the developing countries. There were several reasons for this. Firstly, it was not among the Bank's priorities at the time. In 1957, the majority of the loans made by the Bank (52.7 per cent) still went to the industrialized countries.[1] Secondly, the theoretical framework of the Bank's economists and directors was of a neoclassical bent, and neoclassical theory did not assign any particular place to the developing countries.[2] Finally, it was not until 1960 that the Bank came up with a specific instrument for granting low-interest loans to the developing countries, with the creation of the International Development Association (IDA).

---

1   'The period during which the Bank held firm views on the nature of the development process but did little to reach into it extended roughly up to the late 1950s, and coincided with a phase in Bank lending in which most lending was still made to developed countries (by 1957, 52.7% of funding still went to such countries).' Stern and Ferreira, 'The World Bank as "intellectual actor"', p. 533.

2   'The instruments of neo-classical analysis can be applied in a general way, quite unspecifically, to the questions posed by under-development. Under-development or blocked development is not subjected to systematic analysis in neo-classical theory.' Gerard Azoulay, *Les théories du développement* (Rennes : Presses Universitaires de Rennes, 2002), p. 38 (translation CADTM).

An ethnocentric and conservative vision of the world

The World Bank's vision is marked by several conservative prejudices. In the reports and speeches of the first 15 years of its existence, there are regular references to 'backward' and 'underdeveloped' countries. The Bank sees the reasons for underdevelopment from an ethnocentric point of view. In the World Bank's eighth annual report, we read that: 'There are many and complex reasons why these areas have not been more developed. Many cultures, for instance, have placed a low value on material advance and, indeed, some have regarded it as incompatible with more desirable objectives of society and the individual'.[3] One of the causes of backwardness identified in the report is the lack of desire or absence of will to make material progress and to modernize society. Hindus' deep respect for cows becomes shorthand for the inherent backwardness of India. As for Africa, World Bank president Eugene Black declared in 1961: 'Even today the bulk of Africa's more than 200 millions are only beginning to enter world society.'[4] The reactionary nature of the World Bank's vision has by no means been attenuated by the passing years. In the *Global Development Report* of 1987, the Bank wrote:

In his *Principles of Political Economy* (1848), John Stuart Mill mentioned the advantages of 'foreign trade'. Over a century later, his observations are as pertinent as they were in 1848. Here is what Mill had to say about the indirect advantages of trade:

A people may be in the quiescent, indolent, uncultivated state, with all their tastes either fully satisfied or entirely undeveloped, and they may fail to put forth the whole of their productive energies for want of any sufficient object of desire. The opening of a foreign trade, by making them acquainted with new objects, or tempting them by the easier acquisition of things which they had not previously thought attainable, sometimes works a sort of industrial revolution in a country whose resources were previously undeveloped for want of energy and ambition in the people: inducing those who were satisfied with scanty comforts and little work to work harder for the gratification of their new tastes, and even to save and accumulate capital, for the still more complete satisfaction of those tastes at a future time.[5]

The massive return of the neoconservatives in the administration of US President George W. Bush (2001–08) greatly exacerbated the Bank's deeply materialistic and reactionary tendencies. The appointment of Paul Wolfowitz, one of the leading neocons, to the presidency of the Bank in 2005 further entrenched this orientation.

3   World Bank (IBRD), *Eighth Annual Report 1952–1953* (Washington, DC: IBRD), p. 9.

4   Eugene Black, 'Tale of Two Continents: Africa and South America', Ferdinand Phinizy Lectures, delivered at the University of Georgia, 12 and 13 April 1961, in Kapur, Lewis and Webb, *The World Bank: Its First Half Century, Volume 1*, p. 145. Eugene Black was president of the World Bank from 1949 to 1962.

5   World Bank, Global *Development Report 1987* (Washington, DC: World Bank, 1987), p. 3 <open-knowledge.worldbank.org/bitstream/handle/10986/5970/WDR%201987%20-%20English.pdf> [accessed 6/12/2021].

However, the fact that the Bank had no ideas of its own did not prevent it from criticizing others. For example, in 1949 it criticized a report by a United Nations commission on employment and economics which argued for public investment in heavy industry in the developing countries. The Bank declared that the governments of the developing countries had enough to do in establishing a good infrastructure, and should leave the responsibility for heavy industry to local and foreign private initiative.[6]

According to World Bank historians Mason and Asher, the Bank's position stemmed from the belief that the public and private sectors should play different roles. The public sector should ensure the planned development of an adequate infrastructure: railways, roads, power stations, ports and communications in general. The private sector should deal with agriculture, industry, trade, and personal and financial services, as it is held to be more effective than the public sector in these areas.[7] What this really meant was that anything which might prove profitable should be handed over to the private sector. On the other hand, providing the infrastructure should fall to the public sector, since the costs need to be met by society, to help out the private sector. In other words, the World Bank recommended privatization of profits combined with socialization of the cost of anything which was not directly profitable.

What is striking about the World Bank's publications and the literature of the time dealing with development issues in the 1950s up to the 1970s is the emphasis on *planning* growth and development (in both industrialized and developing economies). Until the end of the 1970s, planning was considered important for several reasons: first, economic planning emerged during the prolonged depression of the 1930s as a response to the chaos resulting from laissez-faire policies; secondly, the reconstruction of Europe and Japan had to be organized; thirdly, the period was that of the 30 years of continuous economic growth that followed the Second World War, and that growth had to be managed and planned for; fourthly, the success, real or supposed, of Soviet economic planning undoubtedly exercised a great fascination, even for the sworn enemies of the so-called 'communist bloc'. However, from the early 1980s, when neoliberal ideologies and policies came back with a vengeance, the idea of economic planning was completely rejected.

Another major preoccupation in the early days that was also rejected after the 1980s was the decision by several Latin American countries to resort to import substitution and the possibility (seen as a danger by the majority of leaders of the most industrialized countries) that other newly independent countries might follow their example.

Let us briefly review some of the economists whose work had a direct influence on and in the Bank.

---

6   Stern and Ferreira, 'The World Bank as "intellectual actor"'.
7   Mason and Asher, *The World Bank since Bretton Woods*, pp. 458–59.

THE HOS (HECKSCHER–OHLIN–SAMUELSON) MODEL

David Ricardo's theory of comparative advantages gained force in the 1930s through the studies of the Swedish economists Eli Heckscher and Bertil Ohlin, later joined by the American Paul A. Samuelson. It is the synthesis produced by the latter that is known as the HOS model. The HOS model raises the issue of factors of production – these factors are work, land and capital – and claims that each country has an interest in specializing in the production and export of goods which make greatest use of that country's most abundant production factor – which will also be the cheapest. Free trade would then theoretically balance out what the factors earn among all the countries taking part in free-trade agreements. The abundant factor, which would be exported, would grow scarcer and thus more costly; the rare factor, which would be imported, would increase and its price would fall. This system of specialization would bring about optimal distribution of factors in a now homogenous market. This model would enable all economies to aim for maximal integration in the global market with positive outcome for all the trading partners. Various studies carried out later, especially those by Paul Krugman,[8] to test the HOS model have shown it to be inaccurate.

THE FIVE STAGES OF ECONOMIC GROWTH ACCORDING TO WALT W. ROSTOW

In 1960, Walt W. Rostow[9] postulated five stages of development in a book entitled *The Stages of Economic Growth: A Non-Communist Manifesto*.[10] He claimed that all countries fall into one of five categories and that they can only follow this route.

The first stage is traditional society, characterized by the predominance of agricultural activity. Technical progress is nil, there is practically no growth in productivity and minds are not ready for change.

Next, in the stage before 'take-off', exchanges and techniques begin to emerge, people's attitudes become less fatalistic and savings rates increase. In fact, this is how European societies evolved from the fifteenth to the early eighteenth century.

---

8   The predominance of exchanges between economies endowed with similar factors (exchanges of similar products between industrialized economies) was established in the work of Paul Krugman and Elhanan Helpman in the 1980s.

9   Walt Whitman Rostow was an influential economist. He was also a high-ranking political adviser, becoming adviser to Robert McNamara during the Vietnam War. Some of the notes he addressed to McNamara can be consulted online, dealing with the politico-military strategy to follow with regard to the North Vietnamese and their allies in 1964. One note entitled 'Military dispositions and political signals' dated 16 November 1964 is particularly interesting, for it shows quite impressive mastery of the arts of war and negotiation <mtholyoke.edu/acad/intrel/pentagon3/doc232.htm> [accessed 6/12/2021]. It is worth mentioning since it highlights once more the political stakes behind the operations of the IMF and the World Bank in countries of the Periphery. Thus economic policy has to be considered in the light of its political motivation and levers.

10   Walt Whitman Rostow, *The Stages of Economic Growth: A Non Communist Manifesto* (New York: Cambridge University Press, 1960).

The third stage is 'take-off', a crucial stage corresponding to a qualitative leap, with significant increases in savings and investment rates and a move towards cumulative growth.[11]

The fourth stage is the 'drive to maturity', where technical progress takes over in all fields of activity and production is diversified.

Finally, the fifth stage coincides with the era of mass consumerism.[12]

Rostow claimed that at the take-off stage, an influx of external capital (in the form of foreign investments or credit) was indispensable.

Rostow's model is marred by oversimplification. He presents the stage of development reached by the USA after the Second World War both as the goal to aim for and the model to reproduce. Similarly, he considers that the British take-off model, with the agricultural revolution followed by the industrial revolution, should be reproduced elsewhere. He thus completely ignores the historical reality of other countries. There is no reason why each country should go through the five stages he describes.

INSUFFICIENT SAVINGS AND THE NEED TO RESORT TO EXTERNAL FUNDING

In neoclassical terms, savings should precede investment and are insufficient in the developing countries. This means that the shortage of savings is seen as a fundamental factor explaining why development is blocked. An influx of external funding is required. Paul Samuelson, in *Economics*,[13] took the history of US indebtedness in the nineteenth and twentieth centuries as a basis for determining four different stages leading to prosperity: young borrowing nation in debt (from the War of Independence in 1776 to the Civil War of 1865); mature indebted nation (from 1873 to 1914); new lending nation (from the First to Second World Wars); and mature lending nation (1960s). Samuelson and his emulators slapped the model of US economic development from the late eighteenth century until the Second World War onto 100 or so countries which made up the Third World after 1945, as though it were possible for all those countries to quite simply imitate the experience of the United States.[14]

As for the need to resort to foreign capital (in the form of loans and foreign investments), an associate of Walt W. Rostow's, Paul Rosenstein-Rodan, formulated it this way: 'Foreign capital will be a pure addition to domestic capital formation, i.e. it will all be invested; the investment will be productive or "businesslike" and result in increased production. The main function of foreign capital inflow is to increase the rate of domestic capital formation up to a level which could then be maintained

11   Note that Walt Rostow claimed that Argentina had already reached the take-off stage before 1914.

12   Rostow also claimed that the USA had permanently reached the stage of mass consumerism just after the Second World War, followed by Western Europe and Japan in 1959. As for the USSR, it was technically ready to reach that stage but first needed to make some adjustments.

13   Paul Samuelson, *Economics*, 11th edn (New York: McGraw Hill, 1980), pp. 617–18.

14   Payer, *Lent and Lost*, pp. 33–34.

without any further aid'.[15] This statement contradicts the facts. It is not true that
foreign capital enhances the formation of national capital and is all invested. A large
part of foreign capital rapidly leaves the country where it was temporarily directed
and returns in the form of capital flight, debt repayments and repatriation of profits.

Paul Rosenstein-Rodan, who was the assistant director of the economics department
of the World Bank between 1946 and 1952, made another monumental error in
predicting the dates when various countries would reach self-sustained growth. He
reckoned that Colombia would reach that stage by 1965, Yugoslavia by 1966, Argentina
and Mexico between 1965 and 1975, India in the early 1970s, Pakistan three or four
years after India, and the Philippines after 1975. What nonsense that has proved to be!

Note that this notion of self-sustained growth is commonly used by the World
Bank. The definition given in 1964 by Dragoslav Avramović, then director of the
economics department, was as follows: 'Self-sustained growth is defined to mean a
rate of income increase of, say, 5% p.a. financed out of domestically generated funds
and out of foreign capital which flows into the country'.[16]

Development planning as envisaged by the World Bank and US academia
amounts to pseudo-scientific deception based on mathematical equations. It is
supposed to give legitimacy and credibility to the intention of making developing
countries dependent on obtaining external capital. There follows an example,
advanced in all seriousness by Max Millikan and Walt W. Rostow in 1957:

If the initial rate of domestic investment in a country is 5 per cent of national
income, if foreign capital is supplied at a constant rate equal to one-third the
initial level of domestic investment, if 25 per cent of all additions to income are
saved and reinvested, if the capital-output ratio is 3 and if interest and dividend
service on foreign loans and private investment are paid at the rate of 6 per
cent per year, the country will be able to discontinue net foreign borrowing after
fourteen years and sustain a 3 per cent rate of growth out of its own resources.[17]

More nonsense!

CHENERY AND STROUT'S TWO-GAP MODEL

In the mid-1960s, the economist Hollis Chenery, later to become chief economist
and vice-president of the World Bank,[18] and his colleague Alan Strout drew up

15 Paul Rosenstein-Rodan, 'International aid for underdeveloped countries,' in *Review of Economics and Statistics* (Cambridge, MA: MIT Press, 1961), Vol. 43, p. 107.
16 Dragoslav Avramović et al., *Economic Growth and External Debt* (Baltimore: Johns Hopkins Press for the IBRD, 1964), p. 193.
17 Max Millikan and Walt Whitman Rostow, *A Proposal: Keys to An Effective Foreign Policy* (New York: Harper, 1957), p. 158.
18 In 1970, Hollis Chenery became adviser to Robert McNamara, then president of the World Bank. Soon after, in 1972, the post of vice-president linked to that of chief economist was created for Chenery by McNamara. Since then, it has become part of the tradition. Chenery served as chief economist and vice-president of the World Bank from 1972 to 1982. Chenery remains the longest-serving occupant of the post of chief economist. Previous and later incumbents stayed between three and six years. ('The World Bank as "intellectual actor"', p. 538.)

a new model called the 'two-gap' or 'dual-gap' model.[19] Chenery and Strout laid emphasis on two constraints: first, insufficient internal savings, and then insufficient foreign currency. Charles Oman and Ganeshan Wignaraja summarized the Chenery–Strout model as follows:

In essence, the two-gap model hypothesises that whereas in the very early stages of industrial growth insufficient savings may stand as the principal constraint on the rate of domestic capital formation, once industrialization gets well under way the principal constraint may no longer be domestic savings per se, but the availability of foreign exchange required to import capital equipment, intermediate goods and perhaps even raw materials used as industrial inputs. The foreign-exchange gap may thus supersede the savings gap as the principal development constraint.[20]

To resolve this dual gap, Chenery and Strout propose a simple solution: borrow foreign currency and/or procure it by increasing exports.

The Chenery–Strout model is highly mathematical. It was the 'in thing' at the time. For its supporters, it had the advantage of conferring an air of scientific credibility upon a policy whose main aims were, firstly, to incite the developing countries to resort to massive external borrowing and foreign investments, and secondly, to subject their development to a dependency on exports. At the time, the model came under criticism from several quarters. Suffice it to quote that of Keith Griffin and Jean-Luc Enos, who claimed that resorting to external inflow would further limit local savings:

Yet as long as the cost of aid (e.g. the rate of interest on foreign loans) is less than the incremental output-capital ratio, it will 'pay' a country to borrow as much as possible and substitute foreign for domestic savings. In other words, given a target rate of growth in the developing country, foreign aid will permit higher consumption, and domestic savings will simply be a residual, that is, the difference between desired investment and the amount of foreign aid available. Thus the foundations of models of the Chenery–Strout type are weak, since one would expect, on theoretical grounds, to find an inverse association between foreign aid and domestic savings.[21]

INCITING DEVELOPING COUNTRIES TO RESORT TO EXTERNAL AID AS A MEANS OF INFLUENCING THEM

Bilateral aid and World Bank policies are directly related to the political objectives pursued by the USA in its foreign affairs.

---

19 Hollis B. Chenery and Alan Strout, 'Foreign assistance and economic development', *The American Economic Review*, 1966, Vol. 56, No. 4, pp. 679–733 <jstor.org/stable/1813524>.

20 Charles Oman and Ganeshan Wignaraja, *The Postwar Evolution of Development Thinking* (London/Paris: Macmillan/OECD), pp. 13–14.

21 Keith B. Griffin and Jean-Luc Enos, 'Foreign assistance: objectives and consequences', *Economic Development and Cultural Change*, April 1970, Vol. 18, No. 3, p. 320.

Hollis Chenery maintained that 'The main objective of foreign assistance, as of many other tools of foreign policy, is to produce the kind of political and economic environment in the world in which the United States can best pursue its own social goals.'[22]

In a book entitled *The Emerging Nations: Their Growth and United States Policy*, Max Millikan[23] and Donald Blackmer, both colleagues of Walt W. Rostow, clearly described certain objectives of US foreign policy in 1961:

It is in the interest of the United States to see emerging from the transition process nations with certain characteristics. First, they must be able to maintain their independence, especially of powers hostile or potentially hostile to the United States [...] Fourth, they must accept the principle of an open society whose members are encouraged to exchange ideas, goods, values, and experiences with the rest of the world; this implies as well that their governments must be willing to cooperate in the measures of international economic, political and social control necessary to the functioning of an interdependent world community.[24]

Under the leadership of the USA, of course.

Later in the book, it is explicitly shown how aid is used as a lever to orient the policies of the beneficiary countries:

For capital assistance to have the maximum leverage in persuading the underdeveloped countries to follow a course consistent with American and free-world interests [...] *the amounts offered must be large enough and the terms flexible enough to persuade the recipient that the game is worth the effort*. This means that we must invest substantially larger resources in our economic development programs than we have done in our past.[25]

As we shall see further on, the volume of loans to developing countries increased at a growing pace throughout the 1960s and 1970s as the consequence of a deliberate policy on the part of the USA, the governments of other industrialized countries and the Bretton Woods institutions, whose aim was to influence the policies of countries of the South.

---

22   Hollis B. Chenery, 'Objectives and criteria of foreign assistance', in Gustav Ranis (ed.), *The United States and the Developing Economies* (New York: W.W. Norton, 1964), p. 81, cited by Griffin and Enos, 'Foreign assistance: objectives and consequences', p. 316.

23   Max Millikan, of the Central Intelligence Agency (CIA) and its predecessor the Office of Strategic Services (OSS), became director of CENIS (Center for International Studies) at the Massachusetts Institute for Technology, with direct links to the State Department.

24   Max F. Millikan and Donald L. M. Blackmer (eds), *The Emerging Nations: Their Growth and United States Policy* (Boston: Little, Brown and Co., 1961), pp. x–xi.

25   Ibid., pp. 118–19 (emphasis added).

MAKING EXPORTS THE PRIORITY

In one of their main contributions, Chenery and Strout claimed that resorting to import substitution is an acceptable method of reducing the deficit in foreign currency.[26] They later abandoned this position, when the import substitution policies maintained by certain developing countries became one of the main targets of criticism levelled by the Bank, the IMF, the OECD and the governments of the major industrialized countries.

Other studies by economists directly associated with the World Bank turned to measuring the effective rates of protection of economies and the resulting bias in terms of utilization of productive resources and of profitability of investments. They favoured redirecting strategies towards exports, abandoning protectionist tariffs and, more generally, a price-fixing policy more closely related to market mechanisms. Bela Balassa, Jagdish Bhagwati and Anne Krueger systematized this approach and their analyses were to leave their mark on the international institutions and become the theoretical justification for opening up trade during the 1980s and 1990s.[27] Anne Krueger[28] wrote:

When industrial growth is based upon the competitive international market, firms can be of optimal economic size without regard to the size or price and demand characteristics of the domestic market. Low-cost firms in individual industries can expand at their desired rate, unconstrained by availability of raw material or the price elasticity of domestic demand for the product. This leads to greater reduction of costs and expansion of output than that observed under protection. Moreover, industries with comparative advantage can increase their shares of industrial output at a more rapid rate when they can profitably export than when their growth is restricted to their shares of the less dynamic domestic market.[29]

More smoke and mirrors. International markets are in fact subject to shocks, economic recessions periodically impact the economies of the most industrialized countries and the world economy, and actual demand is far from being infinite. What's more, in order to be able to sell on the world market one has to be competitive, and that means strongly limiting increases in wages, or even lowering them.

---

26 Chenery and Strout, 'Foreign assistance and economic development,' pp. 682, 697–700.

27 Bela Balassa, *Development Strategies in Some Developing Countries: A Comparative Study* (Baltimore: Johns Hopkins University Press for the World Bank, 1971); Jagdish Bhagwati, *Anatomy and Consequences of Exchange Control Regime* (Cambridge: Ballinger for the National Bureau of Economic Research, 1978); Anne Krueger, *Foreign Trade Regimes and Economic Development: Liberalization Attempts and Consequences* (New York: National Bureau of Economic Research, 1978).

28 Anne Krueger became chief economist and vice-president of the World Bank in 1982 (when President Ronald Reagan let Chenery go and brought in supporters of his neoliberal orientations) and kept the post until 1987.

29 Anne Krueger, 'Import substitution versus export promotion', *Finance & Development*, 1 June 1985, Vol. 22, No. 2 <elibrary.imf.org/view/journals/022/0022/002/article-A007-en.xml> [accessed 29/03/2022].

THE 'TRICKLE-DOWN' EFFECT

The 'trickle-down' effect is a trivial metaphor which has guided the actions of the World Bank from the outset. The idea is simple: the positive effects of growth trickle down, starting from the top, where they benefit the wealthy, until eventually at the bottom a little also reaches the poor. This means that it is in the interests of the poor that growth should be as strong as possible, if they are to be able to lap up the drops. That is because if growth is weak, the rich will keep a larger part than when growth is strong.

What is the result of this concept for the World Bank's actions? The belief that growth should be encouraged at all costs so that there is something left for the poor at the end of the cycle. That any policy which holds back growth for the sake of (even partial) redistribution of wealth or for the sake of protecting the environment reduces the trickle-down effect and harms the poor. In practice, the actions of the World Bank's directors are conducted in line with this metaphor, despite the more sophisticated discourse of certain experts. Moreover, the World Bank's historians devote about 20 pages to discussions of the trickle-down theory[30] and acknowledge that 'This belief justified persistent efforts to persuade borrowers of the advantages of discipline, sacrifice, and trust in the market, and therefore of the need to hold the line against political temptation.'[31] They maintain that the belief gradually fell into disrepute from 1970, due to attacks from an impressive number of researchers concerning the situation in both the United States and the developing countries.[32] Nevertheless, the historians note that in practice, this did not have much effect[33] – particularly since from 1982 on, the trickle-down theory made a triumphant comeback at the World Bank.[34] There is no question that during the years 2000 to 2020 the trickle-down fairy tale has been re-adopted by numerous governments, including that of French president Emmanuel Macron beginning in 2017. Obviously, the trickle-down issue is inseparable from that of inequality, which will be discussed in the next section.

THE QUESTION OF UNEQUAL DISTRIBUTION OF INCOME

From 1973 on, the World Bank began to examine the question of inequality in the distribution of income in the developing countries, as a factor affecting the chances of development. The economics team under the direction of Hollis Chenery gave

---

30   Kapur, Lewis and Webb, *The World Bank: Its First Half Century*, Volume 1, pp. 215–33.

31   Ibid., p. 218.

32   See especially James P. Grant, 'Development: the end of trickle-down?', *Foreign Policy*, Autumn 1973, No. 12, pp. 43–65.

33   For the period 1974–81, they write: 'Attention began to shift away from direct targeting of Bank investments on the poor to the enhancement of indirect benefits through increased urban employment. In effect, the strategy was falling back on the trickle-down approach.' (Kapur, Lewis and Webb, *The World Bank: Its First Half Century*, Volume 1, p. 264.)

34   On the change of direction of 1981–82, they write: 'Poverty reduction would thus have to depend on growth and trickle-down' (Kapur, Lewis and Webb, *The World Bank: Its First Half Century*, Volume 1, p. 336).

the matter considerable thought. The major World Bank book on the subject, published in 1974, was coordinated by Chenery himself and entitled *Redistribution with Growth*.[35] Chenery was aware that the type of growth induced by the Bank's loans policy would generate increased inequality. The World Bank's main worry was clearly expressed by McNamara on several occasions: if we do not reduce inequality and poverty, there will be repeated outbursts of social unrest, which will harm the interests of the 'free world' under the leadership of the United States.

Chenery did not share the point of view expressed during the 1950s by Simon Kuznets[36] – that after a necessary phase of increased inequality during economic take-off, things would subsequently improve. The World Bank was firmly convinced of the need for increased inequality. This is borne out by the words of its president Eugene Black in April 1961: 'Inequalities in income are a necessary by-product of economic growth [which] makes it possible for people to escape a life of poverty.'[37] Yet empirical studies carried out by the Bank itself in Chenery's day disproved Kuznets's claims.

However, after Chenery's departure in 1982 and his replacement by Anne Krueger, the World Bank completely abandoned its relative concern about increasing or maintaining inequality, deciding not to publish relevant data in the *World Development Report*. Anne Krueger did not hesitate to adopt Kuznets's argument, making the rise of inequality a condition for the take-off of growth, on the grounds that the savings of the rich were likely to feed into investments.

Not until François Bourguignon became chief economist in 2003 did the Bank show any real renewal of interest in the question.[38] In 2006, the World Bank's *World Development Report*, subtitled *Equity and Development*, referred to inequality as a hindrance to development.[39] But at best his approach was considered to be good marketing by James Wolfensohn (president of the World Bank from 1996 to 2005) and his successors.

More recently, in his book *Capital in the Twenty-first Century*,[40] the economist Thomas Piketty presents a very interesting critique of Kuznets's 'Curve'. Piketty

35 Hollis B. Chenery et al., *Redistribution with Growth* (Oxford: Oxford University Press for the World Bank and the Institute of Development Studies, London, 1974).

36 Simon Kuznets, 'Economic growth and income inequality', *American Economic Review*, March 1955, No. 49, pp. 1–28.

37 *IDA Annual Report 1961–1962* cited by Kapur, Lewis and Webb, *The World Bank: Its First Half Century, Volume 1*, p. 171.

38 François Bourguignon, 'The poverty-growth-inequality triangle', paper presented at the Indian Council for Research on International Economic Relations, New Delhi, 4 February 2004 <documents1.worldbank.org/curated/en/449711468762020101/pdf/28102.pdf> [accessed 6/12/2021].

39 'Few [of] today's prosperous societies, if any, developed by excluding the majority of their people from economic and political opportunities' (Paul Wolfowitz, 'Foreword', in *World Development Report 2006: Equity and Development* (Washington, DC: World Bank, 2005), p. xi <openknowledge. worldbank.org/handle/10986/5988> [accessed 08/12/2021].

40 Thomas Piketty, *Capital in the Twenty-first Century*, trans. Arthur Goldhammer (Cambridge, MA: Harvard University Press, 2013).

points out that at first, Kuznets himself doubted the validity of his Curve – a fact that didn't deter him from making it the basis of a theory that has proved stubbornly resistant. Meanwhile inequality has reached the highest level in the history of humanity. That inequality is caused by the inherent operation of global capitalism, which is sustained by the policies of the international financial institutions in charge of 'development' and by governments which act in the interests of the wealthiest 1 per cent at the expense of the overwhelming majority of the population, not only in the Global South but in the North as well.

A feminist critique of development

The sociologist Jules Falquet calls attention to the fact that the five central dimensions of development necessarily impact women:[41]

1. The preference given to *intensive monoculture* to the detriment of family-based agriculture deprives women of their work and forces a great number of people into dependence on expensive industrially produced food.
2. *Extraction of raw materials* from the ground for profit generates conflicts which destroy indigenous communities and the environment.
3. The creation of *free-trade zones* encourages offshoring by multinationals who seek unskilled cheap labour, essentially female, to locate there.
4. Bringing in hard currency by exporting female workers who are allowed to work abroad reinforces their exploitation.
5. *Tourism*, which is strongly encouraged, generates an increase in degrading activities for women whose 'exotic beauty' is one of the attractions promoted by tourist destinations.

'Development' needs to be seen for what it is: no longer a synonym for what is arbitrarily called 'progress', but an ideological apparatus deployed to help promote the generalization of capitalist modes of production and Western cultural norms, perpetuating the neocolonial dynamics of organized spoliation and invariably having numerous impacts on women's lives.

---

41   Jules Falquet, 'Analyzing globalization from a feminist perspective' (English version of 'Penser la mondialisation dans une perspective féministe'), *Travail, genre et sociétés* 2011, Vol. 1, No. 25, pp. 81–98 <academia.edu/38929821/Analyzing_Globalization_from_a_Feminist_Perspective> [accessed 13/01/2022].

11
South Korea: The 'Miracle' Unmasked

What is often presented as South Korea's success story is actually the result of policies that in no way conform to the World Bank's recommendations. Instead of a virtuous accumulation favoured by free trade, South Korea's economic development was made possible by a ruthless primitive accumulation that used the most coercive methods to fabricate 'virtue' by force. Korea achieved the 'miraculous' results we hear so much about under the yoke of a particularly repressive dictatorship that enjoyed US protection in order to counter so-called socialist regimes. It enforced a productivist model of development which was deeply detrimental to the environment. The Korean way is neither commendable nor reproducible, but it deserves to be examined in some detail.

The World Bank claims that South Korea is an undeniable success story. In the World Bank's version, the country's authorities used external loans efficiently, attracted foreign investments and used them to set up a successful development model based on export substitution. The *export* substitution industrialization model represents the World Bank's (and others') alternative to the *import* substitution industrialization model (which implies producing commodities within the country itself that had previously been imported). Instead of producing what it imported, Korea supposedly channelled its export activities towards meeting the demands of the world market while successfully encouraging industries that yield high added value, replacing exportation of unprocessed or minimally processed commodities with exports of commodities whose production requires advanced technology. According to the World Bank, the Korean state intervened in a restrained way to support private initiatives and ensure the free play of market forces. But the actual facts of Korea's progress toward industrialization and sustained growth are largely in contradiction with the Bank's official version.

The so-called Korean success story is the result of several factors: a high degree of intervention by the state (which has steered the process with an iron hand); substantial US technical and financial support (in the form of grants); radical land reform carried out from the start; a 25-year period during which the import substitution industrialization model was gradually converted into export substitution (the latter being impossible without the former); ongoing repression of the labour movement (prohibition of independent unions); overexploitation of peasants and industrial workers; state control of the banking sector; the enforcement of authoritarian planning; strict control of currency exchange and capital flows; state-enforced prices for a wide range of products; and not least, the protection afforded by the US, which allowed Korea to implement policies that it condemned elsewhere. The Korean government has also made great progress in education, thus ensuring a ready supply of highly skilled manpower to private enterprise.

Paradoxically the scarcity of natural resources has been an asset in South Korea's development, in that it has not attracted the greed of transnational corporations or the US. The US saw Korea as a strategic military zone to counter the communist bloc, rather than as a crucial source of supplies (as is the case for Venezuela, Mexico or countries in the Persian Gulf). Had Korea been endowed with large oilfields or other raw materials, the country would have been treated as a supply zone and would not have been allowed the same margin of flexibility to develop its powerful industrial network. The US is not prepared to deliberately promote the emergence of powerful competitors who possess large reserves of raw materials as well as diversified industrial activities.

THE HISTORICAL, POLITICAL AND GEOSTRATEGIC CONTEXT

In an agreement signed in 1905 the United States and Japan defined their respective zones of influence in East Asia. The US would control the Philippines, which they had conquered in 1902. Taiwan (which was annexed in 1895) and Korea fell into the Japanese zone. In 1910 Japan annexed Korea and turned it into a food-producing colony, and later into a kind of all-purpose appendix to Japanese industry. When imperial Japan was defeated at the end of the Second World War and it lost control of the peninsula, it left Korea with modern transport and electricity networks, a significant industrial infrastructure ranging from textiles and armaments to chemicals and mechanical construction, and a fully developed banking system. Yet Korean industry was not a consistent whole, since it had been created to meet Japan's needs. Industrialization was more advanced in the country's north, the part that would become North Korea, while the South was more geared to farming. The middle class had hardly developed at all, since Japan's domination granted it very limited space. Compared with Argentina at the same period Korea was definitely backward in terms of industrial development.

Under the Yalta agreement of February 1945 between the United States, the United Kingdom and the USSR, particularly the section concerning the Soviet Union's participation in the war against Japan, Korea was to be occupied by the Soviet army and by the US army.[1] The Soviet army arrived first, in August 1945, and Soviet soldiers were welcomed as liberators with the support of an anti-Japanese liberation movement that had organized into a network of people's committees and was to be the basis of the state apparatus. That state soon implemented a number of democratic and anti-capitalist reforms. Among the measures that met with powerful popular support was a radical land-reform programme. The later evolution of the

---

1   This section is drawn from David Cameron, 'Corée du Sud, un miracle fragile' ('South Korea – a fragile miracle'), *Inprecor*, 20 October 1986, No. 228, among other sources.

North Korean regime and its bureaucratic and authoritarian degeneration should not blind us to its early economic success.

In the south things turned out differently. US soldiers did not reach Korea's shores until 8 September 1945, six days after Japan's surrender and two days after the proclamation, in Seoul, of the People's Republic of Korea by a national assembly of the anti-Japanese people's committees. By the time the US troops arrived, the new government had disarmed the Japanese, freed political prisoners and arrested collaborators. Yet when the nationalists tried to meet the US staff to propose a form of collaboration, their demand was rejected. On 9 September the US Military Government in Korea (USAMGIK) was set up. It would be the main authority in that part of the country until 1948. In February 1946 the US general staff set up a Korean civilian government under the supervision of the USAMGIK. This civilian government was presided over by Rhee Syng-man, a right-wing politician who had returned to Korea in October 1945 after spending 39 out of the 41 previous years in the US. Washington wanted power to be held by the Korean Democratic Party (KDP) – an anti-communist party that had been legally constituted under the Japanese occupation in order to represent the interests of the Korean upper class. The KDP soon underwent a hasty facelift under the new name of Liberal Party. And so, the Rhee Syng-man government included former collaborators with the Japanese occupying forces and the new state apparatus retained a large number of former colonial officers, particularly in the police forces. A Korean CIA was set up and, significantly, called KCIA (Korean Central Intelligence Agency). It is of sinister memory even today.

The government that the US had set up was most unpopular. In 1946 and 1948 protest took the form of popular uprisings that were harshly repressed. The General Council of Korean Trade Unions (GCKTU), led by activists from the Communist Party, had hundreds of thousands of members and led the protest marches. It was the prime target of repressive actions and was eventually suppressed in 1948. Repression was still powerful after 1948 – the UN commission on Korea reported in August 1949 that within the eight months before 30 April 1949, some 89,710 people had been detained under Rhee Syng-man's National Peace Protection Act. Thousands, if not tens of thousands of people were killed. Several historical leaders of the struggle against Japan, though not related to the communists, were assassinated by the Rhee regime, which came into power in 1948.

When the country's division was made official in 1948 with the creation of the Republic of Korea south of the 38th parallel, a large majority of the country's political forces was against it. At the same time, in reaction, the Democratic Republic of Korea was proclaimed in the north. Both governments claimed sovereignty over the entirety of the peninsula. On 12 December 1948 the UN General Assembly recognized the Government of the Republic of Korea as the only one able to represent the Korean people.[2] It was in this context that the Korean War

---

2   A/RES 195 (III) of 12 December 1948.

broke out in June 1950, and the rapid advance of North Korean troops in the south was only partly related to military factors. It was also a logical consequence of the lack of popular support for the Rhee Syng-man government. According to the US army's official history of the Korean War, the South Korean army 'disintegrated'.[3] There were mass desertions.

The war lasted for three years and brought the world to the brink of a third world war. The US army was massively involved with the support of its Western allies; 300,000 Western soldiers fought on the side of the South Korean army with the authorization of the UN Security Council, which placed responsibility for the aggression on the North Korean forces and requested that UN member states provide the necessary aid to the South Korean government.[4] How could the UN Security Council take such a decision when China and the USSR were permanent members with veto power? Since the People's Republic of China had been banned from the UN and the Security Council after the victory of the revolution in China, China was represented by the delegate for Taiwan's anti-communist government, led by General Chiang Kai-shek from 1949 to 1971. Chiang supported the US intervention in Korea. In the context of the Cold War the Soviet Union had a policy of non-participation in the Security Council meetings and could therefore not exercise its veto power.

The expeditionary corps led by the US fought against the North Korean army and a strong Chinese contingent (estimates vary between 500,000 and 850,000 men). The war resulted in three million dead among the Korean population. During the war the Rhee Syng-man government exercised fierce repression against the South Korean left wing. Some sources speak of 100,000 executions or assassinations of activists who opposed the government.[5] The armistice of 27 July 1953 brought the two armies virtually to their starting point, on either side of the 38th parallel.

THE KOREAN BOURGEOISIE BECOMES A WARD OF STATE

Left as it was with an obsolete industrial structure and a financial system formerly controlled by the Japanese,[6] the Rhee Syng-man government would use them, with the blessing of the USAMGIK, to reward and consolidate the upper class's loyalty, since after all they were the basis of its political power. The new industrialists did thriving business, not thanks to their own investments, for they hardly had any equity, but thanks to tax revenues and above all US subsidies that the dictatorship generously handed out. Moreover, a strict protectionist policy protected them from

---

3   Roy E. Appleman, *South to the Naktong, North to the Yalu* (Washington, DC: Center of Military History, United States Army, 1992, 1961), p. 18.

4   Security Council Resolutions 82, 83 and 84 of 25 June, 27 June and 7 July 1950.

5   The figure of 100,000 deaths is taken from the book *The Politics of the Vortex* (Cambridge, MA: Harvard University Press, 1968) by Gregory Henderson, a diplomat in Korea at the time.

6   Until 1945 over 90 per cent of the money invested in Korea's economy outside farming depended on Japan.

foreign competition. Later the Park Chung-hee dictatorship (1961–79) would create industrial and financial conglomerates called *chaebols*.

Finding 1: The Korean bourgeoisie developed in the shadow of the state, which was its guardian and protector.

US EXTERNAL FINANCIAL AID

The World Bank passes over the fact that Korea did not rely on loans for 17 years after the end of the Second World War, and that later it only contracted limited loans until 1967. From 1945 to 1961 Korea neither borrowed money nor received any foreign investments. According to the criteria of the World Bank and neoclassical economics, such a situation is a complete anomaly.

On the other hand, it received over $3.1 billion in grants from the United States over the same period.[7] No other external aid was received. But the amount is more than significant. It represents twice what the Benelux countries received from the Marshall Plan, one-third more than France received, and 10 per cent more than Britain received. To make the comparison we made with Germany's case in chapter 4, but over a longer period, the grants Korea received from 1945 to 1961 amount to more than the World Bank's total loans to newly independent developing countries (colonies not included).

From 1962 onward Korea would borrow, though only moderately. From 1962 to 1966, US grants still amounted to 70 per cent of inflowing capital, while loans accounted for 28 per cent and foreign investments for 2 per cent. Only from 1967 did capital inflow mainly consist of loans from foreign (mainly Japanese) banks. And foreign investments only became significant in the late 1980s, once Korea had successfully carried out its industrialization.

Finding 2: Korea's initial industrialization was in no way dependent on external loans or foreign investments.

LAND REFORM AND THE STATE'S COERCION OF PEASANTS

At the end of the Second World War southern Korea was still an essentially agrarian country. Until the early 1950s over 75 per cent of its population lived in the countryside.

US military authorities then proceeded to implement a drastic land reform to counter the communist influence.[8] The large estates that had been taken from the

---

7   Mahn-Je Kim, 'The Republic of Korea's successful economic development and the World Bank', in Kapur, Lewis and Webb, *The World Bank: Its First Half Century, Volume 2*, p. 25.

8   'The reform similarly eliminated the last key issue on which the left wing could have hoped to develop substantial rural support in Korea.' David C. Cole and Princeton N. Lyman, *Korean Development: The Interplay of Politics and Economics* (Cambridge, MA: Harvard University Press, 1971), p. 21, cited by Anne O. Krueger, *The Development Role of the Foreign Sector and Aid: Studies in the Modernization of the Republic of Korea, 1945–1975* (Cambridge, MA: Council on East Asian Studies, Harvard University, 1979), p. 21.

Japanese[9] without compensation and from Korean landowners with compensation were broken up and most peasants became owners of small pieces of land[10] (parcels could not exceed eight acres per family![11]). The state's intervention was active and coercive. The rent that peasants had once paid to their landlords was replaced by taxes to be paid to the state. The state took over the farming surplus that formerly went to estate owners. The state made it compulsory for farmers to reach given production quotas for certain products. This quota was to be delivered to state entities at a price determined by the authorities. The price set was very low, often less than the cost of production.[12] It has been estimated that 'until 1961, the price at which rice was bought did not cover farmers' production costs and remained well below market price until 1970. Until 1975, public trading offices controlled at least 50% of the amount of rice and 90% of the amount of barley placed on the market.'[13]

In short, Korean farmers were freed from the grip of estate owners and could farm their own land, but they had to work for the state.

Finding 3: When it imposed a radical land reform largely based on the expropriation of Japanese estates without any compensation, the state interfered in a despotic way. The land reform was meant to co-opt communist influence. Peasants were subjected to strong constraints by the state.

FARMING SURPLUSES USED TO SERVE CITIES AND INDUSTRIALIZATION

Since it set the prices at which products were bought (from farmers) and sold (to consumers), the state was supplying food (and essentially rice) at subsidized (and therefore low) prices to those social sectors that were regarded as strategic, such as the vast state bureaucracy.

Moreover, if the urban population, and particularly the emerging industrial proletariat, could afford a bowl of rice, wages could be kept at a very low level.

In addition, taxes paid by farmers were used by the state to invest in infrastructures for communications, electricity and industry.

As Jean-Philippe Peemans observed, writing about the demands made on farmers, 'It was in no way a virtuous accumulation that relied on the virtues of the market, but a brutal form of primitive accumulation that relied on the most coercive methods to create "virtue" by force.'[14]

---

9   40 per cent of farmland was owned by Japanese.
10 The same kind of reform was implemented in Taiwan.
11 Krueger, *The Development Role of the Foreign Sector and Aid*, p. 20.
12 To increase their income, peasants greatly increased their productivity and the volume of their production, particularly for products where prices remained free, such as fruit.
13 See Jean-Philippe Peemans, *Le développement des peuples face à la modernisation du monde* (*Peoples' Development and Global Modernizaton*) (Louvain-la-Neuve/Paris: Academia-Bruylant/ L'Harmattan, 2002), p. 373 (in French; translation CADTM).
14 See ibid., p. 374.

Finding 4: The state did not allow market forces to determine prices: it fixed them on its own authority.

Finding 5: The state enforced heavy taxes on peasants. Neoliberals regularly inveigh against state 'tax mania'. South Korea is an excellent illustration.

USES OF EXTERNAL FINANCIAL AID

The Korean state's finances relied on two main sources of supply: taxes (principally from farmers) and US external aid. It must be specified that until 1961, about 40 per cent of US aid consisted of US farming surpluses (amounting to 40 per cent of the aid granted). This obviously did not contribute to the state's finances. The remaining part, which was paid in US dollars, was used to pay for imports from the United States. Part of these imports consisted of capital goods used to industrialize the country. A total 71 per cent of investments by the state were financed thanks to US aid until 1961.[15] Military aid, which amounted to more than $1.5 billion, should also be taken into account.[16] A large part of it went into building roads, bridges and other infrastructure that was used for industrial production. Finally, we have to add purchases by the US expeditionary corps in Vietnam – which in the early 1970s amounted to 20 per cent of South Korea's exports.

Finding 6: South Korea benefited from massive US external aid. Only very few other countries have received the same kind of preferential treatment. Taiwan and Israel are two of them.

IMPORT SUBSTITUTION INDUSTRIALIZATION

The industrial development of the 1950s was mainly organized around the production of goods to replace imports so as to meet the needs of the domestic market, particularly in the areas of the food and textile industries. These amounted to 55 per cent of industrial production in 1955. Production focused on the processing of cotton and sugar and rice flour production. The manufacturing industries only accounted for 10 per cent of the GDP in 1955.

Finding 7: In the 1950s Korea developed an industrialization policy that aimed at replacing imports; this was to be reinforced in the 1960s.

---

15   Bank of Korea, National Accounts (1987), quoted by Mahn-Je Kim, 'The Republic of Korea's successful economic development and the World Bank', p. 25.
16   According to Mahn-Je Kim, between 1953 and 1961, United States military aid in the form of grants amounted to $1.56 billion.

ECONOMIC POLICY UNDER PARK CHUNG-HEE'S
MILITARY DICTATORSHIP (1961–79)[17]

Rhee Syng-man's corrupt dictatorship was overthrown by the urban uprising initiated by students in April 1960. A powerful movement of political centralization quickly developed among the urban masses that mobilized under the slogan 'a peaceful unification for the whole of Korea', put forward by the students' movement since the late 1960s.

These mobilizations were stopped by General Park Chung-hee's coup, which set up a military dictatorship, further reinforcing the state's intervention in the economy. The new government nationalized the entire financial system, from the largest bank to the smallest insurance company, to turn it into the instrument of its interventions in the economy.

From 1962, the structure of external financing would gradually change, but grants were still the main supply source until 1966. The United States urged Korea to resume economic relations with Japan. Japan signed a ten-year agreement (1965–75) that included economic aid to the amount of $500 million, $300 million of which was in the form of grants.

Korea contracted its first loan with the World Bank in 1962 and signed its first agreement with the IMF in 1965 (under US pressure). The Korean dictatorship's willingness to cooperate with the World Bank was determined by a political rather than an economic agenda. A posteriori, Mahn-Je Kim, who had been deputy prime minister, finance minister and minister for economic planning under dictator Chun Doo-hwan in the 1980s[18] and who then became CEO of a steel company (POSCO), declared his satisfaction at the government's excellent relations with the World Bank and gave a favourable assessment of the military dictatorship. He did not mince words, writing that the Bank helped dictator Park to gather support on the domestic as well as on the international level: 'Such recognition from the Bank – the world's most authoritative international development organization – positively influenced Korea's international relations, but was even more important domestically. It provided a powerful and persuasive justification to the Korean public for the existence of a dictatorial government devoted to economic development.'[19] The World Bank's complicity with the dictatorship could not be more bluntly stated.

---

17   An analysis of Park Chung-hee's regime can be found in a speech by Paik Nak-chung at the international conference of Korean studies at the University of Wollongong, Australia, 10–13 November 2004 (Paik Nak-chung, 'How to assess the Park Chung Hee era and Korean development', *The Asia-Pacific Journal*, 12 December 2005, Vol. 3, No. 12. See also the *Quarterly Changbi* Web-site (magazine.changbi.com/en/). Paik Nak-chung, former editor of *Quarterly Changbi*, was a victim of the repression under Park's dictatorship. The magazine was closed under the dictatorship of General Chun Doo-hwan, 1980–1987.

18   Mahn-Je Kim also acted as a minister under President Kim Young Sam in the 1990s.

19   Mahn-Je Kim, 'The Republic of Korea's successful economic development and the World Bank', p. 46.

Park Chung-hee tried to win greater autonomy from Washington in his economic policies. Calling on World Bank loans from 1962 onward, then mainly on loans from private foreign banks from 1967, was part of this determination to gradually diminish Korea's dependence on financing by the US government. This also suited Washington since the US administration had started to take measures to limit the outflow of US dollars in 1963.

Finding 8: The World Bank supported Park Chung-hee's dictatorship. The dictator used this support to consolidate his position both in the country and on the international scene.

General Park Chung-hee implemented an accelerated industrialization policy underpinned by the strictest planning. The first five-year plan was launched in 1962. Korea took a firm protectionist stand with regard to its agricultural production (a ban on rice imports) and industrial output. In the mid-1960s, Korea already had a number of light industries supplying the domestic market and winning market share abroad. These industries were basically making products – using a massive cheap labour force – by processing or assembling goods imported from abroad. The dictatorship sought to radically change this situation by consolidating the country's industrialization. It decided to reinforce the import substitution industrialization model. Korea would attempt to produce the products it had previously imported. To achieve this objective, starting from the end of the 1960s Korea concentrated on developing a heavy steel and capital goods industry (machine tools, assembly lines, turbines, etc.) as well as a petrochemical industry. Park's government further wanted to produce for export.

The state favoured the development of *chaebols* – vast conglomerates bringing together a number of private companies selected by Park to spearhead the new industry. These *chaebols* are now known the world over: Samsung, Hyundai, LG Corporation, Daewoo,[20] Kia, etc. Year after year they have benefited from substantial and virtually free financial help from the state. Borrowings made by the government or its banks (at market price), mainly from US banks until Japan took pride of place in the 1970s, provided the *chaebols* with a virtually inexhaustible source of fresh capital at very low interest rates, when not at a loss for the loaning party. Direct subsidies from the state were added to this. In actual fact it took over the

---

20 In 1984 Pierre Rousset described the stunning development of the Daewoo group: 'While it started only 17 years ago as a small textile company it now has 70,000 employees. Thanks to Park Chung Hee's support, Kim Woochong has built an empire in trade, shipbuilding, construction, car manufacturing, textiles, finance, telecommunications, electronics, clothing. He owns the largest textile plant in the world and a ultramodern shipyard. He has launched substantial projects in the Middle East. Now he is investing in semiconductors'. Pierre Rousset, 'La Corée du Sud, second Japon?' ('South Korea – a second Japan?'), in *Croissance des jeunes nations*, No. 265 (Paris: October 1984) (translation CADTM).

management of the country's economy through an Economic Planning Board. And it steered all development choices within the *chaebols* with a steely determination.

Five-year plans followed each other. During the first of these (1962–66) priority was given to the development of energy, fertilizers and cement. The second plan (1967–71) focused on synthetic fibres, the petrochemical industry and electric appliances. The third (1972–76) focused on the steel industry, transport facilities, household appliances and shipbuilding.

Finding 9: The state planned the country's economic development with an iron hand. In a sense, it was the state that created the Korean capitalist class.

THE WORLD BANK'S RELUCTANT SUPPORT

At first the World Bank considered Korea's intention to develop heavy industry as premature and tried to dissuade the authorities.[21] But faced with Seoul's insistence and anxious to safeguard its influence in the country, the World Bank changed tack and supported the import substitution industrialization policy. It should be mentioned that this was when Robert McNamara became World Bank president (1968) and that his chief economist Hollis Chenery was not opposed to developing countries using the import substitution model.

The Korean argument went as follows: 1) we need to have heavy industry (steel, petrochemicals) and to manufacture capital goods so that we can supply our light industries ourselves, reduce imports and improve our balance of payments; 2) on the world market, competitor nations can quickly win market share from us by producing the same goods at a lower cost by using lower-paid labour than ours. We must therefore acquire heavy industries in order to diversify our exports towards higher-added-value products that contain more components produced by ourselves. The other nations will have a hard time competing with us in this area; 3) in addition to the development of heavy industry, we are going to step up the pace in technology and make increasing investments in higher education and research; 4) at the start, our heavy industry will not be competitive compared to foreign competitors who can access our domestic market, so we must protect our young industries and close our borders to foreign competition; 5) the state must use public money to finance and control all this.

In the mid-1970s, when Korea was on the way to developing a powerful heavy-industry sector, the World Bank once again voiced its doubts about the chosen strategy. It felt that Korea was overambitious and suggested that the country scale down its efforts in this sector.[22] The Korean authorities chose not to follow these recommendations.

21   Mahn-Je Kim, 'The Republic of Korea's successful economic development and the World Bank', p. 33.
22   Kim, 'The Republic of Korea's successful economic development and the World Bank', p. 35.

The most dramatic illustration of this policy was the programme for the development of heavy industries in 1977–79. For two years 80 per cent of all state investments were devoted to this end. Financing was supported by a huge increase in the economy's indebtedness – the state's as well as the banks' and private companies' – but also by the immobilization of all pension funds and the enforced use of a part of private savings.[23]

Mahn-Je Kim describes in diplomatic terms, and with a hint of irony, the attitude of the World Bank economists:

The flexibility of the World Bank economists should be emphasized. They were typical neoclassical markets economists, and they contributed greatly to the indoctrination of Korean officials with the ideals of the market economic system. The Bank's economists in general were not dogmatic and knew how to harmonize textbook principles with real-world constraints.[24]

Kim is referring to the period leading up to the early 1980s.

Finding 10: South Korea did not adhere to the World Bank's recommendations.

SOCIAL CHANGE BETWEEN 1960 AND 1980

During Park Chung-hee's dictatorship the structure of South Korean society was deeply modified. The urban population rose from 28 per cent in 1960 to 55 per cent in 1980. In the capital, Seoul, the population doubled between 1964 and 1970, from 3 to 6 million inhabitants. In 1980 it was close to 9 million. The structure of the active population radically changed too. In 1960, 63 per cent worked on the land, 11 per cent in industry and mining, and 26 per cent in services. Twenty years later the proportions had changed as follows: 34 per cent in agriculture, 23 per cent in industry and mining, and 43 per cent in services. In 1963 there were 600,000 industrial workers, in 1973 1.4 million and in 1980 over 3 million, half of whom were skilled workers. They were subjected to extreme exploitation: in 1980 the wage costs of a Korean worker amounted to 10 per cent of the wage costs of a German worker, 50 per cent of a Mexican worker, and 60 per cent of a Brazilian worker. One of the components in the Korean miracle was the exploitation of industrial manpower. A Korean worker's working week in 1980 was the longest in the world. There were no legal minimum wages. After the General Council of Korean Trade Unions was crushed between 1946 and 1948, workers had no right to a genuine trade union any more. In 1946 the Rhee Syng-man government created the Federation of

---

23 See 'Corée du Sud – Du mythique "miracle économique" aux traditions de lutte de la classe ouvrière' ('South Korea – from the mythical "economic miracle" to the traditions of struggle of the working class'), *Lutte de Classe*, March 1997 No. 26 (in French).

24 Mahn-Je Kim, 'The Republic of Korea's successful economic development and the World Bank', p. 35.

Korean Trade Unions (FKTU) with the support of the US and its AFL-CIO trade-union federation. The FKTU was the only legal federation in South Korea until the 1990s. It was a mere relay for the dictatorship and the bosses. The working class was shackled, at least until the 1980s.

In addition to plant workers, other social categories asserted themselves. In 1980 there were 100,000 engineers and 130,000 technicians. The number of students in higher education also rose dramatically to reach about one million students in 1980.

Finding 11: Between 1960 and 1980 the social structure was deeply modified and moved closer to that found in industrialized countries.

Finding 12: The dictatorship prevented the working class from developing independent trade unions and used harsh repressive measures. One of the components of the Korean miracle was the exploitation of workers.

FROM PARK CHUNG-HEE TO CHUN DOO-HWAN

Throughout Park's dictatorship, in spite of repressive measures, large protest movements developed at regular intervals, often ignited by students. For example, there were the 1965 protest marches against the signing of the treaty between Japan and Korea, and those in 1972 against martial law and a new constitution that made it possible for the dictator to stay in power for life.

In October 1979 fiercely repressed student demonstrations in the city of Pusan led to a government crisis that resulted in the assassination of Park Chung-hee on 26 October. Park was shot by his closest collaborator Kim Jae-gyu, who was then at the head of the KCIA. On 16 October a large student march in Pusan led to violent confrontations with the police the following day. Park's government immediately proclaimed a state of emergency in that city and sent an infantry division. However, demonstrations spread to other towns such as Masan, another industrial city with several export companies. Many workers were involved in street protest. Park proceeded to proclaim a state of emergency in Masan. A total of 4,207 people were arrested over the four days of confrontation. Student demonstrations reached the capital city Seoul.[25] The KCIA's chief felt that if he got rid of Park, the situation could be saved.

On the day after the death of General Park the army was divided: one faction of it implied that there might be a liberalization of the regime. Demonstrations were still organized. In early December 1979 most political prisoners (some of whom had to serve long prison sentences) were released. On 12 December Major-General Chun Doo-hwan took everybody by surprise and successfully carried out a coup within the army. He had his main opponent, General Ching, arrested and took complete control of the armed forces. The demonstrations continued. On 14 April

---

25   See Jun Yazaki, 'Kwangju revolt opened new stage in S. Korean class struggle', *Intercontinental Press*, 23 June 1980, Vol. 18, No. 24, p. 653 <archive.org/details/sim_intercontinental-press_1980-06-23_18_24/page/653/> [accessed 9/12/2021].

1980 Chun Doo-hwan was appointed the head of the KCIA while retaining his functions within the army. Demonstrations proceeded apace.

Undisguised military dictatorship was back on 18 May 1980. Brutal repression resulted in all opposition leaders being arrested, which led to violent urban uprisings culminating in the Kwangju insurrection.

Immediately after martial law had been proclaimed anew on 18 May 1980, several thousands of students from the Chonam University in Kwangju took to the streets. Paratroopers were sent out and killed demonstrators (including young girls) with their bayonets. On the following day over 50,000 people were out to face the army. In the ensuing confrontations over 260 of them were killed. After four days of street fighting some 200,000 inhabitants out of 750,000 were out and determined to be heard. They eventually took control of the city. Radio stations were set on fire by demonstrators who were incensed by the fact that censorship imposed by the martial law had silenced all information on their fight. The insurgents took over weapons that the soldiers who had retreated outside had left behind, and organized committees to manage the town administration. On 23 May the province of Cholla in the south of the country was entirely controlled by students and the insurgent population. Kwangju students took over buses and lorries, and fully armed as they now were, travelled from town to town and thus extended the movement through the country. When new paratroopers marched on Kwangju, the insurgents formed a crisis committee in order to negotiate with the authorities in charge of imposing martial law. They demanded that the authorities apologize to the people of Kwangju for the atrocities they had been responsible for, that they pay compensation money for the wounded and the dead, that they promise not to retaliate, that military leaders would not move their troops before an agreement was reached. Yet in spite of those negotiations about 17,000 soldiers marched on the town in the early hours of 27 May and set up military occupation. Several hundred students and inhabitants were killed.[26] Repression was carried out with the blessing of Washington and of the US army.[27] In the following months repression struck all over the country. According to an official report dated 9 February 1981, over 57,000 people were arrested during the 'Social Purification Campaign' that had been launched in the summer of 1980. Some 39,000 of them were sent to military camps for 'physical and psychological re-education'.[28] In February 1981 dictator Chun Doo-hwan was received at the White House by the new US president, Ronald Reagan.[29]

---

26 Estimates as to how many demonstrators were killed vary widely. The lowest figure, put forward by the government, is 240. Other sources mention one to two thousand dead. The 28 May 1980 issue of the *New York Times* claims that 50 paratroopers were killed in one single confrontation (see Kim Chang-soo, 'Le Soulèvement de Kwangju' ('The Kwangju revolt'), *Inprecor*, 16 March 1981, No. 97, pp. 35–39).

27 See Jun Yazaki, 'Kwangju revolt opened new stage in S. Korean class struggle', p. 25 and Kim Chang-soo, 'Le Soulèvement de Kwangju', pp. 35–39.

28 Kim Chang-soo, 'Le Soulèvement de Kwangju', p. 35.

29 Ronald Reagan was US president from 1981 to 1988.

Washington was party to the May 1980 massacres

The armed forces of the Korean Republic were placed under joint US–Korean command, itself under the control of the commander-in-chief of the US forces in South Korea. The only exceptions were a garrison in the capital and a section of paratroopers under direct presidential authority. The greater part of the Korean Republic's armed forces could not be mobilized without the permission of the US forces' commander-in-chief. At the time of the Kwangju uprising in May 1980, the troops from the garrison in the capital had been mobilized to keep order in Seoul and paratroop units had been sent to Kwangju. If there had been further uprisings – on a similar or greater scale than the Kwangju uprising – the government could not have responded, since it had no more reserve forces under its direct command.

It was for this reason that the United States, following a request from the South Korean government, quickly made available some of the troops under the joint command. On 19 May, the 31st division was dispatched to Kwangju. And for the final thrust, four regiments, totalling 7,800 men, were detached from the joint command and sent to Kwangju. In addition, the American aircraft carrier *Coral Sea*, at the time heading for the Middle East, was ordered to change course and make full speed for the Korean peninsula.

When the students of Kwangju sent a desperate message to Democrat president Jimmy Carter[30] asking him to intervene on behalf of their rights, the United States ignored the appeal on the pretext that 'it had not come through the official channels'. What, we may ask, are the 'official channels' in the case of a city under siege?

It should be noted that the Japanese government also sided with Chun Doo-hwan against the Korean people.

Finding 13: A powerful social movement spearheaded by the students challenged the dictatorship. After the assassination of Park in October 1979 and a brief democratic interlude, a brutal new dictatorship was established thanks to the bloody repression of May 1980 supported by Washington and Tokyo.

THE ECONOMIC POLICY OF DICTATOR CHUN DOO-HWAN (1980–88)

After the assassination of dictator Park Chung-hee in 1979 and his replacement by General Chun Doo-hwan, the country's economic orientation remained basically unchanged. Korea, which during the 1970s heavily indebted itself to foreign banks, mainly Japanese, was harder hit than the other developing countries by the sudden hike in interest rates because it had mainly borrowed at variable rates. In 1983,

---

30. Jimmy Carter was president of the United States from 1977 to 1980. During his term of office, several of Washington's allies collapsed or were destabilized: the Shah of Iran fled his country in February 1979, driven out by violent popular protest, the Nicaraguan dictator Anastasio Somoza was ousted in July 1979 by the Sandinista revolution and the Korean dictatorship was under threat from October 1979 to May 1980. Enough was enough – it was vital to keep this valuable strategically. Yet Jimmy Carter was known as a vocal advocate for human rights on the international political scene.

South Korea was fourth on the list of most heavily indebted countries in absolute figures ($43 billion), behind Brazil ($98 billion), Mexico ($93 billion) and Argentina ($45 billion). But once again, its geostrategic position entitled Korea to be treated differently from other developing countries. Japan came to the rescue by paying Korea $3 billion (by way of war reparations), which Korea used to keep up debt repayment to Japanese bankers. In this way Korea avoided having to appeal to the IMF and comply with its strict conditions.[31] In exchange, the Japanese government was able to avoid bankruptcy for some of its banks and obtain more flexible investment facilities from South Korea.

Finding 14: Contrary to the World Bank's version of the story, the massive external debt incurred with private banks came close to costing South Korea very dear. If it had not occupied a key geostrategic position in the eyes of the US and Japan, it might have suffered the fate of countries like Argentina, Brazil and Mexico, all of which had been forced to submit to IMF conditions. As we shall see later, Korea was able to pursue a partially independent course of development until the 1990s.

Korea was also affected by the second oil crisis in 1979 (soaring oil prices caused by the Iranian revolution and the overthrow of the Shah), but managed to absorb its impact. Authoritarian control of the economy was maintained, with the government ordering the various industries to produce certain specific products in preference to others. It decided to reorganize the transport vehicle industry and put two *chaebols* in charge of manufacturing automobiles.

The World Bank objected to this development and recommended that Korea discontinue the production of finished vehicles and focus on the production of spare parts for export. It explained that Korean-made cars would not find buyers.

The Korean authorities stood their ground. And in the mid-1980s, the Korean company Hyundai (wholly controlled by private Korean capital backed by the public authorities) succeeded in exporting its cars to the US and winning substantial market share.

At this period, the World Bank had stopped making concessions for the import substitution industrialization model. In 1981, under the Reagan administration, the last economists in favour of state intervention had been replaced by hardcore neoliberals headed by chief economist Anne Krueger. A few years previously,

---

31   'South Korea also got special help from Japan under the formal guise of reparations. The fact that the postwar treaty had been a dead letter for many years did not worry either party. The Japanese government was aware that putting up USD 3 billion to help Korea service its large foreign debt was going to be in the long term interests of the many Japanese companies with investments and joint ventures in Korea. The result was that in a subsequent phase of the debt crisis, the Korean government never had to negotiate with foreign bankers or with the IMF.' John Stopford and Susan Strange, *Rival States, Rival Firms: Competition for World Market Shares* (Cambridge: Cambridge Studies in International Relations, Series Number 18, 1991), p. 46.

Krueger had written a book on Korea to demonstrate the superiority of export substitution over import substitution.[32] Seoul's determination to produce cars for export was an aggressive example of export substitution, and in theory it should have received the World Bank's full support. However, this was not to be, because Seoul's decision was seen as a threat to the US automobile industry. The flexibility of World Bank economists is quickly stretched to the limits when US interests are at stake.

Finding 15: The Chun Doo-hwan regime once again refused to follow the recommendations of the World Bank and its decision paid off. The Bank nevertheless continued to support the dictatorship because its ultimate aim was to maintain influence over it. At the same time, the United States began to view the appetite of South Korean companies with distrust.

THE LAST YEARS OF THE CHUN DOO-HWAN REGIME (1980–87)

During 1979–80, workers in many companies were seeking to form their own trade unions. The idea was to create new 'independent' unions that would openly challenge the FKTU leadership's policy of collaboration despite being legally obliged to affiliate with the federation. Following the crackdown by Chun Doo-hwan, a hundred or so local sections of the FKTU were disbanded, 191 officials were dismissed and some of them were sent to camps.

The driving force behind the move to create independent unions was the young people, workers and student protesters who had chosen to take to the factories to pursue the political struggle begun in the universities.

The student movement gathered strength in 1983–84 and went through a process of radicalization and intense politicization. From January to May 1986, 166,000 students took part in demonstrations.[33] The scale of the movement in the universities[34] is reflected in the number of students among political prisoners: 800 students out of 1,300 political prisoners.

The factory workers resumed the struggle in 1985. For the first time ever, a major strike broke out in a *chaebol* – in this case Daewoo Motors. It had a successful outcome and a new, independent trade union was founded.

On 12 February 1986, the NKDP (New Korean Democratic Party) launched a petition to change the constitution (the objective being to introduce presidential election by direct suffrage instead of by an electoral college). In the months following, a series of rallies took place, attended by tens of thousands of people in major cities around the country. Students participated independently in the democratic

---

32   Krueger, *The Development Role of the Foreign Sector and Aid*.
33   Figures given by Kang Min Chang, chief of national police. Quoted in *Korea Communiqué Bulletin, special issue July 1986*.
34   For example, the storming of the Konkuk campus on 31 October 1986.

movement with radical slogans such as 'Down with the military dictatorship', 'No to the presence of 40,000 US soldiers in the country' and 'Yes to a popular constitution'.

On 29 November 1986, the regime deployed 50,000 policemen in Seoul to prevent an NKDP rally. The government hoped to forcibly quell the opposition, but this policy misfired as a tide of democratic fervour swept through every level of society. Endless negotiations ensued between the regime and the opposition on electoral procedures. The government's position was weakened by the political fallout following the murder of a student in a police station. It was in this context that a demonstration was organized by all the opposition forces, including the new coalition resulting from a split in the NKDP. The day before the demonstration, due to take place on 10 June 1987, the police arrested 3,000 people, placed 140 opposition leaders under house arrest and sent in an advance guard of thousands of policemen. These precautions were to no avail, and on 10 June and in the days after, the protest spread throughout the country, with clashes of such violence that the regime had to back off. It was a victory for direct presidential elections.[35] This time, Washington finally coerced the regime to loosen its grip. In the factories, the movement went far beyond electoral concerns. The South Korean labour force was quick to move into the breach created by the mass demonstrations of June 1987, which had been largely spearheaded by students.

In the summer of 1987 South Korea's dictatorship was weakened by an unprecedented number of strikes. Between 17 July and 25 August, 1,064 labour disputes were recorded,[36] whereas the annual average over the previous ten years had been a mere 200.[37] All sectors of the economy were affected, including the *chaebols* (24,000 workers in the Hyundai naval shipyards, 15,000 coal miners, etc.) The strikers used forceful measures: occupation of company premises, including directors' offices, blocking of railway lines and occupation of railway stations, rejection of lock-out tactics, and so on. These disputes resulted in substantial pay increases and the recognition of independent, democratic trade unions.

In 1988 there were already 2,799 democratic unions. In 1989, the number rose to over 7,000. January 1988 saw the creation of the Korean Trade Union Congress, which a few years later would become the Korean Confederation of Trade Unions (KCTU). Yet up until 2000 the creation of a trade-union confederation was an unlawful act.

On the political scene, elections by universal suffrage were organized in 1988 – a first for Korea. But the opposition was divided and three candidates were put forward, the 'three Kims': Kim Young-sam, Kim Dae-jung and Kim Jong-pil. General

---

35   David Cameron, 'The working class takes up the struggle', *Inprecor*, 7 September 1987, No. 248, pp. 4–5.

36   Figures from the Ministry of Labour quoted in the *International Herald Tribune*, 26 August 1987.

37   'From July to September 1987, the number of strikes reached 3,372.' Hermann Dirkes, 'The new trade union movement', *Inprecor* 6 February 1989, No. 281.

Roh Tae-woo, the candidate supported by the incumbent and who was by his side at the time of the 1979 putsch and the Kwangju massacre of May 1980, was elected.

Finding 16: Assailed on all sides by protest movements, and faced with the growing strength of a young, combative workforce, the dictatorship loosened its grip and organized the first free elections. Washington had finally brought pressure to bear. Thanks to a divided opposition, the regime's candidate managed to win the elections, but movements within the factories were intensifying.

THE DECISIVE 1990s

From the 1980s to the mid-1990s, Korea went from strength to strength in terms of its position in world industry: from the manufacture of bulldozers and IT equipment to shipbuilding (in the 1980s it rose to second rank worldwide in shipbuilding, after Japan). Korea was shaping up to be a serious competitor for US and European transnationals in several sectors.

During the same period, China drew closer to Washington, having for some time curtailed its support for movements in various countries that threatened the stability of US allies. China joined the World Bank in 1980. Meanwhile in Russia, Mikhail Gorbachev signed geostrategic agreements with Washington in the late 1980s, the Berlin Wall came down in 1989 and the USSR imploded in 1991. The Cold War was at an end.

In the wake of the Second World War, the victory of the Chinese revolution of 1949 and the Korean War of 1950–53, the international politico-military situation had fundamentally changed. Washington took the attitude that it would be better in future to avoid supporting declared dictatorships battling with powerful opposition movements and social unrest. In the face of opposition forces prepared to fight to the end, it would be wise to ease the pressure (as in June 1987) and safeguard what was essential – in other words maintain favourable relations with the regime that was replacing the dictatorship. In addition, it was thought that a democratic government could more efficiently apply a neoliberal agenda, since it reduced the possibility of conflict with a democratic opposition allied with a social movement opposed to neoliberalism.

In 1992, following the merger of the party in power and two opposition parties, Kim Young-sam, a former moderate opposition leader, was elected president with the backing of Roh Tae-woo. Kim Young-sam was the first civilian president in 32 years, but nevertheless depended on the support of the military and sided openly with Washington.[38] His agenda was clearly a neoliberal one.

---

38   In October 1995 there occurred the biggest scandal since the end of the Korean War, implicating three successive presidents. Following an accusation by an opposition member of parliament, the former president of the Republic, Roh Tae-woo (1987–93), was arrested on the grounds of having received $369 million in bribes. His predecessor Chun Doo-hwan (1980–87) suffered the same fate. Kim Young-sam found himself in an embarrassing position, having won his election victory largely thanks to Roh Tae-woo's support. He admitted to receiving money during his electoral campaign. The industrial world also came under fire: many of the *chaebols* were implicated in some way or another in the scandal.

Korea continued to occupy a strategic military position, but the United States government, which had 37,000 soldiers posted in the country, decided it was time to curb Korea's economic appetite. Washington applied pressure, using various measures such as tariff protection against Korean products. Washington requested that Korea comply with the recommendations of the World Bank and the IMF, and was partially successful, as can be seen from the report of the mission sent to Korea by the IMF in November 1996 and from the minutes published after a debate between IMF directors. Here are some extracts:

1. On the removal of trade barriers or other forms of import restrictions: 'Since 1994, the authorities have progressively dismantled import barriers and cut tariffs in accordance with the Uruguay Round;[39] except for a small number of products with potentially adverse health or security effects, import licensing is now automatic.'[40]
2. On privatization: 'Over the past ten years, the authorities had partially implemented two public enterprise privatization programs; the program introduced in December 1993 envisaged privatization of 58 of 133 public enterprises during 1994–98. As of mid-1996, 16 enterprises had been privatized.'[41]
3. On the liberalization of capital movements: '[IMF Board members] also welcomed the recent acceleration of capital account liberalization; although some Directors agreed with the authorities' gradual approach to capital account liberalization, a number of Directors considered that rapid and complete liberalization offered many benefits at Korea's stage of economic development.'[42]

Finding 17: From 1985 on, Washington gradually modified its policy relative to dictator allies in a new climate reflecting the end of the Cold War. This turning point was seen in its relations with Brazil in the second half of the 1980s, the Philippines in 1986, South Korea in 1987, and in the next decade with South Africa in 1994, and gradually with Chile and with Indonesia in 1998. From the US viewpoint, the bottom line was positive: essential interests had been safeguarded. What, one wonders, would have happened if Washington had persisted in supporting its dictator allies in the face of mass opposition and protest? The turning point was not a global one, however. Washington continues to support dictatorships in Arab countries, Saudi Arabia first among them.

---

39 The Uruguay Round is the name of the last round of negotiations of the GATT (General Agreement on Tariffs and Trade). It led, among other developments, to the establishment of the WTO, which replaced the GATT in 1995. The GATT was created in 1948 after the International Trade Organization (created on paper in 1946 at the Havana Conference) was scuttled by the United States.
40 *International Monetary Fund Annual Report 1997* (Washington, DC: IMF, 1997), p. 59.
41 Ibid.
42 *IMF Annual Report 1997*, p. 60.

THE ASIAN CRISIS OF 1997 AND ITS CONSEQUENCES

Between 1990 and 1996, South Korean workers obtained a 67 per cent increase in real wages – an impressive achievement.[43] The neoliberal agenda met with resistance from workers in Korea as elsewhere. On 26 December 1996, the first general strike since 1948 was declared. Workers came out in protest against a reform in the labour code that would make layoffs easier. After 24 days on strike, they got their way: the labour code reform was deferred. The KCTU emerged stronger from this strike.

However, the major advances won by the workers faced a new challenge with the Asian crisis of 1997, and the employer class was quick to take its revenge.

In addition, what the United States and the other industrial powers had obtained by negotiation up to 1996 was heightened by the crisis of 1997, brought on by a wave of speculative attacks on South-East Asian and Korean currencies. This wave was facilitated by the capital-movement liberalization measures mentioned above. After the South-East Asian countries (Thailand was the first to be affected in July 1997), the crisis hit South Korea in November 1997. Between November 1997 and 8 January 1998, the Korean unit of currency, the won, depreciated by 96.5 per cent against the US dollar. In December 1997, the government in Seoul bowed to the conditions forced on it by the IMF (while Malaysia refused to do so).[44]

A veritable restructuring operation was put in place: many financial establishments were closed, there were massive layoffs, the central bank was made independent from government, interest rates shot up (plunging local industries and workers into recession), major investment projects were abandoned, certain *chaebols* were dismantled and certain companies were sold to transnational corporations in highly industrialized countries. The modification of the labour code – deferred following the general strike of January 1996 – was adopted, allowing employers to make massive cuts in the labour force. The neoliberal cure imposed on Korea had radical results. The country sank into deep recession: the GDP fell by 7 per cent in 1998.

The loans granted by the IMF, the World Bank and private banks all carried a risk premium. These institutions were therefore able to collect hefty revenues when repayments came due. The tens of billions of dollars loaned to Korea were immediately channelled into repayment of the banks. All parties to the 'rescue scheme' were refunded thanks to export revenues and drastic cuts in public spending. An increasing slice of tax revenues was used to pay back the external debt. Korea's public debt grew spectacularly after the state took over the debt of private companies. Representing 12 per cent of GDP before the crisis, it almost doubled to 22.2 per cent by the end of 1999.

---

43   United Nations Conference on Trade and Development (UNCTAD), *Trade and Development Report, 2000*, pp. 63–65, quoted by Toussaint, *Your Money or Your Life*, chapter 17, p. 357.
44   I made a detailed analysis of the Asian crisis of 1997–98 in my 2005 book *Your Money or Your Life* (chapter 17).

The increased public debt served as a pretext for making additional drastic cuts in social spending and further promoting the privatization scheme and the opening up to foreign capital.

The enforcement of these measures also aimed at disempowering Korean workers and weakening the labour unions, which had grown stronger over the previous years. The real wages of a Korean worker fell by 4.9 per cent in 1998 as a result of the crisis.

Reinforced measures to open up trade had a brutal effect on the small farmers of South Korea, who stepped up resistance movements throughout the country and regularly sent delegations abroad to attend WTO summits – Cancún in September 2003, Hong Kong in December 2005.

In the opinion of the World Bank, Korea is now a developed country. But many battles remain to be waged.

12
The Debt Trap

In the 1970s the debt of developing countries rose at a tremendous rate because the financial conditions of the loans seemed to be extremely favourable. Developing countries were actively encouraged to take on loans by the World Bank, private banks and the governments of highly industrialized countries. Then there was a radical change at the end of 1979, when the US Treasury imposed a sudden rise in interest rates as neoliberal policies kicked in. This jump in interest rates, combined with the drop in the commodities market, completely changed things. During the 1980s the creditors were making huge profits. Since the 1997 South-East Asia and Korea financial crisis, the net financial transfer on debt in favour of the creditors (including the World Bank) has been growing at a considerable rate, while at the same time debt has continued to soar to peaks never seen before.

Figures 12.1 and 12.2 show the structure of the external debt of developing countries, first from the point of view of the creditors, then from the point of view of the debtors. The figures are those provided by the World Bank for 2004, which have been rounded off here.

Table 12.1 shows the period 1970–2004. This is a long period which includes the 1982 crisis and those which came after it.

The second column shows the change in the *total* external debt stock of all the developing countries the World Bank provides data for (long- and short-term debts owed and guaranteed by the governments of developing countries and also debt owed by private companies in developing countries).[1]

Column 4, with the title 'External public debt', shows the change in the total stock only of that part of the external debt which is *owed and/or guaranteed by the government* of the country. Column 6, entitled 'Debt owed to the World Bank', shows that part of the external debt of developing countries which is *owed to the World Bank* (IBRD and IDA).

Columns 3, 5 and 7 show the net financial transfer on these three types of debt stock.

---

1   Among the countries the World Bank does not provide data for are Cuba, Iraq, Libya, North Korea and South Korea.

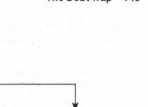

Figure 12.1   External debt of developing countries from the creditors' point of view, 2004
Source: World Bank, *Global Development Finance*, 2005

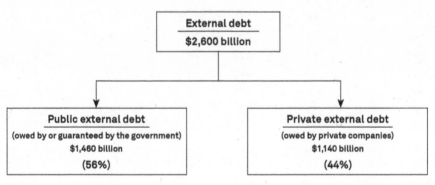

Figure 12.2   External debt of developing countries from the debtors' point of view, 2004
Source: World Bank, *Global Development Finance*, 2005

What is net transfer on debt? It is the difference between what a country receives in the form of loans and what it pays back (capital and interest). If the figure is negative, that means that the country has paid back more than it received.

INTERPRETATION OF TABLE 12.1

From 1970 to 1982, developing countries greatly increased their loans. The total external debt (public and private) in current dollars was multiplied by 10 (from $70 billion to $716 billion). External public debt was also multiplied by 10 (from $45 billion to $442 billion). The public external debt owed to the World Bank was multiplied by 7.5. During this period, the net transfer on debt was consistently positive, which means that developing countries borrowed more than they paid back. They were encouraged to take on more loans since the real interest rates were extremely low.

Table 12.1   Evolution of total external debt of developing countries, 1970–2004 **(USD billion)**

	Total external debt		External public debt		Debt owed to the World Bank	
	Total debt stock	Net debt flows	Total debt stock	Net debt flows	Total debt stock	Net debt flows
1970	70	4	45	4	6	0.3
1971	81	7	53	5	7	0.5
1972	95	10	61	6	9	0.7
1973	113	10	74	8	10	0.9
1974	141	20	92	12	11	1.3
1975	171	27	113	20	13	1.9
1976	209	29	139	20	17	2.0
1977	283	51	177	24	20	2.0
1978	358	39	231	28	23	1.8
1979	427	44	278	31	27	2.6
1980	541	51	339	29	32	3.0
1981	629	41	383	26	38	4.1
1982	716	21	442	30	45	4.6
1983	782	−14	517	17	53	4.9
1984	826	−21	571	9	54	5.0
1985	929	−27	672	−5	71	4.4
1986	1,020	−25	782	−5	91	3.7
1987	1,166	−13	920	−2	116	2.7
1988	1,172	−24	932	−10	116	0.6
1989	1,238	−22	982	−16	120	0.4
1990	1,337	−8	1,039	−14	137	2.4
1991	1,414	−3	1,080	−14	147	−0.8
1992	1,480	31	1,099	−6	149	−2.8
1993	1,632	45	1,193	9	158	−0.8
1994	1,792	0	1,290	−16	174	−2.6
1995	1,972	61	1,346	−16	184	−2.1
1996	2,045	27	1,332	−24	180	−0.9
1997	2,110	4	1,309	−24	179	1.9
1998	2,323	−54	1,395	−7	192	1.6
1999	2,347	−98	1,405	−30	198	0.9
2000	2,283	−127	1,363	−52	199	−0.4
2001	2,261	−114	1,326	−65	202	−0.5
2002	2,336	−87	1,375	−67	212	−7.3
2003	2,554	−41	1,450	−81	223	−7.0
2004	2,597	−19	1,459	−26	222	−6.1

Source: World Bank, *Global Development Finance*, 2005

Furthermore, the export revenue with which they were reimbursing the debt was increasing, since the price of raw materials was high. Consequently, developing countries on the whole did not have repayment problems.[2]

The table does not immediately reflect the downturn which started at the end of 1979 with the sudden increase in interest rates imposed on the world unilaterally by the United States government. Real interest rates exploded at the beginning of the 1980s: 8.6 per cent in 1981, 8.7 per cent in 1982, compared with −1.3 per cent (the real interest rate was actually negative) in 1975, 1.1 per cent in 1976 and 0.3 per cent in 1977.[3] This increase in interest rates, which meant an increase in the sums to be repaid, was compounded by a drop in the commodities market (although initially crude oil was not included in this downturn). When this drop finally brought down the price of crude oil, the main debtors, who were oil-producing nations such as Mexico, were no longer able to pay. This started in 1982.[4]

Going back to the table, one can see that at this point, the developing countries moved into a debt payment crisis and there was a negative net financial flow on the total public and private debt between 1983 and 1991 (nine consecutive years of negative net transfer).

During this time, while the developing countries were paying back more than they were borrowing, their total external debt did not go down at all. Between 1983 and 1991 it went up by $632 billion – that is to say, it increased by 81 per cent. That is explained by the fact that because developing countries were in difficulty due to their drop in revenue and high interest rates, they took on further loans mainly in order to be able to make the payments due, or in other words, to be able to service the debt. In such conditions the new loans were even more expensive (high interest rates and high risk premiums[5]).

It should also be noted that the net transfer on external public debt moved into negative values with a time lag of two years. Why is it that in 1983 and 1984 the net transfer on external public debt was still positive? Clearly because the governments at that point started to borrow considerable amounts (in particular from the IMF and the World Bank) in order to begin to take on debts which had initially been contracted by the private sector but which the governments agreed to take over. These enormous loans, which the public authorities started to pay back a few years later, explain the subsequent negative transfer from 1985

---

2   However, the number of countries with arrears on their payments to the World Bank, and/or who manifested the need to renegotiate their multilateral debt, went up from three to eighteen between 1974 and 1978!

3   See Toussaint, *Your Money or Your Life*. Chapter 8 gives an analysis of the debt crisis which broke out in 1982. See also Damien Millet and Éric Toussaint, *Who Owes Who?: 50 Questions about World Debt* (London: Zed Books, 2004), question 8, p. 34.

4   It was the Latin American countries who had mainly taken out variable-rate loans from private banks who were especially affected by the rise in interest rates combined with the fall in export revenue.

5   For more about risk premiums, see Toussaint, *Your Money or Your Life*, pp. 156–58.

onwards. This was especially true for Argentina, where $12 billion in private debt was transferred to the state by the military junta (through the actions of its servant Domingo Cavallo).[6]

Between 1982 and 1984, external public debt increased by $129 billion (from $442 billion to $571 billion (see column 4) while external private debt went down by $19 billion (from $274 billion to 255 billion).[7]

Looking at the period 1982–88, public debt increased by more than 100 per cent (from $442 billion to $932 billion – see column 4) while private external debt went down (from $274 billion to $240 billion). Capitalists in the developing countries get out of their debt by getting their country's treasury – that is to say, salaried workers, smallholders and the poor, who pay proportionally far more tax than the capitalists – to pay it for them. Furthermore, as will be seen in a later chapter, a very high proportion of these loans go back to the creditor countries through capital flight. That is to say, the capitalists in the developing countries send a large part of the capital they had borrowed straight back to the North!

Looking at column 5 for the period 1985–2004, it can be seen that after 1985, the net transfer on debt was consistently negative except in 1993. Over 20 years, that negative transfer weighed heavily on public finance, reaching a total of $471 billion; in other words, the governments of developing countries transferred to their creditors an amount equivalent to five Marshall Plans. At the bottom of column 5, one can see that between 2000 and 2004, the negative transfer increased. Over that period, the negative transfer totalled $291 billion, or the equivalent of three Marshall Plans paid by developing countries to their creditors in just five years.

After 20 years of negative transfer, economic reasoning would make it logical to suppose that the authorities of a country had paid off their debt. Obviously, if they reimbursed more than they borrowed, one might think that the principal sum was going down or could even reach zero.

However, our table shows that in fact the exact opposite happened: the external public debt of developing countries more than doubled over the period 1985 to 2005 – from $672 billion in 1985, it had gone up to $1,459 billion by 2005.[8]

Thus, we see that what this table shows us is:

1. Management of the external debt of developing countries has taken the form of implementing a powerful mechanism of capital flow from the debtor countries to the various creditors (public and private).
2. Despite enormous and continuous repayment, the total debt has not decreased.

---

6   Ibid., p. 320.
7   In order to obtain the amount of external debt owed by the private sector of a developing country, public debt (column 4) has been subtracted from total debt (column 2).
8   During this period, public treasuries received $2,402 billion in loans and repaid $2,873 billion, or a net negative transfer of $471 billion. (World Bank, *Global Development Finance*, 2005.)

As mentioned above, during the 1960s and 1970s, developing countries were encouraged to contract more and more loans, until the trap finally closed on them. The turning point was 1979, with the sudden jump in interest rates and the start of the drop in the commodities market (which did not affect crude oil at the beginning, but then did from 1981).

The theoretical virtuous circle of contracting external loans to promote development and well-being and which would result in self-perpetuating growth did not work.[9] It turned into a vicious circle of permanent debt with enormous capital flow to the creditors.

If we go back to Table 12.1 and look at column 3 between 1983 and 2004, we see that net transfers were negative up to 1991, and then became positive between 1992 and 1997. From 1998 onwards they were very strongly negative, with a deep trough in 2000 (a negative net transfer of $127 billion for the year 2000). How can this be explained?

During the 1980s, the flow was negative up to 1989, both for the private companies within developing countries and for the governments of these countries.

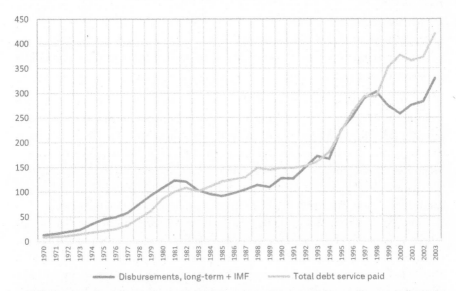

Figure 12.3 Comparison of the sums taken out in loans yearly and amount reimbursed each year (total external debt)

Source: World Bank, *Global Development Finance*, 2004

Comments: Between 1983 and 1991, developing countries repaid more than they borrowed, as was also the case between 1998 and 2004.

---

9   See chapter 10.

As we saw above: 1) the private sector freed itself of its debts by transferring part of its debt to the public sector and was repaying only a part of what remained, and 2) the public sector continued increasing its debt to cover the debts it had taken over from the private sector, and was paying most of the reimbursements. Around 1990, the private sector, having been released from much of its debt, took out new loans, which become massive debts between 1992 and 1997 (the external debt of the private sector rose from $381 to $801 billion, an increase of more than 110 per cent). The loans taken out by the private sector in developing countries were temporarily higher than the repayments made. The low point in 1994 corresponds to the Mexican crisis, which was accompanied by massive capital flight.

The situation changed again from 1998 onwards, when the South-East Asian (Thailand, Malaysia, the Philippines and Indonesia) and South Korean crises occurred, followed by crises in Russia and Brazil in 1999, and in Argentina and Turkey in 2001. Repayments from the private and public sectors were enormous and the negative net flow reached its maximum in 2000–01.

In 2003 and 2004, the net transfer remained negative, but lessened since the private sector and public authorities of developing countries took on new loans under conditions that were temporarily favourable because of:

- relatively low interest rates,
- considerably reduced risk premiums, and
- an increasing export revenue because of an upward trend in the commodities market (oil, gas, etc.).

Instead of taking advantage of this situation to pay off existing loans and radically reduce debt, most medium-income developing countries – with encouragement from the creditors – took on new loans. Those who, like Thailand, Brazil and Argentina, chose advance reimbursement of the IMF,[10] or who like Russia and Brazil reimbursed the Paris Club, simply replaced their debts to public creditors with new debts to private creditors (who were offering temporarily favourable conditions). These countries considerably increased their internal public debt.

The last two columns of Table 12.1 show developing countries' debt to the World Bank. As can be seen, it increased constantly, along with debt to creditors as a whole. But what changes is the final column, which shows the total net transfer. The total net transfer remains positive with regard to the World Bank up to 1990, whereas it becomes negative from 1983 onwards for total external debt (column 3) and from 1985 onwards for external public debt (column 5). This is mainly due to the fact that during the 1980s, the World Bank provided developing countries with loans for repaying private banks of the North who faced bankruptcy without this revenue from debt. Of course it is the IMF which plays the major role at this level, but in close coordination with the World Bank.

---

10   Thailand did so in 2003, and Brazil and Argentina in January 2006.

The net transfer with respect to the World Bank became negative from 1990 to 1996, then positive from 1997 to 1999 before becoming negative again, with the largest negative net flow ever in 2002, 2003 and 2004. The negative transfer over the period 2000–04 alone totals a staggering $21.3 billion. Compare that to the total amount provided in loans each year by the World Bank, which is less than $20 billion.

What is even more serious is that this enormous negative net transfer does not result in the slightest reduction in developing countries' indebtedness. It actually leads to an increase in the debt owed to the World Bank.

This shows the total cynicism inherent in the system, which results in artificially increased debt loads out of all proportion with the amounts actually injected into the economies of these countries.

Figure 12.4 shows that the net transfer was positive from 1970 to 1984. In 1982–83, the years when the debt crisis occurred, it was still positive because public creditors lent a lot of money to allow the governments of the South to keep on reimbursing their debt to private creditors. It became negative in 1985 through to 2004 except in 1993. Over the period 1970–2004, the debt stock spiralled upwards from $45 billion in 1970 to $1,459 billion in 2004.

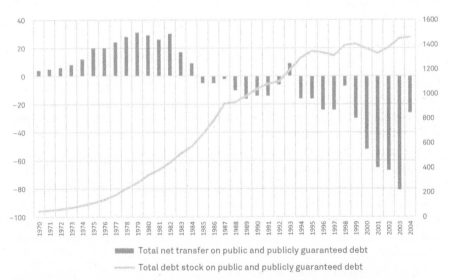

Total net transfer on public and publicly guaranteed debt

Total debt stock on public and publicly guaranteed debt

Left-hand scale: Net transfer on total external public debt of all developing countries together (in USD billion)

Right-hand scale: Change in total external public debt of developing countries (in USD billion)

Figure 12.4 Evolution of total external public debt stock compared with total net transfer on public debt

Source: World Bank, *Global Development Finance*, 2005

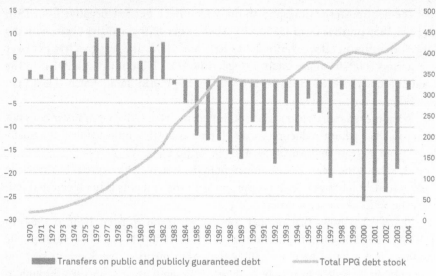

Left-hand scale: Net transfer on the total external public debt of Latin America and the Caribbean (in USD billion)
Right-hand scale: Change in the total external public debt of Latin America and the Caribbean (in USD billion)

Figure 12.5 Evolution of total external public debt stock compared with total net transfer on external public debts in Latin America and the Caribbean

Source: World Bank, *Global Development Finance*, 2005

EVOLUTION OF EXTERNAL PUBLIC DEBT WORLDWIDE

Figures 12.5 to 12.10 illustrate the public external debt of the major regions of the world.

Comments: The net transfer on public debt became negative in 1983 and remained negative through to 2004.

Population of Latin America and the Caribbean in 2004: 540 million

List of countries: [Antigua and Barbuda], Argentina, Barbados, Belize, Bolivia, Brazil, Chile, Colombia, Costa Rica, [Cuba], Dominica, Dominican Republic, Ecuador, Grenada, Guatemala, Guyana, Haiti, Honduras, Jamaica, Mexico, Nicaragua, Panama, Paraguay, Peru, Saint Kitts and Nevis, Saint Lucia, Saint Vincent and the Grenadines, El Salvador, [Suriname], Trinidad and Tobago, Uruguay, Venezuela[11]

Total external public debt in 1970: $16 billion
Total external public debt in 2004: $442 billion

---

11   The countries given in square brackets are not taken into account in the World Bank's statistics concerning indebted nations.

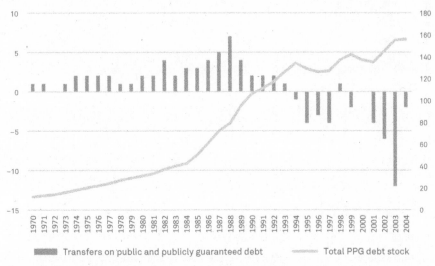

Transfers on public and publicly guaranteed debt   Total PPG debt stock

Left-hand scale: Net transfer on the total external public debt in South Asia (in USD billion)
Right-hand scale: Change in the total external public debt in South Asia (in USD billion)

Figure 12.6 Evolution of total external public debt stock compared with total net transfer on external public debts in South Asia

Source: World Bank, *Global Development Finance*, 2005

This first area, Latin America and the Caribbean, is emblematic of the way debt crises are managed in order to protect creditors' interests.

A quick overview (Figures 12.6 to 12.10) of the evolution of public debt and the net transfer on debt in the other five major developing regions shows that the debt crisis of 1982 which started in Latin America gradually spread to all other regions. Apart from obvious differences, what stands out is that the net transfer became negative everywhere at the end of the 1990s. This illustrates the fact that nowhere in the world has the crisis been resolved. It also shows that at the beginning of the twenty-first century, debt is even more of an obstacle to be overcome than it was in the 1980s.

Comments: The net transfer became negative in 1994 while the total debt stock continued to increase.

Population of South Asia in 2004: 1,450 million

List of countries: [Afghanistan], Bangladesh, Bhutan, India, the Maldives, Nepal, Pakistan, Sri Lanka[12]

Total external public debt in 1970: $12 billion

Total external public debt in 2004: $156 billion

---

12   The country in square brackets, Afghanistan, is not taken into account in the World Bank's statistics concerning indebted nations.

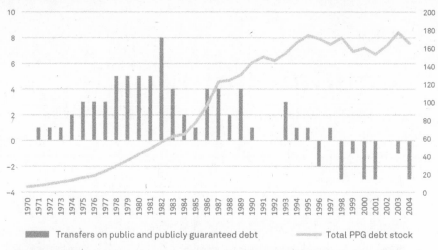

Transfers on public and publicly guaranteed debt   Total PPG debt stock

Left-hand scale: Net transfer on the total external public debt in Sub-Saharan Africa (in USD billion)
Right-hand scale: Change in the total external public debt in Sub-Saharan Africa (in USD billion)

Figure 12.7 Evolution of total external public debt stock compared with total net transfer on external public debts in Sub-Saharan Africa

Source: World Bank, *Global Development Finance*, 2005

Comments: The net transfer became negative in 1996 while the total debt stock rose steadily through to 1995 and dropped slightly in 2004.

Population of Sub-Saharan Africa in 2004: 720 million

List of countries: Angola, Benin, Botswana, Burkina Faso, Burundi, Cameroon, Cape Verde, Central African Republic, Chad, Comoros, Congo (Democratic Republic of), Congo (Republic of), Côte d'Ivoire, Eritrea, Eswatini (formerly known as Swaziland), Ethiopia, Gabon, Gambia, Ghana, Guinea, Guinea-Bissau, Kenya, Lesotho, Liberia, Madagascar, Malawi, Mali, Mauritania, Mauritius, Mozambique, [Namibia], Niger, Nigeria, Rwanda, São Tomé and Princípe, Senegal, the Seychelles, Sierra Leone, Somalia, South Africa, Sudan, Tanzania, Togo, Uganda, Zambia, Zimbabwe[13]

Total external public debt in 1970: $6 billion

Total external public debt in 2004: $165 billion

Comments: The net transfer became negative from 1990 onwards. In spite of these considerable repayments, the total debt has not been noticeably reduced.

Population of North Africa and the Middle East in 2004: 290 million

---

13   The country in square brackets, Namibia, is not taken into account in the World Bank's statistics concerning indebted nations.

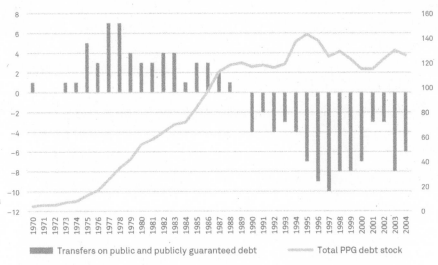

Left-hand scale: Net transfer on the total external public debt in North Africa and the Middle East (in USD billion)
Right-hand scale: Change in the total external public debt in North Africa and the Middle East (in USD billion)

Figure 12.8 Evolution of total external public debt stock compared with total net transfer on external public debts in North Africa and the Middle East

Source: World Bank, *Global Development Finance*, 2005

List of countries: Algeria, Djibouti, Egypt, Iran, [Iraq], Jordan, Lebanon, [Libya], Morocco, Oman, [Saudi Arabia], Syria, Tunisia, Yemen[14]

Total external public debt in 1970: $4 billion

Total external public debt in 2004: $126 billion

Comments: The net transfer was negative between 1988 and 1991, and became massively negative again beginning in 1999, when public debt shot up as a result of the public authorities taking on the burden of private debt and the IMF providing onerous 'emergency' loans. In spite of the large negative net transfer, the debt has not been reduced.

Population of the developing countries in East Asia and the Pacific in 2004: 1,870 million

List of countries: Cambodia, China, Fiji, Indonesia, [Kiribati], [North Korea and *South Korea*[15]], Laos, Malaysia, Mongolia, Myanmar, Papua New Guinea,

---

14   The countries given in square brackets are not taken into account in the World Bank's statistics concerning indebted nations.

15   Since 2003, the World Bank has no longer considered South Korea a developing country since the annual revenue per inhabitant has risen above the ceiling, fixed at present at $9,385. Henceforth, South Korea is considered a developed country.

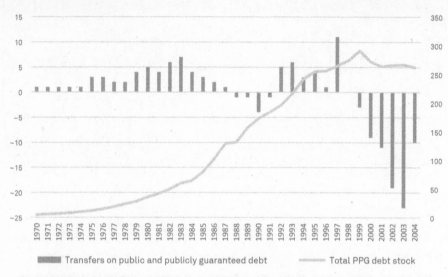

Left-hand scale: Net transfer on total external public debt in East Asia and the Pacific (in USD billion)
Right-hand scale: Change in total external public debt in East Asia and the Pacific (in USD billion)

Figure 12.9 Evolution of total external public debt stock compared with the total net transfer on public external debt in East Asia and the Pacific

Source: World Bank, *Global Development Finance*, 2005

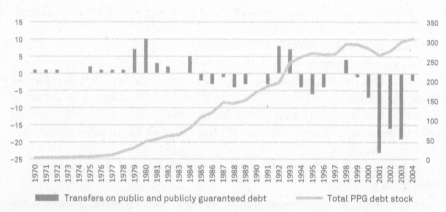

Left-hand scale: Net transfer on the total external public debt in Eastern Europe and Central Asia (in USD billion)
Right-hand scale: Change in the total external public debt in Eastern Europe and Central Asia (in USD billion)

Figure 12.10 Evolution of total external public debt stock compared with total net transfer on external public debts in Eastern Europe and Central Asia

Source: World Bank, *Global Development Finance*, 2005

the Philippines, Samoa, the Solomon Islands, Thailand, [East Timor], Tonga, Vanuatu, Vietnam[16]

Total external public debt in 1970: $5 billion

Total external public debt in 2004: $262 billion

Comments: The net transfer became negative in 1985 and remained negative through to 2004 apart from the years 1992–93 and 1998. In spite of the extremely large negative transfers between 2000 and 2003, the external public debt continued to rise.

Population of Eastern Europe and Central Asia in 2004: 470 million

List of countries: Albania, Armenia, Azerbaijan, Belarus, Bosnia-Herzegovina, Bulgaria, Croatia, Czech Republic, Estonia, Georgia, Hungary, Kazakhstan, Kyrgyzstan, Latvia, Lithuania, Macedonia, Moldova, Poland, Romania, Russia, Serbia and Montenegro, Slovakia, Slovenia, Tajikistan, Turkey, Turkmenistan, Ukraine, Uzbekistan.

Total external public debt in 1970: $3 billion

Total external public debt in 2004: $310 billion

---

16   The countries given in square brackets are not taken into account in the World Bank's statistics concerning indebted nations.

13
The World Bank Sees the Debt Crisis Looming

In 1960, the World Bank already began to see the danger of a debt crisis looming, as the main indebted countries were struggling to keep up with the rising amounts they had to repay. The warning signs increased throughout the 1960s until the oil crisis of 1973. The World Bank's leaders, private bankers, the Pearson Commission and the US General Accounting Office (GAO) published reports warning of the risk of a crisis. However, once the price of petroleum had started to rise in 1973 and huge amounts of petrodollars were recycled through the big commercial banks of the industrialized countries, there was a radical change of tone. The World Bank no longer spoke of a crisis. Yet indebtedness was still increasing faster and faster. The World Bank competed with the commercial banks in granting as many loans as possible, as fast as possible. Until the debt crisis broke out in 1982, the World Bank's discourse was ambivalent. In communications destined for the public and the indebted countries, the Bank claimed there was nothing to worry about and that if there were problems, they would be short-lived. That was what appeared in official documents available to the public. But behind closed doors at internal meetings, the line was different. One internal memorandum reads that if banks see risks rising, they will cut down on loans and 'we may see a larger number of countries in extremely difficult situations'.[1]

AFTER 1960, THERE WERE PLENTY OF WARNING SIGNS

In 1960, Dragoslav Avramović and Ravi Gulhati, two eminent World Bank economists,[2] published a report which clearly highlighted the danger of seeing the developing countries reach an unsustainable level of indebtedness due to the gloomy prospects of earning much in export revenues: 'In several major debtor countries, most of which already have high debt service ratios, service payments are predicted

---

1   'Bank borrowers experiencing debt servicing problems', Memorandum, Surinder Malik and C. Doultsinos to Jean Baneth, 29 October 1979, p. 2, cited in Kapur, Lewis and Webb, *The World Bank: Its First Half Century, Volume 1*, p. 599.

2   The Yugoslav Dragoslav Avramović was chief economist at the World Bank from 1963–64. Thirty years later, he became the governor of the Central Bank of Yugoslavia (1994–96) under the government of Slobodan Milošević.

to rise in the next few years. [...] In some cases uncertain export prospects and heavy debt service schedules constitute a serious obstacle to substantial amounts of further borrowing.'[3] This was just the beginning of a long series of warnings which appeared in different successive World Bank documents until 1973.

On page 8 of the World Bank's 1963–64 annual report we read:

The heavy debt burden that weighs on an increasing number of its member countries has been a continuing concern of the World Bank group. [...] the Executive Directors have decided that the Bank itself may vary some terms of its lending to lighten the service burden in cases where this is appropriate to the project and to the debt position of the country.[4]

THE 20TH WORLD BANK AND IDA ANNUAL REPORT, PUBLISHED IN 1965, CONTAINS A LARGE SECTION ON THE DEBT

The 20th annual report emphasizes that exports of agricultural produce are increasing faster than the demand from the industrialized countries, triggering a drop in prices: 'agricultural export commodities growth has tended to be more rapid than the growth of demand in the industrialized countries. Consequently, the developing countries suffered from a sustained decline in the prices of their agricultural exports during 1957–1962.'[5] For example, while coffee exports *increased* in volume by 25 per cent between 1957 and 1962, the export revenues they brought in *fell* by 25 per cent.[6] Cocoa and sugar prices also fell. The report showed that exports from developing countries were essentially raw materials for which Northern demand was slow and erratic. The prices of raw materials were falling.[7] The report also indicated that financial flows towards developing countries were insufficient – whether aid and loans or foreign investments – because of the large amounts paid out in debt repayments and repatriation of profits on foreign investments.

The report mentions that debt had increased at an annual rate of 15 per cent between 1955 and 1962 and had then accelerated to a rate of 17 per cent between 1962 and 1964. Just over 50 per cent of the debt was concentrated on eleven countries. All were big clients of the Bank (Argentina, Brazil, Chile, Colombia, Egypt, India, Israel, Mexico, Pakistan, Turkey and Yugoslavia).

---

3   Dragoslav Avramović and Ravi Gulhati, *Debt Servicing Problems of Low-Income Countries 1956–58* (Baltimore: Johns Hopkins Press for the IBRD, 1960), pp. 56 and 59.

4   *World Bank and IDA Annual Report 1963–64*, p. 8.

5   *World Bank and IDA Annual Report 1964–1965*, p. 54.

6   Ibid., p. 55.

7   Note that at this time the World Bank was directing its loans towards export crops and raw-materials export activities.

The external public debt of developing countries was growing at a very high rate. Between 1955 and 1963, debt increased by 300 per cent, from $9 billion to $28 billion. In just one year, from 1963 to 1964, debt increased by 22 per cent to reach $33 billion. The total amount of debt service increased fourfold over that whole period (1955–64).

In 1955, debt service absorbed 4 per cent of export revenues. By 1964, that figure had tripled to 12 per cent. And in the case of certain countries, it was almost 25 per cent!

The report places the accent on the need to properly define the conditions under which the World Bank and other creditors granted loans. What was the underlying reasoning?

The harsher the conditions, the higher the repayments. The higher the repayments, the higher the volume of aid would have to be. Consequently, the relative harshness or flexibility of conditions was as important as the volume of aid. Two key factors determined that harshness or flexibility: first, the percentage of aid granted, and secondly, the actual terms and conditions of the loans (repayment periods and interest rates).

The report noted that the share of aid granted (mainly from the USA) had decreased. Interest rates had dropped slightly and the conditions of loans had toughened up. In other words, harshness had been increased on one side and reduced a bit on the other. Note that the USSR lent money at a considerably lower interest rate than that fixed by the 'West'.[8] The UK announced that in future, it would grant interest-free loans to the poorest countries. Canada said much the same. The report pleaded for greater flexibility in the conditions applicable to loans.

None of the 19 annual reports that had preceded this one contained this kind of analysis. How can the particular tone and the original contents of this report be explained?

In fact, the 20th annual report was written under pressure of events. Numerous Third World countries had joined the Non-Aligned Movement. They had a majority within the UN General Assembly and in 1964 they had managed to have the United Nations Conference on Trade and Development founded. UNCTAD is the only UN institution run by representatives of the developing countries.[9] These countries were strongly critical of the attitude of the industrialized countries. The World Bank itself counted 102 member states at the time, most of which were Third World countries. The Bank's leaders were obliged to take account of the recriminations of the South in their analysis.

---

8   'Loans given by the Soviet Union have been made at low interest rates, usually about 2.5%' (*World Bank and IDA Annual Report 1964–1965*, p. 61).

9   For a brief account of the creation of UNCTAD and its subsequent development, see Toussaint, *Your Money or Your Life*, pp. 99–104. See also Samir Amin, Robert Charvin, Jean Ziegler, Anne-Cécile Robert et al., *ONU: Droits pour tous ou loi du plus fort?* (*The UN: Rights for All, or Only for the Strongest?*) (Geneva: Cetim, 2005), pp. 207–19 and Jean-Philippe Therien, *Une voix pour le Sud: le discours de la CNUCED* (*A Voice for the South: UNCTAD's Discourse*) (Paris: L'Harmattan, 1990) (both in French).

The 21st annual report, published in 1966, also discussed loan conditions, pleading for greater flexibility and pointing out that under the present logic, the debt was bound to increase permanently:

While the increasingly heavy debt burden of developing countries points to the need for funds on easier terms [...] the average terms of total bilateral assistance may become less, rather than more, concessionary. [...] A higher level of aid on inappropriate terms, however, could make the external debt problem even more difficult. If aid is not made available on average terms which are more concessionary, the gross volume of assistance will have to be steeply and continuously increased in order to maintain any given level of real resources transfer to the developing countries.[10]

To summarize, the World Bank had clearly detected the persistent danger of a debt crisis breaking out due to countries' inability to sustain rising debt payments. The solutions proposed by the Bank in the texts quoted above consisted of increasing the volume of loans and proposing more favourable conditions: lower interest rates and longer periods for repayment. In fact, the Bank did not see the problem in terms of financial flows. It merely saw that for the indebted countries to be able to repay their debt, they would need to borrow more money on easier terms. Plainly, this was the start of the vicious circle where new debts serve to repay old ones, both in theory and in practice.

In the same reports, the Bank expressed confidence in an increase of private capital flows (loans and investments) towards developing countries. An increase in private loans was considered an important objective. Such an increase would reduce expectations regarding public financing, according to the report cited.

The 20th annual report, published in 1965, states: 'The World Bank group and other international organizations [...] are making strenuous efforts to encourage and enlarge the flow of private capital into the less developed countries. There is no doubt that this flow can be expected to increase [...] thereby accelerating the pace of development and relieving the pressure on public funds.'[11]

In the report published in 1966, the need to free up international movement of capital is highlighted: 'It is to be hoped that conditions can be established in world [private] capital markets which will permit a freer movement of capital internationally.'[12]

---

10 *World Bank and IDA Annual Report 1965–1966*, p. 45.
11 Ibid., p. 62.
12 *World Bank and IDA Annual Report 1965–1966* <documents1.worldbank.org/curated/en/ 786661468765027751/text/multi-page.txt> [accessed 18/01/2022]. Paradoxically, while the World Bank argues for freer movement of capital between the developing countries and developed countries, Washington for its own part has set up severe restrictions on capital flow out of the USA since 1963. These restrictions have accelerated the development in Europe of the market for eurodollars which are recycled as loans to the developing countries. See Toussaint, *Your Money or Your Life*, p. 189 and Philippe Norel and Eric Saint-Alary, *L'Endettement du tiers-monde* (*The Third World's Indebtedness*) (Paris: Syros/Alternatives économiques, 1992), p. 41ff. (in French).

Then, remarkably, after a long discussion of the difficulties of repaying debt, the Bank declares that there should be no reduction in loans: 'None of this, however, should be taken to mean that developing countries cannot afford, and hence should avoid, any increase in debt servicing obligations.'[13]

A crisis predicted several times over

The designation of the Pearson Commission – after Canadian Prime Minister Lester B. Pearson, appointed to head it in 1968 by Robert McNamara, the Bank's new president – is one of the ways in which the US leaders tried to deal with the growing indebtedness and demands of the South. *Partners in Development*, the report published by the Pearson Commission in 1969,[14] predicted that the burden of debt would increase to reach a crisis in the following decade. The percentage of new gross loans used to service existing debt reached 87 per cent in Latin America in 1965–67.

In 1969, Nelson Rockefeller, brother of the president of the Chase Manhattan Bank, explained in a report to the US president about the problems Latin America had to face: 'Heavy borrowings by some Western hemisphere countries to support development has reached the point where annual repayments of interest and amortization absorb a large share of foreign exchange earnings [...] Many of the countries are, in effect, having to make new loans to get the foreign exchange to pay interest and amortization on old loans, and at higher interest rates.'[15]

In 1969, the GAO handed the government an equally alarming report: 'Many poor nations have already incurred debts past the possibility of repayment [...] The US continues to make more loans to underdeveloped countries than any other country or organization and also has the greatest loss ratio. The trend toward making loans repayable in dollars does not ensure that the funds will be repaid.'[16]

Some time later, in 1970, in a report to the US president, Bank of America president Rudolph Peterson sounded the alarm: 'The debt burden of many developing countries is now an urgent problem. It was foreseen, but not faced, a decade ago. It stems from a combination of causes [but] whatever the causes, future export earnings of some countries are so heavily mortgaged as to endanger continuing imports, investment, and development.'[17]

So as can be seen, from the late 1960s on, diverse influential and interrelated sources in the USA considered that a debt crisis could break out in the ensuing years.

---

13   *World Bank and IDA Annual Report 1965–1966*, p. 45.
14   Lester B. Pearson, *Partners in Development: Report of the Commission on International Development* (New York: Praeger, 1969).
15   Nelson Rockefeller, *Report on the Americas* (Chicago: Quadrangle Books, 1969), p. 87, cited by Payer, *Lent and Lost*, p. 58.
16   General Accounting Office, cited by Payer, *Lent and Lost*, p. 69.
17   Task Force on International Development, *U.S. Foreign Assistance in the 1970s: A New Approach. Report to the President* (Washington, DC: US Government Printing Office, 1970), p. 10.

Despite being aware of the danger ...

For his part, Robert McNamara also considered problematic the rate at which Third World indebtedness was growing:

Since the mid-1950's, publicly guaranteed debt has been growing at about 14 per cent a year. At the end of 1972 it stood at about USD 75 billion, and annual debt service exceeded 7 billion. Servicing of debt rose by 18 per cent in 1970 and by 20 per cent in 1971. The average rate of increase since the 1960s has been about twice the rate at which export earnings, from which debt must be serviced, have been growing. Such a relationship cannot continue indefinitely.[18]

...from 1973 on, the World Bank set out to increase debt in competition with the commercial banks

Yet the World Bank presided by McNamara kept up the pressure on the countries of the Periphery to get them even more into debt.

The rise in the price of petroleum products and other raw materials in 1973 led countries to rush blindly into even greater debt. The publications of the World Bank, the IMF and bankers showed less and less pessimism concerning the repayment difficulties that developing countries were faced with.

Take for example the IMF's annual report for 1975, which contained the following dispassionate message: 'investment of the surpluses of oil exporting countries in national and international financial markets – together with the expansion of international financing (through both bilateral arrangements and multilateral facilities) – has resulted in a satisfactory channelling of funds into the financing of the current account deficits of the oil importing countries.'[19]

It needs to be stressed that this diagnosis is at loggerheads with the one that would appear when the debt crisis had arisen. No sooner had the crisis broken in 1982 than the IMF blamed it on the two oil crises of 1973 and 1979. Yet the statement made in 1975 quoted above implies that for the IMF, the recycling of petrodollars combined with public lending had largely solved the problems of oil-importing countries.

WHY DID THE WORLD BANK ENCOURAGE INCREASING INDEBTEDNESS IN THE 1970s?

The World Bank absolutely wanted to increase its influence over the maximum number of countries that clearly positioned themselves in the capitalist camp or at least kept a distance from the USSR (like Yugoslavia) or were trying to

---

18   Robert S. McNamara, *One Hundred Countries, Two Billion People: The Dimensions of Development* (New York: Praeger, 1973), p. 81.
19   IMF, *Annual Report 1975*, p. 1.

(like Romania).[20] To maintain or increase its influence, it needed to strengthen its leverage by constantly upscaling the amounts it lent. But commercial banks also wanted to increase their lending and were ready to offer more competitive rates than the World Bank.[21] This sent the Bank off in search of projects that might require loans. Between 1978 and 1981, the amounts lent by the Bank rose by 100 per cent.

Robert McNamara made a great show of confidence in the 1970s. In 1977 he declared in his annual presidential address that 'the major lending banks and major borrowing countries are operating on assumptions which are broadly consistent with one another' and he concluded that 'we are even more confident today than we were a year ago that the debt problem is indeed manageable'.[22]

Some big commercial banks also showed great serenity.[23] In 1980, Citibank declared:

Since World War II, defaults by LDC's, when they have occurred, have not normally involved major losses to the lending banks. Defaults are typically followed by an arrangement between the government of the debtor country and its foreign creditors to reschedule the debt [...] Since interest rates or spreads are typically increased when a loan is rescheduled, the loan's present discounted value may well be higher than that of the original credit.[24]

This statement is to be taken with the greatest caution as to the motivations of its author. In fact, by 1980 Citibank, one of the most active banks in the 1970s in Third World lending, was beginning to sense that the wind was changing. At the time those lines were being written, it was already preparing to withdraw, and was granting almost no more new loans.

The message was aimed at smaller banks, especially local banks in the USA of the savings and loan type, whom companies like Citibank were trying to reassure so that they would continue to grant loans. In Citibank's view, the money that savings

---

20   It was in this context that the World Bank went to great lengths to persuade China to join its ranks (much to the chagrin of the government of Taiwan, who had occupied China's seat at the Bank from 1949 to 1979). In fact, the People's Republic of China returned to the World Bank at the end of Robert McNamara's presidency.

21   In 1976–78, the commercial banks made loans to Brazil at an average rate of 7.4 per cent while the World Bank was lending at 8.7 per cent (Kapur, Lewis and Webb, *The World Bank: Its First Half Century, Volume 1*, p. 281 and table 15.5, p. 983).

22   Cited by Stern and Ferreira, 'The World Bank as "intellectual actor"', p. 558.

23   In the medium term, they were right. The vision expressed in McNamara's words was confirmed in the 1980s when debt payments were suspended for short periods and rescheduling was agreed between the big US banks and the governments of Latin America with the support of the IMF and the World Bank. As Citibank claimed, interest rates and differentials were usualy revised upwards when a loan was rescheduled. That is exactly what happened. As the next two chapters show, big banks made enormous profits out of the indebted countries.

24   *Global Financial Intermediation and Policy Analysis* (Citibank, 1980), cited in 'Why the major players allowed it to happen', *International Currency Review*, May 1984, p. 22, cited by Payer, *Lent and Lost*, p. 72.

and loans continued to send to the countries of the South would enable them to repay the big banks. In other words, for the indebted countries to carry on repaying the big banks, there had to be other lenders. They could be private (small or middle-sized banks, less well informed than the bigger ones or misinformed by them) or public (the World Bank, the IMF, public export credit agencies, governments, etc.) There had to be lenders of last resort to ensure that the big banks would be fully repaid. In fact, in sending such reassuring messages in the run-up to the crisis, institutions like the World Bank and the IMF were complicit with the big banks that were on the lookout for lenders of last resort. The smaller banks that continued to lend capital to developing countries were forced into bankruptcy after the 1982 crisis and were bailed out by the US Treasury – that is, by US taxpayers.

THE 1979–81 WATERSHED

The second oil crisis of 1979 (after the Iranian revolution) coincided with a fall in prices of other raw materials.

At the end of 1979, two factors forced up the cost of debt: a very sharp rise in interest rates and the appreciation of the dollar. Attempts from the South to revive negotiations for a New World Order failed, and in Cancún in 1981 the North–South Summit on Cooperation and Development produced no results. Moreover, the United States did not apply the budget austerity they imposed on the countries of the South. Instead, they reduced taxes, increased military spending and spent more on consumer goods.

The reorientation towards what the World Bank called 'structural adjustment' was announced in a speech made by Robert McNamara at the UNCTAD conference in Manila in May 1979.

The World Bank's forked tongue

Until the debt crisis broke in 1982, the World Bank's discourse was equivocal. When communicating with the public and the indebted countries in official documents, the Bank claimed that there was nothing to worry about and that if there were problems, they would be short-lived. The other message was heard only behind closed doors at internal meetings.

In October 1978, one of the vice-presidents of the World Bank, Peter Cargill, in charge of finance, addressed a memorandum to the president, McNamara, entitled 'Riskiness in IBRD's loans portofolio'.[25] In it, Cargill urged McNamara and the whole of the World Bank to pay a lot more attention to the solvency of indebted countries. Cargill claimed that the number of indebted countries in arrears on payments to the

---

25   Memorandum, I.P.M. Cargill to Robert S. McNamara, 'Riskiness in IBRD's loan portfolio', 25 October 1978, cited in Kapur, Lewis and Webb, *The World Bank: Its First Half Century, Volume 1*, p. 598.

World Bank and/or which were seeking to renegotiate their multilateral debt had risen from three to eighteen between 1974 and 1978! Robert McNamara himself made his worries known internally on several occasions. And remember that an internal Bank memorandum cited at the start of this chapter had warned that if banks saw risks rising, they would cut down on loans and 'we may see a larger number of countries in extremely difficult situations'.

Yet the *World Development Report* published by the World Bank in 1980 gives an optimistic view of the future, predicting that interest rates would stabilize at the very low level of 1 per cent. This was completely unrealistic, as was proved by real events. It is edifying to learn through the World Bank historians that in the first, unpublished, version of the report, there was a second hypothesis based on a real interest rate of 3 per cent. That projection showed that the situation would eventually be unsustainable for indebted countries. Robert McNamara managed to get that gloomy scenario left out of the final version![26]

And the Bank's *World Development Report* for 1981 says that 'Summing up these various influences on commercial banks, it seems highly probable that both borrowers and lenders will adapt to changing conditions without precipitating any general crisis of confidence.'[27]

Robert McNamara's term as president of the World Bank ended in June 1981, a year before the crisis broke and became common knowledge. US president Ronald Reagan replaced him with Alden William Clausen, president of the Bank of America, one of the major private creditors to the developing countries. Rather like putting a fox in charge of the chicken-run …

---

26 This scenario, though closer to what actually happened, was still too optimistic.
27 World Bank, *World Development Report 1981*, p. 61.

14
The Mexican Debt Crisis and the World Bank

Robert McNamara and Luis Echeverría (1970–76) were as thick as thieves. The Mexican president had cracked down on the radical left. From 1973 on, Mexico's foreign currency revenue soared thanks to the tripling of oil prices. This increase in currency revenue should have prevented Mexico from borrowing. However, the volume of World Bank loans to Mexico rose sharply, quadrupling from 1973 to 1981 (from $118 million in 1973 to $460 million in 1981). Mexico also borrowed from private banks with the World Bank's backing. The volume of loans from private banks to Mexico multiplied sixfold between 1973 and 1981. US banks led the field, followed in decreasing order by banks from the UK, Japan, Germany, France, Canada and Switzerland. The amounts loaned by private banks were ten times those borrowed from the World Bank. When the crisis broke in 1982, the Mexican government owed money to no fewer than 550 banks! Lending money to Mexico was the World Bank's way of keeping its hold on the Mexican authorities. From 1974 to 1976, the predicament of Mexico's public finances seriously worsened. Yet with the alarm signals flashing, the World Bank still insisted that Mexico should contract more debts.

THE BANK URGED MEXICO TO TAKE ON YET MORE DEBT DESPITE UNMISTAKABLE ALARM SIGNALS

On 3 February 1978 the World Bank boldly projected a rosy future:

The Mexican government almost certainly will experience a large increase in the resources at its disposal by the early 1980s. Our most recent projections show that [...] the balance of payments will show a surplus on current account by 1982 [...] large increases in export revenues, mainly from petroleum and products, should make both the foreign debt problem and the management of public finance much easier to manage by the 1980s. The debt service ratio of 32.6% (of export revenue) in 76, will increase progressively to 53.1% in 78, and thereafter will decline to 49.4% in 1980 and about 30% in 1982.[1]

The exact opposite was to occur. Every word of this prediction was contradicted by the facts!

---

1   Kapur, Lewis and Webb, *The World Bank: Its First Half Century*, Volume 1, p. 499.

In October 1979, when Paul Volcker, then chairman of the US Federal Reserve, decided on a steep rise in interest rates that would inevitably lead to a debt crisis (which was to start in Mexico), the World Bank had reassuring words. On 19 November 1979 we read: 'Both the increase in Mexico's external public debt and especially the increase in the debt service ratio, which in 1979 may become as high as 2/3 of its exports [...], suggest a very critical situation. *In fact, the truth is exactly the opposite.*'[2]

This is quite simply stupefying.

The World Bank's message consists of repeating that even when everything suggests there is cause for alarm, actually all is well, the situation is excellent, and you should just contract further debts. What would we think of a crossing-keeper who would tell pedestrians they should cross the railway lines when a red light clearly indicates that a train is arriving? What would a court say if such behaviour had resulted in loss of life?

Private banks of the North loaned exponentially higher amounts to developing countries, starting with Mexico.

THE WORLD BANK KNEW THE GRAVITY OF THE SITUATION

One of the Bank's economists in charge of monitoring the situation sent a most alarming report on 14 August 1981. He explained that he disagreed with the optimistic view held by the Mexican government and its representative Carlos Salinas de Gortari, minister of planning and the budget.[3] He later had serious problems with his hierarchy, and even decided to bring a lawsuit against the World Bank (which he won).[4] In 1981 the World Bank granted Mexico a $1.1 billion loan (scheduled over several years). It was by far the largest loan granted by the World Bank since 1946. In the early months of 1982, the Bank was still claiming that the increase in the Mexican GDP would average 8.1 per cent a year between 1983 and 1985. On 19 March 1982, six months before the crisis, the Bank's president, Alden W. Clausen, sent the following letter to the Mexican president José López Portillo:[5]

Our meetings in Mexico City with your top aides reinforced my confidence in the economic leaders of your country. You, Mr. President, can be rightfully proud

---

2   Ibid. (emphasis added).

3   Carlos Salinas de Gortari became president of Mexico in 1988 as a result of massive electoral fraud to rob the progressive candidate Cuauhtémoc Cardenas of his victory. He left the presidency in 1994, shortly after ratifying the North American Free Trade Agreement (NAFTA). See the next chapter.

4   Here is what the World Bank historians write: 'The economist (at this writing still with the Bank) had taken a much more alarmed view of Mexico's macro prospects in 1981 and wrote up his dissenting economic analysis in the form of a memo to the files. His subsequent career at the Bank was jeopardized; after an embattled few years, he was reinstated after a legal battle. – Pieter Bottelier, interview with the authors, January 19, 1993' (Kapur, Lewis and Webb, *The World Bank: Its First Half Century, Volume 1*, p. 603, note 24).

5   José López Portillo was president of Mexico from 1977 to 1982.

of the achievements of the last five years. Few countries can claim to have achieved such high growth rates, or have created so many jobs. [...] I wish to congratulate you on the many successes already achieved. As I stated during our meeting, the recent setback for the Mexican economy is bound to be transient, and we will be happy to be of assistance during the consolidation process.[6]

Less than a year earlier, Alden W. Clausen had been chairman of the Bank of America, which was busy providing loan upon loan to Mexico.

On 20 August 1982 Mexico, which had paid back considerable amounts over the first seven months of the year, stated that it could not pay any more. The Mexican authorities decreed a six-month moratorium (August 1982 to January 1983). Already in early August they had told the IMF that their currency reserve was down to $180 million, and yet they were expected to pay $300 million on 23 August. At the end of August the IMF convened with the Federal Reserve, the US Treasury, the Bank for International Settlements (BIS) and the Bank of England. The director of the IMF, Jacques de Larosière, told the Mexican authorities that the IMF and the BIS were willing to grant currency loans in December 1982 on the twofold condition that the money be used to refund private banks and that Mexico implement drastic structural adjustment measures. Mexico accepted. It steeply devalued its national currency, considerably increased domestic interest rates, and saved Mexican private banks from bankruptcy by nationalizing them and taking over their debts. In exchange, it seized the $6 billion in cash they had on hand. President José López Portillo presented this measure to the Mexican people as though it were a nationalist move. He of course refrained from divulging that the $6 billion would be used to pay back foreign bankers.

THE CAUSES OF MEXICO'S DEBT CRISIS

Who was really responsible for the Mexican debt crisis? Did Mexico start it?

Generally speaking, the reasons are obvious: a rise in interest rates decided in Washington, plummeting oil revenues and a huge debt are the structural causes. The first two are external factors and Mexico was helpless against them. But the third results from choices made by the Mexican leaders, whom the World Bank and private bankers encouraged to take on enormous debt.

Beyond these structural causes, which are fundamental, an analysis of how one thing led to another shows that private banks of the North started the crisis in that they significantly reduced the loans granted to Mexico in 1982. Aware that almost all available currency in the Mexican treasury had been used to pay back the debt, they considered it was time to reduce their loans. In this way they brought one of

---

6   Letter, A.W. Clausen to His Excellency José López Portillo, president, United Mexican States, 19 March 1982, cited in Kapur, Lewis and Webb, *The World Bank: Its First Half Century, Volume 1*, p. 603.

the world's largest indebted countries to its knees. Seeing that Mexico was facing the combined effects of a rise in interest rates – from which they profited – and a fall in its oil revenues, they chose to act first and move out. An aggravating circumstance was that foreign bankers had aided and abetted Mexican ruling circles (CEOs and leaders of the party-state called the Institutional Revolutionary Party) who were frantically transferring their capital abroad in order to invest it safely. It is estimated that in 1981–82, no less than $29 billion left Mexico as capital flight.[7] After precipitating the crisis private bankers then further benefited from it – and left it for others to mend matters. The evidence can be seen in Tables 14.1 to 14.6.

Table 14.1 traces the evolution of loans granted by private foreign banks without any guarantee by the Mexican state. We note that after a huge increase from 1978 to 1981, loans fell drastically in 1982. On the other hand, repayments did not decrease. On the contrary, they increased by close to 40 per cent in 1982. In 1983 bank loans had completely stopped. Yet repayments were still well underway. Net transfer on debt, which had been positive until 1981, became seriously negative from 1982 on. All in all, between 1978 and 1987, negative net transfer accounted for more than $10 billion in profits for the bankers.

Table 14.2 shows the evolution of loans from foreign private banks that were guaranteed by the Mexican state. We note an increase in loans from 1978 to 1981. In 1982 loans decreased by 20 per cent, while repayments increased rather than decreased. Bank loans decreased sharply until 1986. By contrast, repayments by the Mexican state continued at a very high level. Net transfer on the public debt to foreign banks contracted with a state guarantee, which had been positive from 1978 to 1982, became very strongly negative from 1983. All in all, the net negative transfer between 1978 and 1987 adds up to over $10 billion in profits for the banks.

If we add up negative transfers in the two tables we reach a sum of over $20 billion. Private banks in the North, then, extracted juicy benefits from Mexico's people.

Table 14.3 shows the evolution of World Bank loans to Mexico. We note a sharp increase from 1978 to 1981 – a period when the World Bank was then frantically competing with private banks. In 1982 and 1983 we note a moderate decrease. Loans increased again strongly from 1984 on. The Bank acted as a lender of last resort. Loans were conditioned on the Mexican state repaying private banks, a majority of which were North American. If net transfer remained positive, it is because Mexico used the World Bank loans to repay them.

Table 14.4 shows the evolution of IMF loans to Mexico. There were none between 1978 and 1981. But during those years Mexico repaid old loans to the IMF. From 1982 on, the IMF loaned massive amounts on two conditions: 1) the money had to be used to repay private banks; and 2) Mexico had to implement a

---

7   Morgan Guaranty Trust Co. of New York, 'LDC capital flight', *World Financial Markets*, March 1986, p. 15.

Table 14.1 Foreign banks' loans without any state guarantee and repayments to the banks (USD million)

	1978	1979	1980	1981	1982	1983	1984	1985	1986	1987	Total
Loans from the banks	931	1,565	2,450	3,690	590	0	2,144	1,115	1,700	247	14,432
Repayments	860	1,390	1,450	2,090	2,890	1,546	4,630	3,882	3,490	2,453	24,681
Net transfer	71	175	1,000	1,600	−2,300	−1,546	−2,486	−2,767	−1,790	−2,206	−10,249

Source: World Bank, *Global Development Finance*, 2005

Table 14.2 Foreign banks' loans with state guarantee and repayments to the banks (USD million)

	1978	1979	1980	1981	1982	1983	1984	1985	1986	1987	Total
Loans from the banks	7,235	9,465	7,625	10,063	8,085	5,284	3,134	1,878	198	4,486	57,453
Repayments	5,349	8,582	6,706	7,226	7,260	7,571	7,654	6,922	5,345	5,170	67,785
Net transfer	1,886	883	919	2,837	825	−2,287	−4,520	−5,044	−5,147	−684	−10,332

Source: World Bank, *Global Development Finance*, 2005

Table 14.3 World Bank loans to Mexico and repayments (USD million)

	1978	1979	1980	1981	1982	1983	1984	1985	1986	1987	Total
World Bank loans	167	326	422	460	408	360	682	840	1,016	983	**5,664**
Repayments	184	220	255	283	328	399	485	597	819	1,072	**4,642**
Net transfer	−17	106	167	177	80	−39	197	243	197	−89	**1,022**

Source: World Bank, *Global Development Finance*, 2005

Table 14.4 IMF loans to Mexico and repayments (USD million)

	1978	1979	1980	1981	1982	1983	1984	1985	1986	1987	Total
IMF loans	0	0	0	0	222	1,072	1,234	300	870	786	**4,484**
Repayments	261	178	138	70	0	26	115	202	413	650	**2,053**
Net transfer	−261	−178	−138	−70	222	1,046	1,119	98	457	136	**2,431**

Source: World Bank, *Global Development Finance*, 2005

Table 14.5   Loans from countries of the North to Mexico and repayments (USD million)

	1978	1979	1980	1981	1982	1983	1984	1985	1986	1987	Total
Loans from states	156	229	439	578	673	539	540	446	848	700	5,148
Repayments	171	388	223	286	372	481	583	573	488	377	3,942
Net transfer	−15	−159	216	292	301	58	−43	−127	360	323	1,206

Source: World Bank, *Global Development Finance*, 2005

Table 14.6   Evolution of Mexico's external debt, 1978–87 (USD million)

	1978	1979	1980	1981	1982	1983	1984	1985	1986	1987	Total
Total debt stock	35,712	42,774	57,378	78,215	86,081	92,974	94,830	96,867	100,891	109,471	
Repayment	7,423	11,595	10,962	14,340	15,684	14,825	16,960	15,293	12,944	12,087	132,113
Net total transfer	1,512	3,623	8,757	11,483	−1,799	−15,804	−12,144	−10,932	−6,648	−4,227	−26,179

Source: World Bank, *Global Development Finance*, 2005

structural adjustment policy (reduction of expenditures for social programmes and infrastructures, privatizations, increases in interest rates and indirect taxation, etc.). Net transfer remained positive because Mexico used the IMF loans to repay private banks.

Table 14.5 shows the evolution of loans granted by the most industrialized countries. Like private banks and the World Bank, countries of the North sharply increased their loans to Mexico from 1978 to 1981. Then they did more or less what the World Bank and the IMF were doing. While private banks were reducing their loans, they followed the IMF and the World Bank in lending to Mexico in order to make sure that the country could repay private banks and that it would implement the structural adjustment plan.

Table 14.6 shows the evolution of Mexico's total external debt. It tripled between 1978 and 1987. During this period the amounts that were paid back were 3.5 times the amount owed in 1978. Total negative net transfer amounts to over $26 billion.

Since 1982 the Mexican people have been bled dry for the benefit of their various creditors. The IMF and the World Bank has exacted the last cent back from what they loaned to the country so that it could pay private banks. Mexico has been forcibly subjected to the logic of structural adjustment. The shock of 1982 led to a steep recession, massive layoffs and a dramatic drop in purchasing power. Then the application of structural measures resulted in hundreds of publicly owned companies being privatized. The concentration of wealth and of a large part of the national assets in the hands of a few Mexican and foreign industrial and financial corporations is staggering.[8]

From a historical perspective it is evident that the road to overindebtedness in the 1960s and 1970s, the explosion of the debt crisis in 1982, and the way it was managed in the following years marked a radical break with the progressive policies implemented from the start of the Mexican revolution in 1910 to the 1940s with Lázaro Cárdenas as president. From the revolution to the 1940s, living standards notably improved; Mexico made great strides economically and adopted an independent foreign policy. From 1914 to 1946, Mexico did not pay back any debt and eventually won a resounding victory over its creditors when the latter agreed to write off 90 per cent of the amount owed in 1914, without claiming any interest. But since the 1982 crisis Mexico has lost control of its destiny. Historically, that has been the objective of the US since the nineteenth century.

In 1970, Mexico's external public debt amounted to $3.1 billion. Thirty-three years later, in 2003, it had multiplied by 33, reaching $109.4 billion (public and private external debts together amounted to $158.7 billion). Meanwhile over this period the Mexican government paid back $407.3 billion (122 times the amount owed in 1970). Net negative transfer from 1970 to 2003 amounts to $70 billion.

---

8   The consequences of structural adjustment policies in Mexico are analyzed in the first edition of Toussaint, *Your Money or Your Life*, chapter 15, case study #2.

From 1983 to 2003, a period of 21 years, net transfer on the public external debt was positive only in 1990 and 1995.

In 2004, Mexico's external public debt totalled $112.58 billion. Sixteen years later, in 2019, it was 2.7 times that amount, totalling $307.76 billion (public and private debt together totalled $469.7 billion). Over the same period, Mexico's public authorities repaid $442.81 billion (or close to four times the amount due in 2004). The positive net transfer for the period 2004–19 amounted to $51.5 billion. Between 2004 and 2019, a period of 16 years, the net transfer on external public debt was negative during two three-year periods (2004–06 and 2017–19). The fact that the net transfer has been negative in recent years is related to the new debt crisis in the South since 2015, which has been aggravated by the Covid-19 pandemic.

The day is surely approaching when the Mexican people will be able to win back their freedom to decide their own future.

15
The World Bank and the IMF:
The Creditors' Enforcers

In July 1981, Alden W. Clausen, then president of the Bank of America, was made president of the World Bank. The Bank of America is one of the biggest US banks at risk in case of non-payment of debt by the developing countries. Ronald Reagan, by placing Alden W. Clausen at the head of the World Bank, was sending a strong signal to US banks (and other commercial banks around the world) that their interests would be duly taken care of.

US banks were the most at risk compared to European and Japanese banks because they lent proportionately more. The 1982 crisis particularly affected Latin America, the US banks' preferred hunting ground. The amounts they lent, compared to their capital, were enormous and imprudent. All the US banks taken as a whole had lent the equivalent of 152 per cent of their own capital. Of those, the top 15 had lent the equivalent of 160 per cent of their capital. The nine biggest, including the Bank of America, had committed the equivalent of 229 per cent of their capital.

In August 1982 when Mexico announced that it was unable to pay, the big movers and shakers of world finance got together to bail out the commercial banks. The quartet that orchestrated the strategy was composed of Jacques de Larosière, managing director of the IMF, Paul Volcker, president of the US Federal Reserve, Gordon Richardson, director of the Bank of England, and Fritz Leutwiler, president of the Bank for International Settlements (BIS). The president of the World Bank was not invited to the preliminary meetings.

The strategy adopted may be summarized as follows:

- the crisis should be treated as though it was caused by a short-term liquidity problem that could be solved by the IMF and the major central banks;
- priority should be given to the debts of the three most indebted countries: Brazil, Mexico and Argentina;
- private debt must be converted into public debt for the indebted countries;
- creditors should act collectively while the indebted countries must be dealt with individually, making it impossible for them to present a united front ('divide and rule');
- indebted countries must at all costs continue to repay the interest on their debt;

- no cancellation or reduction of the interest rate should be granted by the creditors – the payments could only be rescheduled; and
- new loans would only be granted by commercial banks on condition that the indebted countries concerned promised to implement austerity policies in agreement with the IMF.

This was basically the strategy that was maintained throughout the 1980s, but it had to be modified to take into account the amplitude of the crisis and the reactions of the commercial banks. The latter, instead of following the last point of the strategy mentioned above, practically stopped all lending and made do with taking in repayments, which sent their profits soaring! The profits that Citibank took from Brazil in 1983 and 1984 alone represented 20 per cent of its total profits. Karin Lissakers (who was later to become the executive director for the USA at the IMF) claimed that the dividends distributed by the big US banks in 1984 came to double what they had been in 1980.[1] In fact, the IMF and the public money-spinners mentioned above, later joined by the World Bank, adopted a tough strategy with regard to the indebted countries in order to protect the commercial banks. They could hardly have done more to promote the interests of big private international finance, or in other words, big international capital. They had become enforcers for the commercial banks, as Karin Lissakers herself points out: 'The IMF was in a sense the creditor community's enforcer.'[2]

Jacques Polak, who was director of research at the IMF then executive director of the IMF for the Netherlands, writes of the strategy outlined above:

In the second half of the 1980s, however, commercial banks began to exploit this approach. No longer afraid of becoming the victims of a generalized debt crisis, the banks began to realize they could insist on favorable terms for themselves by blocking a country's access to Fund credit (and to other credit linked to a Fund arrangement). The Fund was thus pushed increasingly into being used by the commercial banks in the collection of their debts.[3]

What has been said about the IMF goes for the World Bank, too, which behaved in exactly the same way.

The US banks did very well for themselves. So did European banks, by obtaining enormous tax breaks for provisioning large amounts against possible losses on their loans. Furthermore, European and Japanese banks had the advantage of the depreciation of the dollar, which reduced the weight of loans in dollars to indebted countries in their portfolios.

---

1   Karin Lissakers, *Banks, Borrowers and the Establishment: A Revisionist Account of the International Debt Crisis* (New York: Basic Books, 1991), p. 194.
2   Karin Lissakers, *Banks, Borrowers and the Establishment*, p. 194.
3   Cited in Kapur, Lewis and Webb, *The World Bank: Its First Half Century, Volume 1*, p. 636.

The governments of the indebted countries arranged for their country's treasury (and thus its citizens) to take on the burden of the external debt run up by their country's private companies. The case of Argentina was typical: subsidiaries of transnational corporations indebted towards their parent company managed to get their debts paid off by the Argentine treasury![4]

In doing this, governments of the developing countries submitted to the combined pressure of local capitalists, the transnationals implanted in their countries and the big public moneylenders of the North, themselves under the thumb of the big commercial banks of the North.

It was the very same big public moneylenders, particularly the IMF and the World Bank, who gradually replaced commercial banks as creditors to the countries in the greatest distress. Here again, the risks and the costs were transferred from the private sector to the public sector. Table 15.1 shows how commercial banks dissociated themselves from indebted countries encountering repayment difficulties. Their credits to these countries fell from $278 billion in 1982 to $200 billion in 1992, a reduction of 28 per cent. Over the same period, the official creditors (the IMF, the World Bank and states) took over, with their credits increasing from $115 billion to $252 billion between 1982 and 1992, an increase of 120 per cent.

Table 15.1   Real debt of developing countries with debt-servicing difficulties, 1982–92 (USD billion, 1982)

	To commercial banks	To official creditors	Official creditors' share (%)
1982	278	115	29.3
1984	286	143	33.3
1986	278	187	40.2
1988	254	232	47.7
1990	222	251	53.1
1992	200	252	55.7

Source: Michael Dooley, 'A retrospective on the debt crisis', in (),*Understanding Interdependence: The Macroeconomics of the Open Economy* (Princeton: Princeton University Press, 2021), p. 273[5]

4   The Argentine companies with parent companies outside Argentina are: Renault Argentina, Mercedes-Benz Argentina, Ford Motor Argentina, World Bank Argentina, Citibank, First National Bank of Boston, Chase Manhattan Bank, Bank of America and Deutsche Bank. The Argentine state reimbursed the private creditors of the following companies, i.e. their parent companies: Renault France, Mercedes-Benz, Citibank, Chase Manhattan Bank, Bank of America, First National Bank of Boston, Crédit Lyonnais, Deutsche Bank and Société Générale. In short, the Argentine taxpayer repaid the debt incurred by subsidiaries of transnational corporations towards their parent companies or international bankers. According to several authors, those transnationals had created a debt on behalf of their Argentine subsidiaries by 'cooking the books'. The Argentine government had no access to their accounts. See in particular Alejandro Olmos, *Todo lo que usted quiso saber sobre la deuda externa y siempre se lo ocultaron* (Buenos Aires: Editorial de los Argentinos, 1990).

5   In Kapur, Lewis and Webb, *The World Bank: Its First Half Century, Volume 1*, Table 11-5, p. 642.

On the recommendation or at the injunction of the IMF and the World Bank, the indebted countries used loans that they obtained from public creditors (the IMF, the World Bank and states) to repay the commercial banks which had no intention of lending them any more money – not until they had been fully repaid.

However, not only did the loans made by public creditors increase the debt stock which would have to be repaid in any case, but they were far too modest to repay the colossal debts owed to the banks, particularly as the interest rates were extremely high. Concerning the exorbitant interest rates paid by the developing countries, the UNDP had this to say in the *Human Development Report 1992*: 'During the 1980s, when industrial countries were paying 4%, the developing countries were effectively paying 17%. On a total debt of over \$1 trillion, this cost them about \$120 billion of real costs, in addition to a reverse debt-related net financial transfer that reached \$50 billion in 1989.'[6]

The question of negative net transfer on debt mentioned in this UNDP report is fundamental, and deserves closer scrutiny.

THE DEBATE INSIDE THE WORLD BANK ON CALCULATING THE NET TRANSFER ON DEBT

In 1984, the debate over this issue caused a rumpus in the World Bank. For that very year, a team of World Bank economists, led by Sidney Chernick and Basil Kavalsky, produced a report which questioned the Bank's presentation of external debt flows.[7] Hitherto, the Bank had only considered net flows on debt, which it defined as the difference between the capital lent and the capital repaid, without counting the interest. This team of economists took a different stance, declaring that interest payments should be included in the calculation so that the debt problem could be presented more realistically.

Table 15.2 illustrates the crux of the debate, showing how the total amount of external debt of developing countries increased between 1979 and 1987. Using the World Bank's traditional approach, i.e. without including interest payments, the transfer appears positive throughout the period considered. With such a presentation of the transfers, how is one to even realize that a debt crisis broke out in 1982 and continued thereafter?

On the other hand, using the approach advanced by the Bank's team of economists, the result is totally different. It can be clearly seen that the transfer was positive until 1982 and that it became negative as of 1983. It is perfectly justifiable to calculate the net transfer on debt by deducting the amounts repaid both in terms of capital and interest, from the amounts lent. Moreover, since the crisis was caused

---

6   UNDP, *Human Development Report 1992* (New York/Oxford: Oxford University Press, 1992), p. 66.
7   IBRD, Operations Policy Staff, 'Debt and adjustment in selected developing countries', SecM84-698, 1984, in Kapur, Lewis and Webb, *The World Bank: Its First Half Century, Volume 1*, p. 615.

Table 15.2 Net transfer on debt of developing countries with and without counting interest paid, 1979–87 (USD million)

All developing countries	1979	1980	1981	1982	1983	1984	1985	1986	1987
Total external debt	427,424	540,923	628,610	715,788	781,947	826,434	929,186	1,020,494	1,166,248
Net transfer **without** interest payments (i.e. net flow)	67,298	94,821	96,739	83,194	45,366	42,397	38,208	36,327	48,037
Net transfer **with** interest payments	44,247	51,359	40,708	20,341	−14,282	−21,744	−27,614	−24,846	−12,895

Source: World Bank, *Global Development Finance*, 2005.

by a rise in interest rates, it can only become visible and be understood when the interest payments are taken into account.

The report received a very cold reception when it reached the management level of the Bank. Ernest Stern, one of the Bank's senior members and vice-president for operations, sent a fax saying: 'Am not prepared to circulate paper which [is] analytically based on net transfer concept.'[8] In his view, there was no question of presenting the payment of interest as a burden since it was simply the remuneration for capital lent. And that was that.

After a meeting of the New York Federal Reserve to which the Bank had been invited, Ernest Stern wrote a memorandum to the Bank's Managing Committee in which he said: 'the issue of net transfers was raised and was greeted with a veritable firestorm of negative comments, from several governors and other participants. The World Bank was also attacked by several speakers for having endorsed this concept.'[9] The subject was taboo.

Such an outcry clearly shows that this was a particularly sensitive and important issue. It is impossible to grasp the full significance of debt repayment without including the payment of interest as well as repayment of the capital. Table 15.3 uses the same procedure as Table 15.2, this time applied to Latin America and the Caribbean. The Bank's erroneous traditional presentation only reveals a slight problem of negative transfer on debt, limited to 1983, whereas taking the interest paid into account reveals the true situation: that transfers were overwhelmingly negative from 1983 on.

Calculations have shown that between 1982 and 1985, transfers from Latin America to creditors represented 5.3 per cent of the continent's GDP. The burden is enormous when you consider, by way of comparison, that the reparations imposed on Germany by the Treaty of Versailles came to 2.5 per cent of the German GDP between 1925 and 1932.[10]

For the World Bank's directors, the internal debate over net transfers had a direct bearing upon the Bank's interests as a creditor. The Bank (and also the IMF) wanted to maintain its status as a privileged creditor at any cost, since this enabled it to claim a right to prior repayment over other creditors – private or bilateral. Ernest Stern explained, in an internal memorandum made in preparing a speech that the

---

8   Fax message, Ernest Stern to Luis de Azcarate, director, CPDDR, 15 May 1984, in Kapur, Lewis and Webb, *The World Bank: Its First Half Century*, Volume 1, p. 616.

9   Memorandum, Ernest Stern to members of the Managing Committee, 'Conference at the Federal Reserve Bank of New York', 11 May 1984, p. 1, in Kapur, Lewis and Webb, *The World Bank: Its First Half Century*, Volume 1, p. 616.

10   Andres Bianchi, Robert Devlin and Joseph Ramos, 'The adjustment process in Latin America 1981–1986', paper prepared for World Bank–IMF Symposium on Growth-Oriented Adjustment Programs, Washington, DC, 25–27 February 1987, Table 9, in Kapur, Lewis and Webb, *The World Bank: Its First Half Century*, Volume 1, p. 627, note 105, ('By way of comparison, the war reparations imposed on Germany between 1925 and 1932 amounted to 2.5 percent of GDP.')

Table 15.3 Net transfer on debt of developing countries of Latin America and the Caribbean with and without counting interest paid, 1979–87 (USD million)

Latin America and the Caribbean	1979	1980	1981	1982	1983	1984	1985	1986	1987
Total external debt	197,472	242,835	295,301	333,142	361,668	376,004	387,807	406,001	442,010
Net transfer **without** interest payments	35,901	45,710	54,261	37,893	–317	6,211	4,537	2,276	8,515
Net transfer **with** interest payments	23,221	21,359	21,413	299	–34,971	–29,040	–30,204	–27,774	–19,814

Source: World Bank, *Global Development Finance*, 2005

president of the Bank was to give at the World Economic Forum in Davos in January 1984, that the Bank should refrain from asking commercial banks to maintain positive net transfers (including interest paid) as this could cause a backlash for the World Bank. For naturally, such a requirement could also be applied to the Bank. The issue therefore needed be fudged by referring only to net loans, or net flows on debt, thus excluding interest payments from the calculation. Here is an extract from this internal memo:

If we hold the commercial bank responsible for maintaining net transfers [...] then we are saying that [...] the World Bank itself at some future point can be held responsible for not maintaining positive net transfers. We are arguing in other fora that one thing that distinguishes the World Bank from other banks, and justifies our separate treatment in rescheduling, is that we maintain net disbursements − not net transfers. If we accept the net transfer argument in a public speech by the President, our basis for rejecting attempts to draw us into rescheduling when our net transfer payments are no longer positive will be much weaker.[11]

Two important points emerge from the end of this extract. Firstly, that the World Bank's leader already foresaw that the net transfer between the Bank and its clients would also become negative; and secondly, that he was worried that as a result, the Bank would no longer be able to refuse the rescheduling of debts owed it.

Table 15.4 shows transfer on debts owed to the Bank. Using the method preferred by Ernest Stern, transfer appears to remain positive. By applying the alternative approach, the transfer becomes negative as from 1987.[12]

There is one more reason the Bank refused to discuss negative transfers. In the 1980s, middle-income countries like Mexico, Brazil, Argentina, Venezuela and Yugoslavia were the main countries affected by the debt crisis. They were also the World Bank's main clients. These countries funded the Bank through interest payments (added to the repayment of borrowed capital). Indeed, the World Bank owed its positive results to the interest paid by the middle-income countries that made use of its services. The rich countries did not finance the World Bank (the IBRD) since the latter borrowed on the financial markets. The World Bank used its IDA branch to lend to poor countries. In other words, it was the indebted middle-income countries who enabled the Bank to lend to the poor countries at low interest rates without taking a loss. The Bank had to conceal this fact since the

---

11   Memorandum, Ernest Stern to Munir Benjenk, 'Draft speech for Davos', 16 January 1984, p. 2, in Kapur, Lewis and Webb, *The World Bank: Its First Half Century, Volume 1*, p. 616.

12   In drawing up this table, I took into account loans made by the IBRD branch of the World Bank, which grants loans to middle-income countries. I did not take into account loans made by the IDA to low-income countries.

Table 15.4 Net transfer on debt of developing countries to the World Bank with and without counting interest paid, 1979–87 (USD million)

All developing countries	1981	1982	1983	1984	1985	1986	1987	1988	1989
Debt owed to the World Bank (IBRD)	24,356	28,570	33,706	33,426	46,612	63,411	83,372	79,871	80,981
Net transfer **without** interest payments	3,972	4,229	5,144	5,556	5,100	5,667	5,027	3,743	3,329
Net transfer **with** interest payments	2,239	2,217	2,728	2,700	1,838	887	–767	–2,801	–2,738

Source: World Bank, *Global Development Finance*, 2005

middle-income countries, had they been aware of it, could then have demanded the right to examine the Bank's policies towards the poorest countries. But defining that policy is the prerogative of the rich countries that control the Bank.

Intellectual terrorism within the World Bank

The World Bank historians claim that a system of spying was officially set up under the presidency of Alden W. Clausen, with a view to detecting people who deviated from the politico-economic line of the Bank's management. The Bank historians say:

Between early 1983 and 1986, the Bank's Personnel Department informed the institution's senior managers that the Economics Department had adopted an 'intelligence' system to detect staff divergences from establishment positions, that it was categorizing staff by schools of economic thought and openly favouring 'loyalists', and that it was hiring staff on fixed-term contracts to render them more pliable. ERS (Economic Research Staff), the personnel people said, increasingly was seen as a unit selling ideology instead of objective research.[13]

Intellectual terrorism and neoliberal obscurantism were such that, during Anne Krueger's term as vice-president and chief economist, 29 of 37 management-level researchers in the research department left between 1983 and 1986.[14] Even more seriously for the institution's functioning, more than ten posts remained vacant for two years because no-one in the other departments wanted to take the place of those who had left.

The World Bank historians report a crisis that arose between the Bank's leadership, especially Anne Krueger, and the editor of a new Bank review, *World Bank Economic Review*, Mark Leiserson. In 1986, Leiserson, backed by the entire editorial committee, had decided to publish an article by Jeffrey Sachs written in 1985. The Bank's vice-president, Krueger, prevented publication of the article. The editor resigned in protest after having tried in vain to persuade the World Bank leaders to back the editorial committee. This was not an isolated phenomenon since a few months later, the editor of another Bank review, *World Bank Research Observer*, also resigned for similar reasons.

When you consider that Jeffrey Sachs had just finished setting up a very harsh structural adjustment plan for Bolivia, and was thus in the neoliberal camp of the World Bank and the IMF, you can appreciate the degree of intellectual terrorism and obscurantism wielded by Anne Krueger as chief economist on those in the Bank who cautiously tried to give people from outside the institution a chance to make themselves heard. Krueger did not like Jeffrey Sachs' proposal that the World Bank and the IMF should ask commercial banks to cancel debts of extremely

---

13   Kapur, Lewis and Webb, *The World Bank: Its First Half Century, Volume 1*, p. 1194.
14   Ibid., p. 1193, note 47.

indebted countries. In short, Sachs was proposing that the private sector should make an effort, and Anne Krueger found that quite unacceptable! The Bank historians acknowledge that even the Bank's most important publication, *World Debt Tables*, came in for censorship.[15]

Anne Krueger left office in 1987. In 2000, she became number two at the IMF, and occupied that post until August 2006. However, it is important to stress that this is not an issue of individual personalities. Krueger was acting as the representative of the US administration. She is not just an unfortunate accident in the history of the IMF and the World Bank.

RADICAL CHANGES IN WORLD BANK DISCOURSE ON DEVELOPING COUNTRIES AND THEIR LEADERS

Until the debt crisis broke out, the World Bank could not praise the leaders of the developing countries enough, in a desire to encourage them to take on debts and follow the policies it recommended. Some time after the start of the crisis, there was a radical change of tone. The Bank criticized the governments of the developing countries and blamed them for the crisis. On no account was it going to examine its own responsibilities. The change is clearly apparent in the following two quotations.

In 1982, just before the outbreak of the crisis, the Bank wrote in the *World Development Report*: 'The developing countries, despite the rise in their current account deficits from $40 billion in 1979 to $115 billion in 1981, have been much more successful than the industrialized countries in adjusting to the new situation.'[16]

Four years later, it claimed the opposite: 'At the root of the poor performance and debt problems of developing countries lies their failure to adjust to the external developments that have taken place since the early 1970s, coupled with the magnitude of the external shocks.'[17]

In 1984, one of the Bank's economists, Carlos Diaz-Alejandro, produced a qualified analysis of the developing countries' attitudes in the crisis, with emphasis on the fact that they had been subject to powerful external forces. Ernest Stern retorted:

The countries which borrowed $10–15 billion a year are playing in the big league. They thought they had the capacity – they often said so. They did so with their eyes open. They were very proud of what they were doing at the time – and much of what they did was sound. But they miscalculated. That can happen,

15   Ibid., p. 624.
16   World Bank, *World Development Report 1982*, p. 7, in Kapur, Lewis and Webb, *The World Bank: Its First Half Century, Volume 1*, p. 617.
17   World Bank, *World Development Report 1986*, p. 33, idem.

and the cost of miscalculation can be high. But, if they want to be partners in an open and interlinked international economic system, it is time that they equip themselves to do so properly, and you should not put the burden of failure on the shoulders of everyone but themselves – it is not so. I believe it is a view they, in fact, share.[18]

There were several aims behind the Bank's attitude here. Firstly, it sought to avoid criticism for the policy of indebtedness that it had been recommending for decades before the crisis and especially in the 1970s. Secondly, it wished to convince its partners that they should apply radical austerity policies within the framework of structural adjustment without demanding an effort of solidarity on the part of the governments of the rich countries.

Stanley Fisher, who replaced Anne Krueger as the Bank's chief economist in 1987, wrote in an internal memorandum in 1990: 'I very much fear giving them [the less developed countries] any encouragement to believe the international community will do much to help them, and thus tend to emphasize that they have to handle their own problems.'[19]

As the World Bank historians point out: 'Anyone interested in the intellectual history of the debt crisis would be struck by the degree to which the intellectual debate was dominated by voices from the US, in contrast to the virtual absence of voices from the countries bearing the brunt of the crisis.'[20] Later they add that the studies published by the World Bank reflect the political interests of its principal shareholders, especially the USA and major commercial banks.[21]

COMPLICITY BETWEEN BANKERS OF THE NORTH AND THE RULING CLASSES OF THE SOUTH

Several studies show the link between the growing indebtedness of the Latin American countries in the 1970s and 1980s and capital flight from the South to the North. A very large portion of the money lent by Northern bankers returned to their coffers in the form of deposits.

The Bank historians say of this: 'The ratio of capital flight to the increase in external debt in the period 1978–82 is estimated to have ranged from 50 to

---

18 Letter, Ernest Stern to Carlos F. Diaz-Alejandro, 10 September 1984, pp. 3–4, in Kapur, Lewis and Webb, *The World Bank: Its First Half Century, Volume 1*, p. 618.

19 Memorandum, Stanley Fisher to Ibrahim Shibata, 26 May 1990, in Kapur, Lewis and Webb, *The World Bank: Its First Half Century, Volume 1*, p. 618.

20 Kapur, Lewis and Webb, *The World Bank: Its First Half Century, Volume 1*, p. 626.

21 'Be that as it may, during the early years of the crisis, the periodic publicly disseminated formulations of the latest "consensus" on the debt crisis by the Bank (and its Bretton Woods twin), served largely to rationalize the political interests of the major shareholders, especially the United States, and by extension, of the commercial banks.' (Ibid.)

Table 15.5   Argentina, Brazil, Colombia, Mexico, Peru and Venezuela: capital flight, 1973–87 (USD million)

Country	Capital flight (1973–87)	Stock of assets abroad in 1987	Assets abroad as % of external debt (1987)
Argentina	29,469	43,674	76.9
Brazil	1,556	20,634	18.3
Colombia	1,913	2,994	19.5
Mexico	60,970	79,102	73.3
Peru	2,599	4,148	23.0
Venezuela	38,815	48,027	131.5

Source: IFRI, *Ramses 93* (Paris, 1992), p. 235, based on M. Pastor, 'Capital flight from Latin America', *World Development*, January 1990

100 percent for Argentina, Mexico, and Venezuela. In the case of Brazil it was of the order of 10 percent.'[22]

Other studies, one of which is presented in Table 15.5, produce results that corroborate this.

The World Bank historians draw an extremely pertinent conclusion from all this: 'Capital flight increasingly placed private assets in overseas havens, in the very banks that held national debt. The elite of Latin American countries were unlikely to countenance any scheme entailing default that would place their private assets at risk.'[23] Indeed, the affluent elite of the developing countries had clearly no interest in their country suspending payments on its external debt.

To end this chapter, how to resist the pleasure of reproducing the delicate exchange of internal memos between Stanley Fisher of the World Bank and Jacob Frenkel, his colleague at the IMF? The IMF had published a study featuring an optimistic prognosis of the end of capital flight and its return to its country of origin. Stanley Fisher writes to his IMF colleague:

Bank staff are concerned with the Fund's projections of substantial return capital flight in the financial gap analysis for some countries. We are unaware of the economic analysis on which such projections are based, and believe that it would generally be a self-denying prophesy to argue that a financing gap will be closed by return capital flight, which depends above all on confidence in overall macroeconomic and financial stability.[24]

---

22   Kapur, Lewis and Webb, *The World Bank: Its First Half Century,* Volume 1, p. 662. The authors cite as reference Miguel A. Rodriguez, 'Consequences of Capital Flight for Latin American Debtor Countries,' in Donald Lessard and John Williamson, *Capital Flight and Third World Debt* (Washington, DC: Institute for International Economics, 1987), Table 6.1, p. 130.

23   Ibid., p. 678.

24   Memorandum, Stanley Fisher to Jacob A. Frenkel, 'Coordination of forecasts', 27 June 1989, in Kapur, Lewis and Webb, *The World Bank: Its First Half Century, Volume 1*, pp. 611–12, note 45.

Jacob Frenkel replies, 'The issue you raise concerning projections of return capital flight in financial gap analysis is one which, as you are aware, *embraces considerations other than purely analytical ones*.'[25] In other words, the IMF makes optimistic projections for political reasons.

UNBRIDLED STRUCTURAL ADJUSTMENT

In a book published in 1974, the American economist Cheryl Payer, a critic of the IMF and the World Bank, listed the measures that the IMF imposed on developing countries which called on its services:

- abolition or liberalization of control of currency exchange and imports;
- devaluation of the currency;
- restrictive monetary policies to control inflation, as follows: a) raised interest rates and, in some cases, an increase in exchange reserves; b) control of the public deficit: spending cuts; increases in taxes and tariffs for public services and companies; abolition of subsidies on consumer products; c) limits on salary rises in the civil service; d) dismantling of price controls;
- greater hospitality for foreign investments.

In order to define these measures, Payer had analyzed IMF policy as applied in the 1960s in the Philippines, Indonesia, Brazil, Chile, India, Yugoslavia and Ghana.

Beginning in 1981–82 when the debt crisis broke out, a considerable number of countries called upon the services of the IMF (often under pressure from their main creditors, whether public or private) to try to solve the problem of their balance of payments. The IMF then had greater powers at its disposal to generalize the economic measures listed above. The whole set of measures was to become increasingly known by the expression 'structural adjustment policies'.

One of the bitter ironies of history, as was mentioned earlier, was when the price of oil shot up in 1973 and the IMF declared that no structural adjustment was necessary. Yet the oil crisis had considerably modified the international situation. Oil-exporting countries saw a huge increase in their foreign currency revenues, while there was a huge demand for foreign currency on the part of the non-oil-producing developing countries.

When the debt crisis broke out as a consequence of the combined effects of the rise in interest rates decreed by the US Federal Reserve and the fall in prices of raw materials, the IMF and the World Bank completely modified their version of what had happened. They blamed the debt crisis largely on the oil crisis. Suddenly, the adjustment they had deemed unnecessary in the mid-1970s became unavoidable.

The World Bank pioneered the launch of the first structural adjustment loans in 1980. It was on the initiative of Robert McNamara that the Bank initiated these

---

25   Memorandum, Jacob A. Frenkel to Stanley Fisher, ibid. (emphasis added).

new loans. McNamara used the following prediction to justify the policy: after the second oil crisis in 1979, the price of oil would continue to rise throughout the 1980s (in fact he was wrong; the opposite happened). This meant that the developing countries needed to carry out structural adjustment.[26]

The adjustment measures presented by Robert McNamara were those outlined above. Between 1980 and 1983, the Bank granted 14 structural adjustment loans to nine countries.[27]

Throughout the 1980s, there were regular clashes between the Bank and the IMF, who could not seem to manage to coordinate their actions. This led to a concordat between the two institutions in 1989.[28] The following year, in 1990, the concept of the 'Washington Consensus' was born,[29] codifying the policies to be adhered to within the structural adjustment framework. To the measures listed by Cheryl Payer and cited above were added mass privatizations and a policy of cost recovery in sectors like education, health, water distribution, etc. Note that the Washington Consensus includes not only the IMF and the World Bank, but also the US Executive, represented by the Treasury. The novelty of the Washington Consensus was not so much in the economic measures to be applied (most of which were already in effect) as in the *public proclamation* of an agreement between the Bretton Woods institutions and the US government.

The World Bank produces an enormous number of studies and reports that aim to provide a theoretical foundation and codification for structural adjustment policies. Among these, one report is of particular interest: *Accelerated Development in Africa South of the Sahara*,[30] directed by the economist Elliot Berg. It emanated from an order from Robert McNamara. This report was to underpin the World

---

26   Stern and Ferreira, 'The World Bank as "intellectual actor"', p. 540.

27   Ibid., p. 543.

28   In 1989 the two institutions agreed to share responsibilities, as a means of limiting clashes between their recommendations (as occurred for example in Argentina in 1988, when the World Bank backed conditions that the IMF found unsatisfactory). The term 'concordat,' used by the institutions themselves, was significant. It meant that the disagreements and tensions between them were considerable. It was agreed that the IMF would mainly examine the global aspects of macroeconomic policies, particularly concerning budget, prices, currency, credit, interest rates and exchange rates. The World Bank, on the other hand, would concentrate on development strategies, projects and sector-based aspects. Sharing the tasks in this way required various forms of collaboration, but rivalry between the two institutions remains intense. On top of this institutional rivalry there are differences of corporate culture to contend with.

29   The economist John Williamson wrote: 'Ten years ago I invented the term "Washington Consensus". While it is jolly to become famous by inventing a term that reverberates around the world, I have long been doubtful as to whether the phrase that I coined served to advance the cause of rational economic policymaking.' John Williamson, What Should the World Bank Think about the Washington Consensus?, Peterson Institute for International Economics, July 1, 1999 https://www.piie.com/commentary/speeches-papers/what-should-world-bank-think-about-washington-consensus?ResearchID=351 [accessed 06/04/2023].

30   World Bank, *Accelerated Development in Africa South of the Sahara, Indicative Program of Action* (Washington, DC: World Bank, 1981).

Bank's policy line over a long period. Emphasis was placed on the lack of adequate support given to private initiative and over-reliance on the public sector. The report advocated increased aid for cash crops along with even more reduction of subsistence crops. Elliot Berg and his team felt that on no account should countries aim for nutritional self-sufficiency, for, they wrote, 'most African countries have a distinct comparative advantage in the area of cash crops'. Far better to export tropical products and import other foodstuffs, since 'A policy of self-sufficiency based on sacrificing cash crops would prove costly in terms of lost revenue.' The report criticized foreign aid for having reinforced the public sector!

The Berg report blamed African leaders for most of the misfortunes of Africa while exonerating the international financial institutions and the countries of the North. The report might be seen as the World Bank's answer to the Organization of African Unity's (OAU) Lagos Plan, adopted in 1980. The Bank's management was astonished by the negative reactions to the Berg report, particularly as the African officials at the Bank had approved the report without a murmur. The Bank's directorship was caught off guard and had to ask two external experts to sound out the African leaders as to what they thought of the Bank. The results of the survey confirmed their worst fears: the Bank's image was frankly terrible.

The World Bank historians sharply denounce the Bank's theoretical output during the 1980s and the way the Bank and the IMF shared the roles in this field:

The Bank emerged as the headquarters, the fountainhead – some half-jokingly said the Vatican – of neo-orthodox development economics. It was the most authoritative articulation of the longer-term side of the so-called Washington consensus (the IMF dominated the short run) concerning appropriate relations between states and markets, including international and interacting national economic policies.[31]

TIMID ATTEMPTS AT RESISTANCE ON THE PART OF THE DEVELOPING COUNTRIES

The divide-and-rule strategy drawn up in Washington when the crisis broke out was in full spate. Latin American governments did not have the political will to create a united front to deal with the crisis and the creditors.

In January 1984 there was to be a secret meeting in Cuzco, Peru, between the finance ministers of Argentina, Brazil, Colombia, Mexico and Peru. The plan was to try to agree on a common strategy. The meeting was called off at the last minute due to the sudden resignation of the Peruvian minister, Carlos Rodríguez Pastor, who was to have hosted it. The decision to cancel the meeting came so late in the day that

31   Kapur, Lewis and Webb, *The World Bank: Its First Half Century,* Volume 1, p. 1193.

one of the ministers invited actually arrived at the meeting venue, not having been informed in time.[32]

Richard Webb, one of the World Bank historians, had been governor of the Central Bank of Peru. He reported that in June 1984, Peru was confronted with a dilemma: whether to continue servicing its external debt and cancel imports needed for growth, or whether to go ahead with the imports needed to maintain growth and partially suspend debt repayments. The government had just failed to meet the budget austerity goals demanded by the IMF. As governor of the Central Bank of Peru, Webb suggested that Peru should unilaterally declare a partial moratorium, which caused panic in the government. Webb was accused by the prime minister of the time of 'stabbing the country in the back'. Dismissal proceedings were started against him. He was accused of having destroyed Peru's financial credibility abroad.[33]

When Alan García, then president of Peru, announced in 1985 that henceforth his country would devote no more than 10 per cent of export revenues to repaying the debt, the World Bank made an internal study of the issue and concluded that should García carry out this plan, Peru would be able to manage very well, provided it spent the money saved on bolstering its economy. Obviously, the results of this study were never published.[34]

The Argentine economists Alfredo Eric Calcagno and Alfredo Fernando Calcagno summarized the experiment that Peru carried out starting from August 1985:

In August 1985, the government of president Alan García made known its decision to no longer pay more than the equivalent of 10% of its export revenues, giving priority to multilateral financial organisations. Thus the net transfers which had been negative to the tune of −488 million dollars in 1984 and −595 million in 1985 became positive at 112 million dollars in 1986, 89 million in 1987 and 90 million in 1988. Peru was subjected neither to reprisals nor to trade restrictions, and in 1986 and 1987 it increased its imports by an extraordinary amount (by 44% and 18% respectively) in spite of a fall in exports of 15% in 1986 (these showed a slight recovery in 1987). Concerning external finance, non-payment of the major part of the debt largely compensated for the breaking off of loans from private financiers and the reduction in official and multilateral loans. In 1986 and 1987, the gross domestic product increased by 8.9% and 6.5% respectively, sustained by the fact that more domestic demands were met by national productive capacity and by an increase in imports made affordable by the reduction in outpayments on the debt. However there was a shortage of big investments over

---

32   Ibid., p. 620, note 84.
33   Ibid., p. 615, note 64.
34   Ibid., p. 679.

this period and the dynamizing effects had fizzled out by 1988, when the GDP fell by 7.5% and inflation rose sharply. So in fact Peru's crisis over the subsequent years was linked to problems of internal economic policy rather than external trade sanctions or adverse effects of cutting down on debt repayments. On the contrary, the reduced amounts disbursed for external payments opened up an opportunity that the government failed to make the best use of.[35]

During the 1980s, other Latin American countries totally or partially suspended payments of their external debts for several months,[36] but despite the major campaign led by the Cuban government in 1985, no common strategy was adopted. Fidel Castro told numerous delegates from Latin American political and social movements at the end of an international meeting devoted to debt in August 1985: 'We realized [...] that in the final analysis the watchword of debt cancellation was valid for all countries of the Third World.'[37] The campaign led by Castro on the theme 'The debt is unpayable' was sympathetically received by social organizations and left-wing parties of the continent, but less so by its governments.

Nevertheless, Cuba's 1985 initiative found an echo beyond the borders of Latin America – in Sub-Saharan Africa, for example. The young president of Burkina Faso, Thomas Sankara, made the following address to the African heads of state present at the twenty-fifth conference of the OAU on 29 July 1987 in Addis Ababa:

In debt we see neo-colonialism in another guise, with the colonialists recast as 'technical assistants'. In fact, we should say technical assassins. And they are the ones who offered us funding, and financial backers. [...] Those financial backers were recommended to us, we were advised to turn to them. We were shown enticing files and financial packages. We got ourselves into debt for the fifty, sixty years ahead and even more. In other words, we were persuaded to compromise our people for upwards of fifty years.

The debt in its present form is a carefully organised reconquest of Africa, forcing its growth and development to obey norms which are completely foreign to it. So that each of us will become a financial slave, which means a slave, of those who had the opportunity, the cunning, the dishonesty to place funds at our disposal which we would have to repay. [...]

---

35   Alfredo Eric Calcagno and Alfredo Fernando Calcagno, *El universo neoliberal: recuento de sus lugares communes* (Madrid: Ediciones Akal, Pensamiento crítico, 2015), p. 378.

36   This was the case for Brazil, which suspended external debt payments to banks from January 1987 to January 1988. See Éric Toussaint and Arnaud Zacharie, *Le bateau ivre de la mondialisation: escales au sein du village planétaire* (*The Drunken Boat of Globalization: Ports of Call in the Global Village*) (Brussels/Paris: CADTM/Syllepse, 2000), pp. 67–68 (in French).

37   Transcription of a speech by President Fidel Castro Ruz at the Continental Dialogue on the Foreign Debt held at Havana's Palace of Conventions on 3 August 1985 <cadtm.org/Fidel-Castro-The-debt-is-unpayable> [accessed 27/02/2023].

Who, among us here present, does not wish to see the debt quite simply cancelled? Those who do not wish it can leave, take a plane and go straight to the World Bank and pay up. I would not like Burkina Faso's proposal to be seen as coming from young, immature politicians without experience. Neither would I like people to think that only revolutionaries speak in these terms. I would like them to acknowledge that we are motivated merely by obligation and objectivity.

I can give examples of both revolutionaries and non-revolutionaries, among those who have said we should not pay the debt. I will cite, for example, Fidel Castro. He has already said that we should not pay. He is a lot older than me, even if he is a revolutionary.[38]

Three months later, the impetuous Thomas Sankara was assassinated. After that, his country has become a docile pupil of the World Bank, the IMF and the Paris Club under the leadership of Blaise Compaoré, who participated in Sankara's overthrow and murder.[39]

Jean-Philippe Peemans puts in a nutshell the relationship of complicity between the World Bank, the IMF and the governments of the developing countries that show themselves to be good pupils:

For the South, the role of international institutions like the IMF and the World Bank has been essential in this area, as the governments that do as they are told are guaranteed permanent access to multilateral credit. This guarantees them permanent access to global flows, however much their national economy may contract due to adjustment. These external flows enable capital holders to invest their assets abroad with no trouble, while the debt grows in proportion to their withdrawal of capital.[40]

SHOULD DEBTS BE CANCELLED?

In October 1985, James Baker, the new US Treasury Secretary, announced a plan aiming to solve the problems of 15 heavily indebted middle-income countries.[41] The plan was proclaimed with much media coverage during the annual meeting of the IMF and the World Bank in Seoul.[42] Debt cancellation had yet to be mentioned.

---

38   See the complete text reproduced in Millet, *L'Afrique sans dette*, p. 205 (in French).

39   Following a popular uprising, Blaise Compaoré was forced to resign as president of Burkina Faso on 31 October 2014, after 27 years in power. In 2022 he was condemned to a life sentence for the murder of Thomas Sankara <cadtm.org/Conclusion-of-Sankara-and-Companions-Case-A-Salutary-Trial-But-the-demands-for> [accessed 27/02/2023].

40   Peemans, *Le développement des peuples face à la modernisation du monde*, p. 367.

41   Argentina, Bolivia, Brazil, Chile, Colombia, Ecuador, Ivory Coast, Mexico, Morocco, Nigeria, Peru, the Philippines, Uruguay, Venezuela and Yugoslavia. Kapur, Lewis and Webb, *The World Bank: Its First Half Century, Volume 1*, p. 626, note 101.

42   Concerning the issue of who makes the important decisions, it is significant that the US Treasury informed the World Bank of the existence of the 'Baker Plan' only 48 hours before it was made public.

Inside the World Bank, in a small inner circle, the debate had begun over whether or not it was necessary to cancel part of the debt of certain countries, especially Argentina, but no-one would commit themselves publicly to such a measure. In the draft copy of the *World Development Report 1988* there appeared a sentence on the need for partial cancellation of concessional debt. It did not appear in the final version.[43] Among the arguments against cancellation was one that still comes up over and over again. It is that once a country has benefited from cancellation, it will find it hard to regain access to credit. This argument is and always has been totally fallacious – in fact, the opposite happens. Generally, as soon as a country has benefited from debt reduction, the commercial banks offer to lend it money as its subsequent ability to repay has been improved.

In 1992 Stanley Fisher explained that, throughout a large part of the 1980s, the US, British (Margaret Thatcher) and German (Helmut Kohl) governments prevented any discussion about debt cancellation.[44]

The turning point when debt reduction (i.e. partial cancellation) was at last envisaged came in 1988, at the G7 in Toronto, in recognition of the failure of all previous policies. The poorest countries were promised cancellation once the USA had changed its mind on the subject. For the first time, in 1990 in Houston, the G7 extended the possibility of partial cancellation to heavily indebted middle-income countries like Mexico, Argentina, Brazil and the Philippines. This change of heart was initiated by Washington in March 1989 under the George H.W. Bush administration while Nicholas Brady was Secretary of the Treasury. Once again, the US government set the tone. The IMF, the World Bank and the G7 simply went along with it.

The Brady Plan consisted of restructuring part of the debt of a series of middle-income countries through the issue of new debt paper called 'Brady bonds'. When the indebted countries issued their Brady bonds, bankers of the North accepted a reduction of their credit. In exchange, they were guaranteed generous returns. To issue Brady bonds, the countries concerned first had to buy US Treasury bonds as a guarantee. The indebted countries thus found themselves financing the policy of indebtedness of the world's most powerful country.[45]

At first, the Brady Plan seemed to work. The successful outcome for Mexico and its president Salinas de Gortari was much celebrated, to the extent that in 1994 the very neoliberal British weekly, *The Economist*, proclaimed Salinas de Gortari to be one of the great men of the twentieth century. In December of that same year,

---

43 Kapur, Lewis and Webb, *The World Bank: Its First Half Century, Volume 1*, p. 648, note 179.
44 'The US squelched research on this [debt] issue during the mid-80's. One of my reasons for going to the Bank was that I believed the debt issue was about to come to a head. [...] [W]e had to keep research quiet, because the institution was under political orders (not only from the US, also the Germans, and the Brits) not to raise issues of debt relief.' Letter, Stanley Fisher to Nicholas Stern, 19 May 1992, in ibid., p. 1195.
45 This phenomenon has continued to grow.

Mexico was struck down by the Tequila Crisis and went into its deepest recession in 60 years! A few years later, Carlos Salinas de Gortari and his brother Raúl were prosecuted and charged with fraud and massive embezzlement by the Mexican judiciary. Raúl Salinas de Gortari served his prison sentence while Carlos chose exile in Ireland, where he works for the Dow Jones Corporation, which among other things is publisher of the *Wall Street Journal*. The Mexican judicial authorities managed to get their opposite numbers in Switzerland to order Swiss banks to cede back to Mexico the money embezzled by the Salinas brothers and deposited in their coffers.

By the second half of the 1990s, it was clear that the 1982 debt crisis had not been resolved. Measures to reduce the debt had failed. Structural adjustment policies had made countries vulnerable to financial speculation. This led to a succession of financial crises for the major indebted countries. Mexico was the first to be affected at the end of 1994, then the countries of South-East Asia and Korea in 1997–98, Russia in 1998, Brazil in 1999 and in 2000–01 Argentina and Turkey. As for the poorest countries, the partial cancellation of debt conceded to a few good pupils at the G7 summit in Toronto in 1988, and to a few more in London in 1991, Naples in 1994, Lyon in 1996 and Cologne in 1999, has not provided any lasting solution.

16

Presidents Barber Conable
and Lewis Preston (1986–95)

BARBER CONABLE'S TERM OF OFFICE (1986–91)

The Republican congressman Barber Conable succeeded the banker Alden W. Clausen for a term that started in July 1986 and ended in August 1991. James Baker, Secretary of the Treasury, and Ronald Reagan chose Conable because of his thorough knowledge of all the mysteries of the US Congress. At the time, the US Executive had its hands full with its legislative majority since several Republican representatives questioned the weight of the World Bank in US foreign policy (see chapter 5). Barber Conable had 20 years' experience in Congress and had long been the ranking Republican member of the Ways and Means Committee. James Baker and Ronald Reagan wanted Barber Conable to appease the recalcitrant Republicans and persuade them to let the White House steer the World Bank.

The issue was complex and Conable soon found himself in a precarious situation. While he wished to expand the World Bank's activities, the White House made some concessions to the recalcitrant elements, limited the resources granted to the World Bank and demanded that Conable reduce its expenditures. When he did this a number of senior executives and all of the staff turned against him. In 1987 the internal reorganization of the Bank was a veritable game of musical chairs. Several top managers resigned.[1]

Conable also met other obstacles. Several of the Bank's large-scale model projects were challenged by the concerned populations and by environmental associations. The three projects that prompted the most determined protests were the Polonoroeste programme in Brazilian Amazonia,[2] the various dams on the River Narmada in India, and the transmigration project and the Kedung Ombo dam in Indonesia.[3] The largest demonstration occurred in India, where some 50,000 people from all parts of the country marched in the city of Harsud (Madhya Pradesh) in September 1989. A fourth World Bank programme also raised strong opposition from human rights organizations, namely the Ruzizi II hydroelectric project that concerned Zaire (as the DRC was then called) and Rwanda and involved the

---

1   Kapur, Lewis and Webb, *The World Bank: Its First Half Century, Volume 1*, pp. 1199–1201.
2   Chico Mendès, one of the leaders of the Brazilian protest, was assassinated in December 1988 by hired assassins in the pay of big landowners who profited from World Bank subsidies.
3   Rich, *Mortgaging the Earth*, pp. 145–70.

displacement of some 2,500 farmers without any significant compensation.[4] Barber Conable promised that the World Bank would in the future take environmental impacts into account and would see to it that affected people would receive decent compensation.[5] This was truly a titanic task since in India alone the World Bank financed 32 projects involving the displacement of some 600,000 people from 1978 to 1990.[6]

In 1988 the World Bank and IMF annual meeting in West Berlin was greeted by 80,000 demonstrators who denounced their antisocial policies. This was the first mass demonstration against the Bretton Woods institutions.

The uprisings triggered by the policy of structural adjustment and the consequent deterioration in the 'adjusted' peoples' standards of living in the countries concerned led the World Bank to mention the issue of poverty after ten years of silence. The 1990 *World Development Report* is entirely devoted to it.

It was also with Barber Conable as president that the Bank started to systematically refer to 'good governance'. In 1990 Conable told a number of African governors of the Bank:

Let me be frank: political uncertainty and arbitrary rule in so many sub-Saharan African countries are major obstacles to their development. [...] In saying this, I'm not talking politics. Rather, I'm speaking as a defender of increased openness and responsibility, of respect for human rights and the rule of law. Governability is linked to economic development. Donor countries are increasingly indicating that they will cease to back inefficient systems which do not meet the population's basic needs.[7]

This change in the Bank's policy reflects the change in Washington's policy towards the end of the 1980s. It is analyzed in chapter 11 on Korea. The Bank's rhetoric about law and human rights was never an obstacle to its imposing harsh conditionalities on countries under structural adjustment. Nor did its posturing prevent it from supporting dictatorships such as Suharto's in Indonesia until 1998, or the dictatorships of Ben Ali in Tunisia and Mubarak in Egypt until they were ousted by the people in January 2011, or the regime of Marshal Idriss Déby in Chad (in power following a coup in 1990 until his death in April 2021), or that of Paul Biya in Cameroon (in power since 1982 and still in power as these lines are being written).

LEWIS PRESTON'S TERM OF OFFICE (1991–95)

With the appointment of Lewis Preston as president of the World Bank in 1991, President George H.W. Bush again placed a top-shelf banker at the helm of the institution. Lewis Preston had up to then been CEO of J.P. Morgan and Co. He had

---

4   Ibid., p. 150.
5   The World Bank's policy regarding the environment will be analyzed in chapter 21.
6   Rich, *Mortgaging the Earth*, p. 252.
7   Quoted by Carol Lancaster, 'Governance and development: the views from Washington', Institute of Development Studies, *IDS Bulletin*, January 1993, Vol. 24, No. 1, p. 10.

had a remarkable career at the head of this leading New York bank, allowing him to take full advantage of the debt crisis that broke in 1982.

Lewis Preston's term began in June 1991 with the huge political and financial scandal of the Bank of Credit and Commerce International's (BCCI) bankruptcy, which came close to directly implicating the World Bank. Specializing as it did in money-laundering, the BCCI was closed by order of the British authorities in July 1991. Its closure is said to have resulted in the loss of some $20 billion for two million small savers. The BCCI was convicted of the following crimes: involvement in money-laundering, bribery, support of terrorism, arms trafficking, the sale of nuclear technologies, committing and facilitating tax evasion, smuggling, illegal immigration, and illicit purchases in the banking and real-estate sectors. The BCCI was present in 78 countries with over 400 branches, and was closely related to the CIA.[8] Bruce Rich writes that the World Bank had occasionally used the BCCI for the disbursement of loans in African countries. He also establishes that several of the Bank's senior officers had close relationships with the BCCI's senior officers.[9]

Lewis Preston gave his first major speech on the occasion of a huge media circus staged by the World Bank and the IMF in Bangkok for their joint annual meeting in October 1991 (this was the first meeting held in a Third World country since Seoul in 1985). Fifteen thousand bankers and political leaders from all over the world met there for three days. The cost for the Thai authorities amounted to tens of millions in USD. Lewis Preston gave an enthusiastic speech supporting globalization and asserting that the Bank was close to poor people, attentive to environmental issues and committed to improving the lot of women. Here is a short excerpt: 'Poverty reduction, to which I personally am fully committed, remains the World Bank Group's overarching objective [...] The World Bank Group takes into account the interest of the poor so that growth is equitable; environmental aspects so that development is sustainable [...] and the role of women who are vital to the development effort.'[10] The future was bright, since the world had become one after the fall of the Berlin Wall.[11] The challenge posed by the Bank was to include all East European countries in the globalized world. A few hundred yards away from where the meeting was held, 20,000 people demonstrated against the new dictatorship that had been established in Thailand eight months earlier and demanded a return to democracy.[12]

---

8   See the complete report, 'The BCCI affair', devoted to the BCCI in 1992 by Senators John Kerry and Hank Brown: <irp.fas.org/congress/1992_rpt/bcci/> [accessed 14/12/2021]. See also *Wikipedia* on the BCCI.

9   Rich, *Mortgaging the Earth*, pp. 21–22.

10 Address by Lewis T. Preston to the Board of Governors of the World Bank Group, World Bank press release, 15 October 1991.

11 It should be noted that at the time when Lewis Preston was making his address, the end of the USSR was imminent. The final thrust in favour of the dissolution of the USSR came from Boris Yeltsin in August 1991 in Moscow. The USSR was dissolved in December 1991.

12 Rich, *Mortgaging the Earth*, p. 24.

In December 1991 Lawrence H. Summers, the World Bank's chief economist, wrote a confidential memorandum on the 1992 *World Development Report* (which was being drafted). The report was entirely devoted to the environment, in view of the Earth Summit due to be held in May 1992. Summers argued for exporting polluting industries to countries of the South – which, he said, are 'vastly underpolluted' – as a rational means of creating industrial development while alleviating the pressures of pollution in the North. Here are some excerpts from Summers' memorandum:

Just between you and me, shouldn't the World Bank be encouraging MORE migration of the dirty industries to the LDCs [Least Developed Countries]?
[...] the economic logic behind dumping a load of toxic waste in the lowest wage countries is impeccable and we should face up to that.[13]

A favourable wind took this document to the environmental organization Greenpeace, which immediately made it public. The British neoliberal weekly *The Economist* published it at the end of December 1991,[14] just when Lewis Preston was beginning his first tour of Africa. He was set upon by journalists asking whether he approved of his chief economist writing: 'I've always thought that under-populated countries in Africa are vastly under-polluted.'[15]

In February 1992 Willi Wapenhans, the Bank's vice-president, handed Lewis Preston a confidential assessment report on all projects financed by the Bank (almost 1,300 projects in progress in 113 countries). Its conclusions were alarming: 37.5 per cent of projects proved unsatisfactory when completed (as against 15 per cent in 1981), and only 22 per cent of the financial commitments conformed to the Bank's instructions.

In May 1992, a few days before the beginning of the Earth Summit, the Bank's management received the results of the independent survey on the River Narmada dams in India. Lewis Preston had entrusted US Representative Bradford Morse with coordinating the survey. The report considered that the dams and canals would result in 240,000 displaced persons, and not 100,000 as originally foreseen. Such conclusions caused panic among the World Bank's directors. The report had to be kept secret until the Earth Summit was over. That goal was achieved.

The World Bank did very well at the Earth Summit, held in Rio de Janeiro and attended by 118 heads of state. The event was covered by some 9,000 journalists. At its end the Bank was entrusted with management of the Global Environment Facility (GEF) – the global fund for the environment through which the majority

---

13   Lawrence H. Summers, World Bank office memorandum, 12 December 1991, quoted by Rich, *Mortgaging the Earth*, p. 247.
14   The British daily *Financial Times* devoted a long article written by Michael Prowse to the subject on 10 February 1992; its title was 'Save the Planet Earth from economists'.
15   Summers, World Bank office memorandum, 12 December 1991.

of funding related to Agenda 21, adopted at the end of the global meeting, was to transit.

The World Bank would also support the transition of countries from the former Eastern bloc to a capitalist economy. This resulted in a large-scale sell-off of public companies that were privatized and given over to a new class of mostly mafiosi capitalists.

Joseph Stiglitz, the Bank's chief economist from 1997 to 2000, shows very clearly that the Bank's policy in Russia was far removed from the good governance it otherwise advocated. About the time when Lewis Preston was president of the Bank, Stiglitz writes:

It is not surprising that many of the market reformers showed a remarkable affinity to the old ways of doing business: in Russia, President Yeltsin,[16] with enormously greater powers than his counterparts in any Western democracy, was encouraged to circumvent the democratically elected Duma (parliament) and to enact market reforms by decree.[17]

Public companies were sold for peanuts: 'pressured by the United States, the World Bank and the IMF to privatize rapidly, [the Russian government] had turned over its state assets for a pittance'.[18]

Privatization was a large-scale looting of the country for the benefit of oligarchs who invested part of their pilferage in the West in order to launder it and remove it from the reach of the law. 'Privatization accompanied by the opening of the capital markets, led not to wealth creation but to asset stripping. It was perfectly logical. An oligarch, who has just been able to use political influence to garner assets worth billions, after paying only a pittance, would naturally want to get his money out of the country.'[19]

During Lewis Preston's mandate the World Bank and the IMF celebrated their fiftieth anniversary in Madrid in great style. On this occasion a large coalition of social movements (among them the main trade-union federations in Spain, UGT and CCOO), Third World movements, the CADTM and NGOs came together under the name 'Other Voices of the Planet' and organized a four-day conference with many debates and a demonstration by some 20,000 people who chanted 'Fifty years is enough.'

The end of Lewis Preston's term was marked by the Tequila Crisis that hit Mexico from December 1994. Mexico's was the first in a series of financial crises that would hit other emerging countries during the term of the next president, James Wolfensohn.

---

16   Boris Yelstin was president of Russia from 1992 to 1999. The situation that Joseph Stiglitz describes occurred in 1993.
17   Joseph E. Stiglitz, *Globalization and its Discontents* (London: Allen Lane, 2002), p. 136.
18   Ibid., pp. 144–45.
19   Ibid., p. 144.

17

Rwanda: The Genocide's Financiers

It is essential to examine the role played by the international funding bodies in the genocide that occurred in Rwanda in 1994. Everything suggests that the process leading up to the genocide was accelerated by policies imposed by the international financial institutions, the main funding bodies of General Juvénal Habyarimana's dictatorial regime. As a rule, the negative impact of these policies is not taken into consideration in explaining the tragic outcome of the Rwanda crisis.

From 7 April 1994, within less than three months, almost a million of Rwanda's citizens – the exact figure is still to be assessed – were exterminated because they were or were supposed to be of the Tutsi ethnic group, along with tens of thousands of moderate Hutus. It was indeed a genocide, i.e. the planned and targeted destruction of a whole community through mass murder with the objective of preventing it from reproducing itself biologically and socially.

As a rule, the negative impact of the policies recommended by the IMF and the World Bank is not taken into consideration to explain the tragic outcome of the Rwandan crisis. Only a handful of scholars highlight the responsibility of the Bretton Woods institutions, which systematically reject all criticism on this score.[1]

At the beginning of the 1980s, when the Third World debt crisis broke out, Rwanda (like its neighbour Burundi) had an extremely low level of indebtedness. Elsewhere in the world, the World Bank and the IMF jettisoned their policy of active lending, preaching austerity instead. In Rwanda, they adopted a different approach, and began to lend large amounts. Rwanda's foreign debt increased twentyfold between 1976 and 1994. In 1976, it stood at $49 million; by 1994, it had reached more than $1 billion. Most of this increase occurred after 1982. The country's main creditors were the World Bank, the IMF and related institutions (collectively called 'the international financial institutions' or IFI). The World Bank and the IMF played the most active role. In 2001, they held 87 per cent of Rwanda's foreign debt.

---

1   See Michel Chossudovsky, 'Economic genocide in Rwanda,' *Economic and Political Weekly*, 13 April 1996, Vol. 31, No. 15, pp. 938–41; Michel Chossudovsky and Pierre Galand, 'The 1994 Rwandan Genocide – the use of Rwanda's external debt (1990–1994). The responsibility of donors and creditors,' CADTM, 2016 <cadtm.org/The-1994-Rwandan-Genocide-The-Use> [accessed 27/02/2023]; Michel Chossudovsky et al., 'Rwanda, Somalie, ex Yougoslavie: conflits armés, génocide économique et responsabilités des institutions de Bretton Woods' ('Rwanda, Somalia, ex-Yugoslavia: armed conflicts, economic genocide and responsibilities of the Bretton Woods institutions'), in *Banque, FMI, OMC: ça suffit!* (Brussels: CADTM, 1995) (in French); Renaud Duterme, *Rwanda: une histoire volée* (*Rwanda's Stolen History*) (Brussels: Editions Tribord–CADTM, 2013) (in French).

Table 17.1   Evolution of Rwanda's public foreign debt by creditors (USD million)

	1980		1985		1990		1995	
Multilateral debt	91	60%	232	71%	542	82%	814	84%
Bilateral debt	52	35%	85	26%	119	18%	157	16%
Private debt	8	5%	12	4%	4	0.5%	2	0.2%
Total public foreign debt	150	100%	329	100%	664	100%	972	100%
	2000		2010		2019			
Multilateral debt	997	87%	639	84%	2,958	76%		
Bilateral debt	150	13%	120	16%	486	12%		
Private debt	1	0.1%	nc	nc	464	12%		
Total public foreign debt	1,148	100%	759	100%	3,908	100%		

Source: worldbank.org, *International Debt Statistics* <databank.worldbank.org/source/international-debt-statistics> [accessed 23/01/2022]

In 2019, 25 years after the genocide, Rwanda's debt to the IFI had more than tripled (see Table 17.1).

The dictatorial regime in place since 1973 was a guarantee against progressive structural change. For this reason, it received the active backing of Western powers, particularly Belgium, France and Switzerland. Moreover, it acted as a bulwark against those states in the region that sought to protect their independence and effect progressive change (for example neighbouring Tanzania under the progressive president Julius Nyerere, one of the African leaders of the Non-Aligned Movement).

Between 1980 and 1994, Rwanda received large amounts in loan money; the Habyarimana dictatorship channelled a significant share of this money into its own coffers. The loans were meant to help Rwanda participate more fully in the world economy by developing its exports of coffee, tea and tin (its three major export products), to the detriment of crops for domestic consumption. This model worked until the mid-1980s, when tin prices collapsed – soon followed by coffee and tea prices. When the US broke up the coffee cartel in the early 1990s, the Rwandan economy, for which coffee was the main source of hard currency, was devastated.

INTERNATIONAL LOANS USED TO PREPARE THE GENOCIDE

A few weeks before the Rwandan Patriotic Front (RPF) launched its October 1990 offensive, the Rwandan authorities signed an agreement with the IMF and the World Bank to implement a structural adjustment plan.

The SAP was implemented in November 1990, one of the first measures being a 67 per cent devaluation of the Rwandan franc. In exchange, the IMF provided credit in the form of quick disbursing loans to enable the country to maintain the flow of imports. As a result, the country was able to redress its balance of payments. There was a meteoric rise in the price of imported goods; petrol went up by 79 per cent.

Earnings from the sale of imported goods on the domestic market enabled the government to pay the wages of the armed forces, whose ranks were growing rapidly in size. The SAP prescribed a drop in public spending; there were indeed wage freezes and dismissals in the public sector, but part of the savings were transferred over to the armed forces.

While import prices soared, the price at which coffee was bought from local producers was frozen, as required by the IMF. As a result, hundreds of thousands of small coffee farmers were ruined.[2] These farmers, alongside the poorest sectors of the urban population, became a permanent reservoir of recruits for the Interahamwe militia and the army.

The measures imposed by the World Bank and the IMF as part of the structural adjustment plan included increased taxes on consumption and lower business taxes, increased direct taxes on low-income households through a reduction in tax allowances for large families, and cuts in lending programmes for small farmers.

To account for the amounts loaned by the World Bank and the IMF, Rwanda was allowed to present old invoices for imported goods. This system enabled the regime to finance massive arms purchases to be used in the genocide. Military spending tripled between 1990 and 1992.[3] The World Bank and the IMF sent several delegations of experts during this period; they highlighted certain positive features of Habyarimana's austerity policies but nonetheless threatened to suspend credit unless military spending stopped increasing. The Rwandan government then developed ways of hiding rising military spending: lorries imported for the army were put on the Transport Ministry's account; a significant share of the petrol used for militia and army vehicles was put on the Health Ministry's account; and so on. Finally, the World Bank and the IMF suspended credit at the beginning of 1993 – neglecting, however, to freeze the large sums of money held in accounts in foreign banks, which the regime used to buy arms. It can be argued that the Washington-based institutions failed in their duty to monitor the way in which loan money was used. They should have suspended credit in early 1992, as soon as they realized that the money was being used for arms purchases. They should have alerted the UN. By continuing to provide financing until early 1993, they helped a regime that was preparing to commit genocide. Since 1991, human rights organizations had been reporting and condemning the massacres that paved the way to genocide. The World Bank and the IMF systematically helped the dictatorship, since it was an ally of the USA, France and Belgium.

---

2   Jozef Maton, *Développement économique et social au Rwanda entre 1980 et 1993 : Le dixième décile en face de l'Apocalypse* (*Economic and Social Development in Rwanda between 1980 and 1993: The Tenth Decile Facing Apocalypse*) (Ghent: State University of Ghent, Faculty of Economics, Unit for Development Research and Teaching, November 1994) (in French).

3   Marie-Chantal Nduhungirehe, *Les programmes d'ajustement structurel: spécificité et application au cas du Rwanda* (*Structural Adjustment Programmes: Specificity and Application in the Case of Rwanda*), *Licence* thesis, University of Louvain, Faculté de Sciences économiques, 1995.

RISING SOCIAL CONFLICT

For the genocide to be perpetrated, more was required than a regime that had merely developed a blueprint and equipped itself with the necessary hardware. It was also necessary to have an impoverished population, a population that had been 'lumpenized', prepared to go out and kill. In Rwanda, 90 per cent of the population live in the countryside, and 20 per cent of peasant families owned less than half an acre. Between 1982 and 1994, there had been a process of large-scale impoverishment of the majority of the rural population while, at the same time, a tiny section of the population had grown fabulously rich. According to Jozef Maton, in 1982, the wealthiest 10 per cent of the population earned 20 per cent of rural revenues; in 1992, that figure had risen to 41 per cent, in 1993, 45 per cent and by the beginning of 1994, 51 per cent.[4] The disastrous social impact of policies dictated by the IMF and World Bank, and the fall in coffee prices on the global market (a fall linked to the policies of the Bretton Woods institutions and the USA), played a central role in the Rwandan crisis. The massive social discontent was channelled by the Habyarimana regime into implementing its plan for genocide.

THE GENOCIDE'S CREDITORS

Between 1990 and 1994, Rwanda's main arms suppliers were France, Belgium, South Africa, Egypt and the People's Republic of China. China also provided 500,000 machetes. Egypt – whose vice-foreign minister responsible for relations with the African continent was none other than Boutros Boutros-Ghali – granted Rwanda a $6 million interest-free loan in 1991 to purchase arms for its infantry divisions. Once the genocide had begun, France and the British firm Mil-Tec provided arms to the rampaging army via Goma airport across the border in Zaire – violating the 11 May 1994 UN embargo on arms sales to Rwanda. Once the Rwandan capital, Kigali, had been overrun by the RPF opposition, several key leaders of the genocide were received by the French president. Rwandan leaders-in-exile set up the head office of the Banque Nationale du Rwanda in Goma with the help of the French army. Until August 1994, the bank disbursed funds to repay debts for previous arms purchases and to buy new arms. Private banks (Belgolaise, Générale de Banque, BNP, and Dresdner Bank, among others) accepted payment orders from those responsible for the genocide and repaid those who had financed the genocide.

RWANDA AFTER THE GENOCIDE

After the fall of the dictatorship in July 1994, the World Bank and the IMF demanded that the new Rwandan government limit the number of public-sector employees to 50 per cent of the number agreed upon before the genocide. The new government

---

4   Maton, *Développement économique et social au Rwanda entre 1980 et 1993*.

complied. Initial financial assistance provided by the USA and Belgium in late 1994 went towards repaying the Habyarimana regime's debt arrears with the World Bank. Financial aid from the West was barely trickling into a country that urgently needed to be rebuilt. The government took back more than 800,000 returning refugees beginning in November 1996. According to David Woodward's report for Oxfam,[5] while agricultural production did recover somewhat in 1996, it was still 38 per cent lower than normal for first harvests and 28 per cent for second harvests. Industry was taking longer to recover: only 54 out of 88 industrial concerns in operation before April 1994 had resumed activity. Most were operating well below previous levels: by the end of 1995, the total added value of industrial production was 47 per cent of its 1990 levels.

A 20 per cent wage increase in the public sector in January 1996 was the first such rise since 1981. Official estimates, however, are that 80 per cent of public-sector workers lived below the poverty line. It comes as no surprise that Rwandans preferred to work in NGOs as drivers and cooks rather than in the public sector. These poverty statistics were not specific to the public sector: in 1996, the World Bank estimated that 85 to 95 per cent of Rwandans lived below the threshold of absolute poverty. It should be noted that there has been a significant increase in the number of households run by women: from 21.7 per cent before the genocide to 29.3 per cent in 1996, with peaks of 40 per cent in some districts. Their situation is particularly disturbing in view of the profound discrimination against women in such matters as inheritance, access to credit and property rights. Even before the genocide, 35 per cent of women heads of households earned less than 5,000 Rwandan francs (about $15) per month; the corresponding percentage of men was 22 per cent. In spite of a high rate of adoption of orphans (whose parents had been killed in the genocide or died of AIDS), there were between 95,000 and 150,000 children without families. In the education system, only 65 per cent of children were enrolled in primary schools; and no more than 8 per cent in secondary schools.[6] According to the World Bank, the number of pupils completing primary school went down from 34 per cent in 1990 to 28 per cent in 2001.[7] The infant mortality rate remained particularly high (183 per 1,000).

In 1994, Rwanda's foreign debt had reached nearly $1 billion, the totality of which had been contracted by the Habyarimana regime. Ten years later, the debt had increased by about 15 per cent and Rwanda was still under structural adjustment. The debt contracted before 1994 fits the definition of odious debt perfectly; it follows that the new regime should have been totally exonerated from paying it off.

---

5   David Woodward, *The IMF, the World Bank and Economic Policy in Rwanda: Economic and Social Implications* (Oxford: Oxford University Press, 1996).

6   Ibid.

7   World Bank, *World Development Indicators 2003* <openknowledge.worldbank.org/handle/10986/13920> [accessed 17/12/2021].

The multilateral and bilateral creditors knew very well who they were dealing with when they lent money to Habyarimana's regime. After the change of regime, there was not the slightest justification for transferring their claims onto the new Rwanda. Nevertheless, they did it without any misgivings. This is downright outrageous.

The new Rwandan government that came into power in 1994 tried to persuade the World Bank and the IMF to renounce their claims. The two institutions refused, threatening to cut off funding if Kigali persisted. They put pressure on Kigali to keep quiet about the aid they had provided to the Habyarimana regime, in exchange for new loans and a promise of future debt cancellation as part of the initiative in favour of the Heavily Indebted Poor Countries (HIPC), launched in 1996. One can only deplore that the government should have accepted such blackmail. The consequences are pernicious: continued structural adjustment, with its disastrous social and economic consequences, and an unsustainable and odious foreign debt. In complying, the government of Kigali has gained 'good pupil' status in the eyes of the IMF, the World Bank and the Paris Club. Worse still, the Rwandan regime has become the accomplice of the USA and the UK, whose policy is to weaken the Democratic Republic of Congo, by taking part, as of August 1998, in the military occupation of its neighbour country and the plundering of its natural resources.

18
James Wolfensohn Switches on the Charm (1995–2005)

James Wolfensohn became president of the World Bank at a point in time when restoring its public image had become an urgent necessity. Structural adjustment policies were getting very bad press and a series of financial crises were starting to hit the developing countries. It was necessary to quickly draw attention away by again promoting the terms 'poverty reduction' and 'good governance' and providing loans for environmentally responsible projects. There was an onslaught of PR, and Wolfensohn became an expert in dealing with the press. His charm and eloquence made a very good impression.

In 1995, Bill Clinton, then president of the United States, appointed James Wolfensohn, a New York banker, as the World Bank's ninth president.

Wolfensohn (1933–2020), born an Australian, began his banking career in Sydney in 1959. From 1968 to 1977 he was one of the directors of the highly controversial London and New York banking group J. Henry Schroder.[1] According to Patrick Bond,[2] James Wolfensohn was the treasurer of the 'American Friends of Bilderberg', an anti-communist pressure group.[3] He left the Schroder Bank to become an executive partner in the investment bank Salomon Brothers. In 1980–81, Robert McNamara was looking for a successor, and Wolfensohn,

---

1 The Schroder Bank financed Hitler and the SS from the 1920s through to the fall of the Third Reich. The bank later became a base for Allen Dulles, who became director of the CIA. The Schroder Bank was involved in financing several coups d'état – the overthrow of Iranian prime minister Mohammad Mossadegh in 1953, the military putsch against Jacobo Árbenz in Guatemala in 1954, the Bay of Pigs invasion of Cuba in 1961, covert action in Chile between 1970 and 1973, and then Augusto Pinochet's military junta in that country.

2 Patrick Bond, *Elite Transition: From Apartheid to Neoliberalism in South Africa* (London/Sterling, VA: Pluto Press and Pietermaritzburg: University of Natal Press, 2000), p. 164.

3 The Bilderberg Conference is an annual conference that brings together, by invitation only, some 130 of the world's most influential bankers, economists and politicians – who call themselves 'Bilderbergers', or the 'Bilderberg Group'. Their initial aim, in the context of the Cold War, was to reinforce cooperation between the United States and their European allies in their opposition to communism, and also to create a united front to combat nationalist uprisings in the colonies. The aims of the Bilderberg Group have moved on to promoting ultra-liberalism. It is of course resolutely transatlantist. The Bilderberg Group's meetings never reach the media. At its beginnings, the group was financed by the Dutch firm Unilever and the CIA. James Wolfensohn participated in the May 2005 meeting in good company (Pascal Lamy, John Bolton and Robert Zoellick). In 1973, the Trilateral Commission was founded by key members of the Bilderberg Group and of the Council on Foreign Relations, such as David Rockefeller and Henry Kissinger.

who was thought to be on the list, became a US citizen so as to better qualify for the post.[4] However, President Ronald Reagan nominated Alden W. Clausen as president of the World Bank, and Wolfensohn founded his own investment bank, James D. Wolfensohn Inc., which was a very active player in the flurry of mergers and acquisitions of the 1980s and through the first half of the 1990s before being bought by Bankers Trust.

PLAYING TO THE GALLERY[5]

The HIPC Initiative

The Heavily Indebted Poor Countries (HIPC) initiative was launched in 1996, its aim being to offset the increasing demands for cancellation of developing countries' debts. With lavish media support, the Bank announced 'its' solution. There was immediately much criticism of the basic concept of the HIPC initiative and its ability to actually reach the goals or fulfil the aims it announced. At the end of Wolfensohn's tenure, its failure was patently obvious. Instead of the 42 countries which were supposed to benefit from cancellation of up to 80 per cent of their debt as announced in 1996, or even 90 per cent as was said in June 1999 at the G8 in Cologne, by the time Wolfensohn's term of office ended in May 2005, in fact only 18 countries would see some reduction in their debt. While it was supposed to be the ultimate solution to the problem of debt for these 42 countries, the initiative had turned into a fiasco. Their debt decreased from $218 to $205 billion, a reduction of only 6 per cent, between 1996 and 2003.

From SAPs to PRSPs

Wolfensohn introduced the Poverty Reduction Strategy Programmes (PRSPs) to replace the much-discredited Structural Adjustment Plans (SAPs) that had been the Bank's and IMF's main approach to development since the 1980s. But in fact, only the name changed – the macroeconomic framework of privatization and liberalization remained the same. The World Bank and the IMF actually imposed more stringent conditions on their loans, because they were now working hand in hand with the WTO, which came into existence in 1995. At the same time, the much-vaunted 'participation' of civil society – which was presented by the World Bank as a profound policy change – is very difficult to find or observe in reality.

---

4   Global Policy Forum, 'Who is James Wolfensohn?' <globalpolicy.org/socecon/bwi-wto/wolfsohn.htm> [accessed 17/12/2021].

5   The balance of this chapter is based on Walden Bello and Shalmali Guttal, 'The limits of reform: the Wolfensohn era at the World Bank', *Focus on the Global South*, 25 April 2005 <focusweb.org/the-limits-of-reform-the-wolfensohn-era-at-the-world-bank/> [accessed 15/11/2021] (also available at CADTM.org).

The SAPRI initiative

The very first 'constructive engagement' exercise James Wolfensohn committed the Bank to was a three-way assessment of structural adjustment plans between the Bank, civil society and the governments called the SAPRI (Structural Adjustment Participatory Review Initiative) which was launched in 1997. SAPRI was designed as a tripartite field-based exercise, with a Bank team appointed by Wolfensohn to develop a transparent and participatory global methodology for gathering and documenting evidence of the impacts of World Bank–IMF SAPs at local and national levels in seven countries. Walden Bello and Shalmali Guttal are devastating in their criticism:

Despite agreement on the common rules of the exercise and the review methodology, the World Bank team played an obstructionist role throughout the SAPRI process. For example, at public fora, instead of trying to listen to and learn from the evidence presented by civil society representatives about the impacts of SAPs, Bank staff almost always argued points and in the end, claimed that the fora presentations (which were part of the agreed-upon qualitative input) constituted 'anecdotal evidence.' [...]

As the Bank's ability to control country processes decreased, so also did its ability to control the output of the Review. Even before the final and concluding national fora were reached, field investigations already indicated major problems in all aspects of adjustment programmes [...] Reluctant to go public with these findings, the Bank team backed off from an earlier (written) agreement to present all SAPRI findings in a large public forum in Washington DC, with Wolfensohn present. Instead, the Bank team insisted on a closed technical meeting and a small session in Washington DC scheduled when Wolfensohn was not in town. Most important, the Bank now insisted that it and civil society each write separate reports. The Bank report used the Bank's own commissioned research as the basis for its conclusions and barely referred to the five-year SAPRI process. In August 2001, the Bank pulled out of SAPRI and buried the entire exercise, and except to say that it had learned a lot from SAPRI, the Bank did not commit itself to reshaping its lending policies based on the SAPRI findings.

On 15 April 2002, the full SAPRI report (under the name SAPRIN,[6] to include findings from the two countries where civil society conducted investigations without Bank involvement) was released to the public and received immense media coverage. [...]

[Wolfensohn] expressed regrets that he and his staff had not been in touch with SAPRI and promised to read the report and discuss it seriously in the near

---

6   Structural Adjustment Participatory Review International Network.

future. To date, however, neither the Bank, nor Wolfensohn have shown any commitment to review and make changes to their adjustment lending. On the contrary, structural adjustment policies continue to be the mainstay of Bank–Fund lending through PRSPs and the Poverty Reduction and Growth Facility (PRGF).[7]

Corruption scandals

The World Bank's stated aim of promoting 'good governance' was very much contradicted by the revelations which came to the fore following the Asian crisis. The Bank's relationship with the corrupt Suharto dictatorship in Indonesia continued well into the Wolfensohn era. According to Jeffrey Winters, a specialist on Indonesia, the Bank accepted erroneous statistics and tolerated the fact that 30 per cent of every dollar in aid it dispensed to the regime was siphoned off by corrupt individuals.

In Sub-Saharan Africa,

[t]he Bank took more hits as news of corruption and malpractice came to light in Bank supported infrastructure projects. Prominent among these were the Lesotho Highlands Water Project (LHWP) and the Bujagali Falls dam in Uganda. In 2001, the Lesotho High Court started investigating charges of bribery against several major international dam-building companies and public officials in connection with the LHWP. Instead of supporting a nationally accountable legal process, the Bank quietly conducted its own internal investigation of three of the companies charged with paying bribes and concluded that there was insufficient evidence to punish them for corruption. In 2002, the Lesotho High Court eventually succeeded in convicting four companies for paying bribes, among them Acres International, a long term ally and pet contractor of the World Bank and who the Bank had cleared in its internal investigation. It took the Bank well over a year to eventually announce that it would disbar Acres International from World Bank contracts for a period of three years.[8]

The World Commission on Dams (WCD)

Established in 1997, the World Commission on Dams was to conduct a comprehensive and independent global review of the effectiveness of large dams for development and to propose internationally acceptable standards for such projects. Over a period of two and a half years, the WCD commissioned a massive volume of research and received nearly 1,000 submissions from around the world on the environmental, social, economic, technical and institutional aspects around the performance of large dams.

---

7   Bello and Guttal, 'The limits of reform: the Wolfensohn era at the World Bank'.
8   Ibid.

Although the WCD worked independently from the World Bank, the Bank played a more active role in the development of the WCD report than any other institution and was consulted at every stage of the WCD's work programme. James Wolfensohn applauded the WCD process as a model for future multi-stakeholder dialogues. However, the inadmissible happened: the Bank rejected the report's findings because they went too far. The final report, *Dams and Development: A New Framework for Decision-Making*, was presented by Nelson Mandela in London in November 2000. Wolfensohn justified his refusal to follow the report's guidelines by saying that the Bank had to consult its shareholders and the dam-building government agencies in the major dam-building countries. As Bello and Guttal report:

In a March 27, 2001 statement, the Bank said that, 'Consistent with the clarification provided by the WCD [World Commission on Dams] Chair, the World Bank will not "comprehensively adopt the 26 WCD guidelines", but will use them as a reference point when considering investments in dams.' And further that, 'This was an unprecedented and highly productive dialogue between all parties. The World Bank believes that such dialogues are very important for the many controversial development issues, and will continue to engage in them in the future.'[9]

The Bank's tactics are clear. Faced with criticism and opposition, the Bank itself announces the setting up of a participatory mechanism and commissions and actively participates in studies and reports, declaring its intention to take the results into account – and then, when the reports are published, uses evasive rhetoric about the future, while assuring the public that it will continue to engage in such 'highly productive dialogue' in the future.

The Extractive Industries Review

The experience of the WCD was repeated with the Extractive Industries Review (EIR). Challenged in a public meeting by Friends of the Earth, Wolfensohn responded – to the surprise of his staff – that the Bank would undertake a global review to examine whether Bank involvement in extractive industries was consistent with its stated aim of poverty reduction. The Extractive Industries Review was launched in July 2001.

Having learned its lesson from the WCD process, the World Bank kept a much tighter rein on the EIR, which was less independent and less participative than the WCD. However, the EIR's report,[10] published in Lisbon on 11 December 2003,

---

9   Quoted by ibid.
10   Emil Salim, *Striking a Better Balance: The World Bank Group and Extractive Industries – The Final Report of the Extractive Industries Review*, Vol. 1 (Jakarta/Washington: Extractive Industries Review, December 2003) <documents1.worldbank.org/curated/en/222871468331889018/pdf/842860v10WP0St00Box382152B00PUBLIC0.pdf> [accessed 29/12/2021].

turned out to be a surprisingly strong document in spite of the Bank's interference. It firmly recommended that the Bank and its private-sector arm, the
International Finance Corporation (IFC), phase out their involvement in oil,
mining and natural gas. The report called on the Bank to shift its financing to
renewable energy. The report caused an outcry among private financiers (such as
Citibank, ABN AMRO, WestLB and Barclays) for whom Bank involvement in
the oil, mining and gas industries was essential for as long as they were not able
to totally finance such projects themselves. In the 16 June 2004 edition of the
Financial Times, Emil Salim, who presided over the EIR, published an opinion
article in which he stated:

Not only have the oil, gas and mining industries not helped the poorest people
in developing countries, they have often made them worse off. Scores of recent
academic studies and many of the bank's own studies confirmed our findings
that countries which rely primarily on extractive industries tend to have
higher levels of poverty, child morbidity and mortality, civil war, corruption and
totalitarianism than those with more diversified economies.

As with the WCD report, the World Bank decided, in August 2004, to ignore
most of the EIR report's important recommendations. For example, it actually
continued to defend the construction of the Chad–Cameroon pipeline.[11] The Bank
continued to justify its direct involvement in extractive industries on the principle
that its involvement puts it in a position to ensure that the industries comply with
social and environmental standards!

In March of 2004, I had the opportunity to engage in a public debate with
Joseph K. Ingram, Special Representative of the World Bank to the United Nations
and the World Trade Organization, in Geneva. The debate took place in front of an
audience of around 100 educators. I explained that the World Bank's management
was preparing to ignore the recommendations in the EIR review despite having
commissioned it itself. During the debate the Bank's representative categorically
denied the charge, but the following week he mailed me an internal Bank document
asking its representatives to deny that it was preparing to refuse to honour the
conclusions of the report on the extractive industries. In the letter accompanying
the document, dated 26 March 2004, he wrote 'I hope we may find a moment in
the near future to discuss privately your concerns.' When I saw him again a few
months later in his office in Geneva, he had changed his mind and had nothing of

---

11   In December 2005, the World Bank had to withdraw its support from the pipeline, which was
     already in use, in order to try to avoid a scandal; the president of Chad had pocketed the income
     from the oil which the World Bank had promised would benefit future generations (see chapter 20,
     'Chad'). Numerous organizations had warned Wolfensohn of the risk of taking on such a project
     with the dictator Idriss Déby Itno. In the end, however, the World Bank only suspended its support
     to the dictator for a short period. In April 2006, under pressure from the United States, the World
     Bank began to provide loans once again, even accepting the terms fixed by Déby.

any consequence to tell me. He simply said that he planned to resign from his post if Wolfensohn was replaced as Bank president by a hardliner like Paul Wolfowitz. But when Wolfowitz was in fact appointed in 2005, Ingram did not resign.

JAMES WOLFENSOHN STRUGGLES WITH CIVIL SOCIETY

When James Wolfensohn arrived at the World Bank in 1995, the '50 Years is Enough' campaign was in full steam in the US and was gathering momentum throughout the world.[12] Then came the Jubilee 2000 coalition, which was especially strong in predominantly Christian countries, in both the North and the South. The Jubilee 2000 campaign, which started in 1997 and ended in 2000, collected more than 20 million signatures on a petition calling on the Bank to go beyond the HIPC initiative and 'cancel the backlog of unpayable debts of the most impoverished nations'. It also organized several large demonstrations: the human chain of 80,000 people in Birmingham, UK during the G8 summit in May 1998 and the 35,000 demonstrators during the G8 in Cologne in June 1999.

The growing opposition between civil society and Wolfensohn came to the boil during the tumultuous World Bank–IMF annual meeting held in Prague in September 2000, which had to be cut short owing to massive demonstrations. Confronted with a list of thoroughly documented charges at the famous Prague Castle debate, Wolfensohn lost his cool, exclaiming 'I and my colleagues feel good about going to work every day.' It was an answer that was matched only by IMF managing director Horst Köhler's equally famous line at the same debate: 'I also have a heart, but I have to use my head in making decisions.'

The World Bank has implemented a very proactive approach towards NGOs and some local authorities, setting up a strategy of integration/co-optation which it calls 'soft loans'. These soft loans are destined to provide microcredits (especially for NGOs concerned with women), to be used for local education and health initiatives and to manage financial remittances from migrants. The Bank has created a specific structure for loans and donations to help NGOs. This strategy of the Bank to woo civil society and regain some legitimacy in the eyes of the public is producing results. In fact, these financial instruments are part of a system that actually promotes poverty by encouraging indebtedness. In particular, they also do damage to the financial autonomy of women, who are the main targets of loans from microcredit entities.

James Wolfensohn played the open-to-dialogue card in order to defuse criticism of the Bank and to win over some of the contestation movements.

While the initiatives were in three different domains, SAPRI, the WCD and the Extractive Industries Commission were all aimed at bringing the Bank's critics around the table and giving the impression that the Bank was willing to change

12   See <sourcewatch.org/index.php?title=50_Years_Is_Enough> [accessed 17/12/2021].

its way of working and take their criticisms into account. In reality this proved not to be the case. The Bank did not play by the rules; it rejected the results of the commissions. This was above all a lesson for those who were still hanging on to their illusions that negotiation could lead to a change in the Bank's policies and workings.

INTERNAL CRISIS AND THE CRISIS OF LEGITIMACY

During James Wolfensohn's term, in 1999–2000, the Bank's leadership went through an internal crisis resulting in the departure of two key members of staff, namely Joseph Stiglitz – the chief economist and vice-president of the Bank who resigned at the end of 1999, under pressure from US Treasury Secretary Lawrence Summers – and in June 2000 Ravi Kanbur, the director of the World Bank's annual *World Development Report*. Stiglitz and Kanbur were inside reformers whose departure was a clear message that there is no place for reform from within the Bank itself.

The World Bank was also strongly contested in the US Congress, as can be seen from the report of the Meltzer Commission, which was published in February 2000 (see the next chapter).

THE END OF JAMES WOLFENSOHN'S SECOND TERM

The arrival of a conservative administration at the White House in 2001 compli-cated Wolfensohn's presidency. He spent his last four years as president acquiescing to the increasingly aggressive programme of the George W. Bush administration. From time to time he dug his heels in, but invariably ended up doing what Bush and his team required him to do. He himself said in an interview shortly before the end of his mandate, 'I've had the impression from the administration that they are perfectly pleased with what has happened here in recent years.'[13]

In Afghanistan, as well as pledging $570 million and fronting the US effort to raise billions of dollars for reconstruction, James Wolfensohn expressed the Bank's interest in participating in financing a pipeline to channel massive gas reserves through Afghanistan from landlocked Turkmenistan to India and Pakistan, a project greatly desired by US energy corporations backed by US vice-president Dick Cheney.

In Iraq, Wolfensohn, under pressure from Washington, committed between $3 billion and $5 billion for reconstruction and agreed to manage the Iraq Trust Fund to channel money to development projects undertaken by the occupying regime, especially those aimed at 'capacity building' in the private sector, a priority aim of the Bush administration.

---

13   James Wolfensohn press conference, Washington, 12 April 2005.

Despite all his efforts, James Wolfensohn could not stop the erosion of his authority and prestige. No longer appreciated at the White House because of his sympathies with Bill Clinton and John Kerry – the Democrat candidate in 2004 – Wolfensohn was also increasingly mistrusted by those who had believed in his reformist rhetoric. It was perfectly obvious very early on that were George W. Bush to be elected for a second term, there was no chance of Wolfensohn's mandate being renewed in 2005. Sure enough, in March 2005 Bush appointed one of his close collaborators as president of the World Bank, namely Paul Wolfowitz, the Deputy Defense Secretary.

As for James Wolfensohn, in 2005–06 he was charged with a mission in relation to the Bank in the Gaza Strip, in the Palestinian Territories. But he also joined the board of the largest international bank group, Citigroup.

19
Debates in Washington at the Start of the Twenty-first Century

The succession of crises that swept over the so-called emerging countries in the 1990s and the ensuing disastrous IMF and World Bank interventions provoked a worldwide debate concerning the future and the role of these Bretton Woods institutions. A number of establishment intellectuals played a part in these discussions, including Allan Meltzer, Paul Krugman, Joseph Stiglitz and Jeffrey Sachs. All it ended up doing was setting up an ad hoc bipartisan commission.[1] This International Financial Institution Advisory Commission delivered its report at the start of 2000.[2] The report focused on seven multilateral institutions: the IMF, the World Bank, the Inter-American Development Bank, the Asian Development Bank, the African Development Bank, the WTO and the Bank of International Settlements. This chapter is only concerned with the report's conclusions concerning the IMF and the World Bank.

THE MELTZER COMMISSION ON THE IFI AT THE US CONGRESS IN 2000

The International Financial Institutions Advisory Commission (IFIAC) was made up of eleven experts (six Republicans and five Democrats) from Congress, academia and banking. Among them were Allan H. Meltzer (the commission's president), Edwin Feulner (president of the extremely reactionary Heritage Foundation and former president of the Mont Pelerin Society) on the Republican side, and Jeffrey Sachs, C. Fred Bergsten and Jerome Levinson on the side of the Democrats. A large part of the commission's work, including documentation of its internal disagreements, is available on the Internet.[3]

---

1   That is to say, a commission that comprises members of the Democrat and Republican parties.

2   *Report of the International Financial Institution Advisory Commission*, Allan H. Meltzer, Chairman (Washington, DC: US Government Printing Office, March 2000). The full Meltzer Report is available at <cadtm.org/The-Meltzer-Report> [accessed 10/04/2022].

3   The proceedings of Senate Hearing 106-657 (*The Meltzer Commission: The Future of the IMF and World Bank* (Washington, DC: Senate Committee on Foreign Relations, 2000)) are available at <govinfo.gov/content/pkg/CHRG-106shrg66721/html/CHRG-106shrg66721.htm>[accessed 27/02/2023]; Allan H. Meltzer, *The Report of the International Financial Institution Advisory Commission: Comments on the Critics* (Munich: Ifo Institute for Economic Research, 2000) is available at <ifo.de/DocDL/Forum400-focus2.pdf> [accessed 27/02/2023].

All the commission's meetings and hearings were held in public and since its work casts an interesting light on the terms of debate in Washington, it is worth scrutinizing in some detail.

A short resolution was adopted unanimously by the commission while the entirety of the report was approved by eight votes to three. The three votes against were Democrats (Fred Bergsten, Jerome Levinson and Esteban Edward Torres). Two Democrats (including Jeffrey Sachs) voted with the Republicans.

The resolution adopted unanimously reads as follows:

(1) the IMF, the World Bank and the Regional Development banks should write-off in their entirety all claims against heavily indebted poor countries (HIPCS) that implement an effective economic and social development strategy in conjunction with the World Bank and the regional development institutions, and (2) the IMF should restrict its lending to the provision of short-term liquidity. The current practice of extending long-term loans for poverty reduction or other objectives should end.

The report is 188 pages long. Essentially, its recommendation is not that these multilateral institutions be abolished or somehow combined, but, instead, that they should be profoundly reformed. The report contains some extremely critical points concerning the policies of the IMF and the World Bank and also severely lambastes the WTO. It proposes that the World Bank should completely stop its loans to countries that already have access to financial markets and restrict itself to giving aid to countries that do not.

In a similar vein, the report states that the IMF must grant only short-term loans and that it should give up its mission of combating poverty, a mission that should only be the preserve of the World Bank and the regional development banks. It goes on to say that the bank should henceforth be re-named 'World Development Agency'. The report also denounces the governments of the rich countries, the IMF and the World Bank for short-circuiting decision-making bodies and legislative powers. It criticizes the WTO for abusing its powers, commenting that the WTO does not have the automatic right to impose its rules on member states. Instead, each WTO decision must be endorsed by the legislative bodies of each member state.

Below are some of the more salient comments of the report. They start in a congratulatory fashion, praising the role of the US in the world, and go on to confirm the commission's neoliberal credentials.

These institutions, and the US commitment to maintain peace and stability, have had remarkable results. In more than fifty postwar years, more people in more countries have experienced greater improvements in living standards than at any previous time. [...]

Our former adversaries are now part of the expanding global market system. [...]

The United States has been the leader in maintaining peace and stability, promoting democracy and the rule of law, reducing trade barriers, and establishing a transnational financial system. [...]

The Commission believes that to encourage development, countries should open markets to trade, and encourage private ownership, the rule of law, political democracy and individual freedom.[4]

What these Republican and Democrat establishment figures put down in writing here would have caused few raised eyebrows. But what they had to say in the rest of the report is more astonishing. The commission criticized the actions of the IMF and the G7 governments and took issue with the shock policies imposed by the IMF and World Bank.

THE PRINCIPAL CRITIQUES IN THE MELTZER REPORT

Critique of the IMF intervention in the 1982 Mexico debt crisis

In August 1982 the Mexican government announced that it could not service its external debts. The IMF organized and supervised the administration of a plan to reschedule the private commercial debts that the Mexican government had incurred over the previous decade. IMF lending did not channel net new funding to Mexico. *Rather it lent the money to enable Mexico to service the debt. Mexico's debt increased*, but it avoided default.

The IMF made its loans conditional on the implementation of a package of long-term economic reforms. Many of the conditions required sacrifices by the local population, loss of jobs and deep reductions in living standards.

Other developing countries, particularly in Latin America, found that net private capital inflows declined or became negative.[5]

Critique of the SAPs imposed by the IMF

Transformation of the IMF into a source of long-term conditional loans has made poorer nations increasingly dependent on the IMF and has given the IMF a degree of influence over member countries' policymaking that is unprecedented for a multilateral institution. Some agreements between the IMF and its members specify scores of required policies as conditions for continued funding.

---

4   *Report of the International Financial Institution Advisory Commission*, p. 15, p. 22.
5   Ibid., pp. 26–27 (emphasis added).

These programs have not ensured economic progress. They have undermined national sovereignty and often hindered the development of responsible, democratic institutions that correct their own mistakes and respond to changes in external conditions.[6]

The report also says, with regard to the East Asian crisis of 1997–98: 'Cutting government expenditure, raising taxes and interest rates and closing banks aggravated the crises.'[7]

The report criticizes the IFIs' intervention during the 1994 Mexican crisis

After the IMF, the US Treasury, and the foreign creditors had been repaid, however, *the Mexican taxpayer was left with the bill.* The cost of the banking system bailout is currently estimated at roughly 20 percent of Mexico's annual GDP. Real income per capita in 1997, despite ups and downs, was no higher in 1997 than twenty years earlier. *Real wages of the lowest paid workers, those receiving the minimum wage, have fallen 50% since 1985.* [...] *Mexico's total (public and private) external debt, expressed in 1996 U.S. dollars, has grown fivefold over the period since 1973, or fourfold when expressed on a per capita basis.* Real wages are lower and the burden of financing the debt is much higher for each Mexican worker.[8]

Critics also claimed that, by preventing or reducing the losses borne by international lenders, the IMF's 1995 Mexican program sent the wrong message to international lenders and borrowers. By preventing or reducing losses by international lenders, the IMF had implicitly signalled that, if local banks and other firm institutions incurred large foreign liabilities and governments guaranteed private debts, the IMF would provide the foreign exchange needed to honor the guarantees. Economists give the name 'moral hazard' to the incentive inherent in such guarantees.[9]

The commission also criticizes the IMF serving the interests of the G7

[...] The G7 governments, particularly the United States, use the IMF as a vehicle to achieve their political ends. This practice subverts democratic processes of creditor countries by avoiding parliamentary authority over foreign aid or foreign policy and by relaxing budget discipline.[10]

---

6   Ibid., p. 28–29 (emphasis added).
7   Ibid., p. 33.
8   Ibid., p. 30 (emphasis added).
9   Ibid., p. 33.
10   Ibid.

The IMF at the service of the rich

Numerous studies of the effects of IMF lending have failed to find any significant link between IMF involvement and increases in wealth or income. *IMF-assisted bail-outs of creditors in recent crises have had especially harmful and harsh effects on developing countries.* People who have worked hard to struggle out of poverty have seen their achievements destroyed, their wealth and savings lost, and their small businesses bankrupted. Workers lost their jobs, often without any safety net to cushion the loss. Domestic and foreign owners of real assets suffered large losses, while foreign creditor banks were protected. These banks received compensation for bearing risk, in the form of high interest rates, but did not have to bear the full (and at times any of the) losses associated with high-risk lending. The assistance that helped foreign bankers also protected politically influential domestic debtors, encouraged large borrowing and extraordinary ratios of debt to equity.[11]

The commission disapproves of the IMF's policies in Latin America

The Commission does not approve of the IMF's policies in Latin America in the 1980s and in Mexico in 1995, or in many other cases. IMF loans to these countries protected U.S. and other foreign banks, financial institutions, and some investors at great cost to the citizens of the indebted countries. The loans delayed resolution of the 1980s crises by permitting lenders and borrowers to report the debt as fully serviced. [...] *The Commission believes that lenders who make risky loans or purchase risky securities should accept the true losses when risks become unpleasant realities.*[12]

The commission criticizes the interlinked World and regional banks

There is a wide gap between the Banks' rhetoric and promises and their performance and achievements. The World Bank is illustrative. In keeping with a mission to alleviate poverty in the developing world, the Bank claims to focus its lending on countries denied access to the capital markets. Not so; *70% of World Bank non-aid resources flow to 11 countries that enjoy easy access to the capital markets.*[13]

The total resource flow to public-sector activities in countries without capital market access, but with stabilizing policies and institutions, was $2.5 billion for the seven years 1993–1999. This is less than 2% of World Bank Group financing, excluding aid.[14]

---

11 Ibid., p. 40 (emphasis added).
12 Ibid., p. 50 (emphasis added).
13 Ibid., p. 55 (emphasis added).
14 Ibid., p. 68.

The future of the World Bank group according to the Meltzer Commission

The World Bank's role as lender would be significantly reduced.[15]

The commission adds that the Bank should be above all a grant-making institution rather than a lender. Moreover, the commission feels that the World Bank no longer has a raison d'être.

The International Finance Corporation should become an integral part of the redefined World Development Agency. Its capital base would be returned to shareholders as existing portfolios are redeemed.[16]

MIGA[17] *should be eliminated.* Many countries have their own political insurance agencies. In addition, private-sector insurers have entered the market.[18]

The IMF's role as redefined by the Meltzer Report

The mission of the new IMF

The Commission recommends that the IMF be restructured as a smaller institution with three unique responsibilities [...]

1. *to act as a quasi-lender of last resort to solvent emerging economies* by providing short-term liquidity assistance to countries in need [...]
2. to collect and publish financial and economic data from member countries, and disseminate those data in a timely and uniform manner [...]
3. *to provide advice (but not impose conditions) relating to economic policy* as part of regular 'Article IV' consultations with member countries.

[...] The IMF's Poverty and Growth Facility should be closed.

[...] The IMF would not be authorized to negotiate policy reforms.

[...] IMF loans (1) should have a short maturity (e.g., a maximum of 120 days, with only one allowable rollover) [...][19]

THE DEMOCRATS' DISSENTING STATEMENT

The three Democrats who voted against the report (C. Fred Bergsten, Jerome Levinson and Esteban Edward Torres) considered that it was *too* harsh on the IFI and the WTO, regarding it as likely to impinge too greatly on their respective powers and remits. Levinson even went as far as to write a 20-page dissenting statement in which he defended the World Bank, the IMF and the Clinton administration, emphasizing the Democrats' compromise with the leadership of the AFL-CIO labour federation.[20]

---

15   Ibid., p. 95.
16   Ibid.
17   The World Bank's Multilateral Investment Guarantee Agency.
18   *Report of the International Financial Institution Advisory Commission,* p. 96 (emphasis added).
19   Ibid., pp. 42–46 (emphasis added).
20   Ibid., p. 133ff.

He also criticized the World Bank's and the IMF's hostility to workers' rights. Indeed, both institutions have made sure that workers and workers alone have paid the price of financial crises. Levinson should be very well aware of this, having been in Brazil at the time of the military coup backed by the US administration, the World Bank and the IMF.[21] He summarizes correctly how the holders of capital and governments provoke and use crises which have then led to systematic attacks on the working class. The following extract from Levinson's statement in the commission's report is revealing in this respect.

The syndicated bank lending of the decade of the 70's, the tesobono and East Asian financing fiascos, all have common characteristics: in each instance, banks and investors, awash with liquidity, seek a higher financial return than they can obtain in their home bases; without 'due diligence', they invest (tesobonos), or loan (East Asia, 1970's, syndicated bank loans) to governments or banks and corporations in the developing countries; much of the resources are not used for productive investments; a combination of external and internal shocks leads to an international crisis, which is perceived to put at risk the international financial system.

The IMF and the World Bank are charged with overseeing the workout; the financial institutions, who were equally responsible for the crisis by their imprudent lending or investing, are bailed-out and rewarded: they are enabled to buy into local banks and financial institutions at bargain basement prices (Mexico and East Asia); the debtor countries are counseled to export their way out of the crisis, which, in practice, means flooding the U.S. market with goods and services because that is the only market that is effectively open to them; and, in order to make their goods more internationally competitive, the IMF and World Bank require governments in the debtor countries to adopt labor market flexibility measures – making it easier for companies to fire workers without significant severance payments, weakening the capacity of unions to negotiate on behalf of their members, all for the purpose of driving down labor costs and benefits.

Workers in both the industrialized and developing countries, particularly in the unionized part of the labor market, bear a disproportionate part of the burden of adjustment.[22]

Levinson also quotes Joseph Stiglitz (former chief economist at the World Bank) who argues in the same vein:

[e]ven when labor market problems are not the core of the problem facing the country, all too often workers are asked to bear the brunt of the costs of adjustment. In East Asia, it was reckless lending by international banks and other financial institutions combined with reckless borrowing by domestic

---

21   Jerome Levinson was assistant director of USAID in Brazil from 1964 to 1966.
22   *Report of the International Financial Institution Advisory Commission*, pp. 153–54.

financial institutions – combined with fickle investor expectations – which may have precipitated the crisis; but the costs – in terms of soaring unemployment and plummeting wages – were borne by workers.[23]

Jerome Levinson is scathing towards the World Bank's hypocrisy. When this learned institution is asked to promote workers' rights, he notes, it apologizes, saying that it is forbidden by Section 10, Article IV of its statutes to take any political factors into account.[24] Yet when it comes to setting conditionalities, he goes on to argue, it is quick enough to impose the maximum amount of labour flexibility, thus making it easier to cut jobs, weakening the negotiating power of trade unions and reducing the incomes of urban workers.

It must be stressed, however, that Levinson is not an opponent of pro-market economic liberalism and privatization. He regards such measures as necessary, but believes that for them to work, they have to be accompanied by a trade-union counterbalance. Levinson's vision is close to that advocated by Tony Blair in Great Britain or Gerhard Schröder in Germany during the same period.

THE MELTZER COMMISSION'S WORK IN PERSPECTIVE

In a study published in 1998, Anne Krueger, who was chief economist at the World Bank from 1981 to 1987, underlined the differences between the 1970s and the end of the 1990s. Her article is useful for understanding certain terms of the debate. She indicates that at the start of the 1970s, the United States forced the World Bank and the IMF to switch from bilateral to multilateral aid.[25] According to Krueger, from then on, private capital flows, encouraged by the spread of liberalization, proved dominant and reduced the World Bank's and the IMF's room for manoeuvre. Moreover, the Cold War had ended. She notes,

Until the end of the Cold War, political support for development assistance through the IFIs and bilateral agencies originated from two groups: those on the right concerned with security, and those on the left supporting development objectives on humanitarian grounds. With the end of the Cold War, support from

---

23 'Democratic development as the fruits of labor', Keynote Address, Industrial Relations Research Association, Boston, January 2000 <gsb.columbia.edu/faculty/jstiglitz/sites/jstiglitz/files/2000_Democratic_Development_KEYNOTE.pdf> [accessed 17/12/2021].

24 'The Bank and its officers shall not interfere in the political affairs of any member; nor shall they be influenced in their decisions by the political character of the member or members concerned. Only economic considerations shall be relevant to their decisions, and these considerations shall be weighed impartially in order to achieve the purposes stated in Article I.' (International Bank for Reconstruction and Development, *Articles of Agreement* (as amended effective 27 June 2012) <thedocs.worldbank.org>.)

25 Anne Krueger, 'Whither the Bank and the IMF?', *Journal of Economic Literature*, December 1998, Vol. 36, p. 2010, note 85.

the right eroded and the Bank's efforts to spread itself into new issues may reflect a search for a broader political support base.[26]

According to Krueger, the World Bank tends to do too much:

Many of the accusations about the Bank's organizational ineffectiveness may originate from its efforts to extend into all directions in all countries. A strong case can be made that, in getting as involved as it has with environmental matters, cooperation with NGOs, combating corruption, and embracing other 'new issues,' the Bank has moved far beyond its essential competence in addressing many of these issues, and in so doing, has overstretched the capacity of its staff.[27]

As far as the future of the bank is concerned, Krueger believes it has three options:

1) continue to be a development institution, focussing only on those countries that are truly poor and gradually phasing out activities in the middle-income countries; 2) continue to operate in all client countries, focussing on the 'soft issues' of development such as women's rights, preservation of the environment, labor standards, and encouragement of non-governmental organizations (NGOs); or 3) to close down.[28]

While Krueger is not convinced by the latter option and is open to persuasion on the first two, she notes that something must be decided sooner or later. She is also clear as to the Bank's mode of operation: the change to a 'one country – one vote' system must be resisted. Krueger maintains that, though a merger between the World Bank and the IMF cannot be ruled out, it would be unwelcome as it would mean redrafting new statutes along this 'one country – one vote' line, something she believes must be avoided.[29] The major powers, she feels, must retain control.

THE CONTEXT OF THE MELTZER COMMISSION

In order to understand the Meltzer Commission's proposals, one must, of course, put them in their international context: namely the successive financial crises in the peripheral countries and the subsequent catastrophic intervention of the IMF and the World Bank. But this would only be scratching the surface, since the real

---

26   Ibid., p. 2010.
27   Ibid.
28   Ibid, p. 2006.
29   'Merging the IFIs, or any other radical reform, would require the writing of new Articles. Whatever mechanism was chosen to rewrite the Articles of the two institutions would have to be insulated from pressures to politicize the Bank and Fund along the lines of other United Nations agencies. Quite clearly, politicization of staff along nationality lines, moves to one-country one-vote, or a number of other possible changes could render the organizations much less effective.' (Ibid., p. 2015, note 103.)

determining factor was the US *national* context. At the time of the commission, the Republican majority was conducting a fierce guerrilla campaign against Bill Clinton's Democrat administration. This internal political context is crucial in understanding why and how the commission attacked the Executive so ruthlessly for its use of the IMF as an instrument for intervening in world affairs without Congressional approval. Furthermore, the commission's expression of certain social concerns was surely influenced by the need to split the Democrat appointees to the commission in order to win enough of them over to the opinions of Allan Meltzer and his colleagues. It was also a way of attacking the Clinton administration with arguments that would hit home with its electoral and political base.

THE MELTZER COMMISSION'S POSITION TOWARDS WASHINGTON'S POLICY

There are areas of agreement between the Commission and Washington. They can be summed up in eight points:

1. There is fundamental agreement between them over the pursuit of a neoliberal agenda: 'The Commission believes that to encourage development, countries should open markets to trade, and encourage private ownership, the rule of law, political democracy and individual freedom.'[30] These points are considered essential.
2. Both see the necessity of retaining existing international financial institutions: 'These institutions, and the U.S. commitment to maintain peace and stability, have had remarkable results.'[31]
3. There is of course agreement over keeping and strengthening US dominance over these institutions.
4. There is agreement over cancelling all or nearly all the debt of the HIPCs and other indebted poor countries, as long as these nations follow the neoliberal agenda and conform to the interests of the United States. The thinking behind this is quite simple: these countries are of no use to the US if their debts stop them from buying US goods and services. So, in order to prevent this, it would be better to write off or to substantially reduce these debts.
5. It is in the US interest to pressure the World Bank into giving aid to poor countries, and to do so itself, since it is certain that these countries will spend the money on goods primarily from the most industrialized nations. Poor nations immediately spend what they are given on goods from the North because they themselves do not produce enough of what they need. This has been the impact of liberalization and competition over the last 25 years on local producers and firms in developing countries.
6. Corruption in recipient countries must be rooted out in order to ensure that the maximum amount of aid money ends up being spent on products from the North.

---

30   *Report of the International Financial Institution Advisory Commission*, p. 22.
31   Ibid., p. 15.

7. A policy of aid also has the advantage of keeping the elites and the economies of recipient countries in a state of dependence on donor countries.

8. The amounts of money involved in grants and aid are trifling to countries like the United States – far less, for instance, than the $400 billion spent on the 'War on Terror' in Iraq and Afghanistan between September 2001 and April 2006.

HOW THE MELTZER COMMISSION VIEWS THE POLITICS OF AID

The commission concludes that loans should be largely replaced by grants. The example given by the commission, though, clearly shows that the aim of this strategy is for the donor country to become involved in the decision-making processes of HIPCs and thus short-circuit their national policies:

A country with $1,000 per capita income qualifying for 70% grant resources decides that vaccination of its children against measles is a desired goal. If the development agency confirms the need, the government would solicit competitive bids from private-sector suppliers, non governmental organizations such as charitable institutions, and public sector entities such as the Ministry of Health. Suppose the lowest qualifying bid is $5 per child vaccinated, the development agency would agree to pay $3.50 (70%) for each vaccination directly to the supplier. The government would be responsible for the remaining $1.50 (30%) fee. Payments would only be made upon certification by an agent independent of all participants – the government, the development agency and the supplier of vaccinations.

Under a system of user fees, grants are paid after audited delivery of service. No results, no funds expended. Payments would be based upon number of children vaccinated, kilowatts of electricity delivered, cubic meters of water treated, students passing literacy tests, miles of functioning roads. [...] Execution is substantially free of political risk. The supplier of the service, not the government, receives the payment.[32]

And later in the text:

From vaccinations to roads, from literacy to water supply, services would be performed by outside private-sector providers (including NGOs and charitable organizations) or public-sector entities, and awarded on competitive bid. Quantity and quality of performance would be verified by independent auditors. Payments would be made directly to providers. Costs would be divided between recipient countries and the development agency. The subsidy would vary between 10% and 90%, depending upon capital-market access and per capita income.[33]

---

32   Ibid., pp. 89–90.
33   Ibid., p. 91.

THE NEED FOR AN ALTERNATIVE TO THE MELTZER COMMISSION'S APPROACH

Even if the arguments contained in the Meltzer Report are useful in describing the overall effects of the IMF's and the World Bank's actions, the solutions it extols would be as disastrous as they are unconvincing. The use of grants and aid as a new way of entrenching the commodification of essential services such as health, water and education, a policy the report promotes, has to be rejected. It is unacceptable for donor countries to use aid as a way of imposing their demands and wishes on recipient nations.

A very different approach is needed. Some way must be found of breaking the wretched cycle of debt while avoiding a politics of charity that can only perpetuate the current system of global domination by capitalism, the major powers and trans-national corporations. The goal is the creation of an international system that could redistribute wealth so as to compensate for the wholesale plunder which people of the Periphery have endured for centuries and still endure today. Such reparations in the guise of aid should under no circumstances give the more industrialized countries leverage over the internal political affairs of the nations they are compensating. A new strategy is needed, aimed at creating decision-making bodies that would control the destination of aid but leave how it is utilized in the hands of the concerned populations and public authorities. This opens up a huge area for reflection and experimentation.

Furthermore, in opposition to the Meltzer Commission – which wants to retain the IMF and the World Bank, making only slight reforms – these institutions must be abolished outright and replaced with different global institutions that would operate democratically. A 'New World Bank' and 'New Monetary Fund', whatever actual names they might be given, must be created with radically different missions from those of their predecessors. They would, for instance, guarantee the fulfilment of international treaty obligations in terms of political, civil, social, economic and cultural rights as well as in the domains of international monetary and credit relations. These new institutions must play a role in a global institutional system headed by a United Nations that would also be radically reformed. It is an absolute priority that developing countries mobilize as soon as possible into regional entities, with banks and monetary funds in common. At the time of the crisis in South-East Asia and Korea in 1997–98, the establishment of an Asian Monetary Fund for the countries affected was discussed, yet all such talk was quashed under pressure from the US and the IMF. In the Latin America–Caribbean region, at the initiative of the Venezuelan authorities and President Hugo Chávez in particular, discussion of the possibility of building a 'Bank of the South' began in 2005–06. In the end the project did not come to fruition. But clearly, if what is being strived for is emancipation and the attainment of full human rights, these new regional and international financial institutions must be instruments of a social movement that is totally opposed to capitalism and neoliberalism.

20

Structural Adjustment and the Washington Consensus Are Not Abandoned in 2000

During the 1980s, the IMF and the World Bank earned themselves the highly justified but less than enviable reputation of being responsible for very unpopular measures forced upon governments of developing countries – in short, of being the bane of the poor. Admittedly the governments themselves, often in cahoots with the ruling classes, have found it convenient to place the blame on these distant institutions located on 19th St NW in Washington. This unsavoury reputation spread like wildfire and newspapers in the South began to give it ample coverage.[1]

Accustomed to making blunt recommendations for cuts in social expenditures or the privatization of public companies, these two institutions came to realize that plain speaking did not serve their interests. Very quickly, people recognized their leading role in economic and human disasters. Very quickly, the riots that followed price increases in essential goods were referred to as 'anti-IMF riots'. And very quickly, public opinion put pressure on governments to resist the decrees of the IMF and the World Bank. In short, it was becoming more and more difficult to get people to swallow such a bitter pill.

A major public-relations plan was therefore launched in the 1990s to deal with the serious – and rightly deserved – legitimacy crisis that the IMF and the World Bank were then (and still are) facing. The argument focused on debt reduction and the fight against poverty. 'We have learned and we have changed' was the message. But the notorious ultra-liberal conditionalities that marked the structural adjustment plans of the 1980s are still being imposed. A series of examples from the early 2000s, on every continent, clearly expose the contradictions of the two institutions.

SRI LANKA, ECUADOR AND HAITI: BUSINESS AS USUAL FOR NEOLIBERAL POLICIES

Sri Lanka

In Sri Lanka, in 2005, the government refused a $389 million loan conditioned on political reforms such as restructuring of pension schemes and privatization of water resources.[2]

---

1   The source for this chapter is a document co-written by Damien Millet and the author at the beginning of 2006, as well as various CADTM press releases.
2   *Sunday Observer* (Sri Lanka), 6 November 2005.

Ecuador

In Ecuador, in July 2005, the government decided to reform the use of the country's oil resources. Instead of being entirely earmarked for paying back their debt, part of those resources would now fund social programmes, notably for the often underprivileged indigenous communities. To show its displeasure, the World Bank withheld a $100 million loan to Ecuador (see chapter 23).

Haiti

In Haiti, during 2003, the IMF put an end to government-controlled fuel prices, thereby making them 'flexible'. Within a few weeks, fuel prices rose by 130 per cent. The consequences were dramatic: problems boiling water for drinking or cooking food; an increase in transportation costs, which small producers passed on to the market, thus increasing the price of numerous basic commodities. But as inflation is one of the IMF's bugbears, it promptly imposed a wage freeze on the government. The daily minimum wage plummeted from $3 to $1.50 in 1994, which, according to the IMF, was a way of attracting foreign investors. It also served geopolitical interests, weakening President Jean-Bertrand Aristide and leading to his departure from office on 24 February 2004 – something the big powers had been pushing for.

Even in oil-producing countries such as **Iraq** and **Nigeria**, the IMF imposed the same system of flexible pricing. Rates increased, leading to organized protests by the people affected, for example in Basra in December 2005.

IN SUB-SAHARAN AFRICA, THE WORLD BANK PROLONGED THE NEOLIBERAL ATTACKS

Ghana

In Ghana, former President Jerry Rawlings had refused to adopt the Heavily Indebted Poor Countries initiative, but since John Agyekum Kufuor took power in January 2001, Ghana has been complying with conditions imposed by the IMF. One of these conditions – a significant one – concerned the water sector, for which the IMF demanded total cost recovery. In other words, households must bear the total cost of access to water, without the benefit of state subsidies. The price of a cubic metre of water had to be sufficient to recover total operating and management costs. Electricity was next in line and the same principle was applied. The goal was clear: to get the public companies on an even keel before privatization. In May 2001 the price of water rose by 95 per cent, and it did not stop there. The populations seriously affected by this measure formed the National Coalition Against the Privatization of Water. With one out of three Ghanaians having no access to drinking water, the World Bank made another fateful move: in 2004, it granted Ghana a $103 million loan in exchange for the sale of the utility supplying water to the main cities to a private multinational corporation.

Mali

In Mali, it was the cotton industry that was in the line of fire. For decades, the entire cotton sector was controlled by the Compagnie Malienne de Développement des Textiles (CMDT), jointly owned by the Malian government (60 per cent) and the French company Dagris (40 per cent). The CMDT, the real backbone of Mali's economy, was the biggest currency earner for the Malian state through profits and taxes. Its role extended beyond the mere production of cotton. It provided public services, from maintaining rural roads and eliminating illiteracy among rural communities to the purchase of agricultural tools and construction of vital infrastructures. Until 1999, production was constantly on the increase: 200,000 tons in 1988, 450,000 in 1997, 520,000 in 1998, 522,000 in 1999. But the CMDT's questionable management and very low prices triggered unrest among peasants, who refused to harvest in 1999/2000. Production that year fell by almost 50 per cent. The cotton sector's forum, the Etats Généraux de la Filière Cotonnière, was held in April 2001; the Etats Généraux decided to introduce a series of drastic reforms including a 23 per cent reduction in total expenditure on wages, partial or total debt cancellation for smallholders, layoffs (500 to 800 people out of 2,400), the freeze of a planned 7 per cent wage increase, an increase in the guaranteed price paid to farmers from 170 FCFA/kg of cotton to 200 FCFA/kg, opening up of capital, recentring of activities and progressive withdrawal of the Malian state from the CMDT. In spite of the failed privatizations in the neighbouring countries (Benin and Côte d'Ivoire), the World Bank advocated outright privatization, causing great concern among the affected villagers. The first reorganizations, notably in transport and management of fertilizers and pesticides, led to massive disruptions, seriously penalizing Malian producers and putting harvests at risk in 2003 and 2004.[3]

In order to accelerate the process even more, and dissatisfied with the CMDT's guaranteed price, which it found too high, the World Bank put pressure on the government by freezing a $25 million aid payment. By so doing, it disregarded the two factors responsible for the success of Mali's cotton sector: a guaranteed minimum price and vertical integration.

In an article analyzing 'the case of the Compagnie Malienne des Textiles, the parastatal in charge of supervising cotton production since 1974 in Mali', Isaline Bergamaschi sums up the World Bank's actions as follows:

The World Bank has exerted strong financial pressure on the government. Privatization became a conditionality to access debt relief operations in 1998. The government hence adopted a sector rehabilitation plan, a condition to benefit a third structural adjustment credit of $70 million granted

---

3   See Millet, *L'Afrique sans dette.*

in December 2001. In June 2001, the government adopted the Lettre de Politique de Développement du Secteur (LPDSC). In 2002, the IMF makes access to its Facility for Growth and Poverty Reduction conditional to the CMDT privatization. [...] In November 2004, a World Bank delegation suspends aid disbursements until the government takes action to reduce deficits [...]. They ask an amendment of the price mechanism and a 'clear signal' of government will to privatize. The credit is adopted in January 2005 after tense negotiations. In February, the Bank disbursed half of what should have been disbursed in December the previous year, thus depriving the country of greater Bank financial support.[4]

An Oxfam Briefing Paper published in 2006 enunciates the overall problem:

Despite numerous commitments to reform, the World Bank and the International Monetary Fund (IMF) are still using their aid to make developing countries implement inappropriate economic policies, with the tacit approval of rich-country governments. These economic policy conditions undermine national policy-making, delay aid flows, and often fail to deliver for poor people. If the world is to make poverty history, this practice must be stopped. Aid must be conditional on being spent transparently and on reducing poverty, and nothing more.

and adds, in the specific case of Malian cotton:

Given the above climate, donors should be fighting amongst each other to provide aid for Mali. But before providing the much-needed funds, the World Bank and the IMF (and other donors) have required Mali to implement a number of controversial and counter-productive economic conditions: privatisation of the electricity supply, ending government support to cotton farmers by privatising the sector, and liberalising the price of cotton. These conditions have undermined country ownership, actively delayed Mali from receiving greater aid flows, and generally worsened poverty rather than making the situation better.[5]

Niger

In Niger, there was no period of grace following the re-election of President Mamadou Tandja in December 2004. In January 2005, on IMF instructions, a law amending finances was enacted increasing VAT to 19 per cent on basic goods and services (wheat, sugar, milk, water and electricity). Massive social mobilization

---

4   Isaline Bergamaschi, 'Privatizating the African state: uneasy process and limited outcomes: the case of the cotton sector in Mali', British International Studies Association Conference, Manchester, 27–29 May 2011, p. 12ff. <open.ac.uk/socialsciences/bisa-africa/files/bisa-2011-berga-maschi.pdf> [accessed 29/03/2022].

5   *Kicking the Habit: How the World Bank and the IMF Are Still Addicted to Attaching Economic Policy Conditions to Aid*, Oxfam Briefing Paper 96 (Oxford: Oxfam International, November 2006), p. 1; p. 16 <oxfamilibrary.openrepository.com/bitstream/handle/10546/114532/bp96-kicking-habit-011106-en.pdf> [accessed 29/03/2022].

quickly ensued. In March, the population, already impoverished by years of bad harvests (caused by droughts and invasions of desert locusts) and structural adjustment plans (privatizations, cuts in social expenditures, layoffs and salary freezes in the civil service, etc.) took to the streets to express their dissatisfaction. The social movement, organized around three consumer organizations, succeeded in creating a large unified front for a 'coalition against the high cost of living', bringing together 29 organizations and the four trade-union federations. After several days of 'dead town' demonstrations and arbitrary arrests by police, their mobilization forced the government to back down.

Democratic Republic of Congo (DRC)

In the DRC, a parliamentary report published in 2006 denounced the action of the World Bank with respect to the mining industry.[6] Trouble broke out over the operation of a copper and silver mine in Dikulushi controlled by the Australo-Canadian company Anvil Mining. In October 2004, Mai-Mai militiamen occupied the neighbouring town of Kilwa, from where extracted minerals are sent to Zambia. The Congolese army then launched an operation to repress the uprising, causing the death of several dozens of individuals suspected of supporting the rebels (at least 100 people, according to the UN). Summary executions and plunder marked this strong-arm operation. It was against this background that the Anvil Mining company provided vehicles and equipment to the Congolese army, with a view to ensuring unhampered continuation of exports.

This did not prevent the Multilateral Investment Guarantee Agency (MIGA, an affiliate of the World Bank) from approving an insurance contract in April 2005 offering a guarantee of $13.3 million to cover political risks related to the expansion of this mining operation. Thus we see that the World Bank did not hesitate to support Anvil Mining's dubious activities: the aforementioned report by the Congolese Special National Assembly Commission, entrusted with examining the validity of economic and financial agreements, written by 17 Congolese MPs from different parties, and led by Christophe Lutundula, severely criticized 'the policy of splitting up the mining portfolio of the State' in which Anvil Mining was implicated, essentially 'to satisfy the immediate financial needs of governments'.[7] According to the report, collusion between the Congolese authorities and Anvil Mining was flagrant: 'Fiscal, custom, and para-fiscal exemptions were granted in an exaggerated

---

6   National Assembly of the Democratic Republic of the Congo, *Assemblée Nationale – Commission Spéciale Chargée de l'examen de la validité des conventions a caractère économique et financier conclues pendant les guerres de 1996–1997 et de 1998. Rapport des travaux* (*National Assembly – Special Commission to Examine the Validity of Economic and Financial Agreements Entered into during the Wars in 1996–1997 and 1998* ['Lutundula Report']), January 2006 <https://congomines.org/reports/210-rapport-lutundula-version-finale> [accessed 29/03/2022].

7   Translations by CADTM.

way and for long periods of time ranging from 15 to 30 years. [...] As a result, the Congolese State has been deprived of important fiscal resources that are crucial to its development.'[8] But ultimately, any control over Anvil Mining's operations was destined to fail since 'public servants appointed on mining sites are taken care of by the private mining operators that they are supposed to control. These are the cases of Anvil Mining and COMISA; both pay inspectors from DGM, Regional Division of Mining, OCC etc. As a result, public servants completely lack autonomy, independence, and efficiency.'[9] To cap it all, until March 2005 one of Anvil Mining's significant shareholders (17.5 per cent of shares) was First Quantum, a Canadian company exposed in a 2002 UN report on the DRC for not respecting OECD guidelines governing multinationals. How can the World Bank, via MIGA, continue to offer guarantees to a company that has demonstrated how little it respects the fundamental rights of the people of the Kilwa region? In offering a guarantee under such circumstances, MIGA made itself a direct accomplice in Anvil Mining's reprehensible actions.

Chad

In Chad, since the start of construction of a 1,070-kilometre pipeline linking the oil-producing region of Doba (Chad) to the maritime port of Kribi (Cameroon), numerous environmental, human rights and international solidarity organizations have expressed concern over the World Bank's support for the project. From the outset, the environmental, human and financial risks were so great that Shell and Elf preferred to pull out. Still the final consortium consisting of ExxonMobil, ChevronTexaco (USA) and Petronas (Malaysia) was able to complete the $3.7 billion project thanks to powerful strategic and financial support from the World Bank.

To justify its support, the World Bank committed to a pilot programme designed to allow Chadians to benefit from the profits made. In making this investment – the largest in Sub-Saharan Africa – it imposed its conditions: Chad's president Idriss Déby Itno must devote 90 per cent of the revenue earned from oil sales to social projects selected with its approval and to investments in the Doba region. The remaining 10 per cent must be reserved for future generations: they were deposited in a blocked account at Citibank London, under World Bank control.

This arrangement failed since Déby appropriated the sums allocated for future generations: it is estimated that he helped himself to at least $27 million. Moreover, he changed the rules of the game by including security expenditures in the definition of priority sectors to be financed by oil revenue. Weakened by high social tensions, attempts to overthrow him and army desertions, Déby sought to

---

8   Unofficial translation of Lutundula Report <raid-uk.org/sites/default/files/lutundula-excerpts.pdf>
     [accessed 29/03/2022].
9   Ibid.

reinforce his military and repressive machine. In December 2005 the World Bank reacted by blocking existing loans to Chad, pretending to have become aware only then of the authoritative and corrupt nature of the regime, when in fact the Bank's support for the project had allowed Déby to strengthen his power base and bolster his personal fortune for a decade.

All the bombast by World Bank experts on good governance, corruption and reducing poverty is a dismal farce. It was clear from the beginning that this project would end up allowing a notorious dictator to become even wealthier, with total impunity. Each side did just what was expected of it. The World Bank enabled the construction of a pipeline that allows oil multinationals to help themselves to a natural resource and their shareholders to reap juicy profits. And Chad's president helped himself to the wealth that belongs to the people.

Corruption and dictatorship in Chad must be denounced and fought, but that will not be enough. The World Bank was the determining element in a project that placed a heavy burden of debt on Chad, increased corruption and poverty, continues to damage the environment and allows a natural resource to be abusively exploited. In short, in Chad as elsewhere, the World Bank knowingly supports a predatory model and for 30 years has knowingly propped up a corrupt dictatorship. In 2021, Idriss Déby's regime was still in place, and the World Bank financed it to the day he died, on 20 April 2021.

Note that an evaluation commissioned by the World Bank and handed over to its executives in 2009 had considered the project a failure in terms of poverty reduction, environmental protection and good governance: 'In conclusion, the evaluation report states that in the case of Chad, the objective targeted by the WBG through its financing of the program has not been reached, namely poverty alleviation and governance improvement for the best possible use of the oil revenues, in an environmentally and socially sustainable manner.'[10]

Like several other African countries, Chad still struggles under a high level of debt under the combined effects of the Coronavirus crisis and low oil prices (oil being its principal export product).

In 2021, Chad became the first country to request restructuring of its debt. The IMF announced Chad's decision in a declaration concerning a new four-year programme with a value of some $572 million under an Extended Credit Facility and Extended Fund Facility arrangement.[11]

---

10   *The World Bank Group Program of Support for the Chad–Cameroon Petroleum Development and Pipeline Construction Program – Performance Assessment Report, Report No. 50315* (Washington, DC: World Bank Group, 16 September 2009), p. 146 <ieg.worldbankgroup.org/sites/default/files/Data/reports/PPAR_Chad-Cameroon_Petroleum_Dev_Projects.pdf> [accessed 25/01/2022].

11   'IMF reaches staff-level agreement with Chad on a four-year program under Extended Credit Facility (ECF) and Extended Fund Facility (EFF)', International Monetary Fund Press Release 21/26, 27 January 2021 <imf.org>.

21

Climate and the Environmental Crisis: Sorcerer's Apprentices at the World Bank and the IMF

In December 2020, on the occasion of the fifth anniversary of the signing of the Paris Agreement on Climate, the UN Secretary-General sounded the alarm because the climate situation has fundamentally worsened. This chapter will analyze what the World Bank and the IMF have done in connection with the environmental crisis and climate change.

At the end of October 2006 Nicholas Stern, adviser to the UK government on the economics of climate change and development, handed Prime Minister Tony Blair a 500-page report on the consequences of the current climate change and measures to counteract them. In this report, known as the Stern Review,[1] Stern writes: 'Climate change will affect the basic elements of life for people around the world – access to water, food production, health, and the environment. Hundreds of millions of people could suffer hunger, water shortages and coastal flooding as the world warms.' The diagnosis delivered by this report is an implicit condemnation of the policies implemented by the IMF and the World Bank, where Nicholas Stern was chief economist.[2]

The present chapter compares the Stern Review with the positions of major figures in the World Bank, the IMF and the Washington government since 1990. It also offers comments on the report on natural catastrophes the World Bank issued in 2006. The World Bank's analysis contradicted what it had claimed so far. Its current discourse is an attempt to minimize the credibility crisis it suffers from, but this does not change its basic adherence to a market-oriented and productivist model that destroys both people and the environment. While the Stern Review includes interesting views it offers no alternative to the productivist model and the obsession with growth. While the World Bank had announced that it would stop supporting fossil energies from the end of 2019, it is now clear that it has continued to finance the construction and operation of coal-fuelled generating

---

1   Nicholas Stern, *Stern Review: The Economics of Climate Change* (Cambridge: Cambridge University Press, 2007). All quotations from the Stern Review in this chapter are to be found in the Conclusions section. The full text of the Stern Review can be found at: <mudancasclimaticas.cptec.inpe.br/~rmclima/pdfs/destaques/sternreview_report_complete.pdf> [accessed 15/11/2021].
2   Nicholas Stern was chief economist and vice-president of the World Bank from 2000 to 2003.

plants and the exploitation of oil and natural gas. In 2020, several analysts and NGOs exposed its responsibility in the tragic continuation of climate change and the environmental crisis.

THE FORMER ASSERTIONS OF WORLD BANK AND IMF LEADERS

Whereas from the early 1970s many voices have been raised to warn of the dangers of a commitment to limitless growth and the resulting exhaustion of natural resources, World Bank and IMF leaders claimed for a long time that such alarm was unfounded.

Lawrence Summers, chief economist and vice-president of the World Bank from 1991 to 1996 and later Treasury Secretary under US president Bill Clinton, even claimed in 1991:

There are no limits on the planet's capacity for absorption likely to hold us back in the foreseeable future. The danger of an apocalypse due to global warming or anything else is non-existent. The idea that the world is heading into the abyss is profoundly wrong. The idea that we should place limits on growth because of natural limitations is a serious error; indeed, the social cost of such an error would be enormous if ever it were to be acted upon.[3]

In a letter to the British weekly *The Economist* published on 30 May 1992, Summers wrote that even in the worst possible scenario he saw it as sheer demagoguery to claim that failure to attend to global environmental problems would result in terrible problems for our grandchildren, adding that '[t]he argument that a moral obligation to future generations demands special treatment of environmental investments is fatuous.'[4]

Summers' claims roused much protest at the time, and five years later, in 1997, Nicholas Stern (future chief economist at the World Bank and author of the Stern Review) wrote in the book the Bank commissioned to cover its first 50 years:

The Bank's commitment to environmental issues was questioned by some as a result of a leak to the *Economist* magazine, in late 1991, of extracts from an internal memorandum of Lawrence Summers, then chief economist. The memorandum suggested the possibility that environmental issues were being overemphasized in relation to developing countries, and that those countries might actually have lower marginal costs in dealing with or tolerating pollutants.[5]

3   Lawrence Summers, at the World Bank and IMF annual assembly in Bangkok 1991, interviewed by Kirsten Garrett, 'Background briefing', Australian Broadcasting Company, second programme.
4   'Summers on sustainable growth', Lawrence Summers' letter to *The Economist*, 30 May 1992, Vol. 323, No. 7761.
5   Stern and Ferreira, 'The World Bank as "intellectual actor"', p. 566.

Then in the Stern Review, published in 2006, in a scathing if tardy rebuttal of Lawrence Summers' aforementioned reassuring claim that global warming would reduce growth by less than 0.1 per cent a year over the next two centuries:

The Review estimates that if we don't act, the overall costs and risks of climate change will be equivalent to losing at least 5% of global GDP each year, now and forever. If a wider range of risks and impacts is taken into account, the estimates of damage could rise to 20% of GDP or more.[6]

Claims such as those put forward by Lawrence Summers are not isolated. They reflect the US government's dominance over World Bank and IMF decisions. These positions, denying that severe environmental damage was being caused by the productivist model and that climate change was occurring, were taken by Washington until quite recently.

The many speeches delivered by Anne Krueger, chief economist at the World Bank under Ronald Reagan and first deputy managing director at the IMF from 2000 to 2006, testify to this. In one of them, given on 18 June 2003 at the 7th International Economic Forum at Saint Petersburg, Krueger said:

Take the perennial concern that rapid growth depletes our fuel resources and once that happens growth will come to a complete dead stop. World oil reserves today are higher today in 1950 [sic]. Then the world's known reserves of oil were expected to be enough for only 20 more years of consumption. We were expected to run out by 1970. It did not happen. Today, our known reserves are enough to keep us going for another 40 years at our present rate of consumption. There is no doubt that by the time 2040 rolls around research and development will have delivered new breakthroughs in energy production and use.[7]

Krueger continued: 'Nor have we done irreparable harm to the environment. The evidence shows quite convincingly that economic growth brings an initial phase of deterioration in some aspects, but followed by a subsequent phase of improvement. The turning point at which people begin choosing to invest in cleaning up and preventing pollution occurs at a per capita GDP of 5000 dollars.'[8]

When she made this claim, Anne Krueger wanted to convey the following message: growth in the early stages of economic take-off in developing countries leads to environmental degradation, but when they exceed a threshold of $5,000 per capita GDP, people will, to use her words, begin investing in cleaning up and preventing pollution. It follows that there is no need for public authorities to impose restrictive measures to force companies to comply with strong environmental standards; self-restraint will automatically apply as soon as the magic threshold of

---

6   Stern Review, Summary of Conclusions, p. vi.
7   'Supporting globalization, remarks by Anne O. Krueger', 26 September 2002 < imf.org/en/News/Articles/2015/09/28/04/53/sp092602a> [accessed 07/03/2022].
8   Ibid.

$5,000 per capita GDP is reached. This is just smoke and mirrors. It does not rely on any empirical data, and is only meant to promote laissez-faire.

The above quotation from Anne Krueger includes two blatant errors (if not lies). First, facts show that irreparable environmental damage has occurred. Second, it is not true that after 'an initial phase of deterioration' economic growth brings 'a subsequent phase of improvement'. The more industrialized countries have long overreached the per capita GDP $5,000 mark,[9] and yet most of them still implement policies that continue to increase pollution.

It took the aftermath of Hurricane Katrina in August 2005 for the White House to reluctantly start acknowledging the obvious.

Along with other movements, the CADTM did not wait for a catastrophe on the scale of the one suffered by the city of New Orleans in 2005 to expose the World Bank and IMF policies that favoured climate change and weakened developing countries' ability to face natural catastrophes. It notably exposed such policies promoted by the World Bank and the IMF as deforestation and huge power plants as being causes of environmental disasters.[10] Similarly it asked the World Bank to end its support for projects that destroy natural coastal protection such as mangroves, which can absorb part of the impact of tsunamis.[11] The CADTM also demanded that the World Bank stop lending money to the extractive industries. It denounces the World Bank's support of agribusiness, export monocultures, land-grabbing and large seed companies, all of which are responsible for the reduction of biodiversity, the emission of very high levels of greenhouse gases and the impoverishment of those who till the land. Finally the CADTM questioned the decision made at the Rio conference in 1992 to entrust the World Bank with the management of a global environmental protection fund. Again, this amounts to asking the fox to look after the chickens.

A SHIFT IN THE WORLD BANK'S POLICIES

In April 2006, without any attempt at apology, the World Bank's Independent Evaluation Group (IEG) published a report on natural disasters.[12] Its author, Ronald Parker, said at that time: 'There has been an increase in incidents of disaster clearly tied to environmental degradation around the world.'[13] Indeed, while the number of earthquakes has hardly changed, the number and magnitude of natural disasters related to climate have dramatically increased: from an average of 100 in 1975 to

---

9   The per capita GDP is now over $40,000 in North America, Western Europe, Japan, Australia and New Zealand. China's per capita GDP has been over $5,000 since 2010, South Africa's since 2005 and Brazil's since 2006. Yet companies in all those countries are still massively involved in activities that are deleterious to the environment.
10   See for instance Toussaint, *Your Money or Your Life*, chapter 9.
11   Millet and Toussaint, *Tsunami Aid or Debt Cancellation!*
12   *Hazards of Nature, Risks to Development – An IEG Evaluation of World Bank Assistance for Natural Disasters* (Washington, DC: World Bank, 2006) <droughtmanagement.info/literature/WB_hazards_of_nature_natural_disasters_evaluation_2006.pdf> [accessed 25/01/2022].
13   Quoted in the *Financial Times*, 22–23 April 2006.

over 400 in 2005. The Bank acknowledges that global warming, deforestation and soil erosion have made extensive areas more vulnerable. It estimates that developing countries suffer damages of at least $30 billion a year. As Lester Brown, president of the Earth Policy Institute, said, 'This report underlines that although we continue to call these natural disasters, they are sometimes clearly of human origin.'[14]

THE STERN REVIEW ON GLOBAL WARMING

Nicholas Stern is crystal clear: the less industrialized countries, though less to blame for global warming, are also those that will bear the brunt: 'All countries will be affected. The most vulnerable – the poorest countries and populations – will suffer earliest and most, even though they have contributed least to the causes of climate change.'[15]

Completely contradicting the proponents of neoliberal globalization, he adds, 'Climate change is the greatest market failure the world has ever seen, and it interacts with other market imperfections.'[16] This being said, Nicholas Stern does not propose any alternative to the productivist model and to the capitalist market. Quite the opposite: his report is meant to sound the alarm so that sufficient money can be found for industrial conversion and environmental protection so that the mad race to growth can go on. He claims that mankind 'can be "green" and grow'.[17]

Stern explains that the environmental-protection market will represent a new opening for the private sector to make profits. And to crown it all, he suggests that since developing countries pollute less than industrialized countries while suffering more of the consequences of global warming, they could sell polluting rights to the rich countries. With the revenues they would thus bring in, they could then finance the cost of repairing the harm done to their people.

In 2013 Nicholas Stern participated in the creation of the Global Commission on the Economy and Climate, which is both a think tank and a lobbying group dedicated to promoting green capitalism. Stern, who is chair of the commission, sits next to leaders of big private companies that are notorious sources of pollution, such as the cement manufacturer HolcimLafarge and the oil company Shell (whose CEO is a member of the commission). Other participants on the board of this private commission are the IMF's managing director, an executive officer of HSBC, a former governor of the World Bank, a former Mexican president, a former board member of the Development Bank of China and an executive officer of the Asian Development Bank.[18]

---

14   Ibid.
15   Stern Review, Summary of Conclusions, p. vii.
16   Ibid., p. viii.
17   Ibid., Introduction, p. iv.
18   See their website: Members of the Global Commission | New Climate Economy | Commission on the Economy and Climate <newclimateeconomy.net>. Read Daniel Tanuro's critical approach, *Trop tard pour être pessimistes! Ecosocialisme ou effondrement* (*Too Late for Pessimism! Ecosocialism or Collapse*) (Paris: Textuel, 2020), pp. 113–15 (in French).

THE WORLD BANK CONGRATULATES ITSELF ON ITS SUPPOSED
ACTION AGAINST CLIMATE CHANGE

On several pages of the World Bank website we come across bold claims about its remarkable efforts in the struggle against climate change and in support of populations:

Just after the world came together for the landmark Paris Agreement on climate change, the Bank Group unveiled an ambitious Climate Change Action Plan to ramp up financial and technical support to developing countries to step up climate action. The World Bank Group committed to increasing climate finance from 20% of lending in 2016 to 28% by 2020. This target was exceeded each year for the last three consecutive years. [...]

As a result of the Action Plan, all new Bank projects are screened for climate risk. [...]

[T]he Bank's support has branched out beyond sectors traditionally identified with climate action, such as energy, agriculture and environment, expanding the range of climate-smart development to projects that include enhancing digital development and climate resilience. [...]

There is no option but to take climate into account in terms of a recovery from COVID. [...]

There is no doubt that the disruption caused by COVID-19 reinforces the importance of guarding against the environmental risks that have severe and systematic impacts across the economy. [...]

Through the Action Plan, the Bank Group has helped countries reduce the disaster risk through a combination of measures to build resilience in people, infrastructures, and economies. [...]

The Group prioritized investments in renewable energy and energy efficiency as key to helping clients reduce emissions. [...]

[O]ur next Climate Change Action Plan (2020–2025), already underway, aims to boost support for countries to take ambitious climate action by increasing financing for adaptation and supporting increased systemic climate action at the country level.[19]

A HUGE GAP BETWEEN THE WORLD BANK'S
DISCOURSE AND ACTUAL FACTS

There is a huge gap between what the World Bank claims and what it actually does: by promoting fossil and/or polluting energies, the World Bank flouts UN commitments. This is revealed in an investigation carried out by the International

---

19   All these quotations are from the World Bank official website: '5 years of climate leadership: the World Bank Group's first Climate Action Plan' <worldbank.org/en/news/immersive-story/2020/09/08/5-years-of-climate-leadership-the-world-bank-groups-first-climate-action-plan> [accessed 25/01/2022].

Consortium of Investigative Journalists (ICIJ), which includes three German media companies – Norddeutsche Rundfunk, Süddeutsche Zeitung and Deutsche Welle.[20] In 2021, construction of the 'world's largest oil refinery project' was announced in Nigeria.[21] It is being financed by Aliko Dangote, the wealthiest man in Africa.[22] In spite of its global commitments on climate, the World Bank supports Dangote's project: it finances at least five of the banks that granted loans to the businessman. Dangote also received a further credit line of over $150 million from the Bank.

In the context of the International Consortium's investigation, journalist Sandrine Blanchard states that the World Bank justified this loan by claiming that it was meant to help Nigeria improve its activities in the field of natural resources, particularly the production of fertilizers. But Blanchard notes that it is impossible to separate the plant producing fertilizers from the rest of the oil project.[23]

According to the ICIJ, this is but one among many other World Bank investments in fossil energies. Sometimes it even directly invests in coal mining and oil and natural-gas extraction. This is the case in Kenya, Mozambique and Guyana. All in all, the Bank grants more financial support to fossil energies than to renewable energies, which is a source of concern for Uwe Kekeritz, a member of the German parliament (Bundestag) who is in charge of development policies within the German Green Party. Kekeritz is quoted as saying, 'The World Bank's influence is huge and its sustained investments in fossil energies have a disastrous impact on climate, which is unacceptable for a bank that is supposed to support development and should thus have global development as its primary focus.'[24]

The German NGO Urgewald also noted that the World Bank had granted over $12 billion in loans for projects relying on fossil fuel between 2015 – the year of the Paris Agreement – and 2020.[25]

---

20 International Consortium of Investigative Journalists (ICIJ), 'The World Bank is still hooked on fossil fuels despite climate pledge', 10 April 2019 <icij.org/investigations/world-bank/the-world-bank-is-still-hooked-on-fossil-fuels-despite-climate-pledge/> [accessed 25/01/2022].

21 'World's largest oil refinery project to help meet Nigeria's oil demands', World-Energy, 3 June 2021 <www.world-energy.org/article/18091.html> [accessed 25/01/2022].

22 Aliko Dangote, born at Kano, northern Nigeria on 10 April 1957, is a Nigerian businessman who is estimated to be the wealthiest man in Africa. In 2018, when French president Emmanuel Macron went to Lagos, he met with this Nigerian billionaire. Aliko Dangote is fully in favour of the African Continental Free Trade Area. In January 2020 and again in November 2020, Dangote announced that he wanted to buy the British football club Arsenal.

23 Sandrine Blanchard, with Fanny Fascar, Astrid Rasch and Elisabeth Weydt, 'La Banque mondiale investit dans des énergies fossiles, nuisibles au climat' ('The World Bank invests in climate-damaging fossil energy'), Deutsche Welle, 11 April 2019 (in French) <www.dw.com>.

24 'L'influence de la Banque mondiale est gigantesque et ces investissements continus dans les énergies fossiles ont des répercussions catastrophiques sur le climat. C'est inacceptable car il s'agit d'une banque vouée au développement et qui devrait mettre le développement du monde au cœur de sa politique, ce qui n'est pas le cas.' (Cited in ibid. (translation CADTM).)

25 Heike Mainhardt, 'The World Bank drives billions into fossil fuel investments', Urgewald press release, 11 April 2019) <urgewald.org/world-bank-drives-billions-fossil-fuel-investments> [accessed 17/12/2021].

How can the World Bank claim that it stopped financing fossil energies in 2019? The answer is simple enough: officially its loans are meant for 'technical assistance' to the governments of countries that wish to develop the extraction of fossil fuels. The Bank claims that it does not directly finance exploration for and extraction of those fuels; but in fact, through 'technical assistance' loans, it plays a key role in enabling those countries to exploit the fossil fuels present beneath their soil.

If we examine the World Bank website, though these extractivist projects are mixed in with 'environmental' ones, we can see that in 2020 it granted loans to projects that are directly connected to the coal industry, non-renewable energies, and exploitation of gas and oil. The 'green' projects are in fact mere greenwashing for excessive exploitation of nature.

There follow a number of examples that show the negative role played by World Bank technical assistance loans.

MOZAMBIQUE: THE LIQUEFIED NATURAL GAS MEGA-PROJECT CO-FINANCED BY THE WORLD BANK

In an article published in July 2020, Heike Mainhardt of Urgewald wrote:

On July 16, it was widely reported that French oil major Total and partners signed financing agreements worth US$14.9 billion for the massive Area 1 Liquefied Natural Gas (LNG) project in Mozambique.

The deal is being hailed as the largest project financing ever in Africa. It involves 19 commercial banks and public finance from 8 export credit agencies (ECA) and the African Development Bank.

What has not been widely reported is the important role of World Bank public assistance that enabled such a large, unprecedented gas investment to go forward.[26]

The World Bank's contribution consists of a loan of $87 million to finance technical assistance 'with the stated aim of improving governance in order to increase gas and mining investments to bring about broad-based growth'. As Mainhardt reveals, 'Much of the Bank's assistance has focused on supporting Areas 1 and 4, which turn Mozambique into one of the world's largest LNG exporters. The giant LNG development is at the center of growing concerns over displacements [and] loss of fishing livelihoods', as well as exacerbation of the environmental and climate crisis. As Mainhardt says:

---

26 Heike Mainhardt, 'World Bank policy advice boosts oil and gas, undermining climate goals', 21 July 2020 <climatechangenews.com/2020/07/21/world-bank-policy-advice-boosts-oil-gas-industry-undermining-climate-goals/> [accessed 17/12/2021] (all quotes in this section are drawn from this article.)

For many reasons, it is important to understand the role of the World Bank.

In practice, the World Bank's technical assistance funds consultants to advise the government on such things as tax and regulatory policies and the facilitation of large complex financial agreements. Bank-funded consultants have been supporting the government for years to lay the legal groundwork and negotiate the agreements to secure the $14.9 billion finance package.

During the World Bank-sponsored advisory, a new law covering LNG Areas 1 and 4 activities was published in December 2014. According to the law firm Shearman and Sterling, among many concessions, this law includes that no preference needs to be given to Mozambican suppliers for procurement of goods and services [...].

This concession greatly increased opportunities for companies from the countries with participating ECAs at the expense of Mozambican firms. The Export Import Bank of the United States (US Exim) announced its $5 billion loan to Area 1 LNG involves 68 American suppliers and will support an estimated 16,400 American jobs. It is hard to believe this financing agreement structured with the help of World Bank-paid consultants is the optimal outcome for job creation in Mozambique.

Still according to Heike Mainhardt,

Since 2012, the World Bank has funded over $14 million in contracts to at least 12 consulting firms to assist the government on the financial package negotiations involved in LNG Areas 1 and 4. Many of these firms have ties to oil companies and at least two [...] raise substantial conflict of interests. In addition to advising the government of Mozambique, the law firm SNR Denton also advised multiple oil companies involved in Mozambique's LNG Area 1, including Total, ONGC Videsh Limited (OVL), and Bharat PetroResources.

Furthermore, in 2016 ExxonMobil acquired a 25% interest in Mozambique's LNG Area 4. In 2018, the World Bank funded a $2.4 million contract for LNG transaction assistance involving a group of consultants, including ExxonMobil's favored law firm Hunton Andrews Kurth. During this same period, ExxonMobil paid the law firm $500,000 in lobbying fees in the US. It is obvious that instead of promoting governance that would shield the government from the oil industry's influence, the World Bank's assistance is facilitating it.

In addition to favouring oil companies and financiers over the interests of Mozambique:

the World Bank's public assistance undermines its commitment to the goals of the Paris Climate Agreement, which include limiting global warming to 1.5C.

In November 2019, researchers from several expert organizations, including the UN Environment Program, alerted international public opinion as they determined that the world was on track to produce 120% more fossil fuels in 2030 than would be compatible with a 1.5C pathway. Simply put, there is already far too much investment going into fossil fuel production.

As noted earlier, the World Bank announced in 2017 that it would cease financing oil and gas by the end of 2019, but excluded technical assistance and development policy loans. As a result the Bank's loans and advice in fact support oil and gas and thus undermine climate goals. As Mainhardt explains,

One particularly important area the Bank's assistance continues to support is tax incentives for fossil fuel investments. In Mozambique, to attract new investments beyond Areas 1 and 4, the World Bank's $110 million development policy loan in 2014 required the government to approve a new petroleum tax law. The new tax law includes several investment incentives, such as accelerated rates of depreciation for oil and gas exploration.

Accelerated depreciation of new capital investments allows oil companies to quickly write down capital investments that would otherwise depreciate more gradually. In other words, larger tax reductions are taken at the start of the operation, thus making new projects more economic and increasing cash flows that can be put towards more drilling.

SURINAME (SOUTH AMERICA)

As noted by Jacey Bingler of Urgewald in a report published in December 2020,[27] on the eve of the Paris Climate Agreement's fifth anniversary, the World Bank Group 'approved a $23 million technical assistance operation for Suriname in July 2019 aimed at developing the extractive industries, which could include oil and gas'. The Bank thus granted the Suriname government the financial means needed to 'pave the way for big oil companies to exploit the Guyana-Suriname basin's resources at the cost of its people and the environment'. In the light of such actions, Bingler says, the World Bank's 'promises regarding climate responsibility ring hollow. The Bank's warning that the region will be severely impacted by the climate crisis and resulting sea-level rise is beyond cynical.'

One last illustration: in 2019 the World Bank granted Brazil a loan of $38 million for technical assistance contracts to develop oil and gas operations.

DEBTS CLAIMED BY THE WORLD BANK AND THE IMF ARE ODIOUS AND MUST BE CANCELLED

The World Bank and the IMF demand repayment of debts by many developing countries on loans that have resulted in incalculable damage to their populations and to the entire planet. These debts fall under the definition of odious debt because they were contracted against the interest of the populations of the indebted countries. A further condition must be met for a debt to be considered odious:

---

27   This section relies on Jacey Bingler's paper 'Big Oil has set its eyes on Suriname', in *Five Years Lost – How Finance is Blowing the Paris Carbon Budget* (Urgewald, 10 December 2020) <urgewald.org/five-years-lost> [accessed 07/03/2021].

244 The World Bank

that the creditors knew, or cannot provide evidence that they did not know, that their loans were against the interest of the populations.[28] As shown in this chapter and in several studies, including some produced by the World Bank and the IMF themselves, the leaders of those institutions did indeed know that in actual fact their loans were used to support policies that went against the interest of the people and of the environment. Citizens are entitled to demand cancellation of that debt. The same applies to debts claimed by private investors or by creditor governments.

CONCLUSION

The promoters of the dominant productivist model and of the capitalist system initially denied that environmental damage and climate change were a major issue and continued to actively support policies that worsen the situation. When their position became impossible to defend, they made the headlines in international media by publishing a report on the issue, thus attempting to give credence to the idea that international institutions and the governments of the most industrialized countries have taken the measure of this serious problem, while in fact it had been deliberately concealed for decades. At the end of the day, those who defend the current system attempt to perpetuate it by implying that it can provide the solution to a problem it is largely responsible for. It is urgent to understand that environmental damage and ever-increasing inequalities are inherent in the productivist capitalist system and that the only fair and sustainable solution requires that that system be radically called into question.

---

28   A definition of odious debt can be found in the glossary. See also Éric Toussaint, 'A country is entitled to refuse to pay a debt', 18 November 2020, CADTM <cadtm.org/A-country-is-entitled-to-refuse-to-repay-a-debt> and Éric Toussaint, 'The doctrine of odious debt, from Alexander Sack to CADTM', 24 November 2016, CADTM <cadtm.org/The-Doctrine-of-Odious-Debt-from-Alexander-Sack-to-the-CADTM> [both accessed 27/02/2023].

22

Paul Wolfowitz (2005–07): An Architect of the Invasion of Iraq at the Head of the World Bank

The decision of US President George W. Bush to appoint the neoconservative Paul Wolfowitz – as deputy secretary of defense, one of the principal architects of the US invasion of Afghanistan in 2001 and Iraq in 2003– president of the World Bank created much controversy in March 2005. Prior to that decision, media such as the British *Financial Times* had campaigned for a World Bank president chosen for their competence in Third World development and preferably from among citizens of a Southern country. The *Financial Times* had advanced the name of Mexico's president, Ernesto Zedillo, towards the end of the 1990s. Bush's choice of Wolfowitz clearly stated who was running the show. The 24 World Bank governors did no more than rubber-stamp the US choice.

But who was Paul Wolfowitz? He is a pure US state apparatchik, with long experience in the US corridors of power as well as a brief university career. Having graduated with a BA in mathematics, at the age of 23 he went into US government service in the Bureau of the Budget (1966–67). In 1969, he worked for the Committee to Maintain a Prudent Defense Policy, which lobbied Congress in favour of the ABM 'nuclear umbrella', which they said was needed to protect the US from the Soviet Union. They succeeded. As from that moment Wolfowitz was committed to questions of military strategy. A principal theme was identifying adversaries (the USSR, China, Iraq, etc.) and showing them to be more dangerous than they appeared, so as to justify an additional defence effort (a bigger budget, manufacture of new weapons, wider deployment of troops abroad) – up to and including the launch of preventive strikes or wars intended to prevent potential threats rather than respond to actual attacks.

Wolfowitz taught for two years at Yale while working on a doctorate in political science at the University of Chicago, a principal intellectual centre of reactionary conservatism.[1] His doctorate was awarded in 1972. Then for four years he worked at the Arms Control and Disarmament Agency (1973–77) alongside George H.W. Bush

---

1   Milton Friedman, a University of Chicago mandarin, and the so-called Chicago Boys advised Chilean dictator Augusto Pinochet following his US-enabled coup in September 1973. See Toussaint, *Your Money or Your Life*, chapter 14, 'Neoliberal ideology and politics: historical perspectives', pp. 254–69.

(Bush Sr), who at that time was at the head of the CIA. In 1977, during the Carter administration, he went directly to the Pentagon, where he remained until 1980 and where he produced reports claiming falsely that the USSR was building new types of atomic weapons. Despite having worked under a Democrat president, after serving a year of penance at Johns Hopkins University and changing his party affiliation to Republican he joined the Ronald Reagan administration in 1981, becoming director of policy planning at the State Department. From 1983 to 1986, he was Assistant Secretary of State for East Asian and Pacific Affairs under Reagan. From 1986 to 1989 he served as US ambassador to Indonesia. Between 1989 and 1993, he was strategy director for Secretary of State Richard ('Dick') Cheney under the Bush Sr administration, which presided over the First Gulf War. During the Clinton years he served as dean of the Paul Nitze School of International Studies (750 students) at Johns Hopkins. He served the school well, managing to collect $75 million in donations while also acting as a consultant to the giant defence contractor Northrop Grumman.

In 1997, Wolfowitz was one of the founders of the PNAC (Project for a New American Century), a neoconservative pressure group. Other members included Donald Rumsfeld (Secretary of Defense in 2001), Dick Cheney (CEO of Halliburton at the time and US vice-president in 2001), Jeb Bush (son of H.W. Bush and brother of George W. Bush), Richard Perle and Robert Kagan. As from 1998 the PNAC put pressure on Bill Clinton to launch preventive attacks against Iraq and other potentially aggressive states. Following the two Clinton administrations, Wolfowitz became Deputy Secretary of Defense, planning, directing and justifying the invasions of Afghanistan and Iraq alongside Donald Rumsfeld.

During the 1983–89 period when Paul Wolfowitz was involved in US policy in East Asia, he actively supported dictatorships. Indeed, contrary to the image he liked to cultivate, he supported the military dictatorships of Ferdinand Marcos in the Philippines, Chun Doo-hwan in South Korea and Suharto in Indonesia.

In the early 1980s he tried to save Ferdinand Marcos's position by persuading him to implement some democratic reforms. At the time in the Philippines a powerful revolutionary guerrilla movement, allied with a bourgeoisie strongly opposed to the dictatorship under the leadership of Benigno Aquino, was close to bringing about another US defeat similar to that in Nicaragua in 1979, when the Sandinistas allied with the bourgeois opposition led by Violeta Chamorro. It was not Paul Wolfowitz who chased Ferdinand Marcos from power in 1986 but the people's concerted action, with the US securing the dictator's flight to Hawaii.[2]

As for South Korea, Wolfowitz claimed to have persuaded dictator Chun Doo-hwan (who had ordered massacres during the 1980 uprising) to step down

---

2 See Walden Bello, *US Sponsored Low Intensity Conflict in the Philippines* (San Francisco: Institute for Food and Development Policy, 1987).

in 1987. In fact, the dictator's demise was the result of the actions of millions of students, workers and citizens demonstrating against him.

In Indonesia, where actions against the dictatorship were less developed (with good reason too: when he seized power in 1965, Suharto had half a million civilians massacred), the USA supported the dictator as late as early 1998. Paul Wolfowitz, who as will be remembered had been the US ambassador in Jakarta from 1986 to 1989, stated before Congress in May 1997 that 'any balanced judgment of the situation in Indonesia today, including the very important and sensitive issue of human rights, needs to take account of the significant progress that Indonesia has already made and needs to acknowledge that much of this progress has to be credited to the strong and remarkable leadership of President Suharto'.[3]

In the early 2000s Wolfowitz was one of the architects of the 'preventive war' concept used to justify the invasions of Afghanistan and Iraq beginning in October 2001. He was one of the main originators of the lies disseminated through the media about the threat Saddam Hussein represented to the international community. He was also behind the false claims concerning Iraq's supposed 'weapons of mass destruction' and Hussein's alleged support of Al-Qaida and international terrorism. In the early days of the war, he had claimed that US soldiers would always be seen as the liberators of Iraq and therefore welcomed by the Iraqi people. He also asserted that Iraq would pay for its 'liberation' itself thanks to its oil. In fact, Wolfowitz, Donald Rumsfeld, George W. Bush and Dick Cheney used the occupation and so-called 'reconstruction' of Iraq for the greater profit of US transnational corporations. And Wolfowitz did the same using the conditionalities tied to World Bank aid.

As this is being written, with the US completing its withdrawal from Afghanistan, Paul Wolfowitz has joined a chorus of other ideologues of US/NATO unilateralism and militarism who are attempting to 'manage the narrative', as the journalist Caitlin Johnstone puts it,[4] 'spinning' the Afghanistan debacle as proof of the need to continue the same strategy of world domination. These include former British prime minister Tony Blair, former US president George W. Bush and John Bolton, former US ambassador to the UN under W. Bush and national security adviser to Donald Trump. In an op-ed in the *Wall Street Journal* entitled 'The "Forever War" hasn't ended', Wolfowitz referred to the debacle in Afghanistan as 'a wake-up call for many Americans'.[5] Just after 11 September 2001, he was using

3   Tim Shorrock, 'Paul Wolfowitz, Reagan's Man in Indonesia, Is Back at the Pentagon', *Foreign Policy in Focus*, February 2001, p. 3 <fpif.org/paul_wolfowitz_reagans_man_in_indonesia_is_back_at_the_pentagon/> [accessed 19/12/2021].

4   Caitlin Johnstone, 'Bush-era war criminals are louder than ever', CaitlinJohnstone.com, 22 August 2021 <consortiumnews.com/2021/08/24/bush-era-war-criminals-are-louder-than-ever/> [accessed 19/12/2021].

5   Paul Wolfowitz, 'The "Forever War" hasn't ended', *Wall Street Journal*, 27 August 2021 <wsj.com/articles/endless-war-afghanistan-withdrawal-biden-taliban-isis-mass-casualty-terror-attack-taiwan-11630076447> [accessed 19/12/2021].

that exact term, 'wake-up call', to refer to the terrorist attacks.[6] Wolfowitz seems to believe that the patent failure of the Afghanistan and Iraq invasions, of which he was one of the instigators, is a justification for continuing to pursue the same policy of US interventionism that spawned them, just as the 9/11 attacks served as the pretext for those catastrophic invasions. Paul Wolfowitz may well embody better than any single individual the symbiotic relationship between the military and arms manufacturers, political figures bent on maintaining US hegemony, academics who – through the various 'think tanks' often funded by the arms industry and the extractive industries – provide the ideas and the discourse to enable and justify their policies, and the international financial institutions.[7] And if there was any doubt about the latter's role, it has just been dispelled by the announcement that the IMF and World Bank are suspending all operations in Afghanistan.[8] The BBC quotes an IMF spokesperson as saying 'As is always the case, the IMF is guided by the views of the international community.' Of course, we know who the 'international community' really refers to.

WASHINGTON'S OFFENSIVE AGAINST MULTILATERAL ORGANIZATIONS

The appointment of Paul Wolfowitz needs to be seen against the background of the US offensive on several multilateral institutions.

Act One: On 18 January 2005, UN Secretary-General Kofi Annan decided to appoint Ann Veneman, secretary of agriculture in the Bush Jr administration, executive director of UNICEF. It just so happens that the USA and Somalia are the only two countries that have not ratified the UN Convention on the Rights of the Child, or UNCRC (ratified by 189 countries). We can easily imagine the kind of pressure Annan was under to make such a decision.

Act Two: On 7 March 2005, George W. Bush chose John Bolton as US ambassador to the UN. This ultraconservative figure who went on to be President Donald Trump's

---

6   Wolfowitz told the Senate Armed Services Committee, on 4 October 2001, 'These attacks were an assault on our people and our way of life; but they were also a wake-up call – one that we ignore at our peril' <globalsecurity.org/military/library/congress/2001_hr/011004wolf.pdf> [accessed 19/12/2021]. And in an interview with the *San Francisco Chronicle* the following February he said 'There is an opportunity now to really move to a policy that doesn't continue tolerate terrorism as a necessary evil. And I think in that respect that 9/11 really was a wake up call and that if we take proper advantage of this opportunity to prevent the future terrorist use of weapons of mass destruction that it will have been an extremely valuable wake up call.' ('Wolfowitz interview with the San Francisco Chronicle', US Department of Defense News Transcript, 23 February 2002 <w.leadingtowar.com/PDFsources_claims_atta/2002_02_23_dept_defense.pdf> [accessed 19/12/2021].

7   That symbiotic entity has been called the 'MICIMATT' – for Military-Industrial-Congressional-Intelligence-Media-Academia-Think-Tank – Complex, in extension of the term 'Military-Industrial Complex'.

8   Beth Timmons, 'IMF suspends Afghanistan's access to funds', *BBC News*, 19 August 2021 <bbc.com/news/business-58263525> [accessed 1/09/2021].

national security adviser nurtures a deep-seated hatred towards the UN, as testified by his often-quoted statement that if the 38-storey UN building 'lost 10 storeys today, it wouldn't make a bit of difference'.[9] Bolton tried to have Mohamed ElBaradei (head of the UN mission that was to keep track of Iraq's disarmament programme shortly before the 2003 war) sacked. He also managed to see to it that the US did not ratify the treaty that established the International Criminal Court and withdrew from the UN Conference against Racism, convened in Durban in August 2001. The UN, in Bolton's opinion, should never stand in the way of US foreign policy. He even once stated that 'there is no United Nations. There is an international community that occasionally can be led by the only real power left in the world, and that's the United States, when it suits our interests.'[10]

Act Three: On 10 March 2005, George W. Bush announced that Paul Wolfowitz was his candidate for World Bank president. On 31 March the Bank's Board of Governors unanimously approved Wolfowitz. Bush had shown the international community and his supporters that he could and would press direct US leadership on multilateral institutions.

Wolfowitz's appointment is in a way similar to that of Robert McNamara in 1968. McNamara had been Defense Secretary and was withdrawn from that post when the Vietnam War turned into a fiasco. Wolfowitz had to leave his post when it became clear that the war in Iraq was a failure. Like McNamara, Wolfowitz knew how to manage a large administration: the Pentagon. And like McNamara, Wolfowitz was an adviser to the US president on foreign policy issues.

Paul Wolfowitz's hasty resignation from the World Bank

When it was discovered in 2007 that Paul Wolfowitz had increased the salary of his girlfriend, a World Bank employee, by 45 per cent, the Bank's Staff Association considered the favouritism unacceptable and made such a din that Wolfowitz had no choice but to resign. The call for his resignation was backed up by such personalities as the New Zealand executive director Graeme Wheeler, Democrat party leader John Kerry and the European Parliament, among others. Since then, he has never really returned to centre stage. At the age of 64, his political career was over.

---

9   Julian Borger, 'Bush loses another ally as UN ambassador Bolton resigns in face of Senate hostility', *The Guardian*, 5 December 2006 <theguardian.com/world/2006/dec/05/topstories3.usa> [accessed 19/12/2021].

10 Ed Pilkington, 'Who is John Bolton, Trump's new national security adviser?', *The Guardian* 23 March 2018 <theguardian.com/us-news/2018/mar/22/who-is-john-bolton-trump-national-security-adviser> [accessed 25/01/2022].

23

Ecuador: Progress and the Limits of Resistance to the Policies of the World Bank, the IMF and Other Creditors

Ecuador provides an example of a government which officially decided to investigate the process of indebtedness so as to identify illegitimate debt and suspend its repayment. The fact that the government suspended payment of a large part of its commercial debt, only to buy it back at a lower price, shows that it was willing to go beyond mere rhetoric. In fact, it undertook the unilateral restructuring of part of its external debt and thus won a moral victory over its private creditors, who were mainly banks.

In 2007, at the beginning of Rafael Correa's presidency, the government of Ecuador clashed with the World Bank. In this chapter we first analyze the loans granted by the World Bank and the IMF. Then we recount the government's actions mainly regarding the debt audit and the resulting suspension of payment. Finally, we discuss the limitations of the actions of Rafael Correa's government, and briefly evoke the policies of his successor Lenín Moreno (2017–21) and the election of Guillermo Lasso, a former banker, as president in 2021.

The IMF had imposed a programme on Ecuador from 1983 aimed at macroeconomic stability in the short term, so that the country could once again be in a position to repay its debts. The programme took the form of a signed 'letter of intent' between the indebted country and the IMF, imposing antisocial policies such as fiscal and budgetary austerity, devaluation of the currency, price liberalization, etc. Between 1983 and 2003, Ecuador signed 13 such letters of intent. Successive governments of Ecuador did not hesitate to sign these documents, despite the mainly negative impact of the measures they prescribed on the majority of the population. Then in November 2006 Rafael Correa was elected president. Correa was determined to free the country from its debt burden and broke with the Bank, but in the end his government was not willing to take all the necessary steps. Since 2017, Correa's successor Lenín Moreno has returned to the fold of the IMF and the World Bank, triggering massive popular mobilization, especially in October 2019.

The radical neoliberal U-turn was accentuated in the 1990s when the Washington Consensus was enshrined and Ecuador entered the global economy, particularly when Sixto Durán Ballén was president of the Republic, from 1992. That coincided with the World Bank's agenda, as the latter strongly increased its activity and influence in Ecuador from the late 1980s and early 1990s. In Ecuador, as in many developing countries, the Bank granted loans tied to measures aiming to open up markets, reduce the state's role in managing the economy and increase the power of private banks to regulate monetary flows.

The Bank and its accomplices in the country's political class share responsibility for a fraudulent and illegitimate debt that has been incurred at the expense of basic human rights and the sovereignty of the state.

ECUADOR'S DEBT TOWARDS THE WORLD BANK (IBRD)

Between 1990 and July 2007, the World Bank (IBRD) paid $1.44 billion to Ecuador while over the same period, the Ecuadorian government paid $2.51 billion to the Bank. In other words, over the period 1990 to July 2007, the World Bank made a profit of $1.07 billion on the backs of the people of Ecuador. The Bank earned an excellent return on its investment.

By 30 November 2007, Ecuador's total public debt towards the World Bank Group had reached $704.4 million.

Had Ecuador decided, in 2008, to repudiate that entire $704.4 million debt towards the World Bank as recommended by its Debt Audit Commission (see below), that decision would have enabled the country to save over a billion dollars (adding the interest no longer to be paid to the capital to be refunded). Such a sum would have enabled the funding of breakfast and lunch for 1.28 million school-children for 15 years. Or the same amount would have covered five years of health insurance for the country's poor and destitute populations.[1]

THE NEFARIOUS ROLE OF THE WORLD BANK IN TERMS OF FINANCIAL DEREGULATION

The World Bank's intervention in defining the economic and social policies applied in Ecuador was intensive and permanent until 2006 and today, after an interruption of several years during Rafael Correa's term of office, it is back with a vengeance. The Bank had been responsible for the explosion of debt crises since 1993–94. Several large loans from the World Bank that Ecuador must pay back until 2025 and beyond were clearly aimed at financing the adoption of legal reforms that completely deregulate the banking sector. These reforms fostered, when they did not actually trigger, several financial crises throughout the 1990s, including the major banking crisis of 1999, with its terrible consequences for the economy and the country's population.[2]

---

1   The author's calculations are based on the report of the Commission of Inquiry into the Financial Economic Crisis (Comisión Investigadora de la Crisis Económica Financiera), *Síntesis De Los Resultados De La Investigación*, July 2007, p. 45.

2   See Matthieu Le Quang interviewed by Violaine Delteil, 'Entre buen vivir et neo-extractivisme: les quadratures de la politique economique equatorienne' ('Between good living and neo-extractivism: how Ecuadorian economic policy squares up'), *Revue de la Régulation*, 1st semester 2019 (in French only) <journals.openedition.org/regulation/15076> [accessed 19/12/2021].

The World Bank's intervention was clearly damaging and in short constituted a *dol* – a French term meaning fraud by deceit – against the country.

- The 1993 Law Modernizing the State, Privatizations and Management of Public Services by Private Initiative (Ley de Modernización del Estado, Privatizaciones y Prestación de Servicios Públicos por parte de la iniciativa privada) opened up domains hitherto reserved for state management to private-sector participation as well as merging or eliminating public institutions. The law increased the attributions of the National Council for Modernization (Consejo Nacional de Modernización – CONAM), whose function was to privatize public services, particularly in the oil, electricity and water sectors.
- The Law of Monetary Regulation and the State Bank (Ley de Regimen monetario y Banco de Estado) reinforced the independence of the Central Bank and enabled free determination of interest rates and free access to the currency market.
- The 1993 Law of Promotion of Investments (Ley de Promocion de Inversiones) eliminated control of capital flows.
- The 1994 General Law of the Institutions of the Financial System (Ley General de Instituciones del Sistema financiero) continued the liberalization of banking activities – offshore offices, multiplication of financial entities, loans from the Central Bank to private banks (causing inflation to explode), etc. – and limited the scope and reach of banking supervision.

These legal provisions led to the creation of a single account in Ecuador's Central Bank for all the institutions that were to receive transfers from the Ministry of Economy and Finance. This resulted in the use of private banking networks and the reduction of the number of Central Bank accounts held by public institutions. It fulfilled the Ecuadorian government's commitment, in the letter of intent it had signed with the IMF in 1990, to follow the World Bank's lead and make a sweeping reform of the finances of town councils, provincial councils and other government bodies. The goal of this reform was to reduce the amounts transferred from central government and supposedly to improve spending decisions at the local level and make participation in public revenue fairer and more transparent.

As Piedad Mancero, who was a member of the Ecuador Debt Audit Commission in 2007, explains:

It wasn't long before the consequences made themselves felt: an inordinate number of finance companies, the first crisis in 1995, currency speculation, banks failing in 1998–1999. [...] It was obvious: the Central Bank's resources allocated to such loans came from Treasury issues that generated galloping inflation of the mass of currency in circulation, uncontrollable inflationary pressure and speculative demand for currency, which contributed to the great financial crisis of 1999 and the over-hasty adoption of dollarization in January 2000.'[3]

Lastly, in 1998, the Law of the Capital Market (Ley de Mercado de Capitales) and the Law of Reorganization of Economic Matters (Ley de Reordenamiento en Materia Economico) completed the World Bank's destructive work. The Agency for Guaranteeing Deposits (Agencia de Garantía de Depósitos – AGD) was created. It guarantees all deposits, offshore and onshore, without restriction, and made it possible for the Central Bank to grant loans to banks in difficulty and to acquire AGD bonds.[4] Officially created to prevent the crisis spreading and to protect small savers, the AGD was actually set up to further the interests of proprietors and the large borrowers from private banks, especially the banks Filanbanco and FINAGRO.[5]

The financial crisis of 1999 had disastrous consequences for all Ecuadorians. The AGD estimated the total cost of the crisis at \$8.07 billion, or the equivalent of 83 per cent of the general state budget in 2007, or the equivalent of 20 years of health insurance for the entire population. Those state resources, thus used and abused, could not be invested in education, health, job creation, etc. Worse still, the state had to contract more debt to finance the bank bailouts. Poverty levels rose spectacularly, and one million Ecuadorians were forced to emigrate between 1999 and 2005.[6]

The World Bank's responsibility in the Ecuadorian crisis is flagrantly obvious, in view of its active intervention to make the country's government adopt the neoliberal reforms that led to the crisis.

FINANCIAL DEREGULATION CAUSES THE SAME DEVASTATING EFFECTS IN THE NORTH AS IN THE SOUTH

It is important to see the connection between the measures imposed on Ecuador, that led straight to the crisis of 1999, and the effects of the neoliberal policies also applied in the countries of the North – particularly the United States, which has been

---

3   Piedad Mancero, 'El debilitamiento institucional en la decada de los 90 – Presentación de la investigación y análisis del Proyecto Modernización del Estado – BIRF-3822/EC', in Gabriela Weber (ed.), *Sobre La Deuda Ilegítima – Aportes al debate – Argumentos entre consideraciones éticas y normas legales* (Quito: Centro de Investigaciones CIUDAD, 2008), pp. 81–87 (in Spanish; translation CADTM).
4   This last section of the law contravenes Article 265 of Ecuador's constitution. The article stipulates that the Central Bank may not acquire bonds issued by state institutions nor award loans to private institutions except short-term loans of liquidities. The adoption of this law was in fact made possible by Transitional Provision 42 of the 1998 constitution, authorizing the Central Bank, over a period of two years, to make loans to banks in crisis. This Transitional Provision contradicts Article 265 of the same constitution.
5   Report of the Comisión Investigadora de la Crisis Económica Financiera, June 2007.
6   Ibid.

through several financial crises: one in 2001 and another in 2007–08. Deregulation to benefit the financial world in the context of the Washington Consensus, which fulfilled the expectations of the White House and Wall Street (as was denounced repeatedly by Joseph Stiglitz, 2001 Nobel Prize Laureate in Economics), was imposed both in the North and the South, and has produced the same catastrophic effects.

This deregulation was a definitive break from the measures taken in the wake of the crisis of 1929 and the 1930s in the United States. That crisis had been preceded by a wave of deregulation and speculation. The adoption of the Glass–Steagall Act in 1933, during Franklin D. Roosevelt's presidency, was a reaction to that crisis. The law required the complete separation of commercial banks from investment banks. In 1999, during the Clinton presidency, that law was abrogated under pressure from the big banks. The same approach was applied in Ecuador as in the USA.

The radical banking deregulation that began in the 1980s and was completed under the Clinton administration – leading to increasing speculation on financial markets and the development of 'derivatives' and financial institutions free of public control (such as hedge funds[7]) – was a major contributing factor to the US 'subprimes' financial crisis of 2007.

The World Bank has supported the national financial powers in Ecuador who consider themselves the masters of the country and who exploit the state and the government to reach their selfish ends. The Bank has intervened to destabilize governments that have tried to apply social and economic policies aimed at increasing social justice and sovereignty to stand up to the United States.

Such was the case in 2005 when the World Bank intervened against measures taken by Rafael Correa, then minister of the economy in the government of President Alfredo Palacio (see below).

THE STRUCTURAL ADJUSTMENT LOANS GRANTED BY THE WORLD BANK

From the early 1990s, the World Bank awarded loans in key economic and social sectors.[8] The main orientations were reforms of the legal framework to reduce state intervention, privatization of public companies, increased flexibility of the labour market, and financial deregulation and liberalization.

The series of loans awarded by the World Bank – Structural Adjustment Loan (Loan 3819), Debt and Debt Service Reduction Loan (Loan 3820), Public Enterprise Reform (Loan 3821) and Modernization of the State Technical Assistance Project (Loan 3822) – were all designed to reduce the state's influence, clear the way for

---

7   Hedge funds, which are not a form of protection as the name may imply, are non-listed speculative investment funds that seek high returns and make abundant use of derivatives, especially options, often with leverage. The main hedge funds are independent of banks, though banks often endow themselves with hedge funds. They come under the category of shadow banking.

8   Structural adjustment loans, sectoral adjustment loans or poverty reduction and growth facilities (PRGF).

private actors (especially in the telecommunications and electricity sectors) and ensure that Ecuador paid its debt to commercial creditors through the finance guarantees of the Brady Plan (see 'The Brady Plan').

The Brady Plan

Throughout the 1980s, the Brady Plan (named after Nicholas Brady, the US Secretary of the Treasury of the time) meant restructuring the debt of the main indebted countries with exchange of old loans, with reduction of their nominal value or interest rate, for new securities with longer maturity terms and repayment guaranteed by the international monetary authorities. Participant countries were Argentina, Brazil, Bulgaria, Costa Rica, Republic of Côte d'Ivoire, the Dominican Republic, Ecuador, Jordan, Mexico, Nigeria, Panama, Peru, the Philippines, Poland, Russia, Uruguay, Venezuela and Vietnam. At the time, Brady had announced that the volume of debt would be reduced by 30 per cent. In fact, when there was any reduction, it was far less than that; in several significant cases debt even increased. The new securities ('Brady Bonds') guaranteed a fixed interest rate of about 6 per cent, which was highly favourable to the banks. This also ensured the pursuance of austerity policies under the control of the IMF and the World Bank.

The World Bank granted loans to Ecuador so that the latter could align its fiscal and commercial policies with neoliberal globalization and redirect its productive activities towards export, to the detriment of the local market. The first loan (Private Sector Development Project – 3609) to promote these changes was disbursed in 1993,[9] followed in 1998 by a $21 million loan (International Trade and Integration Project – 4346) to support the export capacity of the private sector and remove obstacles to trade by adopting policies in line with WTO decisions and entering into new trade agreements.[10]

By promoting the intensive production of commodities destined for the export market (bananas, shrimp, flowers), these loans have had disastrous, and in some cases irreversible, environmental consequences. One striking example is shrimp farming, of which 90 per cent of production is destined for export. It has led to the destruction of 70 per cent of the mangrove forest biome, a rich ecosystem from which local communities made their living and which forms a natural barrier against flooding and salinization of the soil. The activity has even been developed in zones where the law prohibited the construction of fish-farming pools.

---

9   Conditionalities included continued liberalization of interest rates, the creation of a favourable climate for foreign investments, liberalization of trade and new labour laws.

10   For this, the project provided for a reorganization of the Ministry of Trade, Industry and Fisheries (MICIP in Spanish) and the creation of a new public-private body, the Corporation for the Promotion of Exports and Investment (CORPEI), to promote exports. The project financed the 'training' of MICIP officials and representatives of the private sector in negotiating international trade agreements. Moreover, the World Bank insisted on reducing the staff of the MICIP from 400 to 190 officials. The government had previously adopted a code of good conduct for the adoption and implementation of the norms of a WTO agreement relating to technical barriers to trade.

To complete the environmental disaster, the World Bank has directly financed devastating projects in the domains of agriculture and management of natural resources such as minerals and water. A good example would be the PRODEMINCA (Ecuador Mining Development and Environmental Control Technical Assistance Project, Loan 3655 EC) in 1994, which included the introduction of a new Mining Code and reforms favourable to investors.[11] Two laws (Trole I and II) facilitated the pillage of resources by multinationals by undermining the role of the Ministry of the Environment and permitting mining activities in protected areas.

The World Bank also developed a project regarding indigenous peoples (Indigenous and Afro-Ecuadorian Peoples Development Project – Loan 4277). Once again, the project was aimed at favouring private investments, reducing the role of the state and modifying the legal framework. Not only is the country indebted, but the indigenous communities themselves are also indebted. The project's aim was to increase the dependence of indigenous and peasant communities on seed, herbicides and pesticides supplied by transnational firms. It also had racist and discriminatory characteristics regarding indigenous peoples and Afro-descendants. Moreover, as was denounced by Ecuadorian social movements, it contained a hidden agenda aimed at weakening the powerful indigenous movement, especially the Confederation of Indigenous Nationalities of Ecuador.

These loans had many extremely negative consequences for the majority of Ecuador's population, not least of which was the dramatic reduction of access to public services. Loan 3285 of 1991 for a sum of $104 million to finance decentralization caused a reduction in the amounts awarded to territorial communities. The project gave the IFI more control over the budget and allowed them to pressure the state to increase the share used for debt repayments. The conditions tied to Loan 3821 (Public Enterprise Reform) of 10 February 1995 also reduced electricity subsidies and planned the future privatization of the state power company INECEL.

Public-sector employees have come under constant attack. The Technical Assistance for the Modernization of the State project led to a workforce reduction of 10,000 posts in the civil service. The loss of employment represented a cost to the state of $396.3 million.[12] The government took on another $20 million in debt for a project to restructure the public sector to reduce costs, and it cost them 20 times more than that due to loss of employment!

---

11 The World Bank financed a considerable number of other projects that harm the environment and/or jeopardize food sovereignty and natural resources: Irrigation Subsector Technical Assistance Project (Loan 3730), PROMSA (Agricultural Services Modernization Program, Loan 4075-O-EC), PRAGUAS (Rural and Small Towns Water Supply and Sanitation Project) I and II (Loans 70350 and 74010) and Lower Guayas Flood Control Project (Loan 3276), among others.

12 Mancero, 'El debilitamiento institucional en la decada de los 90'.

In parallel to that, Loan 7174 (Fiscal Consolidation & Competitive Growth Adjustment), awarded in 2003, implemented the emergency austerity decree made by President Gutiérrez at the end of January 2003 with price hikes of 21 per cent for petrol and 3 per cent for diesel. The result was an increase in transport costs and consequently the overall cost of living, since goods have to be transported.

In the area of education, Loan 3425 (First Social Development Project – Education and Training) reduced funding in the education sector, bringing it from 18 per cent of the budget before the loan to 5.8 per cent by the year 2000. The difference, of course, was assigned to servicing the debt and to setting up policies favourable to creditors and Ecuador's ruling class.

These loans tied to conditionalities designed to introduce the aggressive antisocial policies of the Washington Consensus have brought about an increase in poverty and extreme poverty, while increasing the concentration of wealth in the hands of an oligarchy. In 1970, 40 per cent of the population lived below the poverty threshold, and by 2005, the percentage had reached 61 per cent. Impoverishment was particularly acute during the crisis of 1999. Between 1995 and 2000, the numbers of the poor rose from 3.9 million (34 per cent of the population) to 9.1 million (71 per cent) while extreme poverty doubled, affecting 31 per cent of the population by 2000. Meanwhile, the rich became ever richer. In 1990, the richest 20 per cent were taking in 52 per cent of all revenue; ten years later, they were monopolizing 61 per cent of the wealth.[13] Poverty particularly affects the inhabitants of rural areas and small farmers, impacted by the opening up of markets, the increase in the cost of inputs, the instigation of a system of private landowning, etc.

According to a 2003 FAO (UN Food and Agricultural Organization) report, poverty is responsible for malnutrition observed in the country. Although there was enough food to cover the needs of the population, inequality of revenue meant that the poorest could not afford to eat properly.

This increasing poverty also has repercussions on access to health care and education. Job insecurity, increased unemployment, the spread of informal and precarious work, and lower salaries mean that more and more children and adolescents are forced to drop out of the education system to help feed their families.

The 'solutions' proposed by the World Bank to help Ecuador 'emerge' from its crisis consisted in pursuing and even reinforcing the approach that led to the crisis! (7024-EC – Structural Adjustment; 7174-EC – Fiscal Consolidation and Competitive Growth; 4567-EC – Financial Sector Technical Assistance).

---

13 Alberto Acosta, *Ecuador: Deuda externa y migración, una relación incestuosa* (Cuenca: IDIUC, 2002) <bibliotecavirtual.clacso.org.ar/Ecuador/diuc-ucuenca/20121114112219/acosta.pdf> [accessed 03/09/2021].

The population took to the streets on a massive scale on several occasions to demonstrate their discontent, leading to the fall of several presidents during the 1990s and early 2000s, and confounding some of the World Bank's objectives, in particular attempts at privatization. Three right-wing presidents were hounded out of office between 1997 and 2005 through mass mobilization of the population: Abdalá Bucaram in February 1997, Jamil Mahuad in January 2000 and Lucio Gutiérrez in April 2005. It was the mobilizations of indigenous peoples that were decisive in leading to Abdalá Bucaram's resignation in 1997 and Jamil Mahuad's in 2000. In those mobilizations, the CONAIE (Confederation of Indigenous Nations of Ecuador – Confederación de Nacionalidades Indígenas del Ecuador) played a very important role. When Lucio Gutiérrez stood down, it was mainly due to urban mobilizations. Among the many evident signs of opposition to neoliberal policies, one might also add the failure of the 1995 referendum that had aimed notably to privatize the social security system.[14]

WORLD BANK LOANS VIOLATE FUNDAMENTAL HUMAN RIGHTS

The loans made by the World Bank, far from being disinterested gestures, are in fact clearly a means of subjecting the country, politically and economically, to the international order of the most powerful, 'modelling' it to suit their needs and the needs of the local dominant class – in other words, to extract maximum profits. This community of interest between local oligarchies and creditors explains why the country's leaders have so often given in so easily to the Bank's diktats, even if it meant trampling underfoot the rights of Ecuador's citizens.

The Bank's imposition of policies through the programmes it has financed and conditionalities on loans constitutes a denial of sovereignty and flagrant interference in the political affairs of the state, and as such is in violation of Article 2, Paragraph 1 of the United Nations Charter of 1945, which establishes the principle of sovereign equality among states and the right to freely decide economic, social and political regimes. The Bank has also violated the right to development of peoples, set down in the International Covenant on Economic, Social and Cultural Rights of 1966, of which Article 1 states that 'All peoples have the right of self-determination. By virtue of that right they freely determine their political status and freely pursue their economic, social and cultural development', as does the Declaration on the Right to Development of 1986.

Unsurprisingly, these policies dictated by the Bank with total contempt for the will of the people have resulted in serious breaches of fundamental human rights such as the right to a sufficient standard of living, to health, to education and to work. That situation has been met by strong resistance movements, and the

---

14 For the questions voted on, see 'Referéndum de Ecuador de 1995' on <es.wikipedia.org> (in Spanish).

World Bank faced setbacks between 2007 and 2011. Its permanent representative in Ecuador, who was declared *persona non grata*, was expelled from the country. President Rafael Correa and several of his ministers called out the Bank's actions in no uncertain terms and threatened legal proceedings. Ecuador's government, along with those of other Latin American countries, worked to promote a Bank of the South as an alternative to the World Bank. Ecuador announced that it would withdraw from ICSID, the World Bank tribunal.

RESISTANCE AGAINST THE POLICIES IMPOSED BY THE WORLD BANK, THE IMF AND OTHER CREDITORS BETWEEN 2007 AND 2011

I have closely followed the major social struggles that have shaken this country of the Andes. I went to Ecuador for the first time in 1989. I made a second visit in 2000 at the invitation of the Center for Economic and Social Rights (CDES), and at that time I took part in the publication there of a collective work on the issue of illegitimate debt.[15] In the years that followed, I contributed to a campaign aimed at showing that the debt claimed against Ecuador by various creditors was illegitimate. Among other areas we focused on the affair of the fishing boats sold to Ecuador by Norway, which was just one example, but it had the advantage of being particularly eloquent.[16] What happened was that while the country continued to repay the purchase price of these fishing boats, they had in fact been bought for peanuts by an Ecuadorian capitalist oligarch who was using them to export bananas. That campaign was effective, since in 2006 the Norwegian government decided to waive repayment of the debt related to the purchase of the fishing boats.[17] Starting in 2003, CADTM International, in contact with the staff of Ecuador's campaign for the cancellation of illegitimate debts (principally the organization called Jubileo 2000 Red Guayaquil), campaigned for recognition of the need to identify those debts that the country needed to repudiate unilaterally by means of a citizen audit. That approach was an alternative to the priority other movements were giving to the creation of an international debt tribunal. The movements which gave priority to setting up an international tribunal were mainly Jubilee Germany, Jubilee Great Britain and Jubilee United States. The discussion about the two major alternative options took place in several venues where different movements campaigning against the debt globally met and

---

15 Centro de Derechos Economicos y Sociales, *Un continente contra la deuda: Perspectivas y enfoques para la accion* (Quito: Ediciones Abya-Yala, 2000).

16 Hugo Ruiz and Éric Toussaint, 'Deuda externa y auditoria. Aproximacion practica y teorica', in *Donde estan lo que nos prestaron? Deuda externa, deudas ilegitimas y auditorias* (Quito: CDES/ Plataforma Interamericana de Derechos Humanos Democracia y Desarrollo [PIDHDD], 2004), pp. 9–69.

17 'CADTM applauds Norway's initiative concerning the cancellation of odious debt and calls on all creditor countries to go even further', CADTM, 10 October 2006) <cadtm.org/CADTM-applauds-Norway-s-initiative> [accessed 19/12/2021].

debated the orientations to follow beginning in 1999. This was notably the case at the Dakar Conference held in 2000 on the initiative of the CADTM and Jubilee South. A world meeting in Geneva in June 2003 provided the forum where the two major orientations were most thoroughly debated. The annual meetings of the World Social Forum created in 2001 were generally an opportunity to further these debates and for the most radical organizations, that is the CADTM and Jubilee South, to reach agreement on how to conduct actions of international scope.[18]

Ecuador was the place where the approach proposed by the CADTM gained acceptance. Rafael Correa, elected president of Ecuador in November 2006, had campaigned on the basis of four major commitments: to end repayment of illegitimate debt, to call a referendum for a constituent assembly, to close the USA's Manta military base in Ecuador and to refuse to sign a free trade agreement with the superpower. He made good on all four commitments.

Rafael Correa had gained popularity in 2005 when, as finance minister, he came into conflict with the World Bank after he convinced the government that windfall oil revenue should be used for social expenditures rather than for repaying creditors. In July 2005 the government decided to reform the use of petroleum resources. Instead of being used in their entirety for debt repayment, a share was set aside for social spending, and in particular to aid the indigenous peoples, who are often given short shrift. The enraged World Bank took revenge by blocking a $100 million loan it had promised Ecuador. Rafael Correa chose to resign as minister rather than give in to the World Bank's demands. A little more than a year after his resignation he was elected to serve as the country's president.

Four months after he took office, in April 2007, Ecuador expelled the World Bank's permanent representative in Quito from the country. Shortly after, the government informed the permanent representation of the IMF that it would have to leave the facilities it occupied in the central bank's buildings and find offices elsewhere. Rafael Correa was also very active in the campaign to create a Bank of the South as an alternative to the World Bank, the IMF and the Inter-American Development Bank. Two leaders of the movement for the cancellation of illegitimate debt held key posts within the government: Ricardo Patiño was minister of the economy and finance and Alberto Acosta was minister for energy and mines before becoming president of the Constituent Assembly in 2008.[19]

---

18   These debates are referred to in books published by the CADTM, including *History of the CADTM Anti-Debt Policies* (CADTM: 2017) <cadtm.org/History-of-the-CADTM-Anti-Debt> [accessed 27/02/2023] and *En campagne contre la dette* (*Campaigning Against Debt*) (Paris: Syllepse, 2008) (in French) <cadtm.org/En-campagne-contre-la-dette> [accessed 19/12/2021].

19   Detailed biographies of Patiño and Acosta can be found on the Spanish and English *Wikipedia*.

Ecuador also announced in July 2009 that it was withdrawing from ICSID, the World Bank tribunal for investment disputes, following the example given by Bolivia in May 2007. Three months later, the government decided to end a series of bilateral investment protection treaties.[20]

To deal with the question of public debt, in July 2007 Rafael Correa created the Comisión para la Auditoria Integral de la Deuda Pública (CAIC – Comprehensive Public Credit Audit Commission). From March 2007, Ecuadorian activists of the movement for cancellation of illegitimate debt were associated with the authoring of the draft presidential decree setting up the commission, and in April 2007 I was invited to Quito by the finance minister and the anti-illegitimate-debt activists of Red Jubileo 2000 Guayaquil to take part in the preliminary discussions of its content. The commission, created in July 2007, was made up of twelve members representative of Ecuador's social movements (leaders of the indigenous movement, feminist militants, and activists for the cancellation of illegitimate debts), six members of international campaigns for cancellation of illegitimate debts and four delegates of the state (representing the Ministry of Finance, the Comptroller's Office, the Anti-Corruption Commission and the Public Prosecutors' office). I represented the CADTM on the commission, which worked intensively for 14 months, between July 2007 and September 2008.[21] The other international movements represented were Latindadd, Eurodad, Citizen Debt Audit (Brazil) and Jubilee Germany. Rafael Correa's idea was to take action to end repayment of a portion of the debt identified as fraudulent and illegitimate.[22] The CAIC's mandate was to conduct a comprehensive audit of the debts accumulated by Ecuador between 1976 and 2006. The term 'comprehensive' is very important because the audit needed to avoid being limited to an accounting analysis of the country's indebtedness. It was fundamental to measure the human and environmental impacts of the policy of indebtedness. For a rapid overview of the evolution of Ecuador's debt, see 'The evolution of Ecuador's public debt between 1970 and 2008'.

---

20 Later, in 2013, an international commission to audit bilateral investment treaties was set up. An evaluation of that initiative is beyond the scope of this chapter. The commission's report was made public in May 2017. A summary (in Spanish) can be downloaded at <caitisa.org/un-exceso-de-los-tbi/> [accessed 19/12/2021].

21 To participate in the work of the commission, I travelled to Ecuador several times and spent a total of several months there in 2007–08. I did this work on a volunteer basis, for three reasons: to lend the CADTM's support to the Ecuadorian people's struggle against illegitimate debts and neoliberal policies, to maintain my complete freedom and to keep the costs of the commission's work to a minimum. Only my travel expenses (in economy class) and lodgings were covered by the commission.

22 The entire final report of the CAIC is available online in Spanish on the CADTM site: <cadtm. org/Informe-final-de-la-Auditoria>. The part concerning the external commercial debt of which repayment was partially suspended corresponds to chapter 2 – section 1 (pp. 14–88) [accessed 19/12/2021].

The evolution of Ecuador's public debt between 1970 and 2008

Ecuador is one of the many countries that have reimbursed, several times over, debts that were not contracted in the interest of the nation and its citizens. The loans contracted by Ecuador in fact benefited creditors in the North, multinationals, financial speculators and the local ruling classes.

The different stages of the evolution of indebtedness show the illegitimate nature of the debts claimed against Ecuador. All the following constitute illegitimate debt: debts contracted by military dictatorships during the 1970s and which have continued to bloat under the governments that succeeded them; debts to finance projects that in no way benefit ordinary citizens or for projects that have proved destructive to humans and/or the environment; debts contracted through the corruption of public officials; debts contracted at usurious interest rates; private debt converted into public debt; debts stemming from conditionalities imposed by the IMF and the World Bank which violate Ecuador's sovereignty, the right to self-determination and the right of peoples to define their own policies governing commercial development, taxation, spending, energy, and labour legislation and which force drastic reductions in social expenditures and the privatization of strategic sectors; etc.

During the period 1970–2007, despite the fact that the state of Ecuador reimbursed 172 times the amount of external public debt as it stood in 1970,[23] the volume of that external public debt was multiplied by a factor of 53.

During that period of 38 years, the balance between the loans and repayments of external public debt is clearly negative. The accumulated net negative transfer at Ecuador's expense is $9 billion.

Between 1982 and 2007, the net transfer on external public debt was negative for 22 years and positive only four years.

Major public-debt creditors

Total public debt as of 30 August 2008 stood at approximately $13 billion ($10 billion for external public debt and $3 billion for internal public debt). Approximately 40 per cent of external public debt is due to banks and financial markets in the form of securities, called *bonos global* (global bonds); approximately 44 per cent is due to multilateral financial institutions (the World Bank, the Inter-American Development Bank, etc.); approximately 16 per cent consist of country-to-country loans (or bilateral debt), the main creditor countries being Spain, Brazil and Italy.

Meanwhile 95 per cent of internal public debt, amounting to approximately $3 billion, consists of securities (*bonos AGD*).

---

23   According to the World Bank, Ecuador's external public debt came to $195 million in 1970. (Source: World Bank, *Global Development Finance 2007* (Washington, DC: World Bank, 2007).) According to the Ministry of the Economy and Finance (MEF), external public debt had reached $10.38 billion by 3 July 2007. That meant that external public debt had been multiplied by 53 between 1970 and July 2007. Over that same period, the Ecuadorian government had reimbursed $33.47 billion – that is, 172 times the amount of external public debt in 1970.

ECUADOR'S PARTIAL VICTORY AGAINST CREDITORS
OF ILLEGITIMATE DEBTS

Starting in November 2008, Ecuador suspended repayment of a large part of its debt. Concretely, the country ended payment of interest due on the Ecuadorian securities traded on Wall Street that would have come to $3.2 billion.[24] The international financial press raised an enormous stink, since Ecuador had dared to refuse to pay when it had the means to do so. Still, in June 2009, the holders of 91 per cent of the bonds in question accepted a proposal to buy them back at 35 per cent of face value. In broad figures, Ecuador repurchased $3.2 billion worth of debt while disbursing $900 million, which represents a saving of $2 billion on the capital due, to which are added the savings on interest that will no longer have to be paid. Rafael Correa declared in his inaugural speech on 10 August 2009 that this 'means a gain of more than 300 million dollars annually over the next twenty years – amounts that will go not into the creditors' portfolios but will go to national development'.[25] The total amount saved is a little over $7 billion.[26]

The government's energetic action in the area of debt had two consequences:

1. It should be emphasized that the debt reduction enabled the government to greatly increase social expenditures over the years 2009–11, in particular in the areas of health and education, since the state's resources were able to be sharply refocused on those parts of the budget instead of going up in smoke in the form of debt repayment. The living conditions of the population were significantly improved. In parallel, the legal minimum wage was gradually increased by nearly 100 per cent.

2. The unilateral suspension of repayment of the debt of course made the creditors extremely unhappy. But despite predictions of chaotic and painful days ahead by the international financial press and the right, nothing bad happened. Ecuador's victory over its private foreign creditors was total. What is more, when the country decided a few years later to issue new debt securities on the financial markets, the investors crowded in to buy them. That is proof that suspension of payment and debt reduction, far from causing catastrophe, in no way prevent holders of big capital from again lending to the country. That is because they are convinced that the country's situation has improved.[27] It is important to keep

---

24 The global bonds labelled 'Global 2012 and 2030' represent about 85 per cent of external public debt in the form of securities. The other components of Ecuador's external public debt are made up of loans from the World Bank and other multilateral institutions (IMF, Inter-American Development Bank) and of bilateral loans granted by states (Spain, Japan, Italy, Brazil, etc.).

25 Excerpts from Rafael Correa's speech are available in Spanish and French at <cadtm.org/Discours-d-investiture-du> [accessed 19/12/2021].

26 For a concise presentation of the audit in Ecuador, see the excerpt from the film *Debtocracy* devoted to Ecuador: 'The Ecuador debt audit: a seven minute summary' <cadtm.org/Video-The-Ecuador-debt-audit-a> [accessed 19/12/2021].

27 See Éric Toussaint, 'Joseph Stiglitz shows that a suspension of debt repayments can be beneficial for a country and its people', CADTM, 20 January 2015 <cadtm.org/Joseph-Stiglitz-shows-that-a> [accessed 19/12/2021].

this phenomenon well in mind, in order to counter the narratives predicting catastrophe that are used to convince public authorities and the population of indebted countries that they must continue repaying debt at any cost. It is also important to assert the fact that alternatives to a return to the financial markets do exist. A policy of fiscal justice must enable the state to finance itself by forcing the wealthiest individuals and the major corporations to pay much higher taxes, which limits recourse to indebtedness on the backs of the public. Unfortunately, that is not what the Correa government did. There were no such major tax reforms; the increases in tax collection were achieved mainly through the fight against tax evasion and thanks to growth of the economy.

Even if the government's actions in the area of debt were beneficial, as we have just seen, it is important to stress the fact that Ecuador's debt audit commission (CAIC) wanted to go beyond the measures that were in fact taken. It is regrettable that the government and Rafael Correa did not take that path. In its recommendations,[28] the CAIC proposed to end repayment of other very large amounts of debt that correspond to debt claimed by the World Bank, by other multilateral institutions and by bilateral creditors such as Brazil, Japan and European countries. It was also recommended that legal action be brought against the parties, both national and foreign, responsible for illegitimate debt. At that level, based on the work of the CAIC, Ecuador's public prosecutors' office began examining the responsibility of high civil servants who allegedly committed various crimes when entering into or renegotiating debt contracts during the 1990s and early 2000s. However, no strong sentences were handed down and none of the parties guilty of contracting fraudulent debt were jailed, since neither the judicial authorities nor the government chose to pursue matters.

In the end the government followed only one of the commission's recommendations. It nevertheless went further than all the other so-called progressive governments of that period. Rafael Correa and also Ricardo Patiño, who successively held several functions in the government and who chaired the CAIC, tried to persuade other heads of state such as Evo Morales, Hugo Chávez and Fernando Lugo to create comprehensive debt audit commissions in their countries. But to no effect. Ecuador remained isolated where the issue of debt was concerned; the other governments of the region (including Venezuela's and Bolivia's) continued repayments and did not conduct debt audits.

28　See 'Final report of the integral auditing of the Ecuadorian debt – executive summary' <cadtm.org/Final-Report-of-the-Integral> [accessed 27/02/2023].

　　See also (in French) Éric Toussaint, 'Ecuador: La CAIC a proposé à Rafael Correa de suspendre le paiement de près de la moitié de la dette' ('CAIC proposes that Correa suspend repayment of nearly half the debt'), 25 September 2008 <cadtm.org/Equateur-La-CAIC-a-propose-a> [accessed 27/02/2023].

　　See also 'L'Equateur à la croisée des chemins' (Ecuador at the crossroads) in CADTM, *Les Crimes de la dette* (Liège/Paris: CADTM/Syllepse, 2007), part III, pp. 174–265 (in French).

Also, at a meeting held at the presidential palace in January 2011 and to which I was invited along with the other members of the CAIC, Rafael Correa proposed, on the basis of the work we had done in 2008, that Ecuador challenge the debts claimed by another major creditor. After debating the issue, we came to the agreement that repayment should be suspended on the debts claimed by the World Bank. But when came the time to execute the decision, the new minister of the economy and finance opposed it and repayments to the Bank continued. Worse still, starting from 2014 the government began negotiating further loans from the Bank.[29]

RAFAEL CORREA'S U-TURN IN 2011

The year 2011 also marks a turning point in the politics of the Ecuadorian government on several fronts, both in the social arena and regarding the environment, trade and the debt. Conflicts between the government and a series of major social movements such as the CONAIE, and also the teachers' unions and the student movement, became more bitter. The government moved forward with its negotiations with the EU, and made many concessions. Where the debt was concerned, from 2014 Ecuador again began gradually increasing its reliance on the international financial markets, not to mention the debts contracted with China. In the area of the environment, in 2013 the Correa government abandoned its plan not to exploit oil resources in a sensitive part of Amazonia.[30]

Despite his rhetoric about the socialism of the twenty-first century and changing the productive model, in ten years as president Correa did not undertake profound changes to the structure of the country's economy, property relations or relations between social classes. Alberto Acosta, ex-minister for energy in 2007, ex-president of the constituent assembly in 2008 and in opposition to Rafael Correa since 2010, wrote along with his colleague John Cajas Guijarro that:

The absence of structural transformation means that Ecuador remains a capitalist economy tied to exporting raw materials and therefore tied to long-term cyclical behaviour dependent on the demands of the transnational accumulation of capital. This long-term cyclic behaviour is due to the contradictions inherent in capitalism, but is also strongly influenced by dependency on massive exportation of barely

29   Alberto Acosta, 'Lectura sobre el retorno del Ecuador al Banco Mundial', CADTM, 16 December 2014 (in Spanish) <cadtm.org/Lectura-sobre-el-retorno-del> [accessed 27/02/2023].

30   The Yasuní-ITT Initiative had been introduced in June 2007 by Rafael Correa. It consisted of leaving in the ground 20 per cent of the country's oil reserves (some 850 million barrels), located in a region with a high level of biodiversity, the Yasuní National Park in north-eastern Amazonia. For a presentation of the project in 2009, see Alberto Acosta (interviewed by Matthieu Le Quang), 'Le projet ITT: laisser le pétrole en terre ou le chemin vers un autre modèle de développement' ('The ITT Project: leave the oil in the ground – the road towards a new development model'), CADTM, 18 September 2009 (in French and Spanish) <cadtm.org/Le-projet-ITT-laisser-le-petrole-en-terre-ou-le-chemin-vers-un-autre-modele-de> [accessed 27/02/2023].

transformed raw materials (extractivism). In other words, capitalist exploitation – of both labour and nature – following international demands, keeps Ecuador 'chained' to a succession of ups and downs which originate as much within the country as abroad.[31]

LENÍN MORENO (2017–21) OR THE RETURN TO NEOLIBERAL POLICIES AND SUBMISSION TO US INTERESTS

In 2017, at the end of Rafael Correa's presidential term and just when he was succeeded by President Lenín Moreno (the candidate Correa had supported), the country's debt surpassed the level attained ten years earlier. Rapidly Moreno turned once more to the IMF. That led to massive popular protests in September–October 2019, which obliged the government to capitulate to the people's organizations and abandon the decree which had triggered the revolt.[32]

In 2020, Lenín Moreno signed another humiliating agreement with the IMF and in 2021 he tried to have a bill adopted that would make the central bank completely independent of the government and thus even more closely subjected to the interests of private banks.

His popularity faded to nothing: in the last polls, Moreno had a mere 4.8 per cent approval rating. Candidates supported by Moreno in the general elections and in the first round of the presidential election in February 2021 won less than 3 per cent of the votes.

THE ELECTION OF THE FORMER BANKER GUILLERMO LASSO AS PRESIDENT OF ECUADOR IN APRIL 2021

On 11 April 2021, in the second round of the presidential election, Guillermo Lasso (52.4 per cent), the right-wing candidate, defeated Andrés Arauz (47.6 per cent), the candidate supported by Rafael Correa and part of the left. Lasso was in

---

31   Alberto Acosta and John Cajas Guijarro, *Una década desperdiciada: las sombras del correísmo* (Quito: Centro Andino de Acción Popular, 2018) (translation CADTM).

The original quote in Spanish: '*la falta de una transformación estructural provoca que el Ecuador se mantenga como una economía capitalista atada a la exportación de materias primas y, por lo tanto, amarrada a un comportamiento cíclico de larga duración vinculado a las demandas de acumulación del capital transnacional. Tal comportamiento cíclico de larga historia es originado por las contradicciones propias del capitalismo pero, a su vez, es altamente influenciado por la dependencia en la exportación masiva de productos primarios casi sin procesar (extractivismo). Es decir, la explotación capitalista – tanto de la fuerza de trabajo como de la Naturaleza – en función de las demandas internacionales, mantiene al Ecuador "encadenado" a un vaivén de animaciones y crisis económicas que se originan tanto interna como externamente.*'

32   CADTM AYNA, 'Ensemble avec le peuple équatorien' ('With the Ecuadorian people'), CADTM, 15 October 2019 (in French and Spanish) <cadtm.org/Ensemble-avec-le-peuple-equatorien> [accessed 27/02/2023]. See also the collective work Franklin Ramírez Gallegos (ed.), *Octubre y el derecho a la resistencia: revuelta popular y neoliberalismo autoritario en Ecuador* (Buenos Aires: CLACSO). It can be downloaded free of charge at <clacso.org.ar/libreria-latinoamericana/contador/sumar_pdf.php?id_libro=2056> [accessed 27/02/2023].

fact elected due to the left's division, since a large percentage of left-leaning voters, who had given up any trust in Correa, called for a null vote. Lasso's victory was not at all a foregone conclusion, since the two political forces that had won in the first round of the election were the movement supported by Rafael Correa, with 42 National Assembly seats, and Pachakutik, the political arm of CONAIE, who with 27 seats had the best legislative results in the entire history of the indigenous peoples' movement.

The first round of the presidential election, held in February 2021, was clearly favourable to the popular side, since adding Andrés Arauz's votes (slightly over 32 per cent) to those of Yaku Pérez (just under 19 per cent) resulted in a majority, to which a share of the votes of the candidate who was in fourth place – a self-described social democrat who received close to 14 per cent of the vote – can be added. Lasso, the ex-banker, did come in second with 19 per cent of the vote, but was only marginally ahead of Pérez, the Pachakutik candidate, and was 13 points behind Arauz. The votes of the popular camp, which was clearly in the majority in the first round, were divided, which enabled the former banker's election. The resulting situation is serious, since an opportunity to break away from Lenín Moreno's brutal neoliberal policies has been lost. Lasso, while critical of Lenín Moreno for purely political reasons, will continue in the same harmful direction: further extension of neoliberal policies, agreements with the World Bank and the IMF, submission to the private interests of big capital, particularly Ecuador's powerful banking sector and import-export industry, and submission to the United States.

CONCLUSION

Rafael Correa became president of Ecuador in 2007 thanks to the persistence of social movements throughout the period between 1990 and 2005. Without them, his proposals would never have received the attention they did and he would never have been elected. Unfortunately, after a very good start, he clashed with a significant part of those social movements and opted for modernization of extractivist-export capitalism. Then his successor, Lenín Moreno, broke away from Correa's policies and went back to brutal neoliberalism. Guillermo Lasso is sure to further extend those policies. Once again, social mobilization will be needed to overcome these policies and again promote the anti-capitalist structural changes that are indispensable to emancipation. In October 2019 the CONAIE and a wide spectrum of labour organizations, feminist associations and environmentalist collectives put together an excellent platform as an alternative to capitalist, patriarchal and neoliberal policies,[33] and that needs to serve as the foundation of a vast governmental programme.

---

33   CONAIE, 'Entrega de propuesta alternativa al modelo económico y social, 31 octobre 2019' (in Spanish) <conaie.org/2019/10/31/propuesta-para-un-nuevo-modelo-economico-y-social/> [accessed 13/09/2021].

The question of rejecting the policies of the IMF and the World Bank and illegitimate debt is again at the centre of social and political struggles.[34] In a document made public in July 2020 by more than 180 Ecuadorian peoples' organizations is the following demand: 'Suspension of repayment of the external debt and conducting of an audit of the external debt accumulated from 2014 to the present, as well as citizen control over the use of the debts contracted.'[35]

34   Collective declaration signed by Éric Toussaint, Maria Lucia Fattorelli, Alejandro Olmos Gaona, Hugo Arias Palacios, Piedad Mancero, Ricardo Patiño and Ricardo Ulcuango, 'We denounce the renegotiation of the debt by Lenín Moreno's government', CADTM, 3 August 2020 <cadtm.org/We-denounce-the-renegotiation-of-the-debt-by-Lenin-Moreno-s-government> [accessed 21/02/2022].
35   See <rebelion.org/wp-content/uploads/2020/07/PROPUESTA-PARLAMENTO-DE-LOS-PUEBLOS.pdf>, published in July 2020 [accessed 13/09/2021] (translation CADTM).

24

The US President's Men Keep Control of the World Bank

Although several World Bank member countries felt that it was time to choose a Southern-country national as Bank president, the US president nominated a US citizen for the eleventh time in the person of Robert Zoellick. Zoellick was to be succeeded by three more of the president's men.

ROBERT ZOELLICK, ELEVENTH PRESIDENT OF THE WORLD BANK (2007–12), A US BANKER AND BUSINESSMAN

Robert Zoellick had no knowledge whatsoever of development issues. Under the previous Bush administration Zoellick had been the US trade representative – the head of the US delegation to the World Trade Organization (WTO) – where he systematically acted in the sole interests of reinforcing the commercial supremacy of the USA, disregarding the needs of developing countries. During the preparations for the WTO's Ministerial Conference in Doha in 2001 he went around to all the African governments in order to buy their votes. After the WTO, Zoellick specialized in negotiating bilateral 'free-trade' treaties[1] between the US and individual developing countries (Chile, Morocco, El Salvador, Guatemala, Honduras, Nicaragua, Costa Rica, Dominican Republic, Jordan, etc.) which favoured the interests of US transnational corporations to the detriment of the sovereignty of the developing countries. Robert Zoellick was then appointed Deputy Secretary of State under Condoleezza Rice.

As of July 2006, Zoellick had been a senior international adviser and Vice Chairman International at Goldman Sachs. Goldman Sachs is one of Wall Street's principal business banks, deeply implicated in the US private debt crisis that broke out in August 2007. Goldman Sachs was also involved in constructing the huge web of debt that created the disastrous speculative bubble in the real-estate sector. Zoellick quit Wall Street to replace Wolfowitz at the head of the World Bank just in time to avoid being directly involved in the 2007–08 crisis.

During his tenure, Zoellick ensured that a \$3.75 billion World Bank loan to finance the construction of the extremely polluting Medupi coal-fired power plant

---

1   According to Robert Zoellick, 'Trade liberalization itself provides a win–win opportunity to lower barriers and promote economic growth and development. Our new and pending FTA partners represent America's third largest export market – these FTAs are stripping away trade barriers across-the-board, market-by-market, and expanding American opportunities.' USTR Press Release, 1 April 2004 <ustr.gov/archive/Document_Library/Press_Releases/2004/April/USTR_Releases_2004_Inventory_of_Foreign_Trade_Barriers.html> [accessed 16/09/2021].

in South Africa was granted. Over and above the anti-environmental nature of the project, the contracts benefited Eskom and Hitachi Power Africa, two companies owned in whole or in part by leaders of the ruling ANC, allowing them to make money through corruption and embezzlement. The extent of corruption is such that there are many voices calling for the cancellation of this odious debt.[2]

It is also worth noting that one year after the end of his term at the World Bank, Zoellick returned to a position at Goldman Sachs, as Chairman of International Advisors, in 2013.

The World Bank's inconsistencies regarding the number of poor people on the planet

In 2008, under Robert Zoellick's presidency, the World Bank admitted that it had made major errors in its calculations regarding worldwide poverty. While at the same time claiming that its estimations of poverty are becoming more accurate thanks to 'new and better data', the Bank discovered in a working paper that 'an extra 400 million people [are] living in poverty'.[3] An 'extra' 400 million people? That is more than half the entire population of Sub-Saharan Africa at the time!

Such an error, even if admitted, reflects the fact that the statistics published by the World Bank are anything but reliable – which is not surprising since those statistics serve primarily to support the neoliberal policies the Bank's own experts are forcing on countries all over the world.

According to the working paper, 'For 2005 we estimate that 1.4 billion people, or one quarter of the population of the developing world, lived below our international line of $1.25 a day' whereas previous estimations had given a figure of around one billion people.

Yet the Bank still congratulates itself on what it sees as a positive trend, because what is important in its view is not the number of poor people, but the proportion of people who are poor. Why? Because with the soaring world population, a proportional figure hides the truth. If, for example, the number of poor individuals stays the same, the proportion of poor people is automatically reduced as the years pass. Which explains why the stated 'millennium' goal for the period 1990 to 2015 was to reduce the *proportion* of the population whose revenue is below $1.25 per day.

But with the World Bank's enormous miscalculations on poverty, the entire edifice of international poverty reduction policies collapses. The structural adjustment policies imposed by the IMF and the World Bank since the early 1980s – cutting social programmes, recovering costs in the health and education sectors, an agriculture geared towards exportation and reduction of food crops, the abandonment of food sovereignty, etc. – have in fact worsened living conditions for hundreds of millions of people around the world.

---

2   Éric Toussaint, 'South Africa: the odious debts generated by coal-fired power-stations', CADTM, 2 May 2019 <cadtm.org/South-Africa-the-odious-debts-generated-by-coal-fired-power-stations> [accessed 16/09/2021].

3   Shaohua Chen and Martin Ravallion, *The Developing World Is Poorer Than We Thought, But No Less Successful in the Fight against Poverty* (World Bank: Policy Research Working Paper 4703, August 2008) <documents1.worldbank.org/curated/en/526541468262138892/pdf/WPS4703.pdf> [accessed 16/09/2021].

And there has been no lack of criticism of the Bank regarding this. Thomas Pogge of Columbia University, for example, wrote in 2008:

> The World Bank's approach to estimating the extent, distribution and trend of global income poverty is neither meaningful nor reliable. [...] there is reason to believe that the Bank's approach may have led it to understate the extent of global income poverty and to infer without adequate justification that global income poverty has steeply declined in the recent period. A new methodology of global poverty assessment, focused directly on what is needed to achieve elementary human requirements, is feasible and necessary.[4]

The lack of seriousness inherent in the World Bank's methodology is evident in a declaration by Martin Ravallion, one of the Bank's main experts on the issue of poverty: 'The latest poverty estimates draw on 675 household surveys for 116 developing countries, representing 96 percent of the developing world', he explains.[5] How is it possible to claim to be publishing reliable figures on the situation of several billion people on the basis of a survey limited to 675 households? How can such 'experts' expect to be taken seriously! The same author also admits that in the early 1990s, the Bank's sources on poverty were limited to studies conducted in only 22 countries.

Adopting a diplomatic tone, the same Martin Ravallion writes: 'Our latest revision of poverty numbers is the largest revision yet because of important new data revealing that the cost of living in the developing world is higher than we thought.'[6]

As this is being written, the World Bank considers that a person is not living in extreme poverty if they live in a developing country and have more than $1.90 per day to live on. Such a figure is obviously highly debatable. It sets an extremely low borderline for extreme poverty. The figure of $1.90 per day is not a reliable indicator, and the methods used to extrapolate the number of poor people on the planet cannot be taken seriously.

Note that in its recent publications, the World Bank announces that as a result of the crisis related to the Coronavirus, more than 100 million human beings will be added to the ranks of those living in extreme poverty in 2020–21. Referring to a Bank report published in 2020, worldbank.org states: 'Now, for the first time in a generation, the quest to end poverty has suffered a setback. Global extreme poverty rose in 2020 for the first time in over 20 years as the disruption of the COVID-19 pandemic compounded the forces of conflict and climate change'. The authors add: 'New research estimates that climate change will drive 68 million to 132 million into poverty by 2030.'[7]

While these estimates need to be taken with a grain of salt given the methods the Bank uses in making its calculations, they nonetheless point to dramatic developments that urgently call for radical solutions to ensure the protection of human rights.

---

4   Sanjay G. Reddy and Thomas W. Pogge, 'How *not* to count the poor', 29 October 2005 <dx.doi.org/ 10.2139/ssrn.893159> [accessed 05/03/2023]. For an overview of the question see Thomas Pogge, *Politics as Usual: What Lies behind the Pro-Poor Rhetoric* (Cambridge: Polity Press, 2010).

5   'World Bank updates poverty estimates for the developing world', World Bank News Feature, 26 August 2008, updated 17 February 2010 <worldbank.org/en/news/feature/2008/08/26/ world-bank-updates-poverty-estimates-for-the-developing-world> [accessed 17/09/2021].

6   Ibid.

7   World Bank, 'Poverty' (worldbank.org/en/topic/poverty/overview#1) [accessed 29/12/2021].

JIM YONG KIM, ALSO AMERICAN, TWELFTH PRESIDENT OF THE WORLD BANK (2012–19)

Jim Yong Kim, also an American, directed the World Bank between 2012 and 2019, until he resigned suddenly on 7 January 2019, to occupy a better-paid position in an investment fund specializing in infrastructures.

In order to directly defend the interests of American economic superiority, in May 2017 Kim accompanied Ivanka Trump, the daughter of the misogynistic billionaire US president, on a visit to Saudi Arabia, a long-term ally of the USA. The visit was aimed at enabling the ultra-reactionary Saudi monarchy to forge a progressive image for itself as it constantly tramples on women's rights, by donating to the Women's Entrepreneurship Fund. In reality this fund, launched under the aegis of Ivanka Trump, Kim and Canadian prime minister Justin Trudeau, intends to participate in the accumulation of capital at the global level on the pretext of advancing women's emancipation.

Contrary to flattering portraits painted of Kim, he has done nothing to contribute to the reform of the World Bank, which has always defended the interests of capital and the richest and most powerful countries (particularly the United States, Canada, Western Europe and Japan), to the detriment of human rights and the preservation of the planet.

After Kim's resignation Kristalina Georgieva served as interim president until April 2019, when US President Donald Trump appointed one of his trusted lieutenants, David Malpass, president of the World Bank. Georgieva would move on to replace Christine Lagarde as managing director of the IMF in October 2019.

DAVID MALPASS, ANOTHER RIGHT-WING FORMER BANKER, THIRTEENTH PRESIDENT OF THE WORLD BANK SINCE 2019

David Malpass, a Donald Trump favourite, became the thirteenth president of the World Bank in April 2019. He had worked for the US Treasury and State Department during the terms of Ronald Reagan and George H.W. Bush (1989–93), then as chief economist for Bear Stearns, a major investment bank until its bankruptcy in 2008 in the midst of the subprime crisis. In August 2007, Malpass had published an op-ed piece in the *Wall Street Journal* in which he urged his readers not to worry about the state of the financial markets, going so far as to write that 'Housing and debt markets are not that big a part of the U.S. economy, or of job creation. [...] the housing-and-debt-market corrections will probably add to the length of the U.S. economic expansion.'[8] He joined Donald Trump's team in May 2016, where

---

8   Jordan Weissmann, 'Trump taps Bear Stearns economist who said not to worry about credit crisis for key Treasury job', 5 January 2017 <slate.com/business/2017/01/trump-picks-ex-bear-stearns-economist-for-treasury-position.html consulted> [accessed 22/09/2021].

he served as Under Secretary of the Treasury for Foreign Affairs before becoming president of the World Bank.

In February 2023, David Malpass announced his resignation, sparking controversy by failing to say whether he accepted that fossil fuels were driving the climate crisis.

Like Donald Trump, David Malpass is a climate sceptic. Explaining Malpass's demission, *The Guardian* wrote: 'Malpass's departure comes just months after he was forced to push back against claims he was a climate crisis denier. The controversy started after he appeared on a climate finance panel at a conference in New York in September. Asked repeatedly whether he believed "manmade burning of fossil fuels [... are] rapidly and dangerously warming the planet", Malpass tried to dodge the question before saying: "I don't even know. I'm not a scientist." The answer drew condemnation from the White House, and raised pressure on Malpass'.[9]

AJAY BANGA, THE FORMER MASTERCARD CHIEF, NOMINATED BY THE WHITE HOUSE AS THE FOURTEENTH PRESIDENT OF THE WORLD BANK

A few days after David Malpass's resignation, US President Joe Biden announced the appointment of his successor, Ajay Banga. Like his predecessors, the fourteenth head of the World Bank is an American, coming from the world of high finance.

On 23 February 2023, the White House issued a statement: 'Today, President Biden announced that the United States is nominating Ajay Banga, a business leader with extensive experience leading successful organizations in developing countries and forging public–private partnerships to address financial inclusion and climate change, to be President of the World Bank.'[10]

Once again, the president of the World Bank is American, he is a man, and he comes from high finance, which seems to be a guarantee of success for Joe Biden: 'Ajay is uniquely equipped to lead the World Bank at this critical moment in history. He has spent more than three decades building and managing successful, global companies that create jobs and bring investment to developing economies, and guiding organizations through periods of fundamental change.'

Ajay Banga was born in India and took US citizenship, and it is partly for this reason that he could be chosen for the position of president. He was CEO of Citigroup, one of the largest US investment banks, for its Asia–Pacific operations between 2005 and 2009, before becoming CEO of Mastercard. Ajay Banga has no experience in 'development' policies or in climate and environmental issues.

9   Kalyeena Makortoff and agencies, 'World Bank chief resigns after climate stance misstep', *The Guardian*, 16 February 2023 <theguardian.com/business/2023/feb/15/david-malpass-world-bank-president-steps-down> [accessed 05/03/2023].

10   The White House, 'President Biden announces U.S. nomination of Ajay Banga to lead World Bank', 23 February 2023 <whitehouse.gov/briefing-room/statements-releases/2023/02/23/president-biden-announces-u-s-nomination-of-ajay-banga-to-lead-world-bank/> [accessed 05/03/2023].

His track record as a leader of large financial capitalist groups like Citigroup and Mastercard clearly indicates that during his tenure, Ajay Banga will continue to promote an extractivist capitalist system via neoliberal loans and conditionalities imposed by the World Bank.

He is a member of the Trilateral Commission. This commission, founded in 1973 by David Rockefeller, is a private club for consultation and orientation of the international policies of the United States, European countries and Japan. It played an active role in the neoliberal offensive of the 1980s, and it's also important to underline that the appointment of Ajay Banga as the next president of the World Bank is welcomed by the Indian ultra-nationalist right.

25
The World Bank and the Arab Spring

Even as the World Bank and the IMF were praising the authoritarian or dictatorial regimes in power for many decades in the Arab regions, the embers of revolt were ready to flare up.

The main analyses by the two financial institutions concerning Tunisia and Egypt, the two countries where popular revolt arose between December 2010 and January 2011, commended the leadership of Ben Ali and Mubarak (in power for 24 and 30 years respectively). The two despots, who had unfailingly applied the neoliberal policies promoted by the World Bank and the IMF and were faithful allies of the Western powers, were forced to step down in January 2011.

THE WORLD BANK MAKES NO SERIOUS ANALYSIS OF ITS ERRORS

More than a decade later, there is no official World Bank publication that would help to understand the roots of the revolts. The World Bank continues blindly in its errors, while producing half-baked studies trying to justify them.

The World Bank and the IMF clearly have a problem: if, as they say, their recommendations are going in the right direction and they must be pressed harder, how can the popular movements that have rocked the Arab world, from Morocco to Yemen and including Lebanon, be explained? At the time of writing the Arab populations have been expressing their profound discontent with the social, economic and political effects of neoliberal policies for over a decade.

The discrepancies between the World Bank's predictions and the results achieved are such that it could no longer remain silent. The Bank was forced to make unconvincing public-relations declarations to explain its failure to foresee such events.

Several statements from the World Bank, such as the following press release from October 2015, show that they are incapable of understanding where the revolt came from:

Judging by economic data alone, the revolutions of the 2011 Arab Spring should have never happened. The numbers from the decades before had told a glowing story: the region had been making steady progress toward eliminating extreme poverty, boosting shared prosperity, increasing school enrollment, and reducing hunger, child and maternal mortality. Reforms were underway and economic growth was moderate.

And then, in late 2010 and early 2011, millions of people poured onto the streets of major cities in the Middle East and North Africa (MENA), calling for change, and the Arab street began to tell a story that standard quantitative indicators had not foreseen.[1]

The World Bank refuses to admit to its profound misunderstanding of the realities of the Arab region and bends over backwards to try to explain why millions revolted in spite of what the Bank sees as successful policies conducted by the ruling authoritarian regimes.

The Bank's explanation is completely unconvincing. Several of its critics, as shall be seen below, have demonstrated that with rigorous logic. First let us sum up the Bank's explanations.

The title of the aforementioned press release says it all: 'Middle-class frustration fueled the Arab Spring'. The World Bank reaffirms that poverty and inequalities were on a downward trend before 2011; there was progress in 'boosting shared prosperity, increasing school enrollment, and reducing hunger, child and maternal mortality'. According to the World Bank it was the middle classes who were most discontented at not getting what they considered to be their fair share of the abundance.

The Bank says that the poorest 40 per cent of the population were much less discontented than the middle classes and had no need to take to the streets. This is clearly contrary to the circumstances that ignited the street protests in Tunisia, where the movement started. Recall that on 17 December 2010, Mohamed Bouazizi, a young street vendor, set fire to himself in desperation at having his wares confiscated by the police. It was the start of demonstrations that brought together hundreds of thousands from the popular classes, and especially the poorest strata. Contrary to what the Bank claims, it was not only the middle classes that revolted.

The beginnings of the Arab Spring in Tunisia and Egypt

TUNISIA

17 December 2010: Mohamed Bouazizi, a young street vendor in Sidi Bouzid, sets fire to himself in desperation at having his wares confiscated by the police. It was the start of a wave of protests.

    11 January 2011: Confrontations in Tunis.

    14 January 2011: President Ben Ali, in power since 1987, flees to Saudi Arabia.

EGYPT

25 January 2011: First demonstration in Tahrir Square in Cairo. This marks the beginning of several weeks of popular uprising against the regime.

    11 February 2011: President Hosni Mubarak, in power since 1981, resigns.

---

1   'Middle-class frustration fueled the Arab Spring', World Bank News Feature, 21 October 2015 <worldbank.org/en/news/feature/2015/10/21/middle-class-frustration-that-fueled-the-arab-spring> [accessed 15/09/2021].

CRITICISMS OF THE WORLD BANK'S DIAGNOSIS OF THE ARAB SPRING EVENTS

Gilbert Achcar, author of several indispensable books on the Arab region (North Africa and the Middle East) as well as the Arab Spring,[2] demonstrated in a well-documented study published in 2020[3] that the Bank's affirmations are unfounded. Achcar shows that it is untrue to say that inequality was lower in the Arab region than in most of the other developing regions of the so-called developing world. Based on a series of studies, Achcar shows that income inequalities increased greatly in North Africa and the Middle East between 1980 and 2011.

The incomes of the popular classes decreased while the incomes and net worth of the richest increased. Achcar shows that the World Bank's methods of collecting income and household spending data are highly unreliable. In chapter 24 ('The World Bank's inconsistencies regarding the number of poor people on the planet') we discussed the unreliability of the Bank's data in a more general context. In establishing the figures that it wrongly presents as being representative of reality, the Bank uses surveys based on a very limited number of samples. The conclusions drawn are clearly in contradiction with the observed effects of World Bank policies.

THE WORLD BANK BASES ITS FIGURES ON SURVEYS USING A VERY LIMITED NUMBER OF SAMPLES

In works published between 2014 and 2018 that cover the period from 1990 to 2016, Thomas Piketty, Facundo Alvaredo and Lydia Assouad also dispute the World Bank's claims that the Middle East is less unequal than other parts of the World. According to Piketty and his two colleagues: 'the Middle East appears to be the most unequal region in the world, with a top decile income share as large as 64 percent, compared to 37 percent in Western Europe, 47 percent in the US and 55 percent in Brazil.'[4]

---

2   Gilbert Achcar, *Le choc des barbaries: terrorismes et désordre mondial* (*The Shock of Barbarity: Terrorisms and World Disorder*) (Brussels: Éd. Complexe, 2002; Paris: 10/18, 2004); Gilbert Achcar, *Le peuple veut: une exploration radicale du soulèvement arabe* (*The People Want: A Radical Exploration of the Arab Uprising*) (Paris: Sindbad Actes Sud, 2013) (both in French).

3   Gilbert Achcar, 'On the "Arab Inequality Puzzle": the case of Egypt', *Development and Change*, 17 March 2020, Vol. 51, No. 3 <doi.org/10.1111/dech.12585> [accessed 15/09/2021].

4   Thomas Piketty, Facundo Alvaredo and Lydia Assouad, *Measuring Inequality in the Middle East 1990–2016: The World's Most Unequal Region?* (World Inequality Database: Working Paper Series No. 2017/15, 2018) <wid.world/document/alvaredoassouadpiketty-middleeast-widworldwp201715/> [accessed 05/10/2021].

    In this study the authors mention the World Bank thesis: 'A number of papers have argued that national-level income inequality does not seem to be particularly high by international standards, and therefore that the source of dissatisfaction might lie elsewhere (see in particular Halsny and Verne [sic], 2013', Vladimir Hlasny and Paolo Verme have produced several documents for the World Bank. In the Piketty, Alvaredo and Assouad study, the Middle East comprises Turkey and Iran (which are not Arab countries), Egypt, Iraq, Syria, Jordan, Lebanon, Palestine, Yemen and Gulf countries (including Saudi Arabia, Oman, Bahrain, UAE, Qatar and Kuwait). According to Piketty, Alvaredo and Assouad: 'The 1990–2016 period has seen rapid population growth in the Middle East: the total population rose by about 70 percent, from less than 240 million in 1990 to almost 410 million in 2016' (p. 15).

INEQUALITY IS IN FACT GREATER IN THE MIDDLE EAST THAN IN ANY OTHER REGION OF THE WORLD; THE WEALTHIEST 10 PER CENT TAKE IN 64 PER CENT OF ALL REVENUE

According to Piketty, Alvaredo and Assouad, the wealthiest 1 per cent in the Middle East take in a much larger share of total income than in other regions or countries: 'the top percentile income share is about 30 percent in the Middle East, vs. 12 percent in Western Europe, 20 percent in the US, 28 percent in Brazil, 18 percent in South Africa, 14 percent in China and 21 percent in India.'[5]

The studies undertaken by Gilbert Achcar, along with that of Piketty, Alvaredo and Assouad, firmly contradict World Bank declarations that were clearly made in haste to attempt to disqualify intense criticism. The authors of the criticized World Bank studies, Vladimir Hlasny and Paolo Verme, rather than defend their study on a scientific basis, preferred to accuse Achcar and Piketty and his co-researchers of politicizing the question rather than debating it on technical grounds. They write:

Gilbert Achcar's critical review [...] concludes that the research of the protagonists of the 'Arab Inequality Puzzle' debate exhibits a systematic neoliberal bias and a wilful blindness to the fact that 'their recipes were responsible ... for the formidable socio-political explosion of the Arab Spring and the protracted destabilization of the region' (p. 768). We argue that Achcar's conclusion is erroneous and based on a misleading interpretation of evidence, selective review of existing studies, false grouping of scholars and an inadequate understanding of the measurement of income inequality. The review appears to be an attempt to politicize what has otherwise been a healthy technical debate on income inequality in Egypt.[6]

WORLD BANK ANALYSES ARE MADE ON THE BASIS OF DATA FURNISHED BY OFFICIAL SOURCES MONITORED BY AUTHORITARIAN REGIMES

In fact, Achcar's criticisms are directed at the World Bank's own erroneous and misleading analysis of the Arab region and Egypt in particular. He denounces the fact that the Bank relies heavily on data provided by official sources monitored by authoritarian regimes, in particular Egypt's, and replied to the World Bank authors as follows:

It is astonishing indeed that anyone could uphold the claim that the discussion about a topic such as the validity of official data under authoritarian regimes and the causality of major popular uprisings against these same regimes is purely 'technical', and one which econometricians alone should engage in, to the

5   Ibid., p. 17.
6   Vladimir Hlasny and Paolo Verme, 'On the "Arab Inequality Puzzle": a comment', *Development and Change*, Social Studies Institute of The Hague, 2 January 2021 <https://doi.org/10.1111/dech.12626> [accessed 04/10/2021].

exclusion of political economists and all other social scientists – not to mention social and political activists who often know more about their countries than foreign 'experts.'[7]

THE WORLD BANK FEELS THAT INCREASING INEQUALITY IS NECESSARY FOR DEVELOPMENT

It should be noted that the Bank does not consider a rising level of inequality as negative. In fact, the idea of the necessity of rising inequalities is well rooted in World Bank-think. World Bank President Eugene Black said in April 1961: 'Inequalities in income are a necessary by-product of economic growth [which] makes it possible for people to escape a life of poverty.'[8] Indeed, the Bank adopts the theory developed in the 1950s by the economist Simon Kuznets according to which a country whose economy takes off and progresses must necessarily go through a phase of increasing inequality (see chapter 10, 'The question of unequal distribution of income').[9] According to this dogma, inequality will start to fall as soon as the country has reached a higher threshold of development. This is in fact a capitalist version of 'pie in the sky' used by the ruling classes to opiate the oppressed, on whom they impose a life of suffering.

In *Capital in the Twenty-First Century*, Thomas Piketty presents a very interesting analysis of Kuznets's famous Curve. Piketty mentions that at first Kuznets himself doubted the validity of the Curve. Yet his economic theory seems to have taken on a life of its own.

When we analyze the World Bank's position on the Arab Spring, we see that the dogma that inequalities are good for development is still dominant. That is why I say that the World Bank is engaging in equivocation regarding the Arab Spring. The Bank maintains that the level of inequality is less pronounced in the Arab region and that this is a symptom that things are not as they should be in the region's supposed economic success. As faithful disciples of Kuznets's theory, Vladimir Hlasny and Paolo Verme declare that 'low inequality was not an indicator of a healthy economy.'[10]

Gilbert Achcar sums up the position adopted by Paolo Verme[11] as follows:

in the view of the 2014 World Bank study, it is inequality aversion, not inequality per se, that should be deplored, since inequality must inevitably

7   Gilbert Achcar, 'Comment on the "Arab Inequality Puzzle": a rejoinder', *Development and Change*, Social Studies Institute of The Hague, 2 January 2021 <onlinelibrary.wiley.com/doi/10.1111/dech.12625> [accessed 05/10/2021].

8   Cited by Kapur, Lewis and Webb, *The World Bank: Its First Half Century, Volume 1*, p. 171.

9   Simon Kuznets, 'Economic growth and income inequality', *American Economic Review*, March 1955, No. 49, pp. 1–28.

10   Hlasny and Verme, 'On the "Arab Inequality Puzzle": a comment'.

11   Paolo Verme et al., *Inside Inequality in the Arab Republic of Egypt: Facts and Perceptions across People, Time, and Space* (Washington, DC: World Bank, 2014) <worldbank.org/content/dam/Worldbank/egypt-inequality-book.pdf> [accessed 27/12/2021].

rise with development from a Kuznetsian perspective. Had GDP growth been accompanied by a trickle-down effect, the Egyptians would have had a more positive view of inequality, as 'people can hardly appreciate inequality if their own status and the status of their peers do not improve' (Verme et al., 2014: 97). Following the same logic, in order to conform to the Kuznets curve, it is more inequality rather than less that Egypt needs.[12]

ACCORDING TO THE WORLD BANK, THE PROBLEM IS NOT INEQUALITY PER SE, BUT AN AVERSION TO INEQUALITY

It should be added that the World Bank maintains against all evidence that the poorest people were not one of the main social sectors to participate in the action against the authoritarian regimes in place and their antisocial policies. It is important for the Bank to say this because it is supposed to bring assistance to the poor. Given that in the fantasy world as imagined by the World Bank the level of poverty was low, it is not possible that it was the poorest class who rose up in Tunisia and Egypt in January 2011. According to World Bank experts, it was the middle classes who mobilized to protest against the insufficient progress in their living conditions. In the Bank's view, this insufficient progress was due to the state, which was still intervening too much in the economy and mismanaging public affairs.

Also, keep in mind that since the World Bank and IMF need scapegoats, once a regime has fallen, they do not hesitate to denounce and criticize as authoritarian and corrupt the very despots they have upheld to the bitter end.

THE WORLD BANK HAS NOT CHANGED ITS OUTLOOK ON THE ARAB REGION

Ten years after the Arab Spring, the World Bank and IMF are still compelling the countries concerned to apply the policies that were in place before such events: 'The only way to tap into the energy of MENA's youth is to revitalize economies; open more doors to the private sector [...] and have government play its role as a fair regulator.'[13] For them, large sectors of the economy are in need of privatization, free market access and more favourable regulations to attract foreign investment, while the government's role should be merely to regulate the free play of market forces.

---

12   Achcar, 'On the "Arab Inequality Puzzle": the case of Egypt'.

13   Ferid Belhaj, MENA unbound: ten years after the Arab Spring, avoiding another lost decade', World Bank/Al Jazeera, 14 January 2021 <worldbank.org/en/news/opinion/2021/01/14/mena-unbound-ten-years-after-the-arab-spring-avoiding-another-lost-decade> [accessed 06/10/2021]. Note that the author, Ferid Belhaj, is the Bank's vice-president for the Middle East–North Africa region. His official biography on the Bank's website shows that he has represented the Bank in various places around the world and has headed the Bank's activities in Morocco, Lebanon, Syria, Jordan, Iraq and Iran.

Public–private partnerships are also to be encouraged, even though it is well known that such structures are more favourable to investment interests than they are to the interests of the public. The bank says, 'What MENA governments need to do is open markets to competition, introduce public–private partnerships, and revitalize segments of their economies that have been inefficient or dormant altogether.'[14]

In the same document the Bank affirms that 'Governments, playing their rightful role, need to make an immense effort to equip their youth to grow and compete in an ever more globalized world.'[15] In other words, young people must be prepared to compete against each other in offering their work ability to private employers. According to the World Bank, the last thing public authorities should do is to create decent, socially useful jobs, since private enterprise will take care of doing that. In Tunisia in 2021, the rate of unemployment (one of the main factors behind the protests of December–January 2011) is still disastrous, especially among young people and in the country's interior – close to 40 per cent in several regions. And these are the young people who have taken to the streets in Tunisia again since January 2021, the anniversary month of the revolution of 2011.

THE WORLD BANK WANTS THE YOUNG TO BE MORE COMPETITIVE AND CONSIDERS WOMEN FROM THE PERSPECTIVE OF THEIR 'PERFORMANCE'

In this same document we read that women are 'more performing [*sic*]'[16] and that therefore the state should adopt policies that draw more women into employment.[17]

Next, the Bank suggests that social measures are too costly: 'MENA governments must also rethink their approach to social protection, which has been sought through policies that rely on costly, misguided subsidies. For too long, States have chosen the politically easy and economically disastrous path to a flawed social contract, whereby basic goods and services are made available at "protected" prices to buy political allegiances and "social peace".'[18] The Bank's answer is to cut social subsidies.

---

14 Ibid.
15 Ibid.
16 *'Opening more opportunities for women and their economic empowerment is another fundamental axis of progress. In MENA, there remains a gender paradox whereby women are far more educated and performing in academic settings than men, but a fraction of them are economically active.'* Ferid Belhaj, 'MENA Unbound...'
17 Christine Vanden Daelen, 'Quand la Banque mondiale s'intéresse aux femmes ...' ('When the World Bank takes an interest in women ...', CADTM, 26 February 2021 <cadtm.org/Quand-la-Banque-mondiale-s-interesse-aux-femmes> and 'Féminismes et Banque mondiale: un mariage "contre-nature"?' ('Feminism and the World Bank: an "unnatural" marriage?'), CADTM, 11 February 2021 <cadtm.org/Feminismes-et-Banque-mondiale-un-mariage-contre-nature>. Also see Denise Comanne, 'Quelle vision du développement pour les féministes' ('What vision of development should feminists adopt?'), CADTM, 28 May 2020 <cadtm.org/Quelle-vision-du-developpement-pour-les-feministes> (all in French) [accessed 06/10/2021].
18 Belhaj, 'MENA unbound'.

The Bank concludes its neoliberal credo with: 'To avoid another lost decade, a loud wakeup call needs to resonate all across MENA – from the "Ocean to the Gulf." The immediate task is to open the door to private enterprise, win over the resistance to liberalizing economies, and empower youth with opportunities to match their limitless potential.'[19] Amen!

The World Bank needs to be called out for its continuing support for authoritarian regimes in the region. In particular, it supports Egypt's criminal Abdel Fattah al-Sissi regime, in place since 2014, and considers the authoritarian monarchy in Morocco an example to be followed.

INDEBTEDNESS HAS CONTINUED SINCE 2011: THE EXAMPLE OF TUNISIA

Whereas Tunisia's external debt was at 40 per cent of GDP in 2011, it stood at 73 per cent in 2019 and even exceeded 100 per cent of GDP in September 2020. As a result, Tunisia is trapped in the spiral of indebtedness even though the country has undertaken forced reforms that are not suited to its actual economic context. Tunisia is now forced to devote more than twice the amount of resources to repayment of the external debt (25.8 per cent) as it does to health (14 per cent). In April 2020, Tunisia received a loan from the IMF that increased its indebtedness yet again, in the form of a 'Rapid Credit Facility' (RCF) worth $745 million.

Officially this emergency loan is supposed to reinforce the proactive measures taken by Tunisia in reaction to the Covid-19 pandemic. In return, Tunisia has committed to taking emergency austerity measures … as it has been doing since 2011, and even well before – the first IMF loan to Tunisia dates from 1986.

Under the terms of this loan, the Tunisian authorities commit to further extending the neoliberal policies. Two excerpts from the loan announcement clearly indicate that the government is agreeing to increase fuel prices, reduce expenditures for public-sector wages and reduce public investments:

The authorities have also taken steps to limit fiscal pressures, including a mechanism for automatic fuel price adjustment, emergency savings in the civil service wage bill, and a rescheduling of lower-priority public investment. [...]

Macroeconomic stability and debt sustainability hinge on strong policy and reform implementation. The authorities are committed to resuming fiscal consolidation once the crisis abates. These efforts will include a reduction of the civil service wage bill as a share of GDP and further energy subsidy reforms, taking into account the social implications.[20]

---

19   Ibid.
20   'IMF executive board approves a US$745 million disbursement to Tunisia to address the COVID-19 pandemic', IMF Press Release, 10 April 2020, No. 20/144, <imf.org/en/News/Articles/2020/04/10/pr20144-tunisia-imf-executive-board-approves-a-us-745m-disbursement-address-covid19-pandemic> [accessed 06/10/2021].

CONCLUSION

In opposition to the World Bank, the IMF and the governments of the region, the CADTM affirms that to avoid another decade of lost hopes and disillusionment, awareness is needed across the whole region, from the Atlantic to the Gulf. The peoples of the region must continue the action they have undertaken since 2011 by self-organizing and setting up governments that make a radical break with both the capitalist system and its neoliberal version, and carry out profound social reforms in favour of justice and emancipation from all forms of oppression, whether patri-archal, religious or otherwise.

26
The IMF and the World Bank in the Time of Coronavirus: The Failed Campaign for a New Image

Governments and major multilateral institutions like the World Bank, the IMF and the regional development banks have used the repayment of public debt as a tool for generalizing policies that have had a negative impact on public health systems: cutting jobs in the health sector, reducing job security, reducing the number of hospital beds, shutting down local health facilities, increasing the cost of health care and of medicines, underinvestment in infrastructure and equipment, privatization of various health sectors, public underinvestment in research and development of treatments, benefiting the big private pharmaceutical groups, and so on.

Even before the outbreak of the Covid-19 pandemic, these policies had already caused enormous losses of human lives all over the planet.

Criticism of the World Bank and the IMF has grown stronger and stronger. Many protest movements have been organized at the national and international levels, mainly in the early 2000s, on all continents.

This prompted the World Bank and the IMF to attempt to improve their image.

AN END TO STRUCTURAL ADJUSTMENT FOR THE IMF?

In October 2014, in a paper from IMF's Independent Evaluation Office (IEO) entitled *IMF Response to the Financial and Economic Crisis*,[1] the IMF claimed that it had learned from its mistakes and that since the financial crisis in 2008 none of the loans it had granted were based on the drastic conditions it had imposed in the past. From 2009, an economic research centre decided to test this claim.[2] The findings were indisputable: out of 41 countries granted IMF loans, 31 enacted policies of fiscal austerity in a context of recession or slow growth.

---

1   International Monetary Fund, Independent Evaluation Office, *IMF Response to the Financial and Economic Crisis* <elibrary.imf.org/view/books/017/22103-9781498305174-en/front-1.xml> [accessed 27/01/2022].
2   Mark Weisbrot et al., *IMF-Supported Macroeconomic Policies and the World Recession: A Look at Forty-One Borrowing Countries*, Center for Economic and Policy Research (CEPR), October 2009 <cepr.net/documents/publications/imf-2009-10.pdf> [accessed 27/12/2021].

The situation deteriorated from 2010 onward. According to a study by Isabel Ortiz and Matthew Cummins, 'premature expenditure contraction became widespread in 2010, which marked the beginning of a second phase of the crisis, despite vulnerable populations' urgent and significant need of public assistance'.[3] The authors show that in 2013 the contraction of public expenditure significantly intensified and affected 119 countries. They anticipated that 132 countries would be affected by 2015.

According to Ortiz and Cummins,

Regarding austerity measures, a desk review of IMF country reports published since 2010 indicates that governments are weighing various adjustment strategies. These include: (i) elimination or reduction of subsidies, including on fuel, agriculture and food products (in 100 countries); (ii) wage bill cuts/caps, including the salaries of education, health and other public sector workers (in 98 countries); (iii) rationalizing and further targeting of safety nets (in 80 countries); (iv) pension reform (in 86 countries); (v) healthcare reform (in 37 countries); and (vi) labor flexibilization (in 32 countries). Many governments are also considering revenue-side measures that can adversely impact vulnerable populations, mainly through introducing or broadening consumption taxes, such as value added taxes (VATs), on basic products that are disproportionately consumed by poor households (in 94 countries).[4]

The experience of some Arab countries is illustrative (see chapter 25).

Worried that these countries were pulling away from the neoliberal force field starting in 2011 under the impulsion of popular uprisings against dictators, the IMF issued repeated reassuring statements. In its publications that followed the Arab Spring, the institution highlighted the social dimension of the policies it promoted: inclusive growth, social policies for the more vulnerable, etc.

However, when Mohammed Mossallem, a former World Bank analyst, examined the conditions on the loans granted to Tunisia, Morocco, Jordan and Egypt after 2011,[5] he found all the ingredients of the SAPs of the 1980s: lower taxes for the private sector, higher taxes on consumption (the most unfair kind of tax), liberalized investment, fewer state subsidies along with higher energy prices, deregulation of the labour market. And the content of the austerity plans imposed on countries in the eurozone since 2010 strictly follows the same lines as the treatment inflicted upon the North African countries.

---

3   Isabel Ortiz and Matthew Cummins, 'The Age of Austerity – a review of public expenditures and adjustment measures in 181 countries', CADTM, 15 July 2013 <cadtm.org/The-Age-of-Austerity> [accessed 06/04/2023].

4   Ibid.

5   At the time of Mohammed Mossallem's survey, the loan agreement with Egypt was not yet signed. The IMF eventually approved a $12 billion loan agreement in November 2016.

MEA CULPA ON AUSTERITY: GENUINE QUESTIONING OR MAKE-BELIEVE?

In recent years, however, there have been a number of *internal* reports that acutely question IMF policies:

1. January 2013: Olivier Blanchard, IMF chief economist, showed that the IMF had very largely underestimated the negative impact of austerity on economic growth. The error in calculation was anything but marginal: some 300 per cent![6]
2. February 2014: After two students ripped apart a study by a former IMF chief economist that claimed that a public debt of over 90 per cent of a country's GDP automatically resulted in an economic slowdown, IMF experts confirmed that there was no critical threshold for public debt.[7]
3. June 2016: Three IMF economists published a paper entitled 'Neoliberalism: oversold?' in which they affirm that 'Instead of delivering growth, some neoliberal policies have increased inequality, in turn jeopardizing durable expansion.'[8]

Do these repeated critiques point to a change of direction for the institution?

First, while newspaper headlines may suggest that those who draft such reports are thoroughly heterodox in their views, a close reading of their texts shows that they are actually quite moderate. As an illustration, while the paper 'Neoliberalism: oversold?' includes figures that clearly show the limitations of the model, it also claims that 'There is much to cheer in the neoliberal agenda.'[9] We should also emphasize that documents published on the IMF website that are critical or depart from the party line are clearly identified as being the sole responsibility of their authors and not reflections of the institution's position.

Besides, playing with contradictions is not really new with the Bretton Wood institutions. But the point is to know whether this self-criticism, however limited, results in actual changes in the orientations taken by the institution.

The IMF's intervention in Greece from 2010 is illustrative of this continuity in the implementation of neoliberal policies that favour big capital, aggravate social inequalities and destroy essential social gains.[10] As early as 2013, an IMF

---

6   Olivier Blanchard and Daniel Leigh, *Growth Forecast Errors and Fiscal Multipliers* (Washington, DC: IMF, January 2013) <imf.org/external/pubs/ft/wp/2013/wp1301.pdf> [accessed 27/12/2021].
7   Balázs Égert, 'The 90% public debt threshold: the rise and fall of a stylized fact', *Applied Economics*, 2015, Vol. 47, No. 34–35 <tandfonline.com/doi/abs/10.1080/00036846.2015.1021463> [accessed 27/12/2021]; see also Andrea Pescatori, Damiano Sandri and John Simon, *Debt and Growth: Is There a Magic Threshold?* (Washington, DC: IMF, 2014) <imf.org/external/pubs/ft/wp/2014/wp1434.pdf> [accessed 27/12/2021].
8   Jonathan D. Ostry, Prakash Loungani and Davide Furceri, 'Neoliberalism: oversold?', *Finance and Development*, June 2016 <imf.org/external/pubs/ft/fandd/2016/06/pdf/ostry.pdf> [accessed 14/09/2021].
9   Ibid.
10   'Secret IMF documents on Greece commented by Eric Toussaint (CADTM)', CADTM, 16 January 2017 <cadtm.org/Secret-IMF-Documents-on-Greece> [accessed 14/09/2021].

independent evaluation report acknowledged that the first 2010 bailout programme had resulted in 'notable failures'.[11] Yet the same austerity measures have continued to be implemented.

In June 2016, the same 'independent' team produced a report that made the same assessment of the failure of the IMF's action in Greece. This time, however, the IMF experts went as far as to claim that in spite of the limitations of the IMF's action, there was no possibility of an alternative scenario. The notorious TINA ('There Is No Alternative') is still very much present in the corridors of the institution!

In early October 2020, facing the most serious international crisis of capitalism since the 1930s, IMF researchers announced that public investment had to increase.[12]

Clearly, in spite of such declarations, the IMF's leadership has launched yet another round of austerity. The alert was sounded in April 2021 by Isabel Ortiz and Matthew Cummins, the authors cited above, in a new study entitled *Global Austerity Alert – Looming Budget Cuts in 2021–25 and Alternative Pathways*.[13] The authors warn against 'an emerging post-pandemic fiscal austerity shock – one that is far more premature and severe than the one that followed the global financial crisis'.

They go on to say that:

Analysis of expenditure projections shows that austerity cuts are expected in 154 countries in 2021, and as many as 159 countries in 2022. The trend continues at least until 2025, with an average of 139 countries each year, according to IMF projections contained in the October 2020 World Economic Outlook database. Austerity is projected to affect 5.6 billion persons in 2021 or about 75% of the global population, rising to 6.6 billion or 85% of the world population in 2022. By 2025, 6.3 billion people or 78% of the total population may still be living under austerity. [...]

The high levels of expenditures needed to cope with the pandemic and the resulting socioeconomic crisis have left governments with growing fiscal deficits and debt. However, rather than continuing to explore financing options to provide direly-needed support for people and the economy, governments are entering into another period of fiscal austerity.[14]

---

11 IMF, *Greece: Ex Post Evaluation of Exceptional Access under the 2010 Stand-By Arrangement*, Country Report No. 13/156 (Washington, DC: IMF, June 2013) <imf.org/-/media/websites/IMF/imported-full-text-pdf/external/pubs/ft/scr/2013/_cr13156.ashx> [accessed 14/09/2021].

12 Vitor Gaspar, Paolo Mauro, Catherine Pattillo and Raphael Espinoza, 'Public investment for the recovery', *IMFBlog*, 5 October 2020 <blogs.imf.org/2020/10/05/public-investment-for-the-recovery> [accessed 27/12/2021].

13 Isabel Ortiz and Matthew Cummins, *Global Austerity Alert – Looming Budget Cuts in 2021–25 and Alternative Pathways* (New York: IPD/ITUC/PSI/Arab Watch Coalition/BWP/TNW, April 2021) <policydialogue.org/files/publications/papers/Global-Austerity-Alert-Ortiz-Cummins-2021-final.pdf> [accessed 14/09/2021].

14 Ibid., p. 4.

The dramatic events of early May 2021 in Colombia (the repression resulted in over 100 deaths) demonstrated this:

The post-pandemic shock appears to be much more intense than the one that followed the global financial and economic crisis. The average expenditure contraction in 2021 is projected at 3.3% of GDP, which is nearly double the size of the previous crisis, and 1.7% of GDP in 2022. Even more worrisome is the commonplace of excessive budget contraction, defined as spending less than the (already low) pre-pandemic levels. Nearly 50 governments are projected to be spending less in 2021–22 than in 2018–19.[15]

According to Ortiz and Cummins, whose projections are based on the IMF's own data, 'more than 40 governments are forecasted to have budgets that are 12% smaller in 2021–22 than in 2018–19, on average, including countries with high developmental needs like Ecuador, Equatorial Guinea, Kiribati, Liberia, Libya, Republic of Congo, South Sudan, Yemen, Zambia and Zimbabwe'.[16]

IMF AND WORLD BANK DEMOCRATIC REFORM … OR MOLEHILLS PASSED OFF AS MOUNTAINS

Since its founding, the structure of decision-making within the IMF has benefited the US and its victorious allies at the end of the Second World War. The distribution of power flouts any notion of equality since it is based on the rule '1 dollar = 1 vote' (see Annex 2) – a rule questioned by emerging countries that want their share of the cake. To try to establish some pretence of democracy, and to meet the demand of those expanding countries, a reform concerning the increase of quotas[17] and the transfer of voting rights finally came into force at the beginning of 2016.

In fact, adopting a system that would allow all member countries to have a say was never considered; the aim was rather to accommodate 'emerging countries' whose economic weight had become too important to be ignored. While the 6 per cent of voting rights that were newly distributed went to BRICS (South Africa excluded), those who lost out in the operation were predictably the poorest countries, whose voting rights the IMF cynically committed to preserve.[18] Could Bangladesh really feel that its leverage has increased, with its 0.24 per cent voting rights to defend the interests of its 166 million inhabitants?

The USA, on the other hand, scored a twofold victory. Not only did it keep its hold on the voting structure – since, as it had only relinquished 0.3 per cent of its

15   Ibid.
16   Ibid.
17   The quota of a member country determines its maximum financial commitment towards the IMF and its voting power.
18   IMF, 'IMF executive board approves major overhaul of quotas and governance', IMF Press Release, 5 November 2010 <imf.org/en/News/Articles/2015/09/14/01/49/pr10418> [accessed 14/09/2021].

voting rights, it retains its veto power[19] – but the USA is still at the helm of an even bigger international vessel, since the reform also doubled the Fund's resources to nearly $660 billion.

> 'The IMF reforms reinforce the central leadership role of the United States in the global economic system.'
>
> Jacob Lew, US Treasury Secretary, 2015

As regards the World Bank, the last major reform of this kind occurred in April 2010, when the controversial Robert Zoellick was president. As well as a $86.2 billion increase of the capital of the IBRD, countries of the South were granted an increase of 3.13 per cent of their voting rights, reaching 47.19 per cent of total votes. Compared with the USA's 15.44 per cent, this is outrageously little for those 135 countries, who account for 85 per cent of the global population.[20]

'DSRP', 'DOING BUSINESS', 'EBA' ... NEW NAMES FOR THE SAME POLICIES

From the end of the 1990s, a hail of criticism rained down on the World Bank, to the point where it became increasingly difficult for it to promote the structural adjustment policies (SAP) that were at the heart of the polemic. Faced with this crisis of legitimacy, the World Bank executed a flurry of semantic pirouettes without ever touching on the neoliberal logic inscribed in its DNA.

Among these crafty manoeuvres is the Heavily Indebted Poor Countries (HIPC) initiative, which, through limited debt reduction controlled by the international financial institutions, enables them to continue imposing SAP-like policies on the poorest countries and keep them in a spiral of indebtedness. Moreover in 2002, shortly after the World Bank had announced the official end of SAPs, as though by chance, it pulled a new instrument called the Doing Business indicator out of its hat!

> '[T]he World Bank is a human rights-free zone. [...] it treats human rights more like an infectious disease than universal values and obligations.'[21]
>
> Philip Alston, Special UN Rapporteur on extreme poverty and human rights, 2015

The *Doing Business* annual report sets out to classify the 189 member countries of the World Bank according to their ability to create a good 'business climate' for

---

19   IMF, *Acceptances of the Proposed Amendment of the Articles of Agreement on Reform of the Executive Board and Consents to 2010 Quota Increase* (IMF: 24 April 2017) <imf.org/external/np/sec/misc/consents.htm> [accessed 14/09/2021].

20   World Bank, 'World Bank reforms voting power, gets $86 billion boost', WB Press Release, 25 April 2010 <worldbank.org/en/news/press-release/2010/04/25/world-bank-reforms-voting-power-gets-86-billion-boost> [accessed 14/09/2021].

21   Philip Alston, 'Report of the Special Rapporteur on extreme poverty and human rights', A/70/274, 4 August 2015 <undocs.org/A/70/274> [accessed 14/09/2021].

investors based on various criteria: maximum deregulation, taxation favourable to the private sector, and legislation that gives workers' rights as little protection as possible and places them in competition with one another.

As a result the governments of the countries of the South are competing ferociously to offer the private sector the most attractive conditions, aware that the World Bank and bilateral creditors also use the results of the ranking to decide where to place their loans. And the World Bank is overjoyed! In 2014, it was congratulating itself that *Doing Business* had inspired over a quarter of the 2,100 reforms recorded since it was started.[22]

And why stop when you're doing so well? At the request of the G8, which in 2012 solicited the Bank to 'develop options for generating a Doing Business in agriculture index' to benchmark countries on the business climate of their agricultural sector,[23] it developed an instrument called 'Enabling the Business of Agriculture' (EBA).[24] The methodology of EBA, which is financed by the US, British, Danish and Dutch governments and the Bill and Melinda Gates Foundation, is modelled on *Doing Business*.

By promoting access to non-organic inputs and by pushing for contract-driven agriculture, EBA enables the big multinational agribusiness corporations to spread their influence even further.[25] The World Bank's logic conflicts with the realities and interests of the family-based agriculture that is operative in about 80 per cent of the agricultural holdings in the countries of the South.

Limited at first to a pilot project involving ten volunteer countries, the 2016 *Doing Business* report had already spread to include 40 countries with the aim of covering the maximum number of countries as quickly as possible.

In all these new mechanisms, it is hard to see just how the World Bank has become, as it claims, an organization fighting against poverty.

CONTROVERSIES AROUND 'DOING BUSINESS'

Here again, reality soon caught up with the institution. To the numerous accusations from social movements, trade unions and academics have been added those of Paul Romer, then chief economist at the World Bank. In an interview with the *Wall*

---

22 World Bank Group, *Doing Business 2014: Understanding Regulations for Small and Medium-Size Enterprises* (Washington, DC: World Bank Group, 28 October 2013) <doingbusiness.org/reports/global-reports/doing-business-2014> [accessed 14/09/2021].

23 White House, 'Fact sheet: G-8 action on food security and nutrition', Press Release, 18 May 2012, quoted in Oakland Institute, *Unfolding Truth: Dismantling the World Bank's Myths on Agriculture and Development* (Oakland: Oakland Institute, 2014), p. 5 <oaklandinstitute.org/sites/oaklandinstitute.org/files/OurBiz_Brief_UnfoldingTruth_lowrez_0.pdf> [accessed 14/09/2021].

24 World Bank Group, *Enabling the Business of Agriculture 2015: Progress Report* (Washington, DC: World Bank Group, 2015) <hdl.handle.net/10986/21501> [accessed 14/09/2021].

25 Rémi Vilain, 'La nouvelle révolution verte en Afrique subsaharienne' ('The new green revolution in Sub-Saharan Africa'), CADTM, December 2015 (in French) <cadtm.org/La-nouvelle-revolution-verte-en-Afrique-subsaharienne-Partie-1-sur-2> [accessed 14/09/2021].

Street Journal, Romer had criticized the (openly neoliberal) ideological bias in the *Doing Business* report's methodology and the way it is written, using the example of Chile's 23-point decline in the rankings after 'socialist' president Michelle Bachelet was elected.[26] After being reprimanded by President Jim Yong Kim, Romer immediately handed in his resignation in January 2018. In August 2020, the World Bank itself announced, albeit reluctantly, that publication of the 2020 report had been interrupted due to '[a] certain number of irregularities [having] been reported regarding changes to the data in the Doing Business 2018 and Doing Business 2020 reports, published in October 2017 and 2019. The changes in the data were inconsistent with the Doing Business methodology.'[27]

Finally in September 2021, the World Bank officially announced that publication of *Doing Business* would cease. A statement from the World Bank's management said: 'After reviewing all the information available to date on Doing Business, including the findings of past reviews, audits, and the report the Bank released today on behalf of the Board of Executive Directors, World Bank Group management has taken the decision to discontinue the Doing Business report.'[28]

Preferential treatment given to China was exposed in the report on an investigation commissioned by the Bank. According to the report, the president of the Bank (who resigned in 2019) and Chief Executive Kristalina Georgieva (who became managing director of the IMF in October 2019) put pressure on the team in charge of producing the *Doing Business* report to improve China's ranking. Concretely, China moved up seven places in the ranking between 2017 and 2018. The investigative report, conducted by the law firm WilmerHale, criticizes the 'pressure applied by CEO Georgieva and her adviser, Mr. Djankov, to make specific changes to China's data points in an effort to increase its ranking at precisely the same time the country was expected to play a key role in the Bank's capital increase campaign.'[29]

The strained relations between the USA and China are not without bearing on the direction this scandal has taken. It is difficult to imagine this more or less standard practice of the Bank causing such a scandal and ending in the discontinuation of *Doing Business*, had US–China relations been good.

---

26   Reuters Business News, 'World Bank economist Paul Romer quits after Chile comments' <reuters. com/article/us-worldbank-economist-romer-idUKKBN1FD38Y> [accessed 14/09/2021].

27   World Bank, 'Doing Business – data irregularities statement', 27 August 2020 <worldbank.org/en/ news/statement/2020/08/27/doing-business---data-irregularities-statement> [accessed 14/09/2021].

28   World Bank, 'World Bank Group to discontinue Doing Business report', 16 September 2021 <worldbank.org/en/news/statement/2021/09/16/world-bank-group-to-discontinue-doing-business-report> [accessed 19/11/2021].

29   WilmerHale, 'Investigation of data irregularities in *Doing Business 2018* and *Doing Business 2020* – investigation findings and report to the Board of Executive Directors' <thedocs.worldbank.org/en/ doc/84a922cc9273b7b120d49ad3b9e9d3f9-0090012021/original/DB-Investigation-Findings-and-Report-to-the-Board-of-Executive-Directors-September-15-2021.pdf> [accessed 27/01/2022].

THE WORLD BANK, A 'HUMAN RIGHTS-FREE ZONE'

One might reasonably expect of an organization claiming to fight poverty that human rights would be an integral part of its action. Yet even though the World Bank is officially obliged to respect international law,[30] for over 79 years those principles have never passed the threshold of its lush Washington offices.

As we have seen earlier in this book, to 'justify' this refusal to comply with human rights laws, the World Bank hides behind its mission, which, being limited to economic considerations, supposedly prevents it from broaching notions considered too political. It is hard to comprehend why this purportedly technical mission would place it outside or above international law. Moreover the World Bank has never had any problem in finding justifications for dealing with issues such as corruption, money-laundering, financing terrorism or governance, none of which were part of its initial prerogatives.

THE WORLD BANK, A 'NO-GO ZONE'

Considering itself above the law, the World Bank makes no bones about flouting the fundamental rights of the peoples of the South. Among far too many examples, we could cite the field investigation carried out in 14 countries by the International Consortium of Investigative Journalists (ICIJ),[31] which revealed that projects financed by the World Bank had forced nearly 3.4 million people out of their homes since 2004, sometimes using armed police. This is far from being an isolated case; United Nations agencies, national bodies and committees of independent experts confirm that several projects funded by the International Finance Corporation (IFC), part of the World Bank Group, have given rise to serious breaches of human rights – land-grabbing, repression, arbitrary arrests and murders – in order to silence protest movements that oppose certain World Bank projects.

WORLD BANK/IMF AND THE 2020 CRISIS IN
THE CONTEXT OF THE CORONAVIRUS PANDEMIC

As mentioned in the introduction to this chapter, governments and major multi-lateral institutions like the World Bank, the IMF and regional development banks have used repayment of public debt to generalize policies that have damaged public

---

30   The UN Committee on Economic, Social and Cultural Rights recalled in an official statement on 24 June 2016 that the World Bank, like any other international body, must defend and implement the Universal Declaration of Human Rights, the general principles of international law and the 1966 Covenants on Human Rights. See E/C.12/2016/1, 'Public debt, austerity measures and the International Covenant on Economic, Social and Cultural Rights', Statement by the Committee on Economic, Social and Cultural Rights <etoconsortium.org/nc/en/main-navigation/library/docu-ments/?tx_drblob_pi1%5BdownloadUid%5D=189> [accessed 14/09/2021].

31   Sasha Chavkin and Michael Hudson, 'New investigation reveals 3.4m displaced by World Bank', International Consortium of Investigative Journalists, 13 April 2015 <icij.org/inside-icij/2015/04/new-investigation-reveals-34m-displaced-world-bank/> [accessed 14/09/2021].

health systems. This has made them much more vulnerable to pandemics such as the one caused by the Coronavirus.

The outrageous fiasco of 'pandemic bonds' issued by the World Bank

In July 2020, the World Bank abandoned the project of reissuing pandemic bonds after the first issue had been criticized for its tardiness in delivering aid to poor countries affected by epidemics.[32]

In 2017 the World Bank had launched its programme of 'pandemic bonds' in the wake of the 2014 Ebola epidemic in Africa. For a country to access this programme aimed at helping it confront an epidemic, it first had to have registered 2,500 deaths. In 2018, the Democratic Republic of Congo was obliged to wait until the epidemic had wreaked havoc before being granted any aid. This drew fierce criticism.

In 2017 the World Bank issued $320 million worth of bonds, officially destined to help developing countries deal with a serious epidemic of infectious disease.[33]

Investment funds and private banks who had bought these securities in 2017 made ample profits since the World Bank had guaranteed a two-figure return. The owners of the bonds, among whom are the Scottish investment fund Baillie Gifford, Amundi (owned by the French bank Crédit Agricole) and the New York financial firm Stone Ridge Asset Management, were paid interest of up to almost $100 million by the end of February 2020!

Towards the middle of April 2020, over two months after the virus had started spreading across the world, the conditions allowing the release of almost $200 million were finally met. The 64 countries that were to share the meagre sum of $195 million were entitled, according to size, to between $1 million and $15 million – in other words, peanuts. The largest amount available, $15 million, was allocated to Nigeria and Pakistan.

A second version of the 'Pandemic Emergency Financing Facility' (PEF),[34] the name given by the Bank to the 'pandemic bonds', was to have been launched in 2020, after the World Bank had declared in early 2019 that it was making adjustments to the structure before it would be ready to commercialize the new product in May 2020 or thereabouts. Finally, in the face of growing criticism, the World Bank cancelled the new issuance.

---

32 'World Bank ditches second round of pandemic bonds', *Financial Times*, 5 July 2020, <ft.com/content/949adc20-5303-494b-9cf1-4eb4c8b6aa6b> [accessed 06/04/2023].

33 Here is what can be found on the World Bank's website: 'The insurance was obtained in July 2017 in two classes and in both bond and swap form. Class A was composed of US$225 million in bonds and US$50 million in swaps, and Class B was composed of US$95 million in bonds and US$55 million in swaps. The bonds were issued under the IBRD's Global Debt Issuance Facility, under the Capital at Risk Notes supplement which was created in 2014 in part to transfer catastrophe risks to the capital markets.' (World Bank, 'Fact sheet: Pandemic Emergency Financing Facility', 27 April 2020 <worldbank.org/en/topic/pandemics/brief/fact-sheet-pandemic-emergency-financing-facility> [accessed 15/09/2021].

34 Milan Rivié, '6 months after the official announcements of debt cancellation for the countries of the South: where do we stand?' CADTM, 17 September 2020 <cadtm.org/6-months-after-the-official-announcements-of-debt-cancellation-for-the> [accessed 15/09/2021].

Even before the Covid-19 pandemic broke out, these policies had already led to enormous loss of human lives, and all round the world health workers were organizing protests.

If we really want to fight the Coronavirus and, beyond that, improve the health and living conditions of populations, emergency measures must be taken. Immediate suspension of debt payments and better still, cancellation of debt must take priority.

Neither the World Bank nor the IMF have cancelled any debts during the Coronavirus pandemic.[35] They have, however, made endless declarations calculated to give the impression that they are taking very strong measures. This is completely false. The mechanism put in place by the IMF, the World Bank and the G20[36] is identical to the measures taken following the tsunami that hit India, Sri Lanka, Bangladesh and Indonesia in December 2004.[37] Instead of cancellation, public creditors simply postponed the due dates. Note that private creditors are not required to make the slightest effort. As for the IMF, not only does it not end repayments, but it does not even suspend them. It has set up a special fund financed by rich countries into which the IMF can dip to repay itself.

Worse still, since March 2020, the IMF has extended the loan agreements that will only continue the structural adjustment measures enumerated in chapter 15 and summed up in the introduction to this chapter.

As for the World Bank, between March 2020 and April 2021 it received more in debt repayments from developing countries than it paid out to finance either donations or loans.

---

35 Ibid.

36 The G20 or G-20 is an informal structure created by the G7 (Germany, Canada, the USA, France, Italy, Japan and the UK) in 1999 and reactivated in 2008 in the midst of the financial crisis in the North. The members of the G20 are: Argentina, Australia, Brazil, Canada, China, France, Germany, India, Indonesia, Italy, Japan, Mexico, Russia, Saudi Arabia, South Africa, South Korea, Turkey, the USA, the UK and the European Union (represented by the presidents of the Council and of the European Central Bank; the EU Commission is also represented). Spain has become a permanent guest member. International institutions (the IMF and World Bank) are also guests at meetings. The Financial Stability Board (FSB), the Bank for International Settlements (BIS) and the OECD also take part.

37 See Toussaint and Millet, *Tsunami Aid or Debt Cancellation!*

27

The 'Gender Equity' Farce: A Feminist Reading of World Bank Policies

Camille Bruneau

One cannot take an interest in the policies of the World Bank or in the emancipation of peoples without taking into account the issue of gender, which is itself inextricably entwined with other systems of oppression and social inequality.

Despite the fact that officially the World Bank has co-opted 'gender equity' by making 'empowerment' all but an obligation for the debtor countries, in reality its practices do nothing to combat inequalities. As in the case of environmental issues (see chapter 21), the gap between the high-minded rhetoric and any real change is enormous.

The concrete consequences of the projects that are carried out and the macroeconomic recommendations that are made and followed run counter to any hope of emancipation. Furthermore, the Bank's very way of conceptualizing gender (in)equity is fully in line with an overtly neoliberal agenda it makes no effort to hide.

WHY A FEMINIST ANALYSIS OF THE INTERNATIONAL FINANCIAL INSTITUTIONS?

We know that 'The loans made by the World Bank, far from being disinterested gestures, are in fact clearly a means of submitting the country, politically and economically, to the international order of the most powerful, "modelling" it to suit their needs and the needs of the local dominant class – in other words to extract maximum profits.'[1] In other words, debt is one of the central mechanisms of the maintenance of power relations; it is indispensable to the reproduction of neoliberal capitalism and plays a fundamental part in patriarchal, neocolonial, racist and extractivist oppression.

We also know that the policies linked to these loans have a profound and lasting impact on the most vulnerable populations (despite the fact that officially the Bank's 'mission' is to come to their aid), of which a large share are women.[2]

---

1   Éric Toussaint, 'Ecuador: Resistance against the policies imposed by the World Bank, the IMF and other creditors between 2007 and 2011', CADTM, 15 April 2021 <cadtm.org/Ecuador-Resistance-against-the-policies-imposed-by-the-World-Bank-the-IMF-and> [accessed 07/10/2021].
2   Camille Bruneau, the author of this chapter, uses the term 'women' here in a pluralist and non-essentialist perspective: any person who identifies with or is assigned to the 'feminine' gender and/or sex and who thereby is subject to a series of sexist and heteropatriarchal oppressions (cisgender women, transgender people, people who are non-binary, agender, gender fluid, etc.) She uses the 'category' in a political perspective – that is, to analyze social relations of domination.

There is therefore no doubt that women are impacted directly (that is, as 'women' within a patriarchal system) and indirectly (through the general increase in inequalities).

Mainly from the 1990s, studies from all sides have criticized the gender impacts of the World Bank's policies and structural adjustment plans, which forced the international financial institutions to 'react'. One characteristic of the World Bank is its ability to co-opt criticism in order to attempt to renew its image and thus strengthen its power over a multitude of political, social, economic and scientific actors.[3]

Many feminists have long denounced this co-optation by the IFI and the 'development' (a problematic notion in itself)[4] programmes which silence radical feminist and anti-imperialist voices and re-legitimize certain forms of exploitation of women.

After 'greenwashing', 'pinkwashing' or 'genderwashing' has come into vogue – for example with a new conditionality for loans, the 'gender-sensitive budget', which claims to take reduction of gender inequalities into account in budgetary and fiscal policies.

CHRONOLOGY OF RECOGNITION OF INEQUALITIES AND GENDER

As this book shows, the 1980s and the structural adjustment plans (SAPs) are synonymous with the destruction of social protection and the means of subsistence for the peoples of the South. These phenomena contribute to the increase of the various inequalities and have a particular impact on women.

---

3   In addition to this book, see the analysis by Michael Goldman, in particular of environmental questions. He also deals with how the World Bank has historically imposed itself as a repository of knowledge, a fact which has enabled it to consolidate its hegemony. Michael Goldman, *The World Bank and Struggles for Social Justice in the Age of Globalization* (New Haven: Yale University Press, 2005).

4   The notion of development is problematic for many reasons – both the concept itself, which is normative and fashioned by a Western, Eurocentric ideology, and its historical origins, its political intentions, and its social, economic, environmental and cultural consequences. In summary, it is a tool of the neocolonialism and organized looting put in place following the independence of the former colonies in order to continue to control the worldwide organization of production and consumption, and as a result, the distribution of wealth. It is clear that control over women's productive and reproductive capacities (their bodies, their fertility) is an important and sometimes explicit dimension thereof. In addition to the so-called 'post-development' theories and the many decolonial and anti-imperialist critiques, see chapter 10 of this book as well as a few articles that take a feminist view of the notion of development: Falquet, 'Analyzing globalization from a feminist perspective'; Denise Comanne, 'Quelle vision du développement pour les féministes', CADTM, 2005 <cadtm.org/Quelle-vision-du-developpement-pour-les-feministes> [accessed 06/04/2023]; Jules Falquet, 'Femmes, féminisme et "développement": une analyse critique des politiques des institutions internationales' ('Women, feminism, and "development": a critical analysis of the policies of international institutions'), in Jeanne Bisilliat (ed.), *Regards de femmes sur la globalisation: approches critiques* (Paris : Karthala, 2003), pp. 75–112 ; Roger Herla, 'Du Sud au Nord, impacts de mondialisation néolibérale sur le travail des femmes' ('From North to South, impacts of neoliberal globalization on women's work'), CVFE – Publications, 2018 <cvfe.be/sites/default/files/doc/ep-2018-6-du_sud_au_nord._impacts_de_la_mondialisation.pdf> [accessed 06/04/2023]. (All in French.)

Debt is not 'blind' and needs to be perceived in the context of social relations

Patriarchy – which legitimizes day-to-day sexist violence and discrimination – is based on a separation between so-called 'productive' activities and those referred to as 'non-productive' or 'reproductive'. The latter – despite their being essential to the reproduction of life on Earth and of societies – are socially depreciated and assigned to women. And yet the dominant economic system relies on that separation: the accumulation of capital (which mainly benefits wealthy men) is maintained thanks to underpaid or unpaid work done by an overwhelming majority of women who 'naturally' take on care-giving and service tasks.[5]

In case of an economic crisis (in general related to debts), women's marginal status on the labour market means that they are the first to be affected by job cuts or increasingly insecure employment. They are also the first to take up the slack of the disengagement of the social state, being first in line to take on domestic work. These socio-professional inequalities have lasting consequences: on their pension, their social security plan (if it exists), etc. Since they are less able to face crises, they are subject to exploitation. And it should not be forgotten that in many countries these gender norms and inequalities were propagated from Europe by the colonial powers.

Since the 1990s we have witnessed a process of reorganization and reappropriation of (re)productive work on a worldwide scale, in particular around criteria of gender, class and 'race', drawing the contours of a new, globalized, patriarchal and racist capitalism. One of the favourite tools for setting it up is public debt or household debt incurred by households of the working classes, which accelerate this gender and racial division of labour and also sexist violence via the demand for underpaid men and women workers and dependency on wages. Non-white and migrant women are once again the primary 'losers'.[6]

Obviously certain women (often from the higher social classes) escape from this gender bias, as indeed certain men (especially non-whites, migrants and those without secure employment) end up in this category of persons performing work that is socially depreciated and 'invisible'.[7] That is why what must take precedence is an approach that is imbricationist[8] and aware of social relations – which are of concern to all of us – to counter one based on discrimination or individual privilege.

It then becomes evident that the gender- and race-based structure of the dominant economy must be accounted for in our analyses.

---

5   The concept of 'care work' refers to a set of material and psychological practices whose purpose is to provide a concrete response to the needs of others and of a community (or ecosystem). The word 'care' is preferred to 'domestic' or 'reproductive' since it includes the emotional and psychological dimensions (mental load, affection, support) and, for myself and as it is used here, is not limited to 'private' and unpaid aspects but also includes paid activities that are necessary to the reproduction of human life.

6   Camille Bruneau, 'La dette : une arme patriarcale déployée dans les pays du Sud' ('Debt: a patriarchal weapon deployed in the Global South'), *AVP Dettes aux Suds*, 2019, No. 77 (in French) <cadtm.org/La-dette-une-arme-patriarcale-deployee-dans-les-pays-du-Sud> [accessed 8/10/2021].

7   Jules Falquet, 'Neoliberal capitalism: an ally for women? Materialist and imbricationist feminist perspectives', in Christine Verschuur, Hélène Guétat and Isabelle Guérin (eds), *Under Development: Gender* (London: Palgrave Macmillan), 2014, pp. 236–56.

8   Jules Falquet, *Imbrication: Femmes, race et classe dans les mouvements sociaux (Imbrication: Women, Race and Class in Social Movements)* (Vulaines-sur-Seine: Éditions du croquant, 2019) (in French).

Inequalities, to which the World Bank gave little thought (or no thought at all; see chapter 10), were seen as a necessary evil for growth, one that would eventually be lessened by the 'trickle-down effect'. In addition to being completely erroneous, this point of view does not look at what is behind the 'inequalities', which are summed up as the difference in revenue between 'rich' and 'poor'. It took a long time for the question 'Who is poor and why?' to appear. Among the Bank's fundamental texts on inequality, we could cite Kuznets's study published in 1955, in which the word 'women', unsurprisingly, appears exactly zero times.[9] Not until 1982 did the Bank begin to mention 'women', but only in two contexts: unproductive peasant women or backward women with too many children. The 'developing countries' had everything to gain by including women in efforts to increase agricultural productivity (including through the use of chemical fertilizers and commercial seed). And this same vision is still present in many official statements.

During the 1990s, as numerous countries were bearing the brunt of the negative consequences of the SAPs and women specifically were suffering certain types of 'collateral damage', the question of the 'reduction of gender inequalities between men and women' made its appearance. The Beijing conference in 1995 put 'women's rights' and 'reduction of inequalities' on the international agenda, in particular via 'participation in the economy'.[10] But the issue did not really become significant until after 2000.

Whereas in 2001 the World Bank adopted its first basic gender mainstreaming strategy, which was to serve as the basis for its future action plans and evaluations, and the issue of 'empowering women' is mentioned in the Bank's annual report for 2003[11] and in a few other documents, the notion of gender is largely absent from fundamental World Bank documents on reducing inequalities. To give an example from 2004, the famous 'Poverty–Growth–Inequality Triangle'[12] by the Bank's chief economist François Bourguignon, a foundation stone of developmentalist thought in the decade, completely ignores gender issues.

In the 2006 *World Development Report*, on the other hand, we find a few reflections on gender inequalities and discrimination and the need for dealing with them. The World Bank even mentions that it would be possible to reduce them by investing not only in social protection, reproductive health, education for

---

9   Kuznets, 'Economic growth and income inequality'.
10 For a historical and critical analysis of the 'inclusion' of women in 'development' by the major international institutions, and in particular the UN, see the articles by Falquet, 'Femmes, féminisme et "développement": une analyse critique des politiques des institutions internationales' and Comanne, 'Quelle vision du développement pour les féministes', cited above.
11 World Bank, *World Bank Annual Report 2003* <documents1.worldbank.org/curated/en/259381468762619763/pdf/270000PAPER0English0WBAR0vol-01.pdf> [accessed 11/10/2021].
12 World Bank Group, *World Bank Group Gender Strategy (FY16–23): Gender Equality, Poverty Reduction and Inclusive Growth* (Washington, DC: World Bank, 2015) <documents1.worldbank.org/curated/en/449711468762020101/pdf/28102.pdf> [accessed 17/11/2021].

girls and access to water, but also and especially by encouraging private property and productivity.

Year after year, the 'progressive' proposals are invariably counterbalanced by other 'antagonistic interests'. For example, the need to find a 'golden mean' between social protection of women workers and corporate profitability:

in all areas the policy mix needs to be assessed in ways that balance protection (for all workers) with allowances for the restructuring so central to dynamic growth and employment creation. Worker security is often provided by various excessively stringent forms of employment protection legislation, which, in general, make it costly to hire and, in some cases, make it even costlier to hire unskilled, young, and female workers.[13]

Social security, essential for the most precarious persons, which includes women, is seen as an obstacle to the profitability of businesses. So that when positive proposals regarding women are not counterbalanced in this way, the fact is justified by saying that this will encourage risk-taking and thus profitability, or that it will contribute to competitiveness, productivity, growth, an entrepreneurial spirit and so on. When discriminations are attacked as such – for example domestic violence – it is done to enable better integration of women into the labour market! Such measures, then, are not ends in themselves.

The year 2007 saw the Gender Action Plan, entitled: *Gender Equality as Smart Economics*.[14] It made gender a central issue and has since served as a foundation that is regularly updated. It is based on an independent and highly critical evaluation of the 2001 strategy which singled out the failure to take the gender dimension into account beginning in 2003.

Suspecting that the fault lay in the absence of mechanisms for control and evaluation, the new strategy for 2007 accents 'priority' sectors for the emancipation of women: 'agriculture, private sector development, finance and infrastructure'. So it would seem that in 2007, women were not affected by matters of social reproduction, public services, violence, etc.!

The 2012 *World Development Report: Gender Equality and Development* in turn became the conceptual framework for the subsequent strategies.[15]

---

13   World Bank, *World Development Report 2006 – Equity and Development* <openknowledge. worldbank.org/bitstream/handle/10986/5988/WDR%202006%20-%20English.pdf?sequence= 3&isAllowed=y> [accessed 11/10/2021].

14   World Bank, *Gender Equality as Smart Economics: A World Bank Group Gender Action Plan* (Washington, DC: World Bank, August 2006) <documents1.worldbank.org/curated/en/ 295371468315572899/pdf/37008.pdf> [accessed 11/10/2021].

15   World Bank, *2012 World Development Report: Gender Equality and Development* (Washington, DC: World Bank, 2011) <doi.org/10.1596/978-0-8213-8810-5> [accessed 11/10/2021].

Despite increasing recognition of gender norms and the sexual division of labour as the years have passed,[16] the recipe remains increasing revenue via participation in paid labour.

Following the same logic, in 2015 the World Bank launched its strategy for 2016–23 under the banner of 'inclusive growth'. Whereas in the part entitled 'Progress since 2000' the *Gender Strategy* report notes that, despite women being engaged in economic activities, 'gender inequality in the world of work has been stubbornly persistent across multiple dimensions'.[17] Yet the 'Lessons Learned' section contains nothing that calls the Bank's own policies into question. At the end, it even congratulates itself for having shown the way to progress in gender equity in several areas.

Finally, in 2016, a whole series of new indicators were proposed for use in evaluation. Nearly all of them are related to paid labour; we shall return to them later in this chapter.

Briefly:

- The issue of gender has been present in the reports for a little over 20 years, but was not among the central strategies until 2006, whereas recently the Bank has devoted a multitude of reports and projects to it.
- This recent evolution is not the expression of feminist awareness or a desire to end exploitation. It should be understood as:
  o a public-relations effort in response to criticisms and to major protest movements;
  o an attempt to 'incorporate women and the feminist movement in the process of neoliberal globalization'.[18]
- Emancipation is never treated as an end in itself but merely as a tool in the service of the capitalist economy. Women are resources; they are an investment, an 'underutilized asset', and they need to be brought into the productive sphere.

The first paragraph of the introduction to the *World Bank Annual Gender Trust Funds Program Report* for 2015 says it all: 'Failure to fully unleash women's productive potential represents a major missed opportunity, with significant consequences for individuals, families, and economies.'[19]

All this rhetoric has encouraged an institutional and imperialist form of feminism – yet another trump card in the hand of neoliberalism, now hiding behind the mask of 'concern for women's rights'.

---

16 World Bank, *Gender at Work: A Companion to the World Development Report on Jobs* (Washington, DC: World Bank, 2014) <worldbank.org/content/dam/Worldbank/document/Gender/GenderAtWork_ExecutiveSummary.pdf> [accessed 12/10/2021].

17 World Bank, *World Bank Group Gender Strategy (FY16–23): Gender Equality, Poverty Reduction and Inclusive Growth* (Washington, DC: World Bank, 2015) <openknowledge.worldbank.org/bitstream/handle/10986/23425/102114.pdf?sequence=5&isAllowed=y> [accessed 12/10/2021].

18 Vanden Daelen, 'Féminismes et Banque mondiale: un mariage "contre-nature"'.

19 World Bank, *World Bank Annual Gender Trust Funds Program Report* <documents1.worldbank.org/curated/en/465841467999715075/pdf/101061-AR-P133146-PUBLIC-Box393257B-WBG-GenderTrustFunds-Report-2015.pdf> [accessed 16/11/2021].

The World Bank, along with the IMF, continues knowingly to prescribe policies that are prejudicial to women, giving priority to repayment of debt to the detriment of social expenditures. At the centre of these strategies are markets, and human beings; the seemingly progressive rhetoric never calls the fundamental neoliberal credo into question. What all the discourse, all the buzzwords like 'agency' and 'empowerment' and 'mainstreaming' amount to, is nothing more or less than an ambitious genderwashing project.

THE WORLD BANK'S APPROACH TO GENDER IS RHETORIC IN THE SERVICE OF CAPITAL, AND NOT OF THE MAJORITY OF WOMEN!

Since the negative impacts of 'poverty reduction' projects, unaware of gender and aimed at 'heads of families', were recognized, numerous 'development' programmes have begun to focus on reducing workplace inequality, 'gender strategies' and 'empowerment'. Women's rights as an integral part of development have become the stated goal of international institutions and NGOs. Gender budgeting has become de rigueur and is in the continuity of a process oriented towards the needs of investors, using the argument of the miraculous 'trickle-down effect' that is supposed to be favourable to women and the poor.

And yet, in addition to the genderwashing described above, the dominant discourse of the World Bank and its allies reinforces certain gender biases, thus reaffirming a form of patriarchal domination, for two reasons.

Firstly, by presuming to decide for women – especially non-Western women – what is good for them, the Bank takes on the role of father or professor of world economics, acting for the good of individuals who are incapable of knowing for themselves what they need.

Indeed, it is much more common to read and hear what the World Bank considers to be an 'emancipated' woman than to hear the voices of those same women. This discourse is systematically based on one gender norm which is reinforced to serve specific interests. This takes away from the women of the Global South their ability to decide the means of their emancipation for themselves by placing them in prefabricated, homogenous pigeonholes – oblivious of intersectionality[20] and blind to the

---

20   Intersectionality is a concept taken from Black feminism, forged by the American jurist Kimberlé Williams Crenshaw to bring to light the existence of multiple discriminations heretofore invisibilized in the context of law within a segmented and hierarchized approach to discriminations. According to the European Network Against Racism (ENAR), the intersectional approach takes into account those persons who are at the intersection of several sources of discrimination (e.g. being a woman, a Muslim, of foreign origin, etc.) and who are often victims of a new form of discrimination resulting from the accumulation of several characteristics. In sum, 'Our working definition of intersectionality is very simple. We say that intersectionality is about fighting discrimination within discrimination, protecting minorities within minorities and tackling inequalities within inequalities.' (Emilia Roig, Center for Intersectional Justice <intersectionaljustice.org> in 'Intersectionality as a practice: an interview with Emilia Roig' <pocolit.com/en/2020/04/25/intersectionality-as-a-practice> [accessed 12/10/2021]. Decolonial feminists such as Françoise Vergès recall that this notion was already well integrated before the concept itself was recognized, for example within struggles against slavery. See Françoise Vergès, *A Decolonial Feminism* (London: Pluto Press, 2021).

multiple and varied realities of women – which are useful to whatever the economic and conjunctural theory of the moment happens to be: the businesswoman whose enterprising spirit is held back by the local culture; the woman who must see to the needs of a household and who is central to the economy of the family and to resilience in the face of crises; the female skilled worker who is indispensable to economic growth; the poor vulnerable victim, etc. ...

This discourse is self-perpetuating, as can be seen in the IMF report that refers to women as 'one of the most "underutilized assets" in the economy'.[21]

Secondly, empowerment – a multidimensional emancipatory process which should include numerous factors – is measured mainly via women's 'participation in economic and political life', which is much too limited.[22] This rhetoric about emancipation via work is problematic and dangerous for several reasons:

- By promoting increasing participation of women in economic life, this discourse completely hides the reality of how most human societies operate, as if women do not participate in economic life if they do not have declared wage-earning employment! What about the colossal amounts of unpaid work done in caring for loved ones, communities and ecosystems, without which what is called 'the productive economy' would simply collapse? The World Bank is not ignorant of their existence, yet these realities do not enter into the scope of its considerations. At best they are 'obstacles' to paid labour by women. A redistribution which would not reproduce existing exploitative relations, some form of public or collective recognition, or a calling into question of gender norms are simply not on the agenda.
- Denying the importance of care work while placing value on paid work can contribute not only to increasing inequalities of gender (by increasing the total working time), but also between women because it is women of the poorer classes who take on the burden of care in a large percentage of wealthy households (since women who acquire well-paid, full-time employment spurn care work and neither men nor the collectivity take up the burden).
- This simplistic vision of emancipation as being synonymous solely with economic autonomy via paid work ignores the fact that the increase in the number of women on the labour market is generally accompanied by an increase

---

21   Heloisa Marone, *Demographic Dividends, Gender Equality, and Economic Growth: The Case of Cabo Verde*' (IMF: Working Paper WP/16/169, 9 August 2016) <imf.org/-/media/Websites/IMF/imported-full-text-pdf/external/pubs/ft/wp/2016/_wp16169.ashx>, cited in Lovisa Moller and Rachel Sharpe, 'Women as "underutilized assets" – a critical review of IMF advice on female labour force participation and fiscal consolidation', ActionAid International, 2017 <actionaid.org/publications/2017/women-underutilized-assets> [accessed 15/10/2021].

22   Agnès Adjamagbo and Anne-Emmanuèle Calvès, 'L'émancipation féminine sous contrainte' ('Women's emancipation under constraint'), Presses Science Po, *Autrepart*, 2012, No. 61, pp. 3–21 (in French).

in the number of ultra-precarious jobs. In many countries, this entry onto the labour market has been concretized in the form of free-trade zones, making women's devalued labour a prime tool for increasing profitability. In Cambodia, for example, the early 2000s were marked by strong economic growth driven by textile-industry exportation, which employs women almost exclusively. At the same time, from 2004 to 2009, the gender wage gap in the county more than doubled.[23] Unless all forms of exploitation are attacked simultaneously, any expansion of the labour market will always be accompanied by an increase in the exploitation of certain workers.

- Further, the approach is insufficiently founded. Even if there are arguments to indicate a correlation between economic growth and reduction of gender inequalities, others show just as clearly that economic inequality increases with certain forms of growth.

- It also ignores the fact that other possibilities exist for meeting one's needs: the informal economy, self-sufficiency, etc. Since the principal indicators are 'rate of participation' and 'income', emancipation is measured in monetary terms and not in terms of quality of life. It should be stressed that women's entry into the labour market is often accompanied by destruction of the previous means of subsistence and of living space, causing massive migration to the cities to join the ranks of precarious women workers (domestic or industrial work, prostitution, service work, etc.). In numerous cases, while 'monetary poverty' is reduced, material poverty and the arduousness of daily work increase!

The rhetoric is that of a process of putting women's work at the service of financial interests, which makes no apologies for itself and is overlaid with a thin coat of institutional and Western feminism that smells strongly of imperialism and neoliberalism. It takes away the self-determination of the women of the Global South and represses any radical voices that try to move the discussion to the issue of ending overexploitation of the South by the North as a condition of the emancipation of women in all their diversity.

Despite its co-opting of criticism in its official discourse, the World Bank continues to refer to women in nearly exclusively economic terms, closing off the path to real emancipation, which cannot be reduced to the economic dimension alone.

That discourse does not show evidence of a desire to end domination, or to ensure basic human rights; it is all about ensuring profitability. According to the World Bank, then, too much emphasis must not be placed on the notions of patriarchy and unequal social relations because it could weaken the foundation of exploited work on which the system in place rests.

---

23   Juan Pablo Bohoslavsky, 'Impact of economic reforms and austerity measures on women's human rights', CADTM, 14 September 2018 <cadtm.org/Impact-of-economic-reforms-and-austerity-measures-on-women-s-human-rights> [accessed 13/10/2021].

WORLD BANK LOANS, PROJECTS AND POLICIES:
SPECIFIC AND DAMAGING IMPACTS

Whereas several World Bank programmes have surely improved women's access to work and their condition in general (later age for women's first childbirth, access to schooling, formal equality, vocational integration programmes, solidarity-based economies, etc.), criticisms need to be made.

In the name of macroeconomic stability, the institution imposes budgetary austerity and encourages corporate profitability. The very mechanisms that have worsened inequalities are prescribed as remedies.

Following application of the Bank's macroeconomic recommendations, inadequate resources are allocated to public services and social protection, which mainly benefit vulnerable populations, which include women as a whole.

As an example, in the 1990s, when African countries were allocating between 15 and 50 per cent of their budgets to servicing debt, in all cases less than 20 per cent was devoted to social services. In 2013 in Latin America, the figure is often less than 10 per cent for education and less than 5 per cent for health, compared to between 10 and 40 per cent for debt servicing.[24]

The following is a non-exhaustive list of some of the flagship measures promoted by the World Bank and the IMF: currency devaluation, removal of tariff and customs barriers, dismantling of price controls and public subsidies, increased flexibility of labour laws, privatizations, reduction of corporate taxes and taxes on capital, increases in value-added tax (VAT), encouragement of exportations in order to bring in foreign currency, reduction of public spending, and wage freezes and budget cuts for social and public services such as education, health, social protection, non-profit associations, transport, basic infrastructures, etc.

These adjustments of macroeconomic variables, whose purpose is to ensure rapid repayment of creditors, have very concrete consequences for the lives of the most precarious populations. A gender-aware examination shows how women are specifically[25] impacted in six different areas that can occur simultaneously and to varying degrees depending on contexts and regions.

1. Women make up the majority of workers in the sectors concerned.
2. Women are the principal users and beneficiaries of the services and sectors concerned.

---

24   Christine Vanden Daelen, 'La dette, les PAS: analyse des impacts sur la vie des femmes' ('Debt and SAPs: analysis of impacts on women's lives', CADTM, 1 May 2014 (in French) <cadtm.org/La-dette-les-PAS-analyse-des-impacts-sur-la-vie-des-femmes> [accessed 13/10/2021].

25   I stress the term 'specifically' because the point is not to know who is more or less impacted, but to analyze specific impacts according to a person's situation in terms of social relations of gender, class, race, etc.

3. It is mothers, wives, sisters, etc. – that is, women – who compensate for economic shocks and the disengagement of the social state by increasing the amount of unpaid labour they perform.
4. Women are the leading producers and farmers in the world, in particular in the informal economy, whose means of subsistence and production are being destroyed.
5. Women are the first victims of sexist violence, which is increasing under the stress of megaprojects and the precarization of growing fringes of the population.
6. It is women heads of households and small business owners who contract microcredits and consumer credits in order to meet their needs and those of their families.

This reading can be applied systematically to analyses of debt and of austerity. Here we propose to examine four types of measures promoted by the World Bank.

AGRICULTURAL POLICIES AND EXTRACTIVIST PROJECTS: IMPACT ON WOMEN

Far from taking an interest in preserving ecosystems, many of the World Bank's projects and strategies are extractivist in nature: 'development' and growth via the exploitation and destruction of natural resources.[26] I will cite the 'white elephants' – megaprojects that are harmful and often imposed by force: energy production projects, mining projects, infrastructure or logistics projects, of which the INGA dam in the Democratic Republic of Congo is emblematic. I also have in mind the reforms that have come about in the wake of the 'green revolution'[27] and the exportation policies which contribute to the destruction of living organisms, of communities and food sovereignty: monoculture, GMOs, pollution and exhaustion of the soils, biopiracy via intellectual property, land-grabbing, etc.

These projects have in common an obviously ecocidal character, but also the fact that they very often contribute to the destruction of means of subsistence, territories and knowledge possessed by communities, responsibility for whose preservation lies mainly with women. This destruction (deforestation, pollution of the soil, floods) forces them into migration, seeking alternatives in the 'new' forms of employment that are supposedly typically feminine: domestic work, production in free-trade zones, care-giving and even forced prostitution. And it is this 'entry'

---

26 It would be useful to recall that the capitalist system, and Western thought more generally, is based on a series of dualisms ('men' and 'women', for example), one of which is a supposedly distinct frontier between 'human' and 'nature' or the 'wild'. Humans are allowed to draw on, benefit from, exploit, modify, 'make profitable', tame, etc. the non-human as they see fit. Only afterward does the notion of ecology come into play, to repair the damage done to 'the environment', an entity that once again is considered as being fundamentally external to 'ourselves'. At the centre of development, then, we find an objectifying relationship to 'the environment', whether it be to exploit it or to 'protect' it.

27 Falquet, 'Analyzing globalization from a feminist perspective'.

of women into the 'productive economy' that the World Bank is so pleased about. As mentioned above, the International Consortium of Investigative Journalists (ICIJ) reports that 3.4 million persons have been displaced as a result of World Bank projects, and end up in camps for displaced persons.[28] The people the World Bank is supposed to be 'helping' are in reality the ones who are most heavily impacted.

But beyond that, this type of project often involves the presence of armed groups, either assigned to 'protect' the projects in question, or who seek to control territories where raw materials are located. This aggravates the violence, in particular sexual violence, to which women are exposed. Repressive and homicidal violence are also increasing, particularly towards those women who oppose these projects by defending the environment, their land, their culture and their practices.

As for the World Bank's agricultural policies, they aggravate certain inequalities. Agriculture is one of the principal activities of women worldwide. But the planting of monocultures for exportation (which increases the GDP and brings in currency for repaying debt) means that food crops, essential for many families, are pushed onto land that is always further away and less fertile. This increases travel times and risks of aggression while travelling and the arduousness of the work, all the while with harvests diminishing in quantity and quality. It has a direct impact on the income, and also the health and food security of women, including girls, who are the first victims of malnutrition. Lastly, it also threatens national food sovereignty. In certain regions, employment in cash agriculture is offered to men by priority, forcing women into even more precarious activities. Even if, globally, the proportion of women employed in the agricultural sector has diminished over the last 20 years (while increasing in the service sector), it remains their leading source of employment in low- and middle-income countries where they do the most arduous, time-consuming and low-paid work. The agrarian policies promoted by the World Bank therefore impact women especially heavily.[29]

Among the measures imposed is an end to subsidies on agricultural inputs while European products, which are subsidized by Europe's Common Agricultural Policy (CAP), flood the markets – a totally unfair form of competition which directly affects women's means of subsistence and of production.

THE DESTRUCTION OF PUBLIC SERVICES

We saw in chapter 26 that, as confirmed by the UN Human Rights Commission in a 2003 report, structural adjustment plans, the result of a policy knowingly devised and applied by the directors of the IMF and the World Bank, have extremely negative consequences on economic, social and cultural rights, especially in matters of health, education, access to drinking water, food safety, etc.

---

28   Chavkin and Hudson, 'New investigation reveals 3.4m displaced by World Bank'.
29   ILO, *Women at Work Trends 2016* (Geneva: ILO, 8 March 2016) <ilo.org/global/publications/books/WCMS_457317/lang--en/index.htm> [accessed 15/10/2021].

The destruction of these sectors, all of which can be considered to be common goods, has grave consequences for women, both as workers and functionaries who either lose their jobs or suffer wage reductions with no compensation, and also as users of these services, both for themselves and for those they support and care for. Privatization and budget cuts in the health sector reduce access to health services for the poorest women, and seriously affect gynaecological care, maternity services and everything related to sexual and reproductive health. These issues are too often ignored by decision-makers, who are often men.

Further, it is women who compensate for the changes imposed by the World Bank, through the unpaid work they are then forced to perform as a consequence of those policies. The Bank in fact supports the withdrawal of the social state through the privatization of public services or the implementation of public–private partnerships (PPPs). According to neoliberal dogma, private management is more 'competitive' and therefore more efficient. The Bank explicitly and regularly demands that water distribution be privatized, which has had many negative impacts, as proven by the cases of Bolivia and Tanzania, where water privatization resulted not only in increased inefficiency but also higher rates and the closure of public wells, with disastrous consequences for agriculture. Fetching water is a task that generally falls on women and girls. For them, the reduced access to water increases the time necessary for that task, increases the risks to their health – in particular back problems – and increases their exposure to aggression since they have to walk longer distances.[30] PPPs, praised for their supposed better management, are in reality less efficient: they cost the taxpayer up to six times as much and the jobs they provide are more precarious.[31]

TAX REFORMS

The World Bank supports tax reforms that are in reality favourable to big capital – removal of customs barriers, plus reductions in corporate taxes and taxes on large fortunes and very high incomes. To compensate for these losses of revenue, increasing the value-added tax is the most favoured measure of the IFI. This is what is known as regressive taxation, because it has a stronger proportional impact on persons with low income. Thus the 'budgetary efforts' demanded by the World Bank are in fact made by those poorer individuals! Women, who are responsible for many household expenditures despite often having lower incomes, are often the ones who face this day-to-day hell. The fact that essential products such as menstrual protection are not included among the 'basic products' on which the sales tax is

---

30   Bohoslavsky, 'Impact of economic reforms and austerity measures on women's human rights'.

31   Iolanda Fresnillo and Verónica Serafini, 'World Bank and IMF response to debt crisis undermines women's rights', CADTM, 10 April 2020 <cadtm.org/World-Bank-and-IMF-response-to-debt-crisis-undermines-women-s-rights> [accessed 27/12/2021].

lower creates additional difficulties.[32] One adolescent girl in ten in Africa misses a week of school per month as a result.[33]

Another aspect relates to women's principal activity at the worldwide level: informal agriculture, and informal work in general. With prices of agricultural inputs increasing, it costs them more and more to make their living, but they do not benefit from the same tax advantages as do entrepreneurs in the formal economy. For the Bretton Woods Project, women who work in the informal sector and depend on the formal sector for supplies are without doubt the most affected by these measures. In a survey conducted by the International Labour Organization (ILO), women specifically rank 'taxes' among the obstacles to joining the formal economy.

These fiscal measures will always be ineffective in the countries with the lowest revenues, where the majority of the economy is informal. They can only lead to the adoption of new restrictive measures, often in the form of cuts in social protection. It is a familiar vicious circle! Furthermore, these imposed 'adjustments' amount to a direct and repeated violation of the fundamental principle according to which the taxation regime is the foundation of the sovereignty and autonomy of states. Debts contracted in order to implement these measures are therefore totally odious and illegitimate.

ACCESS TO MICROCREDIT

Microcredit has been a favoured vector of the World Bank's 'soft loans' policy and has been greatly praised by the international community. Microcredit consists in granting loans of small amounts to business owners or artisans who do not have access to 'traditional' bank loans. It developed mainly in countries of the South and is aimed at people who are outside the banking system, and therefore often among the poorest.

Worldwide, women account for up to 80 per cent of the clientele for microfinance instruments.[34] Under cover of the principle of encouraging economic autonomy,

---

32   In Kenya, the number of such products was reduced from 400 to 30 in a single year. See Mae Buenaventura and Claire Miranda, *The IMF and Gender Equality: The Gender Dimensions of the IMF's Key Fiscal Policy Advice on Resource Mobilisation in Developing Countries* (Bretton Woods Project, 2017) <brettonwoodsproject.org/wp-content/uploads/2017/04/IMF-and-Gender-Equality-VAT-1.pdf> [accessed 18/10/2021].

33   Frédérique Harrus, 'Scolarité: quand les règles mettent les filles au ban de l'école' ('Schooling: menstruation keeps girls out of school'), Franceinfo, 2015 (in French) <francetvinfo.fr/monde/scolarite-quand-les-regles-mettent-les-filles-au-ban-de-l-ecole_3066825.html> [accessed 18/10/2021].

34   Éric Toussaint and Nathan Legrand, 'Damning testimonies of microcredit abuse', CADTM, 2018 <cadtm.org/Damning-testimonies-of-microcredit>. The CADTM network has long denounced women being the victims of the abuses of microfinance. See also, for example, Nathan Legrand, 'In Sri Lanka, resistance to private indebtedness is a strategic Issue', CADTM, 2020 <cadtm.org/In-Sri-Lanka-Resistance-to-Private-Indebtedness-Is-a-Strategic-Issue>; Milford Bateman, 'How the Bank's push for microcredit failed the poor', CADTM, 2017 <cadtm.org/How-the-Bank-s-push-for>; Éric Toussaint, Sushovan Dhar, Nathan Legrand and Abul Kalam Azad, 'Bangladesh: harsh effects of the Grameen Bank and other microcredit institutions on the rural population', CADTM, 2017 <cadtm.org/Bangladesh-Harsh-effects-of-the-Grameen-Bank-and-other-microcredit-institutions> [all accessed 28/12/2021].

women are directly targeted, in part because of stereotypes concerning their docility in repaying. These microcredits are characterized by significantly higher interest rates than those of 'normal' banks, and of course higher than the zero interest rate which is the norm in most traditional monetary circuits such as tontines.

Jules Falquet stresses that microcredit 'is nothing more than women's right, or their "duty," to go into debt, and at the same time a means of forcing into the banking circuits of the North the immense "deposits of savings," often organized by women, that exist in the South'.[35] This impoverishment of women via debt consolidates the process of transferring wealth from the poor to the rich.

The process of herding the poor into the banking circuit and creating new opportunities for investment is a way of perpetuating the damage caused by neoliberal growth, which continues to exclude collective and macroeconomic solutions in favour of individual and financial ones.

HAS THE BANK CONDUCTED SELF-CRITICISM IN THE MIDDLE OF A MULTIDIMENSIONAL GLOBAL CRISIS?

Despite all this, the Bank still does not seem to engage in any real self-criticism. For example, the Bank's evaluation of its 2007 Gender Equality as Smart Economics (GAP) action plan over a period of three years did not respond to criticism made by civil society.[36] Elizabeth Arend demonstrates this with reference to five areas: failure to consider women's human rights (yes, they also apply to women!); insufficient attention paid to reproductive health; the lack of serious data regarding gender; a narrow vision of emancipation as being limited to attaining economic independence; and the failure to enable gender action at the local level.[37]

In 2012 the Bank finally admitted that reducing inequalities could not be reduced to 'growth' alone, and an impressive report acknowledged that the Bank had placed too much emphasis on the reduction of inequalities as a contributing factor of growth rather than as an end in itself. But we should be wary of hailing a 'change of paradigm'. The analysis remains centred on economics and seeking certain types of growth almost exclusively.[38]

---

35   Jules Falquet, 'Femmes, féminisme et "développement": une analyse critique des politiques des institutions internationales' ('Women, feminism and "development": a critical analysis of the policies of the international institutions') (Canadian Women's Studies/Les cahiers de la femme, 2003) <researchgate.net/publication/279495119_Femmes_feminisme_et_developpement_une_analyse_critiques_des_politiques_des_institutions_internationales> [accessed 18/10/2021] (translation CADTM).

36   World Bank, *Applying Gender Action Plan Lessons: A Three-Year Road Map for Gender Mainstreaming (2011–2013)* (World Bank, 2010) <documents1.worldbank.org/curated/en/782711468012632778/pdf/547520BR0SecM2101Official0Use0Only1.pdf> [accessed 18/10/2021].

37   Elizabeth Arend, 'Critique of the World Bank's "Applying Gender Action Plan Lessons: A Three-Year Road Map for Gender Mainstreaming (2011–2013)"', GenderAction, 2010 <genderaction.org/publications/2010/critique_road_map.pdf> [accessed 18/10/2021].

38   Bretton Woods Project, 'World Bank admits gender equality not just about growth', BWP, 2014 <brettonwoodsproject.org/2014/03/world-bank-admits-gender-equality-just-growth> [accessed 18/10/2021].

Still in 2014, criticism continued to point to the fact that the World Bank neglects the importance of care work. A study established that of some 30 projects, 92 per cent did not explicitly recognize the existence of unpaid care work in their design.[39]

In 2016, while touting '[a] renewed strategy on gender equality' that will 'enhance women's voice and agency', the Bank insisted on the notion of 'build[ing] on past achievements' and 'removing the unique constraints [on economic opportunity] that hold back women and girls'.[40] It also implemented a working group to address sexist violence – an initiative that was criticized for its extremely limited mandate and its silence regarding the violence engendered by the World Bank's own projects.

What, then, is the point of the Bank's poverty and social impact analysis (PSIA) approach, implemented by the debtor countries? Despite the existence of guidelines containing suggestions regarding the inclusion of gender, there are no constraining measures.[41] For example, the programme for 'better management' and 'rationalization' of public administration in Serbia, imposed as a conditionality of a loan granted in 2016, resulted in the loss of nearly 30,000 jobs and a wage freeze in the public sector, where women workers are in the majority. The PSIA mentions no social impact on poverty or on the distribution of wealth.

Although multidimensional analysis seems to be making progress, the years 2020 and 2021 confirm that the macroeconomic measures promoted by the Bank continue to worsen the situation of disadvantaged populations. After several decades of antisocial policies, health systems in particular proved to be in a weakened state in late 2019 on the eve of the global health crisis.

Despite the fact that the share of the budgets allocated to debt service doubled in countries with low and medium income between 2010 and 2018, austerity measures, which have been shown to be ineffective as well as unfair, continue doggedly to be applied. The amount of resources allocated to public services was reduced by 18 per cent in Latin America and in the Caribbean and by 15 per cent in Sub-Saharan Africa between 2014 and 2018. In at least 21 countries with low and medium income, budgets for education have been decreasing since 2015 as expenditures for

39   Bretton Woods Project, 'World Bank criticised for overlooking care work', BWP, 2014 <brettonwoodsproject.org/2014/01/bank-criticised-overlooking-care-work/> [accessed 18/10/2021].

40   World Bank, 'Update of World Bank Group gender strategy: consultations' <consultations. worldbank.org/consultation/update-world-bank-group-gender-strategy-consultations> [accessed 19/10/2021].

41   'In several instances, the Bank did not address the gendered impacts of reforms at all, which, according to its own guidance, would "inform policy interventions", so that staff can "take these gender differences into account" when designing operations. Where the Bank did assess potential negative gendered impacts, the proposed measures to reduce adverse effects were not always sufficient in mitigating these impacts or adequately addressing entrenched gender inequalities.' Ella Hopkins, *The World Bank and Gender Equality: Development Policy Financing* (Bretton Woods Project, 2019) <brettonwoodsproject.org/wp-content/uploads/2019/08/The-World-Bank-and-Gender-Equality-DPF-2.pdf> [accessed 06/04/2023].

debt service increase. As regards health budgets, that is the case for 39 countries,[42] with grave consequences for public health, health-care workers, community care, hospital capacities, etc. To that is added the reduction in access to drinking water in many regions. In such a context, how was the world to face the health crisis that broke out in 2020?

It is immediately evident that the weight of often incoherent political choices falls mainly on women. Women, being particularly numerous in the 'essential' sectors, are on the front lines when it comes to burnout and risk of contamination. They are also in the majority among people for whom teleworking is impossible; in many regions it is the most disadvantaged ethnic groups who are in that situation.[43] Conversely, many women also have professions and occupations that are now prohibited and uncompensated since they are informal (domestic work, sex work, street vending, etc.) That aggravates economic inequalities. And as if that were not enough, their role as care-givers within families increases their exposure to Covid-19 and increases their unpaid workload (caring for out-of-school children, making masks, etc.). Added to all of this, domestic violence and risks stemming from the complete neglect of reproductive and mental health are skyrocketing. The situation is not only dramatic; it was predictable.[44]

In such a context, the announcement of the moratorium by the World Bank, of the IMF's 'aid package' or of the possible restructuring of the G20 are, at best, bad jokes for those whom neoliberalism has left behind. Without calling into question the very structure of the organization of care in our societies, such measures only postpone a debt burden which will have further increased and whose impact on women will be brutal. The World Bank's priority remains the macroeconomic stability of the financial sectors, which is its justification for further austerity and exportation policies.

This crisis is not only the result of economic or health factors, but of our relation to life and to essential activities, our 'taking care' of the world around us. The dominant relation, the one promoted by the World Bank's ideologies, is a world away from being able to conceive of the environmental balance and collective well-being that could enable us to face such crises without always sacrificing the same people, thus turning them into unprecedented social crises.

---

42 Eurodad, 'How public services and human rights are being threatened by the growing debt crisis', European Network on Debt and Development – Eurodad, 2020 <eurodad.org/how_public_services_and_human_rights_are_being_threatened_by_the_growing_debt_crisis> [accessed 20/10/2021].

43 Elise Gould and Heidi Shierholz, 'Not everybody can work from home: Black and Hispanic workers are much less likely to be able to telework', Economic Policy Institute, *Working Economics Blog*, 2020 <epi.org/blog/black-and-hispanic-workers-are-much-less-likely-to-be-able-to-work-from-home/> [accessed 09/03/2022].

44 Taking gendered social relations into account, but also based on earlier experiences such as the Ebola epidemic.

CONCLUSION

In its 2007 report, the World Bank sums up its 'Objective' in these terms: 'empowering women to compete in markets':

- product markets;
- financial markets;
- land markets;
- labour markets.[45]

But what does this vision of equality mean? As anti-capitalist feminists have been saying for a long time, the discourse on equality does not help to fight forms of oppression, but only to move them around. We are being told that equality means equal opportunities to *compete*, to dominate. To excel in areas that have been considered exclusively masculine until now, to appropriate their codes, to break through the 'glass ceiling' (while making the floor even stickier ...) and become agents of the mechanisms of capitalist accumulation.

This vision of 'feminism' is dangerous. Instead of talking about access to the structures of power, we should be discussing a radical questioning of power structures. What is necessary is not the reduction of individual economic obstacles but the creation of a collective dynamics in solidarity; a political force. The Bank does not support feminist demands; it maintains and provides life support to patriarchal, extractivist, racist finance.

The question, ultimately, is not whether or not certain local projects have supported women; nor is it as simple as proclaiming the fact that the World Bank has not done enough to reduce inequalities. The question, rather, is whether or not its political line has contributed to aggravating them. And the answer is yes. The World Bank continues to champion macroeconomic policies that have a negative impact on gender equity and that reinforce structural oppression, as its strategy for 2016 to 2023 clearly illustrates.

In 2016, Elisabeth Prügl referred to the World Bank's new agenda as 'neoliberalism with a feminist face'.[46] In the Bank's new discourse, analysis of gender inequalities is taken further and further, but the analysis is also more and more at the service of markets. In other words, feminist demands, more and more, are being manipulated, co-opted and translated into market terms. For Prügl, while the intent of many of the 'advances' and questionings of gender practices are reprehensible (for example, encouraging governments to invest in day-care facilities so that women can work more), they also open breaches that could be exploited in order to formulate truly feminist demands and alternatives.

---

45   World Bank, *Gender Equality as Smart Economics*.
46   Elisabeth Prügl, 'Neoliberalism with a feminist face: crafting a new hegemony at the World Bank', *Feminist Economics*, 2017, Vol. 23. https://www.tandfonline.com/doi/full/10.1080/13545701.2016.1198043 [accessed 06/04/2023].

All of these considerations add up to one more reason why the majority of debts should be cancelled, since – and this is no accident – they have not served the populations who bear their burden. That is why, as the CADTM and others are urging, what is needed is radical change rather than reforms within these institutions, which – whether it be the G20, the IMF, the World Bank or the UN – continue to sustain the institutionalization of feminism at the expense of the women it is meant to serve.

A feminist, and even an ecofeminist, perspective also leads us to ask the question of 'Who owes what to whom?' in a more general way. If we take into account all the invisible work that is done and the resources that are unscrupulously plundered and devastated, without compensation and with no effort to maintain balance, the equation changes.[47] A significant share of the world's populations, and in particular of the dominant classes, in fact owe an immense debt – environmental, and also reproductive – to women.

---

47   Camille Bruneau, 'An eco-feminist reading of debt to think differently about auditing', *AVP – Les Autres Voix de la Planète*, 4 November 2020, No. 79 <cadtm.org/An-eco-feminist-reading-of-debt-to-think-differently-about-auditing> [accessed 20/10/2021].

28
The World Bank and Human Rights

The question of 'human rights' has never been a priority for the World Bank. Among the conditions the Bank places on its loans, one right supersedes all others: the individual right to private property, which in practice works to the advantage of big property holders, whether they be wealthy individuals or national and transnational corporations. The conditionalities applied by the World Bank in making loans make no reference whatever to the collective rights of peoples and individuals. If there is any consideration of human rights within the World Bank, it is not in the progressive sense expressed in the seminal documents of the United Nations.

Ideologies have their own specific interpretations of the concept of rights. As Jean-Philippe Peemans so rightly points out:

In any case, from the currently predominant Western perspective, human rights are seen first and foremost as concerning individual freedom of action, non-interference in private business, the right to dispose freely of property, and above all, the obligation of the state to refrain from any act that violates the individual freedom to invest time, capital and resources in production and exchange [...]. For neoliberals, social and cultural demands can be seen as legitimate aspirations, but never as rights [...] the neoliberal view rejects any collective approach to the question of rights. The individual is the only entity capable of demanding rights, and even those who violate rights are necessarily individuals who must take full responsibility for their actions. The violation of rights cannot be attributed to organizations or to structures.[1]

The World Bank, like the IMF, takes refuge in this postulate to divest itself of all responsibility in terms of respect for economic, social and cultural rights. Yet these rights are inseparable from civil and political rights: it is impossible to respect individual rights if collective rights are not taken into account. As multilateral institutions, the World Bank and the IMF are bound by international treaties and the rights, both individual and collective, that are declared therein.

Transparency and good governance must be applicable to everyone without exception. Yet the international financial institutions demand them from the

---

1   Peemans, *Le développement des peuples face à la modernisation du monde*, p. 349 (translation CADTM).

governments of indebted countries but feel free to ignore them when it comes to their own affairs. The obligation to evaluate and report on actions taken should not be limited to states but should also extend to the private sector, and even more importantly, to the sphere of international organizations, since their activities, policies and programmes have a major impact on human rights.[2] Structural adjustment plans have such negative consequences for economic, social and cultural rights (particularly among the most vulnerable), as well as for the environment, that these institutions should be obliged to account for their actions.

STRUCTURAL ADJUSTMENT VIOLATES HUMAN RIGHTS

In spite of the international texts that provide the legal framework for the protection of human rights, the IMF and the World Bank 'operate according to the logic of private financial enterprise and world capitalism, with little consideration for the social and political consequences of their actions.'[3]

Already in 2000, in a report presented to the United Nations Commission on Human Rights (UN-CHR), the special rapporteur and an independent UN expert on the effects of external debt on human rights had stated:

For almost 20 years, the international financial institutions and the governments of creditor countries have played an ambiguous and destructive game which consists of remote-controlling the economies of the Third World and imposing unpopular economic policies on powerless countries, on the pretext that the bitter pill of macro-economic adjustment will in the end allow these countries to achieve prosperity and freedom from debt. After two decades, many countries are worse off than when they brought in the structural adjustment programmes enforced by the IMF and the World Bank. These drastically austere programmes have exacted a high social and ecological price and in many countries the human development index has taken a dramatic plunge.[4]

UN-CHR Resolution 2000/82 states that 'the exercise of the basic rights of the people of debtor countries to food, housing, clothing, employment, education,

---

2   Nicolás Angulo Sánchez, *El derecho humano al desarollo frente a la mundialización del mercado* (Madrid: Iepala Editorial, 2006), p. 145 (translation CADTM).

3   Madjid Benchikh, Robert Charvin and Francine Demichel, *Introduction critique au droit international public* (Lyon: Collection Critique du droit, Presse Universitaires de Lyon, 1986), p. 12 (translation CADTM).

4   United Nations Commission on Human Rights (UN-CHR), 'Debt relief and social investment: linking the heavily indebted poor countries (HIPC) initiative to the HIV/AIDS epidemic in Africa, post-Hurricane Mitch reconstruction in Honduras and Nicaragua, and the Worst Forms of Child Labour Convention, 1999 (Convention No. 182) of the International Labour Organization, Common Report by Reinaldo Figueredo (special rapporteur) and Fantu Cheru (independent expert)', 14 January 2000, p. 6 <https://undocs.org/E/CN.4/2000/51> [accessed 29/12/2021].

health services and a healthy environment cannot be subordinated to the implementation of structural adjustment polices and economic reforms arising from the debt.[5]

Yet the policies enforced by the IFI do subordinate human rights and the legitimacy of governments to the dogmatic application of their structural adjustment plans.[6] In practice,

Structural adjustment goes beyond the simple imposition of a set of macroeconomic policies at the domestic level. It represents a political project, a conscious strategy of social transformation at the global level, primarily to make the world safe for transnational corporations. In short, structural adjustment programmes (SAPs) serve as 'a transmission-belt' to facilitate the process of globalization, through liberalization, deregulation, and reducing the role of the State in national development.[7]

The UN-CHR also pointed out that structural adjustment policies have serious repercussions on the ability of developing countries to implement national development policies whose prime objective is to respect human rights, and particularly economic, social and cultural rights, through improved living standards for local populations.[8] According to a UN-CHR report submitted by Bernards Muhdo,[9] an independent expert, structural adjustment plans – the result of a policy knowingly devised and applied by the directors of the IMF and the World Bank – have

---

5   UN-CHR, Commission on Human Rights Resolution 2000/82 – 'Effects of structural adjustment policies and foreign debt on the full enjoyment of all human rights, particularly economic, social and cultural rights', 27 April 2000, E/CN.4/RES/2000/82 <refworld.org/docid/3b00f2af1c.html> [accessed 24/08/2021].

6   Notably, the massive impoverishment of entire strata of populations in Third World countries. We should recall that poverty is considered 'as a state of denial or even of violation of human rights' (UN-CHR, 'Review of progress and obstacles in the promotion, implementation, operationalization, and enjoyment of the right to development – consideration of the sixth report of the independent expert on the right to development – implementing the right to development in the current global context', E/CN.4/2004/WG.18/2, 17 February 2004, para. 12 <https://digitallibrary.un.org/record/516098?ln=en> [accessed 05/03/2023].

7   UN-CHR, 'Effects of structural adjustment policies on the full enjoyment of human rights – report by the independent expert Mr. Fantu Cheru', E/CN.4/1999/50, para. 31 https://digitallibrary.un.org/record/1489663?ln=fr [accessed 06/04/2023].

8   UN-CHR, 'Effects on the full enjoyment of human rights of the economic adjustment policies arising from foreign debt and, in particular, on the implementation of the Declaration on the Right to Development', Commission on Human Rights – Report on the Fifty-Third Session (10 March–18 April 1997) – Economic and Social Council, Official Records, 1997, Supplement No. 3, Draft decision 1, p. 19 <undocs.org/E/CN.4/1997/150> [accessed 25/08/2021].

9   UN-CHR, Effects of Structural Adjustment Policies and Foreign Debt on the Full Enjoyment of Human Rights, Especially Economic, Social and Cultural Rights, report submitted by Mr Bernards Mudho, independent expert, E/CN.4/2003/10, 23 October 2002 <undocs.org/E/CN.4/2003/10> [accessed 18/10/2021].

extremely negative consequences on economic, social and cultural rights, especially[10] in matters of health, education, access to drinking water, food security, etc. The expert further notes that the policies pursued by the IFI have been disputed by citizens through protest movements that have been brutally repressed by governments and public authorities to ensure the success of programmes imposed by these institutions (privatization of water, privatization of energy, privatization of public transport, privatization of hospitals, unrestricted prices for medicines, bread and other basic necessities, and protection of the interests of transnational corporations' investments and their appropriation of common natural resources, etc.): 'Adjustment policies have affected citizens' economic rights in such areas as health care and education, access to water, food security, and viable employment and workers' rights, while related protests have met with government repression in many instances.'[11]

Consequently there is a close link between the massive violation of economic, social and cultural rights and the massive violation of civil and political rights.

Having seen that the public authorities of the states concerned were committing violations, the IMF and the World Bank should have reminded them of their international obligations regarding the protection of civil and political rights and human rights in general. Instead of blocking or suspending the measures undertaken, these institutions continued to apply them even more energetically. Their indifference, and even cynicism, is bluntly revealed in a statement made at the meeting of the independent expert with the IMF directors: 'the IMF did not see blocking a programme because of human rights violations as appropriate'.[12]

This is a very serious state of affairs. The institutions behave as though they were bound by no international obligations whatsoever, unless they be linked to trade or investment agreements. But of course the underlying objective is clear. In 1999, the independent expert designated by the Commission on Human Rights accurately identified the globalization process and the role of the financial institutions as being part of the 'neoliberal counter-revolution'.[13]

---

10   The massive and constant violation of economic, social and cultural rights is indissociable from the entire body of human rights because this violation usually goes hand in hand with serious violations of civil and political rights. See Jacques Fierens, 'La violation des droits civils et politiques comme conséquence de la violation des droits économiques, sociaux et culturels' ('Violation of civil and political rights as a consequence of the violation of economic, social and cultural rights'), *Revue belge de droit international*, 1999, Vol. 1 (Brussels: Éditions Brylant, 1998) (in French) <rbdi.bruylant.be> [accessed 17/11/2021].

11   E/CN.4/2003/10, para. 42, p. 13.

12   UN-CHR, 'Fourth report of the independent expert on the right to development, Mr. Arjun Sengupta, submitted in accordance with Commission resolution 2001/9', E/CN.4/2002/WG.18/2/Add. 1, 5 March 2002, para. 21 [accessed 25/08/2021].

13   UN-CHR, "Effects of structural adjustment policies on the full enjoyment of human rights," paras 28–30.

In international law, whether conventional or customary,[14] there are basic or fundamental legal principles and rules governing the international protection of human rights, whose scope extends to all subjects of international law.

STATES, RESPONSIBILITIES OF INTERNATIONAL FINANCIAL INSTITUTIONS, AND PRIVATE INTERESTS

The World Bank and the IMF are not abstractions. The decisions emanating from these institutions are taken by flesh-and-blood men, and sometimes women, who act on behalf of their states or groups of states. The states are themselves indisputably bound by the United Nations documents. Therefore the member states of the World Bank and the IMF, like any other state, are under the obligation to protect human rights in the decisions they make as members of the international financial institutions.

This must even be taken further. In the process of globalization, as a result of the actions of transnational corporations, the G7 and the IFI,[15] national and local public authorities have been deliberately deprived of their powers in economic and social matters. States intervene more and more frequently to ensure that private interests are served instead of ensuring the full enjoyment of human rights. For the World Bank, the whole problem of underdevelopment and poverty boils down to the fact that public authorities interfere too much in social and economic affairs, often hindering the actions and business of the private sector. A page entitled 'World Bank and private sector' on the Bank's website says that:

Ending poverty and reducing inequality are ambitious goals. But the gap in funding between what is needed and what is available amounts to trillions of dollars each year. The only way to spur this level of investment is by creating new markets and bringing innovative solutions to developing countries. *This is why the private sector must be involved*.

Opportunities have never been greater for owners of capital to get a reasonable return while expanding their investments in developing countries.[16]

The international financial institutions blame the states; yet a report on 'Globalization and its impact on the full enjoyment of all human rights' submitted to the United Nations General Assembly in 2003 affirms:

---

14   *Conventional law* is written law, the rules of which are contained in international agreements and conventions, such as the International Pact on Economic, Social and Cultural Rights. *Customary law* is unwritten law which is binding, such as the prohibition of crimes against humanity, crimes of aggression, the rights of peoples to their natural resources, etc.

15   Alejandro Teitelbaum, in *El papel de las sociedades transnacionales en el mundo contemporáneo* (Buenos Aires: Asociación Americana de Juristas, 2003), describes them as 'instruments and representatives of the major powers and big capital' (p. 104).

16   World Bank, 'World Bank and private sector' <worldbank.org/en/about/partners/the-world-bank-group-and-private-sector/overview> [accessed 29/03/2022] (emphasis added).

There is a general tendency today to ask Governments to carry too many respon-sibilities, without acknowledging that the old-fashioned view of the State's role in development is no longer valid; because of globalization, national Governments no longer have the same tools or resources at their disposal as they once had. Yet, while no mention is made of international responsibilities, or the role played by the current political system and the system of governance in the modern world, responsibilities which these systems do have, Governments are blamed for issues, difficulties and problems that are primarily created in the international arena. This kind of approach is neither objective nor fair, especially to *develop-ing countries, which have very little say in the fundamental decisions taken on the international stage and yet are blamed for hampering the development process*, while underlying international inequities go unmentioned.[17]

It is therefore a fundamental error to consider the states *alone* as being responsible for human rights violations during the application of multilateral trade rules or following the application of measures imposed by the IMF and the World Bank.[18]

Yet this thesis is widely disseminated within the IMF and the World Bank: that the real villains in the human rights story are the member states, taken individually, because it is they who finally decide on the policies these institutions must apply. This denial of responsibility is untenable under international law.

The IMF, the World Bank and the WTO are above all *international organiza-tions* in the strict sense of the term.[19] As such, they possess an international juridical personality,[20] they have their own organs[21] and they are *given jurisdiction* by the treaty or original agreement (absolute jurisdiction).[22] Most importantly, as international organizations they have rights and duties.

---

17 United Nations General Assembly, A/58/257, 'Globalization and its impact on the full enjoyment of human rights', Report of the Secretary-General, 7 August 2003, para. 17 <digitallibrary.un.org/record/501755/files/A_58_257-EN.pdf> [accessed 29/03/2022] (emphasis added).

18 Making the states solely responsible is, in practice 'the implementing entities being held responsible while *the principal institutions that preside over the adoption of such policies enjoy impunity*'. See UN-CHR, 'Economic, social and cultural rights – globalization and its effects on the full enjoyment of human rights', E/CN.4/Sub.2/2003/14, para. 38 <documents-dds-ny.un.org/doc/UNDOC/GEN/G03/147/84/PDF/G0314784.pdf?OpenElement> [accessed 26/08/2021] (emphasis added).

19 See José Antonio Pastor Ridruejo, *Cours général de droit international public*, Collected Courses of the Hague Academy of International Law, 1998, Vol. 274, pp. 193–98 <dx.doi.org/10.1163/1875-8096_pplrdc_A9789041113009_01> [accessed 17/11/2021].

20 See International Court of Justice, 'Reparation for injuries suffered in the service of the United Nations (Bernadotte Case)', *I.C.J. Reports*, 1949, p. 70 <icj-cij.org/public/files/case-related/4/004-19490307-ORA-01-00-BI.pdf> [accessed 17/11/2021].

21 Joe Verhoeven, *Droit international public* (Brussels: Larcier, Précis de la Faculté de Droit de l'UCL, 2000), p. 205.

22 Jean Combacau and Serge Sur, *Droit international public*, 2nd edn (Paris: Montchrestien, 1995), pp. 731–32.

It goes without saying that no serious body, no international organization which claims to act as a subject of international law and which presumes to have jurisdiction and an international juridical personality can reasonably argue that it is excused from international obligations, especially those governing the protection of human rights.[23] As subjects of international law, any and all international organizations are bound by this same international law, including the rules governing the protection of human rights.[24]

In the words of the Advisory Opinion of the International Court of Justice Interpretation of the Agreement of 25 March 1951 between the World Health Organization (WHO) and Egypt: 'there is nothing in the character of international organizations to justify their being considered as some form of "super-State" [...]. International organizations are subjects of international law and, as such, are bound by any obligations incumbent upon them under general rules of international law, under their constitutions or under international agreements to which they are parties.'[25]

While this opinion was handed down with reference to the WHO, clearly any international organization, as a subject of law, must adhere to international law, including internationally recognized human rights (customary international law, general legal principles, etc.). The World Bank, then, is not above the law.

The obligations stemming from international law, therefore, make it incumbent on the international financial institutions to consider the impact of their policies and decisions on individual rights in the borrower countries.

The United Nations Committee on Economic, Social and Cultural Rights (CESCR), in a resolution adopted in June 2016, clearly states that it does not agree that the IMF and the World Bank (IBRD) may deny their obligations regarding human rights:

The Committee is fully aware that, in the case of IMF or IBRD, the relevant Articles of Agreement establishing the organizations have sometimes been interpreted by the organizations as not requiring them to include human rights considerations in their decision-making.[26] The Committee does not agree with such an interpretation.

The CESCR adds:

as specialized agencies of the United Nations, IMF and IBRD are obligated to act in accordance with the principles of the Charter of the United Nations,[27] which sets

---

23 'Globalization and its effects on the full enjoyment of human rights', E/CN.4/Su.2/2003/14, para. 37.
24 Pierre-Marie Dupuy, *Droit international public*, 3rd edn (Paris: Dalloz, 1995), p. 115.
25 ICJ, 'Interpretation of the Agreement of 25 March 1951 between the WHO and Egypt, Advisory Opinion of 20 December 1980', *I.C.J. Reports*, 1980, pp. 89–90, para. 37 <icj-cij.org/public/files/case-related/65/065-19801220-ADV-01-00-EN.pdf> [accessed 02/02/22].
26 See IMF, Articles of Agreement, Art. IV, Sect. 3b), and IBRD, Articles of Agreement, Art. IV, Sect. 10.
27 United Nations Charter, Articles 57 and 63; UN General Assembly Resolution 124 II) of 15 November 1947 approving agreements with the IBRD and IMF.

the realization of human rights and fundamental freedoms as one of the purposes of the Organization, to be achieved in particular through international economic and social cooperation.[28]

THE UNIVERSAL DECLARATION OF HUMAN RIGHTS

Incorporated in the body of customary law,[29] the Universal Declaration of Human Rights is, as its name implies, universal; it binds states and the other subjects of international law in the exercise of their specific actions and their responsibilities. No international organization can hide behind its rules of procedure to avoid having to respect the international agreements ratified by its members.[30]

International institutions therefore have a duty to create conditions favourable to the full enjoyment of all human rights, as well as to the respect, protection and promotion of these rights. However, structural adjustment plans, as shown above, diverge in practice from this theory. Today re-named 'poverty reduction strategies', they stipulate that economic growth in itself will bring about development, a tenet that is contradicted by, among others, the annual reports of the United Nations Development Programme (UNDP). This so-called economic growth, as proposed by the international financial institutions, mainly benefits the most privileged classes and increases Third World countries' state of dependency even further.[31] In addition, economic growth as it is actually practised is fundamentally incompatible with the preservation of the environment.

THE DECLARATION ON THE RIGHT TO DEVELOPMENT

Nor is this view of development, relentlessly maintained by the World Bank in spite of its patent failures, compatible with the eminently social Declaration on the Right to Development adopted by the United Nations in 1986:[32]

Article 1: 1. The right to development is an unalienable human right [...]
2. The human right to development implies the full realization of the right of peoples to self-determination, which includes [...] the exercise of their inalienable right to full sovereignty over all their natural wealth and resources. [...]

---

28   United Nations Charter, Articles 1 3) and 55 c); United Nations, Treaty Body Database, E/C.12/2016/1 <tbinternet.ohchr.org/_layouts/15/treatybodyexternal/Download.aspx?symbolno=E/C.12/2016/1&Lang=en> [accessed 29/12/2021]·

29   ICJ, 'United States diplomatic and consular staff in Tehran' (United States of America v. Iran), *I.C.J. Reports*, 1980, page 42, para. 91.

30   Gustave Massiah, 'La réforme de l'ONU et le mouvement altermondialiste' ('UN reform and the anti-globalization movement'), in Amin, Charvin, Ziegler, Robert et al., *ONU: Droits pour tous ou loi du plus fort?*, pp. 404–05.

31   Sánchez, *El derecho humano al desarollo*, p. 16 (translation CADTM).

32   The full text of the Declaration is given at the end of this chapter.

Article 3: 2. The realization of the right to development requires full respect for the principles of international law [...]
Article 8: 1. States should undertake, at the national level, all necessary measures for the realization of the right to development [...]. Appropriate economic and social reforms should be carried out with a view to eradicating all social injustices.

It was in March 1981 that the United Nations Human Rights Commission proposed to the Economic and Social Council to set up the first working group on the right to development. This group met a dozen or more times during the 1980s,[33] resulting in the adoption on 4 December 1986 of Resolution 41/128 of the UN General Assembly, subsequently to be known as the Declaration on the Right to Development. As Nicolás Angulo Sánchez writes,

Only one country dared vote against it: the United States, on the pretext that this Declaration was confused and imprecise, and rejecting the link between development and disarmament as well as the very idea of a transfer of resources from the developed North to the under-developed South. Eight countries abstained: Denmark, Finland, Federal Germany, Iceland, Israel, Japan, Sweden and Great Britain, insisting on the precedence of individual rights over the rights of peoples and refusing to consider development aid as an obligation under international law.[34]

THE CHARTER OF THE UNITED NATIONS AND SPECIALIZED AGENCIES

Although it is a resolution of the United Nations General Assembly, in practice the Declaration on the Right to Development does not have the binding force of international treaties. But other texts can play this role: the Charter of the United Nations (the Preamble, Paragraph 3 of Article 1 and Articles 55 and 56) is not only the constituent document of the UN, but also an international treaty that codifies the fundamental principles of international relations. The International Covenant on Civil and Political Rights is also an international instrument dealing with the right to development: all the rights stated in the covenants form part of the jurisprudence of the right to development.[35]

---

33 The 1980s were a paradoxical decade. During this period we saw the birth of a potentially marvellous legal instrument on the global level with the adoption of the Declaration on the Right to Development. It is also one of the most negative decades in terms of human rights and the right to development as a result of the explosion of the debt crisis, deteriorating trade terms, and the widening equality gap between the countries of the Centre and the countries of the Periphery, and between people within each country.

34 Sánchez, *El derecho humano al desarollo*, pp. 36–37 (translation CADTM).

35 Ibid., p. 288.

The principal texts of the United Nations concern both individual rights and collective rights, the right to development, and the right of states to political and economic sovereignty. In practice however, not only the World Bank but also the IMF, the WTO and transnational corporations have consistently refused to comply with their terms.

Until now, these institutions have been able to enjoy impunity on an alarming scale, because despite some encouraging progress, present law is far from perfect. Of course, there are instruments and jurisdictions to deal with individual human rights and crimes against humanity, but other crimes that claim numerous victims throughout the world – economic crimes – are not at the present time subject to any international jurisdiction, agreement or international definition.

THE WORLD BANK, A SPECIALIZED AGENCY OF THE UNITED NATIONS

Yet in fact, the World Bank corresponds to the United Nations definition of one of the 'specialized agencies established by intergovernmental agreement and having wide international responsibilities, as defined in their basic instruments, in economic, social, cultural, educational, health, and related fields'.[36] Thus defined, the World Bank is linked to the United Nations system through the Economic and Social Council (known by the abbreviation ECOSOC, which acts under the authority of the General Assembly), as per Article 57, Paragraph 1 of the Charter of the United Nations.

The UN system is based on international cooperation, and more especially on international economic and social cooperation.

The UN Charter's Article 55 states:

With a view to the creation of conditions of stability and well-being which are necessary for peaceful and friendly relations among nations based on respect for the principle of equal rights and self-determination of peoples, the United Nations shall promote:

- higher standards of living, full employment, and conditions of economic and social progress and development;
- solutions of international economic, social, health, and related problems; and international cultural and educational cooperation; and
- universal respect for, and observance of, human rights and fundamental freedoms for all without distinction as to race, sex, language or religion.[37]

---

36   United Nations Charter, Article 57, 1.
37   United Nations Charter, Article 55.

The entire United Nations system is based on the following principles:

1. Sovereign equality for all its Members.
2. Members must in good faith fulfil the obligations they have undertaken by the terms of the Charter.[38]

Consequently, from a historical viewpoint and contrary to their pronouncements, the IMF and the World Bank are specialized agencies of the United Nations. As such, they are bound by the United Nations Charter.

Given this fact, it is impossible to evade the question: are the World Bank and the IMF legally bound to respect the obligations laid down in the United Nations Charter, including the obligation to respect human rights?

The International Court of Justice (ICJ) clearly ruled on this in the cases of Barcelona Traction and East Timor:[39] the Articles of Agreement of the World Bank are permeated with the obligations implied by customary law, in particular *erga omnes* obligations and *jus cogens* laws. These obligations, also called *imperative law*, mean that the rules of international law, whatever their nature, are always legally binding, and that their violation has specific legal consequences with regard to their corresponding obligations and rights. Among these, for example, are the principle of the sovereign equality of states, and the prohibition of the use of force, of torture and of the forced disappearance of persons, all of which are imperative obligations. The *jus cogens* laws are an integral part of international public order from which no subject is exempt, whether or not they have ratified international treaties or agreements. The *erga omnes* obligations, very close to *jus cogens*, concern, as the International Court of Justice has noted, the legal obligation (or more specifically the obligation of prevention and repression) applicable to all subjects of international law, given the importance of the rights at stake, to protect these rights, and in particular the obligation to respect and ensure the respect of human rights at all times and in all circumstances. Subjects of international law are also under the obligation to 'not render aid or assistance' to the continuation of an illegal situation.

While it is true that the World Bank and the IMF are independent of the UN at the operational level, it is nevertheless their duty to respect human rights and customary law in general. This means that they must refrain from lending aid in any form to states which conduct policies contrary to human rights and which have been found guilty of so doing under international law. In this context we should recall the illegality of the loans granted by the Bank to South Africa and Portugal when the policy of apartheid, in the case of South Africa, and Portugal's colonial policies had

---

38   United Nations Charter, Article 2.
39   *I.C.J. Reports*, 1970 and *I.C.J. Reports*, 1996 <icj-cij.org>.

been condemned on several occasions by the UN General Assembly. The obligation to not render aid or assistance was again confirmed by the International Court of Justice in the case concerning the legal consequences arising from the construction of the wall in occupied Palestinian territory, in an Advisory Opinion requested by the General Assembly by virtue of Resolution A/RES/ES-10/14 of 12 December 2003.

The international financial institutions must incorporate this obligation to respect human rights in the implementation of their policies: no subject of international law can escape these obligations by invoking the absence of an explicit mandate or on the pretext of 'non-politicization', let alone by a restrictive interpretation of economic, social and cultural rights as being less binding than civil and political rights. This last aspect has been effectively stressed by Eric David, who writes of the laws applying to the IFI:

the rights more specifically affected by a situation of economic and social deterioration are economic, social and cultural rights. Such a situation in fact threatens the enjoyment of these rights by categories of the population in varying, but usually large proportions. It is not an exaggeration to say that situations of extreme poverty lead to a violation of practically all economic, social and cultural rights'.[40]

David continues: 'if the rights affected by the SAPs are principally economic and social rights, the case also arises where, by a knock-on effect, the violation of these rights also leads to violation of the civil and political rights of the people concerned'.[41]

CONCLUSION

Neither the World Bank nor the IMF should be able to invoke their 'constitutional right' in order to shirk their obligations to protect human rights on the pretext that their decisions must be guided by economic considerations only.

It cannot be too emphatically stated: the policies pursued by the Bretton Woods institutions, whose field of action is planetary, have direct repercussions on the lives and fundamental rights of all peoples.[42]

---

40   Eric David, 'Conclusions de l'atelier juridique: les institutions financières internationales et le droit international', in *Les institutions financières internationales et le droit international* (ULB, Brussels: Bruylant, 1999), para. 2 (translation CADTM).

41   Ibid., para. 4 (translation CADTM).

42   See UN-CHR, *Effects of Structural Adjustment Policies and Foreign Debt*, E/CN.4/2003/10, 'II. Why Debt Relief Alone Is Inadequate to Realize the Human Rights Dimension of Poverty: A Case Study of Bolivia'.

Resolution adopted by the General Assembly
41/128. Declaration on the Right to Development

The General Assembly,

Having considered the question of the right to development,

Decides to adopt the *Declaration on the Right to Development*, the text of which is annexed to the present resolution.

97th plenary meeting
4 December 1986

Declaration on the Right to Development

The General Assembly,

Bearing in mind the purposes and principles of the Charter of the United Nations relating to the achievement of international co-operation in solving international problems of an economic, social, cultural or humanitarian nature, and in promoting and encouraging respect for human rights and fundamental freedoms for all without distinction as to race, sex, language or religion,

Recognizing that development is a comprehensive economic, social, cultural and political process, which aims at the constant improvement of the well-being of the entire population and of all individuals on the basis of their active, free and meaningful participation in development and in the fair distribution of benefits resulting therefrom,

Considering that under the provisions of the Universal Declaration of Human Rights everyone is entitled to a social and international order in which the rights and freedoms set forth in that Declaration can be fully realized,

Recalling the provisions of the International Covenant on Economic, Social and Cultural Rights and of the International Covenant on Civil and Political Rights,

Recalling further the relevant agreements, conventions, resolutions, recommendations and other instruments of the United Nations and its specialized agencies concerning the integral development of the human being, economic and social progress and development of all peoples, including those instruments concerning decolonization, the prevention of discrimination, respect for and observance of, human rights and fundamental freedoms, the maintenance of international peace and security and the further promotion of friendly relations and co-operation among States in accordance with the Charter,

Recalling the right of peoples to self-determination, by virtue of which they have the right freely to determine their political status and to pursue their economic, social and cultural development,

Recalling also the right of peoples to exercise, subject to the relevant provisions of both International Covenants on Human Rights, full and complete sovereignty over all their natural wealth and resources,

Mindful of the obligation of States under the Charter to promote universal respect for and observance of human rights and fundamental freedoms for all without distinction of any kind such as race, colour, sex, language, religion, political or other opinion, national or social origin, property, birth or other status,

Considering that the elimination of the massive and flagrant violations of the human rights of the peoples and individuals affected by situations such as those resulting from colonialism, neo-colonialism, apartheid, all forms of racism and racial discrimination, foreign domination and occupation, aggression and threats against national sovereignty, national unity and territorial integrity and threats of war would contribute to the establishment of circumstances propitious to the development of a great part of mankind,

Concerned at the existence of serious obstacles to development, as well as to the complete fulfilment of human beings and of peoples, constituted, inter alia, by the denial of civil, political, economic, social and cultural rights, and considering that all human rights and fundamental freedoms are indivisible and interdependent and that, in order to promote development, equal attention and urgent consideration should be given to the implementation, promotion and protection of civil, political, economic, social and cultural rights and that, accordingly, the promotion of, respect for and enjoyment of certain human rights and fundamental freedoms cannot justify the denial of other human rights and fundamental freedoms,

Considering that international peace and security are essential elements for the realization of the right to development,

Reaffirming that there is a close relationship between disarmament and development and that progress in the field of disarmament would considerably promote progress in the field of development and that resources released through disarmament measures should be devoted to the economic and social development and well-being of all peoples and, in particular, those of the developing countries,

Recognizing that the human person is the central subject of the development process and that development policy should therefore make the human being the main participant and beneficiary of development,

Recognizing that the creation of conditions favourable to the development of peoples and individuals is the primary responsibility of their States,

Aware that efforts at the international level to promote and protect human rights should be accompanied by efforts to establish a new international economic order,

Confirming that the right to development is an inalienable human right and that equality of opportunity for development is a prerogative both of nations and of individuals who make up nations,

Proclaims the following **Declaration on the Right to Development**:

Article 1

1. The right to development is an inalienable human right by virtue of which every human person and all peoples are entitled to participate in, contribute to, and enjoy economic, social, cultural and political development, in which all human rights and fundamental freedoms can be fully realized.

2. The human right to development also implies the full realization of the right of peoples to self-determination, which includes, subject to the relevant provisions of both International Covenants on Human Rights, the exercise of their inalienable right to full sovereignty over all their natural wealth and resources.

Article 2

1. The human person is the central subject of development and should be the active participant and beneficiary of the right to development.
2. All human beings have a responsibility for development, individually and collectively, taking into account the need for full respect for their human rights and fundamental freedoms as well as their duties to the community, which alone can ensure the free and complete fulfilment of the human being, and they should therefore promote and protect an appropriate political, social and economic order for development.
3. States have the right and the duty to formulate appropriate national development policies that aim at the constant improvement of the well-being of the entire population and of all individuals, on the basis of their active, free and meaningful participation in development and in the fair distribution of the benefits resulting therefrom.

Article 3

1. States have the primary responsibility for the creation of national and international conditions favourable to the realization of the right to development.
2. The realization of the right to development requires full respect for the principles of international law concerning friendly relations and co-operation among States in accordance with the Charter of the United Nations.
3. States have the duty to co-operate with each other in ensuring development and eliminating obstacles to development. States should realize their rights and fulfil their duties in such a manner as to promote a new international economic order based on sovereign equality, interdependence, mutual interest and co-operation among all States, as well as to encourage the observance and realization of human rights.

Article 4

1. States have the duty to take steps, individually and collectively, to formulate international development policies with a view to facilitating the full realization of the right to development.
2. Sustained action is required to promote more rapid development of developing countries. As a complement to the efforts of developing countries, effective international co-operation is essential in providing these countries with appropriate means and facilities to foster their comprehensive development.

Article 5

States shall take resolute steps to eliminate the massive and flagrant violations of the human rights of peoples and human beings affected by situations such as those resulting from apartheid, all forms of racism and racial discrimination, colonialism, foreign domination and occupation, aggression, foreign interference and threats against national sovereignty, national unity and territorial integrity, threats of war and refusal to recognize the fundamental right of peoples to self-determination.

Article 6

1. All States should co-operate with a view to promoting, encouraging and strengthening universal respect for and observance of all human rights and fundamental freedoms for all without any distinction as to race, sex, language or religion.

2. All human rights and fundamental freedoms are indivisible and interdependent; equal attention and urgent consideration should be given to the implementation, promotion and protection of civil, political, economic, social and cultural rights.
3. States should take steps to eliminate obstacles to development resulting from failure to observe civil and political rights, as well as economic, social and cultural rights.

Article 7

All States should promote the establishment, maintenance and strengthening of international peace and security and, to that end, should do their utmost to achieve general and complete disarmament under effective international control, as well as to ensure that the resources released by effective disarmament measures are used for comprehensive development, in particular that of the developing countries.

Article 8

1. States should undertake, at the national level, all necessary measures for the realization of the right to development and shall ensure, inter alia, equality of opportunity for all in their access to basic resources, education, health services, food, housing, employment and the fair distribution of income. Effective measures should be undertaken to ensure that women have an active role in the development process. Appropriate economic and social reforms should be carried out with a view to eradicating all social injustices.
2. States should encourage popular participation in all spheres as an important factor in development and in the full realization of all human rights.

Article 9

1. All the aspects of the right to development set forth in the present Declaration are indivisible and interdependent and each of them should be considered in the context of the whole.
2. Nothing in the present Declaration shall be construed as being contrary to the purposes and principles of the United Nations, or as implying that any State, group or person has a right to engage in any activity or to perform any act aimed at the violation of the rights set forth in the Universal Declaration of Human Rights and in the International Covenants on Human Rights.

Article 10

Steps should be taken to ensure the full exercise and progressive enhancement of the right to development, including the formulation, adoption and implementation of policy, legislative and other measures at the national and international levels.

29
Time to Put an End to World Bank Impunity

Contrary to popular opinion, the World Bank is not entitled to immunity as an institution. Section 3 of Article VII of the Bank's Articles of Agreement explicitly states that the World Bank may be taken to court under certain conditions. For example, the World Bank may be tried by a national court of justice in countries where it is represented and/or has issued bonds.[1]

IS IT POSSIBLE TO SUE THE WORLD BANK?

The possibility of bringing an action against the World Bank has existed since its foundation in 1944 and has never been modified until now, for the simple reason that the Bank's founder countries felt that they would not be able to sell the Bank's bonds unless they guaranteed buyers the right to sue the Bank in case of default. The World Bank finances the loans it grants to member countries by borrowing (by issuing bonds) on the financial markets. Originally, these bonds were bought by the big, mainly North American, private banks. Now, other institutions, including pension funds and trade unions, buy them too.

This is why there is a fundamental difference between the immunity status of the World Bank and the IMF. The Bank does not have immunity because it uses the services of bankers and of the financial markets in general. No banker would grant credit to the World Bank if it were protected by immunity. The IMF can have immunity since it finances its loans itself using the money paid in by its members in the form of pro rata shares. If the World Bank does not enjoy immunity, it is not for humanitarian reasons, but to provide creditors with the requisite guarantees.

It is therefore perfectly possible to sue the World Bank in the numerous countries where it has offices. It is possible in Jakarta or in Dili, the capital of East Timor, just as it is in Kinshasa, Brussels, Moscow or Washington, since the World Bank is represented in all those countries.

The Bank attempts to prevent the victims of its actions from bringing action by entering into bilateral agreements with national governments in which the latter commit to refraining from bringing legal action against the Bank. These same governments are pressured by the Bank to agree to set up obstacles preventing

---

1   IBRD, *Articles of Agreement*, Art. VII, Sect. 3: 'Actions may be brought against the Bank only in a court of competent jurisdiction in the territories of a member state in which the Bank has an office, has appointed an agent for the purpose of accepting service or notice of process, or has issued or guaranteed securities.'

their citizens from bringing any action against the Bank – a situation that is frankly scandalous and which no judge with integrity should accept.

An important detail: no institution, no subject of international law and no individual enjoys immunity if they are implicated in crimes against humanity. And furthermore, no statute of limitations applies. As a result, both the IMF and the World Bank may be brought to justice in cases of crimes against humanity.

WHY SUE?

Since the World Bank has been making loans,[2] a good portion of them have been used to carry out policies that have had a detrimental effect on the welfare of hundreds of millions of citizens. What do we mean by that? The World Bank has systematically given priority to loans for big infrastructures such as huge dams,[3] investments in industries that extract raw materials (for example strip mines and numerous pipelines),[4] agricultural policies that favour 'all-export' at the expense of food security and food sovereignty, and power stations which devour tropical forests.

Moreover, the World Bank has frequently come to the aid of dictatorships known to be guilty of crimes against humanity: there were the dictatorships of the Southern Cone of Latin America from the 1960s to the 1980s; numerous African dictatorships (Mobutu from 1965 until his fall in 1997, the apartheid regime of South Africa); regimes of the former Soviet bloc such as the Ceaușescu dictatorship in Romania; those of South-East Asia and the Far East, such as that of Marcos from 1972 to 1986 in the Philippines, Suharto from 1965 to 1998 in Indonesia, South Korea (1961–87) and Thailand (1966–88); up to and including the dictatorship of Abdel Fattah al-Sissi in today's Egypt, that of his predecessor Hosni Mubarak from 1981 to 2011, and that of Zine El Abidine Ben Ali in Tunisia from 1987 to 2011.

At the same time the World Bank, along with other actors, has contributed to the systematic destabilization of progressive and democratic governments by withdrawing all aid. Such was the case with Sukarno's government in Indonesia until he was overthrown in 1965, the governments of Juscelino Kubitschek (1956–60) followed by João Goulart (1961–64) in Brazil, finally overthrown by a military coup d'état, Salvador Allende's government in Chile (1970–73), and others.

---

2   The first loan was granted in 1947.
3   According to the report of the World Commission on Dams, as many as 80 million people have been displaced as a result of the construction of large dams. In many cases, the rights of these people regarding compensation and resettlement have not been respected. IDMC (International Displacement Monitoring Centre), 'Dams and internal displacement: an introduction', 2017 <internal-displacement.org/sites/default/files/publications/documents/20170411-idmc-intro-dam-case-study.pdf> [accessed 21/10/2021].
4   According to the Extractive Industries Review report published in December 2003, a large portion of the projects financed by the World Bank have had negative effects on the populations of the countries concerned. See chapter 18.

Next there are all the loans made by the World Bank to the colonial powers (Belgium, Great Britain, France, Italy, the Netherlands, etc.) to enable those powers to exploit the natural resources of the countries they ruled until the 1960s. All those loans were later included in the external debt of the states when they became independent. For example, the independent state of Congo (Kinshasa) had to finish paying off the debt incurred by Belgium in the former Belgian Congo. The same thing happened for Kenya, Uganda, Nigeria, Gabon, Mauritania and Somalia for the debts contracted by the colonial governments in those countries.

Then there are the structural adjustment loans that the World Bank has granted since the 1980s. These loans are not designed for any particular economic project, but rather are intended to help implement global policies with the ultimate aim of completely opening up the economies of the 'beneficiary' countries to investments and imports, mainly from the Bank's principal shareholders. This means that the World Bank supports policies denationalizing the assisted countries to the advantage of a few of its members. A handful of industrial powers thus impose their wishes on the majority of the inhabitants and the countries of the planet. The fact that all their remedies – whether long-term structural remedies or of the short, sharp shock type – do more harm than good has been demonstrated repeatedly in the string of crises that began with the 'Tequila' crisis that hit Mexico in 1994. The Bank's new priorities, such as the privatization of water and land, along with its refusal to apply the recommendations of its own Extractive Industries Review, clearly indicate that the Bank has no intention of changing its course and that new social, health and environmental catastrophes are in preparation – powerful tsunamis caused by the cataclysmic interventions of the World Bank!

WHO MIGHT BRING LEGAL ACTION?

Associations representing the interests of people adversely affected by World Bank loans and/or by its support for dictatorships could bring an independent action and sue the World Bank for damages in national courts.

In Common Law countries, class actions – legal actions brought by a large number of persons (physical or moral) – can appeal to the courts regarding the abusive practices of certain companies. In Civil Law countries which lack such a system, a number of fairly strict conditions (including the requirement to 'prove standing') need to be met before bringing litigation. However, certain collective procedures such as the Total trial in France resemble class actions and are an example to be followed in bringing action against the World Bank and other international financial institutions.

Holders of World Bank bonds – who include not only bankers, but also some trade unions – could sue the Bank over the use it makes of the money it borrows from them. There is no guarantee that such lawsuits would be successful, but it is hard to see why citizens' movements should not use their right to hold the World

Bank accountable for its acts. It is inconceivable that the nefarious practices of an institution like the World Bank should not one day be sanctioned by a decision of justice.

WHY HAVE NO SUCH PROCEDURES EVER BEEN INITIATED?

The clause of the World Bank's Articles of Agreement (Article VII, Section 8) which grants immunity to the decision-makers and to officials in the exercise of their duties has tended to obscure the possibility of suing the World Bank as a legal entity (Article VII, Section 3 – see chapter 30). Yet it is more important to be able to demand that the World Bank answer for its actions as an institution than to simply hold its executives to account. Indeed, the same clause (Article VII, Section 8) enables the World Bank to decide to remove the immunity protecting its directors and officials. Actions could also be envisaged against high-ranking officials after they have left office.

Another reason why there were no actions brought against the World Bank for so long is that it has taken a very long time for the truth to emerge, and for people to realize just how systematic and generalized the reprehensible practices of the World Bank are. In the eyes of citizens, it is often their national governments who are responsible for the policies demanded by the World Bank, so that its true role passes unnoticed.

But in recent years, several actions have been brought against the World Bank by groups of victims, in particular against the International Finance Corporation (IFC), the World Bank Group's extension into the private sector. In 2017, farmers in Honduras sued two representatives of the World Bank Group for having encouraged serious violations of human rights by financing the activities of a palm-oil company who had murdered opponents to its projects.

In 2019, the populations of 13 villages in western Guinea brought action against the IFC for its financing of a harmful bauxite mine. The complaint filed with the IFC's independent mediator points to systematic violations of environmental and social standards – confiscation of land and destruction of the environment and means of subsistence.

In 2012, fishers and farmers in Gujarat (India) appealed to the same mediator to denounce the Mundra Ultra Mega Power Project, a coal-fired power plant using coal extracted from sub-bituminous deposits that has resulted in deterioration of air quality and of their living and working conditions. When the IFC denied the findings of its own mediator, the victims filed suit with courts in the USA. As it does every time it is sued, the IFC tried to convince the US justice system that it is entitled to immunity. Fortunately, in February 2019, the Supreme Court of the USA removed the immunity the Bank claimed it was entitled to from liability for damages resulting from its commercial activities.[5] It was the first setback for an institution which flouts international law.

---

5   United States Supreme Court, Budha Ismail Jam et al., Petitioners v. International Finance Corporation <https://caselaw.findlaw.com/us-supreme-court/17-1011.html> [accessed 06/01/2023].

DOES THE UN CONVENTION OF 1947 NOT GIVE FULL IMMUNITY
TO THE SPECIALIZED AGENCIES OF THE UNITED NATIONS,
OF WHICH THE WORLD BANK IS ONE?

A United Nations Convention on the Privileges and Immunities of the Specialized Agencies[6] was approved by the General Assembly on 21 November 1947.[7] Article X Section 37 of the convention, concerning the annexes and the application of the convention to every specialized institution, states that the convention 'becomes applicable to each specialized agency when it has transmitted to the Secretary-General of the United Nations the final text of the relevant annex and has informed him that it accepts the standard clauses, as modified by this annex'. The Bank sent its copy back.

Annex VI concerns the International Bank for Reconstruction and Development, and thus the World Bank. And what does it contain? This is where the Bank has actually inserted those of its statutes which specify the circumstances under which it loses its immunity! Within the United Nations, the World Bank thus prefers to conform to its status as a bank rather than take advantage of the immunity given to the United Nations agencies. Here is the relevant paragraph of the convention:

In its application to the International Bank for Reconstruction and Development (hereinafter called the Bank), the convention (including this annex) shall operate subject to the following provisions: 1. The following shall be substituted for section 4: 'Actions may be brought against the Bank only in a court of competent jurisdiction in the territories of a member of the Bank in which the Bank has an office, has appointed an agent for the purpose of accepting service or notice of process, or has issued or guaranteed securities.'

It is therefore possible to sue the World Bank under the terms of the 1947 United Nations Convention and its annexes.

6   UN, *Convention on the Privileges and Immunities of the Specialized Agencies* (United Nations, 1947) <biicl.org/files/4292_un_convention_on_the_p&i_of_specialized_agencies.pdf> [accessed 22/10/2021].

7   In Article I of the Convention, entitled 'Definitions and Scope', Section 1, the specialized institutions mentioned by name are the following: International Labour Organization (ILO); the United Nations Food and Agricultural Organization (FAO); the United Nations Educational, Scientific and Cultural Organization (UNESCO); the International Civil Aviation Organization; the International Monetary Fund (IMF); the International Bank for Reconstruction and Development (IBRD); the World Health Organization (WHO); the Universal Postal Union; and the International Telecommunications Union.

30

The Case for Abolishing and Replacing the IMF and the World Bank

THIRTY-TWO INDICTMENTS OF THE WORLD BANK AND THE IMF

1. Since their creation in 1944, the World Bank and the IMF have actively supported all the dictatorships and all the corrupt regimes of the US-allied camp.
2. They trample the sovereignty of states underfoot in flagrant violation of the right of peoples to self-determination, in particular through the conditionalities they impose. These conditionalities impoverish populations, increase inequalities, deliver countries up to transnational corporations and change states' legislation (completely rewriting labour codes and mining and forestry codes, abrogating collective-bargaining agreements, etc.) in favour of creditors and foreign 'investors'.
3. Despite having detected massive misappropriations of funds, the World Bank and IMF have maintained, and even increased, the amounts loaned to corrupt and dictatorial regimes allied with the Western powers (see the classic case of Congo-Zaire under Marshal Mobutu after the Blumenthal report in 1982).
4. Through their financial support they helped prop up the dictatorial regime of Habyarimana in Rwanda until 1992, thus allowing the army to increase its strength fivefold. The economic reforms imposed in 1990 destabilized the country and aggravated the latent contradictions. The genocide that the Habyarimana regime had been preparing since the end of the 1980s was effectively perpetrated from 6 April 1994, leading to almost one million deaths among the Tutsis (and moderate Hutus). Subsequently, the World Bank demanded that the new authorities in Rwanda repay the debt contracted by the regime responsible for the genocide.
5. They supported a number of dictatorial regimes in the other camp (Romania from 1973 to 1982, China from 1980) in order to weaken the USSR before its collapse in 1991.
6. They have supported the worst dictatorships until they were overthrown. For example: the emblematic cases of their supporting Suharto in Indonesia from 1965 through to 1998; Marcos in the Philippines from 1972 to 1986; and Ben Ali in Tunisia and Mubarak in Egypt until their overthrow in 2011.
7. They have actively sabotaged progressive experiments in democracy. (Jacobo Árbenz in Guatemala and Mohammad Mossadegh in Iran in the first half of the

1950s; João Goulart in Brazil in the early 1960s; the Sandinistas in Nicaragua in the 1980s and of course Salvador Allende in Chile from 1970 to 1973. The full list is much longer.)

8. The Bank and the IMF finance tyrants and then demand that their victims repay the odious debts contracted by their oppressors.

9. In the same way, the Bank has forced the people of countries who gained independence at the end of the 1950s and early 1960s to repay odious debts contracted by the former colonial powers for the purpose of colonizing their countries. A prime example is the colonial debt contracted by Belgium with the World Bank to complete the colonization of the Congo (Kinshasa) in the 1950s. This is despite the fact that such transfers of colonial debts are forbidden by international law.[1]

10. In the 1960s the Bank and the IMF gave financial support to countries such as South Africa under apartheid and Portugal, which was maintaining domination over its colonies in Africa and in the Pacific despite these countries being under a UN-decreed international financial boycott. The World Bank also supported a country (Indonesia) that had forcibly annexed another country (East Timor) in 1975.

11. On the environmental front, the Bank continues to pursue productivist and extractivist policies that are disastrous for populations and detrimental to nature. It massively underwrites the construction of coal-fired power plants that have disastrous effects in terms of pollution and climate change. It has even managed to put itself in charge of managing the market for permits to pollute. The World Bank also finances the construction of large dams that cause enormous environmental damage. The Bank encourages the development of agribusiness to the detriment of family farming, supporting the massive use of pesticides, herbicides and chemical fertilizers that are responsible for the dramatic loss of biodiversity and impoverishment of the soil. The World Bank promotes privatization and commercialization of land for the benefit of large landowners.

12. The World Bank finances projects that flagrantly violate human rights. Among the projects least respectful of human rights and directly supported by the Bank is the 'transmigration' project in Indonesia in the 1970s and 1980s, many components of which may well be classified as crimes against humanity (destruction of the natural environment of native populations, forced

---

1   Article 38-1 of the Vienna Convention on Succession of States in respect of State Property, Archives and Debts of 1983 reads 'When the successor State is a newly independent State, no State debt of the predecessor State shall pass to the newly independent State, unless an agreement between them provides otherwise in view of the link between the State debt of the predecessor State connected with its activity in the territory to which the succession of States relates and the property, rights and interests which pass to the newly independent State' <legal.un.org/ilc/texts/instruments/english/conventions/3_3_1983.pdf> [accessed 25/10/2021].

displacement of populations). In the 2000s, the World Bank fully financed the ironically named 'Voluntary Departure' project in the DRC, a layoff plan which violated the rights of 10,655 agents of Gécamines, the public mining company located in Katanga. These workers are still waiting for payment of their back wages and the compensation they are entitled to under Congolese law.

13. The World Bank (like the IMF) aided the emergence of factors that caused the outbreak of the debt crisis of 1982. To sum up: a) the World Bank encouraged countries to contract debts under conditions that led to overindebtedness; b) it drove, and even forced, countries to remove capital movement and exchange controls, thereby increasing the volatility of capital and significantly facilitating its flight; and c) it drove countries to abandon import substitution industrialization and replace it with a model based on promotion of exports.

14. The World Bank and the IMF concealed risks they had actually detected (overindebtedness, payment crises, negative net transfers, etc.).

15. As soon as the crisis broke out in 1982, the World Bank and the IMF systematically favoured the creditors and weakened the debtors.

16. The World Bank and the IMF recommended, and even imposed, policies by which the burden of debt was borne by the people, while favouring the most powerful.

17. The World Bank and the IMF have continued the 'generalization' of an economic model that systematically increases inequality between countries and within countries.

18. In the 1990s, the World Bank and the IMF, with the complicity of the governing authorities, extended structural adjustment policies to the majority of the countries of Latin America, Africa, Asia, and Central and Eastern Europe (including Russia).

19. In the aforementioned countries, massive privatizations have been carried out to the detriment of the common good, hugely enriching a handful of oligarchs.

20. The World Bank and the IMF have strengthened large private corporations and weakened both governing authorities and small producers. They have heightened the exploitation of workers and small producers and increased their precarity.

21. Their self-proclaimed fight against poverty fails to conceal a policy that in practice reproduces and aggravates the very causes of poverty.

22. The World Bank's rhetoric concerning 'gender equity' coincides in practice with policies that in fact reinforce certain aspects of patriarchal domination. The policies financed by the Bank and by the IMF have negative consequences for women's lives.

23. The liberalization of capital flows, which they have systematically encouraged, has increased the incidence of tax evasion, capital flight and corruption.

24. The liberalization of trade has strengthened the strongest economies and further weakened the weaker ones. The majority of small and medium producers in

developing countries are unable to withstand competition from large corporations, whether in the North or the South.

25. The World Bank and the IMF operate in close cooperation with the WTO to enforce an agenda that is radically opposed to the fulfilment of basic human rights.

26. Since the crisis struck the European Union, the IMF, beginning in 2010, has been on the front lines to impose the same policies on the people of Greece, Portugal, Ireland, Cyprus and others as were imposed on the peoples of developing countries and of Central and Eastern Europe in the 1990s.

27. The World Bank and the IMF, who preach about good governance in report after report, actually engage in dubious practices within their own walls.

28. The World Bank and the IMF have contributed systematically to undermining public health services. This has greatly weakened the capability of public authorities and of peoples to face traditional diseases like malaria and tuberculosis as well as new epidemics such as Covid-19.

29. The two institutions keep most developing countries marginalized even though they represent the majority of its members, thus favouring a handful of governments in wealthy countries.

30. To sum up, the World Bank and the IMF are despotic instruments in the hands of an international oligarchy (a handful of major powers, their governments and their transnational corporations) who bolster an international capitalist system that is detrimental to mankind and the environment.

31. The harmful practices and activities of the World Bank and the IMF must be exposed and denounced so that they can be stopped. The debts whose repayment these institutions demand must be cancelled, and the institutions and their directors must be brought to justice.

32. It is urgent that a new, democratic international architecture be set up, one that would promote redistribution of wealth and support the efforts of peoples to achieve a form of development that is socially just and respectful of nature.

BUILD A NEW INTERNATIONAL ARCHITECTURE

Proposed alternatives must radically redefine the very foundations of the international architecture (its missions, its operation, etc.) Let us look at the case of the WTO, the IMF and the World Bank.

The aim of the new world trade organization should be to guarantee that a series of fundamental international covenants are established in the area of trade, beginning with the Universal Declaration of Human Rights and all fundamental treaties regarding human rights (individual or collective) and environmental rights. Its function would be to supervise and regulate trade so that it is strictly in conformity with social norms (the conventions of the International Labour Organization) and environmental norms. Such a definition is in direct opposition to the current WTO's goals. This of course implies a strict separation of powers:

there is no question of the WTO, or any other organization for that matter, having its own tribunal. The Dispute Settlement Body must therefore be abolished.

The organization that replaces the World Bank should be highly region-alized (banks of the South could be connected with it) and its function would be to provide loans at very low or zero interest, and aid which would not be granted unless it is used in strict accordance with social and environmental standards and, more generally, fundamental human rights. Unlike the existing World Bank, the new bank the world so sorely needs would not attempt to represent the interests of creditors while forcing debtors into submission to the all-powerful market; its priority mission would be to defend the interests of the peoples who receive the loans and grants and whose labour repays them.

As for the new IMF, it should return to a part of its original mandate to guarantee the stability of currencies, fight speculation, control movements of capital and act to prohibit tax havens and tax evasion. To attain this goal, it could contribute – along with national authorities and the regional monetary funds that also need to be created – to collecting various international taxes.

All of these ideas require a new global architecture that is coherent, hierar-chized and in which there is a division of powers. Its keystone could be the United Nations, provided that the UN General Assembly becomes a true decision-making body – which implies the elimination of the status of permanent member of the Security Council (and the veto power that goes with it). The General Assembly could delegate specific missions to ad hoc organizations.

Another question that has not yet advanced far enough is that of an international legal system, an international judicial power (independent of other international bodies holding power) that would complement the current system consisting mainly of the International Court at The Hague and the International Criminal Court. With the neoliberal offensive that began during the 1970s and 1980s, trade law has gradually gained dominance over public law. International institutions such as the WTO and the World Bank operate with their own judicial organs – the Dispute Settlement Body within the WTO and the World Bank's ICSID – whose role has taken on disproportionate scope. The Charter of the United Nations is regularly violated by the permanent members of its Security Council. We have pointed to the limits of international law and the systematic violations of the UN Charter, and in particular of the prohibition of the use of force set down in Article 2 of Chapter I.[2] New lawless zones are being created (one example is the United States' holding of prisoners without rights at Guantanamo). The United States, after having recused itself from the International Court at The Hague (which had found the US guilty

---

2   'All Members shall refrain in their international relations from the threat or use of force against the territorial integrity or political independence of any state, or in any other manner inconsistent with the Purposes of the United Nations.' Charter of the United Nations, Chapter I, Article 2 <legal.un.org/repertory/art2.shtml> [accessed 29/10/2021].

of aggression against Nicaragua in 1985), now rejects the International Criminal Court. Such a situation is cause for great concern and initiatives for putting a true international legal system in place are urgently needed.

Meanwhile, institutions such as the World Bank and the IMF must be held accountable before national jurisdictions and the debts whose repayment they demand must be cancelled. Action must be taken to prevent application of the harmful policies they recommend or impose.

ANNEXES
Annex 1: The World Bank: An ABC

What we call 'the World Bank' is in fact two bodies, the International Bank for Reconstruction and Development (IBRD) and the International Development Association (IDA). The World Bank is a subsection of the World Bank Group, which includes three more bodies: the International Finance Corporation (IFC), the Multilateral Investment Guarantee Agency (MIGA) and the International Centre for Settlement of Investment Disputes (ICSID). Let see what is hiding behind those names and acronyms.

The International Bank for Reconstruction and Development (IBRD) was created at Bretton Woods (USA) in July 1944, by 45 countries that had met for the United Nations Monetary and Financial Conference. In 2022, it consists of 189 member countries, with Nauru the most recent new member (since April 2016).[1]

The Bank's initial objectives were to provide public money for the reconstruction of Western Europe after the Second World War, to be a reliable ally of Washington and thus to provide an outlet for goods produced by US companies. Later it turned to financing the development of countries of the South, playing the part, in its own words, of 'a vital source of financial and technical assistance to developing countries'.[2] The financing choices are in fact very selective and questionable.

Four other bodies were created to become the 'World Bank Group'; they are assigned the following missions:

- 1956: The International Finance Corporation (IFC): financing the private sector in the South;
- 1960: The International Development Association (IDA): lends to the poorest countries;
- 1966: The International Centre for Settlement of Investment Disputes (ICSID): supranational tribunal where a corporation may take legal proceedings against a state if it considers that a decision is unfavourable;
- 1988: The Multilateral Investment Guarantee Agency (MIGA): guarantees the interests of private companies in the Southern countries.

Further mentions of the World Bank will include the IBRD and IDA.

---

1   To become members of the IBRD, countries first have to be members of the IMF.
2   World Bank, *World Bank GRI Index 2020* <openknowledge.worldbank.org/bitstream/handle/10986/34529/Global-Reporting-Initiative-GRI-Index-2020.pdf?sequence=1&isAllowed=y> [accessed 29/10/2021], and many other World Bank documents.

AN UNDEMOCRATIC LEADERSHIP

Each of the member countries names a governor, usually its finance minister, to represent it. They meet once a year (in autumn, two years out of three in Washington) as the Board of Governors, the senior decision-making body, to set the main policies. The Board makes the important decisions (admitting new members, preparing the budget, etc.) Also, the spring meeting in Washington (in common with the IMF) assesses the action of the World Bank and IMF.

For the day-to-day management of World Bank missions, the Board of Governors delegates its authority to 25 executive directors. Eight countries – the USA, Japan, Germany, France, the UK, Saudi Arabia, China and Russia – name their own executive directors. The other 17 directors are appointed by 17 surprisingly heterogeneous groups of countries: a rich country is grouped with Southern countries and of course it is the rich country that names the executive director to represent the whole group.

The executive directors normally meet three times a week and their meetings are chaired by a president elected for five years. Contrary to all democratic principles, it is understood that the post is reserved for the representative of the United States, chosen by the president of the United States. The executive directors do no more than rubber-stamp the choice.

The connivance between business, US big capital and the World Bank is immediately perceptible when we become aware of where all the 14 US citizens who have succeeded each other at the post have come from.

Eugene Meyer, the first president, lasted no longer than eight months. He was publisher of the *Washington Post* and was formerly tied to Lazard Frères. The second, John J. McCloy, was a big corporate lawyer well established on Wall Street. He went on to be American High Commissioner for occupied Germany and Chairman of the Chase Manhattan Bank. The third, Eugene R. Black, was vice-president of Chase National Bank and went on to be special adviser to President Lyndon B. Johnson. The fourth, George D. Woods, also a banker, was president of the First Boston Corporation. Robert S. McNamara had been the CEO of the Ford Motor Company, then Defense Secretary for Kennedy and Johnson. His successor, Alden W. Clausen, afterwards became president of the Bank of America (one of the biggest US banks, deeply involved in the Third World debt crisis). In 1986 the post went to Barber Conable, former Republican member of Congress, then in 1991 to Lewis T. Preston, former CEO of the J.P. Morgan bank.

The ninth president of the World Bank, between 1995 and 2005, was James D. Wolfensohn, former director of the investment banking section of Salomon Brothers in New York. After leaving the World Bank, in March 2005, Wolfensohn joined Citibank-Citigroup, one of the world's biggest banks. He was succeeded by Paul Wolfowitz, formerly second in command at the Pentagon, who was involved in the 2003 invasion of Iraq by a coalition under US orders. Wolfowitz was forced to resign over questions concerning his influence on the career of his girlfriend, who was on the World Bank payroll. He was replaced by Robert Zoellick, who had been the White House deputy chief of staff under George H.W. Bush, United States trade representative, deputy secretary of state, and a top executive of the bank Goldman Sachs. In this latter capacity Zoellick was heavily involved in the July 2007 subprimes crisis. From 2012 to 2019, Jim Yong Kim, also a US citizen, was at the head of the World Bank before resigning to join a private investment fund.

David Malpass took over from Kim in April 2019. Malpass had worked for the US Treasury Department and the State Department under Ronald Reagan and Bush Sr before becoming chief economist at the big investment bank Bear Stearns, up to its failure in 2008 as a consequence of its role in creating the subprimes speculative

Annex 1.1   The 14 presidents of the World Bank since 1946

Name	Period in office	Antecedents
Eugene Meyer	June 1946 – December 1946	Wall Street investment banker and publisher of the *Washington Post*
John McCloy	March 1947 – June 1949	Director of the Chase National Bank (which became Chase Manhattan)
Eugene Black	July 1949 – December 1962	Vice-president of the Chase Manhattan Bank
George Woods	January 1963 – March 1968	President of First Boston
Robert McNamara	April 1968 – June 1981	CEO of the Ford Motor Company and Defense Secretary for Kennedy and Johnson
Alden W. Clausen	July 1981 – June 1986	President of the Bank of America
Barber Conable	July 1986 – August 1991	Congressman, member of the House Ways and Means Committee
Lewis Preston	September 1991 – May 1995	President of J.P. Morgan and Co.
James Wolfensohn	June 1995 – May 2005	J. Henry Schroder & Co., then Salomon Brothers and President Wolfensohn & Company
Paul Wolfowitz	June 2005 – June 2007	Assistant Secretary of State
Robert Zoellick	July 2007 – June 2012	Deputy Secretary of State under George W. Bush
Jim Yong Kim	July 2012 – February 2019	Medical doctor, president of Dartmouth College; head of the WHO's HIV/AIDS department; joined Global Infrastructure Partners
David Malpass	February 2019 – May 2023	Chief economist at the investment bank Bear Stearns, Under Secretary of the Treasury for International Affairs under Donald Trump
Ajay Banga	June 2023–	CEO of Mastercard

bubble. In August 2007, Malpass published an article in the *Wall Street Journal* reassuring readers on the well-being of the financial markets, going so far as to claim that 'Housing and debt markets are not that big a part of the U.S. economy, or of job creation.' In May 2016 he joined the Donald Trump election campaign. He was rewarded by being given the posts of Under Secretary of the Treasury for International Affairs and then president of the World Bank.

AN UNEQUAL DISTRIBUTION OF VOTING RIGHTS

All member countries are allocated a number of votes that determines the weight of their influence. A basic right of 250 votes is allocated to each country plus a supplementary share determined by a precise and complex calculation. Unlike the UN General Assembly, where each country has one vote (which is not the case with the Security Council, where five countries hold vetoes), this system grants voting power directly related to financial participation. However, unlike a shareholder in a corporation, one country cannot unilaterally increase or decrease its funding level to increase or decrease its voting rights and weigh more. The system is watertight.

The Southern countries simply do not measure up against the Northern countries, who maintain their controlling influence and systematically impose their viewpoint.

Countries' demographic weight and their influence are flagrantly incommensurate.

On top of this unfair allocation of voting rights the US has imposed an 85 per cent majority vote for all major decisions. Being the only country to wield more than 15 per cent of the voting rights, that gives them a built-in veto on major decisions.

Annex 1.2 Voting rights of IBRD directors, January 2020[3]

Country	%	Group presided by	%	Group presided by	%
USA	15.44	Austria	4.87	Switzerland	3.05
Japan	7.77	Mexico	4.74	Iceland	3.05
China	4.79	The Netherlands	4.08	Pakistan	3.01
Germany	4.08	South Korea	3.99	Thailand	2.88
France	3.80	Canada	3.98	Kuwait	2.75
UK	3.80	Brazil	3.71	Uruguay	2.28
Russia (+ Syria)	2.82	India	3.54	Cameroon	2.03
Saudi Arabia	2.70	Italy	3.34	Uganda	1.92
				Nigeria	1.61

Source: World Bank[4]

3 Voting rights have changed frequently since 2010 following a reform of the calculation method and an increase in capital, but the countries of the South will always hold less than 50 per cent of votes.
4 World Bank, 'Voting Powers' <https://www.worldbank.org/en/about/leadership/votingpowers> [accessed 10/03/2022].

Annex 1.3 Voting rights of IBRD directors compared to population, January 2020

Country or group	Estimated population in 2020 (in millions)	Voting rights at IBRD in January 2020 (%)
Group presided by India	1,566	3.54
China	1,439	4.79
Group presided by Uganda	480	1.92
USA	331	15.44
Group presided by Cameroon	326	2.03
Russia (+ Syria)	163	2.82
Japan	127	7.77
France	65	3.80
Saudi Arabia	34	2.70

Source: World Bank, United Nations

The European Union countries, who between them could make up 15 per cent, generally stay in line with Washington. On the one occasion when they did threaten to use their bloc vote, it was in their own selfish interest.[5] It is imaginable that one day a group of Southern countries might manage to build a bloc vote to oppose a US candidate for the presidency of the Bank. However, up to now the US Treasury has been the uncontested master on board, with the power to block any change that runs counter to its interests. That the World Bank's headquarters is in Washington, a stone's throw from the White House, is no coincidence. Over time, adjustments of the voting rights have allowed China to gain a little more weight. But while the US have agreed to a reduction in their share of voting rights, they have made sure that their share stays above 15 per cent, thus maintaining their veto.

DUBIOUS FINANCING CHOICES

The IDA (International Development Association) is officially an ordinary association, but woven into the IBRD, which directs it. In 2020, the IDA had 173 member countries, of which 77 met the conditions for being granted loans – that is, an annual income per head of population less than $1,175 in 2019 (the figure is updated annually).[6] These countries take on long-term low-interest loans (30 to 40 years with grace periods of 5 to 10 years). The funding comes from the rich countries that replenish the available resources every three years and also from gains on loans made to middle-income countries.

---

5   See Éric Toussaint and Damien Millet, 'IMF threat on G8 proposal of debt cancellation' on the threat of a coalition between Belgium, the Netherlands, Switzerland and Norway in June 2005, CADTM, 17 July 2005 <cadtm.org/IMF-threat-on-G8-proposal-of-debt> [accessed 01/11/2021].

6   India must be added to these 77 countries; it is no longer eligible for IDA support since the end of the financial year 2014, but received exceptional transitional support for the period covered by the IDA 17 allocation round (2015–17).

Other Southern countries' borrowing may be from the IBRD at close to financial-market rates to fund projects that strict banking practices would approve as potentially profitable, just like an ordinary bank. The World Bank's creditworthiness is guaranteed by the rich countries who are the biggest stakeholders; this makes it possible for it to borrow funds on the financial markets at favourable interest rates. The IBRD then lends those funds in 15- to 20-year loans.

This privileged situation allows the IBRD to cover running costs and even to make a good profit: between $680 million and $1 billion for the 2011–15 period. Of the $44.6 billion granted in 2015, $19 billion was granted by the IBRD.[7]

With indebtedness growing, the World Bank has, in coordination with the IMF, developed its action in a macroeconomic perspective to impose ever more structural adjustment policies. When providing direct funding of these reforms through its specific loans, the Bank liberally 'advises' countries subjected to IMF therapy.

THE GROWING INFLUENCE OF NATIONAL AND INTERNATIONAL DEVELOPMENT BANKS

Aside from the World Bank, other multilateral development institutions exist, such as the China Development Bank (CDB) and the Brazilian Development Bank (BNDES).

Their influence is not to be neglected, as they are now doing more lending than the World Bank. Between 2005 and 2013 the CDB granted more than $78 billion to Latin American countries alone. In 2017, the total of CDB outstanding loans reached the gigantic sum of $1,427 billion. The total for BNDES was $175 billion.[8]

And like World Bank loans, these loans are open to much criticism. CDB loans have higher interest rates than World Bank loans, and come with tied aid and payments in commodities. A majority of BNDES-assisted projects have caused displacement of populations and have had a negative impact on the environment. In other words, these institutions have no regard for human rights, either.

Then there is the New Development Bank (NDB), formerly the BRICS Development Bank, created in 2014. Unfortunately its actions are inspired by the self-interest of the five powers – Brazil, Russia, India, China and South Africa – that founded it.

REGIONAL DEVELOPMENT BANKS ARE ALIGNED WITH THE WORLD BANK

Numerous regional banks exist: the African Development Bank (AfDB), the Asian Development Bank (AsDB),[9] the Inter-American Development Bank (IADB) and also the European Investment Bank (EIB). These banks are in no way alternatives

---

7   See World Bank, 'The World Bank Group A to Z', 2015 <openknowledge.worldbank.org/handle/10986/20192> [accessed 01/11/2021].

8   William N. Kring and Kevin P. Gallagher, 'Strengthening the foundations? Alternative institutions for finance and development', Wiley Online Library, *Development and Change*, 13 January 2019, Vol. 50, No. 1 <onlinelibrary.wiley.com/doi/10.1111/dech.12464> [accessed 01/11/2021].

9   The African Development Bank and the Asian Development Bank have the same acronym; the lower-case 'f' and 's' are used to distinguish them.

to the World Bank. They are almost perfectly aligned with the same policies and the same criteria, and their results are just as negative.

THE WORLD BANK GROUP: A WEB OF EVER TIGHTER WEAVE

The World Bank's subsidiaries – the International Finance Corporation (IFC), the Multilateral Investment Guarantee Agency (MIGA) and the International Centre for the Settlement of Investment Disputes (ICSID) – have been designed to weave a web of ever tighter weave.

Let us take a theoretical example to illustrate the effects of their policies. The World Bank grants a loan to the government of a country on condition that it privatize its water distribution and purification system. The public company is thus sold to a private consortium including the IFC, a World Bank subsidiary.

Then the population affected by the privatization protests against the sudden sharp increase in rates and the deterioration of the quality of the service provided, and the government turns against the predatory transnational company. The dispute is dealt with by the ICSID, which thus finds itself on both sides of the judge's bench.

A situation has been reached where the World Bank Group is present at every level: it imposes and finances privatization via the IBRD and IDA; it invests in the privatized company through the IFC; it provides the company with guarantees covering it against political risk, through the good offices of the MIGA; and it judges any disputes that may arise through the ICSID.

This is exactly what happened in El Alto, in Bolivia, between 1997 and 2005 (see 'The example of El Alto in Bolivia').

The example of El Alto in Bolivia

On 13 January 2005, after three days of mobilization by the inhabitants of El Alto, Bolivia's president promised the population that he would terminate the 30-year concession granted to the transnational company Suez.

What caused the popular uprising of January 2005 in El Alto?
On 24 July 1997, under pressure from the World Bank and the IMF, the Bolivian government granted a 30-year concession to the company Aguas del Illimani – Suez, for the distribution of drinking water and the treatment of sewage in the town of El Alto and the capital, La Paz. Aguas del Illimani is controlled by the Suez company, a world leader in the commercialization of water, along with Vivendi of France and Thames Water of Great Britain. The concession was attributed fraudulently, as the normal rules of calling for public tender were not respected. The call for tender was launched after a study carried out by the French bank BNP Paribas. Only one company responded: Aguas del Illimani – Lyonnaise des Eaux (Suez). Instead of issuing a second call for tender in order to have several offers, the contract was hastily signed. This concession made to a transnational corporation was the result of the privatization of the public municipal company Samapa, imposed by the World Bank, the IMF and the Inter-American Development Bank (IDB) when Bolivia's debt was rescheduled in 1996.

The World Bank was furthermore a direct receiver of the privatization since it holds 8 per cent of Aguas del Illimani's shares through its private investment instrument, the International Finance Corporation. As for Lyonnaise des Eaux – Suez, it holds 55 per cent of the shares.

In El Alto, Suez deprived 200,000 inhabitants of drinking water

Although Aguas de Illimani claimed that the whole population of El Alto had access to clean drinking water, the reality was quite a different story. Around 70,000 people lived in houses which were not connected to the water mains, as the cost of connection was exorbitant. It came to the astronomical sum of $445, i.e. approximately eight months of the minimum wage. Moreover, 130,000 people living on the territory of the Aguas del Illimani concession were outside the area covered by the transnational corporation.

Insufficient investment in the maintenance and improvement of the installations

According to the contract signed in 1997, Aguas del Illimani was under obligation to guarantee the maintenance and improvement of the water pipes and the sewers. In fact, their investments fell far short of meeting these requirements. Between 1997 and 2004, Aguas del Illimani only invested $55 million, mainly raised by loans from the Bank and the IDB or donations from foreign governments as part of their Official Development Assistance. This was the case for donations from Switzerland destined to guarantee access to clean drinking water for the poor. Insufficient investments resulted in pockets of contamination in certain areas due to the distribution of insalubrious water.

Increased water rates

At the beginning of the contract, in 1997, water rates increased by 19 per cent. The cost of connection to the mains rose by 33 per cent. Despite the fact that Bolivian law prohibited the dollarization of prices (Law 2066 of 11 April 2000, art. 8), Aguas del Illimani indexed its rates against the dollar.

Stealing from both the poor and the government

With its exorbitant rates, Suez redeemed its low investments and made a profit of 13 per cent. As if that were not enough, it used Article 26 of the contract to obtain the guarantee that in case of non-renewal of the concession in 2027, the government would have to reimburse the company for all the investments it had made. Furthermore, while Suez had agreed to pay Samapa $8 million per year, that company claims that it has only received $3.5 million per year.

World Bank: the judge and the judged

For these reasons, the entire population of El Alto took to the streets for three days running, demanding that Aguas del Illimani – Suez leave and that water distribution be returned to the public sector. After the Bolivian president's decree, Suez announced that it would lodge a complaint with the ICSID (the International Centre for the Settlement of Investment Disputes), one of the five branches of the World Bank Group.

Annex 2: The International Monetary Fund: An ABC

Like the World Bank, the International Monetary Fund (IMF) was created in 1944 at Bretton Woods. Its official purpose was to stabilize the international financial system by regulating the circulation of capital. What it has become is the main international institution whose task is to impose inhuman neoliberal policies all over the planet. It is clearly an anti-democratic entity at the service of the interests of the major powers and large private corporations. The conditional granting of credits to countries in difficulty is one of its principal means of exerting pressure. In 2022, 190 countries were members.

UNDEMOCRATIC LEADERSHIP

The IMF's organization is similar to that of the World Bank: each country appoints a governor, usually its finance minister or the governor of its central bank. Together they form the Board of Governors, the IMF's sovereign instance; meetings take place once a year in October. The Board of Governors makes the major decisions (such as admitting new countries and preparing the budget).

For the day-to-day operation of the IMF's missions, it delegates its power to an executive board, which consists of 24 members. The following eight countries – the same as for the World Bank – are entitled to one board member each: the US, Japan, Germany, France, the UK, Saudi Arabia, China and Russia. The other 16 board members are appointed by groups of countries that may differ slightly from those at the World Bank.

The third managing body is the International Monetary and Financial Committee (IMFC), which includes the 24 governors of the countries sitting on the executive board. It meets twice a year (in spring and autumn) and advises the IMF on the functioning of the international monetary system.

The executive board elects a managing director for a five-year term. Acting as a counterpart to the unspoken rule in force at the World Bank, this post is held by a European. The Frenchman Michel Camdessus held this position from 1987 to 2000, before resigning as a consequence of the economic crisis in South-East Asia. The IMF had helped creditors who had made risky investments and imposed economic measures that resulted in more than 20 million people losing their jobs, leading to strong popular protests and the destabilization of several governments. The Spaniard Rodrigo Rato took over in 2004 before resigning in 2007 to join the international department of the Lazard Bank in London.[1] In 2017, Rato was sentenced to four years in prison by a Spanish court for embezzlement at the Bankia Bank. Frenchman Dominique Strauss-Kahn, the socialist former finance minister, became managing director in 2007, before having to resign in 2011 after being charged with sexual assault by a hotel chambermaid.[2] In July 2011, Christine Lagarde, who had up until then been the French finance minister, stepped in. Lagarde was sued in the Crédit Lyonnais case, which cost French taxpayers a great deal of money. She left her position in 2019 to become president of the European Central Bank. A great deal could be said about the IMF under her leadership. After Lagarde's departure, the Europeans and Washington again agreed on a European at the head of the institution. She is Kristalina Georgieva, a Bulgarian economist and former number two at the World Bank.

In 2019, the IMF's staff consisted of 2,765 senior executives from 148 countries, most of them based in Washington, DC. The IMF 'number two' (first deputy managing director, FDMD) is always a representative of the US, which has paramount influence within the institution. During the Asian crisis in 1997–98, FDMD Stanley Fischer bypassed Michel Camdessus on several occasions. Anne Krueger played a very active part in the Argentine crisis of 2001–02. From 2006 to 2011, John Lipsky, former chief economist at J.P. Morgan, one of the main US business banks, played a leading role. As early as March 2010 he had warned that, in the words of a Reuters article, 'developed countries with big budget deficits must start now to prepare public opinion for the belt-tightening that will be needed, starting next year'.[3] Twelve years later, we can only conclude that the neoliberal agenda has been enforced everywhere, with Greece, Ireland and Portugal having been monitored by the IMF since 2010. The IMF has also developed its damaging influence in many countries of the South. In 2018, it granted the biggest loan in its history to Mauricio Macri's neoliberal regime in Argentina, a docile ally of the US. This resulted in a huge fiasco. Fortunately the measures imposed by the IMF on countries such as Ecuador and Haiti led to huge popular mobilizations in 2019 (in the case of Ecuador, the measures had to be abandoned under the pressure of the mass demonstrations).

OPERATION ON THE PRIVATE-ENTERPRISE MODEL

Since 1969, the IMF has had its own accounting system that governs its financial activities with member countries, based on units known as Special Drawing Rights (SDR). This was devised at a time when the system established at Bretton Woods,

1   The Lazard Bank specializes in financial counselling and asset management, notably with governments that face financial problems. For instance, it advised the Greek government in 2015, and we know how successful that was. It also advises the predatory regime in Congo-Brazzaville.
2   See Éric Toussaint and Damien Millet, 'FMI : la fin de l'histoire?' ('IMF: the end of the story?'), CADTM, 20 May 2011 (in French only) <cadtm.org/FMI-la-fin-de-l-histoire?debut_articles_mot=45> [accessed 01/11/2021].
3   Reuters Business News, 'IMF paints grim picture of fiscal tightening needs', 21 March 2010 <reuters.com/article/cbusiness-us-imf-lipsky-idCATRE62K04S20100321> [accessed 01/11/2021].

based on fixed exchange rates, was faltering. Its aim was to remedy shortfall in reserve assets at the time, especially in gold and the US dollar. It was not able to prevent Bretton Woods from collapsing in the wake of President Nixon's decision to terminate the free convertibility of the US dollar to gold in 1971. With a system of floating exchange rates, the SDR has mainly become just another reserve asset. According to the IMF: 'The SDR is neither a currency nor a claim on the IMF. Rather, it is a potential claim on the freely usable currencies of IMF members. SDRs can be exchanged for these currencies.'[4]

Originally valued at 1 USD, it is now revalued daily from a basket of hard currencies (the US dollar, the yen, the euro, the pound sterling, and since 2016 the Chinese renminbi).[5]

Quite unlike any democratic institution, the IMF functions almost exactly like a business. Any country that becomes a member must pay an entry fee known as a 'quota share' and thus becomes a shareholder. The quota share is calculated according to the country's economic and geopolitical importance. Twenty-five per cent of it must normally be paid in SDR or one of its component currencies (or in gold, until 1978) and the rest in the country's local currency. The IMF is thus one of the largest holders of gold reserves, third in line after the United States and Germany, since countries used the precious metal to pay their subscription to the IMF. In addition, in 1970–71, South Africa – which the IMF saw no reason to rebuff despite its notorious violations of human rights under the apartheid regime – sold it huge quantities of gold.

Annex 2.1   Distribution of voting rights among IMF board members, January 2020

Country	%	Group chaired by	%	Group chaired by	%
United States	16.52	Belgium	5.43	Brazil	3.07
Japan	6.15	Colombia	5.31	India	3.05
China	6.09	Thailand	4.34	Eswatini (ex-Swaziland)	2.97
Germany	5.32	Italy	4.13	Switzerland	2.89
United Kingdom	4.03	Australia	3.79	Iran	2.54
France	4.03	Canada	3.38	Egypt	2.53
Russia (+ Syria)	2.68	Sweden	3.29	Mauritania	1.62
Saudi Arabia	2.01	Turkey	3.23	Argentina	1.59

Source: IMF[6]

---

4   'Special Drawing Rights (SDR)', IMF Factsheet <imf.org/en/About/Factsheets/Sheets/2016/08/01/14/51/Special-Drawing-Right-SDR> [accessed 29/12/2021].

5   On 01/11/2021, 1 USD was valued at 0.708807 SDR; see <imf.org/external/np/fin/data/param_rms_mth.aspx>.

6   IMF, 'IMF executive directors and voting power' <imf.org/external/np/sec/memdir/eds.aspx> [accessed 29/12/2021].

In the early twenty-first century, when all its major clients had paid what they owed in advance or ceased to call on its resources, the IMF went through a delicate financial period and in April 2008, its executive board approved the sale of 403 tons of gold at a price of $11 billion, to replenish its coffers. Although those reserves are not used for IMF loans, they nevertheless give it the stability and stature it needs to retain the consideration of international financial actors.

In April 2009, the G20 summit decided to triple the IMF's lending capacity from $250 billion to $750 billion. After a significant decrease in outstanding credits from the IMF to member states, the international crisis which erupted in 2007–08 provided the ideal pretext for resuming the attack, multiplying loans, especially to European countries, using them as a justification for imposing draconian antisocial measures and harsh austerity on populations.

Annex 2.2 Timeline of credits granted by the IMF and repayments it received, 1998–2019 (USD billion)

	Total volume of credit held by the IMF for all member countries	Credit paid out over the year	Payments received by the IMF over the year
1998	93.4	30.1	10.2
1999	78.8	14.7	27.4
2000	64.1	10.0	20.6
2001	74.9	30.8	17.6
2002	95.1	35.9	21.6
2003	106.4	31.3	29.2
2004	96.3	7.7	22.9
2005	49.3	3.8	42.8
2006	20.5	4.3	35.9
2007	15.5	2.0	8.1
2008	33.1	21.7	3.7
2009	66.0	34.4	1.9
2010	93.1	32.6	4.7
2011	141.7	52.9	3.7
2012	146.6	24.4	19.5
2013	138.7	22.1	30.9
2014	108.5	16.1	37.3
2015	79.1	12.7	37.6
2016	74.7	8.6	10.7
2017	65.5	8.1	21.8
2018	85.9	35.4	13.5
2019	99.0	23.9	9.7

Source: IMF

'The G7 governments, particularly the United States, use the IMF as a vehicle to achieve their political ends. [...] Numerous studies of the effects of IMF lending have failed to find any significant link between IMF involvement and increases in wealth or income. IMF-assisted bailouts of creditors in recent crises have had especially harmful and harsh effects on developing countries. People who have worked hard to struggle out of poverty have seen their achievements destroyed, their wealth and savings lost, and their small businesses bankrupted. Workers lost their jobs, often without any safety-net to cushion the loss. Domestic and foreign owners of real assets suffered large losses, while foreign creditor banks were protected.'

Report of the International Financial Institution Advisory Commission of the US Congress, or Meltzer Commission, 2000

Unlike the World Bank, the IMF uses states' subscriptions to constitute its reserves for lending to countries with a temporary deficit. These loans are granted on condition of signing an agreement dictating the measures the country must enforce. The money is released in tranches, after verification that the measures demanded have effectively been applied.

As a general rule, a country in difficulty can borrow up to 100 per cent of its quota share from the IMF annually and up to 300 per cent in all, barring emergency procedures. The loan is short-term and the country is expected to repay the IMF as soon as its financial situation is back to normal.

As with the World Bank, a country's quota share determines the voting rights it has within the IMF, which corresponds to 250 votes plus one vote per tranche of 100,000 SDR of quota share. This is how the executive board of the IMF gives the United States its predominant position (with over 16.5 per cent of voting rights). By way of comparison, in January 2020, Mauritania chaired a group of 23 African countries representing 339 million individuals – 8 million more than the United States – yet had only 1.62 per cent of voting rights, or less than a tenth of the number held by the USA.

Annex 2.3 Voting rights of some FMI board members

Countries or groups	Estimated population in 2020 (in millions)	Voting rights at the IMF in January 2020 (%)
Group chaired by India	1,566	3.05
China	1,439	6.09
Group chaired by Eswatini (ex-Swaziland)	766	2.97
Group chaired by Mauritania	339	1.62
United States	331	16.52
Russia (+Syria)	163	2.68
Japan	127	6.15
France	65	4.03
Saudi Arabia	34	2.01

Source: IMF; United Nations

In 2016, under pressure from emerging countries, a reform of the transfer of voting rights came into force, but it was in fact a masquerade.

It is clear that within such a system, countries of the North easily manage to muster a majority and effectively run the IMF.

Their actual power is disproportionate compared with that of countries of the South, whose voting rights are ludicrously low in comparison with the number of inhabitants.

As for the World Bank, an 85 per cent majority is required for all major decisions affecting the future of the IMF, and the United States is the only country with more than 15 per cent of the voting power – giving it a de facto veto.

THE IMF, A PUBLIC DANGER

The IMF's purpose, as defined by Article I (ii) of its Articles of Agreement is 'To facilitate the expansion and balanced growth of international trade, and to contribute thereby to the promotion and maintenance of high levels of employment and real income and to the development of the productive resources of all members as primary objectives of economic policy.'[7]

In fact, the policies of the IMF are in contradiction with its statutes. The institution does not promote high levels of employment and income. Under the influence of the US Treasury and backed up by the other Northern countries, the IMF has taken it upon itself to become a major player in defining the economic and financial policies of its member countries. And to do so, it does not hesitate to go far beyond its mandate.

The IMF has thus facilitated the current complete freedom of capital movements throughout the world, one of the major causes of the financial crises that have so cruelly hit the countries of the South. Lifting all controls on capital movements favours speculation and is in contradiction with Section 3 of Article VI of the IMF statutes, which states, 'Members may exercise such controls as are necessary to regulate international capital movements'.[8]

Surveillance, financial aid and technical assistance are the three fields in which the IMF intervenes. However, neither annual monitoring of member countries nor its experts' recommendations have enabled the IMF to foresee and avoid the major crises that have occurred since 1994. The policies dictated by the IMF have in fact aggravated them.

Over recent years, IMF policies aimed at ending public subsidies of staple products (fuel and food) and vital public services (such as public transportation) and reducing social services have triggered popular insurrections, for example in Nicaragua (April 2018), Sudan (December 2018), Haiti (summer 2018 and in 2019) and Ecuador (October 2019). Clearly, the nefarious policies of the IMF have not changed.

---

7   IMF, *Articles of Agreement* (Washington, DC: International Monetary Fund, 2020), p. 2 <imf.org/external/pubs/ft/aa/pdf/aa.pdf> [accessed 2/11/2021].

8   IMF, *Articles of Agreement*, p. 20.

Abbreviations and Acronyms

AfDB	African Development Bank
AsDB	Asian Development Bank
BIS	Bank for International Settlements
DC	developing countries
ECOSOC	Economic and Social Council of the UN
EU	European Union
FAO	Food and Agricultural Organization
GDP	gross domestic product
GNP	gross national product
HDI	Human Development Index
HIPC	Heavily Indebted Poor Countries
IBRD	International Bank for Reconstruction and Development (World Bank Group)
ICSID	International Centre for Settlement of Investment Disputes (World Bank Group)
IDA	International Development Association (World Bank Group)
IFC	International Finance Corporation (World Bank Group)
IFI	international financial institutions
ILO	International Labour Organization
IMF	International Monetary Fund
ISI	import substitution industrialization
LDC	least developed countries
MIGA	Multilateral Investment Guarantee Agency (World Bank Group)
NGO	non-governmental organization
OAS	Organization of American States
OAU	Organization of African Unity, replaced by African Union in 2002
ODA	Official Development Assistance
OECD	Organization for Economic Cooperation and Development
OPEC	Organization of the Petroleum Exporting Countries
PRGF	Poverty Reduction and Growth Facility
PRSP	Poverty Reduction Strategy Papers
SAP	structural adjustment programmes
SDR	Special Drawing Rights

SUNFED	Special United Nations Fund for Economic Development
UN	United Nations Organization
UNCTAD	United Nations Conference on Trade and Development
UNDP	United Nations Development Programme
USSR	Union of Soviet Socialist Republics
WB	World Bank
WHO	World Health Organization
WTO	World Trade Organization

Glossary

Author's note

In this book the following are used interchangeably: Third World, countries of the South, Global South, the South, the Periphery, developing countries (DC).

The terms are generally used in contrast to: (the major) capitalist industrialized countries, countries of the North, Global North, the North, the Centre, imperialist countries, G7 and Triad, also considered as synonymous.

Balance of payments: A country's balance of current payments is the result of its commercial transactions (i.e. imported and exported goods and services) and of its financial exchanges with foreign countries. The balance of payments is a measure of the financial position of that country as regards the rest of the world. A country with a surplus in its current payments is a lending country for the rest of the world. On the other hand, if a country's balance is in the red, that country will have to turn to the international lenders to borrow what funding it needs to regain equilibrium.

Bank for International Settlements (BIS): Founded in Basel as a public company in 1930 to handle German reparations after the First World War, the BIS manages part of the foreign currency reserves of the central banks of the highly industrialized countries and some others.

The BIS plays an important role in gathering data on international banking transactions, published in a quarterly report since the early 1980s. It is responsible for handling financial risks associated with the liberalization of money markets. It also carries out banking transactions, receiving gold and currency deposits mainly from the central banks, selling the currency on the markets and granting loans to certain central banks.

Website: <www.bis.org>

Care: The concept of care work refers to all occupations, material or psychological, that provide a concrete response to the needs of others and of the community (including ecosystems). The term *care* is used in preference to 'domestic work' as it includes emotional and psychological (mental, affective, supportive) dimensions. It is not limited to private, unpaid aspects of such work, but includes the paid activities required for the social reproduction of human life.

Central bank: The establishment which in a given state runs its monetary policy and has the monopoly on issuing the national currency. Commercial banks are obliged to get their currency from it, at a supply price determined by the main rates of the central bank.

Conditionality: Covers a range of neoliberal measures imposed by the IMF and the World Bank on countries that sign an agreement, particularly to get their debt repayments rescheduled. The idea is that the measures will make the country more 'attractive' to international investors while making life harder for the population. By extension, the term is used for any condition imposed before granting aid or a loan.

Convertibility: This term designates the legal possibility of changing from one currency to another or from a currency to the standard by which it is officially backed. In the present system of liberalized exchange rates, where it is supply and demand that determine exchange rates, currencies 'float' with respect to the dollar (dollar-standard).

Currency market or money market: Markets where currencies are exchanged and valued.

Debt

- **Private debt:** Loans contracted by private borrowers, whoever the borrower may be.
- **Public debt:** Loans contracted by governments or other public bodies.
- **Multilateral debt:** Debt due to the World Bank, the IMF, regional development banks such as the African Development Bank, and other multilateral institutions such as the European Development Fund.
- **Odious public debt:** A legal doctrine according to which a debt is deemed odious, and therefore null and void, if it fulfils two conditions:
  1. It must have been contracted against the interests of the nation, or against the interests of the people, or against the interests of the state.
  2. The creditors are unable to show that they could not have known that this was the case.

Note that according to the doctrine of odious debt, the nature of the political regime or government which contracted it is not significant, since what counts is the use that the loan was put to.

If a democratic government should contract a debt contrary to the interests of the population, this debt shall be deemed 'odious', provided it also fulfils the second condition. Consequently, the doctrine of odious debt does not only concern dictatorial regimes, as is sometimes mistakenly claimed.[1]

The propounder of the doctrine of odious debt, Alexander Nahum Sack, clearly says that odious debt may be attributed to a regular government. Sack considered that a loan contracted in a regular way by a regular government may still be deemed odious if the two criteria mentioned above are met.

He adds: 'once these two points are established, the burden of proof that the funds were used for the general or special needs of the State and were not of an odious character, would be upon the creditors'.[2]

Sack defined a regular government as follows:

By 'a regular government' is to be understood the supreme power that effectively exists within the limits of a given territory. Whether that government be monarchical (absolute or limited) or republican; whether it function 'by the grace of God' or 'by the will of the people'; whether it express 'the will of the people', of all the people or only of some or of none; whether it be legally established or not, etc., *none of that is relevant to the problem we are concerned with.*[3]

---

1   See Éric Toussaint, 'The doctrine of odious debt: from Alexander Sack to the CADTM', CADTM, 24 November 2016 <cadtm.org/The-Doctrine-of-Odious-Debt-from-Alexander-Sack-to-the-CADTM> [accessed 05/03/2023].
2   Sack, *Les effets des transformations*, p. 154.
3   Sack, *Les effets des transformations*, p. 25.

There is thus no doubt about Sack's position, that all regular governments, whether despotic or democratic, or variants of these, are liable to incur odious debt.

- **Unsustainable public debt:** Debts whose continued repayment would prevent the government from guaranteeing their citizens the exercise of their fundamental rights, particularly concerning health, education, housing, minimum income and security. If continuing to make debt repayments prevents the government from fulfilling their fundamental obligations towards their citizens, the said repayments may be suspended even if the debt is legitimate and legal.
- **Illegitimate public debt:** Debt incurred by public authorities in order to promote the interests of a privileged minority.
- **Illegal public debt:** Illegal debts are those that were incurred in breach of existing legislation (for example, bypassing parliamentary procedure); those where the creditor was guilty of grave misdemeanour (for example, having recourse to corruption, threats or coercion); or those resulting from loans tied to conditions that break national law (whether of the borrower's or the creditor's country) and/or international law, including the general principles of law.
- **Debt rescheduling:** Modification of the terms of a debt, for example by modifying the due dates or by postponing repayment of the capital and/or of the interest. The aim is generally to give a bit of breathing space to a country in difficulty by extending the period of repayments so that the amounts can be reduced, or by granting a reprieve period when payments are not made.
- **Debt servicing:** Repayment of interest plus amortization of the borrowed capital.
- **Net transfer on debt:** The difference between the new loans contracted by a country or a region and its debt servicing (yearly repayments: interest plus capital).

The net transfer on debt is said to be positive when the country or continent concerned receives more (in loans) than it pays out. It is negative if the sums repaid are greater than the sums lent to the country or continent concerned.

Devaluation: A lowering of the exchange rate of one currency relative to others.

Direct foreign investment (DFI): Foreign investment can take the form of direct investment or portfolio investments. Even though it is sometimes difficult to distinguish between the two, for reasons of accountancy, jurisdiction or statistics, a foreign investment is considered to be a direct investment if the foreign investor holds 10 per cent or more of ordinary shares or voting rights in a company.

Eurodollars: The eurodollar market originated when American capital outflow was high in the second half of the 1960s. In 1963 the US authorities introduced a tax on non-resident borrowing, to slow down capital outflow. The result was a shift in the demand for financial backing in dollars from the US market to the European markets, where American bank subsidiaries could operate more freely.

Export credit agency: When private businesses of the North obtain contracts in a developing country (DC), there is a risk that economic or political problems may prevent payment of bills. To protect themselves, those businesses can take out insurance with an export credit agency such as COFACE in France or Ducroire in Belgium. If there is a problem, the agency pays instead of the insolvent client and the business in the North is sure of getting what is owed.

One of the main criticisms lodged against those credit agencies is that they are not very fussy about the nature of the contracts insured (arms, infrastructure and huge energy mega-projects) nor about their social or environmental consequences. They often give their support to repressive and corrupt regimes.

G7: A group of the most powerful countries on the planet: Canada, France, Germany, Italy, Japan, the UK and the USA. The seven heads of state generally meet annually in late June / early July. The first G7 summit was held in 1975 on the initiative of the French president, Valéry Giscard d'Estaing.

G77: The G77 arose from the group of developing countries which met to prepare the first UN Conference on Trade and Development (UNCTAD) in Geneva in 1964. The group provides a forum for the developing countries to discuss international economic and monetary issues. In 2021, the G77 included over 130 countries.

G20: An informal structure created at the end of the 1990s by the G7 (see above) who then relaunched it in 2008 right in the middle of the financial crisis in the North. The members of the G20 are: Argentina, Australia, Brazil, Canada, China, the European Union (represented by the country holding the EU presidency and the European Central Bank; the European Commission also attends meetings), France, Germany, India, Indonesia, Italy, Japan, Mexico, Russia, Saudi Arabia, South Africa, South Korea, Turkey, the United Kingdom and the United States of America. Spain has been made a permanent guest. Some of the international institutions are also invited to the meetings: the International Monetary Fund and the World Bank. The Financial Stability Board, the BIS and the OECD also attend meetings.

GATT: The General Agreement on Tariffs and Trade was a permanent negotiating forum where states only had the status of 'contractual parties'. It was replaced by the WTO (World Trade Organization) on 1 January 1995.

Gross domestic product (GDP): Measures the total wealth produced in a given territory, estimated as the sum of the total added values of goods and services.

Gross national product (GNP): Represents the wealth produced by a nation, as opposed to a given territory. It includes the revenues of the nation's citizens abroad.

HIPC (Heavily Indebted Poor Countries): The HIPC initiative was set up in 1996 and consolidated in 1999 to reduce the debt burden of heavily indebted, very poor countries, with the modest objective of bringing it to a barely sustainable level.

It functions through several particularly demanding and complex stages.

First of all, the country must conduct economic policies approved by the IMF and the World Bank over a period of three years, in the form of structural adjustment programmes. In this case, it will continue to receive the usual aid from all the lenders concerned. Meanwhile, the country must sign up to a Poverty Reduction Strategy Paper (PRSP), sometimes only as an interim measure. At the end of the three-year period, the decision point is reached. The IMF analyses whether or not the state of indebtedness of the candidate country is sustainable. If the net value of the ratio of foreign debt stock to exports is over 150 per cent after applying the traditional debt reduction mechanisms, the country may be declared eligible. However, this choice of criterion penalizes countries with a high level of exports (i.e. a ratio of exports to GDP of over 30 per cent). Then their fiscal revenue will be taken into account rather than their exports. Thus, if their level of indebtedness is clearly very high despite good tax recovery (fiscal revenues of over 15 per cent of GDP, to avoid any laxity in this area), the objective is fixed at a ratio of net value of debt stock to fiscal revenues of more than 250 per cent. If the country is declared eligible, it will benefit from the first reductions of its debt servicing and must continue to implement the policies agreed with the IMF and the World Bank. This period can last from anything between one and three years, according to how fast the key reforms agreed to at the decision point are implemented. Finally, the completion point is reached. This is when the country has achieved debt reduction.

In 2019 the IMF estimated the cost of this initiative at $76.2 billion, or about 2.54 per cent of present-day Third World public external debt. There are only 39 HIPCs, of which 33 are in Sub-Saharan Africa. To those should be added Afghanistan, Bolivia, Guyana, Haiti, Honduras and Nicaragua. On 31 March 2006, 29 countries had reached decision point, and only 18 completion point. By 30 June 2020, 36 countries had reached completion point. Somalia reached decision point in 2020. Eritrea and Sudan have still not reached decision point.

Instead of fulfilling its purpose of providing a permanent solution to the debt problem of these 39 countries, the initiative has ended in fiasco. Their public external debt has risen from $126 to $133 billion – that is, an increase of 5.5 per cent – between 1996 and 2003.

Faced with these facts, the G8 Summit of 2005 decided on an extra reduction, known as the MDRI (Multilateral Debt Relief Initiative), concerning part of the multilateral debt of countries having reached decision point – that is, countries having subjected their economies to the dictates of the creditors. The $43.3 billion cancelled through the MDRI is of little consequence compared to the public external debt of $209.8 billion of these 39 countries on 31 December 2018.

Human Development Rating (HDR): This instrument is used by the UN to estimate a country's degree of development, based on per capita income, the level of education and the average life expectancy of the population.

Import substitution industrialization (ISI): This strategy mainly refers to a well-documented experiment in Latin America in the 1930s and 1940s, and research carried out by the CEPAL (the UN Economic Commission for Latin America) in the 1950s, especially work published by the Argentine Raul Prebisch (who was to become the first secretary-general of UNCTAD in 1964). The starting point is the observation that when faced with a drastic reduction in foreign exchange, the main countries of Latin America had managed to respond to domestic demand by replacing imported products through the development of local production. The CEPAL theory holds that this process can be fruitfully extended to all sectors of industry, one after the other, and thus enable the country to 'disconnect' from the Centre. A good dose of protectionism and coordinated state intervention are expected to promote the expansion of budding industries. South Korea applied the policy successfully but in special circumstances.

Inflation: The cumulative rise of prices. Inflation implies a fall in the value of money since, as time goes by, larger sums are required to purchase particular items.

Interest rates: When A lends money to B, B repays the money borrowed from A (the capital), but also a further sum known as interest, so that it is in A's interest to carry out this financial operation. A higher or lower interest rate determines the amount of interest paid. Let us take a very simple example. If B borrows $100 million for ten years at a fixed interest rate of 5 per cent, in the first year B will pay back one-tenth of the capital initially borrowed, i.e. $10 million, plus 5 per cent of the capital owed, i.e. $5 million, thus in all $15 million. The second year, B will again repay a tenth of the initial capital borrowed, but the 5 per cent of interest will now be calculated on the remaining amount due of $90 million, so it will only be $4.5 million, making the total amount paid $14.5 million. And so on, until the tenth year when B will repay the last $10 million plus 5 per cent of that remaining $10 million, or $0.5 million, making a total of $10.5 million. Over a ten-year period the total amount repaid will have been $127.5 million. However, the capital is not usually repaid in equal instalments. In the early years, payments are mostly of the interest, and the share of capital repaid gradually increases over the years. Thus, should repayments be interrupted, the remaining capital due is higher than in the example. The nominal interest rate is the rate at which the loan was contracted. The real interest rate is the nominal rate reduced by the rate of inflation.

International Monetary Fund (IMF): The World Bank's sister institution, founded in Bretton Woods in July 1944. Its original purpose was to guarantee the stability of the international financial system based on fixed rates of exchange. After the end of the free convertibility of currencies to gold, decided by the US government in August 1971, the financial markets came into play and interest rates became variable. In the wake of the debt crisis of 1982, the IMF was given the particular responsibility of intervening to help developing countries and certain countries of the North (for example, Greece, Portugal, Cyprus, Ireland in the 2010s) with problems in repaying their debt. However, the IMF also imposes structural economic reforms in the neoliberal sense. Its decision-making process is the same as the World Bank's and is based on distribution of voting rights according to the economic might of the member states. An 85 per cent portion of the vote is required to modify the IMF Charter, so the USA has the power to block measures since they have over 16 per cent of the votes. The rich countries hold the majority of votes.

(See also Annex 2.)

Website: <www.imf.org>

Least developed countries (LDC): This category is defined by the UN on the basis of the following criteria: low per capita income, low human assets and little economic diversification. In 2020, the list included 47 countries, of which the most recently admitted were East Timor and South Sudan. Forty years ago, there were only 26 LDC.

London Club: The counterpart of the Paris Club (see below). Its members are private banks that lend to Third World states. Founded in 1976 in the wake of a request from former Zaire, the London Club is an informal group with no official status or legitimacy. It meets to reschedule sovereign debt for countries having difficulty with payments. As a result of the Third World debt crisis, the Club became more important in the last quarter of the twentieth century.

Faced with the changing debt profile of developing countries from the year 2000, as they abandoned recourse to private banks in favour of the financial markets, it seems that the London Club no longer has much to do. To all intents and purposes, its role has been taken over by the IIF (Institute of International Finance, <https://www.iif.com/>), an association of 500 financial establishments (banks, asset managers, insurance companies, sovereign funds and hedge funds) regularly invited to attend the meetings of the Paris Club.

Marshall Plan: This plan was conceived by the administration of the Democrat president, Harry Truman, under the name of the European Recovery Program. It was later to be known by the name of the Secretary of State of that time, George Marshall (Chief of Staff between 1939 and 1945), who was responsible for its implementation. Between April 1948 and December 1951, the United States granted $12.5 billion, mainly in the form of donations, to 15 European countries and Turkey. This represents a sum that would be over ten times greater in 2022. The aim of the Marshall Plan was to help reconstruct Western Europe, which had been devastated during the Second World War.

Moratorium: A situation where a debt is frozen by the creditor, who foregoes payment until an agreed time. However, as a rule, interest continues to accumulate during the period of the moratorium.

A moratorium can also be decided by the borrower, as was the case of Russia in 1998, Argentina between 2001 and 2005, and Ecuador in 2008–09. In some cases, through the moratorium the country manages to achieve reduction of its debt stock and of the interest it must pay.

New Deal: The measures taken by President Franklin Roosevelt on his election in 1933 to end the deep economic crisis that the USA had been going through since 1929.

Under the New Deal in the United States and with the Keynesian policies that spread to Western Europe after the Second World War following significant popular mobilization, social rights were considerably improved. Wide-reaching social security systems were put in place, commercial banks were made separate from savings banks, and in the United States the highest rate of income tax reached 90 per cent. Added to this, inequality in the distribution of income and property was reduced. At the time, big capital was forced to make concessions to the working classes in the face of mass mobilization. President Roosevelt's government, in a bid to reform capitalism to preserve and consolidate it, had to take on the Supreme Court, which tried to abrogate several of the government's decisions. Roosevelt, under pressure from the radicalized left-leaning working classes, managed to overrule the Supreme Court's decisions and imposed strong measures, some of which gave trade unions more power in factories and enabled workers to go on strike to gain more concessions from management.

Non-Aligned Movement: A group of countries advocating neutrality, starting from the 1950s, towards the two blocs under the superpowers of the USA and the USSR who were locked in the grip of the Cold War. In April 1955, a conference of mainly Asian and African countries took place at Bandung, in Indonesia, in support of Third World unity and independence, decolonization and an end to racial segregation. It was initiated by Sukarno of Indonesia, Tito of Yugoslavia, Nasser of Egypt and Nehru of India. The Non-Aligned Movement really came into being in Belgrade in 1961. Other conferences followed in Cairo (1964), Lusaka (1970), Algiers (1973) and Colombo (1976).

Now made up of 120 countries, the Non-Aligned Movement has its headquarters in Jakarta (Indonesia) but its field of action is currently very limited.

Official Development Assistance (ODA): The name given to gifts or loans granted in financially favourable conditions by the public bodies of industrialized countries. A loan has only to be granted at a lower rate of interest than going market rates to be considered as a concessionary loan, and therefore aid, even if it is then repaid to the last cent by the borrowing country. Tied bilateral loans (which oblige the borrowing country to buy products or services from the lending country) and debt cancellation are also counted as part of ODA, which is inadmissible.

Organization for Economic Cooperation and Development (OECD): The OECD was founded in 1960 and is based in the Château de la Muette in Paris; in 2002 it consisted of the 15 members of the European Union as well as Switzerland, Norway, Iceland; in North America, the USA and Canada; in Asia-Pacific, Japan, Australia and New Zealand. Turkey is the only DC to have been a member from the outset, for geostrategic reasons. From 1994 to 1996, two more Third World countries joined the OECD: Mexico, who formed NAFTA (the North Atlantic Free Trade Agreement) with its two North American neighbours; and South Korea. Between 1995 and 2000, four countries of the former Soviet bloc joined: the Czech Republic, Poland, Hungary and Slovakia. And more countries have joined since then: in 2010, Chile, Estonia, Israel and Slovenia; in 2016, Latvia; in 2018, Lithuania; and in 2020, Colombia became the thirty-seventh member.

Website: <www.oecd.org>

Organization of the Petroleum Exporting Countries (OPEC): In 2020, OPEC was composed of 13 oil-producing countries: Algeria, Angola, the Republic of Congo, Equatorial Guinea, Gabon, Iran, Iraq, Kuwait, Libya, Nigeria, Saudi Arabia, the United Arab Emirates and Venezuela. These 13 countries represent 40 per cent of global oil production and own over 79 per cent of known reserves. Founded in September 1960 and based in Vienna (Austria), OPEC is charged with coordinating and unifying the oil policies of its members, to guarantee them stable revenues. To do this, oil production is subjected to a quota system. Each country, represented by its minister of energy and oil, takes its turn in directing the Organization.

In order to limit production, OPEC initiated the creation of OPEC+, bringing in ten more oil-producing countries including seven DC (in italics): *Azerbaijan*, Bahrein, Brunei, *Kazakhstan*, *Malaysia*, *Mexico*, Oman, *Russia*, *Sudan* and *South Sudan*.

Website: <www.opec.org>

Paris Club: This group of 22 lender states was founded in 1956 and specializes in dealing with non-payment of bilateral loans by developing countries. From its beginnings, there has traditionally been a French president. The member states of the Paris Club have rescheduled the debts of more than 90 developing countries. Having once owned up to 30 per cent of Third World debt stock, the Paris Club members at present own about 10 per cent. However, the fact that member states of the Club are strongly represented within the financial institutions (IMF, World Bank, etc.) and informal international groups (G7, G20, etc.) ensures them considerable influence during negotiations.

Links between the Paris Club and the IMF are extremely close, as witnessed by the observer status enjoyed by the IMF in the Paris Club's otherwise confidential meetings. The IMF plays a key role in the Paris Club's debt strategy, and the Club relies on IMF expertise and macroeconomic judgements in instigating one of its basic principles: conditionality. In return, the IMF's status as privileged creditor and the implementation of its adjustment strategies in the developing countries are bolstered by the Paris Club's actions.

Website: <www.clubdeparis.org>

Poverty Reduction and Growth Facility (PRGF): IMF credit facility endorsed in 1999, made available from the end of 2007 to 78 low-income countries (with GDP of less than $895 per capita in 2003). It carries the idea of fighting poverty, but within a global economic strategy always based on growth. Governments must then draw up a vast document – a Poverty Reduction Strategy Paper (see below) – which is a sort of structural adjustment programme with a slightly social feel, under agreement with the multilateral institutions. If deemed eligible, a country can borrow money within the framework of a three-year agreement. The amount is variable, depending on the country's balance of payment difficulties and past record with the IMF: usually no more than 140 per cent of its IMF quota. The annual rate is 0.5 per cent for a ten-year period, with five and a half years' grace.

In 2008, the PRGF was replaced by the Extended Credit Facility (ECF). This is exclusively for low-income countries (i.e. according to World Bank data for 2020, 29 countries with a per capita GDP of less than $1,035). Following on from the PRGF, the ECF grants loans for a period of three to five years, renewable within a yearly limit of 75 per cent of the quota. This limit may be exceeded under certain circumstances. The repayment schedule is spread over a period of ten years, including five and a half years' grace, with a zero interest rate.[4]

Poverty Reduction Strategy Paper– (PRSP): Set up by the World Bank and the IMF in 1999, the PRSP was officially designed to fight poverty. In fact, it turns out to be an even more virulent version of the structural adjustment policies, trying to win governments' assent and legitimacy in the eyes of the social participants. It is also known as the Poverty Reduction Strategy (PRS).

PRSPs are aimed at countries concerned by the HIPC (Heavily Indebted Poor Countries) initiative, and the pursuance of structural adjustment programmes under a different name.

Recession: egative economic growth in a country or a sector for at least two consecutive quarters.

Risk premium: When loans are granted, creditors take stock of the borrower's economic situation in order to fix the interest rate. If there is a possible risk that the borrower may not be able to honour their repayments, a higher interest rate will be applied. The higher amount of interest that the creditor thus receives is supposed to compensate them for the risk taken in granting the loan.

Speculation: The action of seeking profit by gambling on the future values of goods, property and financial or monetary assets. Speculation leads to a divorce between the financial and the productive spheres. Currency markets are the main source of speculation.

---

4   Source: <https://www.imf.org/external/np/pdr/prsp/poverty2.htm> and <http://www.imf.org/external/np/exr/facts/ecf.htm>.

Stock exchange/Stock market: The place where securities (bonds and shares) are issued and traded. A bond is a loan security while a share gives part ownership in a company. New securities are issued for the first time on the primary financial market. Bonds and shares can then be bought and sold freely on the secondary market.

Structural adjustment programme (SAP): As a reaction to the debt crisis, the rich countries entrusted the IMF and the World Bank with the task of imposing strict financial discipline on over-indebted countries. The first objective of structural adjustment programmes, according to the official discourse, is to restore financial equilibrium. To achieve this, the IMF and the World Bank oblige the country to open up its economy to attract capital investments. The aim for countries of the South that apply SAPs is to export more and spend less, through two sets of measures. Shock measures are measures that take immediate effect: the cancellation of subsidies to essential goods and services, reduction of social budgets and of the number of workers on the civil service payroll, currency devaluation and high interest rates. Structural measures are longer-term economic reforms: specialization in a few export products (to the detriment of subsistence crops), liberalization of the economy by ceasing to control capital movements and by removing exchange control, opening up markets by removing customs barriers, privatization of public companies, generalizing VAT and taxation that preserves capital revenue. All this has dramatic consequences for populations; the countries that apply the programmes experience both disappointing economic results and galloping poverty.

Subsistence crops: Crops intended to feed local populations (millet, manioc, sorghum, etc.), as opposed to crops intended for export (coffee, cocoa, tea, groundnuts, sugar, bananas, etc.).

Trade balance: The trade balance of a country is the difference between merchandize sold (exports) and merchandize bought (imports). The resulting trade balance either shows a deficit or is in credit.

Treasury bonds: Bonds issued by public treasuries to fund government borrowing. They may be issued for periods of a few months to thirty years. (Called GILTs in the UK, India and some other Commonwealth countries.)

United Nations Conference on Trade and Development (UNCTAD): Established in 1964, after pressure from the developing countries, to offset the effects of GATT (see above).
    Website: <http://www.unctad.org>

United Nations Development Programme (UNDP): Founded in 1965, the UNDP, based in New York, is the UN's main body for technical aid. Without any political restrictions, it helps developing countries to equip themselves with basic administrative and technical services, provides managerial staff training, looks for ways to fulfil some of a population's essential needs, initiates regional cooperation programmes and, theoretically, coordinates locally activities of all the United Nations' operational programmes. The UNDP generally relies on Western know-how and technology, but one-third of its experts are from the Third World. The UNDP publishes an annual *Human Development Report* that classifies countries according to the Human Development Index (HDI).
    Website: <www.undp.org>

World Bank: See Annex 1.
Website: www.worldbank.org

World Trade Organization (WTO): Founded on 1 January 1995 to replace the GATT (General Agreement on Tariffs and Trade). Its role is to ensure that none of its members adopts protectionist practices, in order to accelerate the global liberalization of trading and to favour the strategies of transnational corporations. The WTO has an international tribunal (the Dispute Settlement Body) which judges possible violations of its founding Marrakesh Agreement.

The WTO functions via 'one country, one vote', but delegates from the countries of the South don't stand a chance against the tons of documents to be studied, and the army of civil servants, lawyers, etc. wielded by the countries of the North. Decisions are made among the powerful in the 'green rooms'.

Website: <www.wto.org>

Bibliography

Achcar, Gilbert. *Le choc des barbaries: Terrorismes et désordre mondial* (*The Shock of Barbarity: Terrorisms and World Disorder*) (Brussels: Éd. Complexe, 2002; Paris: 10/18, 2004).

Achcar, Gilbert. *Le peuple veut: une exploration radicale du soulèvement arabe* (*The People Want: A Radical Exploration of the Arab Uprising*). (Paris: Sindbad, Actes Sud, 2013).

Achcar, Gilbert. 'On the "Arab Inequality Puzzle": the case of Egypt', *Development and Change*, 17 March 2020, Vol. 51, No. 3 <doi.org/10.1111/dech.12585> [accessed 15/09/2021].

Achcar, Gilbert. 'Comment on the "Arab Inequality Puzzle": a rejoinder', *Development and Change*, Social Studies Institute of The Hague, 2 January 2021 <onlinelibrary.wiley.com/doi/10.1111/dech.12625> [accessed 05/10/2021].

Acosta, Alberto. *Ecuador: deuda externa y migración, una relación incestuosa* (Cuenca: IDIUC, 2002) <bibliotecavirtual.clacso.org.ar/Ecuador/diuc-ucuenca/20121114112219/acosta.pdf> [accessed 03/09/2021].

Acosta, Alberto (interviewed by Matthieu Le Quang). 'Le projet ITT: laisser le pétrole en terre ou le chemin vers un autre modèle de développement' ('The ITT project: leave the oil in the ground – the road towards a new development model'), CADTM, 18 September 2009 <cadtm.org/Le-projet-ITT-laisser-le-petrole-en-terre-ou-le-chemin-vers-un-autre-modele-de> (in French and Spanish).

Acosta, Alberto and John Cajas Guijarro. *Una década desperdiciada: las sombras del correísmo* (Quito: Centro Andino de Acción Popular, 2018).

Aglietta, Michel and Sandra Moatti. *Le FMI: de l'ordre monétaire aux désordres financiers* (*The IMF: Monetary Order and Financial Disorder*) (Paris: Editions Economica, 2000).

Amin, Samir, Robert Charvin, Jean Ziegler, Anne-Cécile Robert et al. *ONU: droits pour tous ou loi du plus fort?* (*The UN: Rights for All, or Only for the Strongest?*) (Geneva: Cetim, 2005).

Appleman, Roy E. *South to the Naktong, North to the Yalu* (Washington, DC: Center of Military History, United States Army, 1992, 1961).

Arend, Elizabeth. 'Critique of the World Bank's "Applying Gender Action Plan Lessons: A Three-Year Road Map for Gender Mainstreaming (2011–2013)"', GenderAction, 2010 <genderaction.org/publications/2010/critique_road_map.pdf> [accessed 18/10/2021].

Avramović, Dragoslav and Ravi Gulhati. *Debt Servicing Problems of Low-Income Countries 1956–58* (Baltimore: Johns Hopkins Press for the IBRD, 1960).

Avramović, Dragoslav et al. *Economic Growth and External Debt* (Baltimore: Johns Hopkins Press for the IBRD, 1964).

Azoulay, Gerard. *Les théories du développement* (*Theories of Development*) (Rennes: Presses Universitaires de Rennes, 2002).

Balassa, Bela. *Development Strategies in Some Developing Countries: A Comparative Study* (Baltimore: Johns Hopkins University Press for the World Bank, 1971).

Balbuena, Hugo Ruiz Diaz. 'Les politiques menées par les IFI et leur responsabilité pour les violations massives des droits humains suite à l'imposition des programmes d'ajustement structurel' ('IFI policies and their responsibility for massive violations of human rights following the enforcement of structural adjustment programmes'), Equipo Nizkor y Derechos Human Rights, 2 November 2004 <www.derechos.org/nizkor/econ/hdb.html> (in French) [accessed 21/02/22].

Bateman, Milford. 'How the Bank's push for microcredit failed the poor', CADTM, 19 December 2017 <cadtm.org/How-the-Bank-s-push-for> [accessed 29/03/2022].

Belhaj, Ferid. 'MENA unbound: ten years after the Arab Spring, avoiding another lost decade', World Bank/Al Jazeera, 14 January 2021 <worldbank.org/en/news/opinion/2021/01/14/mena-unbound-ten-years-after-the-arab-spring-avoiding-another-lost-decade> [accessed 06/10/2021].

Bello, Walden F. *US Sponsored Low Intensity Conflict in the Philippines* (San Francisco: Institute for Food and Development Policy, 1987).

Bello, Walden F. *Deglobalization: Ideas for a New World Economy* (London/New York: Zed Books, 2002).

Bello, Walden and Shalmali Guttal. 'The limits of reform: the Wolfensohn era at the World Bank', Focus on the Global South, 25 April 2005 <focusweb.org/the-limits-of-reform-the-wolfensohn-era-at-the-world-bank/> [accessed 15/11/2021]. Also available at <cadtm.org>.

Benchikh, Madjid, Robert Charvin and Francine Demichel. *Introduction critique au droit international public* (Lyon: Collection Critique du droit, Presse Universitaires de Lyon, 1986).

Bergamaschi, Isaline. 'Privatizating the African state: uneasy process and limited outcomes. The case of the cotton sector in Mali', British International Studies Association Conference, Manchester, 27–29 May 2011, pp. 12ff. <open.ac.uk/socialsciences/bisa-africa/files/bisa-2011-bergamaschi.pdf> [accessed 29/03/2022].

Bhagwati, Jagdish. *Anatomy and Consequences of Exchange Control Regime* (Cambridge: Ballinger for the National Bureau of Economic Research, 1978).

Blanchard, Olivier and Daniel Leigh. *Growth Forecast Errors and Fiscal Multipliers* (Washington, DC: IMF, January 2013) <imf.org/external/pubs/ft/wp/2013/wp1301.pdf> [accessed 27/12/2021].

Bond, Patrick. *Elite Transition: From Apartheid to Neoliberalism in South Africa* (London/Sterling, VA: Pluto Press and Pietermaritzburg: University of Natal Press, 2000).

Bretton Woods Project. 'World Bank criticised for overlooking care work', 2014 <brettonwoodsproject.org/2014/01/bank-criticised-overlooking-care-work/> [accessed 18/10/2021].

Bruneau, Camille. 'La dette: une arme patriarcale déployée dans les pays du Sud' ('Debt: a patriarchal weapon deployed in the Global South'), *AVP Dettes aux Suds*, 2019, No. 77 (in French) <cadtm.org/La-dette-une-arme-patriarcale-deployee-dans-les-pays-du-Sud> [accessed 08/10/2021].

Buenaventura, Mae and Claire Miranda. *The IMF and Gender Equality: The Gender Dimensions of the IMF's Key Fiscal Policy Advice on Resource Mobilisation in Developing Countries* (Bretton Woods Project, 2017) <brettonwoodsproject.org/wp-content/uploads/2017/04/IMF-and-Gender-Equality-VAT-1.pdf> [accessed 18/10/2021].

Bundesrepublik Deutschland, Auswärtiges Amt et al. *Deutsche Auslandsschulden; Dokumente zu den internationalen Verhandlungen Oktober 1950 bis Juli 1951; englisches Sonderheft* (Hameln: C.W. Niemeyer, 1952).

CADTM. 'L'Equateur à la croisée des chemins' ('Ecuador at the crossroads'), in *Les Crimes de la dette* (Liège/Paris: CADTM/Syllepse, 2007), part III, pp.174–265 (in French).

CADTM. *En campagne contre la dette* (*Campaigning Against Debt*) (Paris: Syllepse, 2008) <cadtm.org/En-campagne-contre-la-dette> (in French) [accessed 19/12/2021].

CADTM. *History of the CADTM Anti-Debt Policies* (CADTM: 2017) <cadtm.org/History-of-the-CADTM-Anti-Debt> [accessed 27/02/2023].

CADTM AYNA, 'Ensemble avec le peuple équatorien' ('With the Ecuadorian people'), CADTM, 15 October 2019 <cadtm.org/Ensemble-avec-le-peuple-equatorien> (in French and Spanish) [accessed 27/02/2023].

Calcagno, Alfredo Eric and Alfredo Fernando Calcagno. *El universo neoliberal: Recuento de sus lugares communes* (Madrid: Ediciones Akal, Pensamiento crítico, 2015).

Centro de Derechos Economicos y Sociales. *Un continente contra la deuda: Perspectivas y enfoques para la accion* (Quito: Ediciones Abya-Yala, 2000).

Chavkin, Sasha and Michael Hudson. 'New investigation reveals 3.4m displaced by World Bank', International Consortium of Investigative Journalists, 2015 <icij.org/inside-icij/2015/04/new-investigation-reveals-34m-displaced-world-bank> [accessed 15/10/2021].

Chen, Shaohua and Martin Ravallion. *The Developing World Is Poorer Than We Thought, But No Less Successful in the Fight against Poverty*' (World Bank: Policy Research Working Paper 4703, August 2008) <documents1.worldbank.org/curated/en/526541468262138892/pdf/WPS4703.pdf> [accessed 16/09/2021].

Chenery, Hollis B. 'Objectives and criteria of foreign assistance', in Gustav Ranis (ed.), *The United States and the Developing Economies* (New York: W.W. Norton, 1964).

Chenery, Hollis B. et al. *Redistribution with Growth* (Oxford: Oxford University Press for the World Bank and the Institute of Development Studies, London, 1974).

Chossudovsky, Michel. 'Economic genocide in Rwanda', *Economic and Political Weekly*, 13 April 1996, Vol. 31, No. 15, pp. 938–41.

Chossudovsky, Michel and Pierre Galand. 'The 1994 Rwandan Genocide – the use of Rwanda's external debt (1990–1994). The responsibility of donors and creditors', CADTM, 2016 <cadtm.org/The-1994-Rwandan-Genocide-The-Use> [accessed 27/02/2023].

Chossudovsky, Michel et al. 'Rwanda, Somalie, ex Yougoslavie: conflits armés, génocide économique et responsabilités des institutions de Bretton Woods' ('Rwanda, Somalia, ex-Yugoslavia: armed conflicts, economic genocide and responsibilities of the Bretton Woods institutions'), in *Banque, FMI, OMC: ça suffit!* (Brussels: CADTM, 1995) (in French).

Cole, David C. and Princeton N. Lyman. *Korean Development: The Interplay of Politics and Economics* (Cambridge, MA: Harvard University Press, 1971).

Comanne, Denise. 'Quelle vision du développement pour les féministes' ('What vision of development should feminists adopt?'), CADTM, 2005; 28 May 2020 <cadtm.org/Quelle-vision-du-developpement-pour-les-feministes> (in French) [accessed 06/10/2021].

Combacau, Jean and Serge Sur. *Droit international public,* 2nd edn (Paris: Montchrestien, 1995).

Comisión para la Auditoria Integral de la Deuda Pública (CAIC). 'Final report of the integral auditing of the Ecuadorian debt – executive summary', 12 December 2008 <cadtm.org/Final-Report-of-the-Integral> [accessed 28/03/2022].

Dale, William B. 'Financing and adjustment of payment imbalances', in John Williamson (ed.), *IMF Conditionality* (Washington, DC: Institute for International Economics, 1983), p. 7 <www.iefpedia.com/english/wp-content/uploads/2012/01/chap5.pdf> [accessed 28/03/2022].

David, Eric. 'Conclusions de l'atelier juridique: les institutions financières internationales et le droit international', in *Les institutions financières internationales et le droit international* (ULB, Brussels: Bruylant, 1999).

Debtocracy [film]. Aris Chatzistefanou, Katerina Kitidi and Leonidas Vatikiotis. Extract: 'The Ecuador debt audit: a seven-minute summary' <cadtm.org/Video-The-Ecuador-debt-audit-a> [accessed 19/12/2021].

Department of the Treasury, United States. *Assessment of US Participation in Multilateral Development Banks in the 1980s* (Washington, DC: Department of the Treasury, 1982).

Dupuy, Pierre-Marie. *Droit international public*, 3rd edn (Paris: Dalloz, 1995).

Duterme, Renaud. *Rwanda: une histoire volée* (*Rwanda's Stolen History*) (Brussels: Editions Tribord–CADTM, 2013) (in French).

Égert, Balázs. 'The 90% public debt threshold: the rise and fall of a stylized fact', *Applied Economics*, 2015, Vol. 47, Nos 34–35 <tandfonline.com/doi/abs/10.1080/00036846.2015.1021463> [accessed 27/12/2021].

Eisenhower, Dwight D. *Waging Peace* (Garden City, NY: Doubleday, 1965).

European Network on Debt and Development (Eurodad). 'How public services and human rights are being threatened by the growing debt crisis', 2020 <eurodad.org/how_public_services_and_human_rights_are_being_threatened_by_the_growing_debt_crisis> [accessed 20/10/2021].

Falquet, Jules. 'Neoliberal capitalism: an ally for women? Materialist and imbricationist feminist perspectives', in Christine Verschuur, Hélène Guétat and Isabelle Guérin (eds), *Under Development: Gender* (London: Palgrave Macmillan), 2014, pp. 236–56.

Falquet, Jules. 'Femmes, féminisme et "développement": une analyse critique des politiques des institutions internationales' ('Women, feminism, and "development": a critical analysis of the policies of international institutions), in Jeanne Bisilliat (ed.), *Regards de femmes sur la globalisation: approches critiques* (*Women's Perspectives on Globalization: Critical Approaches*) (Paris: Karthala, 2003), pp. 75–112.

Falquet, Jules. 'Analyzing globalization from a feminist perspective', *Travail, genre et sociétés* (*Labour, Gender and Societies*), 2011, Vol. 25, No. 1, pp. 81–98. (Translated from the French by JPD Systems.)

Falquet, Jules. *Imbrication: femmes, race et classe dans les mouvements sociaux* (*Imbrication: Women, Race and Class in Social Movements*) (Vulaines-sur-Seine: Éditions du croquant, 2019) (in French).

Fierens, Jacques. 'La violation des droits civils et politiques comme conséquence de la violation des droits économiques, sociaux et culturels' ('Violation of civil and political rights as a consequence of the violation of economic, social and cultural rights'), *Revue belge de droit international*, 1999, Vol. 1 (Brussels: Éditions Brylant, 1998) (in French) <rbdi.bruylant.be> [accessed 17/11/2021].

George, Susan and Fabrizio Sabelli. *Faith & Credit: The World Bank's Secular Empire* (New York: Routledge, 1994).

Goldman, Michael. *The World Bank and Struggles for Social Justice in the Age of Globalization* (New Haven: Yale University Press, 2005).

Gould, Elise and Heidi Shierholz. 'Not everybody can work from home: Black and Hispanic workers are much less likely to be able to telework', Economic Policy Institute, *Working Economics Blog*, 2020 <epi.org/blog/black-and-hispanic-workers-are-much-less-likely-to-be-able-to-work-from-home/> [accessed 09/03/2022].

Grant, James P. 'Development: the end of trickle-down?', *Foreign Policy*, Autumn 1973, No. 12, pp. 43–65.

Griffin, Keith B. and Jean-Luc Enos. 'Foreign assistance: objectives and consequences', *Economic Development and Cultural Change*, April 1970, Vol. 18, No. 3, p. 320.

Gwin, Catherine. 'U.S. relations with the World Bank, 1945–1992', in Devesh Kapur, John P. Lewis and Richard Webb, *The World Bank: Its First Half Century, Volume 2: Perspectives*, pp. 195–200.

Harrus, Frédérique. 'Scolarité: quand les règles mettent les filles au ban de l'école' ('Schooling: menstruation keeps girls out of school'), Franceinfo, 2015 <francetvinfo.fr/monde/scolarite-quand-les-regles-mettent-les-filles-au-ban-de-l-ecole_3066825.html> (in French) [accessed 18/10/2021].

Henderson, Gregory. *The Politics of the Vortex* (Cambridge, MA: Harvard University Press, 1968).

Herla, Roger. 'Du Sud au Nord, impacts de mondialisation néolibérale sur le travail des femmes' ('From North to South, impacts of neoliberal globalization on women's work'), CVFE – Publications, 2018 <cvfe.be/publications/analyses/1-du-sud-au-nord-impacts-de-la-mondialisation-neoliberale-sur-le-travail-des-women> [accessed 29/03/2022].

Hlasny, Vladimir and Paolo Verme. 'On the "Arab Inequality Puzzle": a comment', *Development and Change*, Social Studies Institute of The Hague, 2 January 2021 <doi.org/10.1111/dech.12626> [accessed 29/03/2022].

Hopkins, Ella. *The World Bank and Gender Equality: Development Policy Financing* (Bretton Woods Project: 2019) <brettonwoodsproject.org/wp-content/uploads/2019/08/The-World-Bank-and-Gender-Equality-DPF-2.pdf> [accessed 06/04/2023].

IMF. *Greece: Ex Post Evaluation of Exceptional Access under the 2010 Stand-By Arrangement*, Country Report No. 13/156 (Washington, DC: IMF, June 2013) <imf.org/-/media/websites/IMF/imported-full-text-pdf/external/pubs/ft/scr/2013/_cr13156.ashx> [accessed 14/09/2021].

IMF. *Acceptances of the Proposed Amendment of the Articles of Agreement on Reform of the Executive Board and Consents to 2010 Quota Increase* (International Monetary Fund: 24 April 2017) <imf.org/external/np/sec/misc/consents.htm> [accessed 14/09/2021].

IMF. *Annual Report 1997* (Washington, DC: IMF, 1997).

IMF. *Articles of Agreement* (Washington, DC: International Monetary Fund, 2020) <imf.org/external/pubs/ft/aa/pdf/aa.pdf> [accessed 02/11/2021].

Indonesian Ministry of Foreign Affairs. *Asia-Africa Speaks from Bandung* (Jakarta: Indonesian Ministry of Foreign Affairs, 1955).

International Bank for Reconstruction and Development. *Summary Proceedings of the 1972 Annual Meetings of the Boards of Governors* (Washington, DC: IBRD, September 1972).

International Displacement Monitoring Centre (IDMC). 'Dams and internal displacement: an introduction', 2017 <internal-displacement.org/sites/default/files/publications/documents/20170411-idmc-intro-dam-case-study.pdf> [accessed 21/10/2021].

International Labour Organization (ILO). *Women at Work Trends 2016* (Geneva: ILO, 8 March 2016) <ilo.org/global/publications/books/WCMS_457317/lang--en/index.htm> [accessed 15/10/2021].

Kapur, Devesh, John P. Lewis and Richard Webb. *The World Bank: Its First Half Century, Volume 1: History* (Washington, DC: Brookings Institution Press, 1997).

Kapur, Devesh, John P. Lewis and Richard Webb, *The World Bank: Its First Half Century, Volume 2: Perspectives* (Washington, DC: Brookings Institution Press, 1997).

Keynes, John Maynard. *Collected Writings*, Vol. 21 (London: Macmillan, 1982).

Krueger, Anne O. *Foreign Trade Regimes and Economic Development: Liberalization Attempts and Consequences* (New York: National Bureau of Economic Research, 1978).

Krueger, Anne O. *The Development Role of the Foreign Sector and Aid: Studies in the Modernization of the Republic of Korea, 1945–1975* (Cambridge: Council on East Asian Studies, Harvard University, 1979).

Krueger, Anne O. 'Import substitution versus export promotion', *Finance & Development*, 1 June 1985, Vol. 22, No. 2 elibrary.imf.org/view/journals/022/0022/002/article-A007-en.xml> [accessed 29/03/2022].

Krueger, Anne O. 'Supporting globalization, remarks by Anne O. Krueger', IMF, 26 September 2002 <https://www.imf.org/en/News/Articles/2015/09/28/04/53/sp092602a> [accessed 07/03/2022].

Lancaster, Carol. 'Governance and development: the views from Washington', *IDS Bulletin*, January 1993, Vol. 24, No. 1, pp. 9–15.

Le Quang, Matthieu. 'Entre buen vivir et neo-extractivisme: les quadratures de la politique economique equatorienne' ('Between good living and neo-extractivism: how Ecuadorian economic policy squares up'), interviewed by Violaine Delteil, *Revue de la Régulation*, 1st semester 2019 <journals.openedition.org/regulation/15076> [accessed 19/12/2021] (in French).

Legrand, Nathan. 'In Sri Lanka, resistance to private indebtedness is a strategic issue', CADTM, 2020 <cadtm.org/In-Sri-Lanka-Resistance-to-Private-Indebtedness-Is-a-Strategic-Issue> [accessed 28/12/2021].

Lissakers, Karin. *Banks, Borrowers and the Establishment: A Revisionist Account of the International Debt Crisis* (New York: Basic Books, 1991).

Mancero, Piedad. 'El debilitamiento institucional en la decada de los 90 – Presentación de la investigación y análisis del Proyecto Modernización del Estado – BIRF-3822/EC', in Gabriela Weber (ed.), *Sobre La Deuda Ilegítima – Aportes al debate – Argumentos entre consideraciones éticas y normas legales* (Quito: Centro de Investigaciones CIUDAD, 2008), pp. 81–87 (in Spanish).

Marone, Heloisa. *Demographic Dividends, Gender Equality, and Economic Growth: The Case of Cabo Verde* (IMF: Working Paper WP/16/169, 9 August 2016) <imf.org/-/media/Websites/IMF/imported-full-text-pdf/external/pubs/ft/wp/2016/_wp16169.ashx> [accessed 29/03/2022].

Mason, Edward S. and Robert E. Asher. *The World Bank since Bretton Woods* (Washington, DC: The Brookings Institution, 1973).

Massiah, Gustave. 'La réforme de l'ONU et le mouvement altermondialiste' ('UN reform and the anti-globalization movement'), in Samir Amin, Robert Charvin, Jean Ziegler, Anne-Cécile Robert et al., *ONU: droits pour tous ou loi du plus fort? (The UN: Rights for All, or Only for the Strongest?)* (Geneva: CETIM, 2005).

Maton, Jozef. *Développement économique et social au Rwanda entre 1980 et 1993 : le dixième décile en face de l'Apocalypse (Economic and Social Development in Rwanda between 1980 and 1993: The Tenth Decile Facing Apocalypse)* (Ghent: State University of Ghent, Faculty of Economics, Unit for Development Research and Teaching, November 1994).

McNamara, Robert S. *One Hundred Countries, Two Billion People: The Dimensions of Development* (New York: Praeger Publishers, 1973).

Meltzer, Allan H. (Chairman). *Report of the International Financial Institution Advisory Commission* (Washington, DC: US Government Printing Office, March 2000). The full Meltzer Report is available at <cadtm.org/The-Meltzer-Report> [accessed 29/03/2022].

Millet, Damien. *L'Afrique sans dette (Africa Without Debt)* (Liège: CADTM/Paris: Syllepse, 2005).

Millet, Damien and Éric Toussaint. *Who Owes Who?: 50 questions about World Debt* (London: Zed Books, 2004).

Millet, Damien and Éric Toussaint. *Tsunami Aid or Debt Cancellation! The Political Economy of Post Tsunami Reconstruction* (Mumbai: VAK, 2005).

Millikan, Max F. and Donald L.M. Blackmer (eds), *The Emerging Nations: Their Growth and United States Policy* (Boston: Little, Brown and Co., 1961).

Millikan, Max F. and Walt W. Rostow. *A Proposal: Keys to An Effective Foreign Policy* (New York: Harper, 1957).

Moller, Lovisa and Rachel Sharpe. 'Women as "underutilized assets" – a critical review of IMF advice on female labour force participation and fiscal consolidation', ActionAid International, 2017 <actionaid.org/publications/2017/women-underutilized-assets> [accessed 15/10/2021].

Norel, Philippe and Eric Saint-Alary. *L'endettement du tiers-monde (The Third World's Indebtedness)* (Paris: Syros/Alternatives économiques, 1992).

Oakland Institute, *Unfolding Truth: Dismantling the World Bank's Myths on Agriculture and Development* (Oakland: Oakland Institute: 2014) <oaklandinstitute.org/sites/oaklandinstitute.org/files/OurBiz_Brief_UnfoldingTruth_lowrez_0.pdf> [accessed 14/09/2021].

Oliver, Robert W. *International Economic Co-operation and the World Bank* (London: Macmillan Press, 1975).

Olmos, Alejandro. *Todo lo que usted quiso saber sobre la deuda externa y siempre se lo ocultaron* (Buenos Aires: Editorial de los Argentinos, 1990).

Oman, Charles and Ganeshan Wignaraja. *The Postwar Evolution of Development Thinking* (London/Paris: Macmillan/OECD).

Ortiz, Isabel and Matthew Cummins. *Global Austerity Alert – Looming Budget Cuts in 2021–25 and Alternative Pathways* (New York: IPD/ITUC/PSI/Arab Watch Coalition/BWP/TNW, April 2021) <policydialogue.org/files/publications/papers/Global-Austerity-Alert-Ortiz-Cummins-2021-final.pdf> [accessed 14/09/2021].

Ostry, Jonathan D., Prakash Loungani and Davide Furceri. 'Neoliberalism: oversold?', *Finance and Development*, June 2016 <imf.org/external/pubs/ft/fandd/2016/06/pdf/ostry.pdf> [accessed 14/09/2021].

Oxfam International. *Kicking the Habit: How the World Bank and the IMF Are Still Addicted to Attaching Economic Policy Conditions to Aid*, Oxfam Briefing Paper 96 (Oxford: Oxfam International, November 2006) <oxfamilibrary.openrepository.com/bitstream/handle/10546/114532/bp96-kicking-habit-011106-en.pdf> [accessed 29/03/2022].

Payer, Cheryl. *The Debt Trap: The International Monetary Fund and the Third World* (New York/London: Monthly Review Press, 1974).

Payer, Cheryl. *Lent and Lost: Foreign Credit and Third World Development* (London: Zed Books, 1991).

Pearson, Lester B. *Partners in Development: Report of the Commission on International Development* (New York: Praeger, 1969).

Peemans, Jean-Philippe. *Le développement des peuples face à la modernisation du monde (Peoples' Development and Global Modernizaton)* (Louvain-la-Neuve/Paris: Academia-Bruylant/L'Harmattan, 2002).

Pescatori, Andrea, Damiano Sandri and John Simon. *Debt and Growth: Is There a Magic Threshold?* (Washington, DC: IMF, 2014) <imf.org/external/pubs/ft/wp/2014/wp1434.pdf> [accessed 27/12/2021].

Piketty, Thomas. *Capital in the Twenty-first Century*, trans. Arthur Goldhammer (Cambridge, MA: Harvard University Press, 2013).

Piketty, Thomas. *Capital and Ideology* (Cambridge, MA: The Belknap Press of Harvard University Press, 2020).

Piketty, Thomas, Facundo Alvaredo and Lydia Assouad, *Measuring Inequality in the Middle East 1990-2016: The World's Most Unequal Region?* (World Inequality Database: Working Paper Series No. 2017/15, 2018) <wid.world/document/alvaredoassouadpiketty-middleeast-widworldwp201715/> [accessed 05/10/2021].

Pogge, Thomas. *Politics as Usual: What Lies behind the Pro-Poor Rhetoric* (Cambridge: Polity Press, 2010).

Prügl, Elisabeth. 'Neoliberalism with a feminist face: crafting a new hegemony at the World Bank', *Feminist Economics*, 2017, Vol. 23. https://www.tandfonline.com/doi/full/10.1080/13545701.2016.1198043 [accessed 06/04/2023].

Ramírez Gallegos, Franklin (ed.) *Octubre y el derecho a la resistencia: revuelta popular y neoliberalismo autoritario en Ecuador* (Buenos Aires: CLACSO, 2020) <clacso.org.ar/libreria-latinoamericana/contador/sumar_pdf.php?id_libro=2056> [accessed 27/02/2023].

Reddy, Sanjay G. and Thomas W. Pogge. 'How not to count the poor', SSRN, 29 October 2005 <dx.doi.org/10.2139/ssrn.893159> [accessed 29/03/2022].

Rich, Bruce. *Mortgaging the Earth* (Boston: Beacon Press, 1994).

Rivié, Milan. 'Illicit financial flows: Africa is the world's main creditor', CADTM, 5 November 2020 <cadtm.org/Illicit-Financial-Flows-Africa-is-the-world-s-main-creditor> [accessed 29/03/2022].

Rivié, Milan. '6 months after the official announcements of debt cancellation for the countries of the South: where do we stand?', CADTM, 17 September 2020 <cadtm.org/6-months-after-the-official-announcements-of-debt-cancellation-for-the> [accessed 15/09/2021].

Rockefeller, Nelson. *Report on the Americas* (Chicago: Quadrangle Books, 1969).

Rodriguez, Miguel A., 'Consequences of capital flight for Latin American debtor countries', in Donald Lessard and John Williamson, *Capital Flight and Third World Debt* (Washington, DC: Institute for International Economics, 1987).

Roig, Emilia. 'Intersectionality as a practice: an interview with Emilia Roig', Pocolit, 25 April 2020 <pocolit.com/en/2020/04/25/intersectionality-as-a-practice> [accessed 29/03/2022].

Rosenstein-Rodan, Paul. 'International aid for underdeveloped countries', in *Review of Economics and Statistics* (Cambridge, MA: MIT Press, 1961), Vol. 43, p. 107.

Rostow, Walt Whitman. *The Stages of Economic Growth: A Non Communist Manifesto* (New York: Cambridge University Press, 1960).

Rousset, Pierre. 'La Corée du Sud, second Japon?' ('South Korea – a second Japan?'), in *Croissance des jeunes nations*, No. 265 (Paris: October 1984).

Ruiz, Hugo and Éric Toussaint. 'Deuda externa y auditoria. Aproximacion practica y teorica', in *Donde estan lo que nos prestaron? Deuda externa, deudas ilegitimas y auditorias* (Quito: CDES/Plataforma Interamericana de Derechos Humanos Democracia y Desarrollo [PIDHDD], 2004), pp. 9–69.

Sack, Alexander Nahum. *Les effets des transformations des états sur leurs dettes publiques et autres obligations financières (The Effects of the Transformation of States on their Public Debt and Other Financial Obligations)* (Paris: Recueil Sirey, 1927).

Salim, Emil. *Striking a Better Balance: The World Bank Group and Extractive Industries – The Final Report of the Extractive Industries Review, Volume 1* (Jakarta/Washington, DC: Extractive Industries Review, December 2003).

Samuelson, Paul. *Economics*, 11th edn (New York: McGraw Hill, 1980).

Sánchez, Nicolás Angulo. *El derecho humano al desarollo frente a la mundialización del mercado* (Madrid: Iepala Editorial, 2006).

Secretary of State for Foreign Affairs of the United Kingdom. *Agreement on German External Debts of 27 February 1953 [with Annexes and Subsidiary Agreements] London, February 27, 1953* (London: Her Majesty's Stationery Office, 1959).

Shiva, Vandana, *The Violence of the Green Revolution* (Penang, Malaysia: Third World Network, 1991).

Slany, William Z., Charles S. Sampson and Rogers P. Churchill (eds). *Foreign Relations of the United States, 1950, Central and Eastern Europe; The Soviet Union, Volume IV.* (Washington, DC: US Government Printing Office, 1980).

Stern, Nicholas. *Stern Review: The Economics of Climate Change* (Cambridge: Cambridge University Press, 2007).

Stiglitz, Joseph E. *Globalization and its Discontents* (London: Allen Lane, 2002).

Stockman, David A. *The Triumph of Politics: How the Reagan Revolution Failed* (New York: Harper and Row, 1986).

Stopford, John and Susan Strange. *Rival States, Rival Firms: Competition for World Market Shares* (Cambridge: Cambridge University Press, 1991).

Tanuro, Daniel. *Trop tard pour être pessimistes! Ecosocialisme ou effondrement (Too Late for Pessimism! Ecosocialism or Collapse* (Paris: Textuel, 2020).

Task Force on International Development. *U.S. Foreign Assistance in the 1970s: A New Approach. Report to the President* (Washington, DC: US Government Printing Office, 1970).

Teitelbaum, Alejandro. *El papel de las sociedades transnacionales en el mundo contemporáneo* (Buenos Aires: Asociación Americana de Juristas, 2003).

Therien, Jean-Philippe. *Une voix pour le Sud: le discours de la CNUCED (A Voice for the South: UNCTAD's Discourse)* (Paris: L'Harmattan, 1990).

Toohey, Paul. 'East Timorese go begging as foreign advisors rake it in', *The Australian*, 25 April 2009 <etan.org/et2009/04april/26/25forei.htm> [accessed 29/03/2022].

Toussaint, Éric. *Your Money or Your Life: The Tyranny of Global Finance* (Chicago: Haymarket Books, 2005).

Toussaint, Éric. *The World Bank: a Neverending Coup d'Etat. The Hidden Agenda of the Washington Consensus* (Mumbai: VAK, 2007).

Toussaint, Éric. *The World Bank: A Critical Primer* (Toronto: Between the Lines / London: Pluto Press / Cape Town: David Philip Publishers / Liège: CADTM, 2008).

Toussaint, Éric. 'Ecuador: la CAIC a proposé à Rafael Correa de suspendre le paiement de près de la moitié de la dette' ('CAIC proposes that Correa suspend repayment of nearly half the debt'), CADTM, 25 September 2008 <cadtm.org/Equateur-La-CAIC-a-propose-a> [accessed 29/03/2022] (in French).

Toussaint, Éric. *The Debt System: A History of Sovereign Debts and their Repudiation* (Chicago: Haymarket Books, 2019).

Toussaint, Éric. 'South Africa: the odious debts generated by coal-fired power-stations', CADTM, 2 May 2019 <cadtm.org/South-Africa-the-odious-debts-generated-by-coal-fired-power-stations> [accessed 16/09/2021].

Toussaint, Éric. 'Ecuador: resistance against the policies imposed by the World Bank, the IMF and other creditors between 2007 and 2011', CADTM, 15 April 2021 <cadtm.org/Ecuador-Resistance-against-the-policies-imposed-by-the-World-Bank-the-IMF-and> [accessed 07/10/2021].

Toussaint, Éric. 'Debt', in *The Routledge Handbook of Global Development* (New York: Routledge, 2022), chapter 5.

Toussaint, Éric and Nathan Legrand. 'Damning testimonies of microcredit abuse', CADTM, 25 April 2018 <cadtm.org/Damning-testimonies-of-microcredit> [accessed 30/03/2022].

Toussaint, Éric and Damien Millet. 'FMI : la fin de l'histoire ?' ('IMF: the end of the story?'), CADTM, 20 May 2011 <cadtm.org/FMI-la-fin-de-l-histoire?debut_articles_mot=45> [accessed 1/11/2021] (in French).

Toussaint, Éric and Arnaud Zacharie. *Le bateau ivre de la mondialisation : escales au sein du village planétaire (The Drunken Boat of Globalization: Ports of Call in the Global Village)* (Brussels/Paris : CADTM/Syllepse, 2000).

Toussaint, Éric with Christina Laskaridis and Nathan Legrand. 'Historical perpectives on current struggles against illegitimate debt', in *The Routledge Handbook of Financialization* (New York: Routledge, 2020), chapter 40.

Toussaint, Éric, Sushovan Dhar, Nathan Legrand and Abul Kalam Azad. 'Bangladesh: harsh effects of the Grameen Bank and other microcredit institutions on the rural population', CADTM, 11 April 2017 <cadtm.org/Bangladesh-Harsh-effects-of-the-Grameen-Bank-and-other-microcredit-institutions> [accessed 29/03/2022].

Transparency International. *Global Corruption Report 2004* (London/Sterling, VA: Pluto Press, 2004).

UNDP. *Human Development Report 1992* (New York/Oxford: Oxford University Press, 1992).

United Nations Commission on Human Rights (UN-CHR). 'Debt relief and social investment: linking the heavily indebted poor countries (HIPC) initiative to the HIV/AIDS epidemic in Africa, post-Hurricane Mitch reconstruction in Honduras and Nicaragua, and the Worst Forms of Child Labour Convention, 1999 (Convention No. 182) of the International Labour Organization. Common Report by Reinaldo Figueredo (special rapporteur) and Fantu Cheru (independent expert)', 14 January 2000 <https://undocs.org/E/CN.4/2000/51> [accessed 29/12/2021].

United Nations Commission on Human Rights (UN-CHR). *Effects of Structural Adjustment Policies and Foreign Debt on the Full Enjoyment of Human Rights, Especially Economic, Social and Cultural Rights*, report submitted by Mr Bernards Mudho, independent expert, E/CN.4/2003/10, 23 October 2002, 'II. Why Debt Relief Alone Is Inadequate to Realize the Human Rights Dimension of Poverty: A Case Study of Bolivia' <undocs.org/E/CN.4/2003/10> [accessed 29/03/2022].

United Nations Conference on Trade and Development. *Trade and Development Report 2000* (New York/Geneva: UNCTAD, 2000).

United Nations Development Programme. *Human Development Report 1994* (Oxford: Oxford University Press, 1994).

Van de Laar, Aart. *The World Bank and the Poor* (Boston/The Hague/London: Martinus Nijhoff Publishing, 1980).

Vanden Daelen, Christine. 'La dette, les PAS: analyse des impacts sur la vie des femmes' ('Debt and SAPs: analysis of impacts on women's lives'), CADTM, 1 May 2014 <cadtm.org/La-dette-les-PAS-analyse-des-impacts-sur-la-vie-des-femmes> [accessed 13/10/2021] (in French).

Vanden Daelen, Christine. 'Féminismes et Banque mondiale: un mariage "contre-nature"?' ('Feminism and the World Bank: an "unnatural" marriage?'), CADTM, 11 February 2021 <cadtm.org/Feminismes-et-Banque-mondiale-un-mariage-contre-nature> [accessed 29/03/2022].

Vanden Daelen, Christine. 'Quand la Banque mondiale s'intéresse aux femmes …' ('When the World Bank takes an interest in women …'), CADTM, 26 February 2021 <cadtm.org/Quand-la-Banque-mondiale-s-interesse-aux-femmes> [accessed 29/03/2022] (in French).

Vergès, Françoise. *A Decolonial Feminism* (London: Pluto Press, 2021).

Verhoeven, Joe. *Droit international public* (Brussels: Larcier, Précis de la Faculté de Droit de l'UCL, 2000).

Verme, Paolo et al. *Inside Inequality in the Arab Republic of Egypt: Facts and Perceptions across People, Time, and Space* (Washington, DC: World Bank, 2014) <worldbank.org/content/dam/Worldbank/egypt-nequality-book.pdf> [accessed 27/12/2021].

Viner, Jacob. 'Problems of international long-term investment', in *Council on Foreign Relations, Memorandum on Postwar Economic Problems* (Washington, DC: Council on Foreign Relations, April 1942).

Weisbrot, Mark et al. *IMF-Supported Macroeconomic Policies and the World Recession: A Look at Forty-One Borrowing Countries* (Center for Economic and Policy Research, October 2009) <cepr.net/documents/publications/imf-2009-10.pdf> [accessed 27/12/2021].

White House, 'Fact sheet: G-8 action on food security and nutrition', Press Release, 18 May 2012.

Williamson, John (ed.). *Latin American Adjustment: How Much Has Happened?* (Washington, DC: Institute of International Economics, 1990).

Wolfowitz, Paul. 'Foreword', in *World Development Report 2006: Equity and Development* (World Bank: Washington, 2005) <openknowledge.worldbank.org/handle/10986/5988> [accessed 08/12/2021].

Woodward, David. *The IMF, the World Bank and Economic Policy in Rwanda: Economic and Social Implications* (Oxford: Oxford University Press, 1996).

World Bank. *2012 World Development Report: Gender Equality and Development* (Washington, DC: World Bank, 2011) <doi.org/10.1596/978-0-8213-8810-5> [accessed 11/10/2021].

World Bank. *Fourth Annual Report 1948–1949* (Washington, DC: IBRD (World Bank), 1949).

World Bank. *Eighth Annual Report 1952–1953* (Washington, DC: IBRD (World Bank), 1953).

World Bank. *Fifteenth Annual Report 1959–1960* (Washington, DC: IBRD (World Bank), 1960).

World Bank. *Annual Report 1965–1966* (Washington, DC: IBRD (World Bank), 1966.

World Bank. *Accelerated Development in Africa South of the Sahara, Indicative Program of Action* (Washington, DC: World Bank, 1981).

World Bank. *Global Development Report 1987* (Washington, DC: World Bank, 1987).

World Bank. *Global Development Finance 2003* (Washington, DC: World Bank, 2003).

World Bank. *Hazards of Nature, Risks to Development – An IEG Evaluation of World Bank Assistance for Natural Disasters* (Washington, DC: World Bank, 2006).

World Bank. *The World Bank Group Program of Support for the Chad–Cameroon Petroleum Development and Pipeline Construction Program – Performance Assessment Report, Report No. 50315* (Washington, DC: World Bank Group, 2009).

World Bank. *Gender at Work: A Companion to the World Development Report on Jobs* (Washington, DC: World Bank, 2014). <worldbank.org/content/dam/Worldbank/document/Gender/GenderAtWork_ExecutiveSummary.pdf> [accessed 12/10/2021].

World Bank. *World Bank Group Gender Strategy (FY16–23): Gender Equality, Poverty Reduction and Inclusive Growth* (Washington, DC: World Bank, 2015) <openknowledge.worldbank.org/bitstream/handle/10986/23425/102114.pdf?sequence=5&isAllowed=y> [accessed 12/10/2021].

World Bank Group. 'Impact evaluation report: Transmigration I, Transmigration II, Transmigration III. World Bank, Operations Evaluation Department, Report No. 12874-IND', 22 March 1994 <documents1.worldbank.org/curated/en/588091468915015089/pdf/12874-PPAR-PUBLIC.pdf> [accessed 12/01/2022].

World Bank Group. 'Indonesia transmigration program: a review of five Bank-supported projects', World Bank, Operations Evaluation Department, 26 April 1994 <documents1.worldbank.org/curated/en/823551468752430966/pdf/multi-page.pdf> [accessed 12/01/2022].

World Bank Group. *Gender Equality as Smart Economics: A World Bank Group Gender Action Plan'* (Washington, DC: World Bank, August 2006) <documents1.worldbank.org/curated/en/295371468315572899/pdf/37008.pdf> [accessed 11/10/2021].

World Bank Group. *Applying Gender Action Plan Lessons: A Three-Year Road Map for Gender Mainstreaming (2011–2013)* (Washington, DC: World Bank, 2010) <documents1.worldbank.org/curated/en/782711468012632778/pdf/547520BR0SecM2101Official0U-se0Only1.pdf> [accessed 18/10/2021].

World Bank Group. *Doing Business 2014: Understanding Regulations for Small and Medium-Size Enterprises* (Washington, DC: World Bank Group, 28 October 2013) <doingbusiness.org/reports/global-reports/doing-business-2014> [accessed 14/09/2021].

World Bank Group. *Enabling the Business of Agriculture 2015: Progress Report* (Washington, DC: World Bank Group, 2015) <hdl.handle.net/10986/21501> [accessed 14/09/2021].

World Bank Group. *World Bank Group Gender Strategy (FY16–23): Gender Equality, Poverty Reduction and Inclusive Growth* (Washington, DC: World Bank, 2015) <documents1.worldbank.org/curated/en/449711468762020101/pdf/28102.pdf> [accessed 17/11/2021].

World Bank Group. 'Fact sheet: Pandemic Emergency Financing Facility', 27 April 2020 <worldbank.org/en/topic/pandemics/brief/fact-sheet-pandemic-emergency-financing-facility> [accessed 15/09/2021].

World Bank Group. 'World Bank Group to discontinue Doing Business report', World Bank, 16 September 2021 <worldbank.org/en/news/statement/2021/09/16/world-bank-group-to-discontinue-doing-business-report> [accessed 19/11/2021].

World Bank Group. 'Update of World Bank Group gender strategy: consultations' <consultations.worldbank.org/consultation/update-world-bank-group-gender-strategy-consultations> [accessed 19/10/2021].

World Bank Group. 'Voting powers', World Bank <worldbank.org/en/about/leadership/votingpowers> [accessed 10/03/2022].

World Bank and IDA. *Annual Report 1965–1966* (Washington, DC: World Bank, 1966). <documents1.worldbank.org/curated/en/786661468765027751/text/multi-page.txt> [accessed 18/01/2022].

Works by Éric Toussaint Published in English

Your Money or Your Life: The Tyranny of Global Finance (London: Pluto Press, 1999).

Globalisation: Reality, Resistance and Alternative (Mumbai: VAK, 2004).

Your Money or Your Life: The Tyranny of Global Finance (Chicago: Haymarket Books, 2005).

Bank of the South: An Alternative to IMF–World Bank (Mumbai: VAK, 2007).

A Diagnosis of Emerging Global Crisis and Alternatives (Mumbai: VAK, 2007).

The World Bank: A Never-ending Coup d'Etat (Mumbai: VAK, 2007).

The World Bank: A Critical Primer (Toronto: Between the Lines / London: Pluto Press / Cape Town: David Philip Publishers / Liège: CADTM, 2008).

A Diagnosis of Emerging Global Crisis and Alternatives (Mumbai: Vikas Adhyayan Kendra (VAK), 2009).

Glance in the Rear-View Mirror: Neoliberal Ideology from its Origins to the Present (Chicago: Haymarket Books, 2012).

The Life and Crimes of an Exemplary Man (Liège: CADTM, 2014).

Bankocracy (London: Resistance Books / IIRE / CADTM, 2015).

Debt System: A History of Sovereign Debts and their Repudiation (Chicago: Haymarket Books, 2019).

Greece 2015: There Was an Alternative (London: Resistance Books/IIRE/CADTM, 2020).

With Damien Millet

The Debt Scam: IMF, World Bank and Third World Debt (Mumbai: VAK, 2003).

Who Owes Who? 50 Questions about the World Debt (Dhaka: University Press / Bangkok: White Lotus Co. Ltd / Halifax: Fernwood Publishing Ltd / Bangalore: Books for Change / Kuala Lumpur: SIRD / Cape Town: David Philip / London: Zed Books, 2004).

Tsunami Aid or Debt Cancellation! The Political Economy of Post Tsunami Reconstruction (Mumbai: VAK, 2005).

Debt, the IMF, and the World Bank: Sixty Questions, Sixty Answers (New York: Monthly Review Press, 2010).

The Debt Crisis: From Europe to Where? (Mumbai: VAK, 2012).

Index

Thanks to our Patreon subscriber:

Ciaran Kane

Who has shown generosity and comradeship in support of our publishing.

Check out the other perks you get by subscribing to our Patreon – visit patreon.com/plutopress. Subscriptions start from £3 a month.

The Pluto Press Newsletter

Hello friend of Pluto!

Want to stay on top of the best radical books
we publish?

Then sign up to be the first to hear about our
new books, as well as special events,
podcasts and videos.

You'll also get 50% off your first order with us
when you sign up.

Come and join us!

Go to bit.ly/PlutoNewsletter